Queering Representation

Queering Representation
LGBTQ People and Electoral Politics in Canada

Edited by Manon Tremblay

UBCPress · Vancouver · Toronto

© UBC Press 2019

All rights reserved. No part of this publication may be reproduced, stored in a retrieval system, or transmitted, in any form or by any means, without prior written permission of the publisher, or, in Canada, in the case of photocopying or other reprographic copying, a licence from Access Copyright, www.accesscopyright.ca.

28 27 26 25 24 23 22 21 20 19   5 4 3 2 1

Printed in Canada on FSC-certified ancient-forest-free paper (100% post-consumer recycled) that is processed chlorine- and acid-free.

ISBN 978-0-7748-6181-6 (hardcover)
ISBN 978-0-7748-6182-3 (pbk.)
ISBN 978-0-7748-6183-0 (PDF)
ISBN 978-0-7748-6184-7 (EPUB)
ISBN 978-0-7748-6185-4 (Kindle)

Cataloguing-in-publication data for this book is available from Library and Archives Canada.

Canadä

UBC Press gratefully acknowledges the financial support for our publishing program of the Government of Canada (through the Canada Book Fund), the Canada Council for the Arts, and the British Columbia Arts Council.

This book has been published with the help of a grant from the Canadian Federation for the Humanities and Social Sciences, through the Awards to Scholarly Publications Program, using funds provided by the Social Sciences and Humanities Research Council of Canada.

Printed and bound in Canada by Friesens
Set in Helvetica Condensed and Minion by Apex CoVantage LLC
Copy editor: Deborah Kerr
Proofreader: Kristy Hankiewicz
Indexer: Judy Dunlop
Cover designer: David Drummond

UBC Press
The University of British Columbia
2029 West Mall
Vancouver, BC V6T 1Z2
www.ubcpress.ca

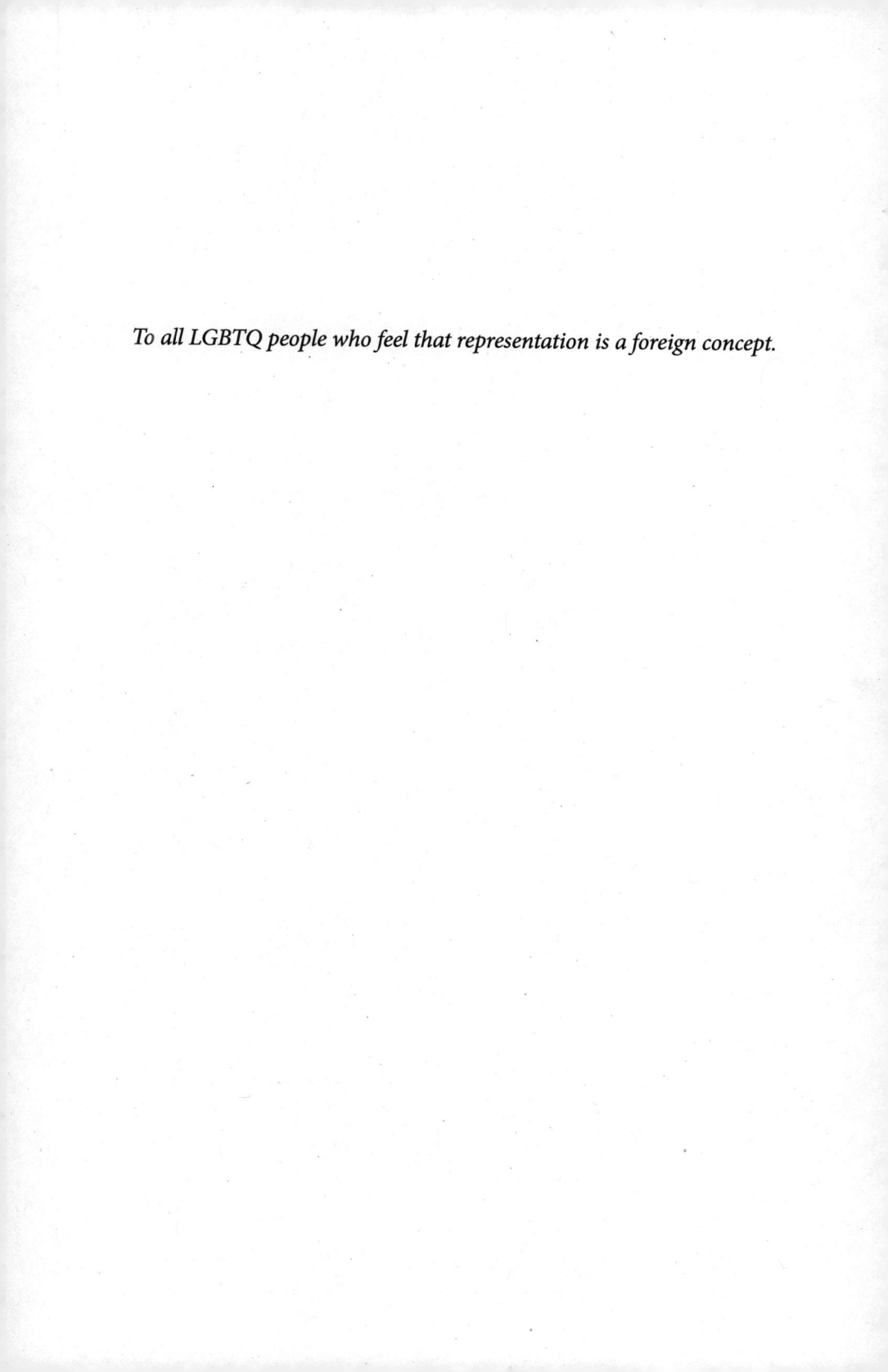

To all LGBTQ people who feel that representation is a foreign concept.

Contents

List of Figures and Tables / ix

Foreword / xi
Rev. Dr. Cheri DiNovo

Acknowledgments / xiii

Introduction / 3
Manon Tremblay

PART 1: LGBTQ VOTERS

1 Profile of the Lesbian, Gay, and Bisexual Electorate in Canada / 51
   Andrea M.L. Perrella, Steven D. Brown, and Barry Kay

2 Winning as a Woman/Winning as a Lesbian: Voter Attitudes toward Kathleen Wynne in the 2014 Ontario Election / 80
   Joanna Everitt and Tracey Raney

3 Media Framing of Lesbian and Gay Politicians: Is Sexual Mediation at Work? / 102
   Mireille Lalancette and Manon Tremblay

4 Electing LGBT Representatives and the Voting System in Canada / 124
   Dennis Pilon

PART 2: LGBTQ REPRESENTATIVES

5 LGBT Groups and the Canadian Conservative Movement: A New Relationship? / 157
   Frédéric Boily and Ève Robidoux-Descary

6 Liberalism and the Protection of LGBT Rights in Canada / 179
  Brooke Jeffrey

7 A True Match? The Federal New Democratic Party and LGBTQ Communities and Politics / 201
  Alexa DeGagne

8 Representation: The Case of LGBTQ People / 220
  Manon Tremblay

9 Pathway to Office: The Eligibility, Recruitment, Selection, and Election of LGBT Candidates / 240
  Joanna Everitt, Manon Tremblay, and Angelia Wagner

10 LGBTQ Perspectives on Political Candidacy in Canada / 259
  Angelia Wagner

11 Out to Win: The ProudPolitics Approach to LGBTQ Electoralism / 279
  Curtis Atkins

12 LGBT Place Management: Representative Politics and Toronto's Gay Village / 298
  Catherine J. Nash and Andrew Gorman-Murray

Afterword: The Champion / 314
Graeme Truelove

Contributors / 329

Index / 334

Figures and Tables

Figures
1.1 LGB support for ROC federal parties in the 2006, 2008, 2011, and 2015 Canadian elections / 66
1.2 LGB support for Quebec federal parties in the 2006, 2008, 2011, and 2015 Canadian elections / 66
1.3 LGB male-female vote differentials, outside Quebec / 67
1.4 LGB male-female vote differentials, Quebec only / 68

Tables
1.1 A comparative socio-demographic profile by sexual orientation and gender / 56
1.2 A comparative electoral engagement profile by sexual orientation and gender / 59
1.3 Regression of electoral engagement variables on LGB membership and socio-demographic background variables / 60
1.4 Regression of electoral engagement variables on LGB membership and socio-demographic background variables, with interactions / 61
1.5 Summary of views on social and political issues, by sexual orientation and gender, 2006–15 / 63
1.6 Sexual orientation and vote choice, outside Quebec / 69
1.7 Sexual orientation and vote choice, Quebec / 70
1.8 Sexual orientation and vote choice, with interactive terms, outside Quebec / 71
1.9 Sexual orientation and vote choice, with interactive terms, in Quebec / 72
2.1 Mean likeability scores for party leaders (standard deviation) / 86
2.2 Mean ratings of leadership traits and issue competencies / 87
2.3 Mean ratings of traits and issue competencies (standard deviation) by respondent's sex / 89
2.4 Determinants of trait attributes and issue ownership for Kathleen Wynne / 91
4.1 Percentage of women's representation in lower houses / 128

4.2 LGBT representation by voting system / 133
4.3 Numbers of LGBT representatives by country and year / 134
4.4 Proportions of LGBT representatives by country and year / 135
4.5 Federal LGBT representation in Canada, 1979–2015 / 140
9.1 Number of out LGBT federal candidates by party and election year, 2004–15 / 248
9.2 Number of out LGBT provincial/territorial candidates by party / 249
9.3 Candidate status and margins of victory at first election / 253

Foreword

Queering Representation: LGBTQ People and Electoral Politics in Canada is a groundbreaking compendium. So very little is known about LGBTQ2S people's involvement in Canadian electoral politics, and so few scholarly works are concerned with our participation.

Of course, one could argue that political representation is a necessity for any minority, including LGBTQ2S people, and that although comparisons can be made with women's involvement or that of racialized minorities, the differences are worth exploring. To that end, *Queering Representation* has assembled a wealth of analytic data, as well as some memorable profiles of LGBTQ2S groundbreakers such as Kathleen Wynne, Kristyn Wong-Tam, and Svend Robinson.

In these pages, the major political parties are critically examined for their contribution or lack of contribution to LGBTQ2S representation, as are their nomination processes and electoral and policy successes. Some chapters confirm long-held assumptions about the involvement of LGBTQ people in politics – that we tend toward the progressive left and away from the conservative right, and that we're less religious than many other Canadians. However, some chapters show that what might intuitively seem valid can be challenged. The jury appears to be out on whether a proportional representation system automatically results in more diversity where we're concerned. And the number of out LGBTQ Tories is increasing. It's possible to be both Conservative and queer. The intersection of partisanship and identity is fascinating.

Historically, all political parties have displayed homo-, bi-, and transphobia, and though some have a better track record than others, none can claim immunity. I remember my own father, not knowing at the time that I identified as queer/bisexual, telling me that Pierre Trudeau's cabinet was "full of homosexuals." He was a passionate NDP-er and unionist, and his words were not intended as a compliment.

This book also traces certain policy changes, such as defining trans rights as human rights (in Ontario in 2012 and federally in 2015) and the legalization of same-sex marriage. We're still waiting for the federal government to act on other issues. In 2015, Ontario banned conversion therapy for minors, but a number of provinces have yet to follow suit. The same is true for Ottawa. Parental rights depend on where you live. British Columbia shines here, followed by Ontario, but lesbian and trans parents in other provinces may be obliged to adopt their own children. Clearly, there's still a great deal of work to be done. *Queering Representation* points to that fact and to the ongoing struggle with representation of the queer community. One example, ProudPolitics, attempts, as Equal Voice does for women, to assist LGBTQ people to run and to win. ProudPolitics challenges aren't minimized. For LGBTQ people, it's still difficult to get nominated and then win, anywhere.

Success in representation is also debated in these pages. Does success have to do with being out, proud, and ardent in championing LGBTQ policy change? Or is it enough simply to have LGBTQ candidates win their seats? In terms of getting elected, does heteronormativity help, even for LGBTQ persons?

Like all explorations, this volume raises as many questions as it answers, which is one of its strengths. How do we represent being LGBTQ politically? What about the intersectional issues, being black, two-spirited, intersex? Should we aim simply to increase the numbers elected and even their degree of (out)spokenness, or should we set our sights on something higher, perhaps something more revolutionary – a non-binary and fluid political presence?

Finally, this is an important book and a pioneering one. Read this and keep on queerying.

Reverend Dr. Cheri DiNovo

(The only woman to sign "We Demand" in 1971, Cheri DiNovo performed the first legalized same-sex marriage in Canada. During her eleven years as a member of the Ontario Legislative Assembly, she managed to have more LGBTQ legislation passed than anyone in Canadian history. This included Toby's Law, which added trans rights to the Ontario Human Rights Code, a first in a major North American jurisdiction; banning conversion therapy for Ontario minors; achieving parental equality for lesbian and trans parents, who are no longer required to adopt their own children; and establishing the Trans Day of Remembrance, on November 20, during which members of the legislature stand and observe a minute of silence.)

Acknowledgments

A NUMBER OF people and organizations made it possible to bring this book to fruition. First, I would like to thank all the authors for agreeing to contribute in 2015, for writing groundbreaking texts, for reviewing their chapters over and over in light of the many rounds of revisions, and for maintaining their confidence in the project despite the many hurdles it has encountered. I remain convinced that *Queering Representation* is worth all the effort!

I am grateful to the reviewers for the time they devoted to reading and commenting on the various drafts of the manuscript. Their comments helped us to produce a book that meets the highest standards.

A special thanks to Reverend Dr. Cheri DiNovo for writing the Foreword of this book. I find it particularly important that she authored the Foreword because her dedication to LGBTQ people and communities for decades is simply exceptional. She signed the "We Demand" brief, submitted to the federal government in 1971 (she is the only woman signatory), and was a member of the Ontario Legislative Assembly from 2006 to 2017. In this respect, she is living proof that any substantial change in the daily citizenship of LGBTQ people requires that social activism and institutional politics work hand-in-hand.

The Introduction and the chapter of which I am the sole author benefitted from Käthe Roth's translation skills. I thank her for this, especially for her constructive guidance, which often goes beyond simple translation.

Some of the chapters in *Queering Representation* were discussed at the 2016 Canadian Political Science Association Congress in Calgary. My thanks go to the colleagues who participated in this event, as well as to the audience for their comments and their enthusiasm for what was then a book project.

I worked on this manuscript while I was a visiting researcher at the Australian National University, School of Politics and International Relations, from January to April 2018. I can never express how much I love being at the ANU, where I can work in utter peace and in a very welcoming environment.

Some parts of *Queering Representation* were supported by the Social Sciences and Humanities Research Council of Canada. I would like to thank the federal agency that has funded my research for more than three decades now.

Finally, I thank the entire team at UBC Press, especially Randy Schmidt and Ann Macklem, who orchestrated the publishing of *Queering Representation*. I am also very appreciative of Judy Dunlop's masterful work in compiling the index to this book. She has a rare talent!

Queering Representation

Introduction

Manon Tremblay

ONE OF THE most important social changes to have occurred in the Western world since the 1960s concerns "homosexuals." Once labelled sinners by the church, perverts by medicine and psychiatry, and criminals by the legal system, today LGBTQ people (and, more precisely, lesbians and gays) enjoy (almost) equal rights under the law.[1] According to Kees Waaldijk (2000), rights respecting homosexuality in the West evolved in three waves. First, homosexuality was decriminalized, though often only partially. This occurred in 1933 in Denmark, 1944 in Sweden, 1951 in Greece, 1967 in England and Wales, 1969 in Canada, 1972 in Norway, 1986 in New Zealand, 1993 in Ireland, and as late as 2003 in the United States (Carroll and Ramón Mendos 2017, 26–36).[2] Second, laws were passed to prohibit discrimination on the basis of sexual orientation. Anti-discrimination laws for employment were adopted between 1983 and 2003 in Australia, Canada, France, the Netherlands, Spain, and the United Kingdom (Carroll and Ramón Mendos 2017, 48–53). Third, lesbians and gays gained the same equality rights as their heterosexual fellow citizens. For example, same-sex couples have had access to civil marriage since 1999 in the Netherlands, 2003 in Belgium, 2005 in Spain and Canada, 2010 in Iceland, 2013 in France, 2015 in the United States, and 2017 in Finland and Australia (Carroll and Ramón Mendos 2017, 68–69).

Another aspect of the "homosexual revolution" that has swept through the Western world over the last half-century is a change in social attitudes. Support by the (presumed straight) population for LGBTQ people is important: it conditions, at least in part, how straight politicians will represent them and their communities (Hansen and Treul 2015; Snell 2017). Increasing support for LGBTQ rights has been observed in Western democracies, although with substantial variations from country to country (Andersen and Fetner 2008; Garretson 2017; Gerhards 2010; Langstaff 2011). An aspect of these attitudinal changes that is of primary interest to the authors in this book is support for lesbians and gays in politics, which has grown steadily since about 1975. In 1978, 26 percent of Americans declared that they would vote for a lesbian or gay presidential candidate; this proportion increased to 59 percent in 1999, 68 percent in 2012 (Jones 2012), and 74 percent in advance of the 2016 presidential election campaign (McCarthy 2015). Support for LGBTQ candidates has also expanded in Canada – and it is stronger than in the United States. According to an Angus Reid poll published in June 2017, Canadians say they would vote for a candidate who is a lesbian (84 percent) or gay (85 percent), compared with 62 percent and 63 percent, respectively, of Americans.

The corollary of this trend is that more out LGBTQ people are elected to political office (and parties are more likely to select them; see de la Dehesa 2010; Marsiaj 2006; Chapters 9 and 10 in this volume). The LGBTQ Representation and Rights Research Initiative at the University of North Carolina at Chapel Hill is a unique research endeavour that compiles data on the descriptive representation of LGBTQ people in national legislatures.[3] According to the initiative, 298 out LGBTQ people sat in various parliaments from 1976 to February 2016 (when the most recent data were collected). Of these, 249 sat in a lower house and 49 – 19 elected and 30 appointed – in an upper house. These individuals were distributed in forty-two countries as diversified as Australia, Bolivia, Canada, Estonia, France, Guatemala, Israel, Lithuania, Mexico, Nepal, Slovakia, the United Kingdom, and the United States. Not surprisingly, paralleling the lopsided proportions of (straight) women and men in politics, there were three and a half times as many gay men as lesbians: of the 249 people who sat in a lower chamber, 50 were identified as lesbians, 178 as gays, 13 as bisexuals, and 4 as trans.[4] The number of LGBTQ MPs sitting in a lower or single house of a national parliament has increased over time: there were 6 in 1983, 8 in 1988, 35 in 1998, 59 in 2003, 78 in 2008, 96 in 2011 (Reynolds 2013, 261), and 147 as of February 2016 (Reynolds 2016). From 1976 to 2016, the British House of Commons included the largest number of out LGBTQ members (51), followed by the Netherlands (24), Germany (23), and Sweden (21) (Reynolds 2016, 13).

These numbers make it possible to put Canada in perspective – in other words, to note its modest performance with regard to the presence of out LGBTQ people in electoral politics. From 1976 to 2016, the Canadian House of Commons had 15 sitting LGBTQ MPs.[5] Following the October 2015 federal election, 6 (1.8 percent) of the 338 seats in the House of Commons were occupied by out lesbian, gay, and bisexual (LGB) members. In comparison, following the May 2015 and June 2017 British elections, the House of Commons had 39 (6.0 percent) and 45 (6.9 percent), respectively, MPs who self-identified as LGBTQ, which was "close to the proportion of Britons estimated to be LGBT" (Reynolds and Magni 2017, 16). As Joanna Everitt, Manon Tremblay, and Angelia Wagner note in Chapter 9, 46 out LGBQ people sat in Canada's federal Parliament from 1979 to 2015 (in the House of Commons or the Senate) or in one of the thirteen provincial and territorial Legislative Assemblies.[6] Several served as cabinet ministers (such as Joanne Bernard in Nova Scotia and Ted Nebbeling in British Columbia), and two were provincial premiers (in Ontario and Prince Edward Island). But many more have been elected at the municipal level as mayor (Glen Murray was mayor of Winnipeg from 1998 to 2004), mayor of a borough (Réal Ménard was mayor of the Montreal borough of Mercier–Hochelaga-Maisonneuve from 2009 to 2017), and city councillor (Kristyn Wong-Tam is currently the councillor for Ward 27 in Toronto; see Chapter 12 in this volume). Although some LGBTQ politicians keep a low profile with regard to their sexual preference and gender identity, even if they are out of the closet, others are fervent advocates of LGBTQ rights and interests. This was certainly the case for Svend Robinson at the federal level (see the Afterword in this volume) and Manon Massé in Quebec provincial politics. By being out and proud (Tremblay develops the meaning of this expression in Chapter 8), these LGBTQ politicians helped to change social attitudes toward "homosexuality" and what is "normal" (Adams 1997; Warner 1999). They also encouraged LGBTQ people to become involved in politics and in their communities, and they brought hope for the future to young and not-so-young LGBTQ people. As Martha Nussbaum (2010, 85) puts it, coming out makes it possible to reverse the "politics of disgust" that plagued the lives of LGBTQ people for years: "The closet had enabled the politics of disgust, making it possible to portray gays and lesbians as unlike ordinary citizens. Coming out ... has a large effect on people's views." Yet, despite these contributions to public life, we know very little about LGBTQ politicians in Canada – or elsewhere in the world. The present volume is intended to fill that gap in knowledge.

Terminology and Scope
Before going farther, I will address some of the notions at the heart of this book. The first is the use of "LGBTQ" rather than "queer," which I employed in my previous book, *Queer Mobilizations: Social Movement Activism and Canadian Public Policy* (Tremblay 2015a). Although "queer" was suitable for a book that focused on social-movement activism, it is not appropriate for one that emphasizes institutional and electoral politics. Today, as in the past, "queer" refers more to civil-society and social-movement politics than to institutional and electoral politics. As Marc Stein (2012, 8–9) notes, it has been used "as a term of derision" and has been associated with radical activism (first, that of lesbian and gay liberationists, then that of Queer Nation). Even today, it is "a negative epithet." It is true that the word is claimed by people who challenge "binary classification systems that treat male and female, masculine and feminine, and heterosexual and homosexual as fixed, innate, and mutually exclusive categories." Yet, although this approach is certainly intellectually fruitful and challenging, it is clearly not commonly used in aspects of institutional and electoral politics such as party

platforms, campaign commitments, and guidelines inspiring the representational role of LGBTQ politicians.

A second issue concerns the false unity that "LGBTQ" seems to promote. In fact, "LGBTQ" is a contested term that encompasses adversarial relationships. Surya Monro and Diane Richardson (2011, 102–3) explain, "There have been longstanding historical tensions between all of the groups included within the acronym 'LGBT' ... Tensions have continued in the sense that there is still misogyny among some gay men, as well as anti-gay sentiment among some lesbians. Some lesbians and gay men refuse to accept that bisexuality exists, and/or attempt to disassociate from trans people" (see also Haider-Markel and Miller 2017; Richardson 2018, 13–14). Stein (2012, 6) warns us not to be fooled by the apparent uniformity of the LGBT label, which, in fact, hides a landscape of oppositions. For instance, he explains that in the 1950s and 1960s, lesbians began naming themselves as such, claiming that "a word other than 'gay' was needed to capture the distinct characteristics and interests of women. In adopting this position, these activists were challenging not only their putative gay male allies, but also community-based 'gay' women." Stein (2012, 6) also states that bisexual activists "have raised compelling criticisms of the gay and lesbian movement for treating their sexual desires, practices, and identities as artificial, illegitimate, and untrustworthy." Today, it seems that although "LGBT" still encompasses a world of diversity, it also expresses something particular in electoral politics. As Andrea Perrella, Steven Brown, and Barry Kay write in Chapter 1, "though the LGB cohort has a distinctive electoral voice, it is certainly not a homogeneous community and should not be conceptualized as a single social or political entity" (page 74).

Third, though the title of this book indicates that LGBTQ people and electoral politics in Canada will be discussed, the primary analytical focus is actually lesbians and gays, as most non-straight politicians in Canada fall into this category. Very few have self-identified publicly as bisexual, trans, or queer. Trans people have become involved in electoral politics only very recently. For example, Jennifer McCreath ran in the 2015 federal election, and Julie Lemieux was elected mayor in a 2017 Quebec municipal election – a first in Canada. Nonetheless, trans individuals are virtually absent from the political class. As noted above, "queer" conveys a sense of derision, radicalism, and transgression (Stein 2012, 8, 9) that is particularly unsuitable to the distinguished nature of institutional and electoral politics. Bisexual people may be more numerous in electoral politics than it seems, but they may refrain from disclosing their sexual preference for fear of arousing prejudices among the electorate, party activists, political elites, the media, or other political actors. Indeed, "bisexuality is a commonly misunderstood identity, and is further complicated by the multiple meanings attached to bisexuality" (McLean 2015, 149; more generally, see Monro 2015). One preconception about bisexual people is that they do not know what they want; sometimes they desire someone of their own sex/gender, sometimes someone of the opposite sex/gender, and sometimes both at the same time! So, the reasoning goes, how can they be trusted – especially – to participate in making decisions that involve the whole community? Similar popular prejudices regarding a perceived unstable and changing gender identity may severely limit the political ambitions of trans people.[7]

Having said that, I think that "LGBTQ" is appropriate for this book. First, although they are mostly invisible and probably few in number, bisexual, trans, and queer people, like their lesbian and gay counterparts, play an active role in Canadian electoral politics, whether as voters (as shown by Andrea Perrella and his colleagues in their article published in 2012 and in Chapter 1 of this volume), party members, activists, or candidates in elections. The addition of "BTQ" to "LGBTQ" takes this fact into account and makes their electoral engagement visible. Second, since the 1990s "LGBT" has been widely used by a reformist stream of sexual-minority activism to frame a broad, public-friendly image of sexual activism (some would describe it as "assimilationist," as Curtis Atkins does in Chapter 11). The bright, colourful rainbow flag contributes to this campaign of seduction. More recently, the "Q" was added to "LGBT" as a strategy of expanded inclusiveness. Third, "LGBTQ" is also increasingly used by mainstream socio-political actors such as politicians and the media to designate the mobilizations and claims of sexual minorities, which is certainly progress in relation to the sadly medical and pathological term "homosexuals." This is especially true of the Trudeau government, which presents itself as being particularly close to LGBTQ people and communities. Finally, I prefer "LGBTQ" to other alternatives because of its relative inclusiveness, its social visibility and public acceptance, and above all, its suitability to the field of electoral politics. To put it simply, unless the context dictates a more appropriate alternative, I use "LGBTQ" throughout this introduction.

A last specification must be made: this book's title announces that it deals with "LGBTQ people," but sometimes the more all-encompassing expressions "LGBTQ communities" and "LGBTQ people and communities" are used. Indeed, an issue related to LGBTQ politics may have more to do with LGBTQ people as they form communities than with LGBTQ people as individuals. The organizing of Gay Pride marches and the dedication of a national monument in memory of an event such as the 1969 Stonewall riots in New York concern first and foremost "LGBTQ communities" because they are the raw materials for the making of cultures, identities, memories, and spaces. Of course, LGBTQ (and straight) people join Pride marches and look at national monuments as individuals, but their participation in a Pride march and their visit to a monument help to form their identities and memories – their sense of belonging to larger social collectives. The very acts by individuals of, say, marching and looking exceed individuality by contributing to something larger: the forming of communities. "LGBTQ communities" are not possible without "LGBTQ people," of course, but the subjectivities of LGBTQ people flow from awareness, the formation of groups, and activism – that is, communities (see, among others, D'Emilio 1998; Miriam Smith 1999). Because LGBTQ people and their communities are intrinsically connected, or because the border between them is blurred, I also use "LGBTQ people and communities."[8]

The authors in this book adopt a "state-centred," as opposed to a "civil-society," approach to electoral politics. Certainly, with its citizens' consultation forums, advocacy groups, boycotts, strikes, demonstrations, and other subtle – and less subtle – tactics of contesting and resisting the state, civil society not only constitutes a fertile ground for nurturing electoral politics but proves to be, in itself, about electoral politics. This is not the approach taken in this book, whose contributors emphasize the structures of the state apparatus that make political representation a reality. Conceptualized in this way, "electoral politics" refers to institutions, actors, processes, and activities. Institutions may be ideological, such as ideas related to political representation and the rights to vote and to run for election, or they may be structural, such as a city council or a parliament. Actors may be individuals, such as candidates and city councillors, or a collective, such as the electorate or a political party. Processes may encompass voting systems as the mechanisms responsible for translating votes into seats, or the electoral process, with all its rules and regulations, various stages, and funding parameters. Activities may include running an election campaign, advocacy by an LGBTQ group to influence a party platform, efforts by an out lesbian mayor to substantively represent LGBTQ constituencies in her city, and holding a leaders' debate. As understood in this book, electoral politics takes place at the municipal, provincial, and federal levels. It includes social-movement activism when the objective of such activism is to influence electoral politics. For example, although ProudPolitics is a social-movement organization firmly rooted in civil-society activism, it is the subject of Chapter 11 because it "focuses on recruiting, training, and electing LGBTQ people to all levels of government in Canada" (page 279). In short, electoral politics is what makes state political representation possible.[9]

The notion of "political representation" provides the background for the relationship between LGBTQ people and electoral politics, which the contributors to this book explore. In her seminal work *The Concept of Representation*, Hanna Pitkin (1967) identifies several forms of political representation: what she calls formalistic views of representation, "standing for" representation, and "acting for" representation. Since Pitkin's book was published, various other conceptions of political representation have been developed (see Dovi 2007; Goodin 2004; Mansbridge 2003, 2011; Rehfeld 2006, 2009; Runciman 2007; Severs 2010, 2012; Squires 2008). Yet, Pitkin's conceptualization is a proven general canvas against which to interpret political representation and has been widely and convincingly used to evaluate the political representation of minorities (notably women). Many recent works on political representation, such as Emanuela Lombardo and Petra Meier's *The Symbolic Representation of Gender* (2014) and Michael Saward's *The Representative Claim* (2010), are based on Pitkin's book, even when they adopt a critical stance on her reflections.

Formalistic views of representation refer to institutional arrangements (such as rules, institutions, and behaviours) surrounding the process of representation: the rights to vote and to run for office, electoral law, the voting system, political parties, and so on (Pitkin 1967, 38–59). The formalistic approach is exemplified in several chapters of this book. In Chapter 4, Dennis Pilon evaluates voters' influence in electing LGBTQ candidates through the various electoral systems. In Chapters 5, 6, and 7, Frédéric Boily and Ève Robidoux-Descary, Brooke Jeffrey, and Alexa DeGagne examine the role of political parties as an intermediary structure between civil society and state apparatus. Political parties aggregate claims expressed by the former – especially by the LGBTQ movement – translate them into a language understandable by the state, and transmit them to the political class. Another role that parties play in representation is to recruit and select candidates for legislative positions. In Canada, it is almost impossible to win a federal, provincial, or territorial seat as an independent candidate; one needs to run under the label of a competitive party.

"Standing-for" representation focuses on the embodiment of representation – "being" versus "doing." It encompasses two variants: descriptive and symbolic. The descriptive version of standing-for representation defends the view that the demographic makeups of the representatives and the represented should resemble each other as much as possible. As John Adams famously put it, a representative legislature "should be an exact portrait, in miniature, of the people at large, as it should think, feel, reason and act like them" (quoted in Pitkin 1967, 60). The authors of several chapters illustrate the descriptive approach to representation. In Chapter 1, Andrea Perrella, Steven Brown, and Barry Kay draw a political profile of the LGB electorate in Canada; in Chapter 9, Joanna Everitt, Manon Tremblay, and Angelia Wagner paint a socio-demographic portrait of out LGBTQ candidates and legislators in Canada. In Chapter 3, Mireille Lalancette and Manon Tremblay look at another interpretation of descriptive representation – how out LGBTQ politicians are depicted by the media. Symbolic representation focuses on the meaning that the represented attribute to their representatives. In Chapter 8, Manon Tremblay reflects on the symbolic dimensions of political representation by assessing the role that emotions play in the representation of LGBTQ people.

"Acting-for" representation puts the emphasis on the activity of representing: the representative's actions and/or opinions "must correspond to or be in accord with the wishes, or needs, or interests, of those for whom he acts, that he must put himself in their place, take their part, act as they would act" (Pitkin 1967, 114). In other words, acting-for representation "means acting in the interest of the represented, in a manner responsive to them" (ibid., 209). In their analysis of how Kathleen Wynne was perceived by voters in the 2014 Ontario election in Chapter 2, Joanna Everitt and Tracey Raney find that she was seen as "best positioned to speak for the LGB community" (page 94). In Chapter 12, which discusses Kristyn Wong-Tam, city councillor for Toronto's Ward 27, Catherine Nash and Andrew Gorman-Murray argue that queer politicians must meet several challenges to substantively represent LGBTQ people because they are required to be responsive to a large array of wishes, needs, and interests expressed by various constituencies, not just those related to LGBTQ communities. That said, Angelia Wagner reminds us in Chapter 10 that not all LGBTQ politicians in Canada have publicly revealed their sexual orientation and that not all of those who have done so see themselves as being responsible for substantively representing LGBTQ communities.

Review of the Literature

As mentioned above, the literature on LGBTQ people's political representation is quite limited, which is merely a reflection of the fact that out LGBTQ people have been present in politics for a short time and are still very few in number.[10] The works on out LGBTQ people and electoral politics have concentrated either on the LGBTQ electorate or on LGBTQ representatives. Both groups of studies can be analyzed through the formalistic, descriptive, and substantive approaches to representation. However, before I review this literature, it might be worth reflecting on the strengths and weaknesses of how LGBTQ people's representation has been studied up to now – mainly as a copy-paste of research on women's political representation.

Can what we know about the political representation of women be used to study the political representation of LGBTQ people? On the one hand, the two groups have much in common. Both are gendered minorities that are typically deprived of socio-political influence and power. Both are markedly underrepresented in politics due to political regimes with formal and informal rules that impede their electability. In this regard, Joanna Everitt (2015, 186) reasons that provincial party regimes in Canada may cause the under-representation of LGBTQ people and women similarly:

> Perhaps the most useful explanation in understanding the patterns of gender and LGB representation across [Canada] comes from structural arguments around the nature of the party system in the various provinces, the electoral success of parties of the left, and internal party rules governing candidate recruitment ... Provinces with the highest levels of women elected tended to also have the highest number of LGB politicians in their legislative assemblies.

Finally, both LGBTQ people and women have developed vibrant social movements since the late 1960s to improve their day-to-day (or substantive) citizenship so that the election of some LGBTQ people and women is a reminder that their citizenship is incomplete and offers the hope that it will be improved in a foreseeable future.

However, LGBTQ people and women differ enough that it is doubtful whether they can be studied as a single entity. For instance, both are gendered minorities, but of a different nature: LGBTQ people carry a legacy of criminalization and social stigma that was not experienced by women, who were, instead, infantilized by laws, cultural customs, and social institutions. Although LGBTQ people and women suffer a deficit of descriptive representation in politics, it remains to be demonstrated that majoritarian voting systems impede, or proportional representation systems enhance, their chances at election. In Chapter 8, Manon Tremblay argues that the first-past-the-post system may favour the election of LGBTQ candidates in ridings where LGBTQ people are geographically concentrated, whereas in Chapter 4, Dennis Pilon displays more confidence that proportional representation systems will increase their presence in politics. The notion of "critical mass" is central to works on women in politics, but Andrew Reynolds (2013, 260) suggests that this concept may not have the same heuristic scope for research on LGBTQ politicians:

> Enhancing gay rights through gay MPs does not necessarily require such a critical mass ... The impact that out gay elected officials have on the voting behavior of their colleagues and resulting public policy may be higher than that of female and minority MPs precisely because their visibility in office is such a new and, in some cases, jarring phenomenon.

Graeme Truelove's observations about Svend Robinson's political career support this point (Truelove 2013; see also his Afterword in this volume). Another example is that although LGBTQ people and women do not form homogeneous voting groups, research by Perrella, Brown, and Kay (2012; Chapter 1 in this volume) shows an underlying trend among the LGB electorate to refrain from voting for the Conservative Party, whereas women are less unanimous in turning their backs on the political right (Schreiber 2008). Last but not least, women can hardly hide their sex/gender, whereas LGBQ politicians can pass as heterosexual and cisgender if they choose – and in so doing downplay the corrosive effects of their minority status but also eradicate the positive effects of their role-model embodiment. In both the past and the present, several LGBQ politicians in Canada have opted to remain in the closet, which proved very effective for some of them (one example is Richard Hatfield, premier of New Brunswick during the 1970s and 1980s). It should be added that this option was possible in part because the Canadian LGBTQ movement had not widely adopted the controversial strategy used in the United States of "outing" closeted politicians who worked behind the scenes against LGBTQ rights and equality (Stein 2012, 187–88; for the United Kingdom, see Donna Smith 2012).[11]

Therefore, although researchers on LGBTQ people in politics may draw several lessons from studies on women in politics, they should exercise caution when they consider applying a copy-paste research approach to studies on political representation by women and by LGBTQ people. Researchers on LGBTQ people in electoral politics must develop their own dynamic, especially with regard to theories and concepts.

The LGBTQ Electorate

The first trend in research on LGBTQ people and electoral politics is related to the electorate, notably its demographics and voting behaviours. Descriptive, formalistic, and substantive conceptions of political representation prove to be meaningful categories within which to organize works in this field. Descriptive representation focuses on the identity of political actors – in this case, LGBTQ voters. What does an LGBTQ constituency look like? Do LGBTQ voters differ from their straight counterparts, and, if so, how? How are LGBTQ-related concerns perceived when it comes to elections? The most comprehensive (and groundbreaking) study undertaken to date on LGBTQ voters is Mark Hertzog's *The Lavender Vote* (1996). Basically, analyzing data from diverse national and local exit polls conducted with self-identified lesbians, gays, and bisexual women and men (LGB people) in the early 1990s, Hertzog concludes that a "lavender vote" exists in the United States – that is, the socio-demographic and ideological profile of self-identified LGB people differs from that of the average heterosexual voter. This thesis cannot fail to remind us of the numerous studies on the "women's vote" that painted a portrait of the female voter and her voting behaviours.

Research conducted on the LGBTQ electorate from a descriptive perspective embraces two broad directions. Certain authors have described the LGBTQ electorate according to some of its socio-demographic traits; others have evaluated the role that sex/gender stereotypes ultimately play in the election context. In terms of demographics, Hertzog (1996, 53–54) estimates the electoral weight of LGB self-identifiers at somewhere between 1.2 and 1.5 percent of the electorate, which is comparable to that of many ethnic, racial, and religious groups in the United States. Gary Gates (2011) estimates that 3.5 percent of adult Americans identify as lesbian, gay, or bisexual and 0.3 percent as transgender. Analyzing the political representation of LGB citizens in the US House of Representatives, Eric Hansen and Sarah Treul (2015) observe that LGB people's weak demographic weight does not prevent straight members from representing them. Indeed, though modest, the electoral presence of LGB voters cannot be ignored, not least because their support may be decisive in close elections. In the United States, Paul Snell (2017) argues that for straight congresspersons, joining the Congressional LGBT Equality Caucus is a way to signify that they represent LGBTQ constituents in their electoral districts. Hertzog (1996, 54–59) also writes that LGB voters tend to be slightly younger, better educated, employed in higher occupational positions, living in a medium- to large-sized city, and much less religious than their straight counterparts. The income of LGB self-identifiers is not markedly higher than that of straight people, challenging the widespread "pink money" stereotype.[12]

Several other researchers have confirmed and added details to Hertzog's findings regarding the demographics of LGB voters. Robert Bailey (1998, 2) observes the increasing proportion of self-identified non-straight voters in the American electorate, from 1.3 percent in 1990 to 5.0 percent in 1996. In his *Gay Politics, Urban Politics*, Bailey (1999, 101–10) contends that self-identified LGB voters tend to be young, highly educated, and urban. Patrick Egan, Murray Edelman, and Kenneth Sherrill (2008, 6) estimate that in 2007, LGB voters represented 2.9 percent of the American electorate. They also note that self-identified LGB voters were younger and better educated than the average American (Egan, Edelman, and Sherrill 2008, 1, 7). Like Hertzog (1996), they disprove the "pink money" assumption: a majority of LGB people have an annual household income of $49,999 or less, whereas a majority of non-LGB American adults earn at least $50,000 annually (Egan, Edelman, and Sherrill 2008, 7). Using data from an American national probability sample of LGB self-identifiers, Gregory Herek et al. (2010) report similar trends: compared with the general population, self-identified LGB people are younger, more highly educated, and not as religious. In Europe, François Kraus (2012) finds that between 2006 and 2010, the LGB electorate represented 6.5 percent of the French adult population; this electorate was younger and better educated than the heterosexual electorate, and its members worked in top-position jobs.

Other studies have looked at the descriptive representation of LGBTQ voters through the lens of stereotypes. This perspective is interesting mainly because of its original and broad reading of descriptive representation: one's identity is determined by "objective" (or measurable) traits, such as age and level of education, but also by subjective (or evaluative) perceptions. Perceptions are never neutral; they are affected by a wide array of factors, including stereotypes. As Charles Stangor (2009, 2) explains, "Stereotypes represent the traits that we view as characteristic of social groups, or of individual members of those groups, and particularly those that differentiate groups from each other. In short, they are the traits that come to mind quickly when we think about the groups." Although stereotypes are ubiquitous in social life and individuals' perceptions, their apparent negativity and overgeneralization make them problematic in light of the goals of equality and justice that Western societies under democratic governments are supposed to pursue. Stereotypes may be seen as one of the devices that contribute to defining and structuring power relations in any society, whether they are based on gender, sexual orientation and gender identity, race/ethnicity, social class, language, or other criteria. For instance, stereotypes contribute to the construction of gender, which Amy Mazur and Gary Goertz (2008, 1) define "as a complex process that involves the social construction of men's and women's identities in relation to each other." Gender rules determine how a woman should feel, look, and behave. She is expected to be sexually and emotionally attracted to men, must have long hair, and should cross her legs when sitting (no womanspreading on public transit!). Stereotypes are disseminated by several vehicles, including the media. Many works have demonstrated their detrimental impact on the election of women to office (among others, see Lawless and Fox 2010; Sanbonmatsu and Dolan 2009; on how gender influences partisanship, see McDermott 2016).

Since heterosexuality stands at the heart of gender (this is a core idea of Judith Butler's 1990 *Gender Trouble*), and since LGBTQ people do not conform to the lifelong diktat of sexual desire for and acts with the opposite sex, as prescribed by the heteronormative component of gender, it is reasonable to expect that stereotypes may dampen their participation in politics. For instance, commenting on the new sex education curriculum in February 2015, Tory MPP Monte McNaughton openly questioned the competence of Ontario premier Kathleen Wynne to legislate on this matter: "It's not the Premier of Ontario's job, *especially Kathleen Wynne*, to tell parents what's age-appropriate for their children [in terms of sex education]" (quoted in Morrow 2015, emphasis added). Instead of accusing McNaughton of lesbophobia, Wynne responded by emphasizing that her personal and political experiences qualified her to act on sex education:

> What is it that especially disqualifies me for the job that I'm doing? Is it that I'm a woman? Is it that I'm a mother? Is it that I have a master's of education? Is it that I was a school council chair? Is it that I was the minister of education? ... What is it exactly that the member opposite thinks disqualifies me from doing the job that I'm doing? What is that? (ibid.)

We cannot know what, according to McNaughton, made Wynne incompetent, but his words conveyed the shadow of pedophilia: homosexuals, the stereotype goes, are child molesters who need to recruit children because they themselves cannot reproduce.[13] In her research on lesbian and gay activism in municipal politics in 1980s England, Davina Cooper (1994, 161–63) points out that lesbians do not escape the stereotype that they need to recruit girls to satisfy their uncontrollable lust. In Cooper's view, such a conception of lesbians (and gays) is grounded in the idea that they are repulsive – dirty, smelly, and contagious. In *From Disgust to Humanity,* Nussbaum (2010, 206) argues that the idea of recruiting is central to the politics of disgust that once publicly demonized lesbians and gays by suggesting that recruiting means contaminating. It was to mock this "sinful" stereotype that Harvey Milk, the first openly gay man elected to public office in California, started his speeches with "My name is Harvey Milk, and I'm here to recruit you." By so doing, Nussbaum (2010, 206) states, Milk turned on its head the stereotype of lesbians and gays as "child molesters/recruiters," moving from a politics of disgust ("I am here to sicken you and spread my contagion") to a politics of humanity ("I am here to ask you to join a movement for freedom and inclusion").

How do stereotypes, which are certainly amplified by the media, influence the involvement of LGBTQ people in electoral politics? In other words, how do straight voters evaluate out LGBTQ candidates and elected officials? By and large, three findings may be drawn from the research: that stereotypes have no effect, negative effects, or positive effects. Ewa Golebiowska and Cynthia Thomsen (1999) show that stereotypes do not influence voter evaluations of lesbian and gay candidates who disclose their non-heterosexual status late in their electoral campaign. Andrew Reynolds and Gabriele Magni (2017, 26) confirm this observation in a recent analysis of candidates' vote share in the May 2015 UK general election: "On average, sexual orientation does not have a negative impact on candidates' vote share. In other words, the electorate does not punish LGBT candidates over straight ones because of their sexual orientation." In reality, sexual orientation has a positive effect, as "LGBT Labour candidates do better than their straight colleagues" (ibid., 35) in terms of vote share. That being said, stereotypes may also have a negative impact on LGBTQ people who contemplate a political career. For instance, Rebekah Herrick and Sue Thomas (1999, 2001) find that straight voters perceive lesbian and gay candidates as more interested in LGBTQ people's rights than are non-LGBTQ candidates and therefore as less electorally viable. It is certainly no coincidence that people are less willing to vote for LGBTQ candidates than for straight ones; indeed, according to Donald Haider-Markel (2010, 149), "About 25 percent of the electorate is unlikely to vote for a gay or lesbian candidate for nearly any office. These individuals are more likely to be conservative, Republican, male, religious, and have less education and live in rural areas." This finding illuminates, at least in part, why several LGBTQ politicians come out after their first election – that is, after having built a reputation as "good politicians," which, they hope, will compensate for potential negative effects arising from the disclosure of their non-heterosexual sexuality.

Even so, Ewa Golebiowska (2001, 557) finds that voter evaluations of lesbian and gay candidates vary according to the gender of both the electors and the candidates:

> Female "voters" evinced a preference for the masculine candidate (gay candidate who did not fit his group's stereotype over the gay stereotype-consistent candidate and the lesbian candidate who fit her group's stereotype over her stereotype-inconsistent counterpart). Male "voters," in contrast, were less willing to vote for the stereotype-consistent candidate, regardless of his or her gender, than [for] his or her stereotype-inconsistent counterpart.[14]

Alesha Doan and Donald Haider-Markel (2010) obtain similar results, as do Everitt and Raney in Chapter 2 of this volume: the gender of both voters and candidates plays a key role in shaping opinions regarding lesbian and gay would-be elected officials. More specifically, women voters express more-liberal opinions than do their male counterparts about lesbian and gay candidates, and they are significantly less likely than men to attribute negative traits to lesbian candidates. Consistent with gender stereotypes, lesbian candidates are perceived as better suited to handle compassion issues (such as education). Yet, contrary to gender stereotyping, female voters evaluate lesbians more positively on military issues than they do gay candidates. In a sense, this supports Golebiowska's (2001) finding that female voters express a preference for masculine-typed candidates. Lesbian candidates do not suffer double discrimination because of their gender and sexual orientation (Haider-Markel and Bright 2014; but for a different opinion, see Bailey and Nawara 2017). Furthermore, it is possible that the intersection of gender and sexual orientation stereotypes benefits lesbians in politics. As Doan and Haider-Markel (2010, 86) explain, "The masculine characteristics stereotypically associated with lesbians by heterosexual women interact to offset, and even compliment [sic], the gender stereotypes associated with female political candidates, particularly regarding the less tangible (but masculinized) dimensions of political capital, such as a candidate's strength of character and ability to handle the military." To put it simply, gender- and sexual-orientation-based stereotypes intersect to shape voter perceptions of LGBTQ candidates.

In sum, research undertaken from a descriptive representation perspective reveals that self-declared LGB voters, first, hold an electoral weight that political parties ignore to their peril, and second, are distinguished from heterosexual voters by their demographics. In addition, voters rely on stereotypes that are based on gender and sexual orientation (sometimes popularized in the media) to assess lesbians and gays in politics, which may create a distorted descriptive picture of their electoral involvement.

The substantive conception of representation concentrates on interests: electing is a means of defending and promoting the perceived interests of a community. This approach to political representation has inspired a huge number of studies that explore whether women in politics substantively represent women (among others, see Celis et al. 2008; Childs and Krook 2009; Escobar-Lemmon and Taylor-Robinson 2014). A rich literature suggests that the political left ("liberal" in the North American context) is more supportive of LGBTQ rights than is the political right ("conservative" – even if the right and conservatism are not necessarily synonymous; see Chapter 5 in this volume). As a consequence, political attitudes and partisan preferences of LGBTQ voters should be congruent with the political left/liberal. An underlying trend that emerges from studies is that LGBTQ voters describe themselves as liberals, adopt liberal positions on socio-political issues, and, in the United States, strongly support the Democratic Party. In some ways, these ideological and partisan stances are not a surprise since they reflect the demographics of LGBTQ voters (young, highly educated, urban). However, it is troubling that American LGBTQ voters are electorally captured by the Democratic Party (Charles Smith 2007; see also Bishin and Smith 2013). The "electoral capture" theory suggests that when a party holds a monopoly on the representation of a group, it can take the group's electoral support for granted. Electoral capture is not without unfortunate consequences, as Snell (2017, 314) observes: "LGBTQ voters' allegiance to the Democratic Party means that the Democratic Party may ignore their interests without electoral retribution."

Hertzog (1996, 84, 86; see also Lublin 2005) finds that self-declared LGB voters, more than straight voters, identify with and vote for the Democratic

Party. More specifically, Donald Haider-Markel and Patrick Miller (2017, 271) observe that since the 1990s, "roughly 20–25 percent of LGBT Americans identify as politically conservative and tend to vote Republican." However, the unity of LGB voters behind the Democrats appears to be less convincing than is their "general aversion to the Republican Party" (Hertzog 1996, 60; see also Bailey 1999, 117–18).[15] Self-identifying LGB electors are very liberal (Hertzog 1996, 60–68). More specifically, they are more likely than are straight voters with similar demographics to self-declare as liberals and to support liberal positions on socio-political issues; for instance, more of them oppose the death penalty and see the environment as a top electoral issue (ibid., 84–85). A highly interesting observation concerns the cutting-edge issue of abortion, for which gaps exist among both non-LGB people and LGB self-identifiers. About 40 percent of the former and 60 percent of the latter think that abortion should "always" be legal (ibid., 84). More tellingly, among gay men, nonfeminist lesbians, and feminist lesbians, 9 percent, 18 percent, and 48 percent, respectively, consider abortion a top electoral issue (ibid., 87). This leads Hertzog (ibid., 69) to state that there is "a strong 'feminism gap' within the lesbian and gay community ... Nonfeminist gays and lesbians are far closer on many issues to the heterosexual population than are lesbian feminists." Lesbian feminists have been at the vanguard of both the women's movement and the gay liberationist movement. As Lilian Faderman (1991, 209) notes, "Lesbian-feminist revolutionaries wanted a restructuring of the entire system of heterosexuality, which, they declared, was at the root of women's oppression." Cracks are numerous in the "LGBTQ" label.

Again, several studies support Hertzog's pioneering observations. In France, Kraus (2012) finds that the LGB electorate mostly supports the political left. In the United States, by and large, studies show that a plurality (if not a majority) of self-declared LGB voters are liberal (they self-identify as such and endorse liberal positions on socio-political issues). They also support the Democratic Party (Bailey 1999, 103, 117–18; Egan, Edelman, and Sherrill 2008, 15; Herek et al. 2010). Gregory Lewis, Marc Rogers, and Kenneth Sherrill (2011) not only find greater political liberalism among LGB self-identifiers than among straight voters, but also that the former are more likely than are similarly liberal heterosexual electors of the same sex to vote for Democratic candidates. The authors also confirm Hertzog's (1996) finding that self-identified LGB people hold more liberal positions on socio-political issues than do average straight Americans (for instance, they opposed war in Iraq earlier and more strongly; Lewis, Rogers, and Sherrill 2011, 674). Eric Swank and Breanne Fahs (2013) suggest that ideas (being liberal) and demographics (being young and highly educated) mix with and influence each other to fuel the electoral activism of LGB people. A recent study by Reynolds and Magni (2017), however, compels us to mitigate the picture of LGBT voters as almost blindly supporting the political left. In the 2015 British election, the Conservatives and Labour shared an equal proportion (26 percent) of the LGBT votes.

Both LGB and non-LGB electors cast their votes for diverse reasons, including structural factors (such as a sense of political duty) and temporal situation (such as a referendum on gay rights). In a book whose subject straddles electoral politics and social-movement activism, Amy Stone (2012) highlights how anti-gay ballot initiatives in the United States have both mobilized the LGBT movement and influenced its goals and claims, its tactical repertoire, and its interpretations of victory and defeat. These interpretations are vital not only to sustaining the morale of LGBT activists and keeping their collective identity alive, but also to responding better to the specificities of each local struggle.[16] Many authors have demonstrated that debates over gay-rights issues during an electoral campaign prompt LGBTQ people to vote. For instance, Ellen Riggle, Sharon Rostosky, and Sharon Horne (2009, 86) point out that "having a marriage amendment on the ballot was associated with LGB individuals' increased political participation and voting." This finding also holds true for Canada. During the 2006 federal election, the issue of same-sex marriage was, for lesbians and gays living outside of Quebec, a definitive factor in both how they voted – against the Conservative Party – and how their votes differed from those of heterosexuals with similar demographics and ideological stances (Perrella, Brown, and Kay 2012; see also Chapter 1 in this volume).[17]

In sum, using a substantive representation approach to analyze LGB voters reveals that lesbians, gays, and bisexual women and men form a distinctive constituency that is characterized by a progressive electoral voice. However, we cannot be certain that all voting systems have an equal capacity to transform this progressiveness into effective representation.

Formalistic representation targets institutions that govern the process of electoral representation, such as the rights to vote and to run for office, the electoral system, and political parties. Although electoral institutions may seem neutral, they are certainly not; they express power relations among citizens according to a plethora of factors such as gender, age, social class, residency, and race/ethnicity. Setting the voting age at eighteen, for instance, precludes those aged sixteen and seventeen from participating in public decisions, the consequences of which they will have to live with. Requiring a $1,000 deposit from candidates impedes the poorest citizens from running for office. Using a majoritarian voting system contributes to generating parliaments that are less diversified than those resulting from a proportional voting system. Provision of public financing to political parties is a way of reducing corruption by limiting the power of the richest to influence politicians and their decisions.

There is almost no research analyzing the LGBTQ electorate from a formalistic perspective of political representation (unlike for women voters); even Hertzog's study is silent on this topic. Two essays by Darren Rosenblum (1995, 1996) and one by Manon Tremblay (2019) are notable exceptions here. Rosenblum argues that proportional representation systems promote lesbian and gay interests. Electoral activism by lesbians and gays in Mexico confirms this point: "Closed proportional representation candidate lists determined electoral success by permitting activists to make their case for a favorable spot on candidate lists to a relatively narrow audience of party leaders rather than appealing to the electorate at large" (de la Dehesa 2010, 99). However, "closed proportional representation candidate lists" also require that LGBTQ people trust the parties to represent LGBTQ-related concerns and interests, which may be risky, as discussed below.

Rosenblum acknowledges that in certain contexts, a single-member district-based voting system may assist lesbians and gays to elect one of their own. This is a stark contrast with the situation of women: the literature reaches near consensus about the negative effects of majoritarian voting systems on their election (although the results of recent research mitigate this widely accepted idea; see Fortin-Rittberger and Rittberger 2014; Moser and Scheiner 2012, 208–35; Roberts, Seawright, and Cyr 2013; Rosen 2013; Salmond 2006; Schmidt 2009). Yet, Rosenblum (1996, 121) states, "Only geographically defined lesbian and gay communities have the opportunity to elect officials who represent their interests." Geographical concentration was an argument put forward to support proposals aimed at drawing electoral boundaries so as to permit representation of LGB people in Los Angeles, New York, Philadelphia, and San Francisco (Hertzog 1996, 12). More specifically, in the Manhattan borough of New York, Rosenblum (1995, 194) explains how, to meet electoral districting exigencies, advocates of lesbian and gay representation advanced diverse pieces of evidence to geographically map their communities: "Maps depicting previous electoral support for lesbian and gay interests; maps reflecting community group member lists; and maps reflecting the locations of lesbian and gay businesses and community institutions." James Button, Kenneth Wald, and Barbara Rienzo (1999) suggest, however, that a cluster of lesbian and gay constituents in a city is not necessarily associated with the election of lesbian and gay politicians. The presence of an identifiable and sizable LGBTQ community within a riding does not guarantee that an out LGBTQ candidate will be elected, as exemplified by the defeat of Svend Robinson in Vancouver Centre in the 2006 federal election (Truelove 2013, 287–88).

Most LGBTQ voters do not live in geographically identified LGBTQ communities, and consequently they cannot benefit from the electoral influence that a district-based voting system may provide to spatially concentrated minorities. Indeed, LGBTQ people have characteristics that make their political representation difficult: amid the challenges arising from their geographical dispersion, their belonging to a sexual minority is not always clear, as they can pass as heterosexuals, and their identities, like those of other citizens, are complex and intersectional. As in the case of women, whose representation benefits from proportional voting systems (see Rule and Zimmerman 1994; Tremblay 2012), Rosenblum (1996, 120) argues, "A proportional representation system can effectively serve the interests of communities that have otherwise been unable to elect sufficient numbers of representatives."

For several reasons, the aforementioned traits of lesbian and gay voters do not preclude their representation under a proportional voting system. First, as such systems are based on ideas, not location, lesbian and gay voters do not need to be geographically concentrated to be represented: "Proportional representation does not require that a group be officially identifiable. Political positions rather than place of residence determine representation" (Rosenblum 1996, 143). Thus, a proportional voting system allows the representation of lesbians and gays who choose to reside outside geographically defined lesbian and gay communities because, for example, they are not open about their sexuality or "because they could not afford to live in expensive gay neighborhoods" (ibid., 144). This argument is particularly convincing for lesbians, who, in addition to suffering greater poverty than gays, may find it hard to deal with the "gay/male/testosterone culture" of gay ghettos (see Nash 2001). Second, because ideas are more relevant than residency, proportional representation encourages like-minded citizens from different backgrounds to unify around common interests and to form coalitions and constituencies. Therefore, reasons Rosenblum (1996, 154), "In a proportional system, lesbians and gay men would form constituencies that candidates would court. In order to gain the votes of these active constituencies, representatives would advocate for the advancement of lesbian and gay interests." Analyzing LGBT electoral activism in Latin America, Rafael de la Dehesa (2010, 152–53) explains how sectors of the Mexican feminist and LGBT movements coalesced and formed political alliances to gain legislative representation. Third, proportional voting systems can advance lesbian and gay interests by "weaken[ing] majority rule and empower[ing] minorities ... Although a proportional system preserves the ability of a group that constitutes a majority to exercise its power, that majority does not succeed to the exclusion of minorities" (Rosenblum 1996, 141). Whereas majoritarian voting systems are designed to form a majority party government, proportional "systems intend to reflect, as exactly as possible, the social forces and political groups in the population" (Nohlen 1984, 87). The principle of representation inspiring proportional voting systems is therefore better suited to the advancement of lesbian and gay interests. Last but not least, Rosenblum (1996, 145) takes up an argument that Harvey Milk made in his Hope Speech (see Chapter 8 in this volume): the election of lesbians and gays will command respect from the larger community, reduce the political self-alienation of lesbians and gays, strengthen their confidence in the political regime, and encourage other minorities to be involved in politics. According to Dieter Nohlen (1984, 87), a voting system that is purposed to represent "the social forces and political groups in the population" (including the LGBTQ electorate) is more likely than are majority/plurality electoral systems to reach these ideals.

In her essay "Uncovering the Gendered Effects of Voting Systems," Tremblay (2019) reflects on the interaction between sexuality and voting systems. As a rule, researchers who study electoral systems have assumed that electoral actors (that is, voters and candidates) are heterosexuals and that sexuality and voting systems do not influence each other. However, Tremblay (2019) states that there is every reason to believe that voting systems are not immune to the candidates' sexuality and that sexuality provides varying electoral assets, depending on the type of voting system. For instance, it is well known that in multi-member constituencies a party has an electoral incentive to field a diversified list of candidates. Yet, as Tremblay (2019, 106) notes, "It remains to be demonstrated that LGBT people offer the same 'electoral appeal' as do women." Another example: in Peru each voter has two votes, and activists who hope to increase the presence of women in politics have used this feature to promote the slogan, "Of your two preferential votes, cast one for a woman." Yet, it is hard to imagine applying this rationale to LGBTQ candidates: "Of your two preferential votes, cast one for a lesbian"! Tremblay (2019, 108) concludes, "This discursive resource is simply not available to the LGBT movement."

Although at first glance there is every reason to believe that proportional voting systems are conducive to the representation of LGBTQ constituencies, the examples above show the need for caution. Indeed, in his comparative study of national parliaments, Reynolds (2013, 263) observes, "The expectation that LGBT members are clearly more likely to be elected from list PR systems than from majoritarian systems is confounded by the data ... The number of gay MPs elected under single-member district systems has tracked closely the number elected by the list system" – an observation that Dennis Pilon challenges in Chapter 4 of this volume.

LGBTQ Representatives
A second line of research on LGBTQ people and electoral politics focuses on out LGBTQ representatives. Here again, formalistic, descriptive, and substantive

conceptions of political representation are useful to organizing the knowledge in this field: how LGBTQ people get elected (formalistic representation), who they are (descriptive representation), and what they do once in office (substantive representation). Donald Haider-Markel addresses these concerns in *Out and Running* (2010), the most in-depth study conducted on LGBTQ representatives. Using a wide range of qualitative and quantitative methods, he explores "whether a candidate's sexual orientation influences electoral support and election outcomes in state legislative elections, and whether increased description [sic] representation for the LGBT community increases the representation of the community's interests in the state policy process" (ibid., x). He also examines whether the greater visibility of out LGBT representatives engenders anti-LGBT policy backlashes, an issue of clear relevance considering the strong anti-gay activism in the United States since the 1980s (see also Fetner 2008; Stone 2012). A major finding of Haider-Markel (2010, 63) is that "potential LGBT candidates are strategic in choosing when, where, and how they run." Billy Kluttz (2014) adds to this observation that LGBT candidates are also strategic in selecting when, where, and how they disclose their non-heterosexual identity.

A major topic of studies on LGBTQ representation undertaken from a formalistic perspective concerns interactions between political parties and LGBTQ movement activists, including how the movement has lobbied parties for representation and how parties have responded to these claims. According to the formalistic reading of political representation, parties play key roles in the process of legislative representation. They contribute to the political socialization of the population and encourage its participation in the polity: for instance, they bring certain issues into the public square and encourage debate on them. They identify citizens who are interested in activism by recruiting them as party members or as volunteers in election campaigns, as well as in other ways. Parties propose a vision of society – what its collective values are, how they can be reached, what model of redistribution of collective wealth should be privileged, how social relations should be organized, and so on. Parties select and train future political elites and, eventually, provide a team of politicians that is ready to govern. In other words, parties are central actors in bringing representation to daily life, and therefore the LGBTQ movement cannot ignore them – at the risk of suffering the consequences.

By and large, studies on LGBTQ people and political parties fall into two areas: parties as spaces of LGBTQ activism and parties as vehicles of LGBTQ representation. LGBTQ activism may occur within parties or outside of them. Michael Hanagan (1998, 4) synthesizes these relationships in five basic models: articulation, permeation, alliance, independence, and competition. In articulation, social-movement organizations (SMOs) "are organized around the party program and articulate the policy positions of parties to constituencies where parties hope to mobilize support and to recruit members." In permeation, SMOs work inside parties to gain their support for their goal, an example being the LGBT Commission in the New Democratic Party of Canada (NDP). In alliance, SMOs and parties maintain their independence but work together on an ad hoc basis on specific issues. In independence, SMOs remain independent from parties and put pressure on them. In competition, SMOs themselves become parties. In *Queering the Public Sphere in Mexico and Brazil*, the most extensive study of LGBT activism regarding party politics conducted to date, de la Dehesa (2010) amply illustrates each of these models. His thorough analysis of LGBT activists' engagements with the state in Brazil and Mexico from the 1970s onward, with a particular focus on parties, delivers several important findings – notably that LGBTQ electoral activism in parties entails both dangers and gains.

On the "dangers" side, playing into the hands of party politics may seriously limit LGBTQ activists' autonomy of thought and action. They may be forced to compromise on their principles, be used to attain the party's alleged superior interests, or be sidelined or even hidden on the grounds that they may irritate the sensitivities of certain voters and thus undermine the party's vitality and electoral fortunes. To illustrate, de la Dehesa (2010, 93) underlines that although they are important, alliances involve trade-offs that can be costly to LGBT activism: "The extent to which activists should commit to issues that many did not see as directly relevant to sexual politics as well as the sometimes extensive sacrifices that potential allies often demanded in the movement's own agenda, particularly in terms of visibility." In Chapter 7 of this volume, Alexa DeGagne describes "moments of co-operation as well as those of compromise, exclusion, and acrimony" (page 202) in the relations between LGBTQ people and the New Democratic Party of Canada.

On the "gains" side, as parties are the antechamber to state power, they are vital allies of LGBTQ people, and activism within their ranks is an indispensable tactic in advancing the LGBTQ agenda. Indeed, as political actors in an intermediary position between the state and civil society, parties offer forums in which LGBTQ activists can mobilize and voice their claims, which eventually will be included in the party program and influence the public decision-making process. Yet, as Juan Marsiaj (2006, 167) puts it, "Parties matter in generating policy and legislative change in favour of sexual minorities." They may also take a more diffuse role in supporting LGBTQ activism – for instance, by legitimizing the cause. At the 1981 national convention of the Brazilian Workers Party, the leader at the time, Luiz Inacio "Lula" da Silva declared, "We do not accept that homosexuality be treated as an illness in our party, much less as a police matter. We defend the respect that these people deserve and invite them to join the greater effort of building a new society" (de la Dehesa 2010, 62). In other words, parties can be conceived of as a two-way (bottom-up and top-down) discursive bridge between state and civil society that fuels LGBTQ electoral activism.

The capacity of parties to be vehicles for LGBTQ representation is conditioned by a number of factors, starting with ideological orientations. As is the case for women's interests, the willingness of parties to advance LGBTQ interests varies according to their ideological posture: by and large, left-leaning parties are more welcoming than their right-leaning counterparts to LGBTQ electoral activism. Together, Chapters 4, 5, 6, and 7 in this volume confirm this general observation for Canada. In addition, Joanna Everitt and Michael Camp (2014, 242) observe that "the NDP is the party that has run the greatest number of LGBT candidates," and de la Dehesa (2010, 61–177) and Marsiaj (2006) give many examples of this left-right split in Mexico and Brazil, respectively (for a recent example in Australia, see Williams and Sawer 2017). Haider-Markel (2010) notes that in the United States, not only do out LGBT candidates disproportionately run under the banner of the Democratic Party (see also Snell 2017) but those who run as Republicans choose districts whose ideological profile resembles the Democratic profile. Haider-Markel (2010, 81) states that

> the distribution of LGBT candidates across state legislative districts is not random – LGBT candidates are more likely to run for office in districts where more citizens have a college education, more residents are Hispanic or LGBT, average income is somewhat lower, and there are fewer African Americans and Protestant fundamentalists. In addition there is some evidence that candidates are more likely to run in more urban districts with high Democratic Party registration.

Hence, it appears that ideology is more than a party label. It also encompasses a socio-political ecology that, in turn, conditions party ideology (for instance, a right-leaning party can water down its ideological stances in a progressive riding). Finally, the sole international comparative study that examined out LGBT legislators finds that the majority were elected for left-wing or Green parties (Reynolds 2013).

Yet, things are not black or white; that is, right-wing parties may manifest sympathy to LGBTQ representation, and left-wing parties may resist it. Analyzing Conservative, Labour, and Liberal Democrat election manifestos in the United Kingdom from 1979 to 2010, Paul Chaney (2013) shows that although

LGBT issues were virtually absent from Conservative programs throughout this period, their number increased dramatically in the 2010 election. Certainly, from the turn of the century onward, debates on same-sex marriage in the Western world have made it possible for a panoply of LGBTQ issues to gain social legitimacy and be discussed politically – a social legitimacy that may have helped to divert attention from other, more sensitive issues that challenge sex and gender norms in a more substantive way (Haider-Markel and Miller 2017). According to Peter Kerr, Christopher Byrne, and Emma Foster (2011, 195), this increased social legitimacy can also be interpreted as a strategy to promote a vision of a Conservative Party that has turned the page on the Thatcher era and is now "pluralistic and willing to embrace groups that were heretofore seen as alien to traditional Tory voters, including gays and lesbians." In addition, several LGBTQ groups that are dedicated to electoral politics are formally or informally associated with conservative-leaning parties. These include Gay Liberals, which is linked to the Liberal/National Party in Australia; GaySVP, to the Swiss People's Party; LGBTory, to the Conservative parties in Canada and the United Kingdom; and the Log Cabin Republicans, to the Republican Party in the United States (see Chapter 5 in this volume). Another argument to support the idea that right-wing parties may not be systematically hostile to LGBTQ electoral activism and representation is that out LGBTQ candidates run under the banner of conservative parties, and several have been elected. For instance, in the 2017 UK general election, forty-two lesbians and gays ran as Conservative candidates, and nineteen of them were elected to the House of Commons (Reynolds 2017; on the 2015 UK election, see Carey 2016, 14; Reynolds 2015).

If it is not possible to describe right-wing parties as necessarily averse to LGBTQ people and communities, neither has it been possible to form an idyllic image of the relationship between left-leaning parties and LGBTQ people and communities. Indeed, Chaney's (2013) study of the election manifestos of UK parties reveals that the Labour Party was not particularly committed to LGBT issues from 1979 to 2005 (though it was more so than its Conservative rival). For instance, Stephen Jeffery-Poulter (1991, 166) notes that the Labour Party's "Campaign Document" for the 1983 general election restricted its commitment to protecting homosexuals "from unfair discrimination." In the same vein, Cooper (1994, 19–38) observes that when the British Labour Party was in control of some local governments during the 1980s, it manifested an unconvincing – at best – commitment to promoting lesbian and gay equality. Three more authors temper the idea that left-wing parties are heaven for LGBTQ electoral activism. Recounting her activist experience in the British Labour Party during the 1970s and 1980s, Ann Tobin (1988, 1990) highlights several instances of sexism, heterosexism, anti-feminism and anti-lesbianism, uneasy coalitions, and disturbing compromises that made her feel alienated as a lesbian and a feminist activist:

> The cultural and social life of the Labour Party is built around the pub or club, the cultural realm of the white working-class [heterosexual] male. If you don't fit into that culture – because you choose not to, or because your own culture and background is in opposition to this lifestyle – then the Labour Party and trade union movement is doubly inaccessible. (Tobin 1988, 257)

Also writing about Great Britain, Simon Edge (1995) documents the incapacity of the Socialist Workers' Party to envisage gay issues as having value in themselves – that is, as independent from class struggle or petit bourgeois deviance. Analyzing the relationship between the Workers Party and the lesbian and gay movement in Brazil from the 1970s to the mid-1990s, James Green (2000) cites several examples of heterosexist prejudices, homophobic attitudes, disappointing alliances, and the bitter feeling of having been snookered. Yet, these three authors agree that the political left, for all its flaws, "provides the most viable political forum for legislative approaches to guaranteeing equal rights [to LGBTQ people]" (ibid., 68). All of this disproves the view that left-wing parties are wholeheartedly sympathetic to representing LGBTQ-related concerns and interests.

In sum, the formalistic conception of political representation teaches us that institutions matter to the representation of minorities, be they women or LGBTQ people (see also the definitive works by Miriam Smith 2008, 2010, 2015a, 2015b on this issue). A striking example of this is the Ladlad Party in the Philippines. The Constitution of 1987 establishes that one-fifth of the representatives will be elected by a party-list system. The Philippine Supreme Court has interpreted that these list seats are for the sole use of parties that represent "marginalized" and "underrepresented" sectors of society (Cardozo 2014, 40). LGBT Filipinos have seized this institutional opening to create a specifically LGBT political party, with candidates running under the party-list tier (ibid., 39–63). Thus, whether or not the voting system empowers LGBTQ people to elect "one of their own," parties act as a screening device between the civil society and the state with which LGBTQ electoral activism must deal to achieve political representation – that is, for LGBTQ people to be elected to office and to participate in the decision-making process.

The two broad orientations used to describe studies conducted from a descriptive approach to political representation on the LGBTQ electorate can also be employed to understand works on LGBTQ representatives: who they are and how they are depicted. A third orientation should be added: What do LGBTQ politicians embody? But before I address these questions, it is interesting to reflect on Haider-Markel's (2010, 150) argument that LGBT people have better descriptive representation in legislative politics than do women: "The six LGBT legislators in Washington constituted 4 percent of the state's legislative seats in 2009. Meanwhile, there is no state legislature in the country where women make up even 40 percent of legislators, even though they constitute more than 50 percent of the population in most states." The problem with this way of reasoning is that it is not clear who is an LGBTQ person. What happens if someone who has defined herself or himself in a certain way does not act according to her or his self-definition? For instance, what about a self-identified heterosexual woman, married to a man, who has also engaged for years in a relationship with a woman? What about a self-declared heterosexual man who regularly has sex with men? Is a self-defined bisexual woman who is in a long-term exclusive opposite-sex relationship not actually a heterosexual woman? In short, counting LGBTQ people is not as easy as it may seem – a challenge that inevitably jeopardizes the descriptive representation of them and their communities.

Little information is available on the demographics of LGBTQ representatives (aside from the picture painted of out LGB legislators in Canada in Chapter 9 of this volume), although some academic biographies focus on particular lesbian and gay politicians, such as David Rayside's *On the Fringe* (1998) and Ken Yeager's *Trailblazers: Profiles of America's Gay and Lesbian Elected Officials* (2000). Despite this paucity of scholarship, there is no doubt that out LGBTQ representatives are overwhelmingly male. In his analysis of legislators in about a hundred national parliaments between 1976 and 2011, Reynolds (2013) identifies 151 out LGBT MPs in twenty-seven countries, including 32 lesbians, 111 gays, 5 bisexuals, and 3 transgender persons.[18] These numbers confirm de la Dehesa's (2010, 124) observation regarding the invisibility within Brazilian LGBT electoral activism of the "L" and the "T" to the benefit of the "G": "While lesbian and more recently some trans activists have certainly played a significant role in legislative activism in Brazil since the movement's resurgence in the 1990s, the public face of the LGBT movement in these efforts ... is, tellingly, still predominantly *G*" (emphasis in original). Reynolds and Magni (2017, 40) welcome the good news that the British House of Commons counts more out LGBT MPs than ever before; yet, as a group, they strikingly lack diversity. On a positive note, more lesbians than ever before are involved in politics as both candidates (Smith and Haider-Markel 2002, 196) and officeholders (Haider-Markel and Bright 2014). Unsurprisingly, Reynolds (2013) also states that a very small minority of out LGBT MPs belong to an ethnic minority. More surprisingly, however, he observes that about a third of the LGBT individuals elected in a single-member district represent an urban and liberal constituency; in other words, an overwhelming majority came from predominantly rural or suburban ridings. Reynolds and Magni (2017, 28) also find that LGBT candidates have a better electoral performance in rural districts than in urban ones. This contradicts the conventional wisdom that non-urban voters are hostile to electing LGBTQ candidates. Yet, Everitt and Camp (2014) offer a more nuanced picture of the impact that the nature of a constituency can have on electoral success of out LGBT would-be politicians. Analyzing the factors that shaped the success (or lack thereof) of all out LGBT candidates in a federal, provincial, or territorial election in Canada prior to November 2013, the authors note that first-time candidates had a better chance of winning in urban ridings than if they ran in non-urban ridings, but that this urban bonus was less significant for candidates who were not "rookies." Another element that adds to the complexity of this picture is that in a study conducted by Haider-Markel (2010, 150), the LGBT aspiring officeholders were "quality candidates," meaning that they held a local political position or worked for a politician in the past (see also Smith and Haider-Markel 2002, 196). The limited information available on the demographics of LGBTQ representatives may in part explain their stereotypical treatment by media.

The descriptive representation of LGBTQ politicians has also been examined through media presentation – that is, how out LGBTQ representatives are depicted in the media. A major study that used this approach is Donna Smith's *Sex, Lies and Politics* (2012). Smith pursues two objectives: to see how out gay politicians (to use her expression) in the United Kingdom have been portrayed in the newspapers since the 1950s and to understand how this press coverage has changed over time. Her results show that whereas gay politicians "have moved closer to recognition over the years" (ibid., 206), full recognition has yet to come. Indeed, although media coverage of gay politicians is more positive today than in the past, prejudices and stereotypes persist. For instance, anal sex, a central feature of gay male sexuality, is still viewed negatively by some people (notwithstanding its prevalence among heterosexuals) and may thus help to promote a negative mediated persona of gay politicians as not worthy of respect and trust. This is a great illustration of Nussbaum's politics of disgust. Donna Smith's (2012) analysis also demonstrates that even today, LGBTQ people in politics continue to be evaluated according to desperately simplistic polarizations, such as good versus bad, out versus in, private sex versus public sex, safe versus dangerous, and clean versus dirty. Thus, the "good" LGBTQ politician is out (and therefore honest and trustworthy) and engaged in a long-term monogamous relationship (in which sex is private and considered to be safe and clean). In Chapter 3, Mireille Lalancette and Manon Tremblay's analysis of three gay or lesbian political leaders (André Boisclair, Wade MacLauchlan, and Kathleen Wynne) illustrates how the media have the power to create "good" (MacLauchlan and Wynne) and "bad" (Boisclair) lesbian and gay politicians. In their analysis of the press coverage of the campaign by Allison Brewer (an out lesbian) for leadership of the New Brunswick NDP in 2005, Joanna Everitt and Michael Camp (2009a, 2009b) find that the media portrayed her through her gender (woman), sexuality (lesbian), and ideas (feminist): "She was a radical feminist whose views were inconsistent with mainstream public norms in the province" (Everitt and Camp 2009b, 140). In a certain way, Brewer was framed as a dangerous sexual stranger (Phelan 2001) because, as a feminist and a lesbian, she threatened heteronormativity. As Everitt and Raney show in Chapter 2 of this volume, even when a lesbian holds a high-profile political position, as did Premier Kathleen Wynne, she never completely escapes media stereotyping.

A third concern has inspired the descriptive analysis of LGBTQ representatives: the impact of their presence in politics. As Raymond Smith and Donald Haider-Markel (2002, 193) summarize it, "Only open LGBT people can serve as role models and speak to LGBT issues convincingly from personal experience." The role-model function of LGBTQ politicians has important effects on both LGBTQ people and the general population. Indeed, the presence of LGBTQ individuals in politics sends a message to the woman and man on the street that straight (and, it can be added, white middle-aged male) citizens do not hold a monopoly on the decision-making process concerning "living together" – that minorities also have a say in the organizing and functioning of society. In other words, the presence of LGBTQ people in politics constitutes a plea for a style of democracy that is inclusive and diversified. It also sends the message to LGBTQ people that heterosexism and homophobia are not definitive barriers to their participation in the polity and that to be involved in politics can change and improve their daily citizenship. In turn, seeing LGBTQ politicians may help to strengthen the trust that LGBTQ people have in politics. But more importantly, LGBTQ politicians embody the hope that LGBTQ people will receive the respect that they deserve as much as every straight citizen. As Harvey Milk stated in his Hope Speech, "A gay person in office can set a tone, can command respect not only from the larger community, but from the young people in our own community who need both examples and hope" (Bull 2001, 166). An out LGBTQ individual in office signals a profound shift away from the politics of disgust that has humiliated LGBTQ people and communities over the years. Robert Bailey (1999, 349) points out, "Once police felt free to raid gay bars and clubs under the pretext of state liquor laws and criminal statutes on vagrancy and sodomy, but today lesbians and gay men – free and firm in expressing their identities – sit on city councils and serve on the staffs of mayors. They have become officials to whom police departments report." In Chapter 8 of this volume, Manon Tremblay further explores the symbolic dimension of descriptive representation.

In sum, although much research remains to be conducted on LGBTQ politicians through a descriptive conception of political representation, existing studies indicate that to have out LGBTQ people in politics is important: as descriptive representatives, they perform the symbolic function of role models, but their presence also greatly enables the substantive representation of LGBTQ people and communities. In *Out and Running*, by far the most detailed study on representation activities by LGBT officeholders, Haider-Markel (2010, 152, 153) clearly demonstrates that increased descriptive representation brings increased substantive representation:

> As LGBT legislators take office, the number of pro-LGBT bills introduced and passed increases ... Even when controlling for other factors such as state and legislature characteristics, higher LGBT representation in state legislatures leads to greater substantive representation in terms of LGBT-related bills that are introduced and adopted. I also find that a greater number of LGBT legislators is associated with a higher probability of adopting antidiscrimination laws based on sexual orientation.

This finding, which challenges the critical mass theory, according to which a minority must make up about one-third of the membership of an organization to achieve substantive representation (Kanter 1977) – LGBTQ representation never reaches this threshold – is consistent with results drawn from other studies. For instance, Donald Haider-Markel, Mark Joslyn, and Chad Kniss (2000) observe that the presence of lesbian and gay legislators significantly raises the likelihood that same-sex registered partnership will be adopted. In the view of these authors, same-sex sexual orientation is the most influential factor in adopting registration policies. Rebekah Herrick (2009) concludes that LGB politicians have a "dramatically larger" probability of representing LGBTQ-related issues than do their straight counterparts, even after factors that may interact with their willingness to represent LGBT concerns (such as receiving support from religious groups) are taken into account. Reynolds (2013) also identifies a consistent and strong relationship between the presence of out LGBT MPs and the adoption of progressive laws on LGBTQ-related concerns (such as a ban on discrimination based on sexual orientation, an equality clause in laws, and registered partnership or same-sex marriage). Finally, Hansen and Treul (2015, 966) conclude their study on the representation of LGB Americans with the following plea: "While broad support from the majority can help the minority achieve broad societal support and eventual policy change, minority incorporation into political institutions is essential for making sure that issues important to the minority find a place on the agenda."

To substantively represent LGBTQ concerns, LGBTQ politicians deploy a wide range of legislative and extra-legislative tactics, such as participating in grassroots electoral activism, building coalitions with other LGBTQ politicians and straight allies, backroom lobbying, "deLGBTQing" LGBTQ issues and framing them in media-friendly language, strategically manoeuvring through legislative procedures, sponsoring and co-sponsoring pro-LGBTQ bills, and blocking anti-LGBTQ legislation (see, for example, Haider-Markel 2010, 84–117; Herrick 2010). The decision to mobilize a particular tactic depends on ideological and socio-political contexts that may be broader (the political culture of a polity or social-movement mobilizations to support or oppose an issue) or more specific (a position in a party platform or an alliance's achievement on a particular LGBTQ issue).

The equation that Donald Haider-Markel (2007) establishes – that more LGBT legislators result in the introduction and adoption of more pro-LGBT bills – does not work by magic. LGBTQ politicians do not operate in a vacuum; the capacity to substantively represent LGBTQ concerns depends on a favourable ideological and socio-political context. More specifically, Haider-Markel (2007, 126) argues, "The LGBT population, religious conservative population, public support for LGBT civil rights, the ideology of political elites, and institutional characteristics drive the introduction and adoption of LGBT-related legislation." In other words, institutions matter, but so do actors and contexts. According to James Button, Barbara Rienzo, and Kenneth Wald (1997, 108–12), the legislative branch of government may, of course, adopt pro-"gay rights" decisions, but its executive counterparts (the civil service, the police, and other bodies) must be willing to implement and enforce them. Unfortunately, the power of LGBTQ politicians to act in this matter is limited at best.

How This Book Is Organized

Because very little is known about LGBTQ people's involvement in Canadian politics, the objective of *Queering Representation* is to explore the relationships between electoral politics and lesbians, gays, bisexuals, and trans and queer people in Canada, using a state-centred approach. Such a goal makes this book innovative, as it is the first to deal extensively with electoral politics and LGBTQ people in Canada. The authors in *Queering Representation* first and foremost adopt an exploratory and descriptive tone. They carry out a first-step examination of the state of relationships between electoral politics and LGBTQ people and communities, in the hope that further comprehensive investigations will follow. "Electoral politics" is defined in a fairly narrow perspective: it refers to state structures (institutions, actors, processes, and activities) that make political representation a practical reality. LGBTQ movement activism is not systematically excluded from the book, but it is considered only when it contributes to political representation as proceeding from and embodied in state structures.

An overarching argument of this volume is that political representation matters to LGBTQ people and communities. Of course, this general stance underplays not only that LGBTQ people and communities are diversified (as discussed above) but also that LGBTQ communities encompass conflicting views. For instance, some sectors of the LGBTQ movement reject state politics. However, focusing on political representation, and notably on electoral politics, should in no way be interpreted as a disavowal of other LGBTQ political concerns, approaches, and strategies. In representative democracies, political representation requires participating in elections. For example, the LGBTQ electorate can support out LGBTQ candidates by voting for them, thus fuelling symbolic and descriptive representation of LGBTQ people and communities. By participating in party politics, LGBTQ citizens can influence party platforms, thus promoting the substantive representation of LGBTQ people and communities. By being elected, LGBTQ people can act as role models for young and not-so-young LGBTQ citizens and can advocate for LGBTQ issues, thus contributing to the symbolic and substantive representation of LGBTQ people and communities. Ultimately, the chapters in this book substantiate the idea that the political representation of LGBTQ people through electoral politics strengthens Canadian democracy.

Mirroring the state of knowledge outlined above, *Queering Representation* is divided into two parts: one on LGBTQ voters and the other on LGBTQ representatives. The descriptive, formalistic, and substantive conceptions of political representation offer the theoretical backdrop with which the chapters dialogue and in light of which their observations make sense.

Composed of four chapters, Part 1 focuses on the LGBTQ electorate's characteristics, its voting behaviours, and its empowerment through voting systems. This portion of the book also examines how straight voters perceive out LGBTQ politicians and the role that the media play in framing such views.

In Chapter 1, which is clearly rooted in a descriptive conception of representation, Andrea Perrella, Steven Brown, and Barry Kay paint a socio-demographic and civic portrait of the LGB community in Canada. They show that "Canadians who publicly identify as lesbian, gay, or bisexual are sufficient in number to represent a potentially significant electoral force" (page 73). More specifically, the LGB community has a demographic weight comparable in size (between 2.0 and 5.5 percent) to those of several ethnic and religious minorities in Canada, and its socio-demographic profile differs from that of the heterosexual community on several dimensions. For instance, LGB people are more politically involved than are their straight fellow citizens, and they are much more likely to be on the left side of the political spectrum.

Chapter 2, by Joanna Everitt and Tracey Raney, overlaps the descriptive and substantive conceptions of representation. Its authors examine how stereotypes based on gender and sexual orientation intersected to shape voter assessment of out lesbian premier Kathleen Wynne during the 2014 provincial election campaign in Ontario. They hypothesize that because Wynne was an established politician who had been well known to the public for several years before the 2014 election, stereotypes based on gender and sexual orientation played a minimal role in voter evaluations of her. Although their findings support this expectation, the authors also show that some stereotypes linked to gender and sexual orientation remained in voter appraisals of Wynne. Furthermore, they observe a gender gap in how voters evaluated Wynne's leadership.

In Chapter 3, Mireille Lalancette and Manon Tremblay pursue a line of thought much like that of Everitt and Raney, as they evaluate the role played by the media in framing voter perceptions, notably through gender- and sexual-orientation-based stereotypes. The authors assess coverage by the press, both LGBTQ and straight, of three out politicians: André Boisclair (former leader of the Opposition, Quebec), Wade MacLauchlan (premier of Prince Edward Island), and Wynne. They argue that the press deployed three overlapping frames to inform voter perceptions of the politicians: "the first lesbian/gay elected in politics" frame, "the representative of LGBT communities and interests" frame, and "the respectability of lesbian/gay politicians" frame. These depictions affected Boisclair, MacLauchlan, and Wynne very differently.

In Chapter 4, Dennis Pilon tackles the crucial yet little-considered question of the role of voting systems in the political representation of LGBT people and communities. Firmly set in the formalistic conception of representation, his discussion illuminates why LGBT people must be concerned with institutions and their influence on electoral representation: voting systems are not neutral – they play a primary role in who is elected (and, more importantly, who is not). Pilon takes a clear position in favour of proportional representation voting systems. Of course, countries that use majoritarian systems do elect out LGBTQ politicians, as exemplified by the high number of out MPs in the British House of Commons. But majoritarian systems – Pilon argues – respond more slowly, in an unequal manner, and in smaller proportions to claims for diverse representation. In contrast, proportional systems deliver diversified descriptive representation more quickly, at an evener pace, and with a higher proportion of representation.

Part 2 of this volume puts the emphasis on elected LGBTQ officials – notably, their representational role and their pathway to power. However, being elected to office in Canada is almost impossible without the support of a political party. According to the formalistic view of representation, parties shape political representation in a manner similar to orchestra conductors interpreting a composition. Therefore, this section of the book opens with a cluster of three chapters on parties and their ideologies.[19] It continues with five chapters on the long journey to seeking elected office and the representational roles of LGBTQ politicians.

Before I go farther, I need to point out that federal political parties and their ideologies are given analytic priority here – in other words, parties and ideologies at the provincial level are not thoroughly discussed.[20] The book focuses on federal parties and ideologies as a consequence of its exploratory and descriptive look at the relationships between electoral politics and LGBTQ people and communities in Canada. As stated above, we hope that further comprehensive studies will follow from this first-step examination. There is no doubt that a book based on a province-by-province approach is much justified. Indeed, provincial governments are constitutionally responsible for areas of jurisdiction that have major impacts on what I call LGBTQ people's substantive citizenship. Of course, these encompass the daily living conditions of LGBTQ people, as they are defined by rights, but also as moulded by discourses, practices, social representations, and interrelations among people in civil society, as well as between citizens and state and private sector institutions – in sum, citizenship as processes of social interactions (Tremblay 2016). In addition, several provincial parties have adopted clear stances in support of or against LGBTQ people and communities. The Parti Québécois has long been associated with struggles for the rights of LGBTQ people and their communities, and Quebec was the first province, in 1977, to amend its charter of human rights and freedoms to include sexual orientation as a prohibited ground of discrimination (for details, see Tremblay 2015b). In Ontario, the NDP introduced Bill 167 in 1994, which, had it been adopted, would have granted mostly the same rights and obligations to lesbian and gay couples as those enjoyed by heterosexual common-law couples. Conversely, the Progressive Conservative Association of Alberta, which formed the government from 1971 to 2015, had a long legacy of LGBTQ-phobic statements, decisions, and public policies. Thus, there is a strong case for focusing on provincial politics.[21] In fact, the case is so strong that the subject must be dealt with in a book of its own.

It will come as no surprise that conservatism is reputed to be hostile to LGBTQ people and communities. Yet, in Chapter 5, Frédéric Boily and Ève Robidoux-Descary forcefully challenge this idea. They begin by describing the two broad ideological trends that drive conservatism in Canada and that are significant in light of recognizing sexual minorities' rights: the neoliberal right and social conservatism. This nuance illuminates the fact that it is indeed possible to self-identify as conservative and to support equal rights for LGBTQ people – even to be an LGBTQ person oneself. Now that the Harper era is over and the Conservative Party has a new leader, the position of the Conservatives toward LGBTQ people and communities remains to be defined. Although Harper-style antagonism no longer seems as likely, the space of possibilities and dilemmas is huge between ignoring LGBTQ people and communities and welcoming them fully to party ranks.

Chapter 6, in which Brooke Jeffrey discusses the Liberal Party of Canada, tells a very different story. According to Jeffrey, the party has historically been closely associated with the recognition of LGBT people and communities. Of course, the Charter of Rights and Freedoms, adopted in 1982, has proved highly effective in promoting non-discrimination and equality rights for LGBTQ people. That being said, the debates and manoeuvrings that paved the way to the legalization of same-sex marriage in 2005 reveal that, like the Conservative Party of Canada, the Liberal Party is not a homogeneous entity that speaks with one voice. More specifically, just as the Conservative Party includes some progressive voices on LGBTQ-related issues, the Liberal Party features some elements of social conservatism.

In Chapter 7, Alexa DeGagne focuses on how the federal NDP's understanding of complex and intersectional LGBTQ issues has evolved from its founding, in 1961, to 2016. By and large, she argues that in interacting mainly with assimilationist members of the LGBTQ movement, the NDP adopted a politics of mainstreaming into heterosexist society, promoting slow and incremental changes by denouncing economic inequality and claiming liberal rights and freedoms for all LGBTQ people. In so doing, it failed to acknowledge the diversity and complexity of LGBTQ communities and disregarded radical, grassroots, and marginalized voices. DeGagne puts forward a somewhat provocative but convincing thesis: in a manner not so different from its Conservative and Liberal counterparts, the NDP "instrumentalizes" LGBTQ people and communities to promote a homonational agenda in which Canada is celebrated as a haven for LGBTQ people.

Adopting the theoretical posture that people from a given community are best suited to represent that community, Manon Tremblay reflects in Chapter 8 on why it is essential that LGBTQ individuals enter politics. Her principal idea is that lesbian and gay politicians are best positioned to represent lesbians and gays descriptively, symbolically, and substantively. In addition, Tremblay underlines the centrality of emotions in the representation of LGBTQ people:

although allies are essential to the substantive representation of LGBTQ interests, only LGBTQ politicians feel the emotions that drive a politics of representation of LGBTQ people in a descriptive and symbolic perspective.

In Chapter 9, Joanna Everitt, Manon Tremblay, and Angelia Wagner analyze descriptive representation of LGBT people in Canadian legislative bodies. They suggest that although no formal barrier disallows the election of LGBT people, cultural and social prejudices still impede their access to legislative representation. Unlike sex/gender, sexual orientation has never been a formal disqualifying criterion for eligibility to run for office. However, recruitment, selection, and election may raise obstacles to LGBT people. The good news is that LGBT candidates are competitive: most run in winnable ridings and take their seats by comfortable margins (although some gender-based differences do exist), confirming similar observations made by Haider-Markel (2010) for the United States and by Reynolds and Magni (2017) for Great Britain.

In Chapters 10 and 11, Angelia Wagner and Curtis Atkins scrutinize particular aspects of the election funnel. Wagner concentrates on the LGBTQ candidate-recruitment process, whereas Atkins examines training LGBTQ candidates to run for election. The decision to compete in an election depends on a plethora of factors, including an evaluation of the challenges that the campaign may entail. Wagner explores one of these potential difficulties: the role that LGBTQ candidates *expect* their sexual orientation and/or gender identity to play in their electoral endeavour and the role that it *actually* plays. She identifies three strategies that candidates use in their campaign communications to deal with the former. Wagner concludes that although things have improved in recent years, non-normative sexuality or gender identity certainly adds to the complexities of an election campaign, although many candidates feel that it does not bring an end to their political ambitions.

Atkins analyzes a unique LGBTQ social-movement organization: ProudPolitics. Created early in 2012, it intends to elect LGBTQ candidates. More specifically, ProudPolitics is an assimilationist-oriented, election-focused, and multi-partisan body that is dedicated to recruiting and training LGBTQ people and electing them to federal, provincial, territorial, and municipal office in Canada. According to its "lived equality" philosophy, ProudPolitics seeks to align equality on the books and equality in everyday life in the field of electoral politics. ProudPolitics is election-focused because it aims to improve both the descriptive and the substantive representation of LGBTQ people, claiming "a place at the table." It is multi-partisan because it works across party labels, with all political parties, and with LGBTQ people of all political stripes.

Chapter 12, by Catherine Nash and Andrew Gorman-Murray, deals with municipal politics. Its position at the end of the book reflects a certain hierarchical, though contested, conception of the levels of government in Canada. Above all, however, it highlights the fact that although municipal politics has a major impact on LGBT people's substantive citizenship, it is not necessarily more accessible and friendlier to them and their communities than is parliamentary politics. In other words, municipal politics should not be thought of as involving fewer challenges to LGBT representation than does legislative politics. In their case study of Kristyn Wong-Tam, a self-identified openly queer municipal politician in Toronto, Nash and Gorman-Murray illustrate this point: they show that in their activities of representation, queer municipal politicians encounter specific challenges that do not confront their straight counterparts. There are several reasons for this. First, they are suspected of being "one-issue representatives" – of speaking only for the local LGBT community. Second, LGBT people and communities are diversified and – therefore – fraught with tensions and oppositions. This is not to say that heterosexual politicians encounter no resistance, but to question the stereotype that LGBT people and communities form a single bloc against heterosexual society. Third, some of Wong-Tam's decisions were criticized as homonormative and neoliberal, illustrating that LGBT people and communities are complex and intersectional in their political values, social practices, and visions for the future.

The book closes with an Afterword by Graeme Truelove, who recounts the political career of Svend Robinson, the first out LGBTQ politician to sit in the Canadian Parliament. Truelove illustrates several of the theoretical elements highlighted elsewhere in the book. For instance, there is no doubt that by coming out of the closet in 1988, Robinson became a role model for Canadian society as a whole and for young LGBTQ people in particular. He also demonstrated the power of institutions: how it is important to have "a place at the table," to use Curtis Atkins's expression, and to know how to turn the formal rules of the parliamentary and legislative game into resources. However, this is not sufficient: as Truelove demonstrates, Robinson's ability to advance LGBTQ rights relied on a rich synergy between state institutions of political representation and the lesbian and gay movement and, occasionally, strategic uses of informal rules such as deploying an emotional performance. In the end, his journey on Parliament Hill offers evidence that electoral politics may serve LGBTQ people – at least, some of them.

Notes

1 I use "LGBTQ" as the default initialism in this chapter, and I explain why below. For the moment, suffice it to say that depending on the context, I sometimes use "lesbians and gays," sometimes "lesbians, gays, and bisexuals" (LGB), and sometimes "lesbians, gays, bisexuals, trans (for transsexual and transgender persons), and queer" (LGBTQ).

2 Before the United States Supreme Court decision in *Lawrence v. Texas* (2003), which struck down the sodomy law in Texas, a majority of states had already made same-sex sexual acts legal between 1972 and 2003.
3 For more on the LGBTQ Representation and Rights Research Initiative, see https://lgbtqrepresentationandrights.org/.
4 Sexual orientation or gender identity was not identified for four persons.
5 This total does not include Charles Lapointe (Liberal), who was elected in Charlevoix in the 1974 federal election.
6 "LGBQ" does not include a "T" here because although some trans persons have run in Canadian legislative elections, none have won a seat. The presence of the "Q" indicates that some legislators identify as queer.
7 This may also be true of those in the midst of transitioning and those who identify as being fluid with regard to their sexual orientation or gender expression.
8 However, the contributors to this book use whatever acronym they think best suits their argument.
9 I use "state political representation" to make a distinction with other forms of representation occurring in civil society via social movements, the media, and even celebrities (Saward 2010).
10 As a rule, I use "LGBTQ" in this section, except when the authors cited use other alternatives, such as "lesbians and gays," "LGB," and "LGBT."
11 On outing closeted politicians, see the 2014 film *The Normal Heart*, directed by Ryan Murphy and produced by HBO films, which portrays the indifference of the American political class, including some in-the-closet gay politicians, toward the HIV/AIDS pandemic in the early 1980s.
12 This stereotype claims that LGBTQ people (particularly gay men) are wealthier than heterosexuals because they do not have to support children and a female partner who typically earns a small salary. Therefore, they enjoy a whirlwind lifestyle, with expensive dining out, luxurious cars, and fabulous vacations. Sean Waite and Nicole Denier (2015) show the inaccuracy of the stereotype using data from the 2006 Census of Canada; they observe that lesbians earn more than their heterosexual counterparts but gay men less than straight men (see also Chapter 1 in this volume). Research remains to be done on this topic, notably the disposable income of LGBTQ versus straight households.
13 This stereotype was particularly promoted by Anita Bryant, the founder of the American social conservative group Save Our Children. In her autobiography, Bryant states that "homosexuals cannot reproduce – so they must recruit. And to freshen their ranks, they must recruit the youth of America" (Bryant quoted in Fetner 2008, xiii).
14 Golebiowska placed "voters" in quotation marks because her method was experimental and not part of a real election.
15 Things may change in the future, as illustrated by the metamorphosis of the British Conservative Party from a profoundly anti-LGBTQ party under Margaret Thatcher to an LGBTQ-friendly one under David Cameron (Reynolds and Magni 2017, 9–12). According to Laurie Rhodebeck (2015, 724), writing about the United States, "The GOP can no longer define a clear line of cleavage between itself and the Democratic Party on gay rights policies." Thus, it is possible to envisage that the "general aversion [of LGB voters] to the Republican Party" may erode over time, as happened with the British Conservative Party.
16 On the same topic, but in a resolutely social-movement approach, see Tina Fetner (2008).
17 Of course, the federal and provincial Conservative parties have LGBTQ constituencies, as reflected in the existence of LGBTory (see Chapter 5 in this volume).

18 As mentioned at the beginning of this introduction, in February 2016 the total was 298 out LGBTQ MPs in forty-two countries. It is intriguing how quickly the numbers have increased: there were 96 out LGBT MPs in office in 2011 (Reynolds 2013, 261), and almost double the number five years later (180 in 2016; Reynolds 2016).
19 Readers may wonder why the book contains a chapter on the New Democratic Party, which has never formed a federal government, unlike the Conservative and Liberal Parties. The NDP has always been a strong ally of LGBTQ people and communities, and it is impossible to ignore this fact in a book on LGBTQ people and electoral politics in Canada. Readers may also wonder why there is no chapter on the Green Party, which has also been a significant supporter of LGBTQ people and communities and has been established for some years. The reason is that the Green Party remains on the fringes of the federal political landscape, and until a political cataclysm occurs, it has no chance of forming the government or even the Opposition (unlike the NDP, which has assumed the latter role).
20 Chapter 5 is an exception.
21 The argument for concentrating on the municipal level is just as strong, if not stronger.

References

Adams, Mary Louise. 1997. *The Trouble with Normal: Postwar Youth and the Making of Heterosexuality*. Toronto: University of Toronto Press.

Andersen, Robert, and Tina Fetner. 2008. "Economic Inequality and Intolerance: Attitudes toward Homosexuality in 35 Democracies." *American Journal of Political Science* 52 (4): 942–58. https://doi.org/10.1111/j.1540-5907.2008.00352.x.

Angus, Reid. 2017. "Could Our National Leader Be: ____? Most in Canada, U.S. Say They'd Vote for More Diverse Candidates." June 26. http://angusreid.org/who-could-be-prime-minister-president/.

Bailey, Mandi Bates, and Steven P. Nawara. 2017. "Gay and Lesbian Candidates, Group Stereotypes, and the News Media." In *LGBTQ Politics: A Critical Reader*, ed. Marla Brettschneider, Susan Burgess, and Christine Keating, 334–49. New York: New York University Press.

Bailey, Robert W. 1998. *Out and Voting: The Gay, Lesbian and Bisexual Vote in Congressional Elections, 1990–1996*. Washington, DC: Policy Institute of the National Gay and Lesbian Task Force.

–. 1999. *Gay Politics, Urban Politics: Identity and Economics in an Urban Setting*. New York: Columbia University Press.

Bishin, Benjamin G., and Charles Anthony Smith. 2013. "When Do Legislators Defy Popular Sovereignty? Testing Theories of Minority Representation Using DOMA." *Political Research Quarterly* 66 (4): 794–803. https://doi.org/10.1177/1065912913475875.

Bull, Chris, ed. 2001. *Come Out Fighting: A Century of Essential Writing on Gay and Lesbian Liberation*. New York: Thunder's Mouth Press/Nation Books.

Butler, Judith. 1990. *Gender Trouble: Feminism and the Subversion of Identity*. New York: Routledge.

Button, James W., Barbara A. Rienzo, and Kenneth D. Wald. 1997. *Private Lives, Public Conflicts: Battles over Gay Rights in American Communities*. Washington, DC: CQ Press.

Button, James W., Kenneth D. Wald, and Barbara A. Rienzo. 1999. "The Election of Openly Gay Public Officials in American Communities." *Urban Affairs Review* 35 (2): 188–209. https://doi.org/10.1177/10780879922184356.

Cardozo, Bradley. 2014. "A 'Coming Out' Party in Congress? LGBT Advocacy and Party-List Politics in the Philippines." Master's thesis, University of California. http://escholarship.org/uc/item/49v8j2wx.

Carey, Craig David. 2016. "'Out' in Parliament." Bachelor's thesis, University of Lincoln. http://www.academia.edu/28462948/Out_in_Parliament.

Carroll, Aengus, and Lucas Ramón Mendos. 2017. *State Sponsored Homophobia 2017: A World Survey of Sexual Orientation Laws: Criminalisation, Protection and Recognition.* 12th ed. Geneva: ILGA. https://ilga.org/downloads/2017/ILGA_State_Sponsored_Homophobia_2017_WEB.pdf.

Celis, Karen, Sarah Childs, Johanna Kantola, and Mona Lena Krook. 2008. "Rethinking Women's Substantive Representation." *Representation* 44 (2): 99–110. https://doi.org/10.1080/00344890802079573.

Chaney, Paul. 2013. "Institutionally Homophobic? Political Parties and the Substantive Representation of LGBT People: Westminster and Regional UK Elections, 1945–2011." *Policy and Politics* 41 (1): 101–21. https://doi.org/10.1332/030557312x645793.

Childs, Sarah, and Mona Lena Krook. 2009. "Analysing Women's Substantive Representation: From Critical Mass to Critical Actors." *Government and Opposition* 44 (2): 125–45. https://doi.org/10.1111/j.1477-7053.2009.01279.x.

Cooper, Davina. 1994. *Sexing the City: Lesbian and Gay Politics within the Activist State.* London: Rivers Oram Press.

de la Dehesa, Rafael. 2010. *Queering the Public Sphere in Mexico and Brazil: Sexual Rights Movements in Emerging Democracies.* Durham: Duke University Press.

D'Emilio, John. 1998. *Sexual Politics, Sexual Communities: The Making of a Homosexual Minority in the United States, 1940–1970.* 2nd ed. Chicago: University of Chicago Press.

Doan, Alesha E., and Donald P. Haider-Markel. 2010. "The Role of Intersectional Stereotypes on Evaluations of Gay and Lesbian Political Candidates." *Politics and Gender* 6 (1): 63–91. https://doi.org/10.1017/s1743923x09990511.

Dovi, Suzanne. 2007. *The Good Representative.* Malden: Blackwell.

Edge, Simon. 1995. *With Friends Like These: Marxism and Gay Politics.* London: Cassell.

Egan, Patrick J., Murray S. Edelman, and Kenneth Sherrill. 2008. *Findings from the Hunter College Poll of Lesbians, Gays and Bisexuals: New Discoveries about Identity, Political Attitudes, and Civic Engagement.* New York: Hunter College.

Escobar-Lemmon, Maria C., and Michelle M. Taylor-Robinson, eds. 2014. *Representation: The Case of Women.* New York: Oxford University Press.

Everitt, Joanna. 2015. "Gender and Sexual Diversity in Provincial Election Campaigns." *Canadian Political Science Review* 9 (1): 177–92.

Everitt, Joanna, and Michael Camp. 2009a. "Changing the Game Changes the Frame: The Media's Use of Lesbian Stereotypes in Leadership versus Election Campaigns." *Canadian Political Science Review* 3 (3): 24–39.

—. 2009b. "One Is Not Like the Others: Allison Brewer's Leadership of the New Brunswick NDP." In *Opening Doors Wider: Women's Political Engagement in Canada*, ed. Sylvia Bashevkin, 127–44. Vancouver: UBC Press.

—. 2014. "In versus Out: LGBT Politicians in Canada." *Journal of Canadian Studies* 48 (1): 226–51. https://doi.org/10.3138/jcs.48.1.226.

Faderman, Lilian. 1991. *Odd Girls and Twilight Lovers: A History of Lesbian Life in Twentieth-Century America.* New York: Columbia University Press.

Fetner, Tina. 2008. *How the Religious Right Shaped Lesbian and Gay Activism.* Minneapolis: University of Minnesota Press.

Fortin-Rittberger, Jessica, and Berthold Rittberger. 2014. "Do Electoral Rules Matter? Explaining National Differences in Women's Representation in the European Parliament." *European Union Politics* 15 (4): 496–520. https://doi.org/10.1177/1465116514527179.

Garretson, Jeremiah J. 2017. "The How, Why, and Who of LGBTQ 'Victory': A Critical Examination of Change in Public Attitudes Involving LGBTQ People." In *LGBTQ Politics: A Critical Reader*, ed. Marla Brettschneider, Susan Burgess, and Christine Keating, 252–69. New York: New York University Press.

Gates, Gary J. 2011. "How Many People Are Lesbian, Gay, Bisexual, and Transgender?" Williams Institute, Faculty of Law, University of California, Los Angeles. https://williamsinstitute.law.ucla.edu/wp-content/uploads/Gates-How-Many-People-LGBT-Apr-2011.pdf.

Gerhards, Jürgen. 2010. "Non-Discrimination towards Homosexuality: The European Union's Policy and Citizens' Attitudes towards Homosexuality in 27 European Countries." *International Sociology* 25 (1): 5–28. https://doi.org/10.1177/0268580909346704.

Golebiowska, Ewa A. 2001. "Group Stereotypes and Political Evaluation." *American Politics Research* 29 (6): 535–65. https://doi.org/10.1177/1532673X01029006001.

Golebiowska, Ewa A., and Cynthia J. Thomsen. 1999. "Group Stereotypes and Evaluations of Individuals: The Case of Gay and Lesbian Political Candidates." In *Gays and Lesbians in the Democratic Process: Public Policy, Public Opinion, and Political Representation*, ed. Ellen D.B. Riggle and Barry L. Tadlock, 192–219. New York: Columbia University Press.

Goodin, Robert E. 2004. "Representing Diversity." *British Journal of Political Science* 34 (3): 453–68. https://doi.org/10.1017/S0007123404000134.

Green, James N. 2000. "Desire and Militancy: Lesbians, Gays and the Brazilian Workers Party." In *Different Rainbows*, ed. Peter Drucker, 57–70. London: Gay Men's Press.

Haider-Markel, Donald P. 2007. "Representation and Backlash: The Positive and Negative Influence of Descriptive Representation." *Legislative Studies Quarterly* 32 (1): 107–33. https://doi.org/10.3162/036298007x202001.

–. 2010. *Out and Running: Gay and Lesbian Candidates, Elections, and Policy Representation*. Washington, DC: Georgetown University Press.

Haider-Markel, Donald P., Mark R. Joslyn, and Chad J. Kniss. 2000. "Minority Group Interests and Political Representation: Gay Elected Officials in the Policy Process." *Journal of Politics* 62 (2): 568–77. https://doi.org/10.1111/0022-3816.00026.

Haider-Markel, Donald P., and Chelsie Lynn Moore Bright. 2014. "Lesbian Candidates and Officeholders." In *Women and Elective Office: Past, Present, and Future*, 3rd ed., ed. Sue Thomas and Clyde Wilcox, 253–72. New York: Oxford University Press.

Haider-Markel, Donald P., and Patrick R. Miller. 2017. "Equality or Transformation? LGBT Political Attitudes and Priorities and the Implications for the Movement." In *LGBTQ Politics: A Critical Reader*, ed. Marla Brettschneider, Susan Burgess, and Christine Keating, 270–94. New York: New York University Press.

Hanagan, Michael. 1998. "Social Movements. Incorporation, Disengagement, and Opportunities – A Long View." In *From Contention to Democracy*, ed. Marco G. Giugni, Doug McAdam, and Charles Tilly, 3–30. Lanham: Rowman and Littlefield.

Hansen, Eric R., and Sarah A. Treul. 2015. "The Symbolic and Substantive Representation of LGB Americans in the US House." *Journal of Politics* 77 (4): 955–67. https://doi.org/10.1086/682699.

Herek, Gregory M., Aaron T. Norton, Thomas J. Allen, and Charles S. Sims. 2010. "Demographic, Psychological, and Social Characteristics of Self-Identified Lesbian, Gay and Bisexual Adults in a US Probability Sample." *Sexuality Research and Social Policy* 7 (3): 176–200. https://doi.org/10.1007/s13178-010-0017-y. Medline:20835383

Herrick, Rebekah. 2009. "The Effects of Sexual Orientation on State Legislators' Behavior and Priorities." *Journal of Homosexuality* 56 (8): 1117–33. https://doi.org/10.1080/00918360903279361. Medline:19882430
–. 2010. "The Legislative Effectiveness of Gay and Lesbian Legislators." *Journal of Women, Politics and Policy* 31 (3): 243–59. https://doi.org/10.1080/1554477x.2010.496690.
Herrick, Rebekah, and Sue Thomas. 1999. "The Effects of Sexual Orientation on Citizen Perceptions of Candidate Viability." In *Gays and Lesbians in the Democratic Process: Public Policy, Public Opinion, and Political Representation*, ed. Ellen D.B. Riggle and Barry L. Tadlock, 170–91. New York: Columbia University Press.
–. 2001. "Gays and Lesbians in Local Races: A Study of Electoral Viability." *Journal of Homosexuality* 42 (1): 103–26. https://doi.org/10.1300/j082v42n01_06. Medline:11991562
Hertzog, Mark. 1996. *The Lavender Vote: Lesbians, Gay Men, and Bisexuals in American Electoral Politics*. New York: New York University Press.
Jeffery-Poulter, Stephen. 1991. *Peers, Queers, and Commons: The Struggle for Gay Law Reform from 1950 to the Present*. London: Routledge.
Jones, Jeffrey M. 2012. "Atheists, Muslims See Most Bias as Presidential Candidates." June 21. http://www.gallup.com/poll/155285/Atheists-Muslims-Bias-Presidential-Candidates.aspx?utm_source=tagrss&utm_medium=rss&utm_campaign=syndication.
Kanter, Rosabeth Moss. 1977. "Some Effects of Proportions on Group Life: Skewed Sex Ratios and Responses to Token Women." *American Journal of Sociology* 82 (5): 965–90. https://doi.org/10.1086/226425.
Kerr, Peter, Christopher Byrne, and Emma Foster. 2011. "Theorising Cameronism." *Political Studies Review* 9 (2): 193–217. https://doi.org/10.1111/j.1478-9302.2011.00232.x.
Kluttz, Billy. 2014. "Outness and Identity in Context: Negotiating Sexual Disclosure in LGBT Campaigns." *Sexuality and Culture* 18 (4): 789–803. https://doi.org/10.1007/s12119-014-9221-x.
Kraus, François. 2012. "Les études électorales. Gays, bis et lesbiennes: Des minorités sexuelles ancrées à gauche." Centre de recherches politiques, Paris. http://www.cevipof.com/rtefiles/File/AtlasEl3/NoteKRAUS.pdf.
Langstaff, Amy. 2011. "A Twenty-Year Survey of Canadian Attitudes towards Homosexuality and Gay Rights." In *Faith, Politics, and Sexual Diversity in Canada and the United States*, ed. David Rayside and Clyde Wilcox, 49–66. Vancouver: UBC Press.
Lawless, Jennifer L., and Richard L. Fox. 2010. *It Still Takes a Candidate: Why Women Don't Run for Office*. Rev. ed. New York: Cambridge University Press.
Lewis, Gregory B., Marc A. Rogers, and Kenneth Sherrill. 2011. "Lesbian, Gay, and Bisexual Voters in the 2000 U.S. Presidential Election." *Politics and Policy* 39 (5): 655–77. https://doi.org/10.1111/j.1747-1346.2011.00315.x.
Lombardo, Emanuela, and Petra Meier. 2014. *The Symbolic Representation of Gender: A Discursive Approach*. Farnham, UK: Ashgate.
Lublin, David. 2005. "The Strengthening of Party and Decline of Religion in Explaining Congressional Voting Behavior on Gay and Lesbian Issues." *PS: Political Science and Politics* 38 (2): 241–45. https://doi.org/10.1017/s1049096505056374.
Mansbridge, Jane. 2003. "Rethinking Representation." *American Political Science Review* 97 (4): 515–28. https://doi.org/10.1017/s0003055403000856.
–. 2011. "Clarifying the Concept of Representation." *American Political Science Review* 105 (3): 621–30. https://doi.org/10.1017/s0003055411000189.
Marsiaj, Juan P. 2006. "Social Movements and Political Parties: Gays, Lesbians, and *Travestis* and the Struggle for Inclusion in Brazil." *Canadian Journal of Latin American and Caribbean Studies* 31 (62): 167–96. https://doi.org/10.1080/08263663.2006.10816905.

Mazur, Amy G., and Gary Goertz. 2008. "Introduction." In *Politics, Gender, and Concepts: Theory and Methodology*, ed. Gary Goertz and Amy G. Mazur, 1–13. Cambridge: Cambridge University Press.

McCarthy, Justin. 2015. "In U.S., Socialist Presidential Candidates Least Appealing." June 22. http://www.gallup.com/poll/183713/socialist-presidential-candidates-least-appealing.aspx?utm_source=Politics&utm_medium=newsfeed&utm_campaign=tiles.

McDermott, Monika L. 2016. *Masculinity, Femininity, and American Political Behavior*. New York: Oxford University Press.

McLean, Kirsten. 2015. "Inside or Outside? Bisexual Activism and the LGBTI Community." In *The Ashgate Research Companion to Lesbian and Gay Activism*, ed. David Paternotte and Manon Tremblay, 149–62. Farnham, UK: Ashgate.

Monro, Surya. 2015. *Bisexuality: Politics and Theories*. Basingstoke, UK: Palgrave Macmillan.

Monro, Surya, and Diane Richardson. 2011. "Intersectionality and Sexuality: The Case of Equalities Work in UK Local Government." In *Theorising Intersectionality and Sexuality*, ed. Yvette Taylor, Sally Hines, and Mark Casey, 99–118. Basingstoke, UK: Palgrave Macmillan.

Morrow, Adrian. 2015. "Wynne Suggests Tory MPP Homophobic after Sex-Ed Comments." *Globe and Mail*, February 24. http://www.theglobeandmail.com/news/politics/wynne-accuses-tory-mpp-of-homophobia-over-sex-ed-opposition/article23189536/.

Moser, Robert G., and Ethan Scheiner. 2012. *Electoral Systems and Political Context: How the Effects of Rules Vary across New and Established Democracies*. Cambridge: Cambridge University Press.

Nash, Catherine. 2001. "Siting Lesbians: Urban Spaces and Sexuality." In *In a Queer Country: Gay and Lesbian Studies in the Canadian Context*, ed. Terry Goldie, 235–56. Vancouver: Arsenal Pulp Press.

Nohlen, Dieter. 1984. "Two Incompatible Principles of Representation." In *Choosing an Electoral System: Issues and Alternatives*, ed. Arend Lijphart and Bernard Grofman, 83–89. New York: Praeger.

Nussbaum, Martha C. 2010. *From Disgust to Humanity: Sexual Orientation and Constitutional Law*. New York: Oxford University Press.

Perrella, Andrea M.L., Steven D. Brown, and Barry J. Kay. 2012. "Voting Behaviour among the Gay, Lesbian, Bisexual and Transgendered Electorate." *Canadian Journal of Political Science* 45 (1): 89–117. https://doi.org/10.1017/s000842391100093x.

Phelan, Shane. 2001. *Sexual Strangers: Gays, Lesbians, and Dilemmas of Citizenship*. Philadelphia: Temple University Press.

Pitkin, Hanna Fenichel. 1967. *The Concept of Representation*. Berkeley: University of California Press.

Rayside, David. 1998. *On the Fringe: Gays and Lesbians in Politics*. Ithaca: Cornell University Press.

Rehfeld, Andrew. 2006. "Towards a General Theory of Political Representation." *Journal of Politics* 68 (1): 1–21. https://doi.org/10.1111/j.1468-2508.2006.00365.x.

–. 2009. "Representation Rethought: On Trustees, Delegates, and Gyroscopes in the Study of Political Representation and Democracy." *American Political Science Review* 103 (2): 214–30. https://doi.org/10.1017/s0003055409090261.

Reynolds, Andrew. 2013. "Representation and Rights: The Impact of LGBT Legislators in Comparative Perspective." *American Political Science Review* 107 (2): 259–74. https://doi.org/10.1017/s0003055413000051.

–. 2015. "LGBT MPs and Candidates in the UK General Election May 2015: Results." May 13. http://global.unc.edu/news/lgbt-mps-and-candidates-in-the-uk-general-election-may-2015/.

—. 2016. "LGBTQ MPs (Updated February 2016)." LGBTQ Representation and Rights Research Initiative. https://lgbtqrepresentationandrights.org/data/.

—. 2017. "A Record Number of LGBTQ People Were Just Elected to the British Parliament." *Washington Post,* June 11. https://www.washingtonpost.com/news/monkey-cage/wp/2017/06/11/a-record-number-of-lgbtq-people-were-just-elected-to-the-u-k-parliament/?utm_term=.e6b6141f6689.

Reynolds, Andrew, and Gabriele Magni. 2017. "Does Sexual Orientation Still Matter? The Impact of LGBT Candidate Identity on Vote Share in the UK Elections of 2015." https://lgbtqrightsrep.files.wordpress.com/2017/04/uk-lgbt-workingpaperargmapr17.pdf.

Rhodebeck, Laurie A. 2015. "Another Issue Comes Out: Gay Rights Policy Voting in Recent U.S. Presidential Elections." *Journal of Homosexuality* 62 (6): 701–34. https://doi.org/10.1080/00918369.2014.998954. Medline:25530286

Richardson, Diane. 2018. *Sexuality and Citizenship.* Cambridge: Polity.

Riggle, Ellen D.B., Sharon S. Rostosky, and Sharon G. Horne. 2009. "Marriage Amendments and Lesbian, Gay, and Bisexual Individuals in the 2006 Election." *Sexuality Research and Social Policy* 6 (1): 80–89. https://doi.org/10.1525/srsp.2009.6.1.80.

Roberts, Andrew, Jason Seawright, and Jennifer Cyr. 2013. "Do Electoral Laws Affect Women's Representation?" *Comparative Political Studies* 46 (12): 1555–81. https://doi.org/10.1177/0010414012463906.

Rosen, Jennifer. 2013. "The Effects of Political Institutions on Women's Political Representation: A Comparative Analysis of 168 Countries from 1992 to 2010." *Political Research Quarterly* 66 (2): 306–21. https://doi.org/10.1177/1065912912449698.

Rosenblum, Darren. 1995. "Overcoming 'Stigmas': Lesbian and Gay Districts and Black Electoral Empowerment." *Howard Law Journal* 39 (1): 149–200.

—. 1996. "Geographically Sexual? Advancing Lesbian and Gay Interests through Proportional Representation." *Harvard Civil Rights – Civil Liberties Law Review* 31: 119–54.

Rule, Wilma, and Joseph F. Zimmerman, eds. 1994. *Electoral Systems in Comparative Perspective: Their Impact on Women and Minorities.* Westport: Greenwood Press.

Runciman, David. 2007. "The Paradox of Political Representation." *Journal of Political Philosophy* 15 (1): 93–114. https://doi.org/10.1111/j.1467-9760.2007.00266.x.

Salmond, Rob. 2006. "Proportional Representation and Female Parliamentarians." *Legislative Studies Quarterly* 31 (2): 175–204. https://doi.org/10.3162/036298006X201779.

Sanbonmatsu, Kira, and Kathleen Dolan. 2009. "Do Gender Stereotypes Transcend Party?" *Political Research Quarterly* 62 (3): 485–94. https://doi.org/10.1177/1065912908322416.

Saward, Michael. 2010. *The Representative Claim.* Oxford: Oxford University Press.

Schmidt, Gregory D. 2009. "The Election of Women in List PR Systems: Testing the Conventional Wisdom." *Electoral Studies* 28 (2): 190–203. https://doi.org/10.1016/j.electstud.2008.08.002.

Schreiber, Ronnee. 2008. *Righting Feminism: Conservative Women and American Politics.* New York: Oxford University Press.

Severs, Eline. 2010. "Representation as Claims-Making. Quid Responsiveness?" *Representation* 46 (4): 411–23. https://doi.org/10.1080/00344893.2010.518081.

—. 2012. "Substantive Representation through a Claims-Making Lens: A Strategy for the Identification and Analysis of Substantive Claims." *Representation* 48 (2): 169–81. https://doi.org/10.1080/00344893.2012.683491.

Smith, Charles Anthony. 2007. "The Electoral Capture of Gay and Lesbian Americans: Evidence and Implications from the 2004 Election." *Studies in Law, Politics, and Society* 40 (2): 103–21. https://doi.org/10.1016/s1059-4337(06)40004-1.

Smith, Donna. 2012. *Sex, Lies and Politics: Gay Politicians in the Press.* Brighton, UK: Sussex Academic Press.

Smith, Miriam. 1999. *Lesbian and Gay Rights in Canada: Social Movements and Equality-Seeking, 1971–1995*. Toronto: University of Toronto Press.

—. 2008. *Political Institutions and Lesbian and Gay Rights in the United States and Canada*. New York: Routledge.

—. 2010. "Federalism and LGBT Rights in the US and Canada: A Comparative Policy Analysis." In *Federalism, Feminism and Multilevel Governance*, ed. Melissa Haussman, Marian Sawer, and Jill Vickers, 97–109. Farnham, UK: Ashgate.

—. 2015a. "LGBTQ Activism: The Pan-Canadian Political Space." In *Queer Mobilizations: Social Movement Activism and Canadian Public Policy*, ed. Manon Tremblay, 45–63. Vancouver: UBC Press.

—. 2015b. "Political Institutions and LGBTQ Activism in Comparative Perspective." In *The Ashgate Research Companion to Lesbian and Gay Activism*, ed. David Paternotte and Manon Tremblay, 181–94. Farnham, UK: Ashgate.

Smith, Raymond A., and Donald P. Haider-Markel. 2002. *Gay and Lesbian Americans and Political Participation: A Reference Handbook*. Santa Barbara: ABC-Clio.

Snell, Paul. 2017. "Equality in the House: The Congressional LGBT Equality Caucus and the Substantive Representation of LGBTQ Interests." In *LGBTQ Politics: A Critical Reader*, ed. Marla Brettschneider, Susan Burgess, and Christine Keating, 309–33. New York: New York University Press.

Squires, Judith. 2008. "The Constitutive Representation of Gender: Extra-Parliamentary Representations of Gender Relations." *Representation* 44 (2): 187–204. https://doi.org/10.1080/00344890802080464.

Stangor, Charles. 2009. "The Study of Stereotyping, Prejudice, and Discrimination within Social Psychology. A Quick History of Theory and Research." In *Handbook of Prejudice, Stereotyping, and Discrimination*, ed. Todd D. Nelson, 1–22. New York: Psychology Press.

Stein, Marc. 2012. *Rethinking the Gay and Lesbian Movement*. New York: Routledge.

Stone, Amy L. 2012. *Gay Rights at the Ballot Box*. Minneapolis: University of Minnesota Press.

Swank, Eric, and Breanne Fahs. 2013. "Predicting Electoral Activism among Gays and Lesbians in the United States." *Journal of Applied Social Psychology* 43 (7): 1382–93. https://doi.org/10.1111/jasp.12095.

Tobin, Ann. 1988. "Somewhere over the Rainbow ..." In *Radical Records: Thirty Years of Lesbian and Gay History*, ed. Bob Cant and Susan Hemmings, 248–58. London: Routledge.

—. 1990. "Lesbianism and the Labour Party: The GLC Experience." *Feminist Review* 34: 56–66. https://doi.org/10.2307/1395305.

Tremblay, Manon. 2012. "Conclusion." In *Women and Legislative Representation: Electoral Systems, Political Parties, and Sex Quotas*, ed. Manon Tremblay, 239–54. New York: Palgrave Macmillan.

—, ed. 2015a. *Queer Mobilizations: Social Movement Activism and Canadian Public Policy*. Vancouver: UBC Press.

—. 2015b. "Social Movements and Political Opportunities: Lesbians, Gays and the Inclusion of Sexual Orientation in the Québec Charter of Human Rights." *World Political Science* 11 (1): 47–73. https://doi.org/10.1515/wps-2015-0005.

—. 2016. "Citoyenneté substantielle des lesbiennes et des gais et politiques publiques au Canada: réflexions autour de la notion d'"homofédéralisme."" *Zeitschrift für Kanada-Studien* 36: 9–27.

—. 2019. "Uncovering the Gendered Effects of Voting Systems: A Few Thoughts about Representation of Women and of LGBT People." In *Gender Innovation in Political Science:*

New Norms, New Knowledge, ed. Marian Sawer and Kerryn Baker, 91–114. [Cham, Switzerland]: Palgrave Macmillan. http://dx.doi.org/10.1007/978-3-319-75850-3.

Truelove, Graeme. 2013. *Svend Robinson: A Life in Politics.* Vancouver: New Star Books.

Waaldijk, Kees. 2000. "Civil Developments: Patterns of Reform in the Legal Position of Same-Sex Partners in Europe." *Canadian Journal of Family Law* 17 (1): 62–88.

Waite, Sean, and Nicole Denier. 2015. "Gay Pay for Straight Work: Mechanisms Generating Disadvantage." *Gender and Society* 29 (4): 561–88. https://doi.org/10.1177/0891243215584761.

Warner, Michael. 1999. *The Trouble with Normal: Sex, Politics, and the Ethics of Queer Life.* Cambridge: Harvard University Press.

Williams, Blair, and Marian Sawer. 2017. "Rainbow Labor and a Purple Policy Launch: Gender and Sexuality Issues in the 2016 Federal Election." In *Double Disillusion: The 2016 Australian Federal Election,* ed. Anika Gauja, Peter Chen, Jennifer Curtin, and Juliet Pietsch, 641–59. Canberra: ANU Press.

Yeager, Ken. 2000. *Trailblazers: Profiles of America's Gay and Lesbian Elected Officials.* New York: Haworth Press.

Part 1
LGBTQ Voters

1

Profile of the Lesbian, Gay, and Bisexual Electorate in Canada

Andrea M.L. Perrella, Steven D. Brown, and Barry Kay

POLITICAL RESEARCH ON lesbian, gay, and bisexual (LGB) people has focused for the most part on issues of equal rights and identity and on the evolution of the LGB movement since the 1980s. (see, for example, Bailey 1998, 2013; Rayside 1998; Rimmerman, Wald, and Wilcox 2000).[1] Until recently, research about LGB *voters* has been relatively rare, due largely to the lack of appropriate survey data. In the United States, that situation has improved considerably since about 1995, resulting in a growing body of research on the subject (see, for example, Cook 1999; Egan, Edelman, and Sherrill 2008; Hertzog 1996; Smith and Haider-Markel 2002). In Canada, however, progress has been slower, and the electoral character of the LGB constituency remains seriously understudied. In this chapter, we take steps to address this situation.

Why is the electoral behaviour of LGB people of interest? As we discuss below, their numbers have not been established with confidence, but even the lowest estimates (about 2 percent of the adult population) make this voting group a potentially potent force in elections nationally and perhaps a pivotal one in some urban contests. We say "potentially" because not all social or demographic groupings in society speak with a distinct and cohesive voice in the electoral arena. The extent to which LGB persons constitute an electoral community is one of the central questions we pose.

Our objective here is to use available survey data to profile the electoral engagement of LGB citizens in Canada. In doing so, we ask the following questions about the LGB constituency:

1. What is its size and socio-demographic profile?
2. Is it distinctive in its level of electoral engagement?
3. Is it distinctive in its political orientations?
4. Is it distinctive and cohesive in its partisan choices?

Data

Data resources for our investigation are limited. Developing a political profile of LGB people would require a mass survey that asked respondents to identify their sexual orientation, but that's not enough. We also require a sample that is large enough to produce a workable subsample of this population. In addition, such a survey should measure political orientations, civic engagement levels, and partisan choices. To our knowledge, there is no one survey in Canada that accomplishes all these objectives, but there are two data sources that, together, may suffice.

The first of these is the General Social Survey (GSS), a series of surveys undertaken annually by Statistics Canada. These surveys employ very large probability samples, have included a sexual orientation question in recent years, and periodically focus on social and civic engagement. In this series, GSS cycles 22 (Statistics Canada 2008) and 27 (Statistics Canada 2013) include both the sexual orientation question and a battery of items dealing with the respondent's participation in civic and electoral affairs. These probability samples, reweighted to reflect a range of population parameters, provide perhaps the strongest available basis for profiling the socio-demographic and civic character of LGB persons.

However, the GSS are state-sponsored surveys and hence do not deal with issues of a partisan nature – vote choices, assessments of the parties, and policy preferences. To address these questions, we draw on a series of Ipsos Election Day surveys. Beginning with the 2006 federal election, the Ipsos Public Affairs Division has administered a survey to the company's online Canadian panel that participants complete after casting their ballot on election day.[2] Hence, four such surveys are currently available (LISPOP 2006, 2008, 2011, 2015), with sample sizes ranging from twelve thousand (LISPOP 2015) to thirty-nine thousand (LISPOP 2011). The surveys are limited in scope, but each provides respondent assessments of the parties and issues, vote choice, and reasons for that vote. Although the major limitation of these studies is that they are not probability samples of the voting electorate, they have been reweighted to reflect the socio-demographic and political character of the country. Furthermore, they provide a sizable subsample of our target population. Online panel samples have proved useful for achieving our main task, which is comparing the behaviour of groups (LGB with non-LGB) within the electorate (Borges and Clarke 2008; Stephenson and Crête 2011).

The GSS and Ipsos studies employed somewhat differing questions to identify LGB persons. The GSS studies asked respondents: "Do you consider yourself to be ... heterosexual (sexual relations with people of the opposite sex), homosexual, that is lesbian or gay (sexual relations with people of your own sex), bisexual (sexual relations with people of both sexes)?" The GSS questions allow us to distinguish bisexual from homosexual respondents, but segmentation at that level of analysis reduces cell counts precipitously, so we will do so sparingly. The Ipsos surveys posed the following question: "Are you a member of the gay, lesbian, bisexual or transgender community?" Inclusion of the transgender category here means that the GSS and Ipsos sexual-minority populations differ from each other. However, because the difference is modest – US estimates of the transgender population are less than 0.5 percent (Conway 2002; Egan, Edelman, and Sherrill 2008; Olyslager and Conway 2007) – we will confine our discussion to the LGB rather than the LGBT populations. (See the Appendix on page 75 for numbers of target respondents on which we base our analyses.)

Size of the LGB Constituencies

The "constituency" explored here is not the LGB population, but the subset of it that has chosen to identify as such. Estimating the size of this subset is complicated by the fact that survey researchers ask the sexual orientation question only infrequently. As a result, there are few data points with which to work, and some of those are based on nonprobability samples. As well, the willingness of LGB respondents to self-identify in these surveys seems to be affected by the survey's mode of delivery and its sponsor. Interactive Voice Response (IVR) and web-based surveys tend to generate higher estimates than do face-to-face or telephone interviews (Kreuter, Presser, and Tourangeau 2008). Estimates are also higher for commercial surveys than for those sponsored by governments (Tourangeau and Smith 1996). Third, as the social stigma associated with LGB identification lessens, the size of the constituency appears to be a moving target. For example, US researchers report that the size of the constituency in that country doubled during the 1990s (Bailey 1998; Lewis, Rogers, and Sherrill 2011). Fourth, though much of the literature treats the LGB constituency as a single electoral community, this may not be warranted. Research in the United States suggests that people who identify as bisexuals are not as politically distinct as those who identify themselves as lesbians or gays (Herek et al. 2010; Lewis, Rogers, and Sherrill 2011). Further, Andrea Perrella, Steven Brown, and Barry Kay (2012) find that LGB males and females in Canada, though equally averse to the Conservative Party in their 2006 voting, exhibited different patterns in choosing among the non-Conservative alternatives. As a result, where data permit, we will test for differences among these subgroups.

With these caveats in mind, evidence suggests that LGB persons currently comprise between 2.0 percent and 5.5 percent of the adult Canadian population.[3] The lower bound of this range is based on Canadian probability samples, estimates from which have grown steadily since the question was first posed in 2003 – from 1.7 percent (Canada 2003) to 2.1 percent in 2008 (Statistics Canada 2008) and to 2.7 percent in 2013 (Statistics Canada 2013). However, the opt-in panel samples of voters used by Ipsos have produced much higher estimates, ranging from 4.2 percent in 2006 to 5.5 percent in 2015. A 2012 Forum poll using IVR technology reported levels in the same 5 percent range (*National Post* 2012).

It is not clear what explains these differences. To be sure, the GSS samples are of the *adult* population, whereas the Ipsos samples are of the *voting* population, and the Ipsos question included the transgendered category. However, estimating LGB numbers using only the *voting* subsets of the GSS samples does not narrow the gap, and as we noted above, size estimates of the transgender or transsexual population would not account for the difference. Because the GSS studies are government-sponsored projects that employ telephone interviews, respondents may be more reluctant to disclose their sexual orientation; however, we are not in a position to explore this possibility.

As noted, the GSS studies allow us to segment the Canadian LGB grouping in terms of both gender and the proportions who consider themselves bisexual rather than homosexual. Regarding gender mix among LGB respondents, both GSS surveys indicate that males marginally outnumber females (52 percent versus 48 percent in 2008 and 53 percent versus 47 percent in 2013). There is reason for caution when considering this gender split. It is roughly consistent with that reported by Patrick Egan, Murray Edelman, and Kenneth Sherrill (2008) in a recent US study, but it is at odds with most other research on the question. Both in the United States (Bailey 2013; Black et al. 2000; Herek et al. 2010) and elsewhere (Wellings et al. 1990; Wilson 2004), most studies estimate male-to-female ratios in the neighbourhood of two to one. As well, all four Ipsos studies report ratios of at least two males for every female LGB person.

Regarding the relative size of the bisexual subset, the 2008 and 2013 GSS tell somewhat different stories. Whereas the 2008 GSS suggests that bisexuals constitute about 39 percent of the sexual-minority community, they slightly outnumber homosexuals (52 percent versus 48 percent) in the 2013 GSS. Such differences are not uncommon in the comparative literature on this question (see Gates 2011). More consistent in that literature is the finding that males and females have quite different splits. For males in both the comparative literature and our GSS data, gays far outnumber bisexuals, frequently by a factor of two. For females, on the other hand, most studies report that bisexuals constitute a majority (Gates 2011; Herek et al. 2010). The Canadian GSS data are in the same ballpark: there are as many bisexuals as lesbians in 2008 and fully twice as many bisexual females as lesbians in 2013.[4]

A Comparative Socio-Demographic Profile

Although we have no reason to believe that sexual orientation is anything but randomly distributed, at least within gender population groups, the same cannot be said for individuals who have publicly identified as LGB. As a preliminary step to our analysis, then, it is essential to sketch their socio-demographic character so we can assess their political distinctiveness apart from their social or demographic one.

Table 1.1 displays relative frequency distributions for an array of socio-demographic variables, broken down by LGB versus non-LGB status and by gender. For the purposes of this analysis, we have pooled the 2008 and 2013 GSS samples. The LGB subgroup is strikingly distinctive on several dimensions – age, urban residency, and religion. Regarding age, LGB respondents are more likely to fall into the eighteen to thirty-four age group than the rest of the sample and much less likely to be aged fifty-five or older. They are similarly distinctive in their residency pattern: relative to others, they are much more likely to live in metropolitan areas. In terms of religious affiliation, the most notable distinction is in the proportion of LGB respondents who are unaffiliated with any organized religion. Whereas 21.5 percent of the total sample claim no religion, 38.0 percent of the LGB group do so. And LGB respondents who acknowledged an organized religious affiliation are significantly less likely to attend services on a regular basis. In addition to these very notable differences, there are modest distinctions regarding education, income, and visible-minority status. Gay/bisexual males (but not females) are more likely to hold a university degree and to be from a visible minority. On income, LGB respondents are generally modestly over-represented in the lowest income group (less than $60,000) and under-represented in the highest one ($100,000 and higher), which challenges some popularly held notions that LGB people command some degree of "pink economic power" (see, for example, Green 2016; Morris 1999).

How does this profile compare with those from other countries and other times? For the most part, it tells a similar story: age, education, urban-rural residency, and income differences are a consistent pattern in American (Bailey 2013; Egan, Edelman, and Sherrill 2008; Herek et al. 2010) and Australian (Wilson 2004) research on the question. The socio-demographic profile of the LGB cohort as a whole (see Table 1.1) masks intriguing differences between gays/lesbians and those who self-identify as bisexuals. Specifically, there are significant differences in age profiles (bisexuals, especially bisexual females, tend to be younger), educational levels (the gay and lesbian subgroups tend to be much better educated, with over half of each group holding a university degree), and income levels (gays and lesbians are both more likely to be in the $100,000-plus group).

Table 1.1

A comparative socio-demographic profile by sexual orientation and gender

		All LGB	All Non-LGB	Male LGB	Male Non-LGB	Female LGB	Female Non-LGB
LGB size	All	2.39%		1.26%		1.13%	
	Homosexual	1.27%		0.82%		0.46%	
	Bisexual	1.14%		0.45%		0.67%	
Age	18–34	48.20%	29.00%	43.50%	29.90%	53.60%	28.10%
	35–54	31.5	37.3	32.5	37.8	30.5	36.9
	55+	20.2	33.7	24	32.3	15.9	35.1
	Chi-sq.	199.2***		49.8***		171.9***	
Education	HS or less	34.20%	34.60%	32.70%	35.10%	36.00%	34.00%
	Some post-sec.	23.9	26.1	22.1	25.7	25.9	26.4
	U. degree	41.8	39.4	45.2	39.1	38.1	39.6
	Chi-sq.	3.5		8.9*		0.834	
Household income	Up to $60K	46.50%	39.80%	44.40%	35.90%	48.80%	43.80%
	$61K–$99K	25.1	27.3	25.2	28.4	25.1	26.2
	$100K+	28.4	32.8	30.4	35.6	26.1	30
	Chi-sq.	16.8***		15.0**		4.61†	
Region	Atlantic	6.20%	7.00%	6.70%	6.90%	5.90%	7.10%
	Quebec	24.6	23.6	28.9	23.6	19.7	23.6
	Ontario	41	38.4	39.1	38.1	43.1	38.8
	Prairies	14.5	17.3	13	17.7	15.9	16.9
	BC + North	13.8	13.7	12.3	13.7	15.4	13.6
	Chi-sq.	7.7†		14.5**		8.0†	

Urban-rural	% Rural	10.70%	17.50%	9.80%	17.60%	11.50%	17.30%
	Chi-sq.	33.9***		23.7***		11.76**	
Employment status	Employed	56.26%	59.50%	58.61%	67.61%	53.65%	51.64%
	Retired	10.9	19	12.3	17.6	9.5	20.4
	Student	17.6	8.2	18.1	7.8	17	8.6
	Other	15.2	13.3	11	7	19.9	19.4
	Chi-sq.	150.8***		101.0***		69.8***	
Religion	None	37.80%	21.50%	38.20%	25.30%	37.40%	17.80%
	Chi-sq.	162.6***		47.7***		127.3***	
Religiosity	Mean religiosity	0.17	0.26	0.16	0.24	0.18	0.28
	t-test	$t=6.9$***		$t=4.6$***		$t=4.9$***	
Born in Canada	% Native-born	77.70%	77.40%	76.30%	77.00%	79.10%	77.70%
	Chi-sq.	.10 NS		.10*		.50 NS	
Visible minority	% Visible minority	17.80%	14.80%	19.70%	15.10%	15.60%	14.40%
	Chi-sq.	7.4**		9.3**		.52 NS	
Language	% French	20.60%	20.70%	25.10%	20.60%	15.60%	20.90%
	Chi-sq.	.01 NS		6.7**		8.5**	

Note: † $p < .10$, * $p < .05$, ** $p < .01$, *** $p < .001$

Source: Pooled 2008 and 2013 GSS (Statistics Canada 2008, 2013).

The Electoral Distinctiveness of the LGB Constituency

Our central question concerns the significance of the gay and lesbian constituency in electoral politics. As large as it is, the constituency takes on political importance to the extent that it is distinctive and cohesive in its political behaviour – distinctive in the sense that, after other relevant variables are controlled for, its members behave in a unique fashion, and cohesive in that there is an apparent consensus within the cohort on how to achieve electoral objectives. Early voting studies sensitized us to the importance of group memberships in predicting both attitudes and behaviour, but they also showed that some group memberships matter more than others in this respect – the critical variables being the strength of members' identity with the group, the group's effectiveness in transmitting its political norms, and the salience of the group's political issues for members (Berelson, Lazarsfeld, and McPhee 1954; Campbell et al. 1960; see also Chapter 8 in this volume). Although some evidence suggests that Canadian LGB voters are indeed distinctive in their political orientations and partisan choices (Perrella, Brown, and Kay 2012), that evidence is based on data collected from the 2006 federal election, when same-sex marriage had unprecedented salience as a campaign issue. Hence, it would be premature to generalize from patterns associated with that time. Indeed, the 1990–2010 period for Canadian LGB interest groups involved an intense struggle for political, legal, and social change, such as recognition of same-sex marriage – a bundle of issues requiring state actions and affected by the partisan character of the government (see Chapters 5 and 6 in this volume). With notable successes on all fronts, one might expect the political salience of the group's agenda to wane and with it, the distinctiveness of its electoral choices. We address this as one of our questions below.

Electoral Engagement

As noted above, LGB interest groups have been involved in an intense civil rights struggle over the past several decades that might make the political process both highly salient and personally relevant for its members. Indeed, Patrick Egan (2008) notes in his US study that "coming out" was a transformational experience for many of his respondents, resulting in dramatically greater interest in politics. It is reasonable to ask, then, whether LGB persons are more engaged with the political process than are other citizens, whether they follow politics more closely, and whether they are more likely to vote and engage in other forms of political expression.

The GSS surveys explored the political engagement of respondents from a number of perspectives: recollected voting in recent federal, provincial, and municipal elections, extent of involvement in various political activities, level of attention to media news, and (for 2013 only) level of political interest (see the Appendix on page 75 for item wordings and construction of measures). Table 1.2 compares LGB respondents with other respondents on these dimensions.

Table 1.2

A comparative electoral engagement profile by sexual orientation and gender

	Voting index	Political involvement	Attention to media news	Political interest
All LGB	.74 (.36)	1.26 (.89)	.57 (.39)	.60 (.30)
All non-LGB	.74 (.37)	.93 (.88)	.56 (.40)	.58 (.31)
Sig.	$p < .70$	$p < .000$	$p < .34$	$p < .04$
LGB males	.74 (.35)	1.28 (.89)	.61 (.39)	.64 (.30)
Non-LGB males	.74 (.37)	.98 (.88)	.57 (.40)	.61 (.31)
Sig.	$p < .84$	$p < .000$	$p < .05$	$p < .04$
LGB females	.74 (.37)	1.23 (.88)	.53 (.39)	.55 (.30)
Non-LGB females	.75 (.37)	.88 (.88)	.54 (.40)	.54 (.30)
Sig.	$p < .47$	$p < .000$	$p < .41$	$p < .66$

Notes: See Appendix for the construction of these measures. Cell entries are group means for each measure, with standard deviations in parentheses. The "political interest" question was asked only in the 2013 GSS.

Source: Pooled 2008 and 2013 GSS (Statistics Canada 2008, 2013).

It can be seen that the LGB respondents tend to display greater political engagement on all but the propensity to vote measure. Quite striking in the table is the group's relative level of political involvement, measured here by a battery of ten survey items (see Appendix). Respondents are assigned a score of 0 for no political involvement, 1 for engaging in one political activity, and 2 for engaging in more than one. LGB individuals generally indicated involvement in substantially more political activities than did non-LGB respondents. Other differences in the table tend to be gender-specific in that gay/bisexual males attend more to media news than other males and to indicate greater interest in political affairs.

Are these differences simply a function of the constituency's distinctive socio-demographic profile? If not, are they equally descriptive of both gay/lesbian and bisexual subgroups? To address these questions, we performed multivariate analyses in which the four engagement measures were regressed on LGB status (with gays/lesbians distinguished from bisexuals) as well as a range of socio-demographic control variables. In Tables 1.3 and 1.4, the control variables are all dummies, coded as follows: two age groups, one for eighteen- to thirty-four-year-olds, the other for

Table 1.3

Regression of electoral engagement variables on LGB membership and socio-demographic background variables

		Voting index Coef.	S.E.	Political interest Coef.	S.E.	Political involvement Coef.	S.E.	Media attention Coef.	S.E.
LGB	Gay/lesbian	.06	.04	.09***	.02	.11***	.03	.01	.01
	Bisexual	.05	.05	.01	.02	.11***	.02	−.04**	.02
Gender	Female	.03***	.01	−.08***	.01	−.05***	.01	−.04***	.01
Age	18–34	−.37***	.01	−.04***	.01	.03***	.01	−.08***	.01
	55 and older	.24***	.01	.09***	.01	−.02*	.01	.10***	.01
Education	HS diploma	−.06***	.01	−.06***	.01	−.14***	.01	−.01***	.01
	U. degree	.10***	.01	.09***	.01	.12***	.01	.01	.01
Income	$60K or less	−.10***	.01	−.04***	.01	−.06***	.01	−.00	.01
	$100K or more	.05***	.01	.02***	.01	.05***	.01	.02***	.01
Region	Atlantic	−.04*	.02	−.02*	.01	−.06***	.01	.01	.01
	Quebec	−.07***	.02	.03***	.01	−.04***	.01	.01	.01
	West	−.07***	.01	.00	.01	−.03***	.01	−.01**	.01
Language	Francophone	.14***	.02	.01	.01	−.03**	.01	.00	.01
Residency	Urban/rural	.01	.01	−.01	.01	.01	.01	−.01***	.01
Employment	Employed	.03**	.01	−.04***	.01	−.02***	.01	−.03***	.01
Born	Native-born	.30***	.02	.02***	.01	.06***	.01	.00	.01
Minority status	Visible minority	−.08***	.02	−.05***	.01	−.09***	.01	.00	.01
Survey year		1.39***	.01	NA		−.07***	.01	−.62***	.01
	Intercept	.49***	.02	.618***	.01	.53***	.01	.85***	.01
	Adj. R^2	.50***	.75	.10***	.29	.09***	.42	.65***	.23
	N	27,148		20,919		27,148		27,148	

Note: * $p < .05$, ** $p < .01$, *** $p < .001$

Source: Pooled 2008 and 2013 GSS (Statistics Canada 2008, 2013).

Table 1.4

Regression of electoral engagement variables on LGB membership and socio-demographic background variables, with interactions

		Voting index Coef.	S.E.	Political interest Coef.	S.E.	Political involvement Coef.	S.E.	Media attention Coef.	S.E.
LGB	Gay/lesbian	.08	.06	.07***	.02	.12***	.03	.01	.02
	Bisexual	.00	.08	.01	.03	.10*	.04	−.03	.02
Gender Interactions	Female	.03***	.01	−.08***	.01	−.05***	.01	−.04***	.01
	Female × gay/lesbian	−.07	.09	.02	.04	−.03	.05	.01	.03
	Female × bisexual	.08	.1	−.01	.03	.01	.06	−.02	.03
Age	18–34	−.36***	.01	−.04***	.01	.03***	.01	−.08***	.01
	55 and older	.28***	.01	.09***	.01	−.01	.01	.10***	.01
Education	HS diploma	−.06***	.01	−.06***	.01	−.13***	.01	−.01***	.01
	U. degree	.10***	.01	.09***	.01	.11***	.01	.01	.01
Income	$60K or less	−.10***	.01	−.04***	.01	−.06***	.01	−.00	.01
	$100K or more	.05***	.01	.02***	.01	.05***	.01	.02***	.01
Region	Atlantic	−.04*	.02	−.02*	.01	−.06***	.01	.01	.01
	Quebec	−.07***	.02	.03***	.01	−.04***	.01	.01	.01
	West	−.07***	.01	.00	.01	−.03***	.01	−.01**	.01
Language	Francophone	.14***	.02	.01	.01	−.03**	.01	.00	.01
Residency	Urban/rural	.01	.01	−.01	.01	.01	.01	−.01***	.01
Employment	Employed	.03**	.01	−.04***	.01	−.02***	.01	−.03***	.01
Born	Native-born	.30***	.02	.02***	.01	.06***	.01	.00	.01
Minority status	Visible minority	−.08***	.02	−.05***	.01	−.09***	.01	.00	.01
Survey year		1.39***	.01	-		−.07***	.01	−.62***	.01
	Intercept	.49***	.02	.62***	.01	.53***	.01	.85***	.01
	Adj. R^2	.50***	.75	.10***	.29	.09***	.42	.65***	.24
	N	27,148		20,919		27,148		27,148	

Note: * $p < .05$, ** $p < .01$, *** $p < .001$

Source: Pooled 2008 and 2013 GSS (Statistics Canada 2008, 2013).

age fifty-five and older; two education groups, one for those who did not go beyond a high school diploma and one for those with a university degree; two income groups, one for those with incomes below $61,000 and the other for incomes above $99,000; three region dummies, one each for Atlantic Canada, Quebec, and the West; a francophone dummy; an urban/rural residency dummy (1 = rural); a gender dummy (1 = female); a native-born dummy; a visible-minority dummy; and an employment status dummy (1 = employed).

The results in Table 1.3 confirm some of the differences from our zero-order analyses but qualify others. As in the original analysis, neither gay/lesbian nor bisexual respondents are distinctive regarding their likelihood of voting, and both demonstrate greater political involvement, even with controls for their unique socio-demographic character. Table 1.4 contains the same analysis with the addition of two interactive variables: female × homosexual and female × bisexual. With these additional variables, the male and female subgroups of the LGB community appear somewhat more distinct. First, there are no gender differences among LGB respondents with respect to voting or media attention. But the same is not true for the other two models. Distinctiveness in political interest probably applies only to the gay male subgroup, whereas both gay and bisexual males appear distinct with respect to political involvement.

Political Orientations

One of the most consistent findings in the US literature is that LGB persons tend to be leftist in their political leanings (Bell and Weinberg 1978; Edelman 1993; Egan, Edelman, and Sherrill 2008; Herek et al. 2010; Hertzog 1996; Schaffner and Senic 2006). Indeed, Brian Schaffner and Nenad Senic (2006) acknowledge that the so-called sexuality gap is larger than the gender gap, and Egan, Edelman, and Sherrill (2008) label LGB voters as the most distinctive voting group in the United States. The Ipsos surveys pose only a limited number of questions that might usefully tap general ideological perspectives. The most direct of these was whether respondents considered themselves to be on the "left," "centre," or "right" on most issues, and it was asked only for the 2011 and 2015 surveys.[5] The first two rows of Table 1.5 report the relative frequency with which LGB and non-LGB males and females opted for the "left" label. As in the United States, LGB respondents are much more likely than others to self-place on the left, and that is true for both genders. To determine whether these effects are simply a function of the socio-demographic character of the group, we employed binary logistic regression to control for variables on which the group is distinctive (age, gender, education, urban residence, and no religious affiliation). Although most of these control variables are significant predictors of a self-placement on the left, sexual orientation also remains a highly significant predictor in each year's equation (results not shown).

Table 1.5

Summary of views on social and political issues, by sexual orientation and gender, 2006–15

	LGB–Non-LGB comparisons			LGB gender comparisons			Non-LGB gender comparisons		
	LGB	Non-LGB	Sig.	Males	Females	Sig.	Males	Females	Sig.
Ideological position: % saying "left" (2011)	51	23	p < .001	46	59	p < .001	20	26	p < .001
Ideological position: % saying "left" (2015)	49	25	p < .001	40	69	p < .001	22	29	p < .001
Abortion: % saying legal in all cases (2006)	59	42	p < .001	57	65	p < .03	39	44	p < .001
Capital punishment: % saying should never be used (2011)	38	22	p < .001	39	38	NS	20	24	p < .001
Capital punishment: % saying should never be used (2015)	45	27	p < .001	45	44	NS	25	28	p < .001
Government role: % saying government should be doing more rather than less (2006)	75	57	p < .001	76	74	NS	52	61	p < .001
Government role: % saying government should be doing more rather than less (2008)	75	62	p < .001	75	74	NS	58	65	p < .001
Government role: % saying government should be doing more rather than less (2011)	78	67	p < .001	76	82	p < .01	62	72	p < .001
Government role: % saying government should be doing more rather than less (2015)	80	66	p < .001	80	80	NS	60	72	p < .001

Notes: The ideological positioning and capital punishment questions were asked only in 2011 and 2015; the abortion question was asked only in 2006; the "government role" question was asked each year.

* $p < .05$, ** $p < .01$, *** $p < .001$

Source: Ipsos Election Day surveys, 2006, 2008, 2011, 2015 (LISPOP 2006, 2008, 2011, 2015).

Also interesting in these comparisons are gender effects. As is the case in previous research (e.g., Everitt 2002), there is evidence here of a modest gender gap among non-LGB respondents, with women somewhat more likely to place themselves on the left. However, the gap between gay/bisexual males and lesbian/bisexual females is much more pronounced. Indeed, in 2015, almost seven in ten LGB women opted for the left label, compared to only four in ten gay/bisexual men. However, when we factor in policy views that typically bundle on the left – a pro-abortion stance, opposition to capital punishment, and approval for a government role in solving societal problems – the other rows in Table 1.5 show only modest differences between these LGB gender groups. On these issues, both groups are decidedly more leftist than non-LGB males and females, but the LGB gender differences are statistically significant only on the abortion question and the 2011 "government role" item. It appears, then, that the difference in self-placement has more to do with labelling than with substantive policy differences. The reason for this is unclear, but it may be rooted in the developmental path that each gender group took during the 1970s, 1980s, and 1990s. Specifically, the lesbian feminist movement had a clear ideological message and positioning on the left, whereas the gay male movement was less organized around a larger ideological project and hence less identified with the "left" label (Cook 1999; Echols 1989; Faderman 1991; Johnston 1973). For the most part, the political orientations of Quebec LGB gender groups resemble those of their counterparts in the rest of Canada (ROC) (data not shown).

Partisan Choices

From their study of the 2006 Canadian election, Perrella, Brown, and Kay (2012) made four general observations about the partisan choices of LGB voters. First, gay and lesbian voters were decidedly and distinctively averse to supporting the Conservative Party in that election (see Chapter 5 in this volume). Stephen Harper's Conservatives formed a minority government, garnering 36.3 percent of all votes in the country, but fewer than one in ten LGB voters were part of that support base. Second, because the partisan options and party histories of gay and lesbian voters in Quebec differed from those in the ROC, the two regions had different support patterns. Outside Quebec, LGB support was divided fairly evenly between the Liberal and New Democratic (NDP) Parties, whereas in Quebec, the Bloc Québécois (BQ) received 60 percent of the LGB vote, with the Liberals and the NDP sharing most of the rest. Third, in the ROC at least, there were substantial gender differences in the way that LGB voters distributed their non-Conservative votes. Specifically, gay/bisexual males were significantly more likely to opt for the Liberal Party than for the NDP, whereas lesbian/bisexual females exhibited the reverse pattern. Fourth, in the ROC, the importance of the same-sex marriage issue was the factor that distinguished the voting choices of LGB voters from those of electors with similar socio-demographic and ideological inclinations. In Quebec, however, the LGB cohort was not distinct in the sense that its pattern of choices could be explained in terms of these general socio-political and demographic factors.

As we have noted, the 2006 election was highly unusual in that LGB rights issues were front and centre, both before and during the campaign. In 2005, the Liberal minority government had passed the Civil Marriage Act to legalize same-sex marriage in Canada, but the Official Opposition – the Conservative Party of Canada (CPC) – opposed that legislation and campaigned in 2006 on a promise to reverse the act if it were elected (see Chapters 5 and 6 in this volume). The CPC, with Stephen Harper as prime minister, did win the election, but as a minority government, it failed in its attempt to reopen the question in Parliament. The Harper Conservatives were returned with another minority government in the 2008 election and with a majority government in 2011, but despite pressure from some members of its caucus, the party did not resurrect the issue in those elections. Indeed, in May 2015, it formally abandoned its definition of marriage as a union between a man and a woman. Given this history, it is reasonable to ask whether the LGB vote patterns reported for 2006 are emergent and persisting properties of the constituency or if they are products of an anomalous period. We address this question below by reconsidering Perrella, Brown, and Kay's (2012) four observations from 2006 in light of LGB patterns in the following three elections.

Figures 1.1 and 1.2 track LGB party support over the four elections, separately for Quebec and the ROC. Easily the most distinctive feature of the LGB vote in 2006 was its rejection of the CPC alternative at a time when that party was ascendant in much of the rest of the country. The figures show that this feature of their support pattern remained quite constant over the four elections in both regions. There has been a slight narrowing of the sexuality gap in CPC support in the ROC, but it is still fair to say that in 2015 the party was anathema to the vast majority of LGB voters. This is not likely to change under Andrew Scheer, whose ascendency to the CPC leadership may be attributed in no small part to socially conservative delegates (Boutilier and Tulk 2017). Support for the other major parties has fluctuated widely over these elections, largely, it seems, reflecting the broader period effects associated with each election. In Figure 1.1, LGB voting trends in 2011 and 2015 mirror the broader political climate in those elections: strongly favouring the NDP in 2011 and strongly favouring the Liberals in 2015. But the effect has been accentuated by the precipitous general decline in support for the BQ.

Figure 1.1

LGB support for ROC federal parties in the 2006, 2008, 2011, and 2015 Canadian elections

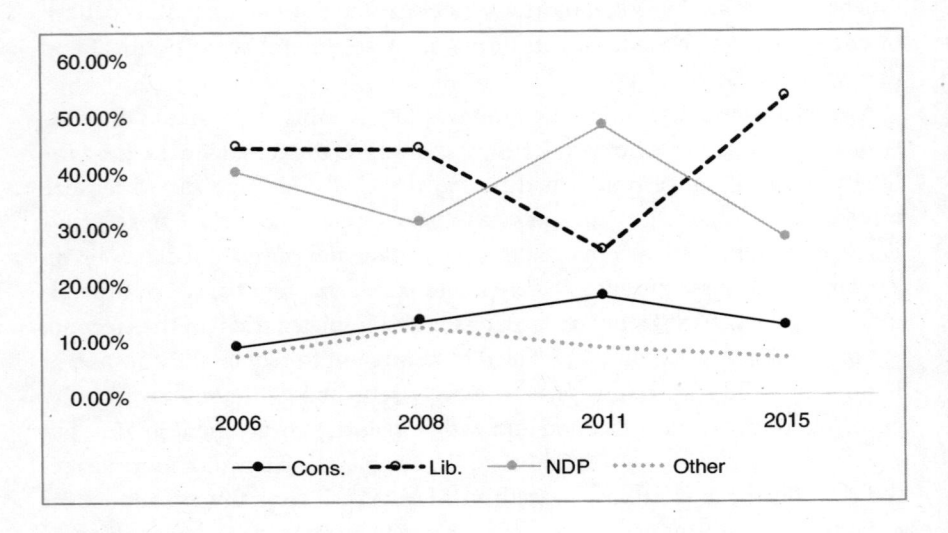

Figure 1.2

LGB support for Quebec federal parties in the 2006, 2008, 2011, and 2015 Canadian elections

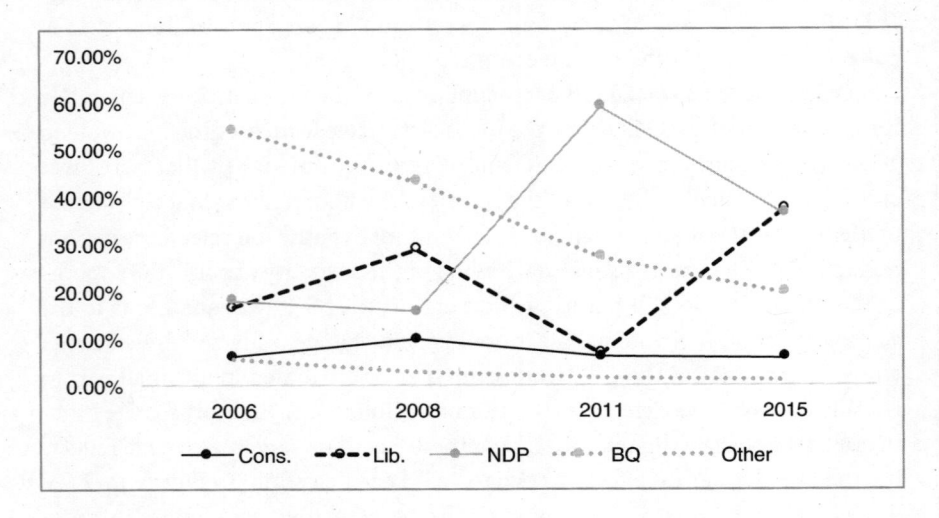

Although it is not apparent from these figures, it is worth noting that the strong period effects in 2011 and 2015 do not entirely account for the swings in LGB vote proportions that favour the NDP in 2011 and the Liberals in 2015.

Specifically, if the non-LGB vote proportions were overlain on these graphs (data not shown), the LGB swings to and from the NDP and the Liberals would appear as more dramatic in each case. In their study of the 2006 election, Perrella, Brown, and Kay (2012) found strategic voting to be more prevalent among LGB respondents than among non-LGB respondents and directionally consistent with efforts to defeat Conservative candidates. It may be the case, then, that a similar sensitivity within the constituency continued to influence partisan choices in subsequent elections.

Although LGB voters were cohesive in their rejection of the Conservative Party in 2006, they were much less cohesive in the distribution of their non-Conservative votes in that election. In particular, there was evidence of significant gender effects, especially among males in the ROC, who tended to vote Liberal, whereas females opted more for the NDP. Figures 1.3 and 1.4 allow us to examine whether any male-female differential is an enduring feature of LGB voting or a function of circumstances specific to the 2006 campaign. It suggests that the pattern in the ROC has persisted through subsequent elections. In Quebec (see Figure 1.4), a similar pattern holds, although gender differences are not as apparent. At least since 2008, lesbian/bisexual women have been more likely than gay/bisexual men to support the NDP and, for the most part, somewhat less likely to support the other non-Conservative alternatives.

Analysis to this point has identified a number of patterns associated with the LGB vote, but some of these may not be distinctive of the group as they

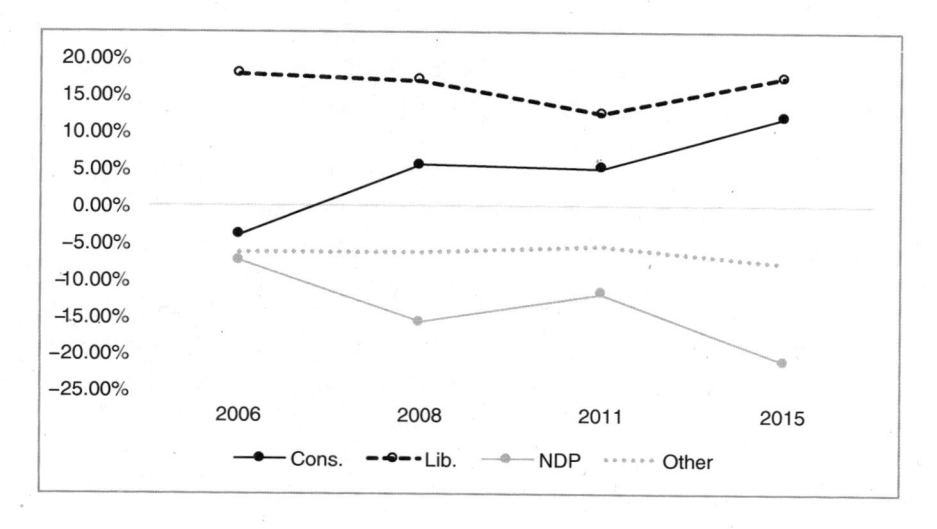

Figure 1.3

LGB male-female vote differentials, outside Quebec

Figure 1.4

LGB male-female vote differentials, Quebec only

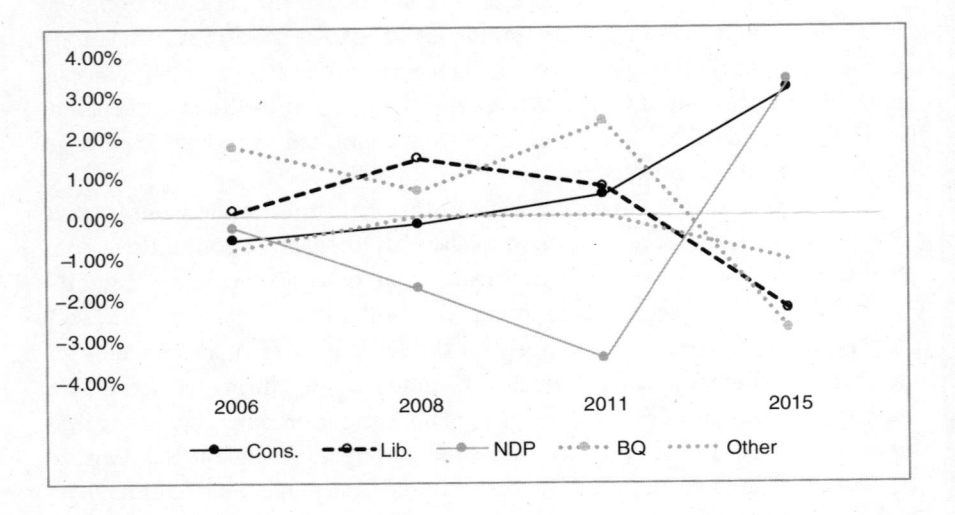

[Line chart showing vote differentials from 2006 to 2015 for Cons., Lib., NDP, BQ, and Other, with y-axis ranging from -4.00% to 4.00%]

may be a function of its socio-political or demographic character. To assess this possibility, we employ multinomial logistic regression, testing separate models for Quebec and the ROC. We include in the models a series of dummy variables to serve as socio-demographic controls. Some of these are identical to the variables in Tables 1.3 and 1.4: the female dummy, the two age dummies, the two education dummies, and the no-religion dummy. Additional variables are community size (1 = city greater than 100,000); two income variables reflecting the lowest (under $55,000) and highest ($100,000 or more) household income cohorts; a variable to reflect those who self-identified as "liberal" (2006 and 2008) or "left" (2011 and 2015) in terms of ideological position; a set of regional dummies for Atlantic Canada, the Prairies, and British Columbia; and a "year" variable that measures the number of years since 2006, ranging in value from 0 (2006) to 9 (2015). In addition, we include two interactive terms in the equations. The first, LGB × election year, tests whether there is any trend apparent in the distinctiveness of the LGB vote. That is, the 2006 election was extraordinary in the sense that there appeared to be much at stake for the LGB community. Did its distinctive pattern of reactions to that election carry over to the subsequent elections when the community's rights agenda was not as politically salient? The second interactive term, LGB × female, throws additional light on the gender effects that are apparent in

Table 1.6

Sexual orientation and vote choice, outside Quebec

	Liberal Coef.	S.E.	NDP Coef.	S.E.	Other Coef.	S.E.
LGB	1.18***	.06	1.26***	.06	1.02***	.08
Years	.03***	.00	.04***	.00	−.010	.01
Female	.17***	.02	.34***	.02	.23***	.03
Age						
18–34	−.06*	.03	.15***	.03	.29***	.04
55 and older	.09***	.02	−.34***	.02	−.37***	.04
Education						
Less than HS diploma	−.20***	.03	−.020	.03	−.24***	.04
More than HS	.44***	.02	.13***	.03	.33***	.04
Income						
Below $55,000	.16***	.02	.43***	.02	.28***	.04
Above $100,000	.010	.03	−.40***	.03	−.17***	.04
Urban	.33***	.02	.32***	.02	−.12***	.03
Ideology (left)	2.78***	.03	2.20***	.03	1.87***	.04
No religion	.23***	.03	.52***	.02	.63***	.04
Region						
Atlantic	.63***	.04	.74***	.04	.24***	.06
Prairies	−1.10***	.03	−.44***	.03	−.27***	.04
British Columbia	−.53***	.03	.25***	.03	.12**	.04
Intercept	−1.52***	.03	−1.71***	.03	−2.36***	.05
N	77,095					
Pseudo-R^2	.31					
−2 log likelihood	50836.53					

Note: * $p < .05$, ** $p < .01$, *** $p < .001$

Source: Ipsos Election-Day Surveys (LISPOP 2006, 2008, 2011, 2015).

Figures 1.3 and 1.4. Are those effects a function of socio-demographic differences between lesbian/bisexual women and gay/bisexual men, or are there possibly cultural differences that go beyond socio-demographics?

Tables 1.6–1.7 and 1.8–1.9 report the results of the regressions. In each case, the Conservative Party serves as the base category. Tables 1.6 and 1.7 exclude the interactive terms, whereas these are included in Tables 1.8 and 1.9. It can be

Table 1.7

Sexual orientation and vote choice, Quebec

	Liberal Coef.	S.E.	NDP Coef.	S.E.	Bloc Québécois Coef.	S.E.	Other Coef.	S.E.
LGB	.92***	.12	1.11***	.11	1.01***	.11	.290	.18
Years	.10***	.01	.25***	.01	−.06***	.01	−.010	.01
Female	.44***	.04	.40***	.04	.35***	.04	.17**	.07
Age								
18–34	−.25***	.06	.25***	.05	.040	.04	.060	.08
55 and older	.13*	.05	−.43***	.05	−.31***	.04	−.66***	.09
Education								
Less than HS diploma	−.39***	.06	−.030	.05	−.020	.04	.030	.09
More than HS	.40***	.05	.10*	.05	.18***	.05	.46***	.08
Income								
Below $55,000	.21***	.05	.19***	.05	.30***	.04	.34***	.08
Above $100,000	.090	.07	−.080	.07	−.16**	.06	−.020	.11
Urban	.25***	.05	.30***	.05	−.11**	.04	−.030	.07
Ideology (left)	2.23***	.06	1.33***	.06	.87***	.05	1.25***	.08
No religion	−.070	.07	.63***	.06	.69***	.05	1.04***	.08
Intercept	−1.48***	.07	−1.62***	.07	.20***	.05	−2.2***	.10
N	24,760							
Pseudo-R^2	.24							
−2 log likelihood	20501.43							

Note: * $p < .05$, ** $p < .01$, *** $p < .001$

Source: Ipsos Election-Day Surveys (LISPOP 2006, 2008, 2011, 2015).

seen from the tables that the socio-political and demographic variables are predictably important in most cases but do not account for the distinctiveness of LGB voting in these four elections. In all but one model (vote for "Other" in Quebec), LGB membership remains a strong and significant predictor in explaining party support.

Table 1.8

Sexual orientation and vote choice, with interactive terms, outside Quebec

	Liberal Coef.	S.E.	NDP Coef.	S.E.	Other Coef.	S.E.
LGB	1.63***	.12	1.50***	.10	1.07***	.14
Years	.03***	.00	.04***	.00	−.010	.01
Female	.20***	.02	.34***	.02	.20***	.03
Interactive terms						
LGB × years	−.07**	.02	−.08***	.02	−.06*	.03
LGB × female	−.59***	.14	.010	.13	.35*	.17
Age						
18–34	−.06*	.03	.14***	.03	.29***	.04
55 and older	.09***	.02	−.34***	.02	−.38***	.04
Education						
Less than HS diploma	−.20***	.03	−.020	.03	−.24***	.04
More than HS	.44***	.02	.13***	.03	.33***	.04
Income						
Below $55,000	.16***	.02	.43***	.02	.28***	.04
Above $100,000	.010	.03	−.40***	.03	−.17***	.04
Urban	.33***	.02	.32***	.02	−.12***	.03
Ideology (left)	2.78***	.03	2.20***	.03	1.87***	.04
No religion	.24***	.03	.52***	.02	.63***	.04
Region						
Atlantic	.63***	.04	.74***	.04	.23***	.06
Prairies	−1.10***	.03	−.44***	.03	−.27***	.04
British Columbia	−.53***	.03	.25***	.03	.12**	.04
Intercept	−1.54***	.03	−1.71***	.03	−2.35***	.05
N	77,095					
Pseudo-R^2	.310					
−2 log likelihood	50755.200					

Note: * $p < .05$, ** $p < .01$, *** $p < .001$

Source: Ipsos Election-Day Surveys (LISPOP 2006, 2008, 2011, 2015).

More than half of the interactive terms in Tables 1.8 and 1.9 are significant. In both the ROC and Quebec, the LGB × election years term is negative, suggesting that, with distance from 2006, voters in the LGB community were less averse to the Conservative Party. This suggests that the distinctiveness of the

Table 1.9

Sexual orientation and vote choice, with interactive terms, in Quebec

	Liberal Coef.	S.E.	NDP Coef.	S.E.	Bloc Québécois Coef.	S.E.	Other Coef.	S.E.
LGB	1.04***	.21	1.40***	.20	1.35***	.19	1.03***	.32
Years	.10***	.01	.26***	.01	−.06***	.01	.000	.02
Female	.44***	.05	.40***	.04	.35***	.04	.17*	.07
Interactive terms								
LGB × years	−.040	.04	−.08*	.04	−.08*	.04	−.27**	.09
LGB × female	.040	.30	.070	.28	−.240	.27	.230	.44
Age								
18–34	−.25***	.06	.24***	.05	.040	.04	.060	.08
55 and older	.13*	.05	−.43***	.05	−.31***	.04	−.66***	.09
Education								
Less than HS diploma	−.39***	.06	−.030	.05	−.020	.04	.030	.09
More than HS	.40***	.05	.100	.05	.18***	.05	.46***	.08
Income								
Below $55,000	.21***	.05	.19***	.05	.30***	.04	.34***	.08
Above $100,000	.090	.07	−.080	.07	−.16**	.06	−.030	.11
Urban	.25***	.05	.30***	.05	−.12**	.04	−.030	.07
Ideology (left)	2.23***	.06	1.33***	.06	.86***	.05	1.25***	.08
No religion	−.080	.07	.63***	.06	.69***	.05	1.04***	.08
Intercept	−1.47***	.07	−1.62***	.07	.19***	.05	−2.21***	.11
N	24,760							
Pseudo-R^2	.24							
−2 log likelihood	50755.20							

Note: * $p < .05$, ** $p < .01$, *** $p < .001$

Source: Ipsos Election-Day Surveys (LISPOP 2006, 2008, 2011, 2015).

2006 LGB vote has weakened somewhat over subsequent elections, although, as noted above, it is still highly distinctive in its support patterns. In no way did LGB voters flock to the Harper Conservatives. In 2006, about 8 percent of LGB respondents indicated support for the Conservatives, whereas in 2015 this level expanded to under 11 percent.

The other interactive term testing the distinctiveness of gender effects within the LGB community tells a more varied story. Curiously, the LGB × female term is highly significant and negative, suggesting that LGB female respondents are *more likely* to have voted Conservative rather than Liberal, compared to all others. The coefficient is not large, and it may simply reflect relative support levels of other groups of voters. For example, from 2006 to 2015, 28 percent of female LGB voters supported the Liberals, compared to 45 percent of their male counterparts. It should be noted that when the multinomial logistic model sets the NDP as the base category, the LGB × female interactive term turns negative for the Conservative and Liberal models. In other words, there is no evidence here to suggest that LGB women are partisans of the Conservatives. In effect, then, the LGB gender differences in party support observed in Figures 1.3 and 1.4 are mostly explicable in terms of their social or demographic composition. However, the LGB gender gap in ROC Liberal Party support, apparent in Figure 1.3, is the exception; the significant negative coefficient for the interactive term suggests that lesbian/bisexual women are less likely to support the Liberal Party in the ROC, even after accounting for social, political, and demographic differences.

Summary and Conclusion

We have learned much in recent years about the struggle of the LGB constituency for rights and respect in Canada and elsewhere, but we know considerably less about its character as an electoral force or even the extent to which it constitutes a political community. Our analysis mined newly available data to throw some light on these questions.

Our research suggests, first, that Canadians who publicly identify as lesbian, gay, or bisexual are sufficient in number to represent a potentially significant electoral force. Size estimates of the group range between 2 and 5 percent of the population, a proportion comparable in sheer numbers to most of the country's ethnic and religious minorities.

Our socio-demographic profile of the group is consistent with cross-national findings in most respects. The LGB cohort tends to be younger and somewhat better educated than the general population, to report less household income, to live in Canada's larger metropolitan centres, and to eschew organized religion. However, within the cohort, there are differences by gender and especially by sexual orientation. For example, relative to heterosexuals, gays and lesbians tend to be much better educated and to report higher household incomes, whereas bisexuals tend to be less educated and to report less income.

Our main task in this chapter has been to assess the distinctiveness and cohesiveness of the LGB cohort as an electoral and political constituency. Our analyses revealed that LGB citizens are indeed distinctive on a number of dimensions. First, we suspected that Canada's recent same-sex marriage debate would render the political process of particular relevance to LGB people. Our analyses showed that gay males (but not bisexuals) claimed more interest in political affairs than did others with similar social and demographic characteristics, and that gays, lesbians, and bisexuals engaged in a greater number of political activities than others.

Second, we assessed the distinctiveness of the cohort's general political orientations. Again, we suspected from US and earlier Canadian studies that it would not reflect the same level of ideological diversity found in the general population. Although we had limited means to test this conjecture, what evidence we had strongly supported that thesis: LGB citizens are almost twice as likely as others to self-place on the left side of the ideological continuum. They were also more likely to adopt a left-wing stance on certain policies. In addition, there were intriguing gender differences in this analysis, with lesbian/bisexual women much more likely than gay/bisexual men to position themselves on the left.

Third, we examined voting patterns of the LGB cohort over four elections. We were particularly interested in whether the large sexuality gap in partisan support found for the 2006 election was replicated in subsequent elections. In general, we found that it was. At least over these four elections, LGB voters remained mostly steadfast in their aversion to the Conservative Party. However, how they distributed their non-Conservative votes was much more variable and reflected changes in the broader partisan political climate. As a consequence, it seems that the partisan disposition of the cohort is defined much more by what it is not than by a positive affiliation with one party or another. That being said, there are again gender differences in partisan affinities within the LGB group. Lesbian/bisexual women are consistently more likely than are gay/bisexual men to support the NDP and less likely to support the Liberal Party.

Although this chapter goes some distance in addressing our central research question, there remain significant gaps that should shape future inquiry. One of these concerns the appropriate group unit on which to focus (LGB or some combination of the cohort's subgroups). Our analysis suggests that though the LGB cohort has a distinctive electoral voice, it is certainly not a homogeneous community and should not be conceptualized as a single social or political entity.

APPENDIX

General Social Survey, Cycles 22 (2008) and 27 (2013)

GSS data are based on the following unweighted LGB subsets: for the 2008 GSS, 396 LGB respondents composed of 140 gay males, 63 bisexual males, 100 lesbian females, and 93 bisexual females; for the 2013 GSS, 683 LGB respondents composed of 223 gay males, 128 bisexual males, 128 lesbian females, and 204 bisexual females. Our analyses are based on data from these two surveys, normalized, reweighted to reflect the Canadian adult population on selected sociodemographic variables, and pooled to form one data file.

Sexual Orientation
  Do you consider yourself to be ...?
  Interviewer: Read categories to respondent.

  1. Heterosexual (sexual relations with people of the opposite sex)
  2. Homosexual, that is, lesbian or gay (sexual relations with people of your own sex)
  3. Bisexual (sexual relations with people of both sexes)

  Don't know
  Refusal

Political Engagement Measures

Mean Voting Index Score (range 0–1 reflecting proportion of elections across the three levels in which respondent was both eligible and recalled voting)

Interest in Politics (converted to 0–1 range with 1 = "very interested") (only in 2013 GSS)

  Generally speaking, how interested are you in politics (e.g., international, national, provincial, or municipal)?

  1. Not at all interested. 2. Not very interested. 3. Somewhat interested. 4. Very interested.

Political Involvement (range 0–10 reflecting number of activities "done")

  In the past 12 months, have you done any of the following activities:

  - Searched for information on a political issue?
  - Volunteered for a political party?
  - Expressed your views on an issue by contacting a newspaper or a politician?

- Expressed your views on a political or social issue through an internet forum or news website?
- Signed a petition on paper?
- Signed an internet petition?
- Attended a public meeting?
- Spoke out at a public meeting?
- Participated in a demonstration or march?
- Worn a badge or T-shirt, or displayed a lawn sign in support or opposition to a political or social issue?

Media Attention (converted to 0–1 range with 1 = "daily")

How frequently do you follow news and current affairs (e.g., international, national, regional, or local)?

1. Daily. 2. Several times a week. 3. Several times a month. 4. Rarely. 5. Never.

Ipsos Election Day Surveys

Ipsos data are based on the following unweighted respondent subsets: LGB subsamples of 1,317 in 2006, of which 767 are male; 1,353 in 2008, of which 743 are male; 1,394 in 2011, of which 814 are male; and 518 in 2015, of which 311 are male. Our analyses are based on these data, reweighted to reflect the Canadian adult population on selected socio-demographic variables.

Sexual Orientation

Are you a member of the gay, lesbian, bisexual or transgender community?
1. Yes   2. No   3. DK/Not specified   4. DK/Refused/Not Stated

Notes

1. In most cases, we will use the standard acronym, LGB, to describe people who identify as lesbian, gay, or bisexual. However, we will also use such phrases as gay, gay/bisexual, lesbian, lesbian/bisexual, and sexual-minority persons as the context dictates and to enhance readability.
2. Recruitment to the Ipsos panel is ongoing and is conducted by a variety of means. Some panellists are invited from online sources, such as websites and email, and others from offline sources, such as telephone interviews. The size of the panel varies over time, but it ranged between 130,000 and 200,000 for the 2006–15 period of our study. Response rates to these election day surveys have ranged between 10 and 20 percent of the panel, but because only voters are eligible to participate, the response rate of the panel's voter subset of the panel is greater than 10 to 20 percent.
3. Size estimates of the LGB population in the United States similarly range between 2.0 and 5.6 percent of the adult population. Gary Gates (2011) finds that, across five studies using probability sampling, the average was 3.5 percent. An additional 0.3 percent identified as transgendered. The Hunter College poll of 2008 reported an estimate of 2.9

percent (Egan, Edelman, and Sherrill 2008). Shaun Wilson (2004) reports size estimates for Australia of 3.9 percent overall (1.6 percent gay men, 1.0 percent bisexual men, 0.5 percent lesbian women, and 0.9 percent bisexual women). Another Australian survey (Grulich et al. 2003) reported an estimate of 4.7 percent overall.

4 Indeed, the increase in LGB proportions between 2008 and 2013 – from 2.1 percent to 2.7 percent of the sample – is mostly an increase in those identifying as bisexual.

5 The 2006 and 2008 Ipsos surveys asked a different question: whether respondents considered themselves to be "liberal," "moderate," or "conservative" on most issues. Because the question confounds ideological positioning with partisan labels, interpretation of responses is problematic. Indeed, within the LGB cohort, there were no gender effects when the "liberal" option was offered, but as we show below, there were dramatic effects when it was labelled "left."

References

Bailey, Robert W. 1998. *Out and Voting: The Gay, Lesbian and Bisexual Vote in Congressional Elections, 1990–1996*. Washington, DC: Policy Institute of the National Gay and Lesbian Task Force. Copy on file with the author.

–. 2013. *Gay Politics, Urban Politics: Identity and Economics in the Urban Setting*. New York: Columbia University Press.

Bell, Alan P., and Martin S. Weinberg. 1978. *Homosexualities: A Study of Diversity among Men and Women*. New York: Simon and Schuster.

Berelson, Bernard, Paul F. Lazarsfeld, and William McPhee. 1954. *Voting: A Study of Opinion Formation in a Presidential Campaign*. Chicago: University of Chicago Press.

Black, Dan, Gary Gates, Seth Sanders, and Lowell Taylor. 2000. "Demographics of the Gay and Lesbian Population in the United States: Evidence from Available Systematic Data Sources." *Demography* 37 (2): 139–54. https://doi.org/10.2307/2648117

Borges, Walter, and Harold D. Clarke. 2008. "Cues in Context: Analysing the Heuristics of Referendum Voting with an Internet Survey Experiment." *Journal of Elections, Public Opinion and Parties* 18 (4): 433–48. https://doi.org/10.1080/17457280802305243

Boutilier, Alex, and Cameron Tulk. 2017. "Social Conservative Candidates Got Strong Support from Toronto Suburbs, Leadership Data Says." *Toronto Star*, May 29.

Campbell, Angus, Philip E. Converse, Warren E. Miller, and Donald E. Stokes. 1960. *The American Voter*. Chicago: University of Chicago Press.

Canada. 2003. "Canadian Community Health Survey." *The Daily*, Statistics Canada, June 15. http://www.statcan.gc.ca/daily-quotidien/040615/dq040615b-eng.htm

Conway, Lynn. 2002. "How Frequently Does Transsexualism Occur?" Unpublished paper. http://www.conseil-lgbt.ca/wp-content/uploads/2013/12/How-Frequently-Does-Transsexualism-Occur.pdf

Cook, Timothy E. 1999. "The Empirical Study of Lesbian, Gay, and Bisexual Politics: Assessing the First Wave of Research." *American Political Science Review* 93 (3): 679–92. https://doi.org/10.2307/2585582

Echols, Alice. 1989. *Daring to Be Bad: Radical Feminism in America, 1967–1975*. Minneapolis: University of Minnesota Press.

Edelman, Murray. 1993. "Understanding the Gay and Lesbian Vote in '92." *Public Perspective* 4 (3): 32–33.

Egan, Patrick J. 2008. "Explaining the Distinctiveness of Lesbians, Gays, and Bisexuals in American Politics." http://papers.ssrn.com/sol3/papers.cfm?abstract_id=1006223

Egan, Patrick J., Murray S. Edelman, and Kenneth Sherrill. 2008. *Findings from the Hunter College Poll of Lesbians, Gays and Bisexuals: New Discoveries about Identity, Political Attitudes, and Civic Engagement*. New York: Hunter College.

Everitt, Joanna. 2002. "Gender Gaps on Social Welfare Issues: Why Do Women Care?" In *Citizen Politics: Research and Theory in Canadian Political Behaviour*, ed. Joanna Everitt and Brenda O'Neill, 110–25. Toronto: Oxford University Press.

Faderman, Lilian. 1991. *Odd Girls and Twilight Lovers: A History of Lesbian Life in Twentieth-Century America*. New York: Columbia University Press.

Gates, Gary J. 2011. "How Many People Are Lesbian, Gay, Bisexual and Transgender?" Williams Institute, Faculty of Law, University of California, Los Angeles. http://williamsinstitute.law.ucla.edu/research/census-LGB-demographics-studies/how-many-people-are-lesbian-gay-bisexual-and-transgender/

Green, Jeff. 2016. "LGBT Purchasing Power Near $1 Trillion Rivals Other Minorities." Bloomberg. https://www.bloomberg.com/news/articles/2016-07-20/lgbt-purchasing-power-near-1-trillion-rivals-other-minorities

Grulich, Andrew E., Richard O. Visser, Anthony M.A. Smith, Chris E. Rissel, and Juliet Richters. 2003. "Sex in Australia: Homosexual Experience and Recent Homosexual Encounters." *Australian and New Zealand Journal of Public Health* 27 (2): 155–63. https://doi.org/10.1111/j.1467-842x.2003.tb00803.x

Herek, Gregory M., Aaron T. Norton, Thomas J. Allen, and Charles L. Sims. 2010. "Demographic, Psychological, and Social Characteristics of Self-Identified Lesbian, Gay, and Bisexual Adults in a US Probability Sample." *Sexuality Research and Social Policy* 7 (3): 176–200. https://doi.org/10.1007/s13178-010-0017-y. Medline:20835383

Hertzog, Mark. 1996. *The Lavender Vote: Lesbians, Gay Men, and Bisexuals in American Electoral Politics*. New York: New York University Press.

Johnston, Jill. 1973. *Lesbian Nation: The Feminist Solution*. New York: Simon and Schuster.

Kreuter, Frauke, Stanley Presser, and Roger Tourangeau. 2008. "Social Desirability Bias in CATI, IVR, and Web Surveys: The Effects of Mode and Question Sensitivity." *Public Opinion Quarterly* 72 (5): 847–65. https://doi.org/10.1093/poq/nfn063

Lewis, Gregory B., Marc A. Rogers, and Kenneth Sherrill. 2011. "Lesbian, Gay, and Bisexual Voters in the 2000 US Presidential Election." *Politics and Policy* 39 (5): 655–77. https://doi.org/10.1111/j.1747-1346.2011.00315.x

LISPOP. 2006, 2008, 2011, 2015. *Ipsos Election Day Surveys*. Laurier Institute for the Study of Public and Policy (LISPOP). http://lispop.ca/content/ipsos-canada-election-surveys.

Morris, Chris. 1999. "Now Meet the Real Gay Mafia." *New Statesman*, February 12, 22–23. https://www.newstatesman.com/now-meet-real-gay-mafia

National Post. 2012. "The True North LGBT: New Poll Reveals Landscape of Gay Canada." July 6. http://news.nationalpost.com/news/canada/the-true-north-LGB-new-poll-reveals-landscape-of-gay-canada

Olyslager, Femke, and Lynn Conway. 2007. "On the Calculation of the Prevalence of Transsexualism." Paper presented to the WPATH Twentieth International Symposium, September 5–8, Chicago. http://citeseerx.ist.psu.edu/viewdoc/download?doi=10.1.1.692.8704&rep=rep1&type=pdf

Perrella, Andrea M.L., Steven D. Brown, and Barry J. Kay. 2012. "Voting Behaviour among the Gay, Lesbian, Bisexual and Transgendered Electorate." *Canadian Journal of Political Science* 45 (1): 89–117. https://doi.org/10.1017/s000842391100093x

Rayside, David. 1998. *On the Fringe: Gays and Lesbians in Politics*. Ithaca: Cornell University Press.

Rimmerman, Craig A., Kenneth D. Wald, and Clyde Wilcox. 2000. *The Politics of Gay Rights*. Chicago: University of Chicago Press.

Schaffner, Brian, and Nenad Senic. 2006. "Rights or Benefits? Explaining the Sexual Identity Gap in American Political Behavior." *Political Research Quarterly* 59 (1): 123–32. https://doi.org/10.1177/106591290605900111

Smith, Raymond A., and Donald P. Haider-Markel. 2002. *Gay and Lesbian Americans and Political Participation: A Reference Handbook*. Santa Barbara: ABC-CLIO.

Statistics Canada. 2008. *General Social Survey – Social Networks (SN) (master file)*. Statistics Canada (producer). Using University of Waterloo Research Data Centre (distributor). https://uwaterloo.ca/southwestern-ontario-research-data-centre/

–. 2013. *General Social Survey – Social Identity (SI) (master file)*. Statistics Canada (producer). Using University of Waterloo Research Data Centre (distributor). https://uwaterloo.ca/southwestern-ontario-research-data-centre/

Stephenson, Laura B., and Jean Crête. 2011. "Studying Political Behavior: A Comparison of Internet and Telephone Surveys." *International Journal of Opinion Research* 23 (1): 24–55. https://doi.org/10.1093/ijpor/edq025

Tourangeau, Roger, and Tom W. Smith. 1996. "Asking Sensitive Questions: The Impact of Data Collection Mode, Question Format, and Question Context." *Public Opinion Quarterly* 60 (2): 275–304. https://doi.org/10.1086/297751

Wellings, K., J. Field, J. Wadsworth, A.M. Johnson, R.M. Anderson, and S.A. Bradshaw. 1990. "Sexual Lifestyles under Scrutiny." *Nature* 348 (6299): 276–78. https://doi.org/10.1038/348276a0. Medline:2250696

Wilson, Shaun. 2004. "Gay, Lesbian, Bisexual and Transgender Identification and Attitudes to Same-Sex Relationships in Australia and the United States." *People and Place* 12 (4): 12–21.

2

Winning as a Woman/Winning as a Lesbian
Voter Attitudes toward Kathleen Wynne in the 2014 Ontario Election

Joanna Everitt and Tracey Raney

ONTARIO'S PROVINCIAL ELECTION of June 12, 2014, resulted in two historic firsts when Kathleen Wynne became the first elected female and first openly gay premier in the province's history. Although Wynne had inherited the premier's office in January of 2013 when she was chosen as the Liberal Party leader, the 2014 election represented the first chance for the voters of Ontario – Canada's largest and most urban province – to confirm their willingness to vote for a gay politician in such an elite role. Although other lesbian, gay, or bisexual (LGB) politicians had led their provincial parties and governed as premier before, Wynne was the first out politician to take her party to electoral victory.[1] As a result, the 2014 Ontario election presents an important opportunity to explore public attitudes toward a high-profile LGB politician in an electoral context.

Using data from an original survey of Ontario voters collected as part of the Comparative Provincial Election Project (CPEP), we assess how and whether voters relied on gender- and sexual-orientation-based stereotypes in their evaluations of Kathleen Wynne in the 2014 election. Canadian research has considered media stereotyping of relatively new LGB candidates (e.g., Everitt and Camp's 2009 work on Allison Brewer in New Brunswick; see also Chapter 3 in this volume). However, less attention has been paid to how voters might rely on stereotypes in their assessments of more established out LGB politicians. In electoral settings in which voters have more information about candidates and their policies, we might expect that they would be less inclined to rely upon group-based stereotypes to form their opinions.

Given that Kathleen Wynne had been well known to voters for some time before the 2014 election, our research expectation was that voter stereotypes based on gender and sexual orientation would be minimized in her campaign, and this is supported by our findings. At the same time, we also discovered that stereotypes of Wynne did not fully disappear and that they were utilized in specific ways: men were more likely than women to stereotype her according to gender and sexual orientation, and all voters believed that, more so than the other party leaders, she spoke for the LGB community as a whole. Thus, we argue that whereas some established and openly LGB politicians may be less susceptible than newer LGB candidates to group-based stereotypes, voter stereotyping can persist. These findings have relevance for future intersectional research on voter stereotypes and for out LGB politicians as they seek higher political office over the course of their careers.

Voter Stereotyping Literature

Throughout her political career, Wynne has been open about her sexual orientation; she came out as a lesbian in the early 1990s, years before she first ran for office.[2] Although she has never actively campaigned on a "gay agenda," early in her career Wynne was involved in several local LGB organizations and activities and has acknowledged her status as a role model and gay-rights supporter (on these aspects of the representational roles of out LGBT politicians, see Chapter 8 in this volume). In her maiden speech after being elected, she noted, "As far as I know, I am the first openly lesbian MPP in Ontario. As such, I have a responsibility to young lesbians who are looking for examples of hope and success" (Ontario 2003). In 2013, while running for the leadership of her party, Wynne also addressed her sexuality during a speech to the Liberal convention delegates: "When I ran in 2003, I was told that the people of North Toronto and Thorncliffe Park weren't ready to elect a gay woman. Well, apparently they were ... I do not believe the people of Ontario judge their leaders on the basis of race, colour or sexual orientation – I don't believe they hold that prejudice in their hearts" (*CBC News* 2014).

In addition to her status as an out LGB politician, Wynne's extensive political record has made her a high-profile figure in the province. She was elected as a Toronto school board trustee in 2000 and then to the Ontario Legislative Assembly in 2003. In the provincial cabinet, she held several portfolios beginning in 2006 (Education, Transportation, Municipal Affairs and Housing, and Aboriginal Affairs), and she finally became Liberal leader and provincial premier in 2013. These experiences meant that she entered the 2014 election as a well-known figure with an extensive political résumé that extended beyond her identity as a lesbian or a gay-rights activist. Yet how much of her identity was constructed by voter expectations of her, not just as a woman, but as a lesbian?

To answer this question, we turn to the extensive literatures in psychology and political science on the role that stereotypes play in evaluations of leaders, and political leaders in particular. Stereotypes serve as heuristic shortcuts in impression formation (Chang and Hitchon 2004; Fiske et al. 1987; Jussim et al. 1995; LaMar and Kite 1998; Sandfort 2005), enabling voters to collect and process specific information about individuals (Chang and Hitchon 2004). Although not all stereotypes are negative, those that are (and even those that are not) can reduce a voter's effort to gather more information about a person (Fiske et al. 1987; Golebiowska and Thomsen 1999). Stereotypes become problematic when they are grounded in false, exaggerated, or misleading assumptions about individuals who come from particular backgrounds. Research also suggests that voters make assumptions about new politicians based on their beliefs about other politicians or about others from similar demographic groups. And these assumptions are often held by journalists who reproduce them in their coverage. For example, in their work on Allison Brewer's bid for the New Democratic Party (NDP) leadership in New Brunswick, Joanna Everitt and Michael Camp (2009) find that the media framed her candidacy by relying upon stereotypes of lesbians, activists, and women in politics.

An established basis for stereotyping candidates relates to the political party that they represent. Party cues provide valuable sources of information about the policies and concerns that a candidate might champion (Conover and Feldman 1989; Popkin 1993; Rahn 1993). Those who run for right-wing parties tend to be seen as conservative and as concerned with the economy, national security, and crime, whereas candidates who represent more left-wing parties are seen as being competent on social issues such as health, welfare, child care, and education (Gordon and Miller 2005; Sanbonmatsu and Dolan 2009). These assumptions can offset other stereotypes in shaping candidate evaluations (Dolan 2014; Gidengil, Everitt, and Banducci 2009; Hayes 2011).

Researchers have also examined the role of gender-based stereotypes in voter assessments of candidates (Alexander and Andersen 1993; Huddy and Terkildsen 1993; McDermott 1997; Rosenwasser and Dean 1989). These studies found that when information is scanty, male candidates tend to be seen as more agentic (tough, aggressive, and assertive) than women, whereas female candidates are often perceived as more communal than men (warm, people-oriented, gentle, kind, passive, caring, and sensitive). To better understand the gendered nature of these dynamics, we draw upon role congruity theory, which focuses on the interplay between gender and leadership stereotypes and expectations (Eagly and Karau 2002). In assessments of leaders, agentic qualities are frequently associated with strength, whereas communal qualities are valued – but deemed less important (Miller, Wattenberg, and Malanchuck 1986). The fact that men are perceived as more agentic than women makes it easy for voters to assume that they would make the best leaders. This poses significant challenges to women who enter leadership positions in traditionally masculine fields such as politics. When they do display the assertive and confident manner that is demanded by the field, they end up challenging traditional expectations about gender roles, which can lead to more critical or negative assessments than a man would garner (Butler and Geis 1990; Eagly and Karau 2002).

Although these results persist in experimental studies in which information other than a candidate's gender is sparse, most real-world politicians and leadership contenders find themselves in situations in which much more information is available to the electorate. As a result, studies focusing on actual, as opposed to fictional, candidates reveal that stereotypes are less present when more is known about a candidate (Banducci, Everitt, and Gidengil 2002; Gidengil, Everitt, and Banducci 2009). If stereotypes are at play, they are nuanced by other identities (Dolan and Lynch 2014), such as a candidate's race (McDermott 1998), party affiliation (Alexander and Andersen 1993; Hayes 2011), and sexual orientation (Doan and Haider-Markel 2010).

There is also some indication that the view of women as lacking in agentic traits has declined over time, as more of them assume positions of political influence (Dolan 2010; Eagly and Carli 2007; Fridkin and Kenney 2009). This finding remains true in lab-based environments when respondents are informed that the woman holds a leadership position. In such cases, positional stereotypes may be trumping gender stereotypes, as participants assume that a woman who has already been chosen to fill a leadership role must possess a certain degree of competency (Everitt, Best, and Gaudet 2016). Nonetheless, even when conditioned by other factors, stereotypes can limit and circumscribe the expectations that voters may have about a politician's character and ability to lead.

Stereotyping is not limited to beliefs about a candidate's qualities and characteristics. It can also structure expectations about his or her areas of policy expertise and priorities and concerns. For example, female politicians are frequently perceived as being expert in policy areas such as health, social welfare, and education, whereas male politicians are viewed as expert in "harder" areas such as the economy, trade, and defence (Alexander and Andersen 1993; Dolan 2010; Huddy and Terkildsen 1993; Koch 1999; Rosenwasser and Dean 1989). In addition, respondents in experimental studies clearly assumed that women would be better prepared than men to deal with issues of concerns to other women, to speak for them, and to protect and promote their rights.

One area that has received relatively little attention is the role that sexual orientation plays in political evaluations. This is because until recently, few LGB politicians have run for office (Everitt and Camp 2014; Golebiowska and Thomsen 1999; Herrick and Thomas 2001; Riggle and Tadlock 1999; Tadlock and Gordon 2003). Although public opinion surveys show that more and more people in Canada and elsewhere are willing to vote for LGB politicians (Doan and Haider-Markel 2007), this does not necessarily mean that they are unlikely to use stereotypes in assessing the candidates. Historically, homosexuals have faced stereotypes steeped in social disapproval and contempt (LaMar and Kite 1998; Sandfort 2005; Simon 1998; Viss and Burn 2001). Recent legal, social, and cultural changes have resulted in a growing public acceptance of sexual diversity, and this, in turn, has reduced much of the blatant homophobia and stigmatization that politicians encountered in the past, particularly if they came out before having developed a strong public persona. However, stereotypes can be deeply entrenched in cultural understandings of the world and are often subtler and more difficult to combat than are homophobic attitudes.

This reality is reinforced by the fact that attitudes toward gays and lesbians are fundamentally gendered and therefore influenced by underlying beliefs about how men and women should behave (Viss and Burn 2001). If, as noted above, men are perceived as agentic and women as communal, what are our expectations about LGB politicians? Most experimental studies show that gay men tend to be seen as having female qualities and that gay women are likewise seen as having masculine characteristics (Everitt forthcoming; Tadlock and Gordon 2003). The limited research on real-world campaigns is now several years out of date, but it indicates that LGB candidates are evaluated more negatively than heterosexual ones; they also tend to receive fewer votes and lower evaluations of electoral viability than do heterosexual candidates (Golebiowska 2001; Golebiowska and Thomsen 1999; Herrick and Thomas 2001). Additionally, as members of an identifiable group, LGB politicians are thought to be more concerned than other individuals with promoting the interests of gays and lesbians. This is accentuated by media coverage that presents them as part of a singular movement, or ideology, with a focus on gay-rights issues or a small cluster of left-wing issues, known collectively as the "gay agenda" (Everitt and Camp 2009; Golebiowska 2002).

Although most forms of stereotyping can negatively affect the public's evaluation of specific groups (see also Jussim et al. 1995), the images associated with homosexuality are particularly problematic for lesbian and gay candidates who seek public support (Fogarty and Pettis 2005; Golebiowska 2001; Herrick and Thomas 2001). Part of their difficulty is that popular ideas about gays and lesbians clash with traditional gender role expectations, creating schema incompatibilities. If individuals are penalized in the public mind when they challenge gender role expectations, to what degree are gays and lesbians punished? How might these stereotypes be complicated when these individuals seek political office, which possesses its own series of stereotypes?

Most studies of gay and lesbian politicians have focused more on the experiences of the former than on those of the latter, and there is no doubt that expectations of gay men are difficult to reconcile with common images of the typical mainstream politician – male, white, and heterosexual (Golebiowska and Thomsen 1999). But what is the situation for lesbians who run for political office? How do stereotypes based on their gender intersect with stereotypes that link to their sexual orientation? Do they benefit from being seen as masculine, or are they simply marginalized due to both their sex and their sexual orientation? Furthermore, there is the question of whether male voters are more likely than female voters to be influenced by stereotypes when they evaluate LGB politicians. Although both sexes see women in stereotypical terms (Glick and Fiske 2007), men can hold more traditional views than women in connection with women and their prescribed gender roles (Glick and Fiske 2007; Twenge 1997). This is particularly true when they assess female leaders who operate in traditionally masculine environments (Carli 2001; Eagly 2007; Eagly and Karau 2002). It should be noted, however, that women who held traditional opinions regarding women and gender roles also tended to see female leaders in a negative light. As a result, men and women with traditional views on gender role identities can be particularly discriminating toward women who do not display conventionally feminine qualities. This situation may produce attitudinal conflicts when gender role stereotypes collide with stereotypes based on sexual orientation.

Methodology and Data Analysis

The 2014 Ontario election provided an excellent opportunity for us to explore the role that stereotypical views of gender and sexual orientation play in leadership evaluations. During this election, Kathleen Wynne – a high-profile out lesbian – ran for elite office. Although such a candidate could be expected to evoke stereotypical reactions, the fact that the public was very familiar with her and with her strengths and weaknesses due to her incumbency as Liberal Party leader and provincial premier suggests that stereotyping could be minimized in her campaign. Additionally, the leaders of the rival parties – Tim Hudak (Progressive Conservative) and Andrea Horwath (NDP) – were also relatively well known, as they had led their parties in the 2011 election. As a result, this election and the data it generated enabled us to explore the role that gender and sexual orientation play in voter evaluations of leaders.

To do so, we used data from the CPEP for the Ontario 2014 election, administered by Abacus Data Research, that were collected shortly after the election (see Appendix on page 96 for methodological details). These data enabled us to compare Wynne's evaluations with those of her competitors to assess the degree to which voter stereotyping occurred across perceived leadership traits and issue competencies for each individual. Furthermore, we scrutinized the degree to which any stereotypes that did appear were shared by differing segments of the electorate, including male and female voters, those with high levels of education and political knowledge, those who held traditional values about gender roles, and those who paid a high level of attention to the election.

As people are most likely to embrace stereotypes when their knowledge of an individual is low, we first assessed voter knowledge of and awareness about

Table 2.1

Mean likeability scores for party leaders (standard deviation)

Mean like/dislike scale of leaders	Overall	Women	Men
Wynne	45.7 (34.7)	49.8 (34.1)	41.5*** (34.8)
Horwath	42.5 (27.4)	46.3 (27.6)	38.5*** (26.6)
Hudak	24.7 (28.2)	23.1 (27.4)	26.2 (29.0)

Note: Scale: 0 "strongly dislike," 100 "strongly like."

Independent samples t-test: *** $p \leq .001$, ** $p < .01$, * $p \leq .05$

the three leaders. Not surprisingly, voters were best acquainted with Wynne, the incumbent premier, although her awareness levels were only slightly higher than Tim Hudak's. Seventy-eight percent of respondents knew either a lot (23.4 percent) or quite a bit (55.0 percent) about Wynne, whereas 73 percent knew either a lot (23 percent) or quite a bit (50 percent) about Hudak. Interestingly, the awareness levels for Andrea Horwath were the lowest. Only 18 percent of respondents had a lot of prior knowledge regarding her, and 43 percent had quite a bit. This may be due to the fact that, as leader of the third-most popular party, the NDP, she received less coverage than her competitors.

Asked to rate the degree to which they liked or disliked the three leaders, respondents indicated that Wynne was the most likeable, with a mean score of 45.7 on a 100-point scale (see Table 2.1). Horwath was the second-most popular, with a score of 42.5, and Hudak trailed considerably with a score of only 24.7. Although no statistically significant differences appeared between male and female respondents with regard to the likeability of Hudak, gender gaps appeared for the female leaders. Female voters were more likely than male voters to like the two female leaders (by about 8 percentage points).

We next examined the degree to which stereotyping occurred in voter assessments of the leaders (see Table 2.2). The presence of such stereotyping became clear in the mean score results of the communal and agentic scales and in the responses to questions regarding the issue competencies of the leaders and their ability to speak for women or gays and lesbians (see Appendix for variable coding).

With respect to the traits scales, voters' views of the two female leaders differed from their perceptions of Hudak. As might be expected, both Wynne and Horwath were perceived as far more communal than Hudak. Surprisingly, however, they were also seen as more agentic. These results show that although

Table 2.2

Mean ratings of leadership traits and issue competencies

	Hudak	Wynne	Horwath
Traits			
Communal	.36	.50	.55
Agentic	.41	.58	.52
Issues			
Social	.34	.47	.57
Economic	.47	.32	.36
Protect rights of women and children	.37	.60	.62
Speak for women	.24	.61	.66
Protect rights of lesbians and gays	.30	.72	.57
Speak for gays and lesbians	.19	.75	.42

Note: Trait and issue competency scales: 0 "not at all"; .33 "not very much"; .66 "quite a lot"; 1 "a great deal."

gender stereotyping occurs with regard to communal traits, it is not as prevalent with agentic characteristics. This supports studies that find that agentic stereotyping is declining and that women are no longer viewed as less capable than men when in leadership roles (Dolan 2010; Eagly and Carli 2007; Fridkin and Kenney 2009).

The findings on the communal scale also suggest a certain degree of stereotyping for sexual orientation. Such stereotypes would predict that Wynne, as a lesbian, would be perceived as more masculine than a heterosexual woman, and thus her scores should fall somewhere between those of Hudak and Horwath, which was indeed the case.

The differences between Wynne and Horwath on the agentic scale may also support arguments about stereotyping on sexual orientation. In this case, Wynne was perceived as more agentic than Horwath, as might be expected, if as a lesbian she was presumed to be more masculine than Horwath. However, Hudak's low agentic scores make this claim difficult to sustain. Conclusions about the presence of stereotyping based on sexual orientation in these leader evaluations become even more complicated when we factor in the role of party stereotypes. Hudak, as leader of the right-wing party, was perceived as notably less communal than the other two leaders, and Horwath, the leader of the left-wing party, was seen as most communal. Wynne, as leader of the more centrist Liberal Party, fell in between. These results mirror established stereotypes based on partisanship, as discussed in the literature on voter behaviour.

Although the assessments of the leaders' competencies on social and economic issues did give hints of stereotyping based on gender and sexual orientation, it is clear that party stereotypes had an impact on these evaluations as well. Again, the Progressive Conservative leader was viewed as more competent in dealing with economic issues, whereas the NDP leader was seen as more capable of dealing with social issues. On economic issues, perceptions of Wynne did not differ significantly from those of Horwath, and opinions of her strength in dealing with social policies fell between those of Horwath and Hudak. These results suggest that although women and sexual minorities may face some stereotyping, the image of an established leader's party is likely to have an even greater impact on overall evaluations of his or her issue competencies.

Stereotypes regarding gender and sexual orientation did appear to shape assessments of the candidates' ability to protect the rights of women and children or lesbians and gays and to speak for these groups. Table 2.3 reveals the stark contrast in responses regarding who looked after the interests of women and children. The two female leaders were perceived as almost twice as likely as Hudak to look after women's and children's rights; they were also almost twice as likely to have the phrase "speaks for women and children" applied to them. Similarly, questions with respect to gays and lesbians produced the highest ratings for Wynne; however, Horwath's scores were notably better than Hudak's, probably because the NDP has a strong history of supporting LGB rights (see Chapter 7 in this volume).

When we controlled for the sex of respondents, significant gender gaps appeared. Women voters viewed both Wynne and Horwath as slightly more communal than men voters did, however no statistically significant gender differences appeared in the communal scores for Hudak. Similarly, the female leaders were ranked higher on the agentic scale by female voters than male voters; however, male voters ranked Hudak higher on this scale than female voters. This speaks to past findings that women are more likely than men to take a positive view of women in leadership positions and that men are more likely than women to draw on gender stereotypes in their evaluations (Carli 2001; Eagly 2007; Eagly and Karau 2002).

Statistically significant gender differences also appeared in voter assessments of the leaders' abilities to deal with economic issues, although not with social issues. Male voters were more likely than female voters to stereotype the male leader as strong on the economic front. They were also less likely

Table 2.3

Mean ratings of traits and issue competencies (standard deviation) by respondent's sex

	Hudak		Wynne		Horwath	
	Women	Men	Women	Men	Women	Men
Traits						
Communal	.35 (.24)	.37 (.25)	.53 (.29)	.47 (.31)**	.57 (.23)	.53 (.23)**
Agentic	.39 (.23)	.43 (.25)**	.62 (.28)	.54 (.29)***	.54 (.23)	.50 (.23)**
Issues						
Social	.32 (.26)	.35 (.26)	.47 (.25)	.47 (.25)	.57 (.23)	.58 (.24)
Economic	.42 (.30)	.53 (.30)***	.35 (.26)	.29 (.26)***	.40 (.23)	.32 (.23)***
Protect rights of women and children	.34 (.29)	.40 (.29)**	.59 (.26)	.61 (.26)	.61 (.24)	.62 (.24)
Speak for women and children	.22 (.25)	.26 (.25)**	.60 (.31)	.61 (.32)	.65 (.27)	.67 (.29)
Protect rights of gays and lesbians	.29 (.26)	.32 (.26)	.72 (.25)	.73 (.26)	.56 (.25)	.59 (.25)*
Speak for gays and lesbians	.18 (.22)	.20 (.21)	.75 (.28)	.75 (.29)	.42 (.27)	.42 (.26)

Note: Sig. at: *** $p > .001$, ** $p > .01$, * $p > .05$.

to perceive the female leaders as being competent in this realm. Interestingly, they were more likely than women to perceive Hudak as speaking for women and children and as protecting the rights of this group. Gender differences in voter responses to these questions and the questions on lesbians and gays did not reach statistical significance except in the case of Horwath's ability to protect gay and lesbian rights, again perhaps due to the NDP record on this issue.

Factors Accounting for Evaluations of Kathleen Wynne

One advantage of the 2014 survey collected in Ontario as part of the CPEP is that it provides us with data to better understand the factors that contribute to evaluations of Wynne. To the best of our knowledge, this is the only Canadian survey to measure voter attitudes about such a high-profile LGB politician. We performed a series of regressions on the trait and issue competency evaluations to learn more about why voters perceived Wynne as they did. Along with the variables included in Table 2.4, we tested variables measuring income, union membership, public sector employment, job status, and visible-minority status. As none of these measures reached statistical significance in the models, we did not include them in the final model.

As can be seen from the ordinary least squares (OLS) regressions presented in the first two columns of Table 2.4, evaluations of Wynne as either agentic or communal were positively related to respondents' levels of education, identification as Liberal partisans, feminist or pro-LGB beliefs, positive perceptions of the economy, and exposure to television news (see the Appendix for coding information). Age and affiliation with a religious institution were also important, although their impacts were smaller. Finally, women voters held more positive assessments of Wynne's agentic qualities than men. Interestingly, having a high level of pre-election knowledge regarding Wynne did not affect these assessments. In Chapter 1 of this volume, Andrea Perrella, Steven Brown, and Barry Kay show that the socio-demographic profile of LGB voters differs from that of the general population. This observation may also hold true for those who support out LGBT politicians.

Similar patterns appeared in the factors that were correlated with perceptions of Wynne's issue competencies, with the exception that religious affiliation was not important, and age was not significant for attitudes toward economic issues. As was the case with the stereotypically masculine/agentic assessments, women were more likely than men to view Wynne as having strengths in dealing with stereotypically masculine economic issues.

Perhaps the best evidence of stereotyping is located in the last two columns of Table 2.4, which measure the factors that contributed to perceptions about Wynne's ability to protect or speak for the rights of gays and lesbians. These models produced R^2 values of only .03 and as a result have very little explanatory power. When we compared these results with similar models for Andrea Horwath and Tim Hudak, we found that they, too, produced R^2 values that were much lower than one might expect, yet were larger than those for Wynne. This suggests that, compared to those of her rivals, Wynne's evaluations on these scores may have been particularly driven by stereotypes. In other words, since little in the model explained why Wynne was seen as so much more able than Horwath and Hudak to represent gays and lesbians (see Table 2.2), we are left to conclude that these evaluations were based on stereotypes regarding her identity as a lesbian.

Table 2.4

Determinants of trait attributes and issue ownership for Kathleen Wynne

	Agentic	Communal	Social issues	Economic issues	Protects women and children	Speaks for women and children	Protects gays and lesbians	Speaks for gays and lesbians
Constant	6.48 (1.00)***	6.01 (1.04)***	4.17 (.95)***	.63 (.94)	4.97 (1.11)***	3.04 (1.31)*	1.07 (1.16)	3.37 (1.33)*
Female	.04 (.01)*	.02 (.02)	−.02 (.01)	.04 (.01)**	−.04 (.02)*	−.04 (.02)*	−.01 (.02)	−.02 (.02)
Education	.02 (.04)***	.02 (.00)***	.02 (.00)***	.01 (.00)*	.01 (.00)**	.02 (.01)***	.01 (.00)	.01 (.01)*
Age	−.00 (.00)***	−.00 (.00)***	−.00 (.00)***	.00 (.00)	−.00 (−.00)***	−.00 (.00)*	.00 (.00)	−.00 (.00)*
Urban	−.02 (.01)	−.01 (.02)	−.02 (.01)	.01 (.01)	−.02 (.02)	−.04 (.02)*	−.01 (.02)	−.03 (.02)
Religious	.05 (.02)*	.04 (.02)*	.03 (.02)	.02 (.02)	.02 (.02)	.03 (.02)	.00 (.02)	.01 (.02)
Pre-election knowledge of Wynne	.04 (.03)	.02 (.03)	.01 (.03)	−.00 (.03)	.01 (.03)	−.00 (.04)	.14 (.03)***	.07 (.04)†
Television exposure	.09 (.04)*	.12 (.05)**	.13 (.04)***	.08 (.04)*	.01 (.05)	.13 (.06)*	.09 (.05)†	.05 (.06)
Economic perception	.25 (.02)***	.29 (.02)***	.24 (.02)***	.27 (.02)***	.15 (.03)***	.18 (.03)***	.04 (.03)	.01 (.03)

(Continued)

Table 2.4 (Continued)

	Agentic	Communal	Social issues	Economic issues	Protects women and children	Speaks for women and children	Protects gays and lesbians	Speaks for gays and lesbians
Partisanship	.16 (.02)***	.19 (.02)***	.12 (.02)***	.14 (.02)***	.09 (.02)***	.13 (.02)***	.03 (.02)	.06 (.02)**
Feminist ideology	.23 (.04)***	.25 (.04)***	.13 (.04)***	.26 (.04)***	.04 (.05)	.15 (.06)**	.04 (.05)	.13 (.06)*
Gay ideology	.17 (.03)***	.17 (.03)***	.12 (.03)***	.08 (.03)**	.17 (.03)***	.19 (.04)***	−.03 (.03)	.03 (.04)
Adj. R^2	.44	.47	.35	.42	.17	.23	.03	.03

Note: Column entries are unstandardized OLS coefficients, with standard errors in parentheses. Partisanship is a dummy: Liberal = 1, all other parties = 0.
† $p < .06$, * $p < .05$, ** $p < .01$, *** $p < .001$

Discussion

Our analyses indicate that in real-world settings with an established, out lesbian politician, stereotyping occurs, but that differing identities (partisan, gender, and sexual orientation) generate these stereotypes in complex and overlapping ways. This is particularly the case when politicians are well known and have a public history, factors that may affect opinions of their personalities or issue strengths, thereby minimizing the need for voters to rely on stereotypes to shape their evaluations. In the case of Wynne, voters in 2014 relied upon a mix of stereotypes based on her party, gender, and sexual orientation. Overall, perceptions of her leadership placed Wynne somewhere between Horwath on the left and Hudak on the right. This makes sense from a partisan standpoint, as she was the leader of a centrist political party who ran a fairly centrist campaign. Similar partisan stereotypes were also applied to Horwath and Hudak. A potential consequence of a long political career for out LGB politicians may be that as the novelty of their gender and/or sexual orientation wears off, voters will rely less on the traditionally negative stereotypes linked to this identity and base their assessments on more policy-related cues, including those grounded in partisanship.

Other factors probably contributed to why gender- and sexual-orientation-based stereotypes were not as pronounced for Wynne, or potentially for other, better-known LGB politicians as compared to those found in experimental studies. For example, some candidates make a point of downplaying their sexuality, hoping to avoid being stereotyped in the first place. Although Wynne was not afraid to speak out about LGB issues during the early part of her career, she has been careful to distance herself from the perception that as a lesbian, she is interested solely in gay issues. Shortly after inheriting the premiership, she made it clear that although she was a lesbian, she was "not a gay activist ... That's not how I got into politics" (Ferguson and Benzie 2013). This explicit delinking of her sexuality from her politics can be viewed as an effort to neutralize the stereotype that she might have a hidden "gay agenda" (Golebiowska 2002). In combination with her extensive political record, her efforts to nullify this particular stereotype may have been moderately successful. Another possibility is that Wynne may be perceived as a "feminine" lesbian (rather than "butch"). The fact that she was once married to a man and is a grandmother may have made her a "respectable" political candidate, as her personal history could be seen as gender conforming (on this issue, see also Chapter 3 in this volume). Future research should consider the relevance of these and other heteronormative expectations of LGB politicians.

The media also play a role in shaping voter attitudes toward political leaders (Everitt and Camp 2009). Throughout the 2014 Ontario election, issues of gender and sexual orientation were noticeably muted. In a rare moment during a campaign stop, Wynne mentioned the importance of the Charter of Rights and Freedoms to same-sex marriage, saying that it enabled her and her partner to "live without fear" (Brennan 2014). Aside from this lone statement, neither Wynne nor her competitors discussed questions of gender or sexual orientation throughout the race, and the traditional media followed suit. This low visibility of gender and sexual orientation prompted some media observers and political scientists to claim that they were "non-issues" during the election (Loriggio 2014; see also Chapter 3 in this volume). When traditional media focus on other aspects of political campaigns, it is likely that gender and sexual-orientation stereotypes of leaders become less salient to voters overall.

At the same time, some stereotyping of Wynne persisted in the 2014 election. Our study reveals the emergence of a gender gap in voter evaluations of Wynne's leadership, with male respondents rating her lower than female respondents on agentic and communal traits and on her ability to handle economic issues. Since male voters also viewed Horwath in a similar way, our results show that voter stereotypes based on gender (even when overlapped with sexual orientation and partisanship) can and do persevere for established female politicians, and that they are most pronounced among male voters specifically. Additionally, voters assessed Wynne as best able to speak for, and protect the rights of, gays and lesbians. Partisanship and an extensive political résumé did not completely wash away the stereotype that as a lesbian, Wynne was best positioned to speak for the LGB community. The fact that her sexual orientation was not the focus of the campaign lends credence to the reality that voters knew she was an out lesbian and applied stereotypes based on her homosexuality to some of their evaluations of her, in the same way that they applied gender-based stereotypes to her evaluations (and Horwath's). Although this stereotype may have had little electoral consequence for Wynne (she may have simultaneously lost some votes on the right and picked up some votes on the left because she was seen as able to speak for LGB issues), it is clear that her gender and sexual orientation were factors in voters' minds despite her muted approach to these issues and the length of her career. This finding probably has implications for gender-non-conforming political candidates, including transgender, LGB, and non-LGB candidates, especially in the early stages of their career.

Conclusion

The rights of gays and lesbians have improved considerably in Ontario during the last few decades. In 1995, Ontario became the first province to legalize the adoption of children by same-sex couples, and in 2003, it became the first province to recognize same-sex marriage as legal. In 1999, George Smitherman was elected as its first openly gay MPP; fifteen years later, the electoral victory of Kathleen Wynne as Canada's first out premier added another achievement along the path toward equality. Our findings suggest that progress has also been made in political campaigns: Ontario voters liked Wynne, evaluated her leadership relatively highly across several categories, and ultimately gave her party a majority government, an outcome that seemed far from certain at the start of the campaign. At the same time, our findings also suggest that some caution is in order, in that some voters still relied upon stereotypes of gender and sexual orientation when they assessed Wynne. These negative stereotypes may have been somewhat offset by partisanship and a positive "positional stereotype" due to her incumbency as the sitting premier, a finding that supports recent work by Joanna Everitt, Lisa Best, and Derek Gaudet (2016). The good news in this final observation is that as more out LGB politicians assume leadership positions over time, negative leader stereotypes tied to group characteristics may diminish. The less encouraging news is that some stereotypes appear quite stubborn and challenging to uproot, even for fairly well-established, high-profile, openly LGB politicians.

APPENDIX

Methodological Details

The Comparative Provincial Election Project was administered by Abacus Data Research for the Ontario 2014 election on June 16–24, 2014 (n = 1,000). Probability-based sampling techniques using comparable sample sizes would typically yield error margins of well below 5 percent. Respondents were randomly selected from a randomly recruited hybrid internet-phone panel, which supports confidence intervals and error testing. Data are weighted by gender, age, education, and region according to census data. The questions used in this study are described below.

Traits

We would like to know how well the following words or phrases describe each of the provincial party leaders. How well do the following words or phrases describe [leader's name]? A great deal, quite a lot, not very much, not at all: compassionate, able to build a consensus, honest, moral, in touch with the people, competent, strong leader, intelligent, commands respect, can really speak for women, can really speak for gays and lesbians.

The order of the leaders' names was randomized. Mean composites of agentic (competent, strong, intelligent, and commands respect) and communal traits (compassionate, able to build a consensus, honest, moral, and in touch with people) were created. All variables were rescaled from 0 = not at all to 1 = a great deal.

Issues

We'd like to ask you about how well the leaders deal with political issues. For [leader's name], how well does she or he deal with the following issues: poverty, education, health care, the economy, Ontario's debt, lowering taxes, protecting the rights of women and children, and protecting the rights of gays and lesbians.

Here too, leaders' names were presented in random order. Mean composites of economic issues (economy, Ontario's debt, lowering taxes) and social issues (poverty, education, health care) were created. All variables were rescaled from 0 = not at all to 1 = a great deal.

Leader Likeability

Using a 100-point scale, where zero means that you really dislike the leader and 100 means that you really like the leader how do you feel about the following leaders? Please enter value between 0 (really dislike) and 100 (really like): Kathleen Wynne, Andrea Horwath, Tim Hudak.

Female
A dummy variable, coded 1 = female, 0 = male.

Education
What is the highest level of education you have completed?
We coded responses as 1 = some elementary/secondary/high school, 2 = completed secondary/high school, 3 = some technical/community college, 4 = completed technical/community college, 5 = some university, 6 = bachelor's degree, 7 = master's degree, 8 = professional degree or doctorate.

Age
Year of birth.

Urban
Do you live in an urban, suburban, or rural environment?
This dummy variable was coded 1 = urban, 0 = else.

Religious
Which of the following best describes your religious affiliation?
A dummy variable, coded 1 = for any identified religion or the "other" religion category and 0 = atheist or no affiliation.

Pre-Election Knowledge of Candidate
Prior to the most recent provincial election, how much did you know about each of the following leaders: a lot, quite a bit, not a lot, not at all? Kathleen Wynne, Tim Hudak, Andrea Horwath.
Variables were recoded for each leader: 0 = not at all to 1 = a lot.

Television Exposure to Politics/Elections
How often do you turn to the following sources to gain information about politics and elections? CTV television, Global, CBC television, Sun News network, TVO.
A mean score composite was created and coded 0 = never to 1 = all the time.

Economic Perception
Over the past year, has Ontario's economy improved, worsened, or stayed about the same?
Recoded as 0 = worsened, .5 = stayed the same, 1 = improved.

Partisanship
In provincial politics, do you usually think of yourself as: [party]?

Dummy variables were created for the party of each leader (Liberal = 1, else = 0; Progressive Conservative = 1, else = 0; NDP = 1, else = 0).

Feminist Ideology
Now a few questions about your beliefs. For each of the following statements, please indicate if you strongly agree, somewhat agree, somewhat disagree, or strongly disagree: Society has reached the point where women and men have equal opportunities for achievement; This country would have many fewer problems if there were more emphasis on traditional family values; Most men are better suited to politics than are most women; Society would be better off if more women stayed at home with their children.

A mean composite score was created and rescaled to 0 = anti-feminist to 1 = pro-feminist beliefs.

Gay Ideology
Now a few questions about your beliefs. For each of the following statements, please indicate if you strongly agree, somewhat agree, somewhat disagree, or strongly disagree: Same-sex marriage is weakening traditional family values in this country; Gays and lesbians should not be allowed to adopt children.

A mean composite score was created and rescaled from 0 = traditional to 1 = non-traditional beliefs on gay equality.

Notes
The preparation of this essay was supported with an Arts Accelerator Grant provided by the Office of the Dean of Arts, Ryerson University. Research assistance was provided by Andrea Spender, a PhD candidate in policy studies at Ryerson University.

1 These leaders include Richard Hatfield, who governed New Brunswick from 1970 to 1987 as a closeted gay man; Allison Brewer, who led the New Democratic Party in New Brunswick; André Boisclair, who led the Parti Québécois in Quebec; and Wade MacLauchlan, who became premier of Prince Edward Island in 2015.
2 She came out of the closet in 1991 at the age of thirty-seven, after being married to a man and having three children.

References
Alexander, Deborah, and Kristi Andersen. 1993. "Gender as a Factor in the Attribution of Leadership Traits." *Political Research Quarterly* 46 (3): 527–45. https://doi.org/10.2307/448946

Banducci, Susan, Joanna Everitt, and Elisabeth Gidengil. 2002. "Gender Stereotypes and Political Candidates: A Meta-Analysis." Paper presented at the International Political Psychology Association annual meeting, July 16–19, Berlin.

Brennan, Richard J. 2014. "Kathleen Wynne Says Charter Allows Her to 'Live without Fear.'" *Toronto Star*, May 23. https://www.thestar.com/news/ontario_election/2014/05/23/kathleen_wynne_says_charter_allows_her_to_live_without_fear.html

Butler, Doré, and Florence Geis. 1990. "Nonverbal Affect Responses to Male and Female Leaders: Implications for Leadership Evaluations." *Journal of Personality and Social Psychology* 58 (1): 48–59. https://doi.org/10.1037//0022-3514.58.1.48

Carli, Linda L. 2001. "Gender and Social Influence." *Journal of Social Issues* 57 (4): 725–41. https://doi.org/10.1111/0022-4537.00238

CBC News. 2014. "Profile: Liberal Leader Kathleen Wynne." March 7. http://www.cbc.ca/news/canada/toronto/profile-liberal-leader-kathleen-wynne-1.2564220

Chang, Chingching, and Jacqueline C. Bush Hitchon. 2004. "When Does Gender Count? Further Insights into Gender Schematic Processing of Female Candidates' Political Advertisements." *Sex Roles* 51 (3–4): 197–208. https://doi.org/10.1023/b:sers.0000037763.47986.c2

Conover, Pamela J., and Stanley Feldman. 1989. "Candidate Perception in an Ambiguous World: Campaigns, Cues, and Inference Processes." *American Journal of Political Science* 33 (4): 912–40. https://doi.org/10.2307/2111115

Doan, Alesha, and Donald Haider-Markel. 2007. "Public Attitudes towards Gay and Lesbian Candidates: The Dynamics of Gender and Religion." Paper prepared for the Midwest Political Science Association, Chicago.

–. 2010. "The Role of Intersectional Stereotypes on Evaluations of Gay and Lesbian Political Candidates." *Politics and Gender* 6 (1): 63–91. https://doi.org/10.1017/s1743923x09990511

Dolan, Kathleen. 2010. "The Impact of Gender Stereotyped Evaluations on Support for Women Candidates." *Political Behavior* 32 (1): 69–88. https://doi.org/10.1007/s11109-009-9090-4

–. 2014. "Gender Stereotypes, Candidate Evaluations, and Voting for Women Candidates: What Really Matters?" *Political Research Quarterly* 67 (1): 96–107. https://doi.org/10.1177/1065912913487949

Dolan, Kathleen, and Timothy Lynch. 2014. "It Takes a Survey: Understanding Gender Stereotypes, Abstract Attitudes, and Voting for Women Candidates." *American Politics Research* 42 (4): 656–76. https://doi.org/10.1177/1532673x13503034

Eagly, Alice H. 2007. "Female Leadership Advantage and Disadvantage: Resolving the Contradictions." *Psychology of Women Quarterly* 31 (1): 1–12. https://doi.org/10.1111/j.1471-6402.2007.00326.x

Eagly, Alice H., and Linda Carli. 2007. *Through the Labyrinth: The Truth about How Women Become Leaders*. Cambridge, MA: Harvard Business Press.

Eagly, Alice H., and Steven Karau. 2002. "Role Congruity Theory of Prejudice toward Female Leaders." *Psychology Review* 109 (3): 573–98. https://doi.org/10.1037//0033-295x.109.3.573. Medline:12088246

Everitt, Joanna. Forthcoming. "Stereotyping Gender and Sexual Orientation: Media Coverage's Impact on Voters' Evaluations." In *Gendered Mediation: Identity and Image Making in Canadian Politics*, ed. Angelia Wagner and Joanna Everitt. Vancouver: UBC Press.

Everitt, Joanna, Lisa Best, and Derek Gaudet. 2016. "Candidate Gender, Behavioral Style, and Willingness to Vote: Support for Female Candidates Depends on Conformity to Gender Norms." *American Behavioral Scientist* 60 (14): 1737–55. https://doi.org/10.1177/0002764216676244

Everitt, Joanna, and Michael Camp. 2009. "One Is Not Like the Others: Allison Brewer's Leadership of the New Brunswick NDP." In *Opening Doors Wider: Women's Political Engagement in Canada*, ed. Sylvia Bashevkin, 127–44. Vancouver: UBC Press.

–. 2014. "In versus Out: LGB Politicians in Canada." *Journal of Canadian Studies* 48 (1): 226–51. https://doi.org/10.3138/jcs.48.1.226

Ferguson, Rob, and Robert Benzie. 2013. "Ontario Liberal Leadership: Kathleen Wynne Vows to Work with Opposition." *The Star*, January 27. https://www.thestar.com/news/canada/2013/01/27/ontario_liberal_leadership_kathleen_wynne_vows_to_work_with_opposition.html

Fiske, Susan, Steven Neuberg, Ann Beattie, and Sandra Milberg. 1987. "Category-Based and Attribute-Based Reactions to Others: Some Informational Conditions of Stereotyping and Individuating Processes." *Journal of Experimental Social Psychology* 23 (5): 399–427. https://doi.org/10.1016/0022-1031(87)90038-2

Fogarty, Brian, and Gregory Pettis. 2005. "Measuring Gay and Lesbian Group Affect." *Journal of Homosexuality* 49 (2): 145–56. https://doi.org/10.1300/j082v49n02_09. Medline:16048899

Fridkin, Kim, and Patrick Kenney. 2009. "The Role of Gender Stereotypes in U.S. Senate Campaigns." *Politics and Gender* 5 (3): 301–24. https://doi.org/10.1017/s1743923x09990158

Gidengil, Elisabeth, Joanna Everitt, and Susan Banducci. 2009. "Do Voters Stereotype Female Party Leaders? Evidence from Canada and New Zealand." In *Opening Doors Wider: Women's Political Engagement in Canada*, ed. Sylvia Bashevkin, 167–93. Vancouver: UBC Press.

Glick, Peter, and Susan Fiske. 2007. "Sex Discrimination: The Psychological Approach." In *Sex Discrimination in the Workplace: Multidisciplinary Perspectives*, ed. F. Crosby, 155–87. Malden, MA: Blackwell.

Golebiowska, Ewa A. 2001. "Group Stereotypes and Political Evaluation." *American Politics Research* 29 (6): 535–65. https://doi.org/10.1177/1532673x01029006001

–. 2002. "Political Implications of Group Stereotypes: Campaign Experiences of Openly Gay Political Candidates." *Journal of Applied Social Psychology* 32 (3): 590–607. https://doi.org/10.1111/j.1559-1816.2002.tb00232.x

Golebiowska, Ewa A., and Cynthia Thomsen. 1999. "Group Stereotypes and Evaluations of Individuals: The Case of Gay and Lesbian Political Candidates." In *Gays and Lesbians in the Democratic Process*, ed. Ellen Riggle and Barry Tadlock, 192–219. New York: Columbia University Press.

Gordon, Ann, and Jerry L. Miller. 2005. *When Stereotypes Collide: Race/Ethnicity, Gender, and Videostyle in Congressional Campaigns*. New York: Peter Lang.

Hayes, Danny. 2011. "When Gender and Party Collide: Stereotyping in Candidate Trait Attribution." *Politics and Gender* 7 (2): 133–65. https://doi.org/10.1017/s1743923x11000055

Herrick, Rebekah, and Sue Thomas. 2001. "Gays and Lesbians in Local Races: A Study of Electoral Viability." *Journal of Homosexuality* 42 (1): 103–27. https://doi.org/10.1300/j082v42n01_06. Medline:11991562

Huddy, Leonie, and Nayda Terkildsen. 1993. "Gender Stereotypes and the Perception of Male and Female Candidates." *American Journal of Political Science* 37 (1): 119–47. https://doi.org/10.2307/2111526

Jussim, Lee, Thomas Nelson, M. Manis, and S. Soffin. 1995. "Prejudice, Stereotypes, and Labeling Effects. Sources of Bias in Person Perception." *Journal of Personality and Social Psychology* 68 (2): 228–46. https://doi.org/10.1037//0022-3514.68.2.228

Koch, Jeffrey W. 1999. "Candidate Gender and Assessment of Senate Candidates." *Social Science Quarterly* 80 (1): 84–96.

LaMar, Lisa, and Mary Kite. 1998. "Sex Differences in Attitudes toward Gay Men and Lesbians: A Multidimensional Perspective." *Journal of Sex Research* 35 (2): 189–96. https://doi.org/10.1080/00224499809551932

Loriggio, Paola. 2014. "Sexuality a 'Non-Issue' during Wynne's Election Campaign: Expert." *National Post*, June 14. http://news.nationalpost.com/news/canada/sexuality-a-non-issue-during-wynnes-election-campaign-expert

McDermott, Monika. 1997. "Voting Cues in Low-Information Elections: Candidate Gender as a Social Information Variable in Contemporary United States Elections." *American Journal of Political Science* 41 (1): 270–83. https://doi.org/10.2307/2111716

—. 1998. "Race and Gender Cues in Low-Information Elections." *Political Research Quarterly* 51 (4): 895–918. https://doi.org/10.1177/106591299805100403

Miller, Arthur, Martin Wattenberg, and Oksana Malanchuck. 1986. "Schematic Assessments of Presidential Candidates." *American Political Science Review* 80 (2): 521–40. https://doi.org/10.2307/1958272

Ontario. 2003. *Debates and Proceedings: The Legislative Assembly of Ontario*, December 15. http://hansardindex.ontla.on.ca/hansardeissue/38-1/l015b.htm

Popkin, Samuel. 1993. "Information Shortcuts and the Reasoning Voter." In *Information, Participation, and Choice: An Economic Theory of Democracy in Perspective*, ed. Bernard Grofman, 17–36. Ann Arbor: University of Michigan Press.

Rahn, Wendy M. 1993. "The Role of Partisan Stereotypes in Information Processing about Political Candidates." *American Journal of Political* Science 37 (2): 472–96. https://doi.org/10.2307/2111381

Riggle, Ellen, and Barry Tadlock. 1999. "Gays and Lesbians in the Democratic Process: Past, Present and Future." In *Gays and Lesbians in the Democratic Process*, ed. Ellen Riggle and Barry Tadlock, 1–21. New York: Columbia University Press.

Rosenwasser, Shirley M., and Norma Dean. 1989. "Gender Role and Political Office: Effects of Perceived Masculinity/Femininity of Candidate and Political Office." *Psychology of Women Quarterly* 13 (1): 77–85. https://doi.org/10.1111/j.1471-6402.1989.tb00986.x

Sanbonmatsu, Kira, and Kathleen Dolan. 2009. "Do Gender Stereotypes Transcend Party?" *Political Research Quarterly* 62 (3): 485–94. https://doi.org/10.1177/1065912908322416

Sandfort, Theo. 2005. "Sexual Orientation and Gender: Stereotypes and Beyond." *Archives of Sexual Behavior* 34 (6): 595–611. https://doi.org/10.1007/s10508-005-7907-8. Medline:16362245

Simon, Angela. 1998. "The Relationship between Stereotypes of and Attitudes toward Lesbians and Gays." In *Psychological Perspectives on Lesbian and Gay Issues. Vol. 4, Stigma and Sexual Orientation: Understanding Prejudice against Lesbians, Gay Men and Bisexuals*, ed. Gregory M. Herek, 63–81. Thousand Oaks, CA: Sage.

Tadlock, Barry, and Ann Gordon. 2003. "Political Evaluations of Lesbian and Gay Candidates: The Impact of Stereotypic Biases in Press Coverage." Paper presented at the annual meeting of the American Political Science Association, August 28, Philadelphia.

Twenge, Jean M. 1997. "Attitudes toward Women, 1970–1995: A Metaanalysis." *Psychology of Women Quarterly* 21 (1): 35–51. https://doi.org/10.1111/j.1471-6402.1997.tb00099.x

Viss, Denise, and Shawn Burn. 2001. "Divergent Perceptions of Lesbians: A Comparison of Lesbian Self-Perceptions and Heterosexual Perceptions." *Journal of Social Psychology* 132 (2): 169–77. https://doi.org/10.1080/00224545.1992.9922969. Medline:1501484

3

Media Framing of Lesbian and Gay Politicians
Is Sexual Mediation at Work?

Mireille Lalancette and Manon Tremblay

THE MEDIA ARE the central information source for both political actors and the public; they are an important component of citizens' relationship with politics. In this sense, their presentation of political issues and actors – from candidates and their families and entourage to elected officials and their advisers – plays a significant role in shaping the perception of how politics works, how it is defined, and what is important. The media are gatekeepers, framing and selecting stories. As Erin Tolley (2016, 15) explains, "This selection of stories is framed by a particular – often narrow – set of interpretative lenses." One of these lenses is sex/gender, which has generated several studies in recent years. Another is sexual orientation, which has been much less thoroughly explored by researchers.

The objective of this chapter is to look at media coverage of three openly lesbian and gay politicians – André Boisclair, Wade MacLauchlan, and Kathleen Wynne – through the concept of sexual mediation (on voter assessments of Wynne, see Chapter 2 in this volume).[1] These politicians are important because they reached high office as provincial premiers (MacLauchlan and Wynne) and leader of the Opposition (Boisclair). We argue that the concept of sexual mediation sheds light on meaningful media framings and thus provides an interpretation of how openly LGBT politicians are covered in the press. First, we examine some studies on gendered literature to build on the concept of sexual mediation. Then we present our methodology and results. We conclude with some thoughts on the scope of our results and the importance of expanding research on the media image of LGBT politicians.

Literature Review

Scholars in Canada, and elsewhere, have devoted a great deal of energy to better comprehension of gendered coverage. Researchers have underlined a double bind for women politicians (Bashevkin 2009; Jamieson 1995; Trimble 2007; Van Zoonen 2006). They have also discovered that distinctive coverage (Banducci, Gidengil, and Everitt 2012; Heldman, Carroll, and Olson 2005) often presents women as "outsiders" in the political world, as "the first," and as alien to politics (Goodyear-Grant 2013; Van Zoonen 2006). More specifically, sexist frames and gender stereotypes are often used in discussions of female candidates (Bashevkin 2009; Lawrence and Rose 2010; Reiser 2009; Trimble et al. 2013). When women's candidacies are evaluated, criteria such as their private lives are often employed (Lalancette and Lemarier-Saulnier 2013; Lalancette, Lemarier-Saulnier, and Drouin 2014; Langer 2011; Lemarier-Saulnier and Lalancette 2012). Gendered coverage depicts the male politician as the norm through the use of masculine vocabulary and metaphors (Gidengil and Everitt 2003; Norris 1997). In Tolley's (2016) view, this gender mediation is deeply rooted in patriarchal ideology.

Research on gendered coverage offers insights on media treatment of LGBT people. Indeed, in light of this research, we hypothesize that, like gendered coverage, media discussions of LGBT politicians highlight specific aspects of their life experiences, bring to light a heteronormative code of conduct, and use stereotypical assumptions when examining their candidacies. In other words, the media will depict LGBT politicians through a sexually oriented framing. Following Tolley (2016, 25–46), we suggest the concept of sexual mediation, which we define as how "sexual orientation" (being homosexual, heterosexual, or bisexual) inspires the ways in which the media portray openly LGBT politicians – more specifically, how their depictions are imbued with heteronormative assumptions.[2] Media framing is gendered – and so is sexual mediation. Alesha Doan and Donald Haider-Markel (2010, 86) suggest that sexual orientation and gender intersect in such a way that "the masculine characteristics stereotypically associated with lesbians by heterosexual women interact to offset, and even compliment [sic], the gender stereotypes associated with female political candidates." It follows that lesbian candidates (who are often perceived as masculine) may be evaluated as more competent than gay men to deal with military issues (because gay men are often stereotyped as effeminate). That being said, it is also possible that stereotypes do not serve lesbians well. For example, they may lower the likelihood that they receive votes (Bailey and Nawara 2017).

Moreover, sexuality, like gender, race, and other markers of identity and otherness, may be used as a tool for exclusion and oppression (Tolley 2016, 29). Sexual mediation is based on heteronormativity, a hegemonic ideology in Western culture that permeates the conceptions of relationships between women and men and the organization of civil society and political life (Ludwig 2011). It is not necessary for sexual mediation to be overtly hostile to LGBT people; instead, it is often discreet and implicit – for instance, talking about family life and children subtly communicates judgments about what "normal" life is. Jamie Landau (2009, 95) demonstrates that despite the growing presence of LGBT families in the United States, print news stories and photographs continue to frame them and the well-being of their children according to "homophobic, (hetero)sexist, and heteronormative" assumptions. Words, images, and stereotypes about LGBT politicians may cast them as having a "lifestyle" that is unsuitable for politics or as "one-issue representatives," which may undermine their potential for election and leadership skills – at least to the straight electorate. In addition, as is the case for women and visible minorities, the presence of LGBT people in politics is not illustrative of their presence in the general population.

Therefore, by emphasizing their particular status (for example, the "first lesbian to be elected"), sexual mediation brings the question of their sexual orientation to light. In Iceland, Jóhanna Sigurðardóttir was presented as the first openly lesbian prime minister, thus highlighting her sexuality (Mundy 2013). This could be viewed as *explicit* sexual mediation. In contrast, *implicit* sexual mediation would be, for example, to cast doubt on the viability of LGBT candidates because they are engaged in a non-hegemonic sexuality. However, as is the case for gendered or racial mediation, sexual mediation is not necessarily negative. Indeed, it may be used to amplify some positive aspect of a candidate's journey or her or his political stance on certain issues. Moreover, candidates may bring up their sexual orientation themselves – for instance, to underline a sustained involvement with young LGBT people in gay-straight alliances.

In Canada, out-of-the-closet LGBT politicians represent a very small proportion of total elected officials (Everitt 2015; Everitt and Camp 2014; see also Chapter 9 in this volume). With so few LGBT candidates and elected representatives, it is not surprising to find that few studies have examined media coverage of them. In this sense, our case study is innovative because we focus solely on coverage of lesbian and gay politicians, rather than comparing it to the coverage of their straight counterparts. Indeed, by not making heterosexual politicians the norm against which LGBT politicians are assessed (typically to their detriment), this methodological approach offers the benefit of evaluating non-heterosexual politicians for their intrinsic value. In other words, our approach avoids two pitfalls: first, devaluing LGBT politicians because they do not perfectly comply with the heterosexual norm, and second, thereby implicitly praising this norm. We feel that ours is a refreshing approach!

Although the research is limited, some initial evidence suggests that sexual mediation of LGBT politicians is prevalent. In the United Kingdom, Donna Smith (2012, 5, 37, 200–1) finds that media coverage of gay scandals in politics often emphasizes the lifestyle of gay politicians. The overarching question is, are they "good" or "bad" gays? She notes that gay politicians are presented as not being "a threat to the norm" and to heterosexual society if they are "open" and in a "stable and public relationship." In Canada, only a few studies have examined media framing of LGBT politicians. Two of them concern Allison Brewer, who briefly led the New Democratic Party (NDP) of New Brunswick. She was systematically presented through sexual mediation, in a stereotypical way, as a lesbian activist (Everitt and Camp 2009a, 2009b). She was framed as the "first openly gay political party leader," who therefore "made history" (Everitt and Camp 2009b, 140). Brewer's election campaign also raised the question of whether the media treatment of lesbians in politics as lesbians is different from that of gays in politics as gays, and whether they face double discrimination as women and as lesbians.

When gay candidate Svend Robinson ran for the leadership of the federal NDP in 1995, he too was sexually mediated; his sexual orientation was discussed in 31 percent of the *Globe and Mail* stories about him (Trimble et al. 2015, 322; for a general overview of Robinson's political career, see the Afterword in this volume). He was systematically presented as being an "open homosexual" and "openly gay." His sexual orientation was evaluated as a potential problem in terms of political representation, as he was not able "to represent traditional 'family values'" of the party. Moreover, as the "first openly gay" candidate, he was also presented as "testing the party's reputation for tolerance." (On NDP openness to LGBT issues, see Chapter 7 in this volume.) Again, this reveals how sexual mediation works by highlighting the importance of fitting into the heteronormative and patriarchal standard for political leadership.

Certain lifestyle issues may also be part of the "threat to the norm" frame. When André Boisclair ran for the leadership of the Parti Québécois (PQ), television news programs on Société Radio-Canada and Réseau TVA paid much more attention to his cocaine use than to his sexual orientation (Lavallée 2009; see also Gingras 2014). These results mirror conclusions from other work on leadership races and press coverage (Lalancette and Lemarier-Saulnier 2013) and on Boisclair's performance as PQ leader (Lalancette 2010). Two major Quebec newspapers, *La Presse* and *Le Devoir*, systematically questioned his (lack of) judgment when discussing his cocaine consumption as an MP. He was portrayed as not fit for the job, because he used drugs, which is certainly a "threat to the norm" of respectability.

These studies offer insights about media coverage of LGBT politicians – more specifically, their sexual mediation. The novelty of their presence in politics brings a "first (openly) gay" storyline that has similarities with the gendered mediation discussed above. In addition, LGBT politicians are depicted as a threat to the norm, which raises questions about representation and respectability. These frames of sexual mediation inspire our examination of press coverage of Boisclair, MacLauchlan, and Wynne.

Methodology

In line with the studies discussed above, and to better understand how LGBT politicians are portrayed in the press, we conducted a qualitative discourse analysis of media portraits of three politicians during their leadership races and electoral campaigns: André Boisclair became Parti Québécois leader in

November 2005 and ran unsuccessfully for premier in 2007; Kathleen Wynne became leader of the Ontario Liberal Party in 2013 and won the provincial election in 2014; and Wade MacLauchlan, who became leader of the Prince Edward Island Liberal Party in 2015, won the provincial election that same year. We examined the coverage in five newspapers (*La Presse*, *Le Devoir*, the *Globe and Mail*, the *Guardian*, and the *National Post*), two magazines (*L'actualité* and *Maclean's*), and the LGBT press (*Daily Xtra* and *Fugues*).[3] We selected these three politicians not only because they were open about their homosexuality, but also because they had held a position at the highest level of political leadership. Following Norman Fairclough's (2003) approach, we chose discourse analysis. Indeed, we think that, "language [being] an irreducible part of social life" (ibid., 2), discourse analysis allows us to grasp the "oscillating relationship" between specific texts and the "order of discourse" that Fairclough describes as "the relatively durable social structuring of language which is itself one element of the relatively durable structuring and networking of social practices" (ibid., 3). By understanding *how* LGBT political actors are presented, we also reach a deeper understanding of society's power structures.

Except for *Daily Xtra* and *Fugues*, we searched all newspapers and magazines with Eureka and Factiva, using a combination of keywords. In English, still using Eureka and Factiva, we did a search in which our keywords were "surname" and "gay" (for the three politicians) and "lesbian" (only for Wynne), "surname" and "sexual orientation," and "surname" and "homosexual." In French, our keywords were "surname" and "gai" (for all three politicians) and "lesbienne" (only for Wynne), "surname" and "orientation sexuelle," and "surname" and "homosexuelle" or "homosexuel." As *Daily Xtra* and *Fugues* were not indexed by Eureka and Factiva, we employed the search function of their websites, using only the politicians' names. The time period selected was from the launch of the leadership race up to and including the Saturday after it ended and from the beginning of the electoral campaign up to and including the Saturday after the election, since newspapers published overviews of the campaign and electoral analyses in their weekend editions. Boisclair's leadership race spanned June 15 to November 15, 2005, and his electoral period was from February 21 to March 26, 2007 (discussed in eighty-six articles).[4] Wynne's race began on November 5, 2012, and ended on February 26, 2013. The Ontario electoral period ran from May 2 to June 12, 2014 (covered in thirty-nine articles). MacLauchlan was elected leader of his party by acclamation. We selected thirteen articles from the beginning to the end of his election campaign: April 6 to May 4, 2015. Even though he was chosen by acclamation, we nonetheless feel that his sexual orientation and the fact that he was elected could lead to sexual mediation in press coverage. We are aware that MacLauchlan's case differs from those of Boisclair and Wynne because he did not have to debate his candidacy with other candidates, which might have affected his media coverage. In the end, however, we saw the very fact that MacLauchlan became premier as sufficient reason to include him in our study. Finally, because of resource constraints, our analysis encompasses only the articles that referred to the sexual orientation of Boisclair, MacLauchlan, and Wynne – in other words, we did not look at articles that did not mention it. In all, we examined 138 articles.

Our analysis focused on framing and intersectional stereotypes, taking into account both gender and sexual orientation as lesbians or gays (on intersectional stereotypes, see also Chapter 2 in this volume). We concentrated on the discourse about LGBT (especially lesbian and gay) politicians and thus did not consider either the identity or the status (journalist, columnist, editorialist) of the individuals who wrote the articles. In our view, sexual mediation crosses sex/gender identities, as well as newspaper affiliation and language. It has an interdiscursive quality. It is a practice that news producers use – consciously or not – to make sense of the world and to organize their articles, columns, and editorials.

In analyzing the texts, we followed Matthew Miles and Michael Huberman's (1994, 10–12) three stages of qualitative research analysis (data reduction, data display, conclusion drawing/verification). We conducted several inductive and iterative rounds of analytical exploration to identify the recurrent frames used to depict the candidates. We first read the articles and took notes on persistent themes (legitimacy, representation, coming out, and ways of presenting the politicians – for example, lesbian, first out lesbian, gay, openly gay). Our unit of analysis was the "thematic unit," which could comprise a word, phrase, paragraph, or group of phrases related to a specific theme (Allard-Poesi 2003). Inspired by grounded theory principles and informed by our literature review and our expertise, we allowed the categories to emerge from the data (Corbin and Strauss 2008). Our knowledge of the field offered us mindfulness of certain frames, such as "first politician" and gendered stereotypes, and our inductive approach dictated the emergence of the frames from the data set. After several rounds of analysis and frame selection, we maximized the differences and similarities among the themes to find the organizing and most important frames, develop conclusions, and distinguish relations with the literature. These frames are presented below.

Finally, it is important to emphasize that our perspective is qualitative. Hence, we did not intend to produce a statistical analysis of the sexual mediation under study or to compare how it may have differed among the politicians in our sample. Our goal was to offer an overview of sexual mediation. We feel that since it is such an underdeveloped field and we were bringing a new concept forward, we needed to define and characterize the phenomenon under study before we could investigate it with a quantitative perspective. In other words, we attempted to provide a basis for theorization, not a study aiming for generalization (Ford 2004). Our descriptions of the results will thus contain qualitative terms such as "frequently," "often," "rarely," and "usually" in our assessment of how the politicians were framed and whether this frame was important when describing them.[5]

Results

How do the media depict LGBT politicians in Canada? In other words, does sexual mediation of LGBT politicians occur in the LGBT and straight press? First of all, it is noteworthy that being a lesbian or gay person was usually framed as a non-issue. This is not unique to Canada: Dean E. Mundy (2013) found that the non-heteronormative sexuality of the former prime minister of Iceland, Jóhanna Sigurðardóttir, was framed as a non-issue. For instance, the June 14, 2014, edition of the *National Post* stated, "Kathleen Wynne's sexual orientation wasn't on voters' minds during the election campaign that saw her crowned Ontario's first openly gay premier." Furthermore, being lesbian or gay was rarely discussed in negative terms, except in the case of Boisclair.[6]

That being said, keeping in mind the concept of sexual mediation and inspired by observations in the studies discussed above, our readings of the press reports enabled us to identify three frames used to depict Boisclair, MacLauchlan, and Wynne: that they were the first elected lesbian/gay politicians; that they represented LGBT communities and interests; and that lesbian/gay politicians were respectable. These themes are not mutually exclusive, but should be thought of as interacting together within a broader dynamic of sexual mediation. In addition, except for the notion about respectability, they have been used to describe the participation of other minorities in politics (notably women). Thus, they do not express an original contribution that LGBT people would bring to the theories of representation.

The First Lesbian/Gay Elected in Politics

LGBT people are a novelty as elected officials, be it in Canada (Everitt and Camp 2014), the United States (Haider-Markel 2010), or elsewhere (Reynolds 2013). Their presence in politics raises questions about their potential impact on the representation of LGBT communities from both a descriptive and a substantive viewpoint (on conceptions of representation as applied to LGBT people and communities, see Chapter 8 in this volume). Essentially, descriptive representation refers to resemblance at both collective (microcosmic) and individual (symbolic) levels. Microcosmic representation states that a political assembly should be a kind of small-scale version of society. This reading inspires public discourses on the representation of minorities. For instance, it is argued that women should be more numerous in politics because they are under-represented, compared with their demographic weight. However, in the newspaper articles that we studied, this rationale was put forward only once: during a June 18, 2014, interview with *Maclean's*, after she won the 2014 election, Wynne declared, "I think it's very important that we work always to have an inclusive political process. That everyone who lives in this province sees themselves reflected in some way in the decisions that are made by government and the people who represent them." This comment is particularly significant in light of a microcosmic conception of representation. In other words, Queen's Park and the Ontario government should reflect the diversity of society, thereby promoting the population's sense of responsibility for – and maybe also acquiescence in – public decisions. That said, Wynne's words can be interpreted through a substantive conception of representation, for "everyone who lives in this province" should feel that political representatives act in their interests "in a manner responsive to them" (Pitkin 1967, 209).

Whereas the microcosmic conception of descriptive political representation is based on the group (that is, the sample should be a small-scale reproduction of the whole), symbolic representation is based on the individual. This person is interpreted as a role model in electoral and political matters, sometimes as an exceptional individual. By stirring up emotions, symbolic representation encourages identification and a sense of political efficacy, thus contributing to the legitimacy of the political regime (Lombardo and Meier 2014, 33–35). In addition, the election to office of a "first" person from a minority demonstrates that the political system works – that it does not throw up systemic barriers to deprive minorities of their right to representation. Several studies have shown how the election of a first woman generates positive effects for girls and women. It encourages female teenagers to discuss politics and women to vote and to run for office (Campbell and Wolbrecht 2006; Wolbrecht and Campbell 2007). It also sends the message to boys and men that they do not have a monopoly on representative democracy. These positive effects have also been observed in respect to LGBT people. Many authors have noted that the election of a "first" LGBT person helped to provide a role model to LGBT people (notably youths) and to change attitudes toward sexual minorities (Golebiowska and Thomsen 1999, 193; Haider-Markel 2010, 156; Herrick and Thomas 2001).

The symbolic conception (notably the label of "the first lesbian/gay in politics") was very present in the texts that we analyzed, although it varied from politician to politician. Indeed, it was rarely applied to Wade MacLauchlan, whose identity as a former academic or university president received far more attention. Sometimes, the two labels were used in tandem. For example, the May 4, 2015,

Guardian wrote, "the former academic – who is also the province's first openly gay premier – was the perceived front-runner in the race." Here, the prestige of MacLauchlan's academic track record seems almost to minimize, or even neutralize, the fact that he is gay, a hypothesis that we revisit below.

The frame of "the first" also appeared in reports on Boisclair, but not because he was the first openly gay man to sit in the Assemblée nationale or the first openly gay Quebec premier.[7] In the November 28, 2005, issue of *Maclean's*, Paul Wells stated that Boisclair was "the first leader to admit he used cocaine while serving as a cabinet minister." Writing for *Fugues* in November 16, 2005, Yves Lafontaine said that Boisclair was "the first openly homosexual leader of a party in Quebec or in Canada" (our translation).[8]

Wynne was closely associated with "the first lesbian/gay" frame. In her case, it would be more accurate to talk about a "first woman breakthrough" trope (Norris 1997). In fact, she has been awarded several "firsts." As the January 25, 2013, *Daily Xtra* noted, "Wynne was the first out lesbian elected to Queen's Park in 2003. In 2006, she became the province's first lesbian cabinet minister." In January 2013, she became the first woman – and, incidentally, the first lesbian – leader of the Ontario Liberal Party. She became premier at the same time, though not due to a general election. This changed when she led her party to victory in the June 2014 election, thus becoming the first popularly elected openly lesbian or gay premier, not only in Canada, but also in the Commonwealth.[9] The June 13, 2014, issue of *Le Devoir* commented that her rise occurred "with utter indifference from the Ontario press and public [to her sexuality], whereas André Boisclair had to endure homophobic taunting during the 2007 election campaign" (our translation). It is possible that Boisclair was a victim of homophobia.[10] It is also possible, however, that he was criticized for his lack of respectability (we will turn to this point later) and his failure to stand out as a role model, unlike MacLauchlan (a former university president) and Wynne, who saw herself as a role model for youth. The January 28, 2013, *Daily Xtra* wrote, "Wynne is Canada's first lesbian premier. At her press conference, she said she's incredibly proud to be a role model for queer youth, but being gay isn't the only quality that defines her." Symbolic representation by being a role model is passive: by standing at the pinnacle of executive power, Wynne is living proof – whether she wants to be or not – that a lesbian or a gay man may realize the highest political ambitions, thus sending the message that sexual preferences are no longer insurmountable obstacles to the political participation and citizenship of LGBT people. In addition, as the first lesbian premier, Wynne embodies a kind of "two-for-one" role model – for lesbians, of course, but also for all women and girls. During her June 18, 2014, interview with *Maclean's*, she explained, "We have some way to go, but I think it is significant that little girls can see that they can be the premier if they want to be. I will do everything I can to live up to the expectations of being a good premier as well as a female premier." Finally, Wynne's victory was interpreted as a coup for the rights of queer people. The January 25, 2013, *Daily Xtra* reported that "Jules Kerlinger, with the Queer Liberals, says having a lesbian premier is a triumph for queer rights in Ontario ... She will send a message of equality."

The Representation of LGBT Communities and Interests
Whereas the descriptive conception of political representation emphasizes identity, the substantive conception focuses on activity, notably the defence of interests. As Hanna Pitkin (1967, 209) puts it, substantive representation "means acting in the interest of the represented, in a manner responsive to them." Substantive representation is based on the idea that there exist communities of interests that meet the requirements of representation in democracy. Communities may be defined by geography and history; a cultural trait and/or an identity such as gender, language, LGBT identities, or religion; or in other ways. Substantive (and descriptive) representation has been the subject of several works on the representation of minorities in general (among others, Williams 1998; Young 2000) and women more specifically (for example, Childs and Krook 2009; Phillips 1995). Indeed, a very rich literature examines whether female politicians substantively represent women – that is, whether their activities contribute to changing and improving the daily lives of women. Researchers tend to answer this question in the affirmative, and the few works on activities of representation by LGBT politicians tend to concur. For instance, Rebekah Herrick (2009, 1125) writes, "Higher LGBT representation in state legislatures leads to greater substantive representation" (see also Haider-Markel 2010, 118–28). That female politicians are more likely to substantively represent women, and LGBT politicians LGBT people and communities, is very good news, but it does have its down side. These individuals may be suspected of being "single-issue" politicians – of representing only women or only LGBT people and communities at the expense of the "general interest" (Haider-Markel 2010, 62). This is a serious concern, particularly for LGBT people and communities, as the support of heterosexual voters is essential if LGBT candidates are to be elected.[11] It is why the media depiction of LGBT candidates is so central to their election: to obtain the support of straight voters, of course, but also of LGBT voters who look for legitimization from heterosexual society (Hertzog 1996, 152, 159–62, 220, 223).

Like the "first" frame, the "representation" frame that substantiates sexual mediation of Boisclair, MacLauchlan, and Wynne provided unequal results, depending on which of them was under scrutiny. Whereas Wade MacLauchlan was rarely defined by the "first" frame, the "representation" frame was never applied to him: the media simply did not see him in this way. It is unclear why – especially because, at first glance, MacLauchlan did not seem to be less involved than Wynne in LGBT community activities, as exemplified by his participation in the 2017 Prince Edward Island Pride Parade (though, of course, involvement cannot be reduced to attending a Pride Parade). However, the representation frame was generously mobilized in reports on Kathleen Wynne and, even more, on André Boisclair. At least two elements contributed to this sexual mediation. First, though Boisclair and Wynne kept their distance from LGBT communities, the press didn't depict them as suitable representatives of "ordinary" (straight) people. Second, because Boisclair and Wynne were not gay activists and because they did not form alliances with other LGBT people to represent LGBT communities and interests, the press did not see them as threatening the heteronormative regime. In fact, some media outlets reported that in their leadership races, Boisclair and Wynne could not take for granted the support of other openly lesbian and gay politicians. Indeed, Wynne and Boisclair have denied that they are lesbian/gay activists. On January 28, 2013, the *Daily Xtra* wrote, "New Ontario premier says she's proud to be a role model, but 'I'm not a gay activist.'" Nonetheless, the fact remains that Wynne has regularly marched in Pride Parades for years. Of course, this is not enough to prove that she is an activist, but it does indicate that she has not turned her back on LGBT communities and perhaps even that she is an "out and proud" politician (see Chapter 8 in this volume). For his part, Boisclair bluntly rejected LGBT militancy, as reported in the November 9, 2005, *Globe and Mail*: "Asked why he didn't embrace a more militant style, he famously replied that, 'I draw no pride from my sexual orientation.'" This absence of pride may partially explain why certain journalists claim that Boisclair has evaded the LGBT press, whether anglophone or francophone, for years. For instance, the November 23, 2005, *Daily Xtra* stated that he had spent "years ... avoiding the gay press," and the November 10, 2005, issue of *La Presse* noted that Yves Lafontaine, editor-in-chief of *Fugues*, tried for eight years to get an interview with him. It remains to be seen if this impression reflects reality. Nonetheless, it fuels the perception that certain LGBT politicians deliberately avoid being associated with LGBT communities. It also kills the hope that electing openly LGBT candidates is an effective strategy for the substantive representation of sexual minorities. The point is that "pride" is intrinsically associated with the LGBT movement; every year, several parades are organized in its name all over Canada. A number of commentators, both outside and within LGBT communities, criticize these events for their exuberance. Wynne was acting strategically by linking the words "proud" and "role model": Who could reproach her for being "proud to be a role model," especially for young LGBT people?[12] Boisclair's statement about drawing no pride from his sexual orientation was much less elegant, because it was a clear rejection of the foundation on which the LGBT movement is built: claiming publicly (coming out) to be "proud" of what had hitherto remained hidden because considered to be shameful (and thus a source of self-hatred) constitutes a kind of "born-again strategy" whereby a stigma is reinterpreted as a positive identity.

Boisclair and Wynne are not activists, of course, but this does not automatically mean that they can represent the (heterosexual) woman and man in the street. Nonetheless, Wynne was seldom questioned on this subject, maybe due to her respectability, which, among other things, is grounded in the fact that her professional career was oriented toward social matters. But her sexual orientation annoys certain groups, notably the Catholic – and conservative – Ontario school boards, which administer schools attended by the young LGBT people to whom Wynne feels a responsibility as a role model. On May 8, 2014, the *Globe and Mail* pointed out, "As a gay woman in a same-sex relationship, the Premier is persona non grata at many Catholic schools. Her lifestyle could even prevent her from speaking to students, according to rules followed by some boards." It seems that Wynne is caught in the middle. On the one hand, her lesbianism is politely described as a "lifestyle" by a straight newspaper. On the other hand, the liberationist fringe of the LGBT movement strongly criticizes the way in which she and her spouse, Jane Rounthwaite, live their "lesbian lifestyle." These critics see it as homonormalization – the adoption by same-sex couples of a petit bourgeois lifestyle previously monopolized by heterosexual couples and characterized by marital life, children, a family house, and common assets, with the long-term objective of retiring together (Marso 2010). As if this were not enough, Wynne's positioning on this issue was not without ambiguity, for, as premier, she participated in major Catholic events with the archbishop of Toronto, Cardinal Collins, and she refused to consider defunding the Catholic Separate School Board system, even though the majority of Ontarians – as well as numerous LGBT people and groups – would have favoured this move.[13]

These criticisms are minor compared with those directed at André Boisclair. Basically, he was framed as unsuited to represent ordinary (that is, heterosexual) people for a variety of reasons. As *La Presse* explained on March 2, 2007, "What is jarring about André Boisclair is not his sexual orientation, it's his cold and haughty personality. And his wooden, disconnected bureaucratic language" (our translation). The March 5 and 24, 2007, issues of the *Globe and Mail* saw him as "a quintessentially urban man" "who can't connect with small-town voters." The November 21, 2005, *Guardian* stated that he was "anathema to many immigrants." For some voters, as *Le Devoir* suggested on March 31, 2007, he was simply not "credible when he talks about family" (our translation) – not because of his homosexuality, but because he had no obvious support networks (family or otherwise).[14] This image of a "lone wolf" contrasts with media depictions of MacLauchlan and Wynne, in which their partners were visible and true allies in their political career. For instance, reporting on Wynne's election campaign, a June 12, 2014, article in the *Guardian* stated that she and her spouse "were inseparable over the marathon campaign across the province." To put it another way, Boisclair was portrayed as a gay with a very small fig leaf of respectability. Why was this so? Of course, one may advance the threadbare argument of media hostility toward Boisclair – but what prompted the hostility? Another more enlightening option is to envisage that, even in a society in which single-individual households are quite common, Boisclair embodied a lifestyle that generates deep-rooted uneasiness. In a public culture obsessed with romance, dating, couples, marriage, reproductive heterosexual sex, and children, singleness can be interpreted as a sign of personal immaturity and social maladjustment at best, or as a threat to social order and the future of society at worst (Budgeon 2008; Kipnis 2003). How, then, can such people be trusted?

The Respectability of Lesbian/Gay Politicians

The debate over the respectability of LGBT people is not new: the watchword of several homophile organizations in the 1950s and 1960s, "respectability," has caused several divisions within the LGBT movement since the early 1970s (Bernstein 2015; Gallo 2006, 18–24; Stein 2000, 200–58).[15] Furthermore, not only has the issue of respectability been raised by a heterosexist society concerned about homoerotic relations, but it has also generated lively debates among lesbians and gays. Indeed, respectability – the ability to pass as a normal (heterosexual) person with a quiet and proper lifestyle, engaged in a long-term couple relationship if not a family with children, and so on – structures a cleavage that continues to characterize LGBT activism. Should one "homonormalize" to the heterosexist order? Or should one resist and destabilize this order by forcing the recognition of sexualities that are stigmatized as abominable or disgusting (Nussbaum 2010; on critiques of homonormalization as guiding political decisions, see Chapter 12 in this volume)? In a seminal queer studies text, Gayle Rubin (1984) defines the frontier between normal, good, and natural sex, on the one hand, and abnormal, bad, and unnatural sex, on the other hand. These polarizations are spelled out below.

This binary categorization and hierarchization of sexualities makes it possible to locate Wynne, MacLauchlan, and Boisclair along a "good, respectable lesbian/gay"

Normal, good, and natural sex	Abnormal, bad, and unnatural sex
Heterosexual	Homosexual [and bisexual]*
Married [or equivalent]	Unmarried [or equivalent]
Monogamous	Promiscuous
Procreative	Non-procreative [and recreational]
Non-commercial	Commercial
In pairs	Alone or in groups
In a relationship	Casual
Same generation	Cross-generational
Private	Public
No pornography	Pornography
Bodies only	With sex toys
Vanilla sex	Sadomasochist

* Brackets indicate our changes to Rubin's categorization.

versus "bad, not-respectable lesbian/gay" continuum, as suggested by Smith (2012, 1–49). Indeed, Wynne and MacLauchlan are sexually mediated as good, respectable lesbian/gay, whereas Boisclair is firmly located on the bad side of the ledger.

First, and again, MacLauchlan stands alone: the media have little to say about his private life. The *Daily Xtra* of January 30, 2015, noted that "his partner, Duncan McIntosh, is the founding artistic director of a local theatre company." The *Guardian* of May 3, 2015, clarified that McIntosh worked at "the Watermark Theatre in Rustico, P.E.I." Like MacLauchlan, McIntosh is a member of the cultural elite – hence a respectable man. Their relationship is all the more respectable because homoerotic love is not unusual in the cultural professions. As mentioned above, the sexual mediation of MacLauchlan made him eminently respectable, as is obvious in the April 7, 2015, issue of the *Globe and Mail*: "Mr. MacLauchlan, 60, a lawyer and academic who served as president of the University of Prince Edward Island from 1999 to 2011."

Wynne is also a very respectable woman: the June 12, 2014, *Guardian* stated, "Born in Toronto, she married Phil Cowperthwaite in 1977 ... She has a son and two daughters as well as three grandchildren. But the marriage didn't last. Wynne came out as a lesbian at age 37 and in 2005 married Jane Rounthwaite, whom she'd first met in university about 30 years prior." Five criteria in Rubin's classification emerge from this quotation: an ex-heterosexual woman (heterosexual sex), Wynne was married (married [or equivalent]) to a man, a relationship from which three children were born (procreative sex); she continues this engagement (monogamous) with her current partner, whom she met at university three decades before – thus, a woman of her generation (same generation). Another newspaper, *Le Devoir*, January 28, 2013, confirmed the sexual mediation of Wynne as a respectable lesbian: "Kathleen Wynne – 59 years old – is a lesbian, married under the auspices of the statute on same-sex marriage, a grandmother (as a result of a first marriage) of several grandchildren" (our translation). Now open about her homosexuality, Wynne has a definitively homonormative lifestyle: she is one half of a monogamous couple (at least, that is what marriage implies), and more importantly, she remains within the procreative cycle via her grandchildren. She is respectable because she is married, a mother and grandmother, her lesbianism not having broken the rhythm of institutions responsible for the renewal of generations.

The media coverage of Boisclair presented a very different story. His sexual mediation portrayed him as a non-respectable gay; the main argument employed to disseminate this message was that he used cocaine when he was a cabinet minister. Indeed, it was his principal descriptor, as several authors note (Gingras 2014; Lalancette and Lemarier-Saulnier 2013; Lavallée 2009, 30–52). Mentioning in the same breath that Boisclair is gay and that he has taken drugs establishes an association between the two. This strategy is particularly efficient with readers who merely scan the headlines, such as the following example in the March 10, 2005, issue of *Maclean's*: "Better with Coke: Why Quebecers Love Their Gay, Drug-Snorting PQ Leadership Hopeful." The magazine offered this explanation for their approval – with a strong content of homonationalism:

> He's got the looks of a matinee idol, a grin that could melt icebergs, and, at 39, in a political formation made up mostly of white-haired veterans, André Boisclair still passes for young. So what better than a little political striptease to sex up his campaign for the Parti Québécois leadership even more? At the onset, he admitted he is gay, and "proud of living in such a tolerant society."

The picture of a gay man with dissolute sexual mores and "an unruly lifestyle" (as the November 9, 2005, *Globe and Mail* put it) – thus implying that the heterosexual lifestyle is necessarily orderly – was disseminated on the French side by *Le Devoir*, the intellectual newspaper in Quebec. For instance, in its issue of October 8, 2005, journalist Denise Bombardier did not mince her words:

> Who wants to party when it is André Boisclair, the future leader of the Parti Québécois founded by René Lévesque, who defines that party? To justify his cocaine consumption, he has explained, with a slight smile, that he was a party guy, that he liked to party. If partying consists of getting high, filling one's nose with powder, forgetting one's own name and especially, in this case, one's position, who wants to rejoice? Why should it be that partying is synonymous with being stoned, unconsciousness, sex galore, and stupefaction, as so many people believe? (our translation)

Several of Rubin's "bad sex" features combine to make Boisclair a non-respectable gay man. "Sex galore," "party guy," and "striptease to sex up" evoke an image of promiscuous homosexual and non-procreative sex, conducted publicly in groups, and possibly even for commercial purposes (striptease is a for-profit industry). The question arises as to whether Boisclair is a respectable man who is capable of commitment, given that his explanation for consuming cocaine consisted of a little smile and a reference to his taste for partying. In reality, Boisclair is a non-respectable gay man because he snorted coke, enjoyed anonymous sex and parties, and, according to Michel David (writing for *Le Devoir* in September 22, 2005, our translation), "is a homosexual who will never have [children]." In sum, unlike the sexual mediation coverage of MacLauchlan and Wynne, which framed them as eminently respectable, that of Boisclair is strongly negative – at least from a heteronormative point of view. One may hypothesize that MacLauchlan and Wynne's positions as provincial premiers accounts for their presentation as good and respectable – to be a premier invites respect – whereas Boisclair never became premier. This hypothesis needs to be tested.

Conclusion

Our objective in this chapter was to employ a qualitative lens to evaluate press coverage of three openly lesbian or gay high-profile politicians: André Boisclair (Parti Québécois), Wade MacLauchlan (Prince Edward Island Liberal Party), and Kathleen Wynne (Liberal Party of Ontario). Using the concept of sexual mediation, our analyses centred around three complementary frames: the "first"; representation of LGBT interests; and respectability. Each frame interacted with the others in the dynamic of sexual mediation of LGBT politicians – what it means to be a lesbian/gay in politics – albeit with uneven heuristic scope.

The "first" frame was widely used to depict all three politicians, but most especially in the case of Wynne. This is unsurprising, given that the number of out-of-the-closet gays, and particularly lesbians, is very small in Canadian politics. Thus, the opportunities to be first are numerous.

The "representation" frame makes clear that MacLauchlan, Wynne, and Boisclair did not enter politics with the intent of speaking for LGBT people. As a result, they do not threaten the heteronormative order (although there are nevertheless doubts about their capacity to represent heterosexual citizens). It seems, rather, that lesbian and gay politicians are notable for their homonormativity – that is, they fit perfectly within the heterosexual lifestyle, thus confirming their respectability in regard to sexual regimes. In other words, to be a lesbian or a gay in politics is acceptable, provided that the individual is respectable. The homosexual orientation of MacLauchlan and Wynne was a non-issue for journalists; in the case of Boisclair and in light of his cocaine consumption, homosexuality was an aggravating factor.

Our research was entirely qualitative, but a quantitative investigation could also be conducted into how these three frames are used in specific contexts and by differing media outlets. Our study did not examine the nature of the publication (LGBT or straight press), who the writers were, or whether their comments appeared in an article or an editorial. A quantitative analysis could address these areas. Thus, it could assess how often columnists, editorialists, and journalists use sexual mediation to cover out LGBT politicians, or how often they use sexual stereotypes to depict them. If media coverage of out LGBT politicians were revealed as overtly negative, it would then come as no surprise that LGBT people refrain from putting their name on the ballot. They might choose a different career to avoid media stigmatization.

Finally, further research should pay more attention to the "newsworthiness" of lesbian and gay politicians. Indeed, as our analysis of Boisclair and work by Smith (2012) show, the issue of out lesbians and gays in politics seems to attract press scrutiny when their actions deviate from the norm – both homo- and heteronormative. Given this, the self-presentation of candidates should be worth studying, in continuity with the work of Elizabeth Goodyear-Grant (2013) and Tolley (2016). It might be relevant to examine the information that lesbian/gay candidates provide when they campaign and seek office. Our analysis showed that Boisclair, MacLauchlan, and Wynne seldom identified with LGBT issues or took pride in that identity. Part of the explanation for this may reside in our research method. Indeed, using other methodologies may generate different observations on media framing of lesbian and gay politicians. For example, by examining their press releases, accessing the original content of media interviews, and analyzing their social media, outlets could offer a different look at the processes of sexual mediation at stake when LGBT politicians are discussed. Moreover, not all LGBT elected officials hide their sexual orientation; for example, gay Alberta MP Randy Boissonnault has been out of the closet for some time. Why would an out LGBT politician use the media to emphasize her or his sexual orientation? Furthermore, it would be worth examining how gendered and heteronormative news is understood by both the electorate and LGBT people who wish to seek public office. Is press coverage such as that Boisclair received likely to deter LGBT candidates from running for office? Does it encourage the electorate not to vote for them? In any case, LGBT people in politics – and their press coverage in particular – offer a rich field of research for the future.

Notes

We would like to thank Linda Trimble and Erin Tolley for their comments on a preliminary version of this essay. Thanks, too, to Valérie Lapointe (University of Ottawa), who collected material for the chapter. This research was made possible thanks to SSHRC funding (435-2014-0023).

1. Our examination does not include politicians who are openly and self-declared "bi," a category that future studies should analyze, as bisexuality – by definition neither homosexuality nor heterosexuality but a little bit of both – poses an original challenge to media framing. That is, is a bisexual woman presented as a heterosexual woman, a lesbian, neither, or a bit of both? Nor does our examination deal with trans politicians, simply because none has been elected in Canada. As a rule, we use "LGBT" as an umbrella expression, but when we analyze the media framing of Boisclair, MacLauchlan, and Wynne, we use "gay and lesbian."
2. We thank Professor Linda Trimble for suggesting the concept of sexual mediation to us.
3. The national press seldom discussed Wade MacLauchlan, but the *Guardian*, the major newspaper on Prince Edward Island, did so, enabling us to assess coverage of him. *Daily Xtra* and *Fugues* are the two most important LGBT publications in English Canada and Quebec, respectively. Moreover, two candidates represented ridings near Toronto (the North Toronto riding of Don Valley West for Wynne) and Montreal (the Gouin riding for Boisclair), where these publications are produced.
4. The large number of articles about Boisclair reflects the controversial aspect of his candidacy, and the fact that the anglophone and francophone press extensively covered the leadership race and the election. It should be noted that distinct linguistic coverage was not the object of our study and did not come to our attention during the analysis. Put another way, we did not check for any potential differences between the anglophone and francophone coverage, although this certainly would be a valuable approach for future research.
5. We see these terms as qualitative in nature, as opposed to terms referring to quantities, such as "20 percent" and "half of the population."
6. This was true even in the conservative *National Post*.
7. André Boulerice was the first openly gay member of the Assemblée nationale.
8. This assertion is dubious because in September 2005, two months before Boisclair was declared leader of the Parti Québécois, Allison Brewer, an out lesbian, became leader of the New Democratic Party of New Brunswick (Everitt and Camp, 2009a, 2009b). In reality, Chris Lea, who was head of the Green Party of Canada from 1990 to 1996, is credited with being the first openly LGBTQ individual party leader in Canada (see https://www.wireservice.ca/index.php?module=News&func=display&sid=17125).
9. Further study should be done on the use of the terms "lesbian," "gay," "LGBT," and "homosexual" to qualify Wynne (and other out lesbian politicians, such as Manon Massé). These words are neither interchangeable nor neutral; the use of one instead of another bespeaks a political stance within the LGBT movement, notably regarding power relations between lesbians and gays. In other words, to describe Wynne as "gay" is inclusive of men, who can thus feel included in her accomplishments, whereas the word "lesbian" may make it difficult for gay men to identify with both her and her achievements. It is also possible that the media avoid using the word "lesbian" because it can be seen as insulting or even degrading, whereas "gay" resonates positively. Nonetheless, this apparently does not apply to Wynne, as the media refer to her as both "lesbian" and "gay."
10. It should be mentioned that out LGBT people are not alone in being targeted by homophobia. For instance, a cisgender heterosexual man whose gender presentation is perceived as effeminate may also experience homophobic attacks.

11 This does not hold true for women, who, in principle, are sufficiently numerous to elect female candidates, provided, of course, that they strategize appropriately.
12 Examples of critics from outside LGBT communities are Shinder Purewal, who attacked Pride Parades for being too explicitly sexual (Boesveld 2011), and REAL Women of Canada, which sharply denounced the parades: "The parade is about hedonistic exhibitionism and narcissism, promoting a deadly form of sexuality. The parade is designed to shock and titillate and the week-long 'celebration' has become an excuse for partying, drug use and promiscuity" (Forsyth 2009). Within LGBT communities, the Toronto Dyke March was organized "to create a specifically women-focused event" (Burgess 2017, 106), in resistance to a Toronto Pride event that was perceived as male-dominated.
13 We are grateful to one of the reviewers for this insightful comment.
14 In comparison, Linda Trimble et al. (2015, 322) find that media commentators framed Svend Robinson's sexual orientation as a liability for those who valued the traditional (heterosexual) family lifestyle.
15 Applying "LGBT movement" to the 1970s is anachronistic, as "lesbian feminism" and "gay liberationism" certainly better reflect the activism of this period. We use "LGBT movement" as a generic expression – that is, as a trans-historical notion.

References

Allard-Poesi, Florence. 2003. "Coder les données." In *Conduire un projet de recherche: une perspective qualitative*, ed. Yvonne Giordano, 245–90. Paris: Éditions EMS.

Bailey, Mandi Bates, and Steven P. Nawara. 2017. "Gay and Lesbian Candidates, Group Stereotypes, and the News Media." In *LGBTQ Politics: A Critical Reader*, ed. Marla Brettschneider, Susan Burgess, and Christine Keating, 334–49. New York: New York University Press.

Banducci, Susan A., Elisabeth Gidengil, and Joanna Everitt. 2012. "Women as Political Communicators: Candidates and Campaigns." In *Sage Handbook of Political Communication*, ed. Holli A. Semetko and Margaret Scammell, 164–72. London: Sage.

Bashevkin, Sylvia. 2009. *Women, Power, Politics: The Hidden Story of Canada's Unfinished Democracy*. Oxford: Oxford University Press.

Bernstein, Mary. 2015. "LGBT Identity and the Displacement of Sexual Liberation: New York City (1969–1986)." In *The Ashgate Research Companion to Lesbian and Gay Activism*, ed. David Paternotte and Manon Tremblay, 89–103. Farnham, UK: Ashgate.

Boesveld, Sarah. 2011. "Q&A: Why Professor Shinder Purewal Is against Explicit Sexuality at Pride Parades." *National Post*, July 29. http://nationalpost.com/news/canada/qa-why-professor-shinder-purewal-is-against-explicit-sexuality-at-pride-parades

Budgeon, Shelley. 2008. "Couple Culture and the Production of Singleness." *Sexualities* 11 (3): 301–25. https://doi.org/10.1177/1363460708089422

Burgess, Allison. 2017. "The Emergence of the Toronto Dyke March." In *We Still Demand! Redefining Resistance in Sex and Gender Struggles*, ed. Patrizia Gentile, Gary Kinsman, and L. Pauline Rankin, 98–116. Vancouver: UBC Press.

Campbell, David E., and Christina Wolbrecht. 2006. "See Jane Run: Women Politicians as Role Models for Adolescents." *Journal of Politics* 68 (2): 233–47. https://doi.org/10.1111/j.1468-2508.2006.00402.x

Childs, Sarah, and Mona Lena Krook. 2009. "Analysing Women's Substantive Representation: From Critical Mass to Critical Actors." *Government and Opposition* 44 (2): 125–45. https://doi.org/10.1111/j.1477-7053.2009.01279.x

Corbin, Juliet M., and Anselm L. Strauss. 2008. *Basics of Qualitative Research: Techniques and Procedures for Developing Grounded Theory*. 3rd ed. Thousand Oaks, CA: Sage.

Doan, Alesha, and Donald P. Haider-Markel. 2010. "The Role of Intersectional Stereotypes on Evaluations of Gay and Lesbian Political Candidates." *Politics and Gender* 6 (1): 63–91. https://doi.org/10.1017/s1743923x09990511

Everitt, Joanna. 2015. "LGBT Activism in the 2015 Federal Election." In *Canadian Election Analysis: Communication, Strategy, and Democracy/Points de vue sur l'élection canadienne. Communication, stratégie et démocratie*, ed. Alex Marland and Thierry Giasson, 48–49. Vancouver: UBC Press.

Everitt, Joanna, and Michael Camp. 2009a. "Changing the Game Changes the Frame: The Media's Use of Lesbian Stereotypes in Leadership versus Election Campaigns." *Canadian Political Science Review* 3 (3): 24–39.

–. 2009b. "One Is Not Like the Others: Allison Brewer's Leadership of the New Brunswick NDP." In *Opening Doors Wider: Women's Political Engagement in Canada*, ed. Sylvia Bashevkin, 127–44. Vancouver: UBC Press.

–. 2014. "In versus Out: LGBT Politicians in Canada." *Journal of Canadian Studies* 48 (1): 226–51. https://doi.org/10.3138/jcs.48.1.226

Fairclough, Norman. 2003. *Analysing Discourse: Textual Analysis for Social Research*. London: Routledge.

Ford, Nigel. 2004. "Creativity and Convergence in Information Science Research: The Roles of Objectivity and Subjectivity, Constraint, and Control." *Journal of the American Society for Information Science and Technology* 55 (13): 1169–82. https://doi.org/10.1002/asi.20073

Forsyth, Cecilia. 2009. "No Money for Gay Parade." *Montreal Gazette*, July 14. http://www.montrealgazette.com/travel/money+parade/1790111/story.html

Gallo, Marcia M. 2006. *Different Daughters: A History of the Daughters of Bilitis and the Rise of the Lesbian Rights Movement*. New York: Carroll and Graf.

Gidengil, Elisabeth, and Joanna Everitt. 2003. "Conventional Coverage/Unconventional Politicians: Gender and Media Coverage of Canadian Leaders' Debates, 1993, 1997, 2000." *Canadian Journal of Political Science* 36 (3): 559–77. https://doi.org/10.1017/s0008423903778767

Gingras, Anne-Marie. 2014. "Marois, Boisclair et la cocaïne. Une étude des cadres des principaux rivaux de la course à la direction du Parti québécois en 2005." In *Genre et politique dans la presse en France et au Canada*, ed. Anne-Marie Gingras, 55–77. Quebec City: Presses de l'Université du Québec.

Golebiowska, Ewa A., and Cynthia J. Thomsen. 1999. "Group Stereotypes and Evaluations of Individuals: The Case of Gay and Lesbian Political Candidates." In *Gays and Lesbians in the Democratic Process: Public Policy, Public Opinion, and Political Representation*, ed. Ellen D.B. Riggle and Barry L. Tadlock, 192–219. New York: Columbia University Press.

Goodyear-Grant, Elizabeth. 2013. *Gendered News: Media Coverage and Electoral Politics in Canada*. Vancouver: UBC Press.

Haider-Markel, Donald P. 2010. *Out and Running: Gay and Lesbian Candidates, Elections, and Policy Representation*. Washington, DC: Georgetown University Press.

Heldman, Caroline, Susan J. Carroll, and Stephanie Olson. 2005. "'She Brought Only a Skirt': Print Media Coverage of Elizabeth Dole's Bid for the Republican Presidential Nomination." *Political Communication* 22 (3): 315–35. https://doi.org/10.1080/10584600591006564

Herrick, Rebekah. 2009. "The Effects of Sexual Orientation on State Legislators' Behavior and Priorities." *Journal of Homosexuality* 56 (8): 1117–33. https://doi.org/10.1080/00918360903279361. Medline:19882430

Herrick, Rebekah, and Sue Thomas. 2001. "Gays and Lesbians in Local Races: A Study of Electoral Viability." *Journal of Homosexuality* 42 (1): 103–26. https://doi.org/10.1300/j082v42n01_06. Medline:11991562

Hertzog, Mark. 1996. *The Lavender Vote: Lesbians, Gay Men, and Bisexuals in American Electoral Politics*. New York: New York University Press.

Jamieson, Kathleen Hall. 1995. *Beyond the Double Bind: Women and Leadership*. New York: Oxford University Press.

Kipnis, Laura. 2003. "Against Love: A Treatise on the Tyranny of Two." In *Constructing Sexualities: Readings in Sexuality, Gender, and Culture*, ed. Suzanne LaFont, 156–61. Englewood Cliffs, NJ: Prentice Hall.

Lalancette, Mireille. 2010. "Vie privée, vie publique, vie médiatique: sur scène et hors-scène? La performance politique de deux politiciens québécois disséquée." In *Les médias et le politique. Actes du colloque "Le français parlé dans les medias,"* ed. Marcel Burger, Jérôme Jacquin, and Raphaël Micheli, 1–20. Lausanne: Centre de linguistique et des sciences du langage. http://www.unil.ch/clsl/page81503.html

Lalancette, Mireille, and Catherine Lemarier-Saulnier. 2013. "Gender and Political Evaluation in Leadership Races." In *Mind the Gaps: Canadian Perspectives on Gender and Politics*, ed. Tamara A. Small and Roberta Lexier, 116–30. Halifax: Fernwood Press.

Lalancette, Mireille, with Catherine Lemarier-Saulnier, and Alex Drouin. 2014. "Playing along New Rules: Personalized Politics in a 24/7 Mediated World." In *Political Communication in Canada: Meet the Press and Tweet the Rest*, ed. Alex Marland, Thierry Giasson, and Tamara A. Small, 144–59. Vancouver: UBC Press.

Landau, Jamie. 2009. "Straightening Out (the Politics of) Same-Sex Parenting: Representing Gay Families in U.S. Print News Stories and Photographs." *Critical Studies in Media Communication* 26 (1): 80–100. https://doi.org/10.1080/15295030802684018

Langer, Ana I. 2011. *The Personalisation of Politics in the UK: Mediated Leadership from Attlee to Cameron*. Manchester: Manchester University Press.

Lavallée, Hugo. 2009. "Analyse de la couverture médiatique d'un leader émergent: le cas d'André Boisclair." Master's thesis, Université de Montréal.

Lawrence, Regina G., and Melody Rose. 2010. *Hillary Clinton's Race for the White House: Gender Politics and the Media on the Campaign Trail*. Boulder: Lynne Rienner.

Lemarier-Saulnier, Catherine, and Mireille Lalancette. 2012. "La Dame de fer, la Bonne Mère et les autres: une analyse du cadrage médiatique de politiciennes canadiennes." *Canadian Journal of Communication* 37 (3): 461–88. https://doi.org/10.22230/cjc.2012v37n3a2583

Lombardo, Emanuela, and Petra Meier. 2014. *The Symbolic Representation of Gender: A Discursive Approach*. Farnham, UK: Ashgate.

Ludwig, Gundela. 2011. "From the 'Heterosexual Matrix' to a 'Heteronormative Hegemony': Initiating a Dialogue between Judith Butler and Antonio Gramsci about Queer Theory and Politics." In *Hegemony and Heteronormativity: Revisiting 'The Political' in Queer Politics*, ed. María do Mar Castro Varela, Nikita Dhawan, and Antke Engel, 43–61. Farnham, UK: Ashgate.

Marso, Lori Jo. 2010. "Marriage and Bourgeois Respectability." *Politics and Gender* 6 (1): 145–53. https://doi.org/10.1017/s1743923x09990572

Miles, Matthew B., and A. Michael Huberman. 1994. *Qualitative Data Analysis*. New York: Sage.

Mundy, Dean E. 2013. "Framing Saint Johanna: Media Coverage of Iceland's First Female (and the World's First Openly Gay) Prime Minister." *Journal of Interdisciplinary Feminist Thought* 7 (1): Article 5.

Norris, Pippa. 1997. "Women Leaders Worldwide: A Splash of Color in the Photo Op." In *Women, Media, and Politics*, ed. Pippa Norris, 149–65. Oxford: Oxford University Press.

Nussbaum, Martha C. 2010. *From Disgust to Humanity: Sexual Orientation and Constitutional Law*. New York: Oxford University Press.

Phillips, Anne. 1995. *The Politics of Presence*. Clarendon: Oxford University Press.

Pitkin, Hanna Fenichel. 1967. *The Concept of Representation*. Berkeley: University of California Press.

Reiser, Kim. 2009. "Crafting a Feminine Presidency. Elizabeth Dole's 1999 Presidential Campaign." In *Gender and Political Communication in America*, ed. Janis L. Edwards, 41–61. Lanham: Lexington Books.

Reynolds, Andrew. 2013. "Representation and Rights: The Impact of LGBT Legislators in Comparative Perspective." *American Political Science Review* 107 (2): 259–74. https://doi.org/10.1017/s0003055413000051

Rubin, Gayle. 1984. "Thinking Sex: Notes for a Radical Theory of the Politics of Sexuality." In *Pleasure and Danger: Exploring Female Sexuality*, ed. Carole S. Vance, 267–319. London: Pandora.

Smith, Donna. 2012. *Sex, Lies and Politics: Gay Politicians in the Press*. Brighton, UK/Portland, OR: Sussex Academic Press.

Stein, Marc. 2000. *City of Sisterly and Brotherly Loves: Lesbian and Gay Philadelphia, 1945–1972*. Chicago: University of Chicago Press.

Tolley, Erin. 2016. *Framed: Media and the Coverage of Race in Canadian Politics*. Vancouver: UBC Press.

Trimble, Linda. 2007. "Gender, Political Leadership and Media Visibility: Globe and Mail Coverage of Conservative Party of Canada Leadership Contests." *Canadian Journal of Political Science* 40 (4): 976–93. https://doi.org/10.1017/s0008423907071120

Trimble, Linda, Daisy Raphael, Shannon Sampert, Angelia Wagner, and Bailey Gerrits. 2015. "Politicizing Bodies: Hegemonic Masculinity, Heteronormativity, and Racism in News Representations of Canadian Political Party Leadership Candidates." *Women's Studies in Communication* 38 (3): 314–30. https://doi.org/10.1080/07491409.2015.1062836

Trimble, Linda, Angelia Wagner, Shannon Sampert, Daisy Raphael, and Bailey Gerrits. 2013. "Is It Personal? Gendered Mediation in Newspaper Coverage of Canadian National Party Leadership Contests, 1975–2012." *International Journal of Press/Politics* 18 (4): 462–81. https://doi.org/10.1177/1940161213495455

Van Zoonen, Liesbet. 2006. "The Personal, the Political and the Popular: A Women's Guide to Celebrity Politics." *European Journal of Cultural Studies* 9 (3): 287–301. https://doi.org/10.1177/1367549406066074

Williams, Melissa S. 1998. *Voice, Trust, and Memory: Marginalized Groups and the Failings of Liberal Representation*. Princeton: Princeton University Press.

Wolbrecht, Christina, and David E. Campbell. 2007. "Leading by Example: Female Members of Parliament as Political Role Models." *American Journal of Political Science* 51 (4): 921–39. https://doi.org/10.1111/j.1540-5907.2007.00289.x

Young, Iris Marion. 2000. *Inclusion and Democracy*. Oxford: Oxford University Press.

4

Electing LGBT Representatives and the Voting System in Canada

Dennis Pilon

ALMOST EVERYWHERE, LESBIAN, gay, bisexual, and trans (LGBT) representation in Western countries registers in fairly low numbers. It is unclear what impact electoral institutions might have on such levels of representation. Many scholars accept that the choice of voting system between majoritarian and forms of proportional representation (PR) can decisively alter the incentive structures for politicians, parties, and voters in terms of what kind of diversity gets elected. But much depends on the interaction of such institutional rules with a host of other social and political factors. Given this complexity, do claims for diverse representation work the same way for LGBT people as for gender, race, and ethnicity?

In this chapter, I utilize insights from the scholarly comparative literature on diverse representation to assess the degree to which the challenges of gaining LGBT representation are distinct from other diverse representation efforts. Canada has used a single-member plurality (SMP) voting system for most of its elections at the federal and provincial level, and thus it has suffered the rather slow increases in diverse representation that are usually associated with such a system. Still, there have been gains in diverse representation from the 1980s (including, more recently, for LGBT people). By examining the historic emergence of LGBT representatives in Canada, we can establish if there are any identifiable patterns in terms of how such candidates have gained office and whether those patterns differ from those of other groups, and thus contribute to a broader comparative dialogue about representation and voting systems. We can also compare Canadian results with those of other Western countries that use similar and different voting systems. Additionally, I will attempt to assess whether the introduction of a proportional voting system might lead to any meaningful differences for LGBT representation in Canada.

Where Does Diverse Representation Come From?

The term "diverse representation" acts here as a shorthand reference for a broad and diverse category of groups, typically excluded or under-represented in elected legislatures in Western countries. In attempting to assess the general and specific factors contributing to their under-representation, researchers must be sensitive to how the groups in this category may face *both* similar *and* different challenges in attempting to gain representation. A considerable academic literature highlights the interactive effects of a number of key factors that contribute to the presence or absence of diverse representation in any given polity. These can be readily divided into two broad categories of concern: social and institutional.

Social factors refer to the role of culture in stemming or fuelling demands for diverse representation and the influence of various forms of inequality on the claims-making process. For instance, over the twentieth century, Western societies witnessed a considerable shift in public attitudes toward greater acceptance of women's participation in all aspects of public life (Norris and Inglehart 2001). This did not occur naturally or simply at the individual level but through the active work of organized social movements that contested generally accepted collective identities and the assumptions that accompanied them (i.e., the accepted social role of women) (Paxton, Hughes, and Green 2006; Polletta and Jasper 2001). But changing public attitudes alone was not sufficient to alter patterns of gendered representation in legislatures, because women have often lacked the financial resources, time, and social networks to compete for nominations in political parties on the same terms as men and because they faced myriad forms of sexism and exclusion in their attempts to become active in parties (Shvedova 2005, 39–44; Stockemer and Byrne 2012). The lack of female candidacies also tended to reinforce perceptions among the public and party elites that women were not viable electorally.

Institutional factors refer to the role of political organizations or codified procedures in reflecting, channelling, shaping, and/or blocking demands for more diverse representation. Such factors would include political parties, their internal structure and procedures, and the character and design of voting systems. Miki Caul (1999) highlights four factors that influence how a party takes up gendered representation (or not): organizational structure (particularly the degree of institutionalization of its rules and processes), ideology, the level of women's involvement as activists within the party, and the use of gendered rules for representation (i.e., quotas). With evidence from sixty-eight countries at three historical moments, Caul (1999) argues that left-wing parties with strong institutional processes internally and high levels of female involvement throughout the party produced a consistently greater degree of women's legislative representation. Caul (1999) also underlines the key role of the voting system, with proportional systems utilizing some form of party list outperforming majoritarian systems. A number of studies also support the view that proportional voting systems better facilitate diverse representation because they use multi-member districts that allow parties to offer a more diverse range of candidates than do systems relying exclusively on single-member ridings (Matland 2005, 101; Rule 1987).

Just how these various factors interact to produce more diverse representation will be explored in fuller detail below. For the moment, it should be emphasized that the representational challenges facing different groups are not all the same and that numerous paths have been pursued to representation. For instance, although visible minorities share many of the challenges that women experience in gaining representation in SMP voting systems (such as resource and networking issues), they sometimes benefit from being geographically concentrated enough to be courted by political parties as nominees in winnable ridings. Further, it must be stressed that these social and institutional factors work together, not in isolation, a point seemingly misunderstood in recent critiques of this literature (see, for example, Roberts, Seawright, and Cyr 2012).

Three Paths to Diverse Representation

Historically, we can identify at least three distinct paths to diverse representation – districting, party formation, and party quotas – with varied results for differing groups. In countries that use single-member ridings, a districting approach has sometimes been used to pursue diverse representation. In light of the 1965 Voting Rights Act in the United States, various court cases forced legislators to take into consideration the geographic concentration of minority-identified voters in drawing up the boundaries for legislative and municipal districts to prevent the dilution of their vote and facilitate the election of a visible-minority candidate (Davidson and Grofman 1994). This led to rather modest increases in the legislative representation of black and Hispanic people in the United States (Grofman and Handley 1991). In the Canadian context, such districting strategies were adopted to aid in the representation of religious diversity, or at the very least to prevent religion from becoming partisanized. At Confederation and shortly thereafter, a number of dual-member ridings were created to allow the two leading national parties to nominate both a Protestant and a Catholic candidate in a few locales (Courtney 2004, 108–9). Of course, districting has also been used to limit diverse representation. The widespread adoption of "at-large" districts to replace single-member wards in American local elections was often a deliberate effort to reduce or eliminate black and labour representation on city councils, a strategy that was very effective throughout most of the twentieth century (Davidson and Korbel 1981).

Another approach to districting that is not limited by the geographic proximity of voters is the provision of dedicated seats to a particular group, such as the seats set aside for Maori people in the New Zealand legislature. At different points in New Zealand's history, Maori were either mandated to or could choose to elect representatives to specifically Maori seats (Nagel 1996). First introduced in 1867, the dedicated seats did provide the Maori with legislative representation but in a way that under-represented them for most of the country's history, with improvements in representation coming only after the adoption of a mixed-member proportional voting system in 1993 (Geddis 2006). This "dedicated seats" approach has been recommended for use in Canada to supplement Indigenous representation at various times but was never introduced (Marchand 1990; Morden 2016, 26).

Those seeking more diverse representation have sometimes attempted to form their own political party as a means of gaining electoral office. The most successful efforts here were built around class representation, specifically that of working-class voters by labour or socialist parties from the late nineteenth to the mid-twentieth century (farmers also pursued this strategy but were less successful). The marriage of identity and a left-wing or progressive ideology made these ventures very successful (Eley 2003; Moschonas 2002). Other attempts to pursue diverse representation claims through stand-alone political parties in Western countries have not been as fruitful, as the fleeting existence of various women's and visible-minority parties in most Western countries attests (Thorpe 2015; Zaborsky 1987).

Rather than forming a new party, diverse representation claimants in Western countries have seen more success by working within existing parties to gain a share of their representation. Here parties of the left have proven more open to diverse representation appeals, creating internal caucuses for various diverse representation groups and establishing quotas to incentivize the nomination of diverse candidates both within the party hierarchy and among its candidates for office (see Chapter 7 in this volume). But it is important to underline that these gains, even in broadly sympathetic parties from the left, did not come about easily or automatically. Here the interaction of social and institutional factors becomes clearer. For instance, both the British and Norwegian Labour Parties had organized women's caucuses by the 1980s, but the increase in the representation of women accelerated much more rapidly in Norway than in the United Kingdom. When all other factors are held constant – a politically active women's movement, an electorally viable left-wing party, and so on – the key difference between the two polities was the competitiveness of the party systems, fuelled in part by the use of different voting systems. (For a broad comparison of these trends across Western countries, see Table 4.1.)

Norway's party-list PR system was much more competitive and more responsive to shifts in voter opinion, which meant that leadership in a particular policy area could create a contagion effect across parties. When a small left-wing party decided to establish quotas on its list to increase women's representation, it influenced the larger Norwegian Labour Party to follow suit (Matland and Studlar 1996, 717). In Sweden, prominent women's organizations threatened to

Table 4.1

Percentage of women's representation in lower houses

	1965	1970	1975	1980	1985	1990	1995	2000	2005	2010	2015
Majoritarian											
Canada	1.5	0.4	2.9	5.0	9.6	13.2	18.0	20.6	21.1	22.4	26.0
United Kingdom	4.6	4.1	4.3	3.0	3.5	6.3	9.2	18.2	20.0	22.0	29.0
New Zealand	6.2	4.8	4.6	4.3	12.6	16.5	21.2	–	–	–	–
United States	2.5	2.3	4.4	3.7	5.2	6.6	11.7	14.0	15.2	16.8	19.4
France	1.7	1.6	1.6	4.1	5.3	5.7	6.0	10.9	12.3	18.5	26.8
Australia*	1.6	0.0	0.0	2.5	5.7	6.1	15.5	23.0	24.7	24.7	26.7
Proportional											
Australia**	6.7	5.0	9.4	10.9	18.4	22.4	21.1	31.6	35.5	35.5	38.2
Sweden	11.5	13.8	21.1	26.6	28.0	38.4	40.4	42.7	45.3	45.0	43.6
Finland	13.5	21.5	23.0	26.0	31.0	31.5	33.5	36.5	37.5	40.0	41.5
Norway	8.0	9.3	15.5	23.9	34.4	35.8	39.4	36.4	37.9	39.6	39.6
Netherlands	9.0	9.0	9.3	14.0	12.7	21.3	31.3	36.0	36.7	40.7	37.3
Belgium	3.3	3.7	6.6	7.5	7.5	8.5	12.7	23.3	34.7	39.3	39.3
Germany	6.9	6.9	5.8	8.5	9.8	20.7	26.2	30.9	31.8	32.8	36.8
Denmark	9.5	10.6	15.1	24.0	26.0	30.7	33.0	37.4	36.9	38.0	37.4
New Zealand	–	–	–	–	–	–	–	30.8	33.1	33.6	31.4

* Lower house; ** Upper house (Senate)

Sources: World Bank, Inter-Parliamentary Union, various country-specific sources (see the Appendix on page 147).

start their own party if the Social Democrats did not show more leadership in electing women – a threat that moved the party to action, again due to the competitiveness of the voting system (a women's party might not have won any seats, but it could have put a dent in Social Democrat support) (Freidenvall 2003, 21). Leadership from the left eventually prompted other parties across the ideological spectrum to offer more female candidates or risk losing support.

No such dynamic existed in the United Kingdom, where the SMP system made the entry of new parties much more difficult and the competitive relationship between electable parties less clear-cut. Women in the Labour Party typically felt that they had few options but to slowly attempt to shift views within their party (Perrigo 1995). However, they did succeed in pushing for a number of women-only shortlists for some parliamentary riding nominations during the 1990s, but the victory was short-lived, as the courts struck them down (Cutts, Childs, and Fieldhouse 2008). By contrast, when the decision about the voting system was finalized in 1998 and Scotland adopted a form of PR (the mixed-member proportional voting system) for its devolved Parliament, the more competitive dynamic quickly altered the behaviour of the parties concerning gender representation. Suddenly, they appeared to take on a more Scandinavian approach to increasing women's representation, introducing quotas and zippered lists, and the results were immediate and impressive (Russell, MacKay, and McAllister 2002). These regional results, along with the disappointing decline in women's representation at Westminster in the 2001 election (the first without the use of women-only shortlists), motivated the Labour government to pass legislation allowing the use of women-only shortlists in the 2005 UK election. This led to an improvement in women's representation at Westminster, though still well below Scottish and Welsh levels (Childs, Lovenduski, and Campbell 2005).

This dynamic is also illustrated quite clearly in Australia, where voters have consistently elected considerably more women to the upper house, chosen by PR, than to the lower house, elected by a majoritarian voting system in single-member districts (Kaminsky and White 2007). The results underline the impact of the voting system on gender representation because the same group of voters often elect both houses simultaneously.

Whereas left-wing leadership combined with PR may amount to a kind of best practice for advancing diverse representation, it should be noted that gains have occurred under all kinds of voting systems and even where left-wing parties are not dominant players. But in the latter cases, the gains typically emerged much more slowly and in lower proportions, lacked institutional support within parties, and did not necessarily move in one direction. Thus, the question is not really whether one party form or voting system advances or blocks diverse representation – all are porous and responsive to some degree. The issue is over the *velocity of change:* how fast and how solidly demands for diverse representation are translated into results. With that in mind, we can turn to the LGBT case specifically to assess how this form of diverse representation is both similar to and different from the others.

Paths to LGBT Representation
Since the rise of a modern LGBT movement in Western countries during the 1970s, all three paths to diverse representation have been pursued, with varied success. As with America's black and Hispanic communities, there have been a number of attempts to use the apparent geographic clustering of LGBT people in specific urban neighbourhoods (usually downtown) to make claims for special districting to advance their representation or electoral influence (Bell 1991).

Darren Rosenblum (1995) argues that activists were ultimately successful in carving out an LGBT district in Manhattan in the 1990s after a court-ordered redistricting effort by the New York City Council. As early as the 1970s and 1980s, researchers found that even without specially designed districts, identifiable geographic clusters of LGBT voters exerted electoral influence as a distinct minority presence, depending on the locale (Bell 1991; Button, Wald, and Rienzo 1999; Moos 1989). Districting would prove crucial to the election of the first openly gay city councillor in California, Harvey Milk, who had failed to win a seat under San Francisco's at-large voting system in 1973 but won in 1977, when it had switched to local wards (Reynolds 2013). Although Milk's election represented a breakthrough in LGBT representation, the district-level focus did little to give voice to non-geographically concentrated LGBT people (Button, Wald, and Rienzo 1999), a group whose potential influence (and size) was hard to estimate because of the traditional lack of visibility of its members. Attempts to form separate LGBT political parties often raised the profile of local gay activists but were not serious strategies in most Western countries (though for a discussion of success in the Philippines, see Cardozo 2014). Thus, like other efforts to gain diverse representation, working within mainstream political parties would become the key focus for LGBT organizing over time.

Although LGBT people, women, and visible minorities appear to share similar challenges in seeking diverse representation, researchers have long argued that the pursuit of LGBT representation has some distinctive elements. Rosenblum (1996, 124) highlights three factors, arguing that LGBT people as a group are not "officially identifiable," have intersectional identities, and are geographically dispersed. By not "officially identifiable," Rosenblum meant that they could "pass" for heterosexual, if they chose (and several did in Canada; see Chapter 10 in this volume), and that official record keepers (such as census bureaus) did not collect such data, thus making the quantification and geographic specification of LGBT populations difficult to assess (but not impossible; see Chapter 1 in this volume). By "intersectional identities," Rosenblum meant that LGBT people were not merely or solely LGBT, but were also gendered, raced, and classed, and could live in urban, suburban, or rural areas. His key point was that the latter identities might influence the degree to which LGBT people could act on and identify with the former (for instance, a poor lesbian might not be able to leave her extended family's home to live in a more LGBT-identified neighbourhood). Finally, Rosenblum's last point reinforced the second one: the visibility of specific geographic LGBT communities should not be mistaken for the totality of LGBT people in the larger society. Because of their invisibility outside of such neighbourhoods, it was easy to underestimate how dispersed they were.

Although some might dispute Rosenblum's claim that LGBT people are distinguished by their intersectional identity (one could argue that *all* identities are intersectional to differing degrees), the selective visibility of LGBT individuals shapes public perceptions of the scope, location, and potential influence of LGBT people as a voting bloc and a group in need of collective representation. Indeed, research highlights that a sense of proximity to and direct interactions with LGBT people influence voter perceptions of the viability and suitability of LGBT candidates for public office (Barth, Overby, and Huffmon 2009; Lewis 2011). Furthermore, though some researchers argue that a critical mass of women must be elected before gendered policy outcomes change, various studies suggest that even a few elected LGBT politicians and bureaucrats can decisively influence policy mix (Haider-Markel, Joslyn, and Kniss 2000; Lewis and Pitts 2011; Reynolds 2013).

Early efforts to establish some degree of LGBT representation suffered from the classic collective action problem. It was felt that LGBT candidates would be a liability to the party that nominated them – an assumption fuelled by elements of the public or media that had few interactions with LGBT people (Herrick and Thomas 2001). This view discouraged LGBT people from becoming involved politically, especially outside of self-proclaimed gay villages. But research suggests that such public attitudes would change only if voters saw and interacted with more LGBT people (Lewis 2011). Given such disincentives, it was not surprising that many early attempts to elect LGBT politicians occurred in districts that had a perceived strong concentration of LGBT residents. A host of ideographic accounts of LGBT politics at the local level highlights struggles to free commercial establishments catering to the LGBT community from harassment and ill treatment by the police and municipal officials, thus bringing LGBT activists into negotiations with local law enforcement agencies, bureaucrats, and politicians (Knopp 1987). But as the political horizons of LGBT efforts widened from mere tolerance ("leave us alone," "let us do our own thing"), to equality ("don't discriminate against us" in areas such as jobs and housing), and finally to inclusion ("we have a right to the same things as non-LGBT people"), the scope of the political project could not be supported wholly within the bounds of the traditional gay village. (Examples of this process across three Western countries are recounted in Rayside 1998; for a similar characterization of the political shift from tolerance to inclusion, see D'Emilio 2000.) The next challenge would be to find out just how widespread – geographically and numerically – a potential LGBT-supporting electorate might be, recognizing that not all its members would necessarily be LGBT-identifying themselves.

Recent research (such as Reynolds 2013) on the state of LGBT representation around the world both confirms and challenges various aspects of the conventional wisdom about where and how LGBT representatives might get elected. Until recently, researchers argued that potential LGBT candidates were most likely to gain nomination from left-of-centre parties, in districts that were urban and that contained some identifiable group of LGBT people. They would be elected only in areas where the party was traditionally strong. Furthermore, it was thought that out-of-the-closet candidates were most likely to succeed if they had already run and won office without disclosing their sexual orientation first. Andrew Reynolds's (2013) summary of LGBT electoral outcomes over the past forty years confirms many of these trends, but only up to 1999. Whether public attitudes really are rapidly changing or we are just discovering a latent tolerance or enthusiasm for diversity that was previously untapped for other reasons (e.g., parties and media acting as gatekeepers/agenda setters), the patterns of LGBT representation changed decisively after the year 2000. Thus, before 1999, most successful LGBT politicians were initially elected from urban gay village districts, in left-of-centre parties, in areas considered party strongholds, and they did not disclose their sexual identity before they won office. But post-1999 LGBT candidates also succeeded in suburban and rural areas, in districts not necessarily seen as safe seats for their party, and although most stood for left-wing parties, an increasing number came from right-of-centre parties. But perhaps most decisive was the shift to running as out LGBT candidates from the beginning of their political careers, with 93 percent informing the electorate about their sexuality in their first contest (Reynolds 2013, 261).

Reynolds's research seems to spark as many questions as it answers. The changing pattern of electoral support for LGBT candidates suggests that a broad and dispersed LGBT electorate exists, or that an electorate not necessarily limited to LGBT people is nonetheless favourable to their representation, or both. The election of LGBT individuals from right-of-centre parties underscores the intersectional nature of LGBT identity (that is, some LGBT people hold right-wing views; see Chapter 5 in this volume). It is also a confirmation of the contagion effect across parties in a way similar to results seen with women's representation. Reynolds concludes that the voting system appears to be key (see Table 4.2), with much higher levels of LGBT representation stretching across more parties in polities that use proportional rather than majoritarian systems, typically finding twice as many LGBT members elected in the former than in the latter, with a few outliers (such as the United Kingdom from 2005 on).

But there are problems with Reynolds's characterizations of the differences. First, Reynolds (2013) compares the actual numbers of elected LGBT representatives in various locales rather than their proportional share of the total available seats. His approach neglects how the higher numbers of elected LGBT members in PR countries might simply reflect the fact that among countries with voters

Table 4.2

LGBT representation by voting system

	Plurality	Majority	Proportional	Total
1983	2	0	4	6
1988	3	1	3	7
1998	11	1	24	34
2003	18	0	42	60
2008	25	1	54	80
2011	33	2	66	101
2013	36	2	73	111

Source: Reynolds (2013), online appendix.

who might be open to supporting diverse representation, a much higher number use proportional voting systems. In other words, reported in this way, it is hard to analyze what impact the voting systems themselves may have had on the general pattern of outcomes. To get a better sense of which voting systems are performing best in terms of diversity, we need to calculate the proportion of LGBT members elected to each legislature over time. Second, Reynolds includes in his list of countries any that have elected LGBT representatives, regardless of differences in political, economic, and social development. As with work on women's representation, it would be better to limit the focus to countries with broadly similar patterns of development to help discern the factors that contribute to diverse representation. Tables 4.3 and 4.4 mirror Table 4.1, using the same countries as the basis of comparison.

Utilizing Reynolds's (2013) data and updates, Tables 4.3 and 4.4 provide a snapshot of the LGBT members of each county's lower house as of December 31 of the year indicated. If we restrict the focus to comparable Western industrialized countries, the gap between majoritarian and proportional voting systems shrinks somewhat compared to Reynolds's findings, though PR systems generally still perform better. The United Kingdom stands out as leading Western countries from 2000 on in terms of consistently increasing its representation of LGBT members, with its 2015 total of thirty-two MPs almost three times better than its nearest challenger (the number increased to 45 in the 2017 general election). But other countries that use a majoritarian system produced fairly low to moderate results. By contrast, PR-using Sweden, Netherlands, and Germany showed consistent, slow improvement over time, whereas Belgium, Finland, and Denmark performed more poorly. However, when we shift to a comparison of the proportions of LGBT representatives across Western countries, a few more twists emerge.

Table 4.3

Numbers of LGBT representatives by country and year

	1985	1990	1995	2000	2005	2010	2015
Majoritarian							
Canada	0	1	2	2	5	5	6
United Kingdom	2	1	2	9	12	24	32
New Zealand	0	0	1	-	-	-	-
United States	1	1	2	3	3	4	6
France	0	0	0	1	0	0	2
Australia	0	0	0	0	0	0	1
Totals	3	3	7	15	20	33	48
Proportional							
Sweden	0	0	0	1	5	12	13
Finland	0	0	0	0	1	2	4
Norway	1	1	2	2	5	4	3
Netherlands	3	3	5	6	6	8	11
Belgium	0	0	0	0	1	2	1
Germany	1	2	3	5	12	13	10
Denmark	0	0	0	1	2	3	5
New Zealand	-	-	-	3	5	6	6
Total	5	6	10	18	37	50	53

Note: Each year represents a snapshot of the total LGBT members in lower houses as of December 31.

Source: Reynolds (2013), online appendix.

Converting the numbers of elected LGBT members to a proportionate share of their legislative bodies gives a slightly different take on the outcomes, making the results from larger legislative houses (such as those in the United States, Germany, and the United Kingdom) look less impressive, while putting a more positive spin on the efforts from countries with smaller legislatures, such as New Zealand, Sweden, and the Netherlands. Indeed, the United Kingdom now surrenders its leadership to the Netherlands, with New Zealand on par with British results. The proportionate results appear to provide support for the view that PR countries have typically produced a higher velocity of change in terms of advancing LGBT representation (a faster and steadier rate of change) than majoritarian systems.

As with other campaigns for diverse representation, a number of paths have led to the election of LGBT individuals, though not all have produced equal

Table 4.4

Proportions of LGBT representatives by country and year

	1985	1990	1995	2000	2005	2010	2015
Majoritarian							
Canada	0	.3	.7	.7	1.6	1.6	1.8
United Kingdom	.3	.2	.3	1.4	1.9	3.4	5.1
New Zealand	0	0	1	-	-	-	-
United States	.2	.2	.5	.7	.7	.9	1.4
France	0	0	0	.2	0	0	.4
Australia	0	0	0	0	0	0	.7
Proportional							
Sweden	0	0	0	.3	1.4	3.4	3.7
Finland	0	0	0	0	.5	1	2
Norway	.6	.6	1.2	1.2	3	2.4	1.8
Netherlands	2	2	3.3	4	4	5.3	7.3
Belgium	0	0	0	0	.7	1.3	.7
Germany	.2	.4	.4	.7	2	2.1	1.6
Denmark	0	0	0	.6	1.1	1.7	2.8
New Zealand	-	-	-	2.5	4.1	5	5

Note: Each year represents a snapshot of the LGBT members as a proportion of the total members in lower houses as of December 31.

Source: Reynolds (2013), online appendix.

success. For example, exploiting the concentration of LGBT people in downtown gay villages to either influence non-LGBT politicians and city officials or convince parties that nominating an LGBT candidate would be viable has worked in countries that rely on single-member districts but in a limited way. LGBT people and their supporters outside such districts are left without representation or, indeed, any way to register such support. Breakthroughs have occurred in countries that use majoritarian voting systems, such as the United Kingdom from 2000 on, but such results are atypical. Countries that use proportional systems have produced stronger, more consistent results. Determining whether these results were generated by PR's tendency to increase party competition and the potential for a contagion effect across the party system when one party shows leadership on an issue or claim for representation, as was the case with gender representation, requires more context-specific research.

Canada's Voting System and Diverse Representation

Canada's voting systems were designed to suit the competitive electoral needs of its dominant parties. Any serious consideration of reforming them has been motivated by and judged mostly in terms of fending off threats to the perceived interests of those parties. Thus, the use of single- and multi-member plurality at all levels of government, the experiments with majority and proportional voting at the provincial and municipal levels, the creation of an independent commission to supervise the revision of riding boundaries, and indeed, most aspects of election administration more generally reflect the interests of the dominant parties. Even recent provincial referenda on voting system reforms in British Columbia, Ontario, and Prince Edward Island were marred by obvious elite manipulation to maintain the status quo (Pilon 2007, 75–93; Pilon 2017; Ward 1950, 153–271). Responding to social demands for more diverse representation has not been a stated goal or any part of such historic deliberations (though they did figure in the contemporary discussions that failed to produce reform). Nevertheless, such demands have elicited various responses from Canada's parties over time, leading to slow increases in female, visible-minority, Indigenous, and, more recently, LGBT representation.

The Canadian experience mirrors that of other Western countries that employ majoritarian voting systems – fairly slow and intermittent progress compared to similar countries using proportional systems (Trimble, Arscott, and Tremblay 2013). For instance, Table 4.1 compares the pattern of women's representation over time in Canada with that of various Western countries, demonstrating these broad trends. Although, regardless of voting system, Western countries see increased levels of women's representation from the 1970s on, the velocity of change in PR countries differs starkly from that in majoritarian countries, with a steady and rapid increase in the former and an uneven and more shallow degree of change in the latter. However, if we restrict our focus to majoritarian countries, then Canada could be considered a leader in women's representation until the mid-1990s, second only to New Zealand, as Richard Matland and Donley Studlar (1996, 715) reveal.

This was due primarily to the leadership of the left-wing New Democratic Party (NDP), for reasons set out by Caul (1999). The NDP's internal party processes were more institutionalized than those of its rivals, it was open to claims for great diversity (e.g., social justice), it maintained a high level of women's involvement at various levels, and it was willing to use quotas (or "targets," as it called them) to assure an increase in female representation internally and in party candidacies (Bird 2007). This did appear to create a contagion effect across the party system, moving the centrist Liberals to nominate more women post-2000, but the impact of NDP efforts was weak because the party perennially placed a distant third at the national level, with seemingly little chance (until 2011) of displacing the two traditional governing parties. Thus, the effect on the Liberals was ad hoc and subject to the whims of the party leadership. For instance, Jean Chrétien used his power as leader to simply impose female candidacies on select ridings in 2000, but his successor, Paul Martin, declined to do so in 2004 (Carbert 2012, 144–45). Meanwhile, the Liberals did not match the NDP in meeting Caul's criteria around the institutionalization of party rules or the active involvement of women. Still, Louise Carbert (2012) argues that the impact was greater than might first appear and that female candidacies increased noticeably post-2000 across all parties. Nonetheless, this trend did not manifest in appreciable changes in female representation, because of the post-2004 over-representation of the Conservative Party, which lagged behind the others in nominating women in winnable ridings.

The pattern for increasing the representation level for other identity claims in Canada is both similar to and different from that for women. As in the case of women's representation, efforts to increase the representation of visible minorities, people with disabilities, and Indigenous people have produced slow and uneven progress over a long period. But each group is distinguished by some unique attributes and challenges. For instance, while women have always made up roughly half of the Canadian population, the percentage of visible-minority members of Canadian society has not remained constant. So, though visible-minority representation has increased over time, these gains have failed to match the increases in the number of visible-minority Canadians (Black 2013). Recently, some scholars have suggested that Canada's SMP is beneficial to diversity groups that are geographically concentrated. As proof, they point to the 2015 federal election, in which the proportion of elected visible-minority MPs matched the percentage of visible-minority citizens in the country (Tolley 2017). Although such results are welcome and demonstrate the capacity of majoritarian voting systems to accommodate demands for diverse representation, they do not change the fact that producing this result via the SMP voting system took a very long time. More in-depth studies of the performance of SMP in terms of visible-minority representation paint a rather less attractive picture. For instance, in a 2011 study of visible-minority representation across three elections in the Greater Toronto Area (GTA), Myer Siemiatycki (2011) found that visible minorities composed nearly 40 percent of the population but only 11 percent of the total elected officials. Broken down, this amounted to 17 percent of the GTA's members of the House of Commons, 26 percent of its members of the Ontario Parliament, and just 7 percent of local city councillors (Siemiatycki 2011). Jerome Black (2013) highlights the sloth-like performance of SMP in advancing visible-minority representation over time by examining the gap between the numbers of visible-minority MPs elected and the changing levels of visible-minority people in the population as a whole. He notes that, in proportionate terms, there was no real advance between 1993 and 2011 (Black 2013, 22). So, despite the positive results in 2015, Black (2017, 16) reminds us, "Over the 1993 to 2011 period, visible minority MPs were being elected in numbers sufficient to keep up with the growth in the visible minority population at large but insufficiently so as to narrow the representation gap." In other words, it is premature to make too much of these recent results.

Western countries that use PR systems have produced varied results in terms of visible-minority representation. Some, such as the Netherlands, can boast of impressive results. Others, however, such as Norway and Denmark – leaders in women's representation – have failed to reflect their ethnic and racial diversity in the national parliament. According to some commentators, this means that institutional rules may be less important than sheer political will for achieving diverse representation (Bloemraad 2013). Others point to the interaction of social demands with a host of institutional rules, not just the voting system. For instance, Karen Bird (2005) finds that Denmark's low levels of visible-minority representation in the national legislature were related to the stringent rules that made the attainment of Danish citizenship a very difficult and drawn-out process. However, in examining visible-minority representation at the local level – where Danish residents could vote regardless of their citizenship status – she finds much higher levels of diversity represented. Indeed, she determines that the particular mechanics of the PR system were crucial in allowing visible-minority populations to select one of their own to represent them. By contrast, Bird (2005) argues that in comparison with that of Denmark, Canada's SMP voting system has tended to put visible minorities in a clientelistic relationship with the traditional governing parties rather than gaining them direct representation.

Indigenous people in Canada have also been chronically under-represented legislatively, typically being elected only in northern ridings with significant Indigenous populations. But here the challenges are complicated by a host of factors related to colonialism, the failure of the Canadian state to meet treaty obligations, a legacy of destructive residential schools, and a long practice of differential treatment before the law (Ladner and McCrossan 2007). As a result, many Indigenous people do not participate in Canadian elections because they refuse to recognize Canadian sovereignty over their people and lands (Morden 2016). But others fail to participate for reasons similar to those of other subaltern groups (Pilon 2015). Again, some have pointed to the most recent federal election results, with their record levels of Indigenous representation, to suggest that Canada's SMP system is good for Indigenous people because it may benefit them where they are numerically concentrated (Tolley 2017). But this, again, ignores how long it has taken to produce this result. For the bulk of Canadian history, and crucially from 1960, when most Indigenous people were finally allowed to vote federally, their legislative representation has been abysmally low (Hunter 2003, 29). It also ignores the fact that most Indigenous people in Canada do not live in areas where their population numbers dominate. Indeed, most live in urban and suburban areas where their votes are greatly outnumbered by those of the non-Indigenous electorate (Statistics Canada 2017).

Until recently, New Zealand used the same SMP system as Canada and also witnessed low levels of Indigenous representation. However, since switching to a mixed-member form of PR in 1996, the country has seen a dramatic improvement in electing Maori MPs. Prior to that year, the Maori were greatly underrepresented, but since then the proportion of Maori MPs has matched or exceeded their percentage of the population in every election (Pilon 2016; Sparrow 2010, 13). The experience in New Zealand suggests that a shift to a more proportional voting system could be one way to boost Indigenous representation, particularly for non-status and spatially dispersed Indigenous people in Canada's urban and suburban locales.

Improving the diversity of Canada's elected representatives was one reason that Justin Trudeau's Liberal Party promised to change the national voting system when it was running in third place during the 2015 election. Indeed, this promise became a key talking point for Trudeau's government after the surprising Liberal victory, repeated consistently during the consultations that took place across the country throughout 2016. However, when the government proved unable to control the outcome of the all-party consultation process, Trudeau abandoned his reform commitment (Wells 2018).

Paths to LGBT Representation in Canada

The positive news-media coverage of the federal Liberal, NDP, and Green Party leaders who marched in various Gay Pride Parades during the summer of 2015, particularly after the federal election campaign kicked off on August 4, suggests a degree of comfort with LGBT people and issues in Canadian national politics (Dehaas 2015). Indeed, by 2015 all federally competitive parties had nominated openly LGBT candidates, and three of the five parties had elected LGBT MPs during the previous decade (Reynolds 2015; see also Chapter 9 in this volume). But gains in overall representation at the national level have been slow in coming and low in terms of the number of elected LGBT MPs. Examining federal results since Svend Robinson was re-elected in 1988 as the first openly LGBT MP, Table 4.5 shows early leadership from the NDP, with the Bloc Québécois (BQ) and the Liberals following much later. As with the election of Canadian

Table 4.5

Federal LGBT representation in Canada, 1979–2015

	Elected	Out	Party	District
Svend Robinson	1979	1988	NDP	Burnaby (Burnaby–Douglas)
Réal Ménard	1993	1994	BQ	Hochelaga
Libby Davies	1997	2001	NDP	Vancouver East
Scott Brison	1997	2002	PC/Liberal	Kings–Hants
Bill Siksay	2004	2004	NDP	Burnaby–Douglas
Mario Silva	2004	2004	Liberal	Davenport
Raymond Gravel	2006	2006	BQ	Repentigny
Rob Oliphant	2008	2008	Liberal	Don Valley West
Randall Garrison	2011	2011	NDP	Esquimalt–Juan de Fuca
Dany Morin	2011	2011	NDP	Chicoutimi–Le Fjord
Philip Toone	2011	2011	NDP	Gaspésie–Îles-de-la-Madeleine
Craig Scott	2012	2012	NDP	Toronto Danforth
Sheri Benson	2015	2015	NDP	Saskatoon West
Randy Boissonnault	2015	2015	Liberal	Edmonton Centre
Rob Oliphant	2015	2015	Liberal	Don Valley West
Seamus O'Regan	2015	2015	Liberal	St. John's S–Mount Pearl

Sources: Reynolds (2013, 2015); Everitt (2015b).

women, the pattern for LGBT representation shows slow gains contrasted with long periods of stasis. For instance, despite considerable instability in the party system between the elections of 2011 and 2015, the number of LGBT members elected to the federal Parliament remained unchanged (Reynolds 2015).

As in the United States, LGBT activism that emerged during the late 1960s and early 1970s in Canada garnered political responses along civil rights lines, including the partial decriminalization of homosexual activity in 1969, with some attention to non-discrimination, particularly at the municipal level (Smith 2012). A number of high-profile cases that contested the prevention of out LGBT people from participating in various activities actually gained surprising levels of public support in the 1970s (as the 1975 case of Doug Wilson in Saskatoon demonstrated) (Korinek 2003). But, on the whole, mainstream politics and political parties eschewed a positive engagement with out LGBT activists for fear of public disapproval (for details of how this began to change in the 1980s, see Rayside 1998, 120–25; Tremblay 2015). And, unlike for the American experience, there has been little research into the early influence of spatially concentrated LGBT communities on non-LGBT politicians in Canada.

A few specifically LGBT parties were launched during the late 1970s and early 1980s in Canada, but they were largely intended to gain visibility rather than seriously run for public office (Everitt and Camp 2014; Warner 2002, 76). There were also a few early, sporadic attempts by out LGBT people to enter mainstream parties, such as Peter Malone's efforts with the Ontario Liberal Party in the 1970s and Maurice Richard's successful bid for office with the Quebec Liberal Party in 1985. However, these were rare. By the 1980s, some breakthroughs had occurred at the municipal level, such as Gordon Price's successful 1986 campaign for alderman in Vancouver with the right-wing Non-Partisan Association and Raymond Blain's in Montreal during the same year (for Blain, see Podmore 2015). But the biggest impact came from NDP MP Svend Robinson's admission in February 1988 that he was gay and from his subsequent re-election to Parliament later that year, his first time running as an out LGBT candidate.

When LGBT representation in Canada is compared with that in other Western countries, there is a similar pattern of early left-wing party leadership, for reasons like those advanced by Caul (1999) for women's representation, with some spread across the political spectrum over time. Joanna Everitt and Michael Camp (2014) note that the NDP has gone the farthest of the federal parties in institutionalizing its commitment to LGBT inclusion, participation, and candidacies, and has produced the strongest results, whereas others, such as the Liberals, have taken a more ad hoc approach (see Chapters 6 and 7 in this volume). In reviewing the pattern of Canadian LGBT legislative representation, Everitt and Camp argue that LGBT candidates typically run for left-wing parties, primarily in urban spaces (specifically ones with a large LGBT population), and that successful candidates tend to be elected before they come out as LGBT. This mirrors Reynolds's comparative work on pre-1999 patterns of LGBT representation across Western countries but appears at odds with his reported trends post-2000. Indeed, Everitt and Camp's federal conclusions are largely based on the success of just one candidate between 1988 and 2007. The pattern in the 2008, 2011, and 2015 elections, in which national LGBT representation expanded from one to six members, adheres much more closely to that advanced by Reynolds for the post-2000 period (2013, 2015).

Diverse representation in Canada fits the pattern for countries using single-member majoritarian voting systems in that advances for all groups have been slower and more uneven than in countries where proportional systems are the norm. In attempting to gain and increase the representation of LGBT people, Canadian LGBT political activists have eschewed the districting approaches of the United States and made only a few, largely symbolic, attempts to launch an LGBT political party. As with other claims for diverse representation in Canada, those seeking to elect LGBT people have sought to do so through the country's mainstream parties, and here parties of the left have led the way. Even so, they created only a weak contagion effect across the party system, as evidenced in part by the low levels of LGBT representation in Canadian legislatures. Such low levels make looking for patterns problematic, particularly in establishing what may distinguish the efforts to gain LGBT representation from other campaigns for diverse representation. As Everitt and Camp (2014) note, the selective visibility of LGBT people makes the project of representing them complex, as we do not really know the size of this group or its potential voting power. Nor do we know the degree to which increases in LGBT representation should be attributed to a geographic concentration of LGBT people, the potential impact of a dispersed (but unknown) LGBT vote, and/or support from non-LGBT people. Attempts to gauge the size and views of the LGBT community via behavioural methods fall afoul of the same problems encountered in efforts to survey many different kinds of marginal communities: an unwillingness to be surveyed, a lack of fit between the concepts used by the researchers and the more fluid reality of interviewees (e.g., on questions of sexual orientation and identity), and fear (for more on this problem, see Pilon 2015).

Would a Different Voting System Advance LGBT Representation in Canada?

As Andrew Reynolds (2015) demonstrates in his review of the 2015 federal election results, Canadian levels of LGBT representation have remained stalled for four elections. Might a different voting system create new opportunities to break through this plateau? Here comparative evidence can be used to argue both sides of the case. Some might point to the United Kingdom, where LGBT representation skyrocketed to thirty-two members, or 5 percent of all MPs, in 2015, and then increased again to forty-five members, or 7 percent, of the total in 2017, using the same SMP system as Canada. The UK results strongly demonstrate that impressive levels of diverse representation can be achieved under any voting system when the requisite political will is in evidence. But, as Reynolds (2015) also points out, the United Kingdom is a bit of an outlier in comparison with other SMP-using countries, such as the United States and Canada. By contrast, PR-using countries in the West have a more reliable track record on LGBT representation. However, one caveat should be stressed: changing the voting system is not a magic bullet – it cannot create results out of nothing. Arguments about the potential impact of differing institutional rules, such as voting systems, must be anchored in the particular contexts in which they will function. In other words, a case must be made that this or that voting system will interact with specifically Canadian conditions to produce certain kinds of results.

Some argue that LGBT representation in Canada can be effectively advanced through our traditional SMP system by exploiting the geographic concentration of LGBT people in a number of major urban centres. As with those who laud the recent federal gains in visible-minority and Indigenous representation, their argument focuses on the inherent representational bias of SMP systems that privileges proximate over dispersed voters. Voters of like mind who live close together can exercise influence, or so the argument goes. In practice, a host of factors interfere with this theoretical possibility, the most obvious being partisanship, which cuts through the membership of all diversity groups (see Chapters 5, 6, and 7 in this volume), thus diluting their ability to act collectively on the basis of group identity. In the United Kingdom, part of what contributed to the recent breakthrough in LGBT representation was the all-party nature of the commitment, effectively removing partisanship from the equation. However, that relied on British Tory leader David Cameron's ability to marginalize the social conservatives in his party (Barnicoat 2010; Kite 2010; Woolf 2006), something that seems highly unlikely to happen in the Canadian or American settings (Rayside, Sabin, and Thomas 2017; Rayside and Wilcox 2011).

Even when successful, SMP's performance with diverse representation tends to be unrepresentative, as can be seen with visible minorities in Canada: a few dominant groups get most of the representation, whereas others get little or none. And then, there is a less savoury aspect of diverse representation as practised through SMP systems that is rarely acknowledged by its supporters: clientelism (for a general discussion of these problems, see Nagel 1996). For instance, Indigenous senator Len Marchand (1990) warned long ago of the dependent relationship between geographic Indigenous communities and the federal government, which meant that Indigenous people were effectively silenced, even in ridings where they were a majority or a considerable minority. Bird (2005, 453) notes a similar relationship between Canada's two dominant federal parties and various leaders in visible-minority communities.

When we examine arguments that favour SMP as the best way forward to increase LGBT representation, we find that the case is weak for at least two reasons. First, it rests on a view of LGBT people as residing in specific geographic locales, which has become increasingly anachronistic. The post-war suburbanization of North America and the emptying of its urban cores created a historic opening for marginalized groups to take up those spaces and define them culturally. That this historic, geographically rooted LGBT community came into existence does not mean that it will persist. Due to exploding urban property prices across Western countries over the past few decades, relocating to gay villages may be financially untenable for new generations of LGBT people, and such spaces will not necessarily escape their own urban renewal (Ghaziani 2010; Ruting 2008). Second, even in their heyday, such areas never contained the totality of LGBT people. A voting system that focuses on geographic concentrations of constituents leaves more dispersed voters poorly represented. Given the particular conditions affecting our knowledge (or lack thereof) of just where LGBT people live, that could leave a very considerable number of them outside such residential enclaves (Gates 2013).

Until recently, comparative work on diverse representation was fairly consistent in concluding that proportional voting systems were better than majoritarian systems at achieving higher levels of diverse representation at an earlier time and across a broader swathe of the political system. However, a few scholars now challenge this consensus. Some simply revise the scope of previous claims regarding the impact of voting systems on representation (Salmond 2006), whereas others more radically reject the long-held view that voting systems do or can make any difference in the representation of diversity (Fortin-Rittberger and Rittberger 2014; Roberts, Seawright, and Cyr 2012; Ruedin 2012). Limitations of space prevent a full engagement with these critics, but suffice it to say that they represent a distinctly minority view in the literature, for reasons of method if nothing else. Most scholars working in this area have moved into an interactive and contextual approach to gauging voting system effects, one that recognizes the importance of careful case selection based on similar political and economic development to aid comparison (Krook 2010a, 2010b; Moser and Scheiner 2012). By contrast, the critics compare more and less developed countries and Western and non-Western regions with none of this nuance. Not surprisingly, the two approaches produce different results. However, when their various samples are divided along traditional lines (such as Western versus non-Western, developed versus less developed), their results look broadly similar to those in the conventional literature. Meanwhile, scholars continue to produce new research that supports the consensus view that voting systems can matter for diverse representation (Rosen 2013, 2017) and even more broadly for class representation as well (see Bernauer, Giger, and Rosset 2015).

So, the short answer to the question of whether a different voting system might advance LGBT representation in Canada would appear to be yes – if the new system were some form of proportional representation. Many of the factors that connect better LGBT representation with proportional voting are the same as those offered for other diversity groups – namely, some level of political leadership on the issue and some contagion effect across the party system that would then be enhanced and accelerated by the increased political competition encouraged by proportional voting. We have already noted that at both the provincial and federal levels, the NDP has shown considerable leadership in advancing LGBT representation, which created a small degree of contagion, as other parties responded by including at least a token LGBT candidate in their pool of aspirants for office. The moderate leadership of the federal Liberals on the issue and the occasional LGBT candidacy from the federal Conservatives suggest that some room exists for influence from the NDP, if the party were given added leverage through a PR system (for an effective demonstration of this contagion process at the provincial level, see Everitt 2015a). But certain factors are unique to the LGBT community, particularly the ongoing reality of selective visibility. Despite what appears to be growing public tolerance and approval of LGBT people, various sanctions (such as the threat of physical harm or social disapproval) still prompt an unknown number of LGBT-identifying individuals to eschew any public identification with being LGBT. This adds an extra challenge to generating a pro-LGBT voting system, as its designers must assume how the target population might interact with the new system, in this case influencing just which kind of proportional system would be seen as most ideal.

Until recently, scholarship examining diverse representation focused on how proportional systems avoided the zero-sum representational challenges of single-member majoritarian systems. The argument was that because proportional systems usually worked with multi-member districts, parties could offer a diverse ticket of candidates to voters via party lists. But another factor considered important was the fact that such tickets could not usually be altered by the voters themselves, thus preventing voters from countering party efforts to increase diversity (Caul 1999; for recent challenges to this view, see Kunovich 2012; Valdini 2013). Given what were thought to be typical dynamics of LGBT support – that it was primarily urban and restricted to areas with large LGBT populations where strong party support already existed – one could imagine that researchers would call for a closed party-list form of PR to best advance LGBT representation.

But Andrew Reynolds's (2013) comparative work on LGBT representation questions these assumptions and opens the way for a consideration of a broader range of proportional systems. In his analysis of LGBT representation in both majoritarian and proportional systems post-2000, he notes that many traditional views about how and where LGBT representatives gained election did not hold up. LGBT success was not limited to urban settings, or to locales with a visible LGBT population, or to safe ridings (Reynolds 2013, 263). What this means is that other forms of PR besides party list could be considered, such as the single transferable vote and mixed-member proportional variants. Reynolds's research also highlights the unique factor of LGBT experience: selective visibility. Clearly, we don't know just how large or dispersed the LGBT voting bloc is, but his findings suggest that the traditional stereotypes are woefully inadequate in understanding the potential political influence of this group. This is arguably the strongest part of the case for adopting PR to advance LGBT representation:

because we don't know where or how large the LGBT population is, a PR system would do the best job of maximizing its influence.

Conclusion

Canada's majoritarian voting system has not prevented the realization of a range of demands for diverse representation. Over the past thirty years, women, visible minorities, Indigenous people, and LGBT individuals have all been elected at the federal, provincial, and municipal levels. But, as in other Western countries that use majoritarian voting systems, the progress has typically been slow and uneven, especially when compared to Western countries that employ proportional forms of voting. LGBT claims for representation have followed a path taken by other claims for diverse representation – such as districting, party formation, and party participation. The latter, working within existing parties, has proved the main and most successful strategy (but see Chapter 11 in this volume). In Canada, LGBT efforts have mostly focused on participating in parties. In both Canada and abroad, campaigns for LGBT representation have also faced the unique challenge posed by the selective visibility of LGBT people, which has made assessing the location and size of this group, and its potential voting support, very difficult. Finally, because the electoral representational challenges facing LGBT people are both similar to other diversity groups and distinct from them in some ways, it was argued that a shift to a proportional voting system could considerably advance the cause of electing more LGBT candidates in Canada.

APPENDIX

Sources for Table 4.1: Percentage of women's representation in lower houses

Information for all countries was obtained from:

Inter-Parliamentary Union, "Parline Database on National Parliaments," http://www.ipu.org/parline-e/parlinesearch.asp.

–, "Women in National Parliaments," http://www.ipu.org/wmn-e/classif-arc.htm.

World Bank, "Proportion of Seats Held by Women in National Parliaments," http://data.worldbank.org/indicator/SG.GEN.PARL.ZS.

Additional information for specific countries was obtained from:

Australia

Parliament of Australia, *Parliamentary Handbook of the Commonwealth of Australia*, 34th ed., 2017, http://www.aph.gov.au/about_parliament/parliamentary_departments/parliamentary_library/parliamentary_handbook.

Joy McCann and Janet Wilson, "Representation of Women in Australian Parliaments 2014," http://parlinfo.aph.gov.au/parlInfo/download/library/prspub/3269009/upload_binary/3269009.pdf;fileType=application/pdf.

Belgium

Petra Meier, "The Belgian Paradox: Inclusion and Exclusion of Gender Issues," in *State Feminism and Political Representation*, edited by Joni Lovenduski, 41–61 (Cambridge: Cambridge University Press, 2005), https://doi.org/10.1017/CBO9780511490996.004.

Canada

Andrew Heard, "Elections: Women Candidates, Canadian Federal Elections, 1921–2011," http://www.sfu.ca/~aheard/elections/women-elected.html.

France

Assemblée nationale, "Les femmes élues députées depuis 1945," http://www.assemblee-nationale.fr/elections/femmes-deputees.asp.

Germany
Martina Hoffhaus, "The Impact of Institutional Factors on the Representation of Women in Parliament: A Comparison between Britain and West Germany" (PhD diss., London School of Economics, 1990).

New Zealand
New Zealand History, "Female MPs 1933–2014," http://www.nzhistory.net.nz/media/photo/women-mps-in-parliament.

Norway
Richard E. Matland, "The Norwegian Experience of Gender Quotas," in *The Implementation of Quotas: European Experiences: Quota Report Series*, edited by Julie Ballington and Francesca Binda, International Institute for Democracy and Electoral Assistance, 2004, https://www.idea.int/sites/default/files/publications/implementation-of-quotas-european-experiences.pdf.

Sweden, Finland, Norway, Denmark
Elina Haavio-Mannila, "How Women Become Political Actors: Female Candidates in Finnish Elections," *Scandinavian Political Studies* 4 (1979): 351–71, https://onlinelibrary.wiley.com/doi/pdf/10.1111/j.1467-9477.1979.tb00228.x.

United Kingdom
UK Political Info, "Women MPs and Parliamentary Candidates since 1945," http://www.ukpolitical.info/FemaleMPs.htm.

United States
Jennifer E. Manning and Ida A. Brudnick, "Women in Congress, 1917–2019, Service Dates and Committee Assignments by Member, and Lists by State and Congress," Congressional Research Services, CRS Report, April 9, 2019, https://www.senate.gov/CRSpubs/bee42bd4-0624-492c-a3b0-a5436cb9e9a2.pdf.

Note
I would like to thank Karen Bird and Manon Tremblay for helping me locate some of the data on women's representation for various countries and Joanna Everitt for providing me with a copy of her research data on LGBT candidacies and representatives in Canada.

References

Barnicoat, Becky. 2010. "Election 2010: Meet the David Cameron Generation." *Guardian*, March 20.

Barth, Jay, L. Marvin Overby, and Scott H. Huffmon. 2009. "Community Context, Personal Contact, and Support for an Anti-Gay Rights Referendum." *Political Research Quarterly* 62 (2): 355–65. https://doi.org/10.1177/1065912908317033

Bell, David J. 1991. "Insignificant Others: Lesbian and Gay Geographies." *Area* 23 (4): 323–29.

Bernauer, Julian, Nathalie Giger, and Jan Rosset. 2015. "Mind the Gap: Do Proportional Electoral Systems Foster a More Equal Representation of Women and Men, Poor and Rich?" *International Political Science Review* 36 (1): 78–98. https://doi.org/10.1177/0192512113498830

Bird, Karen. 2005. "The Political Representation of Visible Minorities in Electoral Democracies: A Comparison of France, Denmark, and Canada." *Nationalism and Ethnic Politics* 11 (4): 425–65. https://doi.org/10.1080/13537110500379211

–. 2007. "Patterns of Substantive Representation among Visible Minority MPs: Evidence from Canada's House of Commons." Paper presented at "Immigration, Minorities and Multiculturalism in Democracies Conference," Ethnicity and Democratic Governance MCRI project, October 25–27, Montreal.

Black, Jerome H. 2013. "Racial Diversity in the 2011 Federal Election: Visible Minority Candidates and MPs." *Canadian Parliamentary Review* 36 (3): 21–26.

–. 2017. "The 2015 Federal Election: More Visible Minority Candidates and MPs." *Canadian Parliamentary Review* 40 (1): 16–23. http://www.revparlcan.ca/en/vol40-no1-the-2015-federal-election-more-visible-minority-candidates-and-mps-2/

Bloemraad, Irene. 2013. "Accessing the Corridors of Power: Puzzles and Pathways to Understanding Minority Representation." *West European Politics* 36 (3): 652–70. https://doi.org/10.1080/01402382.2013.773733

Button, James W., Kenneth D. Wald, and Barbara A. Rienzo. 1999. "The Election of Openly Gay Public Officials in American Communities." *Urban Affairs Review* 35 (2): 188–209. https://doi.org/10.1177/10780879922184356

Carbert, Louise. 2012. "The Hidden Rise of New Women Candidates Seeking Election to the House of Commons, 2000–2008." *Canadian Political Science Review* 6 (2–3): 143–57.

Cardozo, Bradley. 2014. "A 'Coming Out' Party in Congress? LGBT Advocacy and Party-List Politics in the Philippines." Master's thesis, University of California.

Caul, Miki. 1999. "Women's Representation in Parliament: The Role of Political Parties." *Party Politics* 5 (1): 79–98. https://doi.org/10.1177/1354068899005001005

Childs, Sarah, Joni Lovenduski, and Rosie Campbell. 2005. *Women at the Top 2005: Changing Numbers, Changing Politics?* London: Hansard Society.

Courtney, John. 2004. *Elections*. Vancouver: UBC Press.

Cutts, David, Sarah Childs, and Edward Fieldhouse. 2008. "'This Is What Happens When You Don't Listen': All-Women Shortlists at the 2005 General Election." *Party Politics* 14 (5): 575–95. https://doi.org/10.1177/1354068808093391

Davidson, Chandler, and Bernard Grofman, eds. 1994. *Quiet Revolution in the South: The Impact of the Voting Rights Act, 1965–1990*. Princeton: Princeton University Press.

Davidson, Chandler, and George Korbel. 1981. "At-Large Elections and Minority-Group Representation: A Re-Examination of Historical and Contemporary Evidence." *Journal of Politics* 43 (4): 982–1005. https://doi.org/10.2307/2130184

Dehaas, Josh. 2015. "LGBTQ Community Hopes for More Representation in Next Parliament." *CTV News*, August 29. http://www.ctvnews.ca/politics/lgbtq-community-hopes-for-more-representation-in-next-parliament-1.2538037

D'Emilio, John. 2000. "Cycles of Change, Questions of Strategy: The Gay and Lesbian Movement after Fifty Years." In *The Politics of Gay Rights*, ed. Craig Rimmerman, Kenneth Wald, and Clyde Wilcox, 31–53. Chicago: University of Chicago Press.

Eley, Geoff. 2003. *Forging Democracy: The History of the Left in Europe*. Oxford: Oxford University Press.

Everitt, Joanna. 2015a. "Gender and Sexual Diversity in Provincial Election Campaigns." *Canadian Political Science Review* 9 (1): 177–92.

–. 2015b. "List of Federal LGBT Candidates and MPs to the Fall of 2015." Provided to author by source.

Everitt, Joanna, and Michael Camp. 2014. "In versus Out: LGBT Politicians in Canada." *Journal of Canadian Studies* 48 (1): 226–51. https://doi.org/10.3138/jcs.48.1.226

Fortin-Rittberger, Jessica, and Berthold Rittberger. 2014. "Do Electoral Rules Matter? Explaining National Differences in Women's Representation in the European Parliament." *European Union Politics* 15 (4): 496–520. https://doi.org/10.1177/1465116514527179

Freidenvall, Lenita. 2003. "Women's Political Representation and Gender Quotas – The Swedish Case." Working Paper Series: The Research Program: Gender Quotas – A Key to Equality? Stockholm: Department of Political Science, Stockholm University.

Gates, Gary J. 2013. "Geography and the LGBT Population." In *International Handbook on the Demography of Sexuality*, ed. A.K. Baumle, 229–42. Dordrecht: Springer.

Geddis, Andrew. 2006. "A Dual Track Democracy? The Symbolic Role of the Māori Seats in New Zealand's Electoral System." *Election Law Journal* 5 (4): 347–71. https://doi.org/10.1089/elj.2006.5.347

Ghaziani, Amin. 2010. "Reviews: There Goes the Gayborhood?" *Contexts* 9 (4): 64–66. https://doi.org/10.1525/ctx.2010.9.4.64

Grofman, Bernard, and Lisa Handley. 1991. "The Impact of the Voting Rights Act on Black Representation in Southern State Legislatures." *Legislative Studies Quarterly* 16 (1): 111–28. https://doi.org/10.2307/439970

Haider-Markel, Donald P., Mark R. Joslyn, and Chad J. Kniss. 2000. "Minority Group Interests and Political Representation: Gay Elected Officials in the Policy Process." *Journal of Politics* 62 (2): 568–77. https://doi.org/10.1111/0022-3816.00026

Herrick, Rebekah, and Sue Thomas. 2001. "Gays and Lesbians in Local Races." *Journal of Homosexuality* 42 (1): 103–26. https://doi.org/10.1300/j082v42n01_06. Medline:11991562

Hunter, Anna. 2003. "Exploring the Issues of Aboriginal Representation in Federal Elections." *Electoral Insight* 5 (3): 27–33.

Kaminsky, Jackie, and Timothy White. 2007. "Electoral Systems and Women's Representation in Australia." *Commonwealth and Comparative Politics* 45 (2): 185–201. https://doi.org/10.1080/14662040701317519

Kite, Melissa. 2010. "David Cameron in Row over Black and Gay Candidates." *Telegraph*, February 14.

Knopp, Lawrence. 1987. "Social Theory, Social Movements, and Public Policy: Recent Accomplishments of the Gay and Lesbian Movements of Minneapolis, Minnesota." *International Journal of Urban and Regional Research* 11 (2): 243–61. https://doi.org/10.1111/j.1468-2427.1987.tb00048.x

Korinek, Valere J. 2003. "'The Most Openly Gay Person for at Least a Thousand Miles': Doug Wilson and the Politicization of a Province, 1975–83." *Canadian Historical Review* 84 (4): 1–19. https://doi.org/10.3138/chr.84.4.517

Krook, Mona Lena. 2010a. "Beyond Supply and Demand: A Feminist-Institutionalist Theory of Candidate Selection." *Political Research Quarterly* 63 (4): 707–20. https://doi.org/10.1177/1065912909336275

—. 2010b. "Women's Representation in Parliament: A Qualitative Comparative Analysis." *Political Studies* 58 (5): 886–908. https://doi.org/10.1111/j.1467-9248.2010.00833.x

Kunovich, Sheri. 2012. "Unexpected Winners: The Significance of an Open-List System on Women's Representation in Poland." *Politics and Gender* 8 (2): 153–77. https://doi.org/10.1017/s1743923x12000141

Ladner, Kiera L., and Michael McCrossan. 2007. *The Electoral Participation of Aboriginal People*. Working Paper Series on Electoral Participation and Outreach Practices. Ottawa: Elections Canada. http://elections.ca/res/rec/part/paper/aboriginal/aboriginal_e.pdf.

Lewis, Gregory B. 2011. "The Friends and Family Plan: Contact with Gays and Support for Gay Rights." *Policy Studies Journal* 39 (2): 217–38. https://doi.org/10.1111/j.1541-0072.2011.00405.x

Lewis, Gregory B., and David W. Pitts. 2011. "Representation of Lesbians and Gay Men in Federal, State, and Local Bureaucracies." *Journal of Public Administration Research and Theory* 21 (1): 159–80. https://doi.org/10.1093/jopart/mup030

Marchand, Len. 1990. "Proportional Representation for Native Peoples." *Canadian Parliamentary Review* 13 (3): 9–10.

Matland, Richard E. 2005. "Enhancing Women's Political Participation: Legislative Recruitment and Electoral Systems." In *Women in Parliament: Beyond the Numbers*, ed. International Institute for Democracy and Electoral Assistance (International IDEA), 93–111. Stockholm, Sweden: International IDEA.

Matland, Richard E., and Donley Studlar. 1996. "The Contagion of Women Candidates in Single-Member Districts and Proportional Representation Electoral Systems: Canada and Norway." *Journal of Politics* 58 (1): 707–33. https://doi.org/10.2307/2960439

Moos, Adam. 1989. "The Grassroots in Action: Gays and Seniors Capture the Local State in West Hollywood, California." In *The Power of Geography: How Territory Shapes Social Life*, ed. Jennifer Wolch and Michael Dear, 67–93. London: Routledge.

Morden, Michael. 2016. "Indigenizing Parliament: Time to Restart a Conversation." *Canadian Parliamentary Review* 39 (2): 24–33.

Moschonas, Gerassimos. 2002. *In the Name of Social Democracy: The Great Transformation, 1945–Present*. London: Verso.

Moser, Robert G., and Ethan Scheiner. 2012. *Electoral Systems and Political Context: How the Effects of Rules Vary across New and Established Democracies*. Cambridge: Cambridge University Press.

Nagel, Jack. 1996. "Constitutional Reform and Social Difference in New Zealand." *Cardozo Journal of International and Comparative Law* 4 (2): 373–94.

Norris, Pippa, and Ronald Inglehart. 2001. "Women and Democracy: Cultural Obstacles to Equal Representation." *Journal of Democracy* 12 (3): 126–40. https://doi.org/10.1353/jod.2001.0054

Paxton, Pamela, Melanie M. Hughes, and Jennifer L. Green. 2006. "The International Women's Movement and Women's Political Representation, 1893–2003." *American Sociological Review* 71 (6): 898–920. https://doi.org/10.1177/000312240607100602

Perrigo, Sarah. 1995. "Gender Struggles in the British Labour Party from 1979 to 1995." *Party Politics* 1 (3): 407–17. https://doi.org/10.1177/1354068895001003007

Pilon, Dennis. 2007. *The Politics of Voting: Reforming Canada's Electoral System*. Toronto: Emond Montgomery.

—. 2015. "Researching Voter Turnout and the Electoral Subaltern: Utilizing 'Class' as Identity." *Studies in Political Economy* 96 (1): 69–91. https://doi.org/10.1080/19187033.2015.11674938

—. 2016. "Proportional Representation Will Ensure Indigenous Votes Count." *Huffington Post Canada*, October 14. https://www.huffingtonpost.ca/dennis-pilon/electoral-reform-indigenous-vote_b_12488432.html

—. 2017. "Party Politics and Voting Systems in Canada." In *Canadian Parties in Transition: Recent Trends and New Paths for Research*, 4th ed., ed. Alain-G. Gagnon and A. Brian Tanguay, 217–49. Toronto: University of Toronto Press.

Podmore, Julie. 2015. "From Repression to Incorporation: LGBT Activists and City Politics in Montréal." In *Queer Mobilizations: Social Movement Activism and Canadian Public Policy*, ed. Manon Tremblay, 187–207. Vancouver: UBC Press.

Polletta, Francesca, and James M. Jasper. 2001. "Collective Identity and Social Movements." *Annual Review of Sociology* 27 (1): 283–305. https://doi.org/10.1146/annurev.soc.27.1.283

Rayside, David. 1998. *On the Fringe: Gays and Lesbians in Politics*. Ithaca: Cornell University Press.

Rayside, David, Jerald Sabin, and Paul E.J. Thomas. 2017. *Religion and Canadian Party Politics*. Vancouver: UBC Press.

Rayside, David, and Clyde Wilcox, eds. 2011. *Faith, Politics, and Sexual Diversity in Canada and the United States*. Vancouver: UBC Press.

Reynolds, Andrew. 2013. "Representation and Rights: The Impact of LGBT Legislators in Comparative Perspective." *American Political Science Review* 107 (2): 259–74. https://doi.org/10.1017/s0003055413000051

—. 2015. "LGBTQ Candidates in the 2015 Canadian Federal Election: Stalled Progress?" Bulletin from LGBT Representation and Rights Research Initiative. University of North Carolina, Chapel Hill. https://lgbtqrightsrep.files.wordpress.com/2015/10/canadalgbtmpcoct21.pdf

Roberts, Andrew, Jason Seawright, and Jennifer Cyr. 2012. "Do Electoral Laws Affect Women's Representation?" *Comparative Political Studies* 46 (12): 1555–81. https://doi.org/10.1177/0010414012463906

Rosen, Jennifer. 2013. "The Effects of Political Institutions on Women's Political Representation: A Comparative Analysis of 168 Countries from 1992 to 2010." *Political Research Quarterly* 66 (2): 306–21. https://doi.org/10.1177/1065912912449698

—. 2017. "Gender Quotas for Women in National Politics: A Comparative Analysis across Development Thresholds." *Social Science Research* 66: 82–101. https://doi.org/10.1016/j.ssresearch.2017.01.008. Medline:28705365

Rosenblum, Darren. 1995. "Overcoming 'Stigmas': Lesbian and Gay Districts and Black Electoral Empowerment." *Harvard Law Journal* 49 (1): 149–200.

—. 1996. "Geographically Sexual? Advancing Gay and Lesbian Interests through Proportional Representation." *Harvard Civil Rights - Civil Liberties Law Review* 31: 119–54.

Ruedin, Didier. 2012. "The Representation of Women in National Parliaments: A Cross-National Comparison." *European Sociological Review* 28 (1): 96–109. https://doi.org/10.1093/esr/jcq050

Rule, Wilma. 1987. "Electoral Systems, Contextual Factors and Women's Opportunity for Election to Parliament in Twenty-Three Democracies." *Western Political Quarterly* 40 (3): 477–98. https://doi.org/10.2307/448386

Russell, Meg, Fiona MacKay, and Laura McAllister. 2002. "Women's Representation in the Scottish Parliament and National Assembly for Wales: Party Dynamics for Achieving Critical Mass." *Journal of Legislative Studies* 8 (2): 49–76. https://doi.org/10.1080/714003911

Ruting, Brad. 2008. "Economic Transformations of Gay Urban Spaces: Revisiting Collin's Evolutionary Gay District Model." *Australian Geographer* 39 (3): 259–69. https://doi.org/10.1080/00049180802270465

Salmond, Rob. 2006. "Proportional Representation and Female Parliamentarians." *Legislative Studies Quarterly* 31 (2): 175–204. https://doi.org/10.3162/036298006x201779

Shvedova, Nadezhda. 2005. "Obstacles to Women's Participation in Parliament." In *Women in Parliament: Beyond the Numbers*, ed. International Institute for Democracy and Electoral Assistance (International IDEA), 33–51. Stockholm, Sweden: International IDEA.

Siemiatycki, Myer. 2011. *The Diversity Gap: The Electoral Underrepresentation of Visible Minorities*. Diverse City Counts Research Series. Toronto: Ryerson Centre for Immigration and Settlement.

Smith, Miriam. 2012. "Identity and Opportunity: The Lesbian and Gay Rights Movement." In *Queerly Canadian*, ed. Maureen Fitzgerald and Scott Rayter, 121–38. Toronto: Canadian Scholars' Press.

Sparrow, Jeremy. 2010. "The Truth about Maori Seats." Bachelor's diss., University of Otago, Dunedin, New Zealand.

Statistics Canada. 2017. "Aboriginal Peoples in Canada: Key Results from the 2016 Census." *The Daily*, October 25.

Stockemer, Daniel, and Maeve Byrne. 2012. "Women's Representation around the World: The Importance of Women's Participation in the Workforce." *Parliamentary Affairs* 65 (4): 802–21. https://doi.org/10.1093/pa/gsr063

Thorpe, J.R. 2015. "6 Feminist Political Parties around the World You Should Know About." *Bustle*, May 5. https://www.bustle.com/articles/81055-6-feminist-political-parties-around-the-world-you-should-know-about.

Tolley, Erin. 2017. "The Electoral System and Parliament's Diversity Problem: In Defence of the Wrongly Accused." In *Should We Change How We Vote? Evaluating Canada's Electoral System*, ed. Andrew Potter, Daniel Weinstock, and Peter Loewen, 111–25. Montreal and Kingston: McGill-Queen's University Press.

Tremblay, Manon, ed. 2015. *Queer Mobilizations: Social Movement Activism and Canadian Public Policy*. Vancouver: UBC Press.

Trimble, Linda, Jane Arscott, and Manon Tremblay, eds. 2013. *Stalled: The Representation of Women in Canadian Governments*. Vancouver: UBC Press.

Valdini, Melody Ellis. 2013. "Electoral Institutions and the Manifestation of Bias: The Effect of the Personal Vote on the Representation of Women." *Politics and Gender* 9 (1): 76–92. https://doi.org/10.1017/s1743923x12000700

Ward, Norman. 1950. *The Canadian House of Commons: Representation*. Toronto: University of Toronto Press.

Warner, Tom. 2002. *Never Going Back: A History of Queer Activism in Canada*. Toronto: University of Toronto Press.

Wells, Paul. 2018. "Justin Trudeau on Electoral Reform: Maybe Consistency Isn't the Word." *Maclean's*, February 1.

Woolf, Marie. 2006. "Cameron's gAy List." *Independent*, February 5.

Zaborsky, Dorothy. 1987. "Feminist Politics: The Feminist Party of Canada." *Women's Studies International Forum* 10 (5): 613–21. https://doi.org/10.1016/0277-5395(87)90075-6

Part 2
LGBTQ Representatives

5

LGBT Groups and the Canadian Conservative Movement
A New Relationship?

Frédéric Boily and Ève Robidoux-Descary

> *How can you be gay? You're a conservative!*
>
> – Eric Lorenzen (2016a)

POLITICAL PARTIES OF the right must today confront claims relating to social and sexual inclusion, issues to which they have traditionally been averse. Likewise, Canadian Conservative parties have endured difficult relationships with so-called special-interest groups, notably those that advocate on behalf of sexual minorities and women. For example, Stephen Harper's Conservative Party was said to have maintained "a complex relationship with women" (Bird and Rowe 2013, 165). More generally, right-wing responses to sexual-minority organizations fall somewhere between outright rejection and discomfort or incomprehension – a difficult position to hold, politically speaking. A vivid example of this occurred in Alberta during 2014, when the Progressive Conservative Party led by Jim Prentice was challenged by Liberal MLA Laurie Blakeman's proposed legislation to recognize gay-straight alliances in schools (Bellefontaine 2014). Indeed, some conservative supporters, more specifically those identified as social conservatives, subscribe to a resolutely traditional world view. We will return to this shortly.

To be sure, on many counts, the Conservative Party of Canada stands apart from its right-wing equivalents in other Western countries, notably on issues of diversity and plurality. For example, it is not wholly opposed to multiculturalism, and it seems more tolerant of diversity than are conservative organizations in the United States. Nonetheless, Canadian conservatives remain generally reluctant to embrace theories of recognition.

Against this backdrop, where do Canadian conservatives stand on specifically LGBT-related issues? Do they systematically reject the claims of LGBT advocates? Some provincial conservative leaders do appear more open to sexual diversity. Are isolated instances of openness due to savvy political marketing, or do they signal a profound and long-lasting philosophical reorientation? These questions form the basis of our investigation. Our primary focus is the federal Conservative Party, but we also examine some provincial ones, although it should be noted that LGBT-related issues are not fully integrated into their agendas. We shall see that although the right-wing provincial parties have the skills to generate specific policies, they are reluctant to do so. This shyness seems a deliberate strategy to avoid acting on issues that offend some of their electorate.

We find that while conservatives generally meet sexual-minority movements with more opposition than recognition, right-wing parties and intellectuals hold a range of widely divergent positions. Indeed, it is essential to distinguish between two significant trends in the political right, in order to refine our understanding of the federal and provincial Conservatives' response to LGBT claims. The first, stemming from neoliberalism, is more inclined to recognize LGBT rights; the other, that of traditional conservatism, is much more averse to recognizing sexual-minority rights. This crucial distinction also helps to determine whether some new organizations, such as LGBTory Canada, represent new thinking among conservative organizations or are little more than political marketing operations seeking to modernize the conservative image.

The Right and LGBT Movements in Canada

Generally speaking, political parties instrumentalize a given issue (or a position issue) to distinguish themselves from each other. As Stefano Bartolini (2002, 100) explains, "Position issues are inherently divisive as they involve explicit choices 'for' or 'against.'" More specifically in our case, some studies show that issues related to gender and sexuality serve to differentiate political parties and often to demonstrate how they staunchly oppose each other (Winter 2010). Other authors, however, observe that in recent years this polarizing trend has begun to reverse, as conservative parties increasingly support sexual-minority rights. According to Andrew Reynolds (2016), "In 2016 conservatives around the world are embracing gay and transgender rights as a core part of their belief in individualism, liberty and the family as the foundation of society." One would certainly agree that the right has made obvious efforts to present itself more favourably to the electorate. Nevertheless, significant differences separate the various currents that animate the right, as various contingents may hold widely divergent positions on this issue.

The terms "right" and "conservatism" (or "neoconservatism") are often used interchangeably, especially to describe political organizations that sit at the right end of the spectrum (Boily 2015). Yet these terms do not overlap neatly, and it is difficult to identify which traits reliably define the right (O'Hara 2011, 10–11). Actually, the issue of Canadian neoconservatism seems more appropriate for foreign policy analysis than for identity politics (Bloomfield and Nossal 2013). Moreover, in our particular case, that of recognizing the rights of sexual minorities, the dissimilarities between *neoliberal right* and *conservatism* are crucial and are associated with significantly different political positions. There is a distinctly *liberal* right that favours individual rights (Boily 2009), the so-called neoliberal right, as represented by authors such as Friedrich Hayek and, in a more extreme form, Ayn Rand. In this version of the right, government involvement is mostly if not always decried as excessive or denounced as a kind of statism that stifles economic activity. In this view, nothing is more important than giving unfettered rein to individual initiative, realized mainly through the free market. Supporters of the liberal or neoliberal right have a generally negative view of the state, choosing to place their trust more readily in spontaneous market mechanisms than in state-enforced regulations. For the neoliberal right, the individual is the basic unit of society. Neoconservatives also share certain views with neoliberals, especially because they come together to focus on the free market (Wiseman 2013, 209). The neoliberal right is fundamentally different from the more properly *conservative* right, which sees the protection of social traditions and mores, such as the nuclear family, as central to its political agenda (Malloy 2013, 185–87). For these conservatives, those of the "traditional" or "social" bent, the political community is defined by its own foundational or traditional path that must be preserved above all. Conservatives and traditionalists who espouse this approach regard the family as the vital cell of society, understood as an organic whole. This is especially true for French Canadian Catholic conservatives such as Lionel Groulx, but also for British conservatives. For a recent example, a conservative intellectual writes that "the basic truth remains that the family is a place in which the ends of life are constructed and enjoyed" (Scruton 2015, 142). Contrary to their neoliberal counterparts, social conservatives are willing to admit a greater role for the state when it comes to protecting the traditions or moral foundations of the community. To put it differently, they see the state as the ultimate guarantor of moral order of the organic whole and of the social cells, such as the family, that compose it. Social hierarchies are the building blocks of this organic model. Conservatives believe that when these disappear, liberty disappears along with them (Vincent 2016, 47–48).

The friction between neoliberals and social conservatives can be readily observed around issues such as prostitution. Here, the neoliberal right favours legalization, citing an individual's freedom of choice as either purchaser or provider of a service, whereas social conservatives insist that any given society rests on a moral foundation that must be protected. With regard to prostitution, Danielle Smith, the former leader of the Alberta Wildrose Party, advocated policies that revealed a neoliberal bent (Boily 2013). Similarly, Tom Flanagan, former advisor to Stephen Harper, was critical of the bill to criminalize prostitution (C-36), arguing that its heavy-handed social conservatism strayed too far from the "British legal heritage" (Flanagan 2014).

As we have seen, political parties of the right struggle constantly to contain the tension between two competing currents of conservative thought, and this is especially apparent in matters of morality and sexual diversity. One side proposes a government that respects and protects what it considers essential to the moral salubrity of the community, as was the case, for example, in North Carolina, which is discussed below (Berman 2016). The other side is much more inclined to let individuals decide what they perceive as moral and good. This tension has been a challenge to the Canadian right, especially since the emergence of the Reform Party some years ago. In its early days, Reform attracted mostly religious and social conservatives. And although its leader, Preston Manning, was himself among their number, he chose to "not prioritize opposition to gay rights" in the mid-1990s, when his party first aspired to government (Malloy 2013, 190–91). It is precisely because of this tension between two competing trends within the political right that claims for the recognition of LGBT rights moved front and centre during Stephen Harper's years in government.

Federal Canadian Conservatives: New Warriors for Gay Rights?

In the federal election of October 2015, Justin Trudeau's Liberals won a decisive victory, toppling the Harper Conservatives, who had held office since 2006. A few months later, in January 2016, Rona Ambrose, interim Conservative leader, stated, "I've been clear for a long time that the Conservative Party welcomes all conservatives, regardless of sexual orientation. If you believe in smaller government, lower taxes, balanced budgets and individual freedom, we want you in our party" (Ivison 2016). Her remark may seem surprising, given its obvious break with the party's socially conservative base. In fact, Ambrose was responding to pressure from a conservative group, LGBTory Canada, that was pushing the party to put to rest, definitively, any debate over same-sex marriage (for details on same-sex marriage, see Chapter 6 in this volume). That topic had been a flashpoint in the 2006 election. During that year, "the issue that had the strongest impact on the probability of voting Conservative was same-sex marriage" (Gidengil et al. 2012, 92; see also Chapter 1 in this volume).

According to LGBTory, the 2015 election defeat provided the party with a timely opportunity to update its image, especially since the Conservatives had been "completely shut out of the Island of Montreal, Vancouver and most of the Greater Toronto Area" (Ivison 2016). Such an update would require a profound revision to certain policies, especially that regarding same-sex marriage. This was enshrined in the party's 2013 policy declaration, which stated,

> We believe that Parliament, through a free vote, and not the courts should determine the definition of marriage. We support legislation defining marriage as

the union of one man and one woman. We support the freedom of religious organizations to refuse to perform unions or allow the use of their facilities for events that are incompatible with their faith and beliefs. (Conservative Party of Canada 2013, 28)

LGBTory president Doc von Lichtenberg (2016a) wrote, "This policy is a significant obstacle to the acceptance of the Conservative message by voters who would otherwise be attracted to the party's stance on economic, security, and foreign policy issues. Most of us have had encounters with people for whom the Conservative vision resonates strongly but who are repelled by a social-conservative policy on same-sex marriage."

The marriage clause was duly overturned at the May 2016 Conservative convention in Vancouver. Electoral considerations appear to have animated this move, in a bid to regain urban ridings – precisely those where Liberal victories had been most decisive. Similar motives recently helped elect women to lead provincial parties, as was the case with the Alberta Conservatives (Boily 2014) and the British Columbia Liberals (Robidoux-Descary and Boily 2014). Nevertheless, a rapprochement between Conservative politicians and LGBT groups predates the October 2015 election. According to Jamie Ellerton, an openly gay former staffer for Jason Kenney, Conservatives have had no choice but to alter their policies to better harmonize with Canadian society: "It's no secret that the Conservative Party hasn't always been the biggest champion of gay rights, but public pressure, and quite frankly, society evolving has changed their views" (Hopper 2012).

For some years, conservative Canadians have been paying closer attention to the LGBT movement. Since 2011, for example, Conservative conventions have featured a Blue Tent event, a party at which gay Conservatives are celebrated. Some prominent Tories have attended, including Laureen Harper, wife of Stephen Harper (Levitz 2016). Perhaps more significantly, some cabinet ministers espoused firm and visible positions in defence of gay and lesbian rights outside Canada, such as Minister of Immigration Jason Kenney and Minister of Foreign Affairs John Baird. For example, both strongly criticized anti-gay legislation in Uganda. In a speech delivered in Quebec City, Baird condemned Ugandan laws forbidding same-sex marriage, drawing censure from some Canadian members of the Ugandan diaspora, who resented his meddling in the internal affairs of their country of origin (*Ugandan Diaspora* 2012; for a critical look at this exportation of Canadian-style liberal LGBT rights to developing countries, see Chapter 7 in this volume). But some LGBT activists believe that outright denunciation is not the solution and that acting behind the scenes would have been more profitable:

In Uganda, there was worry in LGBT circles that Baird was doing their cause more harm than good. Frank Mugisha, the diminutive and soft-spoken leader of the Ugandan gay rights group Sexual Minorities Uganda, blitzed Canadian media before an appearance in Toronto last year. His message: instead of public shaming like Baird's, Canada should be using backroom diplomatic channels to pressure Uganda. (McCann 2014)

The Conservatives' advocacy for gay rights outside Canadian borders has some parallels with their defence of religious rights in foreign countries (Chase 2013). Nevertheless, Baird was compelled to reassure the party's base that he was not promoting same-sex marriage:

Same-sex marriage was not something we promoted internationally. When I spoke out about Uganda, I spoke about a gentleman who was bludgeoned to death with a hammer ... What we've talked about are three things: the criminalization of sexuality; violence against sexual minorities and the death penalty against sexual minorities. I don't know any conservative in Canada who supports any of those three things. (Chase 2013)

For the Conservative Party does retain elements, such as REAL Women, that are strongly opposed to any recognition of gay and lesbian rights. This group was quick to criticize Baird's position, which it perceived as disdain for his own supporters: "Mr. Baird's actions are destructive to the conservative base in Canada and causing collateral damage to his party" (MacKinnon 2013). In 2014, when "Russian president Vladimir Putin signed into law a statute against 'homosexual propaganda'" (Paternotte and Tremblay 2015, 1), Baird condemned it. REAL Women accused him of operating behind the scenes to discourage Putin from passing laws to prevent homosexual couples from adopting young Russians. In its view, Baird's actions amounted to "homosexual propaganda" (MacKinnon 2013).

For his part, Jason Kenney sent an unsolicited letter to the LGBT people of Canada in 2012 – not without controversy, it must be added, as it was unclear how he had obtained their email addresses (it was later confirmed that they were from a petition; Lindell 2012). This letter detailed the efforts made by the Conservative Party in support of the LGBT constituency:

We are proud of the emphasis our Conservative Government has placed on gay and lesbian refugee protection, which is without precedent in Canada's immigration history. We have increased the resettlement of gay refugees living abroad as part of our refugee programs. In particular, we have taken the lead in helping gay refugees who have fled often violent persecution in Iran to begin new, safe lives in Canada. We are also helping community groups like the Rainbow Refugee Committee to sponsor gay refugees for resettlement to Canada. (*CBC News* 2012a)

But it was also Jason Kenney who, in 2005, had firmly opposed same-sex marriage and who, as citizenship and immigration minister, refused to include a section on the recognition of gay and lesbian rights in the Guide to Citizenship that was provided to aspiring Canadians (Beeby 2010). That being said, the 2012 version of the guide, also produced under his direction, did mention same-sex marriage by stipulating that gay and lesbian Canadians have access to civil marriage.

All told, there can be no question that some prominent and powerful members of the Conservative Party promoted positions that broke with the party's traditional "anti-gay" image, to the point of being described as "warriors for gay rights." As a *National Post* journalist remarked, "One would think that Canadian gay activists would have little in common with the right-leaning culture warriors who still have a prominent place within the Conservative party. But, in the post-9/11 world, the two groups have found common ground" (Kay 2013). Some observers claim that Conservatives are mostly interested in the "T of LGBTory," casting doubt upon the sincerity of their conversion to LGBT support (Jefferys 2015). Nevertheless, their activism was directed largely at gay rights outside of Canada because they could take a strong position in foreign policy without upsetting social conservatives.

Federal Conservatives do not have an umbrella policy with regard to LGBT issues (unlike the New Democratic Party, for instance; see Chapter 7 in this volume). Although, as we have pointed out, ministers such as John Baird condemned discriminatory policies adopted by foreign regimes, this has not been an integral element of the party's image. To find a conservative movement that truly embraces and promotes LGBT rights, one must turn to LGBTory, which was formed specifically for this purpose. The LGBTory website notes that the group emerged rather recently, in 2015, to enable Toronto conservatives who wished for a visible presence at local Gay Pride events to connect with each other. LGBTory president Doc von Lichtenberg (2016b) describes the organization thus: "We are a network of LGBT Canadians from all walks of life and diverse identities, but we all share a belief in the fundamental conservative principles of individual liberty, personal responsibility, reward for hard work, a free-market economy and democratic government." Clearly, members of LGBTory wish to reconcile their conservative and gay identities.

As discussed earlier, this group pressured Rona Ambrose to discontinue Conservative Party opposition to same-sex marriage. The LGBTory online resources include essays arguing that, in fact, same-sex marriage is a natural extension of traditional conservative values:

> How can it be good conservative policy to advocate excluding gays from the benefits and responsibilities of this institution [marriage]? Allowing gay citizens to marry stabilizes and enriches same-sex relationships while benefiting society and strengthening the institution of marriage. It respects individual rights while minimizing the oppressive intrusion of the state into the lives of a minority of its citizens. Above all, it treats all Canadian citizens as equal under the law. All of these values are deeply rooted in the conservative movement and appeal to lesbians and gays and straights alike. (Lorenzen 2016b)

In addition to promoting same-sex marriage as inherently compatible with conservative principles, LGBTory defends gay and lesbian rights outside of Canada, employing a form of homonationalism in doing so (on how the promotion of LGBT rights in Canada can be interpreted as domestic homonationalism, see Chapter 6 in this volume). Highlighting the intended parallel between this area of advocacy and typical conservative foreign policy, Jonathan Kay (2013) dubs these commentators "Rainbow Hawks." According to him, Stephen Harper made gay and lesbian rights "a centrepiece of Canada's foreign policy," a claim that resonates with the materials posted by LGBTory. We think that Kay overplays this point, as the defence of gay rights is clearly not a centrepiece in Conservative foreign policy. Nevertheless, the issue does have some importance, as LGBTory confirms. Its website features a collection of articles from Canada's major dailies, a typical example calling for stronger human-rights sanctions against homophobic Middle Eastern regimes (Weinthal 2016).

This sort of international advocacy recalls the mandate of the Conservative government's Office of Religious Freedom, established to monitor religious oppression and to protect religious freedoms in authoritarian regimes. LGBTory argues in favour of a similar policy with regard to LGBT rights, which has been described elsewhere in terms of homonationalism (see, for example, Dryden and Lenon 2015). More precisely, "This 'right-wing liberal' approach toward homosexuality could be called 'homonationalist,' because it turns gay rights into a matter of national pride and even chauvinism, often connected with Islamophobia" (Tobin 2017, 5). This ideological convergence facilitates the inclusion of gay and lesbian rights within a traditional conservative foreign policy animated by strong, clear-cut moral positions. This strategy – relegating to external affairs an issue that divides the party internally – seeks to unify the party around a common core of conservative, rightist principles, unfettered by special-interest groups or lobbyists.

LGBTory seems intent on demonstrating that supporting LGBT rights is compatible with firm moral conviction in matters of foreign policy and that it buttresses a strong opposition to tyrannical regimes that trample on human rights. Nevertheless, it is still too early to determine whether this movement will have a significant influence within the party or whether it will effectively counter the accepted wisdom that one cannot be both gay and conservative. At the time of writing, its efforts do not seem to have swayed those voters who are sensitive to issues relating to sexual diversity.

Conservative Provincial Politics

To determine the relationship between right-wing parties and various LGBT issues, we examined four conservative parties that are currently represented in legislative assemblies across the country. We discuss two parties in Alberta, one in Ontario, and one in Newfoundland and Labrador. Some provincial conservative governments have paid so little attention to LGBT issues that we were unable to assess their stances. For example, former Saskatchewan premier Brad Wall – a prominent conservative in Canada – showed limited interest and was rather moderate in setting up neoliberal policies to ensure his province's prosperity (Wiseman 2013, 222). In 2013, when gay-straight alliances were debated in Saskatchewan, Wall stood on the sidelines by stating that his government would not oppose the alliances, while also mentioning a concern about the freedom of religion in the province (*CBC News* 2013).

In Quebec, as in Saskatchewan, right-wing parties – first the Action démocratique du Québec (ADQ) and later the Coalition Avenir Québec (CAQ) – were fairly silent on the issue and never quite defined their position on LGBT concerns (Boily 2008). The ADQ, led by Mario Dumont, mostly eschewed social concerns. Its platform was dominated by public spending, the size of the civil service, *autonomisme*, and national identity, although critics claimed that its family policy was a step backward for working women (Dandurand 2003). It should be mentioned that in 2002, the ADQ voted along with other Quebec political parties on Bill 84, An Act instituting civil unions and establishing new rules of filiation (Tahon 2005). The CAQ, its successor, is likewise more concerned with revitalizing Quebec's economy. Among the candidates who attended a roundtable discussion hosted by the Conseil québécois LGBT, "only Alain Clavet, the Coalition Avenir Québec candidate in Ste-Marie–St-Jacques, a newcomer to politics, did not have a real vision of the issues" (Boullé 2014, our translation). Plainly speaking, the CAQ appears to have a blind spot in this regard, as, like the ADQ, it is preoccupied with the state's role in the economy and with the national question.

Thomas Lukaszuk and the Progressive Conservative Association of Alberta

Thomas Lukaszuk is a former member of the Legislative Assembly of Alberta (MLA) for the Progressive Conservative Association of Alberta (PC Alberta). He served as an MLA for Edmonton-Castle Downs from 2001 to 2015. From 2010 to 2014, he also held various cabinet positions, such as minister of education and deputy premier. When the NDP won the provincial election on May 5, 2015, Lukaszuk lost his seat.

In early 2014, Alberta Liberal MLA Kent Hehr launched a debate over the rights of gay students, with a non-binding motion that called on school boards to create peer-support groups (also known as gay-straight alliances). The motion was defeated. Liberal House leader Laurie Blakeman made a second attempt a few months later, with a private member's bill. In short, Bill 202 would ensure the creation of peer-support groups if they were requested by students (Giovannetti 2014). In response, Premier Jim Prentice introduced Bill 10, which was intended to give Alberta school boards the final word on the creation of peer-support groups. In December 2014, when Bill 10 went to second reading, Lukaszuk was the only PC Alberta MLA who voted against it. In explanation, he stated, "I simply do not believe in incremental granting of human rights" (Braid 2014). Bill 10 passed its second reading and was then put on hold until PC Alberta education minister Gordon Dirks amended it to allow gay-straight alliances for any students in the public and Catholic schools of Alberta. According to Prentice, this change of attitude reflected media coverage "about how students and young people were responding to the difficult debate that was surrounding gay-straight alliances and Bill 10" (*CBC News* 2015a). It was also the result of various consultations. The amended bill passed on March 10, 2015.

Even after his 2015 election defeat, Lukaszuk remained vocal on LGBT rights. For example, in an opinion piece published in the *Edmonton Journal* on March 2, 2016, he discussed school board policies. Among other things, he wrote that the province's NDP government "was correct in requesting that all school boards develop their own policies to comply with Bill 10 and to guarantee LGBTQ children full protection of the law and access to appropriate bathrooms. That's the law and that's the right thing to do" (Lukaszuk 2016).

With regard to his opinions on LGBT issues, Lukaszuk stands out from other conservative politicians in the province. For example, in 2014, PC Alberta leadership candidate Ric McIver participated for the fourth time in the Calgary March for Jesus. McIver later apologized for doing so, claiming he was unaware that the parade organizers condemned homosexuals on their website. This explanation appears questionable, as he had taken part in other events with the group (Gunter 2014). At the time, Lukaszuk, who was also running for the PC Alberta leadership, released this statement:

> My own views on human sexuality are on the record ... I have been an advocate for individual rights, I have initiated ground-breaking projects to end homophobic bullying, I have supported Camp fYrefly and other programs for young people struggling with their own identities, I supported changes to Alberta's birth certificate requirements for transgendered Albertans, and I voted in favour of gay-straight alliances. I am proud of this record. (*CBC News* 2014a)

In April 2016, interim PC Alberta leader Ric McIver and the other members of the caucus launched the Engage campaign, including a thirty-eight-page document to start a public conversation. On the subject of education, the Engage document suggested that

> the government develops a comprehensive sexual health education program that is age-appropriate, science-based and non-judgmental, which includes topics such as sexual health information for persons with disabilities, LGBTQ identities, consent in relationships and sexual abuse, to ensure that our schools are safe and inclusive environments while continuing to respect parents' role in educational delivery that is protected in current legislation. (PC Alberta 2016, 13)

A statement about LGBT issues is not surprising, given that inclusivity was one of the five guiding themes of the conversation. In this respect, the Engage campaign was intended to ensure that future services and policies would meet the needs of historically under-represented citizens.

Danielle Smith and the Wildrose Party of Alberta

Danielle Smith served as leader of the Wildrose Party of Alberta from 2009 to 2014 and as leader of the Official Opposition from 2012 to 2014. She was an MLA for Highwood from 2012 to 2015. Smith crossed the floor and joined the PC Alberta government in December 2014 but lost the PC nomination race in Highwood on March 2015.

During the 2012 provincial election, controversy arose around an anti-gay blog written in 2011 by Allan Hunsperger, the Wildrose candidate in Edmonton South. In his posted comments, Hunsperger stated that gays and lesbians would "suffer the rest of eternity in a lake of fire" (*CBC News* 2012b). When confronted by PC Alberta premier Alison Redford, he defended his remarks: "[They] are my own personal religious views and were given in the capacity as a church pastor. I fully support equality for all people, and condemn any intolerance based on sexual orientation or any other personal characteristic" (Graveland 2012). To a surprising degree, Danielle Smith refused to condemn Hunsperger's anti-gay post or to terminate his candidacy, suggesting that even if she didn't agree with his comments, he had the right to make them. During the previous week, she had also criticized the government decision to reinstate public funding for gender confirmation surgery.

In October 2013, the Wildrose Party voted in favour of a resolution to oppose intolerance against anyone, including LGBT people (Bennett 2013). Still, a year afterward, it voted down a policy that would have promoted equal rights regardless of race, religious beliefs, colour, gender, and sexual orientation. Instead, party members chose to maintain the current policy, which is based on equal rights, privileges, and responsibilities for all. According to Smith, the proposed policy was lacking in fairness as it only prohibited discrimination on the grounds of race, religious beliefs, colour, gender, and sexual orientation: "The nature of the debate was (the members) were concerned that there might be something excluded in that long list" (Bennett 2014). However, the decision represented a backward step, as it put equal treatment of minority groups at risk.

Nevertheless, in 2015, the party blocked potential Calgary Varsity candidate Russ Kuykendall from running for the nomination in the riding of Calgary-Varsity. Wildrose leader Brian Jean did not explain why, but commentators speculated that it was the result of a post written by Kuykendall in 2007, which had denounced a Gay Pride brunch held in a Catholic church hall (Canadian Press 2015). In the party's latest platform, Standing Up for Albertans!, the section on education does include a brief statement on sexual orientation, in which the party promises to "work with all partners to make sure that every child, regardless of gender, disability, race, religion, sexual orientation, appearance or any other characteristic, has a bully-free educational experience" (Wildrose 2015, 14). But it seems that the relationship between Wildrose and LGBT advocates remains strained, as the party struggles to overcome the perception that it doesn't support LGBT people (Gerson 2014).

Now that Wildrose and PC Alberta have merged to form the United Conservative Party, with Jason Kenney at the helm, we will have to wait and see how things evolve. Kenney has already raised concerns within LGBTory (2017b) and among LGBT Albertans by stating that parents should be warned if their children attend a gay-straight alliance (Radio-Canada 2017).

Patrick Brown, Doug Ford, and the Progressive Conservative Party of Ontario

Currently the mayor of Brampton, Patrick Brown was the elected leader of the Progressive Conservative Party of Ontario (Ontario PC Party) between May

2015 and January 2018. The official party website notes, "He ran on a platform of Party renewal, promising to grow the Party to over 100,000 members from every walk of life and every corner of the province" (Ontario PC Party 2016). He was elected to the Ontario legislature for the riding of Simcoe North during a provincial by-election on September 3, 2015.

From 2006 to 2015, Brown represented the riding of Barrie as a Conservative MP in the House of Commons. As an MP, he voted in 2006 to repeal same-sex marriage (Hébert 2015). He did so because he felt that striking down same-sex marriage would enable elected officials to determine whether they wished to revisit the issue. On May 5, 2015, CBC Radio's *Metro Morning* asked him if he supported the traditional definition of marriage, to which he replied, "Any way someone can find love I'm happy, regardless of whether that is a same-sex marriage or a traditional marriage" (*CBC News* 2015b). That said, he also voted against two bills whose purpose was to protect gender identity and expression under the Canadian Human Rights Act and the Criminal Code (Feibel 2015).

Although some opponents have labelled Brown as a social conservative, he describes himself as a "pragmatic" conservative: "Anything that benefits Ontario, anything that helps families, that helps create jobs, that helps enhance the quality of life in Ontario, I would rally behind regardless of where that idea originated" (*CBC News* 2015b). On July 3, 2015, he became the first Ontario PC Party leader to head an official delegation in the Toronto Pride Parade (Taber 2015). Brown also attended other Pride events in Barrie. During the party convention on March 5, 2016, in Ottawa, he made a speech about inclusivity: "It doesn't matter who you are ... It doesn't matter who you love, it doesn't matter if you belong to a union ... It doesn't matter where you worship, you have a home in the Progressive Conservative Party of Ontario" (Ferguson 2016). Nevertheless, we must be careful not to put too much emphasis on Brown's gestures and statements, especially in light of his 2018 expulsion from his party due to accusations of sexual misconduct.

It could be argued that to a large extent, Brown won the Ontario PC Party leadership race by building on inclusivity. His decision to participate in the Toronto Pride Parade could be seen as part of his effort to involve more people in the party, including LGBT people. Of course, in reality, it could also have been a matter of political expediency. The arrival of Doug Ford at the head of the Conservatives could move the party into more overt hostility toward LGBT people. In the platform developed by Brown, called the People's Guarantee, the former Conservative leader said that he wanted to support changes to the sex-education curriculum. However, Ford has expressed the desire to revisit these changes. In fact, it seems that Ford might want to court the social conservatives who backed Tanya Granic Allen's candidacy during the 2018 Ontario PC leadership race, as she built her support based on the position to abolish the Liberals sex-education curriculum (Beattie 2018). This possible reopening of the debate on sex education and parental consent has also been poorly received by LGBTory (Brulé 2018). On the other hand, Granic Allen was expelled from the party after homophobic comments she made in 2014 resurfaced only a few days before the official start of the 2018 provincial election campaign, claiming that her eviction was "another betrayal of social conservatives" (*CBC News* 2018).

After being elected premier on June 7, 2018, at the head of a comfortable majority, Doug Ford was still eager to abolish the sex-education curriculum. That being said, some LGBT people have organized to denounce and counter the abandonment of the curriculum (Goldman 2018). In August 2019, Doug Ford introduced a new curriculum that was similar to the one he had promised to abolish. It will also be interesting to see whether Ford persists in absenting himself from the Toronto Pride Parade. In the summer of 2018, shortly after being elected, he chose not to attend on the pretext that the police were not allowed to participate – a "convenient excuse," according to some (Teitel 2018). As of 2019, Ford had not attended a Pride parade.

Steve Kent and the Progressive Conservative Party of Newfoundland and Labrador

Steve Kent is a member of the House of Assembly (MHA) for the Progressive Conservative Party of Newfoundland and Labrador. He has served as MHA for Mount Pearl North since 2007 and has held a number of cabinet portfolios, including that of deputy premier. In December 2015, he became deputy Opposition House leader until his resignation in 2017.

In 2014, while he was competing for the leadership of his party, Kent pledged to create a dedicated office to deal with and promote LGBT rights if he were elected premier: "The office could also interact with service providers to ensure that concerns from the LGBT community are being addressed and government is doing everything it can to promote diversity and equality and inclusion in our society" (*CBC News* 2014b). He also expressed his desire to start a discussion with other premiers on resources available across the country for trans people who were seeking gender confirmation surgery. At the flag-raising ceremony to launch Pride Week 2015 in Newfoundland and Labrador, he stated, "As a government, we are committed to embracing and celebrating the diversity of all people in the province, regardless of age, gender, or sexual orientation" (Government of Newfoundland and Labrador 2015). Nonetheless, LGBT issues were absent from the policy "Blueprint" of the latest PC leader, Paul Davis, which was released only a few months later, on November 2015 (PC Party of Newfoundland and Labrador 2015).

Provincial Conservative and Inclusion?

With regard to conservative provincial politics, it is clear that there is little to no evidence of LGBT inclusion in party platforms. Tolerance toward sexual orientation and gender identity appears to happen more easily at the individual level. Thus, some politicians, such as Thomas Lukaszuk and Steve Kent, seem more open to sexual diversity. Lukaszuk stands out from his colleagues, not only as an ally of LGBT people but also as an advocate for them. Others, such as Danielle Smith, Ric McIver, and Allan Hunsperger, are still somewhat reluctant to accept LGBT claims or may even oppose them. As for Patrick Brown, it is not entirely possible to determine whether his shift on LGBT issues is genuine or merely part of his desire to get elected, which is why he is often portrayed as an instrumentalizer.

Now that "[most] provinces and territories have included sexual orientation in their human rights legislation as a prohibited ground of discrimination" (Government of Canada 2018), governments are increasingly likely to implement changes in official policy, even if they were traditionally unfriendly to sexual minorities, at least to secure re-election. On the other hand, parties that currently make up the Official Opposition might do little to advance LGBT equality should they take power, regardless of campaign promises. The election of a majority PC government in Manitoba on April 9, 2016, provided an opportunity for leader Brian Pallister to respond to the pressure applied by the citizens of the province. Generally speaking, provincial Conservative governments tend to shy away from prioritizing LGBT issues.

Conclusion: What Path for Canadian Conservatives?

Currently, the Canadian right sits in an uncomfortable position with regard to the recognition of sexual diversity and LGBT rights. We have seen above that conservatives are not wholly opposed to such rights. Nonetheless, Stephen Harper's party remained without a comprehensive policy on these issues.

Now that Harper has been defeated, we can surmise that conservative politics in Canada faces a critical juncture as the party has found a new leader in the person of Andrew Scheer and is in the process of determining its future orientation. This moment in its history bears similarities with that of British conservatism during the early 2000s, in that the party must develop its future ideological bases and policy positions around a number of key issues, among them the environment and, of course, sexual minorities. Given this, the party will have to commit to one of several avenues. It may follow a path opened by David Cameron toward reconciliation with LGBT movements.

It may be argued that, more than in any other country, Great Britain's political parties from across the spectrum have embraced the LGBT constituency. This is particularly evident in the case of the Conservative Party, led by Cameron from 2005 to 2016. It has been repeatedly pointed out that, since the 2015 election, the British Parliament has included a remarkably high number of LGBT MPs, possibly the most of any Western parliament: of the 152 LGBT-identified individuals who ran for office, 27 were elected (13 Labour, 12 Conservative, and 2 Scottish National Party; Gerdes 2015). Here, it would be most accurate to speak of lesbian and gay, as the four trans-identified candidates failed to obtain a seat (Shariatmadari 2015).

The election of 12 LGBT Conservatives follows a sort of *aggiornamento* undertaken by the party during the mid-2000s (Heppell 2014, 127–42), but its beginnings may be traced back to the 1980s, when, in what has been described as a Quiet Revolution, a number of politicians came out as gay (Shariatmadari 2015). Under Cameron's leadership, the Conservative Party sought to distance itself from the Thatcher legacy and began to revamp its image, starting with women's issues (Bird and Rowe 2013, 175), followed by sexual-minority rights – the cornerstone of which was same-sex marriage. Insisting that this approach was indeed consistent with Conservative ideology (Jones 2008, 169), Cameron stated, "I don't support gay marriage in spite of being a conservative. I support gay marriage because I am a conservative" (Reynolds 2016). In our opinion, Stephen Harper would never have made such a declaration, even though his party agreed to hold a free vote in Parliament on the question of same-sex unions. Be that as it may, British conservatives have begun a process of transformation that would perhaps account for the support they now find among LGBT people.

Nevertheless, Canadian Conservatives could follow the example of conservative parties and organizations in the United States, where sexual minorities continue to elicit profound mistrust or outright rejection. Of course, one must guard against conflating Evangelical Christian conservatives, who are hostile to sexual minorities, with the Republican movement as a whole, in which "the antigay animus is slowly dissipating" (Kirchick 2010, 87). Since the 1980s, American political parties appear to have become increasingly polarized vis-à-vis abortion, same-sex marriage, and women's rights in general. This was the period that saw Ronald Reagan, to give but one example, strongly oppose the Equal Rights Amendment and, more forcefully, abortion (Costain 1991, 121–23). The conflicted response of Republicans to sexuality politics forms the basis of conservative author James Kirchick's essay "The Consistency of Gay Conservatives." Quoting Marvin Liebman's open letter to well-known conservative William F. Buckley, Jr., Kirchick (2010, 87) concludes that conservatism "is the logical political home of gay men and women," given its defence of individual rights against the state. Granted, this is something of an overstatement, given the strong opposition that LGBT rights continue to encounter in many jurisdictions, as witnessed recently in North Carolina, where the question of bathroom access for transgender individuals led to fierce debates (Graham 2016). As the North Carolina case makes clear, sexual-minority rights are by no means accepted by some Republicans. Fred Litwin (2015) points out, "There had been splits among conservatives about homosexuality for quite a while, and it shouldn't be surprising that it was an uphill fight for gay rights in the Republican Party." One should not dismiss too quickly the idea that the American rather than British scenario could develop among Canadian Conservatives. Canadian Conservatives need to choose between a position of confrontation and one of collaboration, as was the case with immigration, for which they successfully shifted from the former to the latter (Bird and Rowe 2013, 178).

In conclusion, we suggest that the future offers several possible avenues for Canadian Conservatives. We began this chapter by observing that conservative organizations often prefer to avoid debating LBGT issues, and persisting in this course is certainly an option. Or perhaps they will decide to follow the British model. Will a new generation emerge, more willing to confront the issue head on (Levitz 2016)?

It is now up to Conservative leader Andrew Scheer to answer this question. Perhaps significantly, he has expressed socially conservative views by opposing, for example, same-sex marriage (Macdonald 2017). In fact, he seems reluctant to take a public stand on such topics. Instead, his website highlights national and ethnic events. Furthermore, he chose to not participate in any Pride Parades across the country. For now, it is difficult to predict what position he will adopt during the federal election campaign of 2019. In the aftermath of his 2017 leadership victory, the LGBTory (2017a) website asserted, "We will continue to advocate in the CPC for LGBT people. However, we will be vigilant and will not hesitate to call him out when we feel that the CPC's actions or policies are a threat to LGBT equality." In short, there is uncertainty about the intentions and proposals of the new Conservative leader, just as we do not know what direction will be taken by the Conservative Party leaders in Ontario and Alberta.

References

Bartolini, Stefano. 2002. "Electoral and Party Competition: Analytical Dimensions." In *Political Parties: Old Concepts and New Challenges,* ed. Richard Gunther, José Ramón-Montero, and Juan Linz, 84–112. Oxford: Oxford University Press.

Beattie, Samantha. 2018. "PC Leader Doug Ford Promises to Scrap the Liberals Sex-Ed Curriculum." *Toronto Star,* March 12. https://www.thestar.com/news/queenspark/2018/03/12/pc-leader-doug-ford-promises-to-scrap-the-liberals-sex-ed-curriculum.html.

Beeby, Dean. 2010. "Immigration Minister Pulled Gay Rights from Citizenship Guide, Documents Show." *Globe and Mail,* March 12. http://www.theglobeandmail.com/news/politics/immigration-minister-pulled-gay-rights-from-citizenship-guide-documents-show/article571718/.

Bellefontaine, Michelle. 2014. "Gay-Straight Alliance Bill Leaves Emotions Raw at Alberta Legislature." *CBC News*, December 1. http://www.cbc.ca/news/canada/edmonton/gay-straight-alliance-bill-leaves-emotions-raw-at-alberta-legislature-1.2856866.

Bennett, Dean. 2013. "Wildrose Party Affirms Gay Rights." *CTV News*, October 26. http://www.ctvnews.ca/politics/wildrose-party-affirms-gay-rights-1.1514890.

–. 2014. "Alberta's Wildrose Party Backtracks on Equal Rights Statement." *Globe and Mail*, November 15. http://www.theglobeandmail.com/news/alberta/albertas-wildrose-party-reverts-statement-on-equal-rights/article21604093/.

Berman, Mark. 2016. "North Carolina Governor Says He Wants Bathroom Law Partially Changed after Backlash." *Washington Post*, April 12. https://www.washingtonpost.com/news/post-nation/wp/2016/04/12/deutsche-bank-halts-north-carolina-expansion-due-to-transgender-bathroom-law/.

Bird, Karen, and Andrea Rowe. 2013. "Women, Feminism, and the Harper Conservatives." In *Conservatism in Canada*, ed. James Farney and David Rayside, 165–83. Toronto: University of Toronto Press.

Bloomfield, Alan, and Kim Richard Nossal. 2013. "A Conservative Foreign Policy? Canada and Australia Compared." In *Conservatism in Canada*, ed. James Farney and David Rayside, 139–64. Toronto: University of Toronto Press.

Boily, Frédéric. 2008. *Mario Dumont et l'Action démocratique du Québec. Entre populisme et démocratie*. Quebec City: PUL.

–. 2009. "Un néoconservatisme à la canadienne? Stephen Harper et l'École de Calgary." In *Le conservatisme. Le Canada et le Québec en contexte*, ed. Linda Cardinal and Jean-Marie Lacroix, 35–49. Paris: Presses Sorbonne nouvelles.

–. 2013. *La droite en Alberta. D'Ernest Manning à Stephen Harper*. Quebec City: PUL.

–. 2014. "La droite à visage féminin. Les cas des Albertaines, Alison Redford et Danielle Smith." In *Genre et politique dans la presse en France et au Canada*, ed. Anne-Marie Gingras, 79–100. Montreal: Presses de l'Université du Québec.

–. 2015. "La droite canadienne et l'influence américaine. L'incubateur albertain." *Journal of Canadian Studies/Revue d'études canadiennes* 49 (1): 128–54. https://doi.org/10.3138/jcs.49.1.128.

Boullé, Denis-Daniel. 2014. "Élections québécoises et questions LGBT." *Fugues*, March 24. http://www.fugues.com/239152-article-elections-quebecoises-et-questions-lgbt.html.

Braid, Don. 2014. "For PCs, No Easy End to Debate over Gay-Straight Alliances." *Calgary Herald*, December 3. http://calgaryherald.com/news/politics/braid-for-pcs-no-easy-end-to-debate-over-gay-straight-alliances.

Brulé, Claudine. 2018. "LGBTory inquiet de la victoire de Doug Ford à la tête des progressistes-conservateurs." *Radio-Canada*, March 12. https://ici.radio-canada.ca/nouvelle/1088798/lgbtory-doug-ford-progressistes-conservateurs.

Canadian Press. 2015. "Wildrose Candidate Russ Kuykendall Punted after Anti-Gay Blog Post Surfaces." *Huffington Post*, April 15. http://www.huffingtonpost.ca/2015/04/16/wildrose-looking-for-new-_n_7075328.html.

CBC News. 2012a. "Jason Kenney's Mass Email to Gay and Lesbian Canadians." *CBC News*, September 25. http://www.cbc.ca/news/politics/jason-kenney-s-mass-email-to-gay-and-lesbian-canadians-1.1207144http://www.cbc.ca/news/politics/jason-kenney-s-mass-email-to-gay-and-lesbian-canadians-1.1207144.

–. 2012b. "No Apology from Wildrose Leader for Candidate's Anti-Gay Blog." *CBC News*, June 12. http://www.cbc.ca/news/canada/edmonton/no-apology-from-wildrose-leader-for-candidate-s-anti-gay-blog-1.1278691.

–. 2013. "Gay-Straight Alliances Subject of Debate in Saskatchewan." *CBC News*, April 16. http://www.cbc.ca/news/canada/saskatchewan/gay-straight-alliances-subject-of-debate-in-saskatchewan-1.1357369.

–. 2014a. "Ric McIver Apologizes for Participation in March for Jesus." *CBC News*, June 19. http://www.cbc.ca/news/canada/calgary/ric-mciver-apologizes-for-participation-in-march-for-jesus-1.2681018.

–. 2014b. "Steve Kent Commits to Office for LGBT Issues." *CBC News*, September 1. http://www.cbc.ca/news/canada/newfoundland-labrador/steve-kent-commits-to-office-for-lgbt-issues-1.2752345.

–. 2015a. "Bill 10 to Allow Gay-Straight Alliances for Any Student in Alberta Schools." *CBC News*, March 10. http://www.cbc.ca/news/canada/edmonton/bill-10-to-allow-gay-straight-alliances-for-any-student-in-alberta-schools-1.2989399.

–. 2015b. "Patrick Brown Says Ontario PC 'Establishment' to Blame for Recent Losses." *CBC News*, May 5. http://www.cbc.ca/news/canada/toronto/patrick-brown-says-ontario-pc-establishment-to-blame-for-recent-losses-1.3061740?autoplay=true.

–. 2018. "Granic Allen Says Ford Has Betrayed Social Conservatives." *CBC News*, May 7. http://www.cbc.ca/news/canada/toronto/granic-allen-says-ford-has-betrayed-social-conservatives-1.4652333.

Chase, Steven. 2013. "Baird Belies Conservative Image through Defence of Gay Rights Abroad." *Globe and Mail*, August 8. http://www.theglobeandmail.com/news/politics/baird-belies-conservative-image-through-defence-of-gay-rights-abroad/article13680375/.

Conservative Party of Canada. 2013. "Conservative Party of Canada Policy Declaration." November 2. http://www.conservative.ca/media/documents/Policy-Declaration-Feb-2014.pdf.

Costain, Anne N. 1991. "After Reagan: New Party Attitudes toward Gender." In *"American Feminism: New Issues for a Mature Movement"* Special issue, *Annals of the American Academy of Political and Social Science* 515 (1): 114–25. https://doi.org/10.1177/0002716291515001010.

Dandurand, Renée B. 2003. "Une révolution pour la famille?" In *ADQ, à droite toute! Le programme de l'ADQ expliqué*, ed. Jean-Marc Piotte, 177–93. Montreal: Hurtubise HMH.

Dryden, OmiSoore H., and Suzanne Lenon, eds. 2015. *Disrupting Queer Inclusion: Canadian Homonationalisms and the Politics of Belonging*. Vancouver: UBC Press.

Feibel, Adam. 2015. "Conservative LGBT Group Defends against Call for Ban from Pride Parade." *Ottawa Citizen*, August 21. http://ottawacitizen.com/news/local-news/conservative-lgbt-group-defends-against-call-for-ban-from-pride-parade.

Ferguson, Rob. 2016. "Patrick Brown Sees a New, Inclusive Ontario PC Party." *Toronto Star*, March 6. https://www.nationalnewswatch.com/2016/03/06/patrick-brown-sees-a-new-inclusive-ontario-pc-party/#.XFlgb3nTkkI.

Flanagan, Tom. 2014. "The Prostitution Bill Is a Bizarre Work of Moral Panic." *Globe and Mail*, June 20. http://www.theglobeandmail.com/opinion/prostitution-bill-has-the-makings-of-another-moral-panic/article19256534/.

Gerdes, Stefanie. 2015. "Britain Has Elected the Most LGBTI MPs in the World." *Gaystarnews*, May 8. http://www.gaystarnews.com/article/britain-has-elected-most-lgbti-mps-world080515/#gs.ef=oj7o.

Gerson, Jen. 2014. "Alberta's Wildrose Struggles to Distance Itself from Allegations Party Doesn't Support Gay People." *National Post*, November 17. http://news.nationalpost.com/news/canada/canadian-politics/albertas-wildrose-struggles-to-distance-itself-from-allegations-party-doesnt-support-gay-people.

Gidengil, Elisabeth, Neil Nevitte, André Blais, Joanna Everitt, and Patrick Fournier. 2012. *Dominance and Decline: Making Sense of Recent Canadian Elections*. Toronto: University of Toronto Press.

Giovannetti, Justin. 2014. "What You Need to Know about Bill 10 and Alberta Gay Students' Rights." *Globe and Mail*, December 4. https://www.theglobeandmail.com/news/alberta/what-you-need-to-know-about-bill-10-and-alberta-gay-students-rights/article21964421/.

Goldman, Jordana. 2018. "What Does Doug Ford's Plan to Scrap the Sex-Ed Curriculum Mean for Queer Kids?" *NOW*, June 16. https://nowtoronto.com/lifestyle/class-action/sex-ed-hall-of-justice/.

Government of Canada. 2018. "Rights of LGBTI Persons." https://www.canada.ca/en/canadian-heritage/services/rights-lgbti-persons.html.

Government of Newfoundland and Labrador. 2015. "Provincial Government Recognizes Pride Week 2015." Press release, July 20. http://www.releases.gov.nl.ca/releases/2015/swsd/0720n02.aspx.

Graham, David A. 2016. "North Carolina Overturns LGBT-Discrimination Bans." *The Atlantic*, March 24. http://www.theatlantic.com/politics/archive/2016/03/north-carolina-lgbt-discrimination-transgender-bathrooms/475125/.

Graveland, Bill. 2012. "Alberta Premier Shocked at Wildrose Candidate's Anti-Gay Blog Post." *Toronto Star*, April 15. http://www.thestar.com/news/canada/2012/04/15/alberta_premier_shocked_at_wildrose_candidates_antigay_blog_post.html.

Gunter, Lorne. 2014. "Alberta MLA Ric McIver's Anti-Gay Ties Could End Leadership Hopes." *Edmonton Sun*, June 18. http://www.edmontonsun.com/2014/06/17/alberta-mlas-views-could-end-leadership-hopes.

Hébert, Chantal. 2015. "Is Patrick Brown as Socially Conservative as He Appears: Hébert." *Toronto Star*, May 11. https://www.thestar.com/news/canada/2015/05/11/is-patrick-brown-as-socially-conservative-as-he-appears.html.

Heppell, Timothy. 2014. *The Tories from Winston Churchill to David Cameron*. London: Bloomsbury.

Hopper, Tristin. 2012. "Warriors for Gay Rights: The Conservatives Have Become Unlikely LGBT Supporters." *National Post*, September 22. http://news.nationalpost.com/news/canada/warriors-for-gay-rights-the-conservatives-have-become-unlikely-lgbt-supporters.

Ivison, John. 2016. "Call to Revamp Tory Position on Gay Marriage." *Edmonton Journal*, January 26.

Jefferys, Jenn. 2015. "Rise of the Rainbow Conservative." *Ottawa Citizen*, September 1. http://ottawacitizen.com/news/politics/jenn-jefferys-rise-of-the-rainbow-conservative.

Jones, Dylan. 2008. *Cameron on Cameron: Conversations with Dylan Jones*. London: Fourth Estate.

Kay, Jonathan. 2013. "Rise of the Rainbow Hawks: How Conservatives and Canada's Gay-Rights Activists Made Common Cause." *National Post*, August 23. http://news.nationalpost.com/news/canada/canadian-politics/how-in-a-few-short-years-the-conservative-party-became-gay-rights-warriors.

Kirchick, James. 2010. "The Consistency of Gay Conservatives." In *Proud to Be Right: Voices of the Next Conservative Generation*, ed. Jonah Goldberg, 71–87. New York: Harper.

Levitz, Stephanie. 2016. "LGBT Tories Want Rona Ambrose to End Party's Opposition to Same-Sex Marriage." *CBC News*, January 22. http://www.cbc.ca/news/politics/lgbt-tory-party-policy-ambrose-1.3415699.

LGBTory Canada. 2017a. "Best Wishes, and Caution, to Andrew Scheer." May 28. http://www.lgbtory.ca/2017/05/28/best-wishes-and-caution-to-andrew-scheer/.

–. 2017b. "Jason Kenney Should Reconsider His Stance on Gay-Straight Alliances." April 4. http://www.lgbtory.ca/2017/04/04/jason-kenney-should-reconsider-his-stance-on-gay-straight-alliances/.

Lichtenberg, Doc von. 2016a. "LGBTory's Letter to the Honourable Rona Ambrose." LGBTory, January 10. https://www.lgbtory.ca/2016/01/10/same-sex-marriage-initiative-campaign.

–. 2016b. "Welcome to LGBTory, the Home of LGBT Conservatives." LGBTory. http://www.lgbtory.ca/about-us/.

Lindell, Rebecca. 2012. "Kenney Sparks Privacy Debate with Unsolicited Email on Gay Refugees." *Global News*, September 25. http://globalnews.ca/news/290564/kenney-sparks-privacy-debate-with-unsolicited-email-on-gay-refugees/.

Litwin, Fred. 2015. "Coming Out under the Fabulous Blue Tent." *Ottawa Citizen*, September 17. http://ottawacitizen.com/news/politics/litwin-coming-out-under-the-fabulous-blue-tent.

Lorenzen, Eric. 2016a. "How Can You Be Gay? You're a Conservative!" LGBTory. April 15. http://www.lgbtory.ca/thesymposium/2016/1/8/how-can-you-be-gay-youre-a-conservative.

–. 2016b. "Why Gay Marriage Is Good Conservative Policy." LGBTory. April 17. http://www.lgbtory.ca/thesymposium/2016/1/8/why-gay-marriage-is-good-conservative-policy.

Lukaszuk, Thomas. 2016. "Showdown on School Boards' LGBTQ Policies Failing Kids." *Edmonton Journal*, March 2. http://edmontonjournal.com/opinion/columnists/thomas-lukaszuk-showdown-on-school-boards-lgbtq-policies-failing-kids.

Macdonald, Neil. 2017. "Andrew Scheer Says He Won't Impose His Religious Beliefs on Canadians." *CBC News*, May 30. http://www.cbc.ca/news/opinion/andrew-scheer-leadership-1.4136808.

MacKinnon, Leslie. 2013. "Women's Group Slams Baird over Anti-Gay Laws Stance." *CBC News*, August 8. http://www.cbc.ca/news/politics/women-s-group-slams-baird-over-anti-gay-laws-stance-1.1326628.

Malloy, Jonathan. 2013. "The Relationship between the Conservative Party of Canada and Evangelicals and Social Conservatives." In *Conservatism in Canada*, ed. James Farney and David Rayside, 184–206. Toronto: University of Toronto Press.

McCann, Marcus. 2014. "Principle or Hypocrisy?" *Policy Options/Politiques*, March 3. http://policyoptions.irpp.org/magazines/opening-eyes/principle-or-hypocrisy/.

O'Hara, Kieron. 2011. *Conservatism*. London: Reaktion Books.

Ontario PC Party. 2016. "Patrick Brown, Leader." http://www.ontariopc.com/Leader, accessed April 4, 2016.

Paternotte, David, and Manon Tremblay. 2015. "Introduction: Investigating Lesbian and Gay Activism." In *The Ashgate Research Companion to Lesbian and Gay Activism*, ed. David Paternotte and Manon Tremblay, 1–12. Farnham, UK: Ashgate.

PC Alberta. 2016. "Engage: Connecting with Albertans." PC Alberta. http://www.abpcmla.ca/uploads/5/9/8/2/59829773/16-03-31_pc_caucus_engage_web.pdf, accessed April 7, 2016.

PC Party of Newfoundland and Labrador. 2015. "Davis '15 Blueprint – A Leader You Can Trust." PC Party of Newfoundland and Labrador. https://www.poltext.org/sites/poltext.org/files/plateformes/progress_consv_pc_blueprint.pdf, accessed April 8, 2016.

Radio-Canada. 2017. "La victoire de Jason Kenney inquiète la communauté LGBT." October 30. http://ici.radio-canada.ca/nouvelle/1064261/jason-kenney-inquiete-communaute-lgbt-alberta.

Reynolds, Andrew. 2016. "GOP Out of Touch with World LGBT Views." *Charlotte Observer*, March 29. http://www.charlotteobserver.com/opinion/article68803312.html.

Robidoux-Descary, Ève, and Frédéric Boily. 2014. "Entre réappropriation et neutralisation du genre. Le cas de Christy Clark." In *Genre et politique dans la presse en France et au Canada*, ed. Anne-Marie Gingras, 101–21. Montreal: Presses de l'Université du Québec.

Scruton, Roger. 2015. *How to Be a Conservative*. London: Bloomsbury.

Shariatmadari, David. 2015. "The Quiet Revolution: Why Britain Has More Gay MPs than Anywhere Else." *The Guardian*, 13 May. http://www.theguardian.com/world/2015/may/13/quiet-revolution-britain-more-gay-mps-than-anywhere-else-lgbt.

Taber, Jane. 2015. "Why Ontario PC Leader Patrick Brown Embraced Pride." *Globe and Mail*, July 3. http://www.theglobeandmail.com/news/politics/why-patrick-brown-embraced-pride/article25247192/.

Tahon, Marie-Blanche. 2005. "Mariage homosexuel, bimaternité et égalité: la loi québécoise instituant l'union civile." *Recherches familiales* 1 (2): 115–20. https://doi.org/10.3917/rf.002.0115.

Teitel, Emma. 2018. "Pride Police Ban Gives Ford a Convenient Excuse Not to March." *Toronto Star*, June 15. https://www.thestar.com/opinion/star-columnists/2018/06/15/pride-police-ban-gives-ford-a-convenient-excuse-not-to-march.html.

Tobin, Robert Deam. 2017. "Gays for Trump? Homonationalism Has Deep Roots." *Gay and Lesbian Review Worldwide* 24 (3): 5–7.

Ugandan Diaspora. 2012. "Ugandan Parliamentarian Blasts Canadian Foreign Affairs Minister over Gay 'Marriage' Remark." *Ugandan Diaspora*, October 26. http://www.ugandandiasporanews.com/2012/10/26/ugandan-parliamentarian-blasts-canadian-foreign-affairs-minister-over-gay-marriage-remark/.

Vincent, Jean-Philippe. 2016. *Qu'est-ce que le conservatisme? Histoire intellectuelle d'une idée politique*. Paris: Les belles lettres.

Weinthal, Ben. 2016. "How to Fight Homophobia in the Middle East." LGBTory. https://www.lgbtory.ca/2016/07/15/benjamin-weinthal-how-to-fight-homophobia-in-the-middle-east/.

Wildrose. 2015. "Standing Up for Albertans! Five Priorities." Wildrose. https://d3n8a8pro7vhmx.cloudfront.net/wildrose/pages/223/attachments/original/1429486424/WEB-StandingUpForAlbertans5_Apr19.pdf?1429486424.

Winter, Nicolas J.G. 2010. "Masculine Republicans and Feminine Democrats: Gender and Americans' Explicit and Implicit Images of the Political Parties." *Political Behavior* 32 (4): 587–618. https://doi.org/10.1007/s11109-010-9131-z.

Wiseman, Nelson. 2013. "Provincial Conservatism." In *Conservatism in Canada*, ed. James Farney and David Rayside, 209–30. Toronto: University of Toronto Press.

6
Liberalism and the Protection of LGBT Rights in Canada

Brooke Jeffrey

THEORETICALLY, LIBERALISM ADDRESSES LGBT issues from a rights-based perspective, underpinned by its view of the appropriate role of government in society. The long-standing commitment of liberalism to a clear distinction between public and private spheres of influence and, more importantly, to the separation of church and state is critical to an understanding of its approach to LGBT issues. Equally important is the commitment of modern liberalism to the protection of human rights, a concept that has evolved over time in parallel with liberal thinking on equality of opportunity. In practice, this liberal vision has resulted in the implementation of a wide range of legislation and constitutional guarantees designed to prevent discrimination against minorities of all kinds – of which the LGBT community is viewed as one among many – and to encourage tolerance of diversity in the majority.

In Canada, where the federal Liberal Party was in power for most of the past century, these two key liberal values – ensuring the secular state and prioritizing the human rights of individuals over the powers of the state – have driven the agenda of successive Liberal governments, both legislatively and symbolically. Justice Minister Pierre Trudeau's amendments to the Criminal Code in 1968, for example, are a classic illustration of the concern of liberalism with the separation of church and state, and his introduction of the Charter of Rights and Freedoms as prime minister in 1982 epitomizes liberals' commitment to human rights and equality of opportunity. Subsequent legislative initiatives by the Liberal federal governments of Jean Chrétien, Paul Martin, and Justin Trudeau have reinforced this liberal approach with measures to enhance representation and respect for diversity, an approach that is also reflected in the actions of several provincial Liberal governments, most recently that of Ontario premier Kathleen Wynne.

In this chapter, I argue that the philosophical approach of liberalism, and especially its emphasis on a broad-based conception of human rights rather than a focus on the rights of specific minorities, has had a significant and positive impact on the evolution of rights discourse in Canada. This in turn has resulted in comparatively rapid progress for many equality-seeking minority or disadvantaged groups, including the LGBT community. Even more striking is the fact that this progress has been achieved without deep societal divisions or recourse to violence, in stark contrast with many other jurisdictions, notably the United States. For LGBT individuals, this approach has been particularly important, as federal Liberal government initiatives have placed Canada among the world leaders in the protection and promotion of LGBT rights.

I therefore explore the contribution of Liberal governments to the evolution of LGBT rights through the lens of these two key values of liberalism. The chapter begins with a discussion of the role played by the concept of separation of church and state in Liberal policy making. I then move on to an examination of the impact of Liberal human-rights initiatives on the evolution of LGBT legal rights. In the third section, I outline the competing value claims that emerged during the debate on the Liberals' same-sex marriage legislation, and in the final section I identify the most recent efforts of Liberal governments to enhance social equality for LGBT individuals through increased political representation and the active promotion of tolerance of diversity in society.

Liberalism in Practice: Promoting the Secular State

As mentioned above, the separation of church and state is a crucial element of liberal thinking.[1] In Canada, federal Liberal governments have inevitably confronted numerous "moral" issues that challenged this key value of liberalism, not only because the Liberal Party was in power for so much of the post-war era, but also because both the Criminal Code and the subject of marriage fall under federal jurisdiction. This chapter therefore focuses exclusively on the actions of Liberal governments at the federal level.[2]

Undoubtedly, one of the most dramatic tests of this fundamental tenet of liberalism occurred under the stewardship of Liberal prime minister Lester Pearson, whose minority government introduced an omnibus bill to amend numerous sections of the Criminal Code. Justice Minister Pierre Trudeau described the amendments as "certainly the most extensive revision of the Criminal Code since the 1950's and, in terms of the subject matter it deals with, I feel that it has knocked down a lot of totems and overridden a lot of taboos ... It's bringing the laws of the land up to contemporary society" (*CBC News* 2012). Among them was a measure to effectively legalize abortion, and the rationale outlined by Pearson's government is instructive. In the words of Liberal MP and future solicitor general Mark McGuigan,

> I believe that this omnibus bill reflects an entirely new governmental approach to criminal law ... The bill would bring about a change not only in criminal legislation but also in the philosophy behind it, for it apparently indicates a determination that law shall no longer be thought of as a mirror of morals, and that from now on, crime and sin, law and morals, must be distinguished. (*CBC Television News* 1967)

The abortion amendment was hardly the only one to raise such concerns. Probably the most controversial change proposed in the omnibus bill was the decriminalization of private homosexual acts. Significantly, this measure was defended by the government with precisely the same rationale as that used for abortion. Trudeau, who tabled the legislation, repeatedly defended it in the House of Commons and in numerous media interviews as an issue of private versus public domain. During one such interview, he memorably declared, "There's no place for the state in the bedrooms of the nation" (*CBC Television News* 1967).

Although the bill died on the order paper with the defeat of the Pearson government in 1968, it was quickly reintroduced after the ensuing election by the new Liberal government of Pierre Trudeau. His successor as justice minister, John Turner, adopted the identical approach when defending the provision in Bill C-150 on homosexuality, declaring it to be a private matter between consenting adults. (Similar arguments were also advanced by Trudeau and Turner in 1978, when the new Immigration Act removed homosexuals from the list of inadmissible classes.)

As many observers suggested, this was especially noteworthy as Turner, like Trudeau, was a practising Roman Catholic. Nor did Turner personally sanction homosexuality. Nevertheless, he insisted that it was not the role of the state to adjudicate moral issues that did not affect the public sphere. As he bluntly told one reporter, "There are areas of private behaviour, however repugnant and immoral, if they do not directly involve public order, should not properly be within the criminal law of Canada" (CBC Radio 1969).

The position taken by the Liberal government, framed as an issue of separation of church and state, was supported by a strong minority (some 48 percent) of the general public, but it was not without its ardent political opponents. Indeed, Stuart Chambers (2010, 250) argues that Trudeau's decision to secularize the issue of homosexuality "could have been political suicide when one considers the orthodox view of homosexuality at the time" in Canada and the United States. Meanwhile, similar legislation was being enacted in Great Britain at roughly the same time, although it should be noted that this step came nearly a decade after the Wolfenden Report had first recommended it. Significantly, the report's authors justified their recommendations by using the philosophical approach of Tory conservatism, which closely mirrored the position of Canadian liberalism in this regard. (In fact, the Wolfenden Report relied on the rationale of well-known liberal philosopher John Stuart Mill, whose seminal work "On Liberty" stressed that the state should avoid legislating in areas of private morality.) But this Tory perspective was not shared by the leader of the federal Progressive Conservative Party in Canada, former prime minister John Diefenbaker. Instead, adopting an argument that was more reminiscent of the American conservative philosophy, Diefenbaker categorically rejected the amendments, saying that the bill "undermines the whole concept of a family as a unit" in society (Canada 1967, 4191; on conservatism, see Chapter 5 in this volume).

Despite this ongoing opposition, many observers have seen the Trudeau government's move to decriminalize homosexuality as a landmark decision that "began a process of breaking down the barriers that made homosexuals second-class citizens. More than anything, Bill C-150 provided a neutral framework so that homosexuals could lead more productive lives ... and Trudeau became the symbol for democratic rationalism" (Chambers 2010, 263).

But not all Canadians were convinced. Nearly forty years later, the philosophical debate about the separation of church and state and the distinction between morality and public policy re-emerged when the federal Liberal governments of Jean Chrétien and Paul Martin addressed the question of same-sex marriage. However, the situation in 2003 was considerably different from that faced by the Liberals with Bill C-150 in 1968–69, primarily because the Charter of Rights and Freedoms had been entrenched in the Constitution in 1982. As a result, the Liberal rationale for the same-sex legislation focused on the matter as primarily a question of equality, as discussed in detail below.

Nevertheless, the issue of morality was again raised by many opponents. Indeed, history repeated itself as Chrétien and Martin, both practising Roman Catholics, were warned by local and national Catholic clergy not to proceed with the legislation. (Moreover, the bishops' views were supported by the Vatican, which issued a directive calling on Catholic politicians around the world to reject such legislation; see McIlroy 2003.) Responding to these concerns, Martin said that his responsibilities as a politician meant that he "must take a wider perspective" than his faith (McIlroy 2003).

A new aspect to the philosophical debate was also added with the advent of the Reform/Alliance Parties (and ultimately of Stephen Harper's new Conservative Party). As James Farney (2012) and others point out, the "social" conservatism of these predominantly Western Canadian MPs was heavily influenced by their American counterparts in the Evangelical Christian movement. However, unlike in the United States, where the movement has wielded considerable influence and thwarted the evolution of a rights discourse, the social conservative movement in Canada has always represented a very small minority of popular opinion (see, for example, Adams 2009; Bibby 2011).

The argument favouring morality in public policy was resurrected by these new politicians, who arrived in Ottawa after the collapse of the Progressive Conservative Party in the 1984 election. Nowhere was this more evident than in the comments of Reform leader Preston Manning, an ardent Evangelical Christian, who once declared, "Sure, I believe in the separation of church and state, but I don't think that means the separation of religious values and political values" (Jeffrey 1995, 347). With respect to gay and lesbian rights, this position was made crystal clear when Manning urged one political audience to pray with him "to eradicate the moral bankruptcy of the nation, brought about by ... homosexuality and general moral laxity" (Jeffrey 1995, 312–13). His views were reinforced by his successor, Alliance Party leader and fundamentalist lay preacher Stockwell Day, who, as Alberta education minister a few years earlier, had insisted, "God's law is clear. Standards of education are not set by government but by God, the Bible, the church and the family" (Laird 2000).

Rejecting these arguments, Jean Chrétien in 2003 and then his successor, Paul Martin, in 2004 proceeded to ignore church warnings and introduce the same-sex marriage legislation outlined in the following section. It became law on July 19, 2005, making Canada only the fourth country in the world to legalize same-sex marriages and the first one outside of Europe.

Still the issue continued to generate political controversy. During the House of Commons debate in 2005, newly elected Conservative Party leader Stephen Harper, an Evangelical Christian himself, promised to allow a free vote on the repeal of the legislation if his party were elected, a commitment he repeated during the 2006 federal election. The Conservatives did form a minority government and the vote took place in December 2006, but the motion was defeated by the Liberals and other Opposition parties, and the legislation remained in force.

Liberalism in Practice: Promoting Human Rights and Equality

The protection of minority rights and tolerance of diversity are fundamental values of Canadian liberalism. However, the definition of those rights, and the transition from the narrower concept of civil rights to the broader concept of human rights, has evolved over time. In Canada, as elsewhere, human-rights discourse expanded incrementally but steadily throughout the post-war era, and this is reflected internationally in the implementation of various United Nations conventions and covenants. As a result, the identification of specific individual rights, though proceeding too slowly for some, has ultimately led to widespread recognition and public acceptance.

The Trudeau government's accession to the International Convention on Civil and Political Rights in May 1976, for example, launched a string of federal and provincial legislative anti-discrimination measures. In 1977, Trudeau's government introduced the Canadian Human Rights Act (CHRA), which featured a wide range of prohibited grounds of discrimination, including sex, and was the national complement to provincial human-rights codes that had been introduced across the country.

However, sexual orientation was not included as a ground. (As Clément, Silver, and Trottier [2012] indicate, the term "sexual orientation" was not included in the original prohibited grounds of legislation in *any* jurisdiction at that time.[3]) This occurred for a variety of reasons, despite considerable lobbying by gay and lesbian rights groups. Some Liberal legislators assumed that the inclusion of the word "sex" was sufficient to cover a range of issues, such as marital status or pregnancy, as well as sexual orientation. They were hesitant to add more provisions than necessary to an already lengthy list of prohibited grounds, for fear that their credibility would be diminished. For others, including several Liberal cabinet ministers and Liberal and NDP MPs, as well as most Conservative MPs and a large segment of the general public, the concept of sexual orientation as a ground for discrimination was not yet considered legitimate. To understand how significant the opposition to this proposal was, one need look no farther than comments by NDP leader Ed Broadbent, who declared that his party "has got to stop supporting every fad issue or minority concern that comes along, 'whether it's the homosexual minority or whatever'" (Urquart 1976, 58; on the NDP, see Chapter 7 in this volume).

Regardless of legislative intent, however, a series of rulings demonstrated that Canadian courts were interpreting the term "sex" in the CHRA in a far narrower way than had been anticipated by some politicians, minority groups, and, especially, women's rights activists. Moreover, as a simple statute rather than a constitutional guarantee, the act did not have precedence and could not be used to override any other conflicting legislation that the courts might identify. At the provincial level, this narrow interpretation was reinforced by similar omissions in grounds in provincial acts, as demonstrated by the case of John Damien, the Ontario Jockey Club executive who was fired in 1975 because of his sexual orientation. The Ontario Human Rights Commission declined to hear his case because the provincial Human Rights Act – like all other provincial acts at the time – did not specifically include such grounds.

This situation changed dramatically with the advent of constitutional reform negotiations in 1980, following the unsuccessful Quebec referendum on sovereignty. Over the objections of several premiers, Prime Minister Trudeau made it clear that a human-rights bill would be included in his promised reform package, and it would apply to both federal and provincial governments. Since Canada, unlike most Western democracies, did not have an entrenched bill of rights in its Constitution, the significance of this development can hardly be overestimated. Between 1980 and 1982, a series of parliamentary committee hearings and debates, federal-provincial meetings, and a constitutional reference to the Supreme Court eventually culminated in the adoption of the Constitution Act, 1982.

The act entrenched a wide-ranging (and highly popular) Charter of Rights and Freedoms, whose impact many experts have subsequently described as revolutionary. Perhaps most importantly, it reflected the liberal vision of equality, encompassing the rights of all minority or disadvantaged groups within the broader context of human rights. As Miriam Smith (2008) outlines, this progress is in sharp contrast with the situation in the United States, where a broadly based rights discourse did not evolve, and each disadvantaged group was instead forced to fight for recognition independently, often involving violent confrontation. In particular, Smith (2008, 174–77) notes that it was the Charter's all-encompassing approach, in comparison with the much more limited and hierarchical approach to rights taken under the American Constitution's Fourteenth Amendment, that resulted in the Canadian adoption of LGBT rights as equal and legitimate. Consequently, Smith (2008, 171) argues that the process in Canada has solidified "the policy and partisan discourse of 'Charter values' in ways that have strengthened lesbian and gay rights claims rather than undermining them."

The debate during the drafting of the Charter was not without controversy, however. Here again, the possibility arose of including "sexual orientation" as a prohibited ground, but this time the Liberal government took a different approach. On the one hand, cognizant of ongoing public and political opposition to the very concept of this proposed ground (including within the Liberal caucus), Justice Minister Jean Chrétien again opted not to include the term among the list of specifically proscribed grounds in the equality rights clause (section 15) of the Charter. On the other hand, he declared that the list would be considered "illustrative" rather than "exhaustive." This important legal distinction was clearly a less-than-ideal option in the view of gay-rights activists who had been lobbying for outright inclusion. However, it was a critical turning point, as it meant that the courts could "read into" the provision any other rights that they deemed appropriate. (Unlike many other affected groups, who mounted extensive campaigns and provided comprehensive expert testimony before the parliamentary committee, thereby capturing public attention and raising awareness, the Canadian lesbian and gay movement was relatively weak at the time and was preoccupied with more pressing issues such as the HIV/AIDS pandemic.)

Chrétien reiterated his legal interpretation when he appeared on January 16, 1981, before the Special Joint Committee on the Constitution, whose task was to study the proposed Charter. Responding to NDP MP Svend Robinson's question as to the intent of the legislation, and whether the courts could potentially interpret the list of prohibited grounds to include sexual orientation, Chrétien replied, "Yes, that will be for the courts to decide. It is open-ended ... We say other types of discrimination and we do not define them. That is why I say it will be for the courts to decide" (Fraser 2003; see also the Afterword in this volume). As a result, section 15(1) of the Charter, on equality rights, stated, "Every individual is equal before and under the law and has the right to the equal protection and equal benefit of the law without discrimination and, *in particular*, without discrimination based on race, national or ethnic origin, colour, religion, sex, age or mental or physical disability" (emphasis added).

But the implications of this clause were not felt immediately. Although the Charter came into force in April 1982, the application of section 15 was delayed for a three-year period in agreement with the provinces, which were all expected to use the extension to modify any of their legislation that contravened the Charter. The Trudeau government anticipated that the three-year delay would provide ample time for all levels of government to amend potentially conflicting legislation. Nevertheless, the Liberals also expanded an existing program within the Secretary of State Department (later Canadian Heritage) that was originally designed to provide financial assistance to official language minorities who wished to pursue legal challenges to federal legislation under the Official Languages Act. The program was renamed the Court Challenges Program and was designed to allow minority groups to pursue legal redress on any issues related to section 15 – an expensive undertaking that few volunteer groups could otherwise afford – if any legislation or procedures were believed to be discriminatory.[4]

It was the stated intention of the Trudeau government to avoid the necessity of minority groups having to pursue such court challenges as much as possible, at least with respect to federal legislation. Trudeau had vigorously opposed the inclusion of the notwithstanding clause in the Charter, but he had been forced to accept it as a last-minute compromise to secure the support of Saskatchewan's NDP premier Allan Blakeney and Manitoba's Conservative premier Sterling Lyon, in light of the Supreme Court reference that urged that greater consensus be found among premiers (Behiels 2011). The two premiers saw the Charter as a threat to provincial powers and insisted that provinces be given the capacity to override a court ruling if their legislation were to be struck down. By contrast, Trudeau argued that both levels of government were having their powers constrained only in favour of citizens and their basic rights. As Janet Hiebert (2009, 110) notes, Trudeau "saw its inclusion [the notwithstanding clause] as being inconsistent with the purpose of the Charter" and never accepted its underlying premise. He himself said that its inclusion "violated my sense of justice: it seemed wrong that any province could decide to suspend any part of the Charter, even if the suspension was only temporary" (ibid.). Having declared that Ottawa would never use the clause, he therefore planned to implement required amendments to federal legislation to redress any obvious non-compliance issues as quickly as possible. For this reason, he charged the Justice Department with analyzing all existing legislation and making recommendations to that end (see also Kelly and Manfredi 2009, 86–129).

However, before these amendments could be identified and implemented, the Liberals were defeated in the 1984 election. Almost immediately, a notable change in attitude toward section 15, and the Charter itself, was demonstrated by the Mulroney Progressive Conservative government that succeeded them. Simply put, it soon became clear that the new government's approach was to wait for the courts to make decisions on any Charter issues involving federal legislation. As noted elsewhere, this was due in part to significant opposition in the Conservative caucus to some of the rights enumerated in the Charter, as well as to the potential implications of the "illustrative" caveat. Enjoying a massive majority, the Mulroney government found itself with a large number of first-time MPs who had not been involved in the 1982 constitutional process. Many of them were openly hostile to certain aspects of the Charter, such as official language and multicultural guarantees, and especially section 15 (see Jeffrey 1992, 93–102; on the ideological tenets of conservatism, see Chapter 5 in this volume).

Consequently, the government did not implement the recommendations of the Justice Department but instead established a special all-party House of Commons subcommittee to examine existing federal legislation independently, to ascertain whether any of it failed to comply with section 15, and if it did, to recommend *whether* it should be changed. The subcommittee completed its review by October 1985, when it tabled its unanimous report, *Equality for All*. Unlike a standing committee, whose government members would be obliged to toe the party line on government legislation, this subcommittee was looking at constitutional issues and therefore had more leeway. To the dismay of many backbench Conservative MPs, despite the Conservative majority of members on the subcommittee, the influence of Liberal and NDP MPs – and a progressive chair, Conservative MP Patrick Boyer of Toronto – carried the day. As a result, the all-party report once again asserted that "the prohibited grounds of discrimination enumerated in Section 15 are simply illustrative and do not exhaust the forms of discrimination" covered by the Charter (Canada, Subcommittee on Human Rights and Justice 1985, 5). Among other things, it recommended numerous changes to federal legislation and procedures in order to eliminate potential discrimination on the basis of sexual orientation. The recommendations included adding "sexual orientation" as a specific ground in the CHRA, ending the ban on homosexuals in the Armed Forces and the RCMP, and eliminating relevant security clearance guidelines for the public service (Canada, Subcommittee on Human Rights and Justice 1985, 28–32).

However, none of the recommendations in the report was immediately adopted. Moreover, and despite the assistance of the Court Challenges Program to minimize costs, the process of pursuing a legal challenge was still time consuming. The Mulroney government's decision to "wait and see" exacerbated this situation, since numerous minority groups felt that they had no choice but to pursue legal action in light of the Conservatives' failure to act. The result was a significant backlog of Charter-related cases at the Superior Court level. Some Charter critics then began to portray the high number of Charter challenges as the "Americanization" of the Canadian legal system that they had feared, apparently unaware that the government itself was largely to blame.[5]

Not surprisingly, the next ten years saw a series of court decisions that declared various federal statutes and practices unconstitutional by virtue of the Charter's section 15. Women, the disabled, and Indigenous people all pursued such cases and achieved a considerable measure of success. And it was here that Jean Chrétien's decision to utilize the "illustrative" method proved highly effective for gay-rights activists as well. As Michael Ignatieff (2000, 86) points out, "Rights claiming can also have the positive benefit of helping to realize individual or group recognition. Thus one of the key changes brought about by the Charter is that it increasingly encourages political demands framed as rights."

A string of legal decisions forced the issue of sexual orientation to the forefront of equality rights concerns. As a result, between 1986 and 1995 all provinces (except Quebec, which had made this amendment in 1977) either amended their human-rights acts to specifically include such ground or had the concept "read into" their acts for them by court decisions. (In the case of a recalcitrant Alberta Conservative government, which continued to oppose the concept despite the decisive 1995 ruling in *Egan v. Canada,* it was not until 1998 that a scathing Supreme Court ruling in *Vriend v. Alberta* finally put the matter to rest.)[6]

Meanwhile, at the federal level, the Mulroney government and Justice Minister John Crosbie continued to delay any such move, despite repeated statements between 1985 and 1992 that they would consider introducing some type of amendment. Finally, in 1992 the Ontario Court of Appeal ruled that the absence of such ground in the CHRA violated the Charter. In response, Mulroney's new justice minister, Kim Campbell, did introduce a bill proposing to add sexual orientation to the CHRA, but it did not pass first reading and died on the order paper due to widespread opposition from Conservative MPs. As a result, for the decade in which the Conservatives were in power, little of the anticipated progress in equality rights was achieved at the federal level, and no amendment was made to the CHRA.

Liberalism in Practice: Implementing Equality Rights

When the Chrétien Liberals returned to power in late 1993, they introduced a series of measures in rapid succession to "regularize" federal legislation in light of the many court decisions concerning women, Indigenous Canadians, and numerous other minority groups. Several of these changes related specifically to the issue of sexual orientation. In 1995, for example, the Liberal government extended employment-related benefits to same-sex couples, and the Liberal-dominated House of Commons Board of Internal Economy followed suit with respect to its employees.

This was followed in early 1996 by the Chrétien government's introduction of the long-awaited amendment to the CHRA that added "sexual orientation" as a specific proscribed ground. As David Rayside (1998, 106) notes, "victory" on the CHRA was due to "the massive realignment of partisan forces resulting from the 1993 federal election, which created incentives for socially reformist Liberals to press ahead on gay rights."

The same year, amendments were introduced to the Criminal Code to include "sexual orientation" in hate-crime legislation (for Svend Robinson's activism on this issue, see the Afterword in this volume). Also in 1996, the Liberals instructed Revenue Canada to modify its interpretation of the Income Tax Act to allow same-sex couples to obtain employer-paid medical and dental benefits tax-free, and in 1998 the government introduced legislation allowing a same-sex couple to register each other for survivor benefits in government pension plans.

Then, in 1999, a Supreme Court decision *(M v. H)* led most provincial governments to alter their definition of common-law partners to include same-sex couples – that is, the old wording, "a man and a woman," was changed to "two persons." This ensured that such couples were eligible for all the social and tax benefits that applied to heterosexual couples. The Chrétien government responded similarly, by tabling the Modernization of Benefits and Obligations Act (Bill C-23) in February 2000, a move that required changes to some sixty-eight pieces of federal legislation. The bill passed easily on April 11, 2000, by a vote of 174 to 72, with opposition coming almost entirely from Alliance MPs and their leader, Stockwell Day.

Finally, in 2001, the Liberal government modified the Immigration and Refugee Protection Act once more. (Pierre Trudeau, as mentioned above, had first done so in 1978 to remove homosexuals from the list of inadmissible individuals.) This time, the Chrétien government included "common-law partner" along with "spouse" among the individuals who could be sponsored for immigration to Canada. In addition, and given the increasingly serious human-rights violations reported against LGBT individuals in Africa and Eastern Europe, the refugee determination criteria were modified to allow claims of persecution on the basis of sexual orientation.

Most of the changes listed above were implemented by the Liberals with minimal political opposition in Parliament or the media. However, the Alliance opposition to Bill C-23 foreshadowed the difficulties that lay ahead. With Bill C-23, the Liberals had ensured that in federal law, same-sex unions and opposite-sex common-law unions were offered the same protection and equal status, but the legislation went too far for opponents and not far enough for supporters.

On the one hand, some opponents, such as most Alliance MPs, viewed the issue of same-sex partners as one of morality and rejected the concept of equal treatment. Others who opposed the move – including some Liberal cabinet ministers and Liberal and NDP MPs – were supportive of equal treatment but remained anxious that Bill C-23 would also alter the definition of marriage. This was despite the fact that the government had already allowed a free vote on an Alliance opposition motion a few months earlier, one that saw parliamentarians vote 216 to 55 in favour of preserving the definition of marriage as "the union of a man and woman."

As a result, in an effort to reassure the majority within Parliament and the general public about the implications of this legislation, Justice Minister Anne McLellan introduced a clause in Bill C-23 to reiterate that these measures did not affect the traditional definition of marriage. For those who were concerned only about the definition, this addition was sufficient, but Alliance MPs and others still rejected the bill on moral/religious grounds.

On the other hand, a number of Liberal and NDP MPs, as well as representatives of gay-rights groups, still viewed acceptance of the term "marriage" for same-sex couples as a last but necessary step toward achieving full equality. They acknowledged the significant progress made under the Liberal government during the previous decade and lauded the positive impact of C-23, but they continued to lobby for this change and to pursue redress through the courts in a number of provinces.

Liberalism in Practice: The Groundbreaking Same-Sex Marriage Legislation

Within a few years of the passage of C-23, the Chrétien government found itself obliged to address the issue of same-sex marriage directly. Not surprisingly, the subject proved highly contentious. Significantly, the controversy arose within all political parties and the general public. (An Environics poll in early 2005, for example, indicated that some 55 percent of Canadians still disagreed profoundly with the concept; *CBC News* 2005.)

There were numerous aspects to the debate as it unfolded. It was far more complex than any other issue concerning sexual orientation that the Liberals had handled to date, and it involved both the secular and human-rights values of liberalism. At least four separate concerns arose:

1. Not only was opposition to the use of the term "marriage" very strong, but for many people it remained rooted in views about morality and religious concerns, making such opposition largely intractable.
2. Since religious freedom was guaranteed under the Charter, any attempt to compel religious organizations to authorize same-sex marriages would almost certainly be found unconstitutional. Moreover, given the Liberal commitment to separation of church and state, such an attempt would clearly contravene a key liberal value.
3. With the advent of the Charter of Rights, the Liberals had exchanged their arguments in support of "separation of church and state" for a rights-based "discourse of equality." Nonetheless, many Liberals did not feel that the issue of same-sex marriage fell within the purview of this rights discourse. To put it another way, the Liberal government's numerous moves to guarantee fully equal legal status for same-sex couples, as exemplified by Bill C-23, were seen by many Liberals as appropriate and sufficient redress for any potential discrimination or unequal treatment based on sexual orientation. Thus, the debate over the use of the term "marriage" rather than "union," and "spouse" rather than "partner," was not seen by many progressives as an equality issue. Instead, they perceived it as a question of semantics, a needlessly distracting and counterproductive concern rather than one involving any philosophical rights issue. This viewpoint, it should be noted, was bolstered by a 1993 Ontario court ruling, *Layland and Beaulne v. Ontario*, that had already dismissed a Charter challenge by two gay men who had been denied a marriage licence in Ontario.

    Conversely, proponents maintained that same-sex marriage was a legitimate equality rights issue and that the essentially "separate but equal" approach of many progressive Liberals was discriminatory. In several provinces, new court cases were launched to test the validity of this argument.
4. Jurisdiction proved a major concern. Although the legal definition of marriage falls under federal jurisdiction, the civil legislation that is most likely to affect such couples comes under provincial jurisdiction. (Provinces, for example, are responsible for issuing marriage licences, as *Layland and Beaulne v. Ontario* demonstrated.) As a result, there were serious concerns that Ottawa could not ensure provincial compliance with the intent of any such federal legislation, even if it were introduced. Several provinces, and most notably the Conservative governments of Alberta and Ontario, steadfastly opposed the concept. They

repeatedly refused to register gay "marriages" performed in some churches and even threatened to invoke the notwithstanding clause if Ottawa attempted to alter the definition of marriage. Another important legal point was whether the federal government could unilaterally change the definition of marriage or whether it would require provincial consent, an outcome that would make any amendment difficult if not impossible.

Consequently, the Chrétien government initially took the position that there was no need for any specific legislation to redefine marriage and argued that any attempt to impose it would cause unnecessary and potentially serious divisions within society.[7] However, this stance was soon altered in response to the changing dynamics of the debate. Between 2000 and 2005, the situation evolved rapidly, primarily because of a number of rulings at the provincial Superior Court level.

The transition began with a ruling by the Ontario Superior Court in July 2002, *Halpern v. Canada (Attorney General)*, which declared that Ontario's refusal to recognize gay marriages was unconstitutional and that it violated the Charter of Rights and Freedoms. The Ontario government decided not to appeal the decision, saying that "only the federal government can decide who can marry" (Cauchon, cited in Larocque 2006, 78). Since similar cases were scheduled to be heard by provincial Courts of Appeal in British Columbia and Quebec in 2003, the Chrétien government decided to appeal the Ontario court ruling to expedite the process. McLellan's successor as justice minister, Martin Cauchon (ibid.), declared that in light of the conflicting 1993 and 2002 decisions, "We need to seek further clarity on these issues. At present there is no consensus, either from the courts or among Canadians, on whether or how the laws require change."

On June 10, 2003, the Ontario Court of Appeal provided that clarity, ruling that the "separate but equal" approach *should* be considered discriminatory and that the province must recognize the legality of same-sex marriages. The following day, the Ontario attorney general announced that the province would accept the ruling and begin to register same-sex marriages.

One week after the Ontario ruling, expecting that similar cases in British Columbia and Quebec would produce similar decisions, Prime Minister Chrétien announced that his government would not appeal any other provincial decisions. Instead, it would shortly table legislation "making same-sex civil marriages legal while at the same time permitting churches and other religious groups to 'sanctify marriage as they see it'" (Hurley 2010, 14). Less than a month later, in July 2003, the government referred a first draft of this legislation to the

Supreme Court to ensure its compliance and avoid future conflict, posing three fundamental questions:

(1) Whether the bill fell within the federal government's exclusive jurisdiction,
(2) Whether the extension of the definition of marriage to same-sex couples was consistent with the Charter and, if so,
(3) Whether the religious freedom provision of the Charter shielded religious officials "from being forced to perform same-sex marriages contrary to their religious beliefs." (Hurley 2010, 14–15)

One month later, on August 19, 2003, Chrétien gave a public speech on the issue at a Liberal caucus retreat in North Bay. His stated purpose in delivering the speech nationally was to influence not only the dissident caucus members who continued to resist the draft legislation, but also the general public, where opposition had declined from 75 percent to roughly 55 percent in less than five years, though it remained both substantial and visceral. Noting that he himself had been born in rural Catholic Quebec and found the rapid pace of change surprising, Chrétien went on to say, "I have learned over forty years in public life that society evolves, and the concept of human rights evolves, often more quickly than some of us might have predicted" (Jeffrey 2015, 389). Rejecting opponents' arguments about morality and religious freedom, he then reiterated liberalism's commitment to equality rights and stated, "This is not about weakening traditional religion ... It is about giving force and effect to Canadian values. We need to be guided by how court after court has been interpreting the Charter of Rights. And the courts have been telling us that separate but equal has no place in Canada." Finally, he stressed that a government "must live up to its responsibilities. And none of these are more essential than protecting the constitution and the fundamental rights it guarantees to all Canadians."[8]

Chrétien's arguments were echoed by his justice minister, Martin Cauchon, an early supporter of the concept of same-sex marriage, in a speech to the Canadian Bar Association in Montreal the same day. "We must do better than almost equal," he said. "It is simply a question of equality, human dignity and respect for all" (Clark, Taber, and Thanh Ha 2003). Cauchon also rejected the argument of Conservative MPs (who, under Stephen Harper, had now replaced the Canadian Alliance and Stockwell Day) and other social conservatives that the courts were imposing values on Parliament and on Canadians. "Let us remember that the Charter was not put in place by the judiciary," he said, noting that it had received support from all political parties and that "its adoption in 1982 was a political decision following a heated debate in Parliament" (Clark, Taber, and Thanh Ha 2003).

The Supreme Court reference was heard in October 2004, by which time Paul Martin had replaced Chrétien as prime minister and leader of the Liberal Party. (Responding to the concerns of the Liberal caucus members who continued to question the constitutional need for the term "marriage" – all of whom had supported Martin during the internal leadership struggle that racked the party – Martin had subsequently added a fourth question, asking whether the term "union" would satisfy the Charter, even though this issue had already been addressed by the courts.) The Supreme Court's decision, rendered in December 2004, found that Ottawa did have exclusive jurisdiction to redefine marriage, that the religious freedom clause in the Charter did protect church officials from being compelled by the state to perform same-sex marriages, and that the draft legislation submitted by Chrétien was consistent with the Charter, although it also confirmed provincial jurisdiction over "the solemnization of marriage." (Not surprisingly, the court did not bother to address Martin's additional question.)

Armed with this reference, Martin's government moved quickly to table Bill C-38, the Civil Marriage Act, in February 2005. Despite the fact that Martin personally was ambivalent about the issue, and the fact that he allowed a free vote in his caucus, the vast majority of Liberal MPs, along with the majority of NDP and Bloc Québécois MPs, voted in favour of the bill; the majority of Conservative Party MPs voted against it. Simply put, the human-rights discourse of equality had won the day, even among many Liberal and other MPs who were personally uncomfortable with the specific concept. As mentioned earlier, it became law on July 19, 2005, making Canada the fourth country in the world to legalize same-sex marriage.

Consequently, given that virtually all the legal infrastructure was now in place with respect to sexual orientation, one might assume that the federal government's future role would be minimal. Certainly, this was the case over the next decade, as the Harper Conservatives were in power throughout this period and the issue of equality rights in general largely faded from view, as exemplified by the government's cancellation of the Court Challenges program.

Liberalism in Practice: Promoting Tolerance of Diversity

When the federal Liberals returned to power in the fall of 2015, under leader Justin Trudeau, many voters assumed that they would substantially rethink their approach to a number of long-standing issues, such as climate change and Canada's role at the United Nations. Some minority groups also anticipated positive developments, most notably Indigenous Canadians, and they were not disappointed when the first Throne Speech delivered by the new government identified Indigenous issues as a top priority. Similarly, women were singled out for attention as the new prime minister made good on his promise to establish gender equity in cabinet. Appointments to other government positions soon followed that highlighted Trudeau's commitment to diversity in representation, as signalled by his iconic statement at his swearing-in ceremony that these measures were being taken "because it's 2015."

Perhaps one of the least-anticipated areas of further government action, however, was on LGBT issues, primarily because the same-sex marriage issue had been resolved and full legal equality established under earlier Liberal regimes. Yet the Trudeau Liberals took up a number of initiatives in short order, some of which followed through on election campaign commitments. Most involved measures to enhance social equality, since tolerance of diversity and lack of representation remained areas where the LGBT community continued to express concerns.

With respect to representation, for example, the new Liberal government appointed several noted human-rights and Charter experts to Superior Court posts, along with representatives of the Indigenous and Chinese Canadian communities. These selections were accompanied by the appointment of Lucy McSweeney, formerly the official children's lawyer of the Ontario government, to the province's Superior Court. McSweeney, a nationally known gay-rights activist, had received a leadership award from Out on Bay Street in 2013 for her mentoring work with LGBT law graduates who were transitioning to work life. Her appointment was praised by Toronto lawyer and Pride organizer Paul Saguil as "sending a strong signal" (Fine 2016, A1) about the importance of recognizing diversity. Similarly, Sheila Greckol, a noted Charter specialist who had represented Delwin Vriend in the landmark ruling on sexual orientation, was appointed to the Alberta Court of Appeal.

On July 3, 2016, less than a year after taking power, Justin Trudeau became the first Canadian prime minister to march in the annual Gay Pride Parade in Toronto. Referring to a recent homophobic shooting tragedy in Orlando, Florida, Trudeau effectively summarized the broad-based liberal perspective on equality and tolerance in his short statement: "We can't let hate go by ... We have to speak up any time there is injustice or intolerance" (Andrew-Gee 2016, A1.S). For the LGBT community, his appearance marked another important chapter in the evolution of Canadian society.

Responding to emerging issues identified by LGBT activists, the Trudeau government also proposed a number of legislative measures. (At the same time, it must be noted that many if not most current concerns, particularly for transgender individuals, fall under provincial and/or municipal jurisdiction.) One of the legislative changes announced was a review of the refugee determination process, which had been "streamlined" by the Harper government in 2012. As indicated above, enhancements to the process were made earlier, under Jean Chrétien, to include discrimination on the basis of sexual orientation as a legitimate ground for refugee claims. But an international report by an expert panel found that the emphasis on "credibility" and speed imposed by Harper's 2012 changes had "a particular and disproportionately negative impact on LGBT claimants" (Keung 2015).

This remedial action was followed in May 2016 by the tabling of a bill to protect transgender Canadians against discrimination and violence, a move once again reflecting the evolution of liberal thinking on equality rights. Trudeau announced the legislation on May 16 in Montreal, where he was receiving an award from a leading gay-rights organization for "the unparalleled commitment made by Mr. Trudeau to demystify the realities of lesbian, gay, bisexual and transgender individuals for the general public across Canada" (Leblanc 2016, A11). In his acceptance speech, Trudeau indicated that his government hoped to "lead by example," and he concluded with a classic liberal emphasis on broadly based equality rights, saying, "We must carry on the legacy of those who fought for justice by being bold and ambitious in our actions. We must work diligently to close the gap between our principles and our actions" (Leblanc 2016, A11).

The bill was tabled in the House of Commons on the following day, marking the UN's International Day against Homophobia, Transphobia and Biphobia. Reflecting the mandate letter that Trudeau had given to his new justice minister, Jody Wilson-Raybould, in October 2015, the bill added "gender identity" and "gender expression" as prohibited grounds for discrimination in the CHRA, the Criminal Code, and legislation that specifically targeted hate-crime. One practical consequence of this was the decision to house transgender inmates in federal penitentiaries according to their gender identity.

Finally, in August 2016, it was reported that the Trudeau government was planning to introduce a number of measures when Parliament reconvened in the fall, many of which had been recommended in a brief submitted by the gay activist group Egale. These measures included eliminating the difference in the age of consent for sexual acts between heterosexuals and homosexuals, providing education and training sessions regarding LGBT rights for federal judges, border guards, and the RCMP, and implementing administrative reforms "to protect the dignity of transgender and intersex individuals in federal prisons" (Ibbitson 2016, A3).

Strikingly, supporters of the proposed measures anticipated that they would encounter little or no opposition, thereby demonstrating once more the progress made by the rights discourse approach in Canadian society throughout just a few decades (Ibbitson 2016). Nor was there opposition to the plan to expunge the criminal records of those who were persecuted for their sexual orientation before changes were made to the Criminal Code.

What could have proven the only controversial proposal was a largely symbolic one: a government apology to individual gay and lesbian Canadians who had been imprisoned because of Criminal Code provisions prior to 1968 or fired from their government jobs because of their sexual orientation. But when Trudeau stood in the House of Commons to issue that groundbreaking apology on November 28, 2017, this measure generated little or no disagreement, despite earlier concerns that public resistance to "serial" apologies was mounting and that resistance to compensation payments was also growing. It would appear that the Trudeau government was able to overcome such opposition by framing the apology as an issue of equality rights. Certainly, this was once again the planned strategy. The comments of a spokesperson for the prime minister during the lead-up to the apology demonstrated once more the broad-based liberal approach to human-rights issues: "We have committed to working with Egale and other groups on an ongoing basis," Cameron Ahmad stated, "to bring an end to discrimination and further guarantee equality for all citizens" (Ibbitson 2016, A3). This approach was repeated in Trudeau's statement in the House, which concluded, "We're Canadians, and we want the very best for each other, regardless of our sexual orientation, or our gender identity or expression. We will support one another in our fight for equality" (PMO 2017).

Conclusion

When Justice Minister Pierre Trudeau introduced changes to the Criminal Code in 1968 to decriminalize homosexuality, fewer than 50 percent of Canadians approved. Less than forty years later, some 70 percent of Canadians now support the concept of same-sex marriage. Many observers argue that the steady, albeit incremental, proactive measures taken by Liberal governments and the rights-based discourse of equality that they have encouraged through the entrenchment of the Charter of Rights and Freedoms have been key factors in this remarkable societal progression, which has made Canada a world leader in the protection of LGBT rights. This gradual and peaceful evolution also stands in stark contrast with the path followed by minority groups in the United States, and especially the LGBT community, both historically and in terms of recent events.

With legal equality guaranteed, the Trudeau government has now begun to address issues of social inequality and discrimination that still plague members of the LGBT community, an approach that relies to a considerable extent on enhanced representation and positive symbolism, and that will hopefully result in further progress toward widespread societal acceptance.[9] Nevertheless, Trudeau recognized in his apology that there was more work to be done. As he explained, "The changing of hearts and minds is a collective effort. We need to work together, across jurisdictions, with Indigenous peoples and LGBTQ2 communities, to make the crucial progress that LGBTQ2 Canadians deserve" (PMO 2017).

Notes

1 The phrase "separation of church and state" typically indicates that the state guarantees religious freedom and that there is no state-sponsored religion. Liberalism expands on this concept of the secular state to ensure that perceived moral issues are not adjudicated by the state.
2 It should be noted that not all provincial Liberal Parties have been as progressive as their federal counterpart. In the case of Ontario, for example, although the Liberal government of Kathleen Wynne took some important initiatives in support of LGBT rights, the Opposition Liberals in that same province defeated NDP government legislation on same-sex spousal benefits in 1994.
3 The province of Quebec under the Parti Québécois government of René Lévesque was the first to do so, in 1977. For more details, see Manon Tremblay (2015).
4 For more on the Court Challenges Program, see its website at http://voices-voix.ca/en/facts/profile/court-challenges-program.
5 Many conservative commentators, such as Jeffrey Simpson (1993), lamented what they perceived as the Americanization of the Canadian system in which rights issues determined through the courts took precedence over the legitimate role of legislators. See also Philip Kaye (1998) for an in-depth discussion of the two opposing views.
6 In *Vriend v. Alberta* (1998), the Supreme Court ruled that "sexual orientation" should be read into section 15 and therefore invalidated the Alberta legislation as unconstitutional. The court also stated that arguments made by the provincial government in opposition to this were "nonsensical." Writing for the majority, Justice Frank Iacobucci declared, "Far from being rationally connected to the objective of the impugned provisions, the exclusion of sexual orientation from the (Alberta) IRPA [Individual's Rights Protection Act] is antithetical to that goal. Indeed, it would be nonsensical to say that the goal of protecting persons from discrimination is rationally connected to, or advanced by, denying such protection to a group which this Court has recognized as historically disadvantaged" (ibid., para. 119).
7 Although Ontario had willingly complied with the *M v. H* ruling by changing its Family Law Act to accommodate "spouses or same-sex partners," the Conservative government of Mike Harris was adamant that it would not go farther and recognize same-sex marriages. Meanwhile, the Alberta government had announced that it would invoke the notwithstanding clause if the federal government were to change its definition of marriage.
8 Jean Chrétien, Transcript of speech to the National Liberal Caucus, August 19, 2003, 3, North Bay.
9 It should be noted, however, that some radical LGBTQ groups see the attainment of equality as an insufficient objective that further marginalizes those within the LGBTQ community who wish to diversify from the status quo rather than conform to it.

References

Adams, Michael. 2009. *Fire and Ice*. Toronto: Penguin.
Andrew-Gee, Eric. 2016. "Pride Parade Takes a Political Turn." *Globe and Mail*, July 4, A1.S.
Behiels, Michael. 2011. "Book Review of Ron Graham. *The Last Act: Trudeau, the Gang of Eight, and the Fight for Canada*." *Policy Options*, December 10. http://policyoptions.irpp.org/magazines/the-year-in-review/the-last-act-pierre-trudeau-the-gang-of-eight-and-the-fight-for-canada-book-review/.
Bibby, Reginald. 2011. *Beyond the Gods and Back*. Lethbridge: Project Canada Books.
Canada. 1967. *Debates and Proceedings*. January 24, 4191.

Canada, Subcommittee on Human Rights and Justice. 1985. *Equality for All: Report of the Subcommittee on Human Rights and Justice*. Ottawa: Queens Printer.
CBC News. 2005. "Canadians Deeply Split on Same-Sex Marriage, Poll Suggests." April 10. http://www.cbc.ca/news/canada/canadians-deeply-split-on-same-sex-marriage-poll-suggests-1.527494.
–. 2012. "Timeline: Same-Sex Rights in Canada." January 12. http://www.cbc.ca/news/canada/timeline-same-sex-rights-in-canada-1.1147516.
CBC Radio. 1969. "Second Go-Round for the Omnibus Bill." *Sunday Morning Magazine*, April 20. http://www.cbc.ca/archives/entry/second-go-round-for-the-omnibus-bill.
CBC Television News. 1967. "Trudeau: 'There's No Place for the State in the Bedrooms of the Nation.'" December 21. http://www.cbc.ca/archives/entry/omnibus-bill-theres-no-place-for-the-state-in-the-bedrooms-of-the-nation.
Chambers, Stuart. 2010. "Pierre Elliott Trudeau and Bill C-150: A Rational Approach to Homosexual Acts, 1968–9." *Journal of Homosexuality* 57 (2): 249–66. https://doi.org/10.1080/00918360903489085. Medline:20390992
Clark, Campbell, Jane Taber, and Tu Thanh Ha. 2003. "Chrétien Speech Aims to Sway Caucus, Country on Same-Sex." *Globe and Mail*, August 19. http://www.theglobeandmail.com/news/national/chretien-speech-aims-to-sway-caucus-country-on-same-sex/article4129224/.
Clément, Dominique, Will Silver, and Daniel Trottier. 2012. *The Evolution of Human Rights in Canada*. Ottawa: Ministry of Government Services.
Farney, James. 2012. *Social Conservatives and Party Politics in Canada and the United States*. Toronto: University of Toronto Press.
Fine, Sean. 2016. "Government Appointments Signal Intent to Diversify the Judiciary." *Globe and Mail*, June 21, A1.
Fraser, Graham. 2003. "What the Framers of the Charter Intended." *Policy Options*, October 1. http://policyoptions.irpp.org/magazines/who-decides-the-courts-or-parliament/what-the-framers-of-the-charter-intended/.
Hiebert, Janet L. 2009. "Compromise and the Notwithstanding Clause: Why the Dominant Narrative Distorts Our Understanding." In *Contested Constitutionalism: Reflections on the Charter of Rights and Freedoms*, ed. James B. Kelly and Christopher P. Manfredi, 107–28. Vancouver: UBC Press.
Hurley, Mary. 2010. *Sexual Orientation and Legal Rights*. Background Paper 08-49-E. Ottawa: Parliamentary Information and Research Branch, Library of Parliament.
Ibbitson, John. 2016. "Justin Trudeau to Apologize for Historic Persecution of Gay Canadians." *Globe and Mail*, August 11, A3. http://www.theglobeandmail.com/news/politics/justin-trudeau-to-apologize-for-historic-persecution-of-gay-canadians/article31376155/.
Ignatieff, Michael. 2000. *The Rights Revolution*. Toronto: House of Anansi Press.
Jeffrey, Brooke. 1992. *Breaking Faith: The Mulroney Legacy*. Toronto: Key Porter.
–. 1995. *Hard Right Turn*. Toronto: Harper Collins.
–. 2015. *Divided Loyalties: The Liberal Party of Canada, 1984–2006*. Montreal and Kingston: McGill-Queen's University Press.
Kaye, Philip. 1998. "Parliament and the Courts – Who's Legislating for Whom?" *Canadian Parliamentary Review* 21 (3). http://www.revparl.ca/english/issue.asp?param=68&art=112.
Kelly, James, and Christopher Manfredi, eds. 2009. *Contested Constitutionalism: Reflections on the Charter of Rights and Freedoms*. Vancouver: UBC Press.
Keung, Nicholas. 2015. "Canada's Asylum System Re-Victimizes LGBTQ Refugees." *Toronto Star*, April 3. https://www.thestar.com/news/immigration/2015/09/29/canadas-asylum-system-re-victimizes-lgbtq-refugees.html.

Laird, Gordon. 2000. "Can Stockwell Day Separate Church from State?" *Globe and Mail*, July 17. http://www.theglobeandmail.com/opinion/can-stockwell-day-separate-church-from-state/article768825/.

Larocque, Sylvain. 2006. *Gay Marriage: The Story of a Social Revolution*. Toronto: James Lorimer.

Leblanc, Daniel. 2016. "Ottawa Hopes Gender Bill Will 'Lead by Example.'" *Globe and Mail*, May 17, A11.

McIlroy, Anne. 2003. "Canadian Government to Defy Church on Gay Marriage." *Guardian*, August 11. https://www.theguardian.com/world/2003/aug/11/worlddispatch.gayrights.

PMO (Prime Minister's Office). 2017. "Remarks by Prime Minister Justin Trudeau to Apologize to LGBTQ2 Canadians." November 28. https://pm.gc.ca/en/news/speeches/2017/11/28/remarks-prime-minister-justin-trudeau-apologize-lgbtq2-canadians.

Rayside, David. 1998. *On the Fringe: Gays and Lesbians in Politics*. Ithaca: Cornell University Press.

Simpson, Jeffrey. 1993. "Rights Talk: The Effect of the Charter on Canadian Political Discourse." In *Protecting Rights and Freedoms: Essays on the Charter's Place in Canada's Political, Legal, and Intellectual Life*, ed. Philip Bryden, Steven Davis, and Peter Russell, 52–59. Toronto: University of Toronto Press.

Smith, Miriam. 2008. *Political Institutions and Lesbian and Gay Rights in the United States and Canada*. New York: Routledge.

Tremblay, Manon. 2015. "Social Movements and Political Opportunities: Lesbians, Gays and the Inclusion of Sexual Orientation in the Québec Charter of Human Rights." *World Political Science* 11 (1): 47–73. https://doi.org/10.1515/wps-2015-0005.

Urquart, Ian. 1976. "The NDP Out of Season." *Maclean's*, November 29, 47–62.

Vriend v. Alberta, [1998] 1 S.C.R. 493.

7

A True Match?
The Federal New Democratic Party and
LGBTQ Communities and Politics

Alexa DeGagne

THE NEW DEMOCRATIC PARTY OF CANADA (NDP) and its provincial counterparts are commonly seen as the most supportive advocates of lesbian, gay, bisexual, trans(gender), and queer (LGBTQ) equality and rights in federal and provincial politics.[1] After all, two NDP politicians – Svend Robinson and Libby Davies – were among the first to publicly identify as gay and lesbian, respectively, while holding seats in the House of Commons. The NDP often touts itself as advancing the most progressive legislation regarding LGBT issues. For example, the Ontario NDP introduced same-sex benefits legislation with Bill 167 in 1994. As well, the federal NDP has introduced many versions (in 2005, 2006, 2009, and 2013) of a bill to add gender identity and gender expression to the Canadian Human Rights Act and to the hate-crime provision of the Criminal Code. Thus, the NDP is seen as supporting the values and issues that are most pressing in LGBT communities across Canada, including equality, justice, and non-discrimination. Key issues here involve the inclusion of sexual orientation and gender identity and expression in federal and provincial Human Rights Acts, the legalization of same-sex marriage, the permitting of adoption by homosexual parents, the toughening of hate-crime provisions, and the creation of anti-bullying legislation to protect LGBT students.

In this chapter, I trouble this narrative of a wholly supportive relationship between the federal NDP and LGBT citizens and movements.[2] The political views and needs of LGBTQ citizens, and their support for political parties, are not uniform or consistent. Throughout its history, the broader LGBT movement in Canada has been pulled in various ideological directions as its members engaged in homophile, liberationist, anti-assimilationist, liberal human-rights, queer, and intersectional activisms and political projects. Moreover, LGBTQ people's experiences with inequality, discrimination, and violence are differently conditioned by their gender identity and expression, race, indigeneity, class, occupation, and abilities. Therefore, when considering the issues and needs of LGBTQ citizens, political parties have had to engage with complex, changing, and conflictual LGBTQ communities and movements. Party affiliations are not universal among LGBTQ people. For example, some LGBTQ individuals and movements position themselves to the left of the liberal rights agenda espoused by the federal and provincial NDP. They fight for more radical and community-based solutions to issues such as LGBTQ experiences with poverty, violence, over-criminalization, and police harassment. At the same time, LGBT voters have shown higher support for the Liberals than for the NDP in the past few general elections and are increasingly supporting the Conservative Party (Perrella, Brown, and Kay 2012; see Chapters 1 and 5 in this volume).

Although the federal NDP has historically had a contentious relationship with various social movements, including labour, feminism, and LGBTQ, leftist social-movement activists and advocates tend to gravitate to it (more than to other parties), and the NDP has used this momentum to attract members and voters. In this context, I critically analyze the relationship among LGBTQ voters, the LGBTQ movement, and the federal NDP precisely because the party has a reputation as the strongest ally of LGBTQ people and movements. I look at moments of co-operation as well as those of compromise, exclusion, and acrimony to understand whether LGBTQ citizens and their movement truly were well represented by the party.

I argue that the NDP conceived of LGBT issues predominantly in terms of economic inequality and a denial of liberal rights and freedoms, seldom entertaining more radical perspectives. LGBTQ mainstream and radical groups attempted to establish relationships with the party. When it did embrace the LGBTQ community, it worked with the mainstream, centre, and liberal parts of the movement because the party was conditioned by the confines of party politics and the formal political process. It predominantly advocated a politics of slow, incremental change through inclusion into established legislation, such as the Canadian Human Rights Act (CHRA), and established institutions, such as marriage.

Even so, the NDP did initially differentiate itself from other parties by being the first to engage with and seek to represent the mainstream LGBT community. The Liberals and Conservatives soon followed the NDP's initiatives, which were facilitated by the NDP's strategies for incremental change and by slowly changing public opinion in support of certain LGBT rights. As a result, the NDP no longer stood at the forefront of fighting for LGBT rights and equality. Discrepancies remain in terms of the federal parties' support for transgender rights, for example. Yet, the three parties have supported homonational LGBT politics in various ways, using Canada's LGBT human-rights reputation to interfere in the politics of other countries. Thus, the parties increasingly support mainstream, liberal LGBT priorities and perpetuate homonationalism, calling into question the unique nature of the relationship between the NDP and LGBT people and communities.

The NDP Commitment to Equality, Solidarity, and the LGBT Community, 1961–2005

The NDP was founded in 1961 as a social-democratic party seeking to fill the gap left by the electoral decline of the Co-operative Commonwealth Federation (CCF). The CCF and NDP shared the core ideological concepts of equality, democracy, solidarity, and an active state. David Laycock and Lynda Erickson (2014a) argue that although these core concepts and basic policy objectives remained central to the NDP, the corresponding meaning, discourses, and policy instruments altered over the decades. For example, the party's understanding of equality changed, expanding from class-based economic equality to entail "incorporating solidarity with various disadvantaged groups, including women, ethnic minorities, the LGBT community, and future generations affected by environmental damage" (Laycock and Erickson 2014a, 300). This acknowledgment of the interconnection between equality and solidarity with marginalized people and groups was influenced in large part by social movements that were increasingly interacting with and joining the party (Laycock and Erickson 2014a).

The NDP's Initial Contact with the LGB Community, 1960s

James Farney (2009, 243, 244) argues that personal issues, such as divorce, abortion, and homosexuality, were first brought into formal federal political debate through a joint House of Commons/Senate committee report on divorce law reform, in 1967, and the Liberal Party's omnibus bill of 1968–69 to amend the Criminal Code, which reformed the provisions of buggery and gross indecency. Although the three major federal parties – Liberal, Progressive Conservative, and NDP – negotiated their stances on issues such as homosexual sex, the NDP stood out as the first and most vocal supporter of certain gay rights. The first major interaction between the NDP and gay and lesbian communities came in 1967, in connection with Everett George Klippert. Seven years earlier, he had been convicted and imprisoned for gross indecency and was subsequently declared a dangerous sexual offender, a designation that the Supreme Court of Canada upheld in November 1967. The day after the decision, NDP leader T.C. Douglas referred in the House of Commons to Klippert's case and the decision, asserting that the Criminal Code should be changed. In 1968, Douglas also stated that homosexuality was "a mental illness ... a psychiatric condition" (Ibbitson 2016). Yet throughout the 1960s and 1970s, LGB activists argued that homosexuality should not be classified as a psychological condition because the designation subjected homosexuals to psychiatric and psychological regulation and government intervention.

From Human Rights to Economic Equality, 1970s–1990s

The relationship between the NDP and the gay movement developed incrementally after other social movements were connected to the party – first, the labour movement and then the "second wave" of the liberal feminist movement (Markle and Beuhler 2016). Many gay and lesbian activists were linked to the NDP through the Waffle group and the Revolutionary Marxist Group. A radical wing of the NDP, the former was established during the late 1960s. Its founders, some of whom were gay-rights activists, were predominantly members of socialist, student, and other radical movements. They produced a manifesto that called for a renewed "democratic socialist NDP." The group held that the NDP should engage in consultation and collaboration with grassroots movements (Markle and Beuhler 2016).[3] Lesbian and gay liberationists in the Revolutionary Marxist Group called for solidarity between workers and lesbian and gay liberationists, positing that sexual liberation would occur through revolution, not reform (Kinsman and Gentile 2010, 280). The NDP did not adopt this position regarding sexual revolution. Still, during Ed Broadbent's leadership, 1975–89, the party began to engage with and seek votes from "disadvantaged" groups, including "ethno-cultural" minorities, Indigenous people, and gays and lesbians, although such shifts in focus could not overshadow its economic and labour priorities. The New Democratic Gay Caucus was formed at the 1975 NDP national convention, and shortly afterward the party advocated inclusion of sexual orientation in Canadian human-rights codes, becoming the first national party to do so (Canadian Lesbian and Gay Archives 1997). Yet support for gay-rights issues, such as adding sexuality to the Canadian Bill of Rights, was not uniform throughout the party. During a 1976 interview with *Maclean's* magazine, Broadbent stated that homosexual rights were a minority "fad issue" that the party should not support in lieu of fighting for the economic and social rights of the majority of voters (Urquart 1976). Despite this opposition, the NDP pursued engagement with gay issues as it attempted to attract new voters beyond the labour tradition and began to extend its definition of equality to include liberal group rights and the egalitarian distribution of opportunities and social-economic resources to "disadvantaged" groups (Laycock 2014).

Although the NDP did not connect with the gay and lesbian movement as it did with the liberal feminist movement, select members of the party advocated tirelessly for several gay-rights issues during the 1970s and 1980s. In 1971, a lesbian and gay coalition mounted the first large-scale gay and lesbian protest in Canadian history and presented a list of demands to the federal government, titled "We Demand" (Waite and DiNovo 1971). The We Demand protest and manifesto were ambitious and progressive for their time. Yet their priorities were grounded in liberal rights and equality. In subsequent decades,

"We Demand" was influential in setting the federal political agenda for mainstream lesbian and gay activists and organizations and their allies. To these ends, the NDP, in the person of MP Svend Robinson, supported the "We Demand" call that homosexuals should be permitted to serve in the Armed Forces, the RCMP, and the public service; for reforms to age of consent laws, which discriminated against anal sex; and for the addition of sexuality to the Canadian Bill of Rights, which was promoted by the National Gay Rights Coalition (*CBC News* 2012; Hooper 2014; Warner 2002; on Svend Robinson's activism, see the Afterword in this volume).

In 1981, a month after police raided four bathhouses in Toronto, targeting, assaulting, and arresting hundreds of gay and gender-non-conforming individuals (Guidotto 2011), protesters took to the streets, and Robinson spoke to the crowd, denouncing the raids (*Toronto Life* 2016). Gay-rights activists, motivated by "We Demand" and the bathhouse raids, pointed out that the Criminal Code still retained problematic clauses pertaining to homosexual acts. They concentrated on the ages of consent for vaginal and anal sex, which were not the same; the definition of "indecent"; the bawdy house law; group sex and orgies; and the distinction between public and private (Hooper 2014). In the following years, Robinson introduced five bills to make the age of consent uniform. All five were defeated, but all received unanimous support from the federal NDP caucus (Hooper 2014). Thus, certain members of the NDP were vocal in their support for the gay and lesbian community as they fought for liberal rights issues, such as inclusion in the CHRA and uniformity in age of consent laws.

David Laycock (2014) argues that NDP membership and support were broadened during the 1980s, as the party worked to include women, Indigenous people, gays and lesbians, and environmentalists. The federal and provincial NDP adopted policies to recruit "underrepresented groups," including women, gays and lesbians, and people of colour. Also during this decade, the federal NDP began to reserve seats on its executive body for gays and lesbians (Dehaas 2015). Joanna Everitt (2015) holds that these policies contributed to higher numbers of female, gay, and lesbian candidates for the NDP than for other parties, but neither the provincial nor the federal NDP met their targets. The 1989 election of Audrey McLaughlin as NDP leader was thought to be due, in part, to her support for coalition politics among labour and feminist, Indigenous, and gay and lesbian movements (Laycock 2014). Laycock and Erickson (2014a) state that the NDP did not see class rights and identity-based rights as competing with each other; however, during the mid-1990s, the party struggled with inconsistent messaging and agendas regarding identity-based social movements (Laycock 2014). It continued to emphasize addressing economic equality in order to address identity-based inequality. Thus, party mandates throughout the 1980s and 1990s focused predominantly on the economic inequalities of various marginalized groups and offered relatively less content on issues of recognition, representation and human rights, and discrimination and violence.

Between the 1960s and the 1990s, the party consistently updated its platforms concerning women. In comparison, its platforms did not mention sexual orientation or gay rights until 1997, when the platform of that year stated, "Canada's NDP has a proud history of fighting for the democratic rights of all Canadians, regardless of their gender, skin colour, sexual orientation or religion. Discrimination must be eliminated and equality guaranteed" (New Democratic Party 1997, 9). However, the party's official documents and platforms remained vague about its support for complex and urgent lesbian and gay issues. The 1997 and 2000 platforms focused on the economic standing of lesbian and gay people. The 1997 platform listed one corresponding goal: to establish federal laws that would permit same-sex spousal benefits (New Democratic Party 1997, 9). The 2000 platform listed an additional goal: to create "amendments to the Human Rights Act to recognize same-sex marriages" (New Democratic Party 2000, 17).

Thus, the NDP's initial discussion of sexual orientation as a party priority was vague, and it concentrated on the economic issues of spousal-support and same-sex marriage benefits. Nonetheless, the NDP acknowledgment of gay issues and support for gay rights were unique among federal parties, given that the Progressive Conservatives largely avoided making public decisions or statements on gay-rights issues (Farney 2009). Later, members of the Reform Party took a distinctly social conservative stance and vocally opposed the legalization of same-sex marriage (Farney 2012). Accordingly, Canadian federal parties differentiated themselves in terms of their support for, or derision of, the lesbian and gay community.[4]

Engagement with New Social Movements, 2000s

Despite the NDP's ongoing challenges with representing various complex social movements, left-wing, radical, and social justice communities and movements continued to attempt to work with and influence its priorities. The New Politics Initiative (NPI) was created in 2001 by NDP anti-globalization activists who wanted the party to take a strong stance against neoliberal globalization and the resulting economic inequalities, environmental degradation, and human-rights abuses (Stanford 2011). The NPI also asserted that the party needed to commit itself to challenging "multifaceted forms of inequality and exclusion experienced by so many Canadians: by women; people of colour; lesbians, gays, bisexuals and transgendered people; and the people with disabilities" (Cofounders of the New Politics Initiative 2011). Several former members of the Waffle group endorsed the NPI, as the two movements were alike in many of their concerns and their connections to social movements (Stanford 2011). That said, the NPI, like the NDP, understood inequality and exclusion primarily in economic terms: "We also continue to see class as a crucial axis along which millions of working Canadians are systematically exploited and disadvantaged" (Cofounders of the New Politics Initiative 2011). NDP MPs Libby Davies and Svend Robinson were co-creators of the NPI (Stanford 2011), which demonstrates the social-movement – and practically LGBT – underpinning of the group.

The founding document of the NPI advocated a renewed respect for the role of social movements in the NDP. The NPI contended that the party needed to acknowledge the hard work of activists and social-movement members in helping it attain its human-rights, economic, and environmental victories. It suggested that social movements needed to be given a more meaningful and influential position in the party (Cofounders of the New Politics Initiative 2011). MP Libby Davies saw the founding of the NPI as a missed opportunity for the party to reflect on its respect for social movements and on the role that they played in influencing its policies and strategies, both during and between elections (Markle and Beuhler 2016). Tristan Markle and Sarah Beuhler (2016) state that the NPI failed to attain much support from the party because of a mutual distrust between the NDP and social movements. In part, this stemmed from the grievance that the NDP did not work well with social movements between elections, and yet it assumed that the movements would be its electoral allies. Given this history, tensions persisted between the NDP and various grassroots social movements.

Jack Layton and Same-Sex Marriage, 2000s

NDP leader Jack Layton did not support the NPI, but NPI co-founder Jim Stanford (2011) states that he seemed to be "sympathetic to many of its ideas and goals." Layton's election as leader occurred, in part, through his ability to gain the support of union activists, party operatives, and left-wing MPs such as Davies and Robinson, both of whom were NPI co-founders (Laycock and Erickson 2014b; Stanford 2011). As well, during his time in Toronto civic politics, Layton worked with immigrant, racialized, and LGBT communities, and it was hoped that his experience would help retain and attract a growing range of constituents (Laycock 2014). Because Layton supported the traditional incremental and reformist approach of the NDP, as opposed to the large-scale and revolutionary leftist tactics and goals promoted by various social movements, he retained broad approval among rank-and-file party members during his years as leader. The NDP supported equality through group rights and various policy initiatives that it believed would help marginalized communities. To this end, it was the first federal party to propose adding gender identity to the CHRA, a position it adopted in 2004 (New Democratic Party 2004, 38).

The battle over same-sex marriage dramatically illustrated the parties' differentiating support for gay rights and confirmed the incremental, liberal rights, and equality priorities of the NDP. In 1997, the party had supported federal laws that permitted same-sex spousal benefits (New Democratic Party 1997, 35). The Liberal Party did not support same-sex marriage until the Supreme Court forced its hand in 2005 (Rayside and Wilcox 2011; on the Liberal position, see Chapter 6 in this volume). Finally, in 2016, the Conservative Party voted to discontinue its policy goal of abolishing same-sex marriage should it return to power, but it stopped short of officially supporting its legalization. These developments reveal how far federal parties and public opinion had shifted regarding certain gay and lesbian issues (see Chapter 5 in this volume). During parliamentary debates of the mid-2000s, before the other parties finally rethought their attitudes to such issues, NDP members offered personal, passionate, and powerful speeches in support of same-sex marriage and the gay community, often in the face of harsh anti-gay statements from MPs in other parties. Thus, the NDP stood out in Parliament, and to the media, as an ally of the gay and lesbian community.

The NDP stance on same-sex marriage was seen as progressive in the 2000s, especially in comparison with the attitudes of the other parties. The NDP was the first and most consistent supporter of same-sex marriage, as the majority of the party accepted homosexuality and gay rights, and the mainstream and powerful elements of the LGBT movement were pressuring parties to support same-sex marriage. The willingness (or not) of parties to accept same-sex marriage has been used – by activists, governments, and academics – as a shorthand measure for their receptivity to advancing the equality of LGBT citizens. Yet same-sex marriage was prioritized by elite members of LGBT organizations, which primarily fought for its legalization through the courts (Smith 2010). Although the issue gained traction throughout the LGB community, it was not unanimously accepted, as critics suggested that other subjects were more pressing. Moreover, many LGBT people, specifically trans people, were not included in the consultation or court process, as mainstream LGB organizations shut them out, impeding them from gaining the ear of government, courts, and parties. On the subject of same-sex marriage, the NDP was receiving clear messages from the majority of its adherents and the elites of the LGB movement, and the latter were likely to question their allegiance to the party should it falter in its support. Thus, by advocating same-sex marriage, the NDP was following the wishes of privileged members of the LGBTQ community, who were seeking equality through incremental change.

Clarifying Priorities beyond Marriage, 2006–16

To identify the NDP's post-same-sex-marriage LGBT agenda, I analyzed its public electronic documents – press releases, statements, party platforms, campaign materials, policy books, and speeches – from 2006 to 2016. I searched specifically for documents that discussed LGB issues, homosexuality, trans(gender) issues, and HIV/AIDS.[5]

Beyond same-sex marriage, NDP initiatives focused on a host of equality rights, including youth bullying and the past firing of LGBT public servants. The party's 2010 policy document listed the following priorities: protecting trans rights, promoting LGBT rights internationally, strengthening hate-crime provisions, eliminating justice system discrimination against LGBT people, endorsing artistic freedom, halting discrimination against LGBT individuals in immigration and refugee procedures, and supporting LGBT youth (New Democratic Party 2010b). In 2014, the NDP announced that it would continue fighting for trans rights and added a new set of priorities: to end the ban on gay men donating blood and organs, to "suspend criminal records for gay offences which are no longer illegal," to make the age of consent uniform for heterosexual and homosexual sex, to "revise service records for those discharged from the Canadian Forces on the basis of sexual orientation or gender identity," and to "secure an apology for civil servants fired on the basis of sexual orientation or gender identity" (New Democratic Party 2014a). Finally, the party's "Gay Agenda," which was initiated in anticipation of World Pride 2014 in Toronto, listed the following priorities: "Full equality for trans and gender-variant Canadians[;] No discrimination in blood and organ donations[;] No more unequal age of consent laws[;] Rock-solid rights for LGBTQ people everywhere" (New Democratic Party 2015b). Thus, the NDP raised a wide range of LGBT issues concerning many aspects of LGBT people's experiences with inequality and discrimination.

For the first time, the party's 2015 platform included an entire section devoted to LGBT issues, albeit with the safe, liberal title of "Equal Rights and Opportunities" (New Democratic Party 2015a, 33). The section lauded the party's LGBT record and promised to fight for trans rights in the CHRA and the Criminal Code, and reiterated the 2014 priorities (ibid.). In response to an election survey by the Canadian Centre for Gender and Sexual Diversity, the NDP offered a detailed discussion of its vision for LGBT people. The survey asked federal parties about LGBT suicide rates and mental health, homelessness and poverty, and violence and hate-crimes, among other things, which prompted the NDP to detail its efforts in these areas, including a national suicide prevention strategy, affordable housing, tougher hate-crime and bullying policies, and a plan for LGBT seniors (Canadian Centre for Gender and Sexual Diversity 2015).

The party's LGBT priorities fluctuated over the years, indicating that it updated its agenda, in part, in accordance with the changing priorities of various national, mainstream, human-rights-focused LGBT organizations. The LGBT focus of the NDP, therefore, remained grounded in a liberal human-rights framework, which held that equality is based on the attainment and protection of group rights, be it in terms of non-discrimination, blood donation, job discrimination, or criminal records. Two liberal-rights-based issues dominated the NDP agenda: transgender rights in the CHRA and the Criminal Code, and exporting Canadian-style liberal LGBT rights to developing countries. The 2008 and 2011 NDP platforms, where LGBT issues were concerned, enumerated only these two priorities (New Democratic Party 2008, 2011a). In its 2008 platform, the party promised to "amend the *Canadian Human Rights Act* to include gender identity and gender expression and identity among the prohibited grounds for discrimination[, and] support gay, lesbian, bisexual, trans-gender and transsexual equality internationally, as per the Montreal and Jakarta Declaration on Human Rights" (New Democratic Party 2008, 41). Through the combination of these two priorities, the NDP applauded Canada's LGBT rights record and argued for its exportation to other countries. At the same time, it chastised the federal government for failing trans people by blocking the addition of gender identity and expression to the CHRA and the Criminal Code.

Domestic Concerns: Trans(gender) Rights and Hate-Crime Provisions, 2004–16

Fitting into a liberal rights framework, the issue of trans rights was first mentioned in the party's 2004 platform: "Jack Layton and Canada's NDP will respect equality by [...] following the lead of the Northwest Territories and amending the Canada Human Rights Act to ensure a person cannot be discriminated against because of gender identity" (New Democratic Party 2004, 38). Party platforms in 2008 and 2011 added gender expression and called for the insertion of both terms in the CHRA and Criminal Code sections that pertained to hate-crimes (New Democratic Party 2008, 2011a).[6] In 2005 and 2006, NDP MP Bill Siksay introduced a bill that proposed the addition of gender identity and expression to the CHRA. He reintroduced the bill in 2009, this time also seeking to include gender identity and expression in the hate-crime provisions of the Criminal Code. The 2009 version of the bill made it past a third reading in the House of Commons but failed to be considered in the Senate before the dissolution of Parliament for the 2011 election (Parliament of Canada 2015).

Siksay argued that inclusion in the CHRA would protect trans people from discrimination in housing, employment, and health care, and that inclusion in the hate-crime provisions would deter hate-crimes against trans people, who experience disproportionate levels of discrimination and violence. Siksay, the NDP GLBT critic, explained, "Trans people routinely face violence and discrimination in the workplace, in health care and even in obtaining housing and identity documents ... I believe that explicit protection in the Canadian Human Rights Act (CHRA) and our Criminal Code will go a long way to counter this discrimination and move towards full acceptance and equality for transgender [people] and transsexuals" (New Democratic Party 2009b).

A further iteration of the NDP stance on LGBT rights, Bill C-279, was introduced to the House of Commons by NDP MP Randall Garrison (Parliament of Canada 2015). In July 2015, Bill C-279 was permitted to die on the order paper when government Senate leader Claude Carignan deliberately delayed debate on its passage (Baglow 2015), striking at nearly ten years of attempts to attain these rights for trans people. Relief from this frustrating situation was anticipated in 2016, when the Liberals introduced Bill C-16, which proposed that both gender identity and gender expression be added to the CHRA and the hate-crime section of the Criminal Code (Government of Canada 2016). The bill passed with the support of all Liberal and NDP members. Interim Conservative leader Rona Ambrose stated that she would support it, although she had opposed past iterations, and that she would support a free vote for the Conservative caucus (Mas 2016). Tory MPs and conservative senators opposed the bill, presenting many arguments, ranging from religious beliefs about the divine form of heteropatriarchal families to the confusion that would ensue for children's sports teams to freedom of speech.

Throughout their ten-year fight for recognition, trans activists expressed fear, anger, and disillusionment at the particularly bigoted and hateful debates that surrounded the bills. Although the NDP championed the bills and stated that it was listening to and representing the trans community while doing so, it may not have anticipated the backlash that was hurled at the trans community by MPs, organizations, and voters. Conservative MPs, such as Rob Anders, claimed that the bill would enable male "sexual predators" to access women's washrooms. When Anders produced a petition in opposition to the gender identity bill, citing the bathroom argument, NDP GLBT critic Randall Garrison responded, "Anders' petition is based on ignorance, misinformation, and fear. He is deliberately promoting prejudice against transgendered and transsexual people by portraying them as sexual offenders and pedophiles" (New Democratic Party 2012). Although the NDP stood firm in defence of the bill, refuted the petition, and deprecated the transphobic aspects of the parliamentary debate, the aftermath of harassment and violence was most deeply felt by those who were seeking a remedy to oppression in the first place.

As many activists pointed out, inclusion in the CHRA and hate-crime policies was only one of numerous priorities for their communities and movement, which were dealing with under-representation in political institutions; systemic and daily violence; lack of LGBTQ competence in physical, mental, and addictions health services; inadequate legal and social services for trans refugees and immigrants; and transmisogynistic and racist policing, justice, and prison systems.[7] They argued that exercising one's rights in the CHRA and hate-crimes policies is complicated and costly. Trans activists and academics further noted that relying on the police and criminal justice system for protection through hate-crime provisions reinforces anti-trans and racist institutions that target and criminalize trans and street-involved people, sex workers, Indigenous persons, and people of colour (Vipond 2015). Thus, as with same-sex marriage, the NDP was representing a particular element of the LGBT movement, which was focused on attaining liberal rights through formal political institutions.

Having gender identity and expression included in the CHRA and the Criminal Code would have been a historic accomplishment for the NDP, given the hostility of the Conservative majority governments. Even so, the NDP's ten years of work paved the way for the Liberal government to introduce Bill C-16. By championing inclusion in the CHRA and the Criminal Code as its top priorities for trans people, the NDP appeased some members of the trans community, contributed to changing public discussion of trans rights, and centred the issue enough to make other parties more willing to support trans rights legislation. Although the NDP has contributed to altering the terrain of LGBT politics federally, we must question how the party and the mainstream LGBT movement's prioritization of rights-based issues, such as same-sex marriage and the inclusion of gender identity and expression in hate-crime policies, has affected the nature of political debates about LGBT issues, the future prioritization of LGBT issues, the lives of marginalized LGBTQ people, and the proliferation of homonationalism by various federal parties and the Canadian government.

International Concerns: Exporting Canada's LGBT Rights Record, 2006–16

Throughout the 2000s and 2010s, the NDP claimed that it and its MPs were leaders in fighting for LGBT rights in Canada. As openly gay NDP MP Bill Siksay claimed, "Canada has led the world in ensuring the full equality of gay and lesbian citizens and our full participation in society. New Democrats are proud to have been front and centre in this achievement and we will remain vigilant to prevent any backsliding on these victories" (New Democratic Party 2010a). In 2009, Siksay stated,

In Canada, we've made so many advances in the 42 years since New Democrats first called for the decriminalization of homosexuality, but there's still so much left to do ... As activists in a country with a high standard of LGBTT rights but an unsupportive government, we have a lot to share and a lot to learn about working for LGBTT liberation at home and supporting LGBTT movements abroad. (New Democratic Party 2009a)

As these two passages confirm, the NDP constructed a particular homonational narrative by celebrating Canada as a world leader in LGBT rights and by positioning itself as the party that represented LGBT rights in Canada. Jasbir Puar's homonational theory applies here: "Despite the fact that sexual minorities living within American borders continue to be subjected to multiple forms of discrimination, a homonationalist dialogue allows the state to simultaneously render these inequalities invisible and champion their progressive and 'exceptional' ways on an international stage" (Gaucher and DeGagne 2016, 461).

True, the NDP did acknowledge Canada's shortcomings, such as the denial of gender identity rights in the CHRA. Yet it predominantly blamed such flaws on the "unsupportive" Conservative government and suggested that the Conservatives were not in tune with the human-rights needs of LGBT people. Nonetheless, the NDP still perpetuated a homonational agenda by boasting that it was committed to exporting "full human rights" to LGBT people around the world and by averring that the Conservative government should shoulder this task:

Let us not forget that LGBTT people around the world still suffer prejudice and discrimination, even to the point of violence and death. Our work is not done. New Democrats will continue pressing issues of concern to LGBTT Canadians, starting with the reintroduction of Bill Siksay's Transgender Rights bill by our new LGBTT critic, Randall Garrison. New Democrats will continue to press Canada to be a leader in international forums aimed at establishing full human rights and ending the persecution of LGBTT people around the world. (New Democratic Party 2011b)

The NDP first declared its commitment to international LGBT rights through its official adoption of the 2006 Declaration of Montreal on Lesbian, Gay, Bisexual, and Transgender Human Rights (Everitt and Camp 2014). The Montreal Declaration, which was produced by participants in the International Conference on LGBT Human Rights, focused almost entirely on the proliferation of LGBT rights "around the world" (Declaration of Montreal 2006).

In 2014, the NDP singled out certain countries as particularly hostile toward homosexuality: "In Uganda, Cameroon, Russia, Nigeria and Jamaica LGBTQ people are facing lengthy prison sentences, substantial fines, violence and even death. Today, New Democrats call on all Members of Parliament to take concrete action to eliminate homophobia and transphobia. We call on the government to stand up for the Canadian values of equality and respect" (New Democratic Party 2014b). The party also cited India and Syria as countries in need of LGBT rights (New Democratic Party 2013). The NDP thus asked the Conservative government, which it had long criticized as homophobic and transphobic, to promote the "Canadian values of equality and respect" in countries that it saw as more homophobic and transphobic than Canada. This request could have been an exercise in futility had the Conservatives not been pursuing homonational projects of their own (Troster 2011). They too were using Canada's track record on LGBT rights to justify reprimanding the behaviour of other countries and to position Canada as the saviour of LGBT refugees (Gaucher and DeGagne 2016).

Although the international LGBT politics of the two parties differed, both perpetuated homonationalism. The NDP and the Conservative Party, to different degrees and in different ways, chose the domestic LGBT issues and communities that they wished to support. True, the NDP claimed that liberal rights issues were still unresolved in Canada, whereas the Conservative Party did not officially support trans rights. Yet both used the LGBT community to promote Canada, and themselves, as human-rights leaders and to justify chastising other countries and intervening in their domestic policies.

In 2015, the NDP urged the newly elected Liberal Party to "follow the U.S. example and create a special envoy who would promote lesbian, gay, bisexual, transgender and queer rights around the world ... The NDP say creating a Canadian envoy would mark a return to Canada's 'traditional role as an international defender of diversity and equal rights'" (*Huffington Post* 2015). Perhaps the point of this appeal was to speak to the Liberal Party's own pride in its human-rights record, as it too had supported homonational exportation of LGBT and other human rights (see Chapter 6 in this volume). When the Liberal Party announced its gender identity and expression bill, the NDP used the occasion to reinforce its own commitment to exporting LGBT rights:

> This tireless advocacy comes to fruition today, as we applaud the proposed inclusion of gender identity to the Canadian Human Rights Code, and to the hate crimes section of the Criminal Code. This legislation was proposed most recently in the last Parliament by my colleague MP Randall Garrison and we are pleased that the Government has chosen to introduce it today. And yet, there is still so much to do here in Canada and abroad. There are still too many places

where discrimination, persecution and violence against members of the LGBTQ community are practiced with impunity. (New Democratic Party 2016)

NDP MPs attached their discussion of trans rights and international LGBT rights as they cited only the two issues in many of their public documents, and as they finally used the forthcoming granting of trans rights to further justify intervention in LGBT issues overseas. In doing so, the NDP defined inclusion in the CHRA and the Criminal Code as the most important trans issue; used the trans community to applaud its own LGBT record; entrenched most discussion of LGBT issues, both domestic and foreign, in the liberal values of diversity and equality; and contributed to the silencing of voices, both domestic and international, that sought different, community-based solutions to their intersectional LGBTQ issues.

Conclusion

Since its creation in 1961, the NDP has seen LGBT issues in terms of economic equality, liberal rights, and homonationalism, all while engaging in incremental change through formal political and social institutions. The relationship between the NDP and LGBT people and movements was sometimes tense, as both sides struggled to attain their goals, be it gaining votes or liberal rights, while seeking support and compromise from the other. As the party courted various movements throughout its history, it made connections to all parts of the movements – radicals included. For their part, many radical activists, who often hesitate to engage in party politics for fear of compromising their goals, put their faith in the NDP, only to see the party take up mainstream, liberal issues and perspectives. Still, the NDP was the first major party to support LGBT people and issues, a stance that helped to open up space in federal politics, to the point where other parties were compelled to engage with LGBT issues to varying degrees. All three major parties have courted mainstream LGBT voters. By adhering to the mandate of such voters, they can claim to support the LGBT community while incurring relatively little political risk. The NDP pushed for trans rights, but the Liberal government ultimately passed the relevant bill. The NDP has focused on LGBT rights internationally but so have the Conservatives and Liberals, albeit for different reasons. In this changing political landscape, where mainstream LGBT politics are ever-more supported by the major parties, and LGBT issues are barometers for the human-rights support of countries and parties, I suggest that the NDP may find itself called to abandon homonational politics; to acknowledge the radical, grassroots, and intersectional complexity of Canada's LGBTQ people and movements; and to fight for the current needs of marginalized LGBTQ people.

Notes

1. Throughout this chapter, I shift between "LGB," "LGBT," "LGBTQ," "GLBT," and other acronyms to refer to various organizations and communities. I have respected the identification that they use to describe themselves. If they had not selected one, I chose a description that seem to best suit their politics, location, and time period.
2. Although an analysis of the provincial and federal New Democratic Parties would be a valuable endeavour, I examine the federal NDP for several reasons. First, it is problematic to compare the federal NDP, which has never been in power, to provincial NDP governments, which have. Second, the federal NDP offers a substantive history of engagement with LGBT communities, movement, and issues, which has been insufficiently studied by scholars. Third, I have focused on the federal NDP because of limitations of space but also to achieve consistency with the other chapters in this volume, which deal largely with the federal Liberal and Conservative Parties.
3. The Waffle group was relatively successful as it influenced the NDP to support anti-imperialism, Quebec sovereignty, and women's rights within the party and in Parliament (Markle and Beuhler 2016).
4. At that time, none of the major federal parties expressed any support for transgender people.
5. Employing these criteria, I collected and analyzed fifty-four party documents. They were pulled from both archived and active websites of the party and research institutions, predominantly the Poltext project at Université Laval.
6. Trans activists and organizations suggest that gender identity and expression differ from each other, as the former refers to how individuals understand their gender, and the latter refers to how they present it, through appearance, actions, speech, name, and use of pronouns. The Ontario Human Rights Commission (2016) argues that trans and gender-non-conforming people experience discrimination and violence on the basis of both their identity and their expression.
7. Although the NDP has a relatively strong history of supporting the nomination of gay and lesbian candidates, its record for supporting and fielding trans candidates is weak. In the 2007 federal election, Micheline Anne Montreuil became the first trans person to be nominated as a candidate for a major political party, when she ran for the NDP in a Quebec City riding. However, the party removed her from the nomination, claiming that she was too controversial (Houston 2011). As reported by *Xtra* News, Montreuil stated that she was dropped because of her gender identity: "I was a very attractive candidate when I was chosen to run for the NDP but now, nine months later, I have lost all of my sex appeal" (Rau 2008). As of the 2015 general election, no trans person had been nominated as a candidate for a major party or won a federal seat, meaning that trans people remained represented by cisgender people.

References

Baglow, John. 2015. "Senate Tramples Transgender Rights." *Toronto Star*, July 7. http://www.thestar.com/opinion/commentary/2015/07/07/senate-tramples-transgender-rights.html.

Canadian Centre for Gender and Sexual Diversity. 2015. "Federal Election Survey 2015." Canadian Centre for Gender and Sexual Diversity. http://ccgsd-ccdgs.org/wp-content/uploads/2015/09/LGBTQ-Election-Survey.pdf.

Canadian Lesbian and Gay Archives. 1997. "Victories and Defeats: A Gay and Lesbian Chronology 1964–1982." Canadian Lesbian and Gay Archives. https://arquives.andornot.com/en/list?q=A+Gay+and+Lesbian+Chronology+1964-1982&p=1&ps=20.

CBC News. 2012. "Timeline: Same-Sex Rights in Canada." *CBC News*, January 12. http://www.cbc.ca/news/canada/timeline-same-sex-rights-in-canada-1.1147516.

Cofounders of the New Politics Initiative. 2011. "The New Politics Initiative Vision Statement of 2001: Open, Sustainable, Democratic." *Rabble.ca*. November 28. http://rabble.ca/news/2011/11/new-politics-initiative-vision-statement-2001-open-sustainable-democratic.

Declaration of Montreal. 2006. "Declaration of Montreal on LGBT Human Rights." http://www.declarationofmontreal.org/.

Dehaas, Josh. 2015. "LGBTQ Community Hopes for More Representation in Next Parliament." *CTV News*, August 29. http://www.ctvnews.ca/politics/lgbtq-community-hopes-for-more-representation-in-next-parliament-1.2538037.

Everitt, Joanna. 2015. "Gender and Sexual Diversity in Provincial Election Campaigns." *Canadian Political Science Review* 9 (1): 177–92.

Everitt, Joanna, and Michael Camp. 2014. "In versus Out: LGBT Politicians in Canada." *Journal of Canadian Studies* 48 (1): 226–51. https://doi.org/10.3138/jcs.48.1.226.

Farney, James. 2009. "The Personal Is Not Political: The Progressive Conservative Response to Social Issues." *American Review of Canadian Studies* 39 (3): 242–52. https://doi.org/10.1080/02722010903146076.

–. 2012. *Social Conservatives and Party Politics in Canada and the United States*. Toronto: University of Toronto Press.

Gaucher, Megan, and Alexa DeGagne. 2016. "Guilty Until Proven Prosecuted: The Canadian State's Assessment of Sexual Minority Refugee Claimants and the Invisibility of the Non-Western Sexual Non-Citizen." *Social Politics: International Studies in Gender, State and Society* 23 (3): 459–81. https://doi.org/10.1093/sp/jxu029.

Government of Canada. 2016. "Bill C-16: An Act to amend the Canadian Human Rights Act and the Criminal Code." Parliament of Canada. https://openparliament.ca/bills/42-1/C-16/.

Guidotto, Nadia. 2011. "Looking Back: The Bathhouse Raids in Toronto, 1981." In *Captive Genders: Trans Embodiment and the Prison Industrial Complex*, ed. Eric A. Stanley and Nat Smith, 63–76. Edinburgh: AK Press.

Hooper, Thomas. 2014. "'More than Two Is a Crowd': Mononormativity and Gross Indecency in the Criminal Code, 1981–82." *Journal of Canadian Studies* 48 (1): 43–81. https://doi.org/10.3138/jcs.48.1.53.

Houston, Andrea. 2011. "Trans Candidate Makes Canadian History in Ontario." *Xtra*. September 27. http://www.dailyxtra.com/toronto/news-and-ideas/news/trans-candidate-makes-canadian-history-in-ontario-4749.

Huffington Post. 2015. "NDP to Stephane Dion: Liberals Should Create Envoy to Promote LGBTQ Rights." *Huffington Post*, November-December. http://www.huffingtonpost.ca/2015/12/11/ndp-ask-liberals-to-create-special-envoy-to-promote-lgbtq-rights-around-globe_n_8776250.html.

Ibbitson, John. 2016. "Canada's Swift Shift from Criminality to Acceptance of Homosexuality." *Globe and Mail*, March 1. http://www.theglobeandmail.com/news/politics/canadas-swift-shift-from-criminality-to-acceptance-of-homosexuality/article28990634/.

Kinsman, Gary, and Patrizia Gentile. 2010. *The Canadian War on Queers*. Vancouver: UBC Press.

Laycock, David. 2014. "Conceptual Foundations of Continuity and Change in NDP Ideology." In *Reviving Social Democracy: The Near Death and Surprising Rise of the Federal NDP*, ed. David Laycock and Lynda Erickson, 109–39. Vancouver: UBC Press.

Laycock, David, and Lynda Erickson. 2014a. "Future Scenarios: NDP Evolution and Party System Change." In *Reviving Social Democracy: The Near Death and Surprising*

Rise of the Federal NDP, ed. David Laycock and Lynda Erickson, 299–321. Vancouver: UBC Press.

—. 2014b. "Modernizing the Party." In *Reviving Social Democracy: The Near Death and Surprising Rise of the Federal NDP*, ed. David Laycock and Lynda Erickson, 84–108. Vancouver: UBC Press.

Markle, Tristan, and Sarah Beuhler. 2016. "NDP Must Connect with Social Movements to Prevent History from Repeating." *Rabble.ca*. February 12. http://rabble.ca/news/2016/02/ndp-must-connect-social-movements-to-prevent-history-repeating.

Mas, Susana. 2016. "Transgender Canadians Should 'Feel Free and Safe' to Be Themselves under New Liberal Bill." *CBC News*, May 17. http://www.cbc.ca/news/politics/transgender-bill-trudeau-government-1.3585522.

New Democratic Party. 1997. "Election Platform: A Framework for Canada's Future." New Democratic Party of Canada. https://www.poltext.org/sites/poltext.org/files/plateformes/can2000ndp_plt_en._14112008_173645.pdf.

—. 2000. "The NDP Commitment to Canadians." New Democratic Party of Canada. https://www.poltext.org/sites/poltext.org/files/plateformes/can2004ndp_plt_en.14112008_173645.pdf.

—. 2004. "NDP: New Energy. Positive Choice Platform 2004." New Democratic Party of Canada. https://www.poltext.org/sites/poltext.org/files/plateformes/can2004ndp_plt_en._14112008_171856.pdf.

—. 2008. "Jack Layton and the New Democrats: A Prime Minister on Your Family's Side, for a Change: Platform 2008." New Democratic Party of Canada. https://www.poltext.org/sites/poltext.org/files/plateformes/can2008ndp_plt_eng._14112008_160417.pdf.

—. 2009a. "New Democrats Attend World Outgames and LGBTT Rights Conference." Press release, New Democratic Party of Canada, July 28. http://wayback.archive-it.org/227/20091219002409/http://www.ndp.ca/press/new-democrats-attend-world-outgames-lgbtt-rights-conference.

—. 2009b. "New Democrats Mark International Trans Day of Remembrance." Press release, New Democratic Party of Canada, November 20. http://wayback.archive-it.org/227/20091218204306/http://www.ndp.ca/press/new-democrats-marks-international-trans-day-remembrance.

—. 2010a. "Statement on Pride by Bill Siksay, NDP Critic, Gay, Lesbian, Bisexual, Transgender and Transsexual Issues." New Democratic Party of Canada. June 29. http://wayback.archive-it.org/227/20100803165502/http://www.ndp.ca/press/statement-on-pride-by-bill-siksay-ndp-critic-gay-lesbian-bisexual-transgender-transsexual-issu.

—. 2010b. "Our Vision for Canada." New Democratic Party of Canada. http://wayback.archive-it.org/227/20100803161554/http://www.ndp.ca/vision/rights-and-heritage.

—. 2011a. "Giving Your Family a Break: Practical First Steps." New Democratic Party of Canada. https://www.poltext.org/sites/poltext.org/files/plateformes/can2011ndp_plt_en_12072011_114905.pdf.

—. 2011b. "Statement from New Democrat Leader Jack Layton on Pride." New Democratic Party of Canada. June 30. http://wayback.archive-it.org/227/20111103222652/http://www.ndp.ca/press/statement-from-new-democrat-leader-jack-layton-on-pride.

—. 2012. "Garrison Criticizes Anders' Petition against the Gender Identity Bill." New Democratic Party of Canada. October 5. http://www.ndp.ca/news/garrison-criticizes-anders-petition-against-gender-identity-bill.

—. 2013. "NDP Supports LGBT Equality in India." New Democratic Party of Canada. December 12. http://www.ndp.ca/news/ndp-supports-lgbt-equality-india.

—. 2014a. "New Democrats Release Gay Agenda for Pride Season." New Democratic Party of Canada. June 18. http://www.ndp.ca/news/new-democrats-release-gay-agenda-pride-season.

–. 2014b. "Statement by the Official Opposition on the International Day against Homophobia and Transphobia." New Democratic Party of Canada. May 17. http://wayback.archive-it.org/227/20141107104103/http://www.ndp.ca/news/statement-official-opposition-international-day-against-homophobia-and-transphobia.

–. 2015a. "Building the Country of Our Dreams: Tom Mulcair's Plan to Bring Change to Ottawa." New Democratic Party of Canada. https://www.poltext.org/sites/poltext.org/files/plateformes/can_ndp_2015_plt_en.pdf.

–. 2015b. "Our Gay Agenda Petition." New Democratic Party of Canada. http://petition.ndp.ca/LGBTQ.

–. 2016. "NDP Statement on the International Day against Homophobia and Transphobia." New Democratic Party of Canada. May 17. http://www.ndp.ca/news/ndp-statement-international-day-against-homophobia-and-transphobia.

Ontario Human Rights Commission. 2016. "Gender Identity and Gender Expression (Brochure)." Ontario Human Rights Commission. http://www.ohrc.on.ca/en/gender-identity-and-gender-expression-brochure.

Parliament of Canada. 2015. "Private Member's Bill: C-279: An Act to amend the Canadian Human Rights Act and the Criminal Code (gender identity)." LEGISinfo. https://www.parl.gc.ca/Legisinfo/BillDetails.aspx?Language=E&Mode=1&billId=5122660.

Perrella, Andrea, Steven Brown, and Barry Kay. 2012. "Voting Behaviour among the Gay, Lesbian, Bisexual and Transgendered Electorate." *Canadian Journal of Political Science* 45 (1): 89–117. https://doi.org/10.1017/s000842391100093x.

Rau, Krishna. 2008. "NDP Not so Queer-Friendly: Party Has History of Double-Crosses." *Xtra*, September 15. http://www.dailyxtra.com/canada/news-and-ideas/news/ndp-queer-friendly-53109.

Rayside, David, and Clyde Wilcox. 2011. "The Difference That a Border Makes: The Political Intersections of Sexuality and Religion on Canada and the United States." In *Faith, Politics, and Sexual Diversity in Canada and the United States*, ed. David Rayside and Clyde Wilcox, 3–25. Vancouver: UBC Press.

Smith, Miriam. 2010. "Federalism and LGBT Rights in the US and Canada: A Comparative Policy Analysis." In *Federalism, Feminism and Multilevel Governance*, ed. Melissa Haussman, Marian Sawer, and Jill Vickers, 97–110. Farnham, UK: Ashgate.

Stanford, Jim. 2011. "The History of the New Politics Initiative: Movement and Party, Then and Now." *Rabble.ca*. November 29. http://rabble.ca/news/2011/11/history-npi-movement-and-party-then-and-now.

Toronto Life. 2016. "The 10 Biggest Moments in LGBT Toronto in the Last 50 Years." *Toronto Life*, July 4. http://torontolife.com/city/life/top-10-moments-in-toronto-lgbt/.

Troster, Ariel. 2011. "Unlikely Bedfellows: The Harper Government and Homonationalism." Major research paper, University of Ottawa.

Urquart, Ian. 1976. "The NDP Out of Season." *Maclean's*, November 29, 47–50.

Vipond, Evan. 2015. "Trans Rights Will Not Protect Us: The Limits of Equal Rights Discourse, Anti-Discrimination Laws, and Hate Crime Legislation." *Western Journal of Legal Studies* 6 (1): 1–20.

Waite, Brian, and Cheri DiNovo. 1971. "We Demand." *Body Politic* 1 (November–December): 6–7.

Warner, Tom. 2002. *Never Going Back: A History of Queer Activism in Canada*. Toronto: University of Toronto Press.

8
Representation
The Case of LGBTQ People

Manon Tremblay

IN JUNE 2016, Stéphanie Vallée, the Quebec minister of justice and minister responsible for the fight against homophobia and transphobia, declared that the lack of sexual diversity in the Liberal caucus was not a problem.[1] As she explained, "We do not need to be from the community to be for the community" (Richer 2016, my translation) – a statement that I found deeply offensive. In other words, in Vallée's view lesbians and gays can be satisfactorily represented by proxy through heterosexual allies in government and the legislative caucus, and by LGBTQ people who are present "in the party's bodies ... the ministers' offices ... the PLQ [Parti libéral du Québec] youth commission" (Richer 2016, my translation).[2] Her claim raises fundamental questions concerning the political representation of LGBTQ people: Do there have to be lesbians and gays in politics to represent lesbians and gays? If the answer is yes, why is their presence necessary and why can't this role be delegated to persons who are (or call themselves) allies? Can these allies represent lesbians and gays? If they can, what are the implications with regard to their sexual citizenship? And beyond the issue of "who," Vallée's statement raises broader questions about the representation of LGBTQ people: "where," "how," "what," and "when."

These questions emerge from rich reflections regarding the political representation of women. For example, Karen Celis and her colleagues (2008) maintain that the parameters that framed reflections on substantive representation of women had to be rethought, notably that it was performed by women in legislative spaces, that it was motivated by clearly defined "women's interests," and that it gave rise to public decisions and policies. Celis et al. argue for a broadening, even an explosion, of this frame – in other words, they suggest that the "how," "what," "when," "where," and "who" of women's political representation should be revisited. Maria Escobar-Lemmon and Michelle Taylor-Robinson (2014) examine several aspects of these questions. At the end of their essay, they launch an invitation: "Lessons learned in this volume about the importance of how women's interests are defined and measured, that representation occurs on different women's issues in different venues and by different strategies, can provide a useful base for the study of representation of other historically under-represented groups" (ibid., 246).

In this chapter, keeping in mind the legacy of research on women in politics, I reflect on the representation of lesbians and gays in light of the five queries listed above, which, far from being distinct, overlap on the analytic level. My guiding idea – which may be seen as provocative – is that lesbian and gay politicians are best qualified to represent lesbians and gays, from the descriptive, symbolic, and substantive points of view. That is, although the support of straight allies is indispensable, only out (and proud) lesbian and gay politicians can descriptively and symbolically represent LGBTQ people, and in terms of substantive representation, only they have the legitimacy to perform a politics of emotion with regard to LGBTQ representation.

This raises the question of how to interpret "emotion." Defining it is not easy, and its meaning varies depending on the theoretical perspective through which it is viewed: biological, health-related, psychological and psychoanalytical, behavioural, socio-cultural, and so on. My objective is to speculate on the role of emotions in LGBTQ representative performance, and I understand "emotion" from a socio-cultural and interactionist approach that theorizes it as culturally and socially constructed (Ahmed 2014). This approach pays attention to the rules (social, cultural, and political) that govern the expression of emotions, their management by those who display and witness them, and their socio-cultural and political assessment. In this perspective, emotions are located in time and space, and are shaped by social roles. Thus, although an out lesbian politician may express her proudness by dancing as she marches in the Pride Parade, she must refrain from such exuberance when sitting in a highly disciplined place such as a legislative assembly. In that environment, she must express her emotions more discreetly and subtly – which does not mean less efficiently.

In what is probably the most thorough research on emotions and LGBTQ politics, Deborah Gould (2009, 20) states that "an emotion is one's personal expression of what one is feeling in a given moment, an expression that is structured by social convention, by culture." Yet, despite this resolutely social constructionist and interactionist approach, Gould (2009, 441) recognizes that emotions are not defined solely by social environment but also encompass biological dimensions – what she calls "affect": "the non-conscious, noncognitive, nonlinguistic components of our feelings ... the visceral and bodily components of politics." She goes so far as to argue that "the *movement* in 'social movements' gestures toward the realm of affect; bodily intensities; emotions, feelings, and passions; and toward uprising" (Gould 2009, 3, emphasis in original). Emotions are intrinsic to social movements and eminently political, for they help to instigate involvement in political activism, to manufacture counter-hegemonic historical and political narratives, and to build identities, among other things. Far from escaping this rule, the LGBTQ movement exemplifies it.

Although long ignored, the role of emotions in social movements is better recognized today (see, among others, Flam and King 2005; Goodwin, Jasper, and Polletta 2001b; Jasper 1998). Emotions are also at the heart of social-movement politics and have been used tactically in the anti-abortion, anti-nuclear, environmental, and feminist movements, among others. The LGBTQ movement is no exception here; one of its annual pivotal events is based on an emotion: pride. In fact, the movement juggles with a wide range of emotions. Gould (2009), for instance, discusses the emotions (including anger, anxiety, despair, fear, indignation, and outrage) that fed into HIV/AIDS activism in the United States during the 1980s and 1990s. The present study falls within the research approach that not only recognizes the importance of emotions in examining social movements, but sees them as a strategic resource available to LGBTQ politicians to represent LGBTQ interests. As Jeff Goodwin, James Jasper, and Francesca Polletta (2001a, 9) put it, "Emotions can be strategically used by activists *and* be the basis for strategic thought" (emphasis in original). The objective of this chapter is not, however, to establish whether LGBTQ politicians effectively use emotions strategically, but to reflect on the role of emotions in their representative performance. Of course, straight allies may also deploy emotional performances with regard to LGBTQ issues, as Prime Minister Justin Trudeau eloquently did by manifesting much joy when he appeared at Gay Pride events and by expressing his indignation regarding the discrimination that still targets LGBTQ people in Canada. As important as his performance was, however, it does not confer the legitimacy brought by life experiences of marginalization and exclusion. Only LGBTQ politicians hold this capital of legitimacy, which flows from their life experiences, and only they can mobilize emotions to legitimize their representative performance of LGBTQ interests.[3]

Where?

Since the 1990s, political science has become much more diversified and much more complex. "Classic" theories (structuralist, functionalist, systemic, and company) have been enriched by other approaches – such as post-structuralist, constructivist, and critical. The field of political representation did not escape this upheaval. Thus, though political representation has long been viewed as the purview of parliaments, authors have noted that it might be deployed outside of the political (and even the state) arena and could be performed by individual actors and unelected collectives. Michael Saward (2006) gives the example of the singer Bono, who has declared that he represents people in Africa who have no voice at all. The union movement is said to represent workers; the feminist movement, women; and the LGBTQ movement, LGBTQ people (at least, some of them).

Here, I look mainly at the state aspect of representation, notably the role of lesbian and gay politicians with respect to LGBTQ people. This focus should not be interpreted as a denial of the role played by the LGBTQ movement in representation of LGBTQ people. In fact, it is difficult to imagine that lesbian and gay politicians could represent LGBTQ people and ignore the LGBTQ movement. What remains to be understood is the nature of the relations between lesbian and gay politicians and the LGBTQ movement. Who is responsible for this role of representation? There are various possibilities: people endowed with a strong "LGBTQ social capital" positioned between the state (notably the parliamentary space) and the movement (beyond the legislature's walls); politicians such as Manon Massé in Quebec provincial politics, or Réal Ménard and Svend Robinson in federal politics; or even unelected LGBTQ people who operate in legislative or non-legislative spaces such as "the party's bodies ... the ministers' offices ... the PLQ youth commission," as minister Vallée said (Richer 2016).[4] Or are such roles forged by collective actors, positioned in the gap between legislative and non-legislative spaces? These actors include LGBTQ interest groups (such as Egale Canada and Queer Ontario) and, especially, political parties (to which all elected LGBTQ individuals belong), whose purpose, among other things, is precisely to establish a bridge between the state and civil societies. And what are the roles, successes, and failures of intra-party LGBTQ caucuses, hybrid social-movement organizations that behave like pressure groups within political parties? Although relationships between parties and movements are diversified and complex, some research conducted outside of Canada shows that being in a relationship with a political party is fraught with dangers for a social-movement organization (such as an LGBTQ group) and does not always bring the expected gains (de la Dehesa 2010; Green 2000; Marsiaj 2006; Tobin 1988).

Who?

The "who" corresponds to what Hanna Pitkin (1967) calls descriptive representation: representation depends on presence. It is not neutral: it carries ideas and generates emotions (Lombardo and Meier 2014, 19–38). In this respect, it has a symbolic dimension: the meaning of presence is revealed in the light of ideas and emotions. For example, when Barack Obama was elected in the United States, some saw this as another step in the long march of black Americans toward equality, and many African Americans felt proud. In parades through the streets of Western cities, "LGBTQ pride" manifests a colourful and festive presence on behalf of a value that is pivotal to liberal democracies: equality.

Descriptive representation is divided into collective and individual aspects. At the collective level, it suggests that the demographic makeup of representatives as a group should mirror that of the represented. This argument was the impetus for proposals to redraw the electoral map in Los Angeles, New York, Philadelphia, and San Francisco to facilitate the representation of LGBTQ people (Hertzog 1996, 12). In the debates surrounding the creation of a lesbian and gay electoral district in Manhattan in 1991, the large-circulation lesbian and gay magazine *Outweek* stated "that since lesbians and gay men constituted 10% of New York's population, they deserved at least five [of the fifty-one] seats on the City Council" (Rosenblum 1996, 139n113; see also Chapter 1 in this volume). What voting system would best achieve a proportionate level of representation for the LGBT population? Currently, there is no clear-cut answer to this question, as Andrew Reynolds's (2013) observations reveal. On the one hand, first-past-the-post systems may contribute to the election of minority candidates when they are geographically concentrated. The success of the Bloc Québécois in the 1990s and 2000s is illustrative here. On the other hand, proportional voting systems favour the election of minority candidates if they are placed in eligible positions on lists. It is also possible that a preferential vote contributes to the election of LGBTQ candidates because of its appeal to group identity, encouraging like-minded groups to form alliances. In Chapter 4 of this volume, Dennis Pilon argues that proportional voting systems, more than majoritarian systems, encourage the election of LGBTQ candidates. In short, research remains to be done on the role of voting systems in the election of lesbians and gays.

Considered from an individual point of view, descriptive representation is focused on persons – essentially, their identity. This reading postulates that presence counts: black people are best to represent black people, and women, women (Mansbridge 1999). Similarly, lesbians and gays are better than non-LGBTQ people at representing lesbians and gays (and, as we shall see, out lesbian and gay politicians are better than their closeted counterparts). But why is this so? A number of theorists have answered this delicate question.

Anne Phillips (1995), who has inspired a number of studies on political representation of women, maintains that fair representation of historically marginalized groups necessitates their presence in politics, of course, but also the expression of their ideas. Indeed, life experiences mould ideas, and access to parliamentary spaces offers people from such groups a public arena where their voices can be heard. Interactions between these new political actors and those who are already in place encourages the transformation of democratic deliberations and the process of making public decisions. That said, Phillips (1995, 48–56, 82–83, 163–64) emphasizes that although presence in electoral institutions does not guarantee political representation in terms of ideas and actions, an enhanced process of substantial representation may be triggered – notably in terms of role model effects exerted by the representatives of minority groups and emotional work performed by historically marginalized citizens.

According to Melissa Williams (1998), representation of historically marginalized groups calls upon weighty mechanisms such as identification and trust – which involve emotions. Like Phillips (1995), Williams (1998) believes that the shared experience of being sidelined generates specific perspectives that the people from the sidelined groups are best able to express and convey. This is also the position of Iris Marion Young (2000, 143–44): "To the extent that what distinguishes social groups is structural relations, particularly structural relations of privilege and disadvantage, and to the extent that persons are positioned similarly in those structures, then they have similar perspectives both on their own situation and on other positions in the society." In this perspective, Williams (1998) develops her reading of representation as a process of mediation that is destined, through voice, trust, and memory, to include what the past has excluded: representation as mediation must tend toward discussion rather than confrontation and must admit that the excluded will have the highest trust in representatives who resemble them, because of a shared identity that history (or memory) has shaped as Other. This reading of representation is imbued with emotions.

To the question, "Should blacks represent blacks and women represent women?" Jane Mansbridge (1999) answers "a contingent 'yes.'" She believes that in certain situations, historically marginalized groups will benefit from being represented by those who are similar to them and with whom they share experiences. This is the case, notably, when these groups do not trust the dominant class because of a past marked by oppression. It is also the case when the interests of a historically marginalized group are not clearly defined and written in the political agenda – which is certainly true for LGBTQ people (see the "What" section).

Suzanne Dovi (2002) pushes the argument one notch farther: although black people are best represented by black people, and women, women (and LGBTQ people, LGBTQ people), not all blacks or women (or lesbians and gays) are equally worthy of assuming this role. In Dovi's view, the "preferable descriptive representatives will have strong *mutual* relationships with *dispossessed subgroups*" (ibid., 735, emphasis in original). According to this approach, lesbian and gay politicians who have strong relationships not only with LGBTQ people but with deprived LGBTQ subgroups are better suited to represent LGBTQ people than are (privileged) lesbians and gays who do not have such relationships. Otherwise, it is possible that only the interests of the privileged people in a given minority will be represented.

A basic idea that emerges from these studies (and many others) is that historically marginalized groups share certain life experiences. These inspire perspectives that the members of these groups are best suited to articulate. Their experiences generate emotions that are pivotal to the mandate of representation. This idea was masterfully expressed by Harvey Milk in his Hope Speech, delivered in 1978 shortly before he was assassinated by a homophobe:

Why it is important that gay people run for office and that gay people get elected ... You see there is a major difference – and it remains a vital difference – between a friend and a gay person, a friend in office and a gay person in office. Gay people have been slandered nationwide. We've been tarred and we've been brushed with the picture of pornography. In Dade County, we were accused of child molestation. It's not enough anymore just to have friends represent us ... A gay person in office can set a tone, can command respect not only from the larger community, but from the young people in our own community who need both examples and hope ... The anger and the frustrations that some of us feel is because we are misunderstood, and friends can't feel that anger and frustration. They can sense it in us, but they can't feel it. Because a friend has never gone through what is known as coming out. I will never forget what it was like coming out and having nobody to look up toward. I remember the lack of hope – and our friends can't fulfill that ... I use the word "I" because I'm proud. I stand here tonight in front of my gay sisters, brothers and friends because I'm proud of you. I think it's time that we have many legislators who are gay and proud of that fact and do not have to remain in the closet. (Bull 2001, 165, 166, 167)

I have included this long excerpt because it links some of the theoretical elements mentioned above: Lesbians and gays constitute a historically marginalized group whose members must represent themselves. They cannot delegate the task to allies who have not encountered the ostracism that they themselves have experienced. Nor can closeted lesbians and gays assume this responsibility, as they cannot act on public opinion, offer models, or embody hope, thus reminding us that emotions lie at the heart of LGBTQ representation. In a word, Milk believed that lesbians and gays who were elected to office must be out and proud. I will briefly discuss each of these points.

It is relatively easy to demonstrate that lesbians and gays form a historically marginalized group. As Mark Hertzog (1996, 6) maintains, "No other group of persons in American society today, having been convicted of no crime, is subject to the number and severity of legally imposed disabilities as are persons of same-sex orientation." The same holds true for Canada (see, among others, Kinsman 1996; Millward 2015; Warner 2002).[5] Although this ostracism has been greatly attenuated, traces persist in the state and in society.[6] When all is said and done, society is immersed in a heterosexual culture (Tin 2012) that cannot help but ostracize lesbians and gays, revealing to them that they are sexual strangers (Phelan 2001).[7]

Milk emphasizes that out lesbian and gay politicians are better able to represent LGBTQ people than are allies or closeted LGBTQ politicians, but the contribution of allies to *substantive* representation (see below) of lesbians and gays cannot be ignored or minimized. Without the support of male allies, women would never have obtained the right to vote from legislative assemblies composed solely of men. Without the support of straight allies, lesbian and gay couples would never have obtained the right to civil marriage. However, although this support is fundamental, it does not give allies legitimacy to speak on behalf of lesbians and gays, because their bodies, their life paths, and their ideas do not bear the traces of ostracism that is linked to the fact of being lesbian or gay.

As for closeted LGBTQ politicians, though they may contribute (as do allies) to representation of lesbians and gays, their remaining in the closet is regrettable at best and damaging at worst. It is regrettable because they do not help to change public opinion (and its prejudices) with regard to LGBTQ people, they do not offer positive lesbian and gay models, and they do not embody hope. It is damaging because, in hiding from public view, they maintain the perception that being lesbian or gay is shameful, to the point that it must be concealed.

In Milk's view, lesbian and gay politicians must be out and proud. It is here, I think, that the symbolic aspect of descriptive representation is posed with the greatest force: presence becomes meaningful in the light of ideas and emotions. Being out and proud requires, at minimum, recognizing oneself as and accepting being lesbian or gay, living with one's head high and coming out of the closet, identifying broadly with LGBTQ communities, and seeing in them a source of individual and collective empowerment. This aspect of the equation calls upon group consciousness theories and, more specifically, identity politics theories. Although highly contested in the literature (Bernstein 2005), the notion of identity politics suggests a link between perceptions of discontent gleaned from personal experiences and political activism: it aims to transform these experiences into positive ones. One way to achieve this is to be a role model: indeed, to be present in politics as an out and proud LGBTQ person is a political act guided by ideas (such as rejecting shame and claiming equality), because it embodies a powerful, emotionally driven role model function.

In electoral and legislative politics, the role model function has been discussed mainly in terms of effectiveness, legitimacy, and identity and affinity. Symbolic representation feeds the idea that the election of a member of a minority group contributes to and is sufficient to that group's representation. For instance, the election of a first lesbian becomes symbolic of the proof that LGBTQ people can be elected and that their interests can be represented. Donald Haider-Markel (2010, 156) argues, "As a stigmatized minority, LGBT people – and especially LGBT youth – need role models who make it clear that the political process can be successfully engaged." The election of lesbians and gays not only sends the message that the institutional architecture offers them all of its opportunities, but can also consolidate the view that the political regime has positively responded to LGBTQ struggles for citizenship. Thus, it legitimizes the state's electoral and political institutions as effective in representing all, notwithstanding their socio-political capital. In other words, their presence sends the message that representative democracy works. Reflecting on Afro-descendant women in power in Latin America, Mala Htun (2014, 120) notes, "Merely by being present in power, they prevent people from ignoring or denying this inescapable reality of a diverse society and compel them to take it into account." There is no reason to believe that this does not apply to lesbians and gays in politics.

Symbolic representation also proceeds by identity and affinity – that is, the presence of lesbian and gay politicians might encourage a process of identification and a feeling of proximity between them and LGBTQ people, particularly when token representatives "are highly identified with their own social group" (Kanter 1977, 987). David Rayside (1998, 203) writes about Svend Robinson (the first openly gay MP in Canada), "None was more obviously identified with his candidacy [for leadership of the federal NDP in 1995] than the gay and lesbian movement." In the same vein, identity and affinity may encourage openly lesbian and gay representatives to have a role model effect on young LGBTQ people: "Openly gay and lesbian public officials may provide role models for lesbian and gay youth, a population that appears to be particularly vulnerable to the consequences of membership in this stigmatized group" (Golebiowska and Thomsen 1999, 193; see also Herrick and Thomas 2001). Identity and affinity may also mean overturning historical prejudices against lesbians and gays simply by educating others. In the most in-depth study conducted to date on the involvement of LGBTQ people in US electoral politics, Haider-Markel (2010, 115) states that "LGBT legislators believe that part of their representation role is simply to educate other legislators on LGBT issues. Part of this occurs simply through their presence in the institution." Donald Haider-Markel and Chelsie Bright (2014) make similar comments, and Andrew Reynolds (2013, 260) observes, "The new-found legislative presence and political viability feed into a climate of transformation of values ... There is strong evidence that, in general, heterosexuals become more supportive of gay rights when they know someone who is gay."

In short, from a descriptive and symbolic point of view, out and proud lesbian and gay politicians are best suited to represent LGBTQ people: they alone can embody the historical marginalization of lesbians and gays, and the role model effects of their presence within state power constitute a real strategy for reversing this past ostracism. They are also the best to perform their representational role via emotions.

How?

"How" corresponds to what Pitkin (1967, 114) calls substantive representation – that is, the activity of representation, "the substance or content of acting for others." This aspect comprises two facets: discursive and institutional. In terms of discourse, Pitkin (1967) sees in representation a performance involving a certain amount of creativity, even if it simply entails activities that define the interests of the represented. This idea of political representation as a creative performance has been explored further by Michael Saward (2006). He suggests that the agent (the one representing) is a claim-maker who puts forward a particular idea of the principal (the one represented). Seen in this way, representation is a creative discursive process of "claims-making" in virtue of which the represented and their interests are defined. Thus, for instance, claiming to represent LGBTQ people consists of depicting them in one way and not in another: "At the heart of the act of representing is the depicting of a constituency *as* this or that, as requiring this or that, as having this or that set of interests" (Saward 2006, 301, emphasis in original). Of course, these representative claims, to use Saward's (2006) terms, are not unlimited; they must be inscribed in the historical, cultural, and political opportunity structure of a given community. Above all, as Andrew Rehfeld (2006) stresses, they must be endorsed by the audiences for which they are intended – in the above example, LGBTQ people. In this, representation perceived as a creative discursive process calls upon emotions: representative claims must be shaped so that they find and capture the audiences to whom they are addressed. In this regard, Eline Severs (2012, 179) believes that "representative claims," which she renames "substantive claims," must contain a "substantive core; implying (i) the denunciation of a situation which is negative for the represented, (ii) the formulation of a proposal to improve the situation of the represented and (iii) the formulation of a right for the represented with the same intention." These claims are most likely to find and capture LGBTQ people if they are formulated by out and proud lesbian and gay politicians who position themselves as "critical voices and actors" of LGBTQ representation (Childs and Krook 2009).

I argue that lesbian and gay politicians possess an important asset that straight politicians do not share – their historically anchored experience of being marginalized because of their non-heteronormative sexuality. They can use this to denounce a situation that is negative for the represented or to formulate a proposal or a right to improve the situation. In the view of Phillips (1995), Mansbridge (1999), and Williams (1998), among others, marginalization inspires perspectives that only people who have experienced it can fully articulate. What is more, these experiences explain that the people who live them have unique perspectives on the representation of their group. Furthermore, they legitimize this representation as inscribed in an emotional setting: a lesbian politician speaks of lesbophobia with knowledge and emotion because she has lived through it. Erica Lenti (2015) illustrates this point on the role played by LGBTQ politicians when a bill banning conversion therapy was introduced in Ontario:

> The emotional connection and benefit of having openly queer politicians in government has made all the difference in Ontario. When NDP Parkdale-High Park MPP Cheri DiNovo, who identifies as queer, introduced a bill to ban LGBTQ conversion therapy, it passed with all-party support – despite the fact that it was a private members bill, which seldom become law. During the bill's second reading, openly gay premier Kathleen Wynne, along with other queer MPPs, shared their own coming-out stories and the importance of making the bill law. It was a show of solidarity from those who understand its effects best.

Although there are few out and proud lesbians and gays in politics, they have been "critical voices and actors" for LGBTQ representation by contesting hegemonic discourses and constructing alternative meanings "of what is appropriate, legitimate, authorised, and socially accepted" (Lombardo and Meier 2014, 46; see also Schmidt 2008 on discursive institutionalism). What is more, their discursive performance quickly overflowed the rigid borders that the formal rules of the electoral game reserve for representation to embrace the country as a whole: an out and proud lesbian or gay politician represents LGBTQ people in the entire country, not just those in her or his electoral riding. Svend Robinson represented lesbians and gays throughout Canada – not just those in his riding (see the Afterword in this volume). In this, he was not only a descriptive and symbolic representative for LGBTQ people, but also their surrogate representative – that is, a form of "representation by a representative with whom one has no electoral relationship" (Mansbridge 2003, 522; see also Rubenstein 2007). In his book on Svend Robinson, Graeme Truelove (2013, 133) states that after Robinson revealed that he was gay and proud of it, "thousands of gay Canadians found a hero in Parliament, and that second constituency of Canadians from across the country who saw Robinson as their unofficial MP grew even larger."

Surrogate representation may lead one to believe that political institutions do not matter, but this is not the case (Smith 2015). For instance, Haider-Markel (2010, 90) notes "that although many LGBT legislators may attempt to represent the interests of the LGBT community once elected, the institutional and political context in which they operate may limit or prohibit their opportunities to represent the interests of the LGBT community" (see also Haider-Markel and Bright 2014; Chapter 12 in this volume). Even so, political institutions are not straitjackets that impede all movement; they may be loose enough to allow for representation activities – at least, this is what we should understand from Haider-Markel's (2007, 107) observation that "higher LGBT representation in state legislatures leads to greater substantive representation" (see also Haider-Markel 2010, 118–28; Haider-Markel, Joslyn, and Kniss 2000; Reynolds 2013). What is more, Rebekah Herrick (2009) shows that lesbian and gay politicians are much more likely than non-LGBTQ legislators to substantively represent LGBTQ interests. Examples of representative activities performed by such legislators are denouncing situations of discrimination against lesbians and gays, presenting bills to promote LGBTQ rights, and, seconded by straight allies, working to defeat measures that are contrary to these rights or would slow their adoption (Herrick 2010).

Whereas the American regime of separation of powers confers great freedom on legislators to conduct their own representative agenda, the institutional framework of Canadian parliamentarism has proved much less generous in this regard. In fact, the fusion of legislative and executive powers in the parliamentary system forces the government to count on the support of a majority of MLAs or MPs to stay in power – a majority that it obtains by subjecting the members of its legislative caucus to party discipline. Thus, the executive-controlled Westminster parliamentary regime "creates considerable opportunity for change when the political executive is headed by favorably disposed leadership, and very little when it is not" (Rayside 1998, 108). For example, for various ideological and electoral reasons, the Canadian government was disposed to open civil marriage to same-sex couples; as a consequence, it had to adopt its bill rapidly, before those who opposed it could impede it through institutional means (Johnson and Tremblay 2018; Smith 2008; see Chapter 6 in this volume). The attempts to have sexual orientation added to the Canadian Human Rights Act as a prohibited ground for discrimination encountered many more obstacles (Rayside 1998, 105–39).

Nevertheless, elected lesbian and gay representatives have a wide range of means to advance LGBTQ interests. Rayside (1998, 179–211) identifies a number of these tools in his analysis of Svend Robinson's political career. On the strictly institutional level, lesbian and gay MPs may intervene in Parliament and on committees, make statements in Parliament, submit petitions, lobby ministers, arrange alliances with non-LGBTQ colleagues to promote an LGBTQ interest, or block measures that are hostile to LGBTQ rights. As parliamentarians, they may also form a bridge between the state and civil society: for example, they can encourage LGBTQ people to call upon their representative, denounce discrimination, complain to civil rights commissions, and participate in legislative processes of public consultation. They may also be allies of initiatives such as ProudPolitics, which is dedicated to increasing the political presence of LGBTQ people (see Chapter 11 in this volume). Because they are parliamentarians, lesbian and gay politicians benefit from media visibility, which they can use to represent LGBTQ people. Thus, they can make LGBTQ issues visible in the public space, inform the public of problems, and act as role models for the population and for their colleagues (in Chapter 3 of this volume, Mireille Lalancette and Manon Tremblay demonstrate that media coverage may have a considerable impact on role model effect).

These representative activities are mentioned in other studies (Haider-Markel 2010, 118–28; Herrick 2009, 2010; Reynolds 2013), but what remains a mystery is how they are deployed and adapted to the institutional framework of the political regime to enable the representation of LGBTQ interests by lesbian and gay politicians. For example, Rayside (1998, 193) writes that Svend Robinson "convinced Justice Minister John Crosbie that discrimination on the basis of sexual orientation should be included in the mandate [of the subcommittee inquiry into equality rights just as section 15 of the Charter was coming into force], in part on the strength of the open-ended wording of Section 15 which Robinson himself had originally pressed for." But *how* he did this is not disclosed. Rayside (1998, 109, 193) also writes that Robinson worked "behind the scenes" but, again, how? In fact, how can interests that have historically been marginalized, even repressed, by a political regime be served today by that regime? How is this institutional turnaround possible, and is it attributable to representation activities by lesbian and gay politicians or to other factors? We do not know precisely.

What?

The "what" refers to the object of representation. This difficult question about what is (claimed to be) represented has generated a very rich literature with regard to political representation of women. Most of the studies revealed the difficulty of thinking about "women's interests," because there is no unified subject called "woman" – in reality, women have very diversified living conditions that reflect their inclusion in systems of oppression that are similarly multiple and varied. As a consequence, it is simplistic to believe that a "universal interest" may cover all women (for an overview of these debates, see Smooth 2011).

I think these observations are very fertile when it comes to reflecting on the object of representation of LGBTQ people: What exactly is represented – and, as a consequence, who is represented and who isn't? LGBTQ people form no more unified a subject than does "woman": what has come to be called "sexual orientation" is a category of "Ls," "Gs," and "Bs," and the "gender identity" class of trans (transsexual and transgender) people. What is more, an intersectional analysis quickly reveals the diversity and cleavages that divide these "letters" from each other according to various regimes of oppression, such as social class, ethnicity or race, way of life, and normative or non-normative sexualities, among others. Finally, as Marc Stein (2012, 5–9) notes, many hierarchies tear through the LGBT alphabet: many "Ls" feel that the "Gs" take too much (all of the?) physical and protest space, which has prompted a number of "Ls" to slam the door in the face of the "Gs" to found their own groups (feminist, radical, or separatist lesbians; see Podmore and Tremblay 2015). In addition, lesbian and gay communities are not free of biphobia and transphobia (Weiss 2011).

Like women, LGBTQ people have highly varied living conditions. As a consequence, it is possible that "LGBTQ interests," to paraphrase studies on the political representation of women, benefit from unequal representation by LGBTQ politicians. In other words, certain LGBTQ interests may be better expressed than others in the legislative space of political representation.[8] Perhaps this is because what Pitkin (1967, 38–59) calls formal representation (that which passes through state institutions such as Parliament, the public administration, and the courts) lends itself only to the defence of certain questions (and therefore certain LGBTQ people) – those that can be digested by state logic. In Canada, the civil rights charters – federal, provincial, territorial – have proved powerful assets to the representation of LGBTQ interests. For example, they have protected LGBTQ people against discrimination and have conferred upon them equality rights such as access to civil marriage and full assumption of their parental roles (Rayside 2008, 167–91; Smith 2007, 2013). Certain critical voices have claimed that this form of representation is inscribed in a process of homonormalization of lesbians and gays: "The normal lesbian/gay citizen ... is in the process of being materialized primarily through an adherence to dominant intimate norms coded as heterosexual and monogamous. It is 'the couple,' within a particular domesticated setting, that has become the rights-bearing subject of lesbian and gay claims to citizenship" (Richardson and Monro 2012, 81). In this context, what becomes of representation of the LGBTQ people who reject the prison of coupledom? Aside from reaching very few people on the LGBTQ fringe, does this form of representation based on assimilation with a neoliberal heterosexual lifestyle further marginalize those who resist homonormalization? What becomes of the representation of LGBTQ interests that are less socially acceptable and politically profitable – lesbian and gay S/M sex (Khan 2014) or intergenerational lesbian or gay relations (Paternotte 2014)? Dovi (2002) argues that the "preferable" lesbian and gay representatives are those who maintain links with the most deprived subgroups of the LGBTQ movement, so that "LGBTQ interests" do not become synonymous with "privileged LGBTQ interests."

In the end, the legislative representation of "LGBTQ interests" seems to encounter the same pitfalls as does the representation of "women's interests" or of other minorities: political representation is an elitist and normalizing process that does not reach out well to phenomena on the margin, thus perhaps reinforcing the exclusion of the excluded. This is even more true when the time span of representation is very restricted.

When?

"When" refers to the legislative phase of public decision making. At what point in this process, at either the executive phase (cabinet and administration) or the legislative phase (in Parliament), can lesbian and gay politicians intervene to represent LGBTQ people? If they are ministers, when can they express their substantive representative claims to support LGBTQ interests (for example, during work in cabinet committees)? If they are not ministers, can they make themselves heard when a public policy is being formulated in cabinet – especially if they do not belong to the party in power? If they are backbenchers, can they make their claims known during parliamentary debates or when bills are being studied in parliamentary committees? To refer again to MP Svend Robinson, if it is not clear *how* he "convinced" Justice Minister John Crosbie and "pressed for," it is no clearer *when* he did so. Rayside (1998, 109, 193) states that Robinson worked "behind the scenes," but again, when (and how) did he do that? What about during the weekly parliamentary caucus, the preview to the legislative process, in which lesbian and gay MPs may represent LGBTQ people? These are subjects for future research.

Conclusion

In this chapter, I have reflected on the representational role of lesbian and gay politicians in Canada, suggesting that they are best equipped to represent LGBTQ people because they alone have the legitimacy to do so. Of course, heteronormative allies can contribute here, but they lack the necessary emotions – the anger and frustration that only LGBTQ people can feel, to paraphrase Harvey Milk.

Although I stressed the role of emotions, whether LGBTQ politicians use them strategically during their representative performance remains to be explored. In this sense, the notion of emotional management (Jasper 1998) offers fertile heuristic potential. Do LGBTQ politicians use emotions consciously (and therefore strategically) to represent LGBTQ interests? If they do, what are they hoping to achieve? How do they select the emotions and according to what criteria? Does their choice vary depending on their audience? How do they assess the impact of their performance, as well as its success or failure?

This chapter focuses on LGBTQ politicians, but other research should consider representation from the point of view of LGBTQ people. As the section titled "What?" reveals, they and their communities are diverse. They are subject to various regimes of oppression, resulting in both shared and opposing interests. Thus, representing LGBTQ people and communities entails structural relations of privilege and disadvantage: it may mean further excluding LGBTQ people from representation, especially the most "dispossessed subgroups," to use Dovi's (2002) expression. Such exclusion was masterfully rendered on the screen by director Robin Campillo in *BPM (Beats per Minute)*, a film dealing with AIDS and, more precisely, with the neglect of the French state (like many other Western states) to address the pandemic. The anger and frustration that Milk spoke about are not evenly distributed among LGBTQ people and communities: some LGBTQ people are angrier and more frustrated than others. Perhaps LGBTQ politicians do not address the concerns of LGBTQ people who are most in need because they are unaware of their existence, or because they do not want to be associated with what they see as "hot-potato issues," or because by their very nature the most deprived social groups have difficulty expressing their concerns to the powerful and being heard by them. Many LGBTQ people may be unimpressed by out LGBTQ politicians or may not trust them. It is also possible that they simply do not recognize themselves in their LGBTQ representatives.[9] Much research needs to be done on how LGBTQ people perceive LGBTQ politicians, whether they feel represented by those individuals, and what emotions they arouse in them.

What is certain is that the good intentions expressed by Stéphanie Vallée with regard to representation of LGBTQ people can, in no way, be substituted for the strong emotions of pride hammered out by the LGBTQ movement as an antidote to the anger and frustration experienced daily by lesbians and gays, or for the hope sought by Milk. The transition from childhood to adulthood is marked when children achieve the capacity to speak on their own behalf and by the willingness of their parents to let them do so. As long as allies represent lesbians and gays by proxy, lesbians and gays will remain minors who are refused full citizenship.

Notes

1 The words "homophobia" and "transphobia" indicate that the government's stance is still in the realm of negative rights: "to fight against."
2 This chapter discusses lesbians and gays specifically, rather than LGBTQ people, for three reasons. First, the few studies on LGBTQ people and political representation deal essentially with lesbians and gays, and the other components of the initialism are ignored or mentioned only in passing. Second, at least in Canada, there are no sustained public bisexual mobilizations that demand political representation. Finally, in recent years, trans people have been gaining autonomy with regard to political representation

and have distanced themselves from the LGBT movement. That said, I use "lesbians and gays" and "LGBTQ people" synonymously.
3 One may assert that lesbian and gay politicians cannot necessarily represent bisexual and trans people. This is a compelling argument. Its rebuttal would be that lesbians, gays, bisexuals, and trans people all share experiences of marginalization and exclusion based on their non-conformity with the heteronormative model, which gives them a capital of legitimacy for representing sexual minorities.
4 Here I am adapting the notion of "homosocial capital," as developed by Elin Bjarnegård (2013, 1–51), according to which people who resemble each other form networks that create essential capital for acceding to societal power.
5 Of course, lesbians and gays are certainly not the only historically marginalized group in Canada. Indigenous people, whose lands were stolen and culture stripped away, not to mention being sterilized and disenfranchised, carry a heavy legacy of marginalization. I am indebted to one of the anonymous reviewers for suggesting this important nuance.
6 For instance, in Canada, unlike in similar countries, the age of consent for heterosexual relations still differs from that for homosexual relations, preserving the long-lasting LGBTQ-phobic prejudice that lesbians and gays recruit, pervert, and abuse young people. In November 2016, the Trudeau government introduced Bill C-32 to remove section 159 from the Criminal Code, which sets out the unequal age of consent. However, as of November 2018, the bill was stalled in the legislative process of adoption. Another example: gay men are still banned from donating blood unless they have abstained from homosexual relations for one year, fuelling the prejudice that they are plague-ridden and a source of death because their blood is impure.
7 As I wrote these lines, I was listening to a Radio-Canada program that praised a novel about the love of a woman and a man. This was followed by a Céline Dion song, in which the singer is dying with love for a man. Next, I went to the convenience store and encountered a couple – a woman and a man – walking arm in arm. Heading home, I saw them again, kissing. When I got home, I poured myself a glass of milk – the container featured a picture of a smiling woman and man. As I read my newspaper onscreen, an ad popped up for eye surgery. It showed a woman and a man on a scooter, him driving and her behind, like a trophy wife – which is connected to laser surgery how? And all of this in less than an hour.
8 As is the case for "women's interests," defining "LGBTQ interests" is a contentious process and beyond the scope of this chapter.
9 It is worth mentioning that after recently analyzing the profile of out LGB MLAs and MPs, I discovered that a much higher proportion of them are married than is the case in the general LGBTQ population. I had to wonder if I felt represented by them, as I am single, and more importantly, I maintain a vitriolic critique of homonormative coupledom.

References

Ahmed, Sara. 2014. *The Cultural Politics of Emotion*. Edinburgh: Edinburgh University Press.
Bernstein, Mary. 2005. "Identity Politics." *Annual Review of Sociology* 31 (1): 47–74. https://doi.org/10.1146/annurev.soc.29.010202.100054
Bjarnegård, Elin. 2013. *Gender, Informal Institutions and Political Recruitment: Explaining Male Dominance in Parliamentary Representation*. Basingstoke, UK: Palgrave Macmillan.
Bull, Chris, ed. 2001. *Come Out Fighting: A Century of Essential Writing on Gay and Lesbian Liberation*. New York: Thunder's Mouth Press/Nation Books.

Celis, Karen, Sarah Childs, Johanna Kantola, and Mona Lena Krook. 2008. "Rethinking Women's Substantive Representation." *Representation* 44 (2): 99–110. https://doi.org/10.1080/00344890802079573

Childs, Sarah, and Mona Lena Krook. 2009. "Analysing Women's Substantive Representation: From Critical Mass to Critical Actors." *Government and Opposition* 44 (2): 125–45. https://doi.org/10.1111/j.1477-7053.2009.01279.x

de la Dehesa, Rafael. 2010. *Queering the Public Sphere in Mexico and Brazil: Sexual Rights Movements in Emerging Democracies*. Durham: Duke University Press.

Dovi, Suzanne. 2002. "Preferable Descriptive Representatives: Will Just Any Woman, Black, or Latino Do?" *American Political Science Review* 96 (4): 729–43. https://doi.org/10.1017/S0003055402000412

Escobar-Lemmon, Maria C., and Michelle M. Taylor-Robinson. 2014. "Does Presence Produce Representation of Interests?" In *Representation: The Case of Women*, ed. Maria C. Escobar-Lemmon and Michelle M. Taylor-Robinson, 227–47. New York: Oxford University Press.

Flam, Helena, and Debra King, eds. 2005. *Emotions and Social Movements*. Abingdon, UK: Routledge.

Golebiowska, Ewa A., and Cynthia J. Thomsen. 1999. "Group Stereotypes and Evaluations of Individuals: The Case of Gay and Lesbian Political Candidates." In *Gays and Lesbians in the Democratic Process: Public Policy, Public Opinion, and Political Representation*, ed. Ellen D.B. Riggle and Barry L. Tadlock, 192–219. New York: Columbia University Press.

Goodwin, Jeff, James M. Jasper, and Francesca Polletta. 2001a. "Introduction: Why Emotions Matter." In *Passionate Politics: Emotions and Social Movements*, ed. Jeff Goodwin, James M. Jasper, and Francesca Polletta, 1–24. Chicago: University of Chicago Press.

—, eds. 2001b. *Passionate Politics: Emotions and Social Movements*. Chicago: University of Chicago Press.

Gould, Deborah B. 2009. *Moving Politics: Emotions and ACT UP's Fight against AIDS*. Chicago: University of Chicago Press.

Green, James N. 2000. "Desire and Militancy: Lesbians, Gays, and the Brazilian Workers Party." In *Different Rainbows*, ed. Peter F. Drucker, 57–70. London: Gay Men's Press.

Haider-Markel, Donald. 2007. "Representation and Backlash: The Positive and Negative Influence of Descriptive Representation." *Legislative Studies Quarterly* 32 (1): 107–33. https://doi.org/10.3162/036298007x202001

—. 2010. *Out and Running: Gay and Lesbian Candidates, Elections, and Policy Representation*. Washington, DC: Georgetown University Press.

Haider-Markel, Donald P., and Chelsie Lynn Moore Bright. 2014. "Lesbian Candidates and Officeholders." In *Women and Elective Office: Past, Present, and Future*, 3rd ed., ed. Sue Thomas and Clyde Wilcox, 253–72. New York: Oxford University Press.

Haider-Markel, Donald P., Mark R. Joslyn, and Chad J. Kniss. 2000. "Minority Group Interests and Political Representation: Gay Elected Officials in the Policy Process." *Journal of Politics* 62 (2): 568–77. https://doi.org/10.1111/0022-3816.00026

Herrick, Rebekah. 2009. "The Effects of Sexual Orientation on State Legislators' Behavior and Priorities." *Journal of Homosexuality* 56 (8): 1117–33. https://doi.org/10.1080/00918360903279361. Medline:19882430

—. 2010. "The Legislative Effectiveness of Gay and Lesbian Legislators." *Journal of Women, Politics and Policy* 31 (3): 243–59. https://doi.org/10.1080/1554477x.2010.496690

Herrick, Rebekah, and Sue Thomas. 2001. "Gays and Lesbians in Local Races: A Study of Electoral Viability." *Journal of Homosexuality* 42 (1): 103–26. https://doi.org/10.1300/j082v42n01_06

Hertzog, Mark. 1996. *The Lavender Vote: Lesbians, Gay Men, and Bisexuals in American Electoral Politics*. New York: New York University Press.

Htun, Mala. 2014. "Political Inclusion and Representation of Afrodescendant Women in Latin America." In *Representation: The Case of Women*, ed. Maria C. Escobar-Lemmon and Michelle M. Taylor-Robinson, 118–34. New York: Oxford University Press.

Jasper, James M. 1998. "The Emotions of Protest: Affective and Reactive Emotions in and around Social Movements." *Sociological Forum* 13 (3): 397–424. https://doi.org/10.1023/a:1022175308081

Johnson, Carol, and Manon Tremblay. 2018. "Comparing Same-Sex Marriage in Australia and Canada: Institutions and Political Will." *Government and Opposition* 53 (1): 131–58. https://doi.org/10.1017/gov.2016.36

Kanter, Rosabeth Moss. 1977. "Some Effects of Proportions on Group Life: Skewed Sex Ratios and Responses to Token Women." *American Journal of Sociology* 82 (5): 965–90. https://doi.org/10.1086/226425

Khan, Ummni. 2014. *Vicarious Kinks: S/M in the Socio-Legal Imaginary*. Toronto: University of Toronto Press.

Kinsman, Gary. 1996. *The Regulation of Desire: Homo and Hetero Sexualities*. Montreal: Black Rose Books.

Lenti, Erica. 2015. "Why Canada Needs to Elect More LGBTQ Politicians: Queer Representation in Government Is Necessary for Community-Minded Policy Outcomes." *Torontoist*, November 4. http://torontoist.com/2015/11/why-canada-needs-to-elect-more-lgbtq-politicians/

Lombardo, Emanuela, and Petra Meier. 2014. *The Symbolic Representation of Gender: A Discursive Approach*. Farnham, UK: Ashgate.

Mansbridge, Jane. 1999. "Should Blacks Represent Blacks and Women Represent Women? A Contingent 'Yes.'" *Journal of Politics* 61 (3): 628–57. https://doi.org/10.2307/2647821

–. 2003. "Rethinking Representation." *American Political Science Review* 97 (4): 515–28. https://doi.org/10.1017/s0003055403000856

Marsiaj, Juan P. 2006. "Social Movements and Political Parties: Gays, Lesbians, and *Travestis* and the Struggle for Inclusion in Brazil." *Canadian Journal of Latin American and Caribbean Studies* 31 (62): 167–96. https://doi.org/10.1080/08263663.2006.10816905

Millward, Liz. 2015. *Making a Scene: Lesbians and Community across Canada, 1964–84*. Vancouver: UBC Press.

Paternotte, David. 2014. "Pedophilia, Homosexuality and Gay and Lesbian Activism." In *Sexual Revolutions*, ed. Gert Hekma and Alain Giami, 265–78. Houndmills, UK: Palgrave Macmillan.

Phelan, Shane. 2001. *Sexual Strangers: Gays, Lesbians, and Dilemmas of Citizenship*. Philadelphia: Temple University Press.

Phillips, Anne. 1995. *The Politics of Presence*. Oxford: Clarendon Press.

Pitkin, Hanna Fenichel. 1967. *The Concept of Representation*. Berkeley: University of California Press.

Podmore, Julie, and Manon Tremblay. 2015. "Lesbians, Second-Wave Feminism and Gay Liberation." In *The Ashgate Research Companion to Lesbian and Gay Activism*, ed. David Paternotte and Manon Tremblay, 121–34. Farnham, UK: Ashgate.

Rayside, David. 1998. *On the Fringe: Gays and Lesbians in Politics*. Ithaca: Cornell University Press.

–. 2008. *Queer Inclusions, Continental Divisions: Public Recognition of Sexual Diversity in Canada and the United States*. Toronto: University of Toronto Press.

Rehfeld, Andrew. 2006. "Towards a General Theory of Political Representation." *Journal of Politics* 68 (1): 1–21. https://doi.org/10.1111/j.1468-2508.2006.00365.x

Reynolds, Andrew. 2013. "Representation and Rights: The Impact of LGBT Legislators in Comparative Perspective." *American Political Science Review* 107 (2): 259–74. https://doi.org/10.1017/s0003055413000051

Richardson, Diane, and Surya Monro. 2012. *Sexuality, Equality and Diversity*. Basingstoke, UK: Palgrave Macmillan.

Richer, Jocelyne. 2016. "La diversité sexuelle au gouvernement n'est pas une priorité, juge la ministre Vallée." *Le Devoir*, June 27. http://www.ledevoir.com/politique/quebec/474251/absence-d-elus-liberaux-gais-pas-de-probleme-dit-stephanie-vallee

Rosenblum, Darren. 1996. "Geographically Sexual? Advancing Lesbian and Gay Interests through Proportional Representation." *Harvard Civil Rights – Civil Liberties Law Review* 31: 119–54.

Rubenstein, Jennifer. 2007. "Accountability in an Unequal World." *Journal of Politics* 69 (3): 616–32. https://doi.org/10.1111/j.1468-2508.2007.00563.x

Saward, Michael. 2006. "The Representative Claim." *Contemporary Political Theory* 5 (3): 297–318. https://doi.org/10.1057/palgrave.cpt.9300234

Schmidt, Vivien A. 2008. "Discursive Institutionalism: The Explanatory Power of Ideas and Discourse." *Annual Review of Political Science* 11 (1): 303–26. https://doi.org/10.1146/annurev.polisci.11.060606.135342

Severs, Eline. 2012. "Substantive Representation through a Claims-Making Lens: A Strategy for the Identification and Analysis of Substantive Claims." *Representation* 48 (2): 169–81. https://doi.org/10.1080/00344893.2012.683491

Smith, Miriam. 2007. "The Impact of the Charter: Untangling the Effects of Institutional Change." *International Journal of Canadian Studies* 36: 17–40. https://doi.org/10.7202/040775ar

–. 2008. *Political Institutions and Lesbian and Gay Rights in the United States and Canada*. New York: Routledge.

–. 2013. "Social Movements and Human Rights: Gender, Sexuality, and the Charter in English-Speaking Canada." In *Taking Liberties: A History of Human Rights in Canada*, ed. David Goutor and Stephen Heathorn, 213–32. Don Mills, ON: Oxford University Press.

–. 2015. "Political Institutions and LGBTQ Activism in Comparative Perspective." In *The Ashgate Research Companion to Lesbian and Gay Activism*, ed. David Paternotte and Manon Tremblay, 181–94. Farnham, UK: Ashgate.

Smooth, Wendy. 2011. "Standing for Women? Which Women? The Substantive Representation of Women's Interests and the Research Imperative of Intersectionality." *Politics and Gender* 7 (3): 436–41. https://doi.org/10.1017/s1743923x11000225

Stein, Marc. 2012. *Rethinking the Gay and Lesbian Movement*. New York: Routledge.

Tin, Louis-Georges. 2012. *The Invention of Heterosexual Culture*. Boston: MIT Press.

Tobin, Ann. 1988. "Somewhere over the Rainbow ..." In *Radical Records: Thirty Years of Lesbian and Gay History*, ed. Bob Cant and Susan Hemmings, 248–58. London: Routledge.

Truelove, Graeme. 2013. *Svend Robinson: A Life in Politics*. Vancouver: New Star Books.

Warner, Tom. 2002. *Never Going Back: A History of Queer Activism in Canada*. Toronto: University of Toronto Press.

Weiss, Jillian. 2011. "Reflective Paper: GL versus BT: The Archaeology of Biphobia and Transphobia within the U.S. Gay and Lesbian Community." *Journal of Bisexuality* 11 (4): 498–502. https://doi.org/10.1080/15299716.2011.620848

Williams, Melissa S. 1998. *Voice, Trust, and Memory: Marginalized Groups and the Failings of Liberal Representation*. Princeton: Princeton University Press.

Young, Iris Marion. 2000. *Inclusion and Democracy*. Oxford: Oxford University Press.

9

Pathway to Office
The Eligibility, Recruitment, Selection, and Election of LGBT Candidates

Joanna Everitt, Manon Tremblay, and Angelia Wagner

"A REPRESENTATIVE LEGISLATURE," according to John Adams, "should be an exact portrait, in miniature, of the people at large, as it should think, feel, reason and act like them" (quoted in Pitkin 1967, 60). This reading of political representation is an ideal. Yet its value here is to expose the lack of demographic representativeness of the House of Commons, provincial and territorial legislatures, and municipal councils in Canada. Although several groups are excluded from representation in Canada (people with little education, manual workers, and the poor, among others), women make up the most under-represented social group in political decision-making institutions, a fact that is now well documented and understood (see Trimble, Arscott, and Tremblay 2013). Similarly, lesbians, gays, bisexuals, and transgender people (LGBT people) have historically been invisible in Canadian legislative arenas.

Our objective in this chapter is to explore the legislative representation of LGBT people in Canada. For this purpose, we draw upon the expansive gender and politics literature to develop a four-step analysis of LGBT people's entry into Canadian legislative bodies. Theoretical and empirical insights into women's under-representation offer a useful starting point for one key reason: as for LGBT individuals, many of the barriers that limit women's political advancement are rooted in societal attitudes. But this is not to suggest that women's circumstances neatly map onto those of LGBT people. They differ in important ways. For instance, women form half of the population and are evenly dispersed geographically, whereas the proportion of LGBT people is unclear, and they tend to gravitate to and be concentrated in large urban centres, increasing representational demands in these areas. In addition, women are found in all groups within society, whereas LGBT people (at least, those who self-identify as such) are not randomly distributed: they tend to have higher levels of education and be less religious than the non-LGBT population (Egan 2012; Hertzog 1996, 54–59). Furthermore, claims for women's rights are largely considered legitimate today, whereas this is far from true for LGBT people, who remain an ostracized minority. For proof, we need look no farther than the publicly expressed hate messages that followed the homophobic mass murder of LGBT people in Orlando in June 2016 or the protest against reforms that acknowledged same-sex relationships in Ontario's sex-education curriculum in 2015.

The representation of LGBT people also has much in common with that of women. First, both are based on the concept of gender, and both question the stricture of gender, though differently. For instance, the "women in politics" field underlines the limits that gender roles impose on women's involvement in politics, whereas the "LGBT people in politics" field shows concerns for heteronormativity and homonormativity. Second, both fields are about the representation of minorities, although these minorities differ. Demographically, one human being out of two is female, yet from a sociological viewpoint, women constitute a deprived minority. LGBT people are both a numerical and a social minority. Because of their demographic weight, women can exert electoral influence on politicians and parties, whereas the electoral pull of LGBT people is much more limited, though not inconsequential (Egan 2012; Perrella, Brown, and Kay 2012; see also Chapter 1 in this volume). Third, women and LGBT people have historically been denied representation in politics, though for different reasons. Women were barred because they were seen as similar to minors and as already represented by a male relative (such as a father or a husband), whereas LGBT people were excluded because they were seen as criminals or sinners or as insane. Fourth, women and LGBT people both developed strong social movements to fight against their socio-political marginalization and to gain civil and political citizenship, though with unequal success. By 2017, most countries had adopted laws that recognized women and men as equal (though practices have not necessarily caught up), yet same-sex sexual acts remain illegal in seventy-one countries and are punishable by death in thirteen of them (Carroll and Mendos 2017, 37–40).

In this chapter, we argue that LGBT individuals who aspire to political office in Canada no longer have to overcome legal hurdles, but they still encounter social and cultural obstacles stemming from their identities. Societal attitudes toward sexual minorities have improved but not to the extent that potential candidates do not have to carefully consider the ramifications of publicly revealing their sexual orientation. Differences in party ideologies and recruitment practices also shape the political opportunity structure for LGBT candidates.

Theoretical Framework

Pippa Norris (1996) provides a useful theoretical framework for understanding the environment that confronts anyone who aspires to public office. Her model includes four components. The first refers to the social context – that is, the ideological, economic, socio-cultural, and political megastructures that define and regulate the competition for state power. These encompass the legal framework and traditions, as well as the economic regime (agrarian, industrial, or post-industrial, according to the categorization of Inglehart and Norris 2003). They also consist of political institutions, such as the nature of the state – unitary or federal – or the nature of the electoral and party system, and the social culture (traditional or egalitarian as regards gender roles). Together, and as they interact with each other, these megastructures define the environment of the electoral competition. The second component is the recruitment process – the rules that a political party employs in choosing its electoral candidates. These rules vary greatly from one party to another according to their ideologies. For instance, left-wing parties, such as social democrats and socialists, are more likely than their right-wing counterparts to accept the notion of social or descriptive representation – the idea that a parliament should reflect the demographic of the population. They are also more likely to adopt measures such as quotas to achieve this objective. The third and fourth components go hand in hand – that is, the supply of people who wish to be elected and the demand by party elites for candidates. This supply of, and demand for, candidates is central to the question of who takes the path to political power.[1]

Norris (1996) and Richard Matland and Kathleen Montgomery (2003) identify four steps in the process of being chosen as a legislative representative: eligibility, recruitment, selection, and election. The first two constitute the supply side of the equation and the last two the demand side. That is, individuals who wish to be elected must first comply with legal requirements (eligibility) and then either put forward their candidacy (self-recruitment) or be approached to do so (recruitment). But having a supply of candidates is only part of the story. This supply must respond to a demand from a party, notably by being selected as the candidate in a given constituency, as well as from the electorate by gathering the greatest number of votes in a riding. Thus, the journey to parliament involves a series of personal, organizational, and collective factors. Far from being independent of society, the process by which political elites are designated is an expression of its socio-cultural, economic, and political traits. Examples of the first trait would be heterosexist socialization and the gender regime; of the second, the level of women's participation in professional and managerial positions; and of the third, the nature of the voting system. A society is very likely to count few, or no, women within its political class if it values traditional gender roles, if women cannot vote, if a high electoral deposit is required for running, and if a majoritarian voting system is used, with no positive action measures to support female candidacies.

Analyzing LGBT People's Legislative Representation in Canada

The theoretical framework used to study the under-representation of women in politics has generated fruitful results. If eligibility is no longer an obstacle for women who wish to be elected, and if voters are not opposed to female candidacies (Dolan 2004, 153; Goodyear-Grant 2010), the recruitment and selection steps must clearly hinder their election to parliament. Given the heuristic power of the eligibility, recruitment, selection, and election framework in explaining the unequal presence of women in politics, it makes sense to use it to better understand the under-representation of other social minorities, notably LGBT people.

Eligibility

The rights to vote and to run in legislative elections are protected by section 3 of the Canadian Charter of Rights and Freedoms. A person who wishes to be a candidate must comply with minimal conditions defined by federal, provincial, or territorial election acts: basically, one must be a Canadian citizen and at least eighteen years of age on election day. There are other administrative conditions, such as the requirement to pay a deposit and to provide a letter of endorsement if one runs under the banner of a political party.

What appears today to be a very open process has not always been so. Indeed, the evolution of rules governing candidacies could be described as moving from exclusion to inclusion. In the aftermath of the First World War, several exclusions that targeted groups based on their sex, race, or religion were eliminated as the franchise was expanded. From a numerical point of view, women are the most important group to have benefitted from this development. From Confederation in 1867 to the end of the 1910s, they were forbidden to vote and to stand for election. Although this changed in 1918 and 1919, when women aged twenty-one or older gained these rights federally (and provincially between 1916 and 1940), several were excluded, such as Indigenous women, who were not enfranchised until 1960. Among the arguments put forward to justify the denial of political rights to women were that suffrage for women was contrary to Biblical writings and to female nature, that granting women the vote would threaten gender roles and destabilize marital harmony, that women were already represented by their father or their husband, and that they did not want the vote and would not use it if they had it (Cleverdon 1974, 3–18).

Section 41 of the British North America Act provided for explicit gender exclusion by limiting the right to vote to male citizens (if they were property-owning British subjects who were twenty-one or older). By contrast, exclusion based on sexual orientation has never been enshrined in Canadian electoral law.[2] Nonetheless, their exclusion did arise indirectly, for example, by having a criminal record or being diagnosed as having a mental condition due to being homosexual. Since same-sex acts between men were criminalized until 1969 (when they were partially decriminalized), and social ostracism of homosexuals remained strong until quite recently, it is unlikely that an out "homosexual" person could have been elected until recent decades. Instead, many individuals, such as Richard Hatfield, who was premier of New Brunswick in the 1970s and 1980s, kept their sexual orientation private until after they left office.

To the best of our knowledge, Robert Douglas Cook was the first out individual to run for political office in Canada ("B.C. Candidate Scores Points" 1979). He ran for the Gay Alliance Toward Equality party in Vancouver during the BC provincial election of 1979. However, at an all-candidates meeting hosted by the Society of Political Action for Gay People, two other candidates, Doug Henderson and Keith Eady (both Conservatives), also came out. Although none were elected, their campaigns opened the door for other gay candidates at the provincial level. Yet, not until the mid-1980s did Maurice Richard became the first out politician elected to office, in this case for the Quebec Liberals (Everitt and Camp 2014). Svend Robinson was the first out elected politician at the federal level in Canada, but he disclosed his homosexuality only in February 1988 – almost a decade after his first election win in 1979 (see the Afterword in this volume). He was subsequently re-elected in the November 1988 federal election, but another sixteen years would pass before a non-incumbent out candidate, Bill Siksay, was elected federally (Everitt and Camp 2014). Even though social ostracism of LGBT people has declined considerably in recent years, out LGBT individuals may choose not to run in politics, fearing that their sexual orientation will impede their election. Other LGBT people may decide to run but will conceal their sexual identity.

Recruitment

Although fear of a public backlash might discourage some sexual minorities from seeking elected office, an increasing number are putting themselves forward as candidates at the federal, provincial, and municipal levels. During the early twenty-first century, Canada saw a sharp rise in LGBT candidates (Everitt and Camp 2014, 235). The amount of courage required to run for office should not be underestimated. The decision to do so is the first step in the journey, as the potential for discrimination in the recruitment process is immaterial if a person never contemplates becoming a candidate (Lawless and Fox 2010, 34). Extensive research has found that political ambition in North America is gendered, with women typically expressing less confidence than men in their political abilities or qualifications (Lawless 2010, 54; Lawless and Fox 2010, 116–35; Lee 1976, 307; Thomas 2012) and less interest in running for office (Lawless and Fox 2010, 157). Little is known about the level of political ambition among sexual minorities, but studies suggest that gendered differences might help to explain why men comprise a larger share of LGBT candidates than do women (Everitt and Camp 2014, 245).

This is not to suggest, however, that the path from ambition to recruitment is a linear one. Some individuals consider becoming a candidate only after someone suggests the possibility. Women's groups, government agencies, and non-partisan organizations have been particularly active in trying to encourage more women to run for office (Dittmar 2015, 762; Francia 2010; Guppy 2012). In Canada, Equal Voice, Canadian Women Voters Congress, and the Federation of Canadian Municipalities work to raise awareness regarding women's under-representation in politics and to train women in the practical aspects of political campaigns. Activists in the United States have created several women's political action committees, the most famous of which is EMILY's List, to provide vital financial resources to competitive female candidates (Day and Hadley 2005; Nelson 1994). The Gay and Lesbian Victory Fund offers similar support to LGBT candidates. In Canada, the multi-partisan organization ProudPolitics highlights the candidacies of LGBT individuals at all three levels of government (see Chapter 11 in this volume). LGBT party members have also mobilized within the federal Conservatives and Liberals, and the NDP has a formal LGBT Commission, as well as equality measures enshrined in its constitution. Furthermore, the federal NDP and various provincial branches have adopted rules for their nomination meetings to promote affirmative action for under-represented candidates, including LGBT individuals. As a result, the party has fielded a higher percentage of female or LGBT candidates than other parties (Everitt 2015a, 2015b; Everitt and Camp 2014; see Chapter 7 in this volume). Despite the activities of such bodies, little is known about organized efforts to recruit more LGBT individuals into electoral politics. Media and scholarly attention to improving the diversity of legislators in Canada usually focuses on women and, to a lesser extent, visible minorities.

Regardless of a person's social characteristics, what inspires him or her to become a candidate can take one of three forms. Efforts by women's and LGBT groups to encourage more diverse individuals to seek office are necessary because many people consider running only after being tapped on the shoulder. Susan Carroll and Kira Sanbonmatsu (2013) refer to this group as "pure recruits," whereas those who make the decision on their own are "self-starters." A third group consists of individuals who attribute their decision to a combination of personal ambition and encouragement from others (Carroll and Sanbonmatsu 2013, 125). In their study of American mayors, Carroll and Sanbonmatsu (2013, 125) discovered that many female candidates were pure recruits, one-third were self-starters, and one-quarter were mixed (see also Brodie 1985, 101).

Using their framework, an ongoing study of LGBT political candidacy in Canada found that self-starters slightly outnumbered pure recruits when it came to the decision to run for office at the federal, provincial, or municipal level (see Chapter 10 in this volume). Nine of the sixteen LGBT study participants (56.3 percent) described their first candidacies as primarily self-directed, with some harbouring political aspirations since they were youths and others not entertaining the idea until later in life. Six participants (37.5 percent) largely framed their candidacies as the result of recruitment by party officials, community members, or friends who were active in politics. In just one case (6.3 percent), the first run for office was the product of both internal ambition and external recruitment. Unlike in other research, women-identified individuals in this study were more likely to be self-starters than pure recruits, whereas men-identified participants were more evenly distributed across the two categories. A sharper pattern emerged in terms of race. Caucasian candidates were twice as likely to be self-starters as pure recruits. Non-white candidates, on the other hand, leaned toward being pure recruits (of the five non-white participants, three were pure recruits).[3] The sample size is too small to reach any definitive conclusions about the sources of recruitment for LGBT candidates in Canada, but the experiences of these study participants suggest that sexual minorities do not all necessarily take the same path to political candidacy. Gender and race evidently intersect with sexuality to shape their recruitment experiences.

LGBT candidates also vary in terms of their motivations for seeking office. Like other political hopefuls, they intend to pursue what Melissa Deckman (2007, 542) refers to as "political or professional goals, policy goals, and community or social goals" (see also Rao 2005). The latter two categories – policy and community – were the most popular among the sixteen study participants. In the community category, several individuals indicated that they became candidates due to a desire to contribute something back to society and to help make their communities better. Several others were inspired to run mainly in hopes of advancing specific policy interests, improving government services, or combating the policy actions of incumbent governments. A smaller number primarily saw their candidacy as an opportunity to establish or further their political careers and to represent the interests of various groups. These results, however, must be viewed as broad generalizations. Many participants offered multiple reasons for seeking office, and their rationales sometimes spanned all three categories. Interestingly, few individuals specifically mentioned a desire to represent the LGBT community and/or issues. The desire not to be seen as a single-issue candidate was also reflected in the tendency of American lesbian candidates to campaign on education, environmental, and health care issues rather than on equality or civil rights (Haider-Markel and Bright 2014, 264). One conclusion of these findings is that LGBT candidates are no less complex than their heterosexual counterparts in their reasons for becoming involved in electoral politics and in what they hope to achieve once in office.

Canadian political parties are also slowly becoming more receptive to LGBT candidates. As noted above, the federal New Democratic Party has an affirmative action policy that requires local riding associations to make a concerted effort to find qualified women and minority candidates (Cross 2005, 70). As a result, many out LGBT candidates have run for the NDP (Everitt 2015a, 187). In contrast, the Liberals and Conservatives do not have formal rules on the recruitment of diverse candidates. The Liberals have opted for more informal efforts, such as the Invite Her to Run program in the lead-up to the 2015 federal election, which solicited the public's assistance in identifying potential women candidates. The Conservatives are ideologically opposed to affirmative action and make no special effort to recruit more candidates from under-represented groups (Young 2006, 61–62). Thus, LGBT individuals who wish to run for the Liberals or Conservatives will probably need to be self-starters rather than pure recruits.

Selection

The impact of these varying party approaches regarding recruitment can be seen in the number of LGBT candidates whom they field for both federal and provincial office. Identifying who is an LGBT candidate can be challenging, as not all of them are out to their constituents or even to their riding association. Election agencies do not gather data on sexual orientation. Therefore, we must rely on published sources such as websites and other online materials, newspaper articles, and LGBT magazines, as well as conversations with academics, journalists, and party officials to identify the individuals who should be included in this analysis. On the basis on this information, Joanna Everitt created a data set containing information on all identifiable out LGBT provincial politicians up to the Yukon territorial election of November 2016. This data set may not have captured all LGBT candidates in all parts of the country, but it is the most complete record we have for this information.

As Tables 9.1 and 9.2 reveal, twenty-one LGBT candidates ran in the 2015 federal election, and an additional forty-four have competed in provincial elections since 2013. The NDP has had the most LGBT candidates in recent federal elections, although their numbers have dropped from a high of fifteen in 2004 to only ten in 2015. During this period, the House of Commons increased its number of seats, which is one explanation for the notable decline in the percentage of LGBT candidates. The Liberals fielded the second highest number, followed in recent elections by the Greens. Although the Bloc Québécois (BQ), a Quebec-only party, once nominated a number of LGBT candidates, their numbers have dropped off in recent years. Table 9.1 suggests that the total number of LGBT electoral candidates appears to have stabilized at around twenty.

Of the number of out candidates in the 2015 election, 28.5 percent (six) were women (one of whom was Jennifer McCreath, a trans woman who represented the Strength in Democracy party of Newfoundland and Labrador), matching the roughly 30 percent of all female candidates in that election. Only two of the

Table 9.1

Number of out LGBT federal candidates by party and election year, 2004–15

Election year	2004	2006	2008	2011	2015	Total
Conservatives	2 (0.64%)	0 (0%)	2 (0.65%)	0 (0%)	1 (0.29%)	5
Liberals	4 (1.3%)	2 (0.65%)	3 (1%)	3 (1%)	6 (1.8%)	18
NDP	15 (4.9%)	10 (3.2%)	3 (1%)	10 (3.2%)	10 (2.9%)	48
BQ	1 (1.3%)	2 (2.6%)	0 (0%)	0 (0%)	0 (0%)	3
Greens	0 (0%)	0 (0%)	1 (0.3%)	5 (1.6%)	3 (0.9%)	9
Other					1	1
Total	22	14	9	18	21	84

Note: Percentages vary based on the number of candidates that parties ran in each election.

LGBT candidates were non-white, again reflecting the under-representation of visible minorities in Canadian politics. Five ran in the seat-rich province of Ontario, four in Alberta, three each in Saskatchewan and Quebec, two each in British Columbia and Newfoundland and Labrador, and one in Manitoba and Nova Scotia. To the best of our knowledge, no out candidates ran in New Brunswick, Prince Edward Island (despite having a premier who is openly gay), or the territories in this federal election. With a few exceptions, most were in urban ridings.

Table 9.2 shows that similar party nomination patterns occur at the provincial level. Again, the NDP fielded the highest number of LGBT candidates, followed by the Liberals and the Greens. As was the case federally, right-wing parties such as the Conservatives, or provincial variations such as the Saskatchewan and Wildrose Parties, selected fewer LGBT candidates than the rest. Of the forty-four LGBT candidates who ran in the most recent provincial elections, seventeen (38.6 percent) identified as women (one was a trans woman), and twenty-six were men (59.1 percent). One candidate in the 2016 Saskatchewan election identified as non-binary. In December 2015, half a year after being elected to the Alberta Legislative Assembly, Estefania Cortes-Vargas formally came out as genderqueer. As at the federal level, few candidates can be identified as of minority background (one federal and one provincial), and one can be identified as Indigenous (federal). Similarly, the larger and more urban provinces of Ontario and British Columbia had a greater number of LGBT candidates than the smaller, more rural ones. It is noteworthy, however, that except for Yukon and Nunavut, every province and territory had LGBT candidates. This is an improvement over even the previous 2011 election, when the total number of LGBT candidates was thirty-four and where only five provinces saw LGBT

Table 9.2

Number of out LGBT provincial/territorial candidates by party

Province/Territory	Election	Cons.	Liberals	NDP	PQ	Greens	Other	Total
BC	2013	1 (1.7%)		5 (5.9%)		2 (3.3%)	1	9
Manitoba	2016		2 (3.5%)	3 (5.9%)				5
Quebec	2014				2 (1.6%)		2	4
Nfld & Lab	2015			1 (2.5%)				1
NS	2013		1 (2.0%)					1
Ontario	2014	3 (2.8%)	2 (1.0%)	5 (4.7%)		3 (2.8%)		13
Yukon	2016							0
Alberta	2015		1 (1.8%)	3 (3.4%)				4
PEI	2015		1 (3.7%)			1 (4.1%)		2
Sask.	2016			2 (3.3%)		1 (5.2%)		3
NB	2014			1 (2.0%)				1
Nunavut	2013							0
NWT	2015						1	1
Total		4	7	20	2	7	4	44

Note: Percentages vary based on the number of candidates that parties ran in each election.

candidates run. Furthermore, the successful nomination of three trans candidates (one federal and two provincial) since 2015 and the identification of two other non-binary or genderqueer individuals speaks to the changes that are occurring in Canadian society. These trends suggest that with every election, the doors are opening wider for the nomination of LGBT candidates.

Election

Getting elected is the final step for anyone who aspires to office. This is the procedure by which the electorate of a given constituency designates its representative by voting for one of the candidates listed on the ballot. Research shows that the election process can pose several difficulties to the entry of women into politics. Sexist media coverage (see, for example, Trimble et al. 2015), a voting system based on uninominal representation (Rule 1994; Tremblay 2012), and being selected for a swing or unwinnable riding (Erickson 1993; Tremblay 2008) all represent serious electoral hurdles.

The news media do not report on female candidates or political leaders in a neutral way (Everitt 2003; Goodyear-Grant 2013), and the same is true for sexual orientation. Studying the newspaper coverage of the New Brunswick NDP leader Allison Brewer, Joanna Everitt and Michael Camp (2009) observe that she was depicted with stereotypical descriptors that emphasized her identity as a woman in politics, an activist, and a lesbian. "Brewer's sexual orientation ... became the dominant signifier of her public life," they wrote. "She was the lesbian leader, not the leader who happened to be lesbian" (Everitt and Camp 2009, 36). In Chapter 3 of this volume, Mireille Lalancette and Manon Tremblay suggest the concept of sexual mediation to describe how media framed out LGBT politicians according to heteronormative assumptions. Evidently, sexual mediation can be positive when out politicians fit the homonormative lifestyle (as was the case for Prince Edward Island premier Wade MacLauchlan and Ontario premier Kathleen Wynne), but extremely detrimental when they do not (as for Parti Québécois leader André Boisclair).

A rich literature demonstrates how voting systems favour or hamper the election of women, but no similar information is available for LGBT candidates. At best, our knowledge is vague and certainly inconclusive. On the one hand, we might assume that the plurality/majority voting system facilitates the representation of geographically concentrated minorities, such as the LGBT communities that live in large urban centres (Haider-Markel 2010, 8–9; Chapter 8 in this volume). Indeed, our data seem to confirm this: although in the most recent federal, provincial, and territorial elections, only 33 percent of the LGBT candidates ran in ridings that had high concentrations of LGBT voters (such as a gay village), 54 percent of them won their seats. By comparison, only 27 percent of the LGBT candidates who competed in ridings that lacked a strong and identifiable LGBT constituency were elected. On the other hand, several observers suggest that proportional representation (PR) will promote the nomination of LGBT individuals by ensuring that parties are more inclusive in their lists of candidates (Cardozo 2014, 39–41; Rosenblum 1996). Interestingly, a study of 151 LGBT MPs who sat in the national parliaments of 27 countries between 1976 and 2011 found no convincing evidence of this. As its author, Andrew Reynolds (2013, 263), points out, "The expectation that LGBT members are clearly more likely to be elected from list PR systems than from majoritarian systems is confounded by the data ... The number of gay MPs elected under single-member district systems has tracked closely the number elected by the list PR system." However, in Chapter 4 of this volume, Dennis Pilon critically interrogates this conclusion. What is clear is that PR systems do not automatically generate high levels of LGBT representation: they must be accompanied by activism and the requisite political will. In other words, LGBT activists need to apply pressure on parties to ensure LGBT representation, and list-makers must not only place LGBT candidates on the list but must also put them high enough to ensure their election. Thus, if PR systems fail to satisfy expectations regarding the election of LGBT candidates, this might be due to a lack of LGBT activism and to the reluctance of party elites to increase LGBT representation.

Be that as it may, Canada uses the first-past-the-post system to elect members of the House of Commons (MPs) and of provincial and territorial assemblies (MLAs).[4] Forty-four out legislators won a seat in federal (fifteen), provincial (twenty-seven), or territorial (two) elections between 1979 and 2015. Two others have been appointed to the Senate (Laurier LaPierre and Nancy Ruth), bringing the total to forty-six. Not surprisingly, the first elected LGBT people were not out of the closet. For instance, Richard Hatfield (premier of New Brunswick from 1970 to 1987) was never publicly out, and his homosexuality was disclosed only after his death. He is one of eleven male politicians (three at the federal level and eight at the provincial level) who have been publicly identified as gay either after they retired from office or after their death. Although it is important to acknowledge them, we have not included them in our discussion of out elected officials. The same is true for individuals whose sexual orientation is known to the LGBT community but not to their constituents. Even today, it remains unclear how many closeted LGBT candidates have run for election. That said, their numbers clearly seem to be dropping: Sheri Benson, Randy Boissonnault, and Seamus O'Regan, three new LGBT MPs who were elected in October 2015, were all out of the closet when they launched their campaigns. An increasing number are also doing so at the provincial level.

Thirteen of the forty-four elected LGBT MPs and MLAs were either lesbians or bisexual women, and thirty-one were gay men (29.5 percent versus 70.5 percent). This means that the proportion of lesbians or bisexual women in Canadian legislative politics was slightly higher than the average proportion of women in the House of Commons and the provincial and territorial legislatures (27.2 percent in the summer of 2016). This result suggests that though queer women may face the additional challenge of addressing their sexual orientation during their campaigns (Kluttz 2014), they have no greater difficulty than their straight female counterparts in being elected. LGBT politicians are also highly educated: thirty-two out of forty, or 80 percent, held a university degree (the level of education was unknown for six individuals). It comes as no surprise that they worked at the top of the employment ladder as executives or professionals: this was the case for 82.2 percent of LGBT MPs, MLAs, or senators (thirty-seven out of forty-five; information was missing for one politician).

Not surprisingly, left-wing parties count many more LGBT people in their parliamentary ranks than do their right-wing rivals. Scott Brison, who eventually crossed the floor in 2003 to join the Liberal caucus, is the only out Conservative candidate to have been *elected* at the federal level, although observers have speculated that Conservative caucuses contained more LGBT members who remain closeted. Nancy Ruth is the only out lesbian Conservative to have been appointed to the Senate. No out Conservatives have sat in provincial legislatures, although several came out after they left office. Of the forty-six out LGBT MPs, MLAs, and senators, fifteen (now including Brison) are part of the federal, provincial, or territorial Liberal family.[5] Another twenty-two carry the NDP banner, and two are Bloc Québécois MPs. Provincially, four are Parti Québécois MLAs, one is a Québec Solidaire MLA, one is a Conservative (Nancy Ruth, mentioned above) and one, Julie Green of the Northwest Territories, is an Independent, as there are no political parties in the territory.

As noted above, fifteen out LGBT politicians have sat in the House of Commons and two in the Senate. At the provincial and territorial level, the Legislative Assembly of Manitoba has welcomed one lesbian and one gay man; a lesbian has sat in the Newfoundland and Labrador House of Assembly and in the Nova Scotia and the Northwest Territories legislatures; and a gay man has sat in the legislatures of Prince Edward Island and Yukon. Three provinces stand out for their high number of LGBT MLAs: British Columbia (eight out lesbians and gays), Quebec (six), and Ontario (five). In Alberta, where only six LGBT candidates have ever run (this figure does not take into account the 2019 election), three of the four who competed in the 2015 election won their seats. All three were with the NDP, which toppled the long-governing Progressive Conservatives. As for the six out LGBT MLAs in Quebec, only one (Maurice Richard in 1985) was a Liberal, even though the Liberal Party was the province's main governing power between 1970 and 2016 (during twenty-six out of forty-six years). The remaining five MLAs were from the Parti Québécois (four) or Québec Solidaire (one).

One factor that helps determine whether LGBT politicians win office is whether they run in constituencies that are strongholds for their parties or in a locale that might be considered lost-cause or swing ridings. The federal and provincial Conservative parties, which have chosen a handful of out LGBT candidates over the years, have yet to see one elected, as they tend to run in ridings where the party has little history of success. Similarly, though the Green Party has fielded many LGBT candidates and is relatively open to non-traditional ones, none have won a seat, due to the party's low support among voters. A final example of the relationship between location and the success of candidates occurred in Quebec. In the 2011 election, when the "orange wave" unexpectedly hit the province, two members of the five-person NDP LGBT caucus were swept into office, even though the party had seldom won seats in Quebec. Both were defeated in the 2015 election.

Of course, not all candidates have been relegated to lost-cause ridings. Both the Liberals and the NDP have been strategic in their choice of location. In recent elections, three of the six federal Liberal LGBT candidates and four of the seven provincial ones were victorious. Most ran in constituencies that had substantial LGBT populations. The NDP success rate has been smaller: two of eight federal candidates and eight of eighteen provincial candidates won their seats. It should be noted that these individuals were less likely than the Liberal candidates to compete in a riding with a large LGBT presence.

More precisely, Table 9.3 analyzes candidate status at the time of first election and margins of victory for the forty-four out MPs and MLAs who took office between 1979 and 2015. The table features three types of candidates – challenger, inheritor, and open-seat. A challenger contends with an incumbent for the riding. In the case of an inheritor, no incumbent is running, and the inheritor represents the party that won the last election. In an open-seat race, there is no incumbent. As the table shows, it is difficult to argue that LGBT candidates are sacrificial lambs: fifteen were challengers, but fifteen ran as inheritors, and fourteen competed for an open seat. Lesbians and bisexual women were more likely than gay men to challenge an incumbent: 46.2 percent (or six of the thirteen women) versus 29.0 percent (nine of the thirty-one men). As for margins of victory, again it is difficult to assert that LGBT candidates barely win their first election. On average, inheritors enjoy a margin of 15.7 percent and challengers 11.4 percent. In open seats, the margin is above the 5.0 percent threshold, at 7.6 percent. Once again, we see gender differences: women inheritors won by an average margin of 11.4 percent and men by 17.3 percent; women challengers had an average margin of 8.7 percent and men of 13.2 percent. Finally, in open-seat competitions, the margin for women was 9.6 percent and 7.1 percent for men. More research needs to be done, but even if the proportion of lesbians in politics is higher than that of straight women, lesbians do not seem to escape the negative gendered effects of political institutions.

Out LGBT politicians in Canada apparently have successful political careers. Indeed, twenty-five of the forty-four LGBT candidates have been elected at least twice (this figure does not include the two senators). For instance, Svend

Table 9.3

Candidate status and margins of victory at first election

Candidate status	Number	Margins of victory at first election (mean)		
		All	Women (N)	Men (N)
Challenger	15	11.4	8.7 (6)	13.2 (9)
Inheritor	15	15.7	11.4 (4)	17.3 (11)
Open seat	14	7.6	9.6 (3)	7.1 (11)

Robinson was elected eight times, four of them after coming out as gay. Scott Brison won office seven times, including five times as an out gay man. And Libby Davies and Agnès Maltais triumphed six times each – the former three times as an out bisexual woman and the latter four times as an out lesbian. Eleven of the nineteen LGBT politicians in office in 2016 were first elected between 2012 and 2015, and could therefore be successful in the next election. In addition, almost half (nineteen of the forty-four, or 43.2 percent) took on parliamentary or ministerial responsibilities. For example, Jennifer Howard was minister of finance in Manitoba, Estefania Cortes-Vargas is the government whip for the NDP in Alberta, Randy Boissonnault is parliamentary secretary to the federal minister of Canadian Heritage, and Kathleen Wynne was the premier of Ontario.

Conclusion

Our analysis suggests that the issues facing LGBT politicians at various stages of the election process (eligibility, recruitment, selection, and election) are similar to, but not exactly the same as, the issues encountered by straight female candidates. Like women, LGBT individuals are no longer subject to legal impediments that bar them from running for office. But also like women, they must cope with social and cultural challenges that, though changing, continue to present potential hurdles. At the eligibility stage, many would-be candidates still think carefully about the implications of campaigning as out individuals. In the past, many concealed their sexual identities because of the public hostility they would otherwise experience. As a result, the total number of LGBT candidates and politicians in Canada is probably much higher than the number of out-of-the-closet MPs, MLAs, and senators whom we have presented here. Many early LGBT candidates and politicians came out only after they were elected, and several still do not identify publicly as LGBT even though their sexual orientation is widely known in the LGBT community. Increasingly, however, concealment is not an option for young people, who have lived much, or all, of their lives out of the closet.

Again, as for women, the recruitment of LGBT candidates depends on party ideologies and approaches to the nomination process. For instance, left-wing parties are most likely to seek out candidates in under-represented groups. Thus, the NDP regularly selects more LGBT candidates than any other party, and the Conservatives choose the fewest. Like women, LGBT candidates frequently run in areas where their party has achieved little electoral success. This is true for the Conservatives, the Greens, and, to some extent, the NDP. However, women and LGBT candidates are not necessarily recruited in similar locations. Whereas women are distributed across the country in relatively equal numbers, LGBT individuals often congregate in large metropolitan ridings. In such areas, savvy parties will choose to field an LGBT candidate. An illustrative example of this is the provincial riding of St. George–St. David, which included the largest LGBTQ community in Canada, in downtown Toronto, where six LGBT candidates ran between 1987 and 1995, and which was represented by Ian Scott (a closeted gay man). An additional four ran between 1999 and 2015 after the riding was redistributed into Toronto Centre–Rosedale, which later became Toronto Centre. In these later incarnations, the riding was held first by George Smitherman and then by Glen Murray, both openly gay and high-profile Liberals who were appointed to Dalton McGuinty's cabinet.

A final point of comparison with women is in the type of constituency that LGBT candidates tend to win. For the most part, these are large urban ridings in the more populated provinces of the country. Although not all successful LGBT candidates run in large metropolitan areas (Scott Brison from rural Nova Scotia and Sylvain Gaudreault from northern Quebec are obvious exceptions), a significant majority do. This observation gives credence to Donald Haider-Markel's (2010, 80) conclusion that, in the United States, LGBT "candidates strategically select where and when to run and thereby reduce, and perhaps negate, the role of sexual orientation in elections." It may be hoped that in the future, LGBT people will no longer have to engage in such strategic manoeuvres to win an election.

Notes

1 The supply-and-demand model is largely used to study the route to elective office, but Mona Krook (2010, 711) sheds light on some of its pitfalls. She also suggests an alternative approach based on institutionalist and feminist tenets paying "attention to the role of gender in structuring institutional content and effects." Through her concept of heterosexual matrix, Judith Butler (1990, 1–24) shows that sexuality is vital to gender, and Krook's suggestion that the supply-and-demand model should take gender into account is certainly relevant to the study of LGBT people's pathway to office. In other words, research into how gender influences the competitiveness of LGBT candidacies would yield valuable results.
2 However, the 1952 Immigration Act did target LGBT individuals for exclusion: "Homosexuals, lesbians, and persons coming to Canada for any immoral purpose" (Girard 1987, 7) would not be admitted.
3 The "non-white" category encompasses individuals of non-European origin, including Indigenous people.
4 Here, we use "MLA" in a generic sense to encompass MPPs (Ontario), MNAs (Quebec), and MHAs (Newfoundland and Labrador).
5 Brison left federal politics in January 2019.

References

"B.C. Candidate Scores Points." 1979. *Body Politic* 53: 15.
Brodie, Janine. 1985. *Women and Politics in Canada*. Toronto: McGraw-Hill Ryerson.
Butler, Judith. 1990. *Gender Trouble: Feminism and the Subversion of Identity*. New York: Routledge.

Cardozo, Bradley. 2014. "A 'Coming Out' Party in Congress? LGBT Advocacy and Party-List Politics in the Philippines." Master's thesis, University of California, Los Angeles.

Carroll, Aengus, and Lucas Ramón Mendos. 2017. *State Sponsored Homophobia: A World Survey of Sexual Orientation Laws: Criminalisation, Protection and Recognition*. 12th ed. Geneva: ILGA. https://ilga.org/downloads/2017/ILGA_State_Sponsored_Homophobia_2017_WEB.pdf

Carroll, Susan J., and Kira Sanbonmatsu. 2013. "Entering the Mayor's Office: Women's Decisions to Run for Municipal Positions." In *Women and Executive Office: Pathways and Performance*, ed. Melody Rose, 115–36. Boulder: Lynne Rienner.

Cleverdon, Catherine L. 1974. *The Start of Liberation: The Woman Suffrage Movement in Canada*. Toronto: University of Toronto Press. Originally published 1950.

Cross, William. 2005. *Political Parties*. Vancouver: UBC Press.

Day, Christine L., and Charles D. Hadley. 2005. *Women's PACs: Abortion and Elections*. Upper Saddle River: Pearson Education.

Deckman, Melissa. 2007. "Gender Differences in the Decision to Run for School Board." *American Politics Research* 35 (4): 541–63. https://doi.org/10.1177/1532673X07299196

Dittmar, Kelly. 2015. "Encouragement Is Not Enough: Addressing Social and Structural Barriers to Female Recruitment." *Politics and Gender* 11 (4): 759–65. https://doi.org/10.1017/S1743923X15000495

Dolan, Kathleen A. 2004. *Voting for Women: How the Public Evaluates Women Candidates*. Boulder: Westview Press.

Egan, Patrick J. 2012. "Group Cohesion without Group Mobilization: The Case of Lesbians, Gays and Bisexuals." *British Journal of Political Science* 42 (3): 597–616. https://doi.org/10.1017/S0007123411000500

Erickson, Lynda. 1993. "Making Her Way In: Women, Parties and Candidacies in Canada." In *Gender and Party Politics*, ed. Joni Lovenduski and Pippa Norris, 60–85. London: Sage.

Everitt, Joanna. 2003. "Media in the Maritimes: Do Female Candidates Face a Bias?" *Atlantis* 27 (2): 90–98.

–. 2015a. "Gender and Sexual Diversity in Provincial Election Campaigns." *Canadian Political Science Review* 9 (1): 177–92.

–. 2015b. "LGBT Activism in the 2015 Federal Election." In *Canadian Election Analysis 2015: Communication, Strategy, and Canadian Democracy*, ed. Alex Marland and Thierry Giasson, 48–49. Vancouver: Samara/UBC Press.

Everitt, Joanna, and Michael Camp. 2009. "Changing the Game Changes the Frame: The Media's Use of Lesbian Stereotypes in Leadership versus Election Campaigns." *Canadian Political Science Review* 3 (3): 24–39.

–. 2014. "In versus Out: LGBT Politicians in Canada." *Journal of Canadian Studies* 48 (1): 226–51. https://doi.org/10.3138/jcs.48.1.226

Francia, Peter L. 2010. "Women's Organizations as Leaders in Finding and Supporting Female Candidates." In *Gender and Women's Leadership: A Reference Handbook*. Vol. 1, ed. Karen O'Connor, 151–59. Los Angeles: Sage.

Girard, Philip. 1987. "From Subversion to Liberation: Homosexuals and the Immigration Act 1952–1977." *Canadian Journal of Law and Society* 2 (1): 1–27. https://doi.org/10.1017/s0829320100001137

Goodyear-Grant, Elizabeth. 2010. "Who Votes for Women Candidates and Why? Evidence from Recent Canadian Elections." In *Voting Behaviour in Canada*, ed. Cameron D. Anderson and Laura B. Stephenson, 43–64. Vancouver: UBC Press.

–. 2013. *Gendered News: Media Coverage and Electoral Politics in Canada.* Vancouver: UBC Press.
Guppy, Lynn. 2012. *Canadian Provincial Policies and Programs for Women in Leadership.* St. John's: Leslie Harris Centre of Regional Policy and Development, Memorial University.
Haider-Markel, Donald P. 2010. *Out and Running: Gay and Lesbian Candidates, Elections, and Policy Representation.* Washington, DC: Georgetown University Press.
Haider-Markel, Donald P., and Chelsie Lynn Moore Bright. 2014. "Lesbian Candidates and Officeholders." In *Women and Executive Office: Past, Present, and Future.* 3rd. ed., ed. Sue Thomas and Clyde Wilcox, 253–72. New York: Oxford University Press.
Hertzog, Mark. 1996. *The Lavender Vote: Lesbians, Gay Men, and Bisexuals in American Electoral Politics.* New York: New York University Press.
Inglehart, Ronald, and Pippa Norris. 2003. *Rising Tide: Gender Equality and Cultural Change around the World.* Cambridge: Cambridge University Press.
Kluttz, Billy. 2014. "Outness and Identity in Context: Negotiating Sexual Disclosure in LGBT Campaigns." *Sexuality and Culture* 18 (4): 789–803.
Krook, Mona Lena. 2010. "Beyond Supply and Demand: A Feminist-Institutionalist Theory of Candidate Selection." *Political Research Quarterly* 63 (4): 707–20. https://doi.org/10.1177/1065912909336275
Lawless, Jennifer L. 2010. "Women's Political Ambition." In *Gender and Women's Leadership: A Reference Handbook.* Vol. 1, ed. Karen O'Connor, 50–57. Los Angeles: Sage.
Lawless, Jennifer L., and Richard L. Fox. 2010. *It Still Takes a Candidate: Why Women Don't Run for Office.* Cambridge: Cambridge University Press.
Lee, Marcia Manning. 1976. "Why Few Women Hold Public Office: Democracy and Sexual Roles." *Political Science Quarterly* 91 (2): 297–314. https://doi.org/10.2307/2148414
Matland, Richard E., and Kathleen A. Montgomery. 2003. "Recruiting Women to National Legislatures: A General Framework with Applications to Post-Communist Democracies." In *Women's Access to Political Power in Post-Communist Europe,* ed. Richard E. Matland and Kathleen A. Montgomery, 19–42. Oxford: Oxford University Press.
Nelson, Candice J. 1994. "Women's PACs in the Year of the Woman." In *The Year of the Woman: Myths and Realities,* ed. Elizabeth A. Cook, Sue Thomas, and Clyde Wilcox, 181–96. Boulder: Westview Press.
Norris, Pippa. 1996. "Legislative Recruitment." In *Comparing Democracies: Elections and Voting in Global Perspective,* ed. Larry Leduc, Richard G. Niemi, and Pippa Norris, 184–215. Thousand Oaks: Sage.
Perrella, Andrea M.L., Steven D. Brown, and Barry J. Kay. 2012. "Voting Behaviour among the Gay, Lesbian, Bisexual and Transgendered Electorate." *Canadian Journal of Political Science* 45 (1): 89–117. https://doi.org/10.1017/s000842391100093x
Pitkin, Hanna Fenichel. 1967. *The Concept of Representation.* Berkeley: University of California Press.
Rao, Nirmala. 2005. "The Representation of Women in Local Politics." *Policy and Politics* 33 (2): 323–39. https://doi.org/10.1332/0305573053870176
Reynolds, Andrew. 2013. "Representation and Rights: The Impact of LGBT Legislators in Comparative Perspective." *American Political Science Review* 107 (2): 259–74. https://doi.org/10.1017/s0003055413000051
Rosenblum, Darren. 1996. "Geographically Sexual? Advancing Lesbian and Gay Interests through Proportional Representation." *Harvard Civil Rights – Civil Liberties Law Review* 31: 119–54.

Rule, Wilma. 1994. "Parliaments of, by, and for the People: Except for Women?" In *Electoral Systems in Comparative Perspective: Their Impact on Women and Minorities*, ed. Wilma Rule and Joseph F. Zimmerman, 15–30. Westport: Greenwood Press.

Thomas, Melanee. 2012. "The Complexity Conundrum: Why Hasn't the Gender Gap in Subjective Political Competence Closed?" *Canadian Journal of Political Science* 45 (2): 337–58. https://doi.org/10.1017/s0008423912000352

Tremblay, Manon. 2008. "Des femmes candidates dans des circonscriptions compétitives: le cas du Québec." *Swiss Political Science Review* 14 (4): 691–714. https://doi.org/10.1002/j.1662-6370.2008.tb00117.x

–, ed. 2012. *Women and Legislative Representation: Electoral Systems, Political Parties, and Sex Quotas*. Rev. ed. New York: Palgrave Macmillan.

Trimble, Linda, Jane Arscott, and Manon Tremblay, eds. 2013. *Stalled: The Representation of Women in Canadian Governments*. Vancouver: UBC Press.

Trimble, Linda, Daisy Raphael, Shannon Sampert, Angelia Wagner, and Bailey Gerrits. 2015. "Politicizing Bodies: Hegemonic Masculinity, Heteronormativity, and Racism in News Representations of Canadian Political Party Leadership Candidates." *Women's Studies in Communication* 38 (3): 314–30. https://doi.org/10.1080/07491409.2015.1062836

Young, Lisa. 2006. "Women's Representation in the Canadian House of Commons." In *Representing Women in Parliament: A Comparative Study*, ed. Marian Sawer, Manon Tremblay, and Linda Trimble, 47–66. New York: Routledge.

10
LGBTQ Perspectives on Political Candidacy in Canada

Angelia Wagner

LGBTQ INDIVIDUALS HAVE historically been an invisible minority in politics. Unlike other markers of difference, such as gender and race, sexual orientation can be kept hidden while LGBTQ candidates pursue elected office. But changes in societal attitudes toward sexual minorities, as well as a great deal of personal courage, led a few candidates to run as openly LGBTQ, starting in the 1970s. The numbers of LGBTQ people in electoral politics grew substantially during the early twenty-first century, especially at the provincial level (Everitt and Camp 2014; see also Chapter 9 in this volume), though their rate of candidacy and electoral success remains below their presumed share of the general population. Because out candidates are a relatively recent phenomenon and still few in number, little is known about the obstacles and opportunities they encounter in electoral politics because of their sexual orientation or gender identity (for an exception, see Wagner 2019). Research on LGBTQ people and politics tends to focus on social-movement activities because legal and educational remedies to major issues such as discrimination, family rights, same-sex marriage, and bullying in schools have been more successful than political ones (Everitt 2015b, 131–34; Rayside 2015, 93–100; Swank and Fahs 2011, 2013). The small number of out LGBTQ candidates also makes it difficult to do quantitative research on the factors that influence their attempts to attain office.

In this chapter, I undertake a qualitative investigation of the LGBTQ-related factors that out candidates identify as affecting their recent pursuit of elected office in Canada. The research question that guided this inquiry was the following: What role did LGBTQ individuals expect their sexual orientation or gender identity to play in a bid for office, and what role did it actually play? Determining the answer to this question is crucial in achieving both descriptive and substantive representation of this diverse social group. Despite their limited numbers, LGBTQ politicians have been critical actors inside political institutions, educating their heterosexual colleagues about LGBTQ issues, promoting a pro-LGBTQ legislative agenda, and blocking anti-LGBTQ initiatives (Haider-Markel 2010; Reynolds 2013). The under-representation of LGBTQ individuals in Canadian legislatures therefore has material implications in terms of what issues are placed on the agenda and the manner in which they are addressed.

LGBTQ Dimensions of Politics

All candidates who aspire to elected office must create a campaign team, organize volunteers, raise money, and identify their voter base. But only LGBTQ candidates need to evaluate the risks and rewards associated with disclosing their sexual orientation. In Western societies, public attitudes toward sexual minorities have historically been negative, if not outright hostile, because of the challenges that these groups pose to heterosexist assumptions "that gender and biological sex are binary categories and that individual expressions of gender necessarily correspond to either a male or female bodily form" (Norton and Herek 2013, 740). However, mainstream acceptance of sexual and gender minorities has gradually improved, as LGBTQ activism on sexual discrimination, adoption, and same-sex marriage led to sustained public debate about issues related to sexual orientation. Canadian attitudes toward homosexuality, in particular, have markedly improved since 1981, with each successive generation displaying more liberal opinions than the one before (Andersen and Fetner 2008; Langstaff 2011). American perceptions of homosexuality are slightly less liberalized than Canadian ones (Andersen and Fetner 2008), but they are still more accepting of homosexuality than of transgendered identities, especially among heterosexual men (Norton and Herek 2013). Age is thus an important factor in perceptions of sexual and gender minorities, with older generations less accepting than younger generations of these groups.

In addition, resistance to sexual diversity varies among differing social groups in Western societies. First-generation immigrants in Europe are less accepting of homosexuality than native-born Europeans, though their opposition decreases the longer they live in their host country (Röder 2015). Generational effects are also at work here: second-generation immigrants are more supportive of homosexuality than are their parents. Several studies have also found that religious groups and ethnic-minority communities are less welcoming than secular groups or white individuals toward sexual minorities within their own ranks (Anderson and Koc 2015; Eidhamar 2014; Morales 1989), in some cases because they see homosexuality "as something that only occurs among Whites" (Harris 2009, 435). Canadian polling results, however, indicate that non-European immigrants are only slightly more opposed to homosexuality than are Canadians in general (41 percent versus 36 percent) and, surprisingly, *less* opposed than European immigrants (47 percent). Immigrants' attitudes are also softening over time in Canada (Langstaff 2011, 64).

Even though Canada partially decriminalized homosexuality in 1969, historical disdain for sexual and gender minorities meant that LGBTQ individuals who sought elected office during the late twentieth century probably refrained from disclosing their identities for fear of a voter backlash. Although pressure to provide socially acceptable answers to hot-button issues can lead respondents to downplay their own biases and push responsibility for discrimination onto unnamed others, empirical research demonstrates that voter resistance to LGBTQ candidates still exists. In two American studies, individuals who were asked to evaluate hypothetical lesbian and gay candidates perceived them as less electorally viable than heterosexual candidates, though experiments showed that their own voting intentions were not always swayed by a candidate's sexual orientation (Herrick and Thomas 1999, 2002). A 2003 survey of Americans found that gender, age, religiosity, and partisanship shaped hypothetical voters' support for gay and lesbian candidates for Congress: older Republican males who were born-again Christians and who frequently attended church were least likely to vote for such candidates (Doan and Haider-Markel 2010). Intersecting stereotypes related to gender and sexuality can also produce differential assessments of lesbian and gay candidates, but so far no pattern has emerged in terms of which group enjoys greater support as a result (Doan and Haider-Markel 2010; Golebiowska and Thomsen 1999). What is clear is that religion is an ongoing factor in the electoral fortunes of LGBTQ candidates. Examining American state legislatures, Jennifer Merolla, Jean Schroedel, and Scott Waller (2011) found that states with the highest proportion of politically engaged evangelical Protestants had the fewest gay and female elected officials in their legislatures. Interestingly, even though states in the American south scored highest on the religious measure, they also scored high when it came to the political representation of women and gays. The authors argue this finding indicates that "factors other than evangelical strength may also be important for predicting the electoral prospects of women and gays" (ibid., 172).

The timing of public disclosure is a crucial issue for LGBTQ candidates because of the potential impact of sexual stereotypes on voter evaluations. Stereotypes are widely held assumptions about the traits, abilities, and behaviour of a group of people, however defined (Crawford et al. 2011). Applying an intersectional approach to stereotyping is important when attempting to understand voter perceptions of and responses to LGBTQ candidates, who vary not only by sexual orientation but also by gender identity, race/ethnicity, class, age, and nationality. Alesha Doan and Donald Haider-Markel (2010, 71) define intersectional stereotyping "as stereotyping that is created by the combination of more than one stereotype that together produce something unique and distinct from any one form of stereotyping standing alone." Sexual minorities thus face differing sets of stereotypes based on their particular mix of gender identity, sexual expression, race/ethnicity, class, age, and other characteristics.

Stereotypes play a role in how voters evaluate LGBTQ candidates. A survey of openly gay American politicians who were in office in 1993 and a sample of unsuccessful candidates found that individuals whose sexuality was known when they first ran for office believed that stereotyping was a bigger issue in their campaigns than those who did not reveal their sexuality until a later campaign (Golebiowska 2002). Although American antagonism toward sexual minorities has softened since the early 1990s, the potential for stereotyping, lingering resistance, and organized opposition leads most LGBTQ candidates to run as Democrats and to "select districts where they believe their sexual orientation will be less of an issue" (Haider-Markel 2010, 57). Canada's party-focused political system differs in many respects from the candidate-focused American system, but LGBTQ candidates in both countries are careful about their political choices. Strategic decisions about which party to represent and when and where to run can boost LGBTQ candidates' electoral chances in Canada (Everitt and Camp 2014). Even so, such candidates cannot completely escape stereotyping. The news media remain a potential source of stereotypical treatment. New Brunswick journalists framed Allison Brewer's bid for the NDP provincial leadership, and her early tenure in the position, in terms of her lesbian identity and social activism, suggesting that she was interested only in addressing a limited range of issues (Everitt and Camp 2009a, 2009b). One consequence of this type of coverage is that it could potentially depict an LGBTQ individual as an unviable candidate.

The tendency of out LGBTQ candidates to run for left-wing parties at the provincial and federal levels in Canada further complicates their electoral viability. At the provincial level, the NDP's affirmative action policies regarding the recruitment of diverse candidates have resulted in many out individuals running under its banner, though the strength of this representation varies across provinces depending upon the party's electoral viability (Everitt 2015a; see also Chapters 7 and 9 in this volume). For example, as of late 2017, the NDP was the governing party in Alberta and British Columbia, the Official Opposition in Manitoba and Saskatchewan, and the third party in Nova Scotia and Ontario. It had no members in the New Brunswick, Prince Edward Island, and Quebec legislatures. LGBTQ candidates, in fact, enjoy greater electoral success in provincial elections than in federal ones. Joanna Everitt and Michael Camp (2014) offer several reasons for this difference: LGBT candidates who run provincially have done so more recently, when public attitudes have become more liberal toward sexual minorities; they typically run in urban ridings, where the population is even more accepting of sexual difference; provincial ridings are smaller and their electorates more homogeneous than their federal counterparts; and the NDP, which fields the most LGBT candidates, is most electorally successful at the provincial level.

Publicly out LGBTQ candidates who run for right-wing parties might face additional barriers because of the potential incongruity between party stereotypes and sexuality stereotypes.[1] In relation to gender, American studies have found that party stereotypes mediate the role of gender stereotypes in voter evaluations of Democratic and Republic women candidates, producing differing assessments of their competency on so-called female and male issues (Dolan 2004, 80–81; Dolan 2014, 104; see also Chapter 2 in this volume). In Canada, right-wing parties have traditionally been associated with socially conservative attitudes that support and promote heterosexual gender norms. The federal Conservative Party shifted its position on gay rights only after it lost the 2015 election, controversially dropping its official opposition to same-sex marriage in May 2016 and seeing its leadership contenders march in the Toronto Pride Parade a couple of months later (McGregor 2016; Tasker 2016; see Chapter 5 in this volume). Since their sexual orientation is at odds with socially conservative values, publicly out LGBTQ candidates who run for right-wing parties will have to address strong, and potentially conflicting, notions about who is a typical – and acceptable – conservative candidate *and* LGBTQ candidate.

Data and Methods

The study discussed here is part of a larger research project on the supply-side factors that affect political candidacy in Canada, especially for under-represented groups such as women and ethnic and sexual minorities. This chapter focuses on LGBTQ individuals who ran for office at the federal, provincial, and municipal levels after the year 2000. Since a person's social location naturally shapes his or her perceptions of a career in politics, research participants were recruited according to gender, sexual orientation, and race/ethnicity, as well as from a wide range of professional and personal backgrounds and from various ideological perspectives. This intersectional approach to sampling should produce a complex and nuanced understanding of the factors that LGBTQ individuals expect to encounter when they run for office. Although this approach limits the ability to generalize from the data (Mosley 2013), the purpose of the project is not to determine the *extent* to which perceptions matter in the candidate emergence process, but to discover *what* those perceptions might be. It is designed to build theory, not to test it (Eisenhardt and Graebner 2007).

Ideally, the study would include an equal number of white and non-white LGBTQ individuals, but political realities and methodological issues made this difficult to achieve. First, few openly LGBTQ Canadians have sought elected office, with the result being that the pool of potential research participants is small. Like heterosexual candidates, most LGBTQ candidates are white males, with few women and even fewer ethnic minorities standing for election at any level of government. Low response rates also stymied efforts to reach a quota of six individuals in three of the four gender/race categories: white females, ethnic-minority females, and ethnic-minority males. A key methodological issue was the lack of a complete list of openly LGBTQ candidates. This study drew upon Joanna Everitt and Michael Camp's data set of known out LGBTQ candidates at the federal and provincial levels to identify possible research participants (no such list exists for the municipal level). I identified other potential participants through online news coverage and the Twitter feed of ProudPolitics (@ProudPolitics), which routinely highlights the candidacy of LGBTQ individuals for elected office across Canada (see Chapter 11 in this volume). In all, I recruited sixteen candidates for this study: five white women, one ethnic-minority woman, six white men, and four ethnic-minority men.

All participants agreed to do a semi-structured interview and complete an online questionnaire. During the interview, they were asked a series of questions about political candidacy, including their motives for seeking office, the circumstances that prompted them to do so, the challenges they expected to encounter, and their strategies, if any, for addressing them.[2] This chapter focuses on issues related to sexual orientation. The online questionnaire gathered information about their political, professional, volunteer, and personal backgrounds. Interviews ranged from fifty-one minutes to more than two hours, with most taking about an hour. Four participants were interviewed face-to-face and the rest by telephone. All interviews were recorded using a digital audio recorder. Each participant received a transcript of his or her interview and questionnaire responses for review, and any requested corrections or amendments were made. Because sexual orientation is a personal issue, I kept identities confidential unless a participant provided explicit permission to be named. I also respected the preferred gender pronouns of participants, if specified. Following Erin Tolley (2016, 129–30), I have opted to extensively quote participants not only to illustrate various analytical points but also to emphasize their otherwise marginalized voices in political research.

Findings

Although, as mentioned earlier, public attitudes toward sexual and gender minorities are improving (Andersen and Fetner 2008; Langstaff 2011), pockets of resistance make the coming-out process fraught with difficulty for LGBTQ candidates, even in the early twenty-first century. Because sexual orientation is invisible, LGBTQ individuals must continually engage in the coming-out process as they inform family members, friends, co-workers, and the general public about their sexuality (Morales 1989), though younger generations first reveal their sexuality at an earlier age than did older cohorts (Dunlap 2016). Even out

LGBTQ politicians with a high public profile find themselves having to come out to people whom they encounter on the street. Study participant George Smitherman, a former Liberal deputy premier and cabinet minister in Ontario, was bemused by this fact:

> Who is ever fully out? I have to come out to every taxi driver that I'm in a taxi with. Even if they know who I am, they're like, "Who are these children? Where is their mother?" I'm like, "Don't you read the paper? I'm openly gay and I adopted these kids and then my husband took his own life." What the fuck? How often do I have to come out? *[Laughs]* You're never out fully.

The people in Smitherman's life had long been aware of his sexual orientation, and he had been active in LGBTQ groups before seeking provincial office. Nonetheless, he felt that being authentic and transparent with voters demanded that he come out publicly when he first ran for office. Studies indicate that candidates like Smitherman, who run openly as LGBTQ, serve as role models and educators on LGBTQ issues (Haider-Markel 2010, 115; Haider-Markel and Bright 2014, 271).

Although Smitherman was not concerned about how the voters in his riding would react to news of his sexuality, not all out LGBTQ individuals were as self-assured. Before deciding to run, Paul Harris spoke to an LGBTQ politician to learn what role sexual orientation might play in a political career. The individual urged him not to let the issue prevent him from becoming a candidate. Yet Harris admitted to a certain degree of nervousness based on his experiences of coming out to others throughout his life:

> You build up these monsters in your head, what it's going to be like to come out to your parents or to your friends. How many stories have you heard about people that come out to their dear friends and their friends go, "Okay. Isn't this pasta fabulous? *[Laughs]* What are we doing tomorrow? Did you want to go camping?" It's like, "Really, you needed to tell me this?" Most of the stories are like that now, but there are still a few that are the horror stories, and those are likely from the dysfunctional families and dysfunctional communities.

Harris, who spent seven years as an Alberta city councillor, took a passive approach to disclosure. If someone asked him about his homosexuality, he was willing to reply, but he then followed up with a question of his own: Why did the person need to know the details of his private life?

Overall, LGBTQ individuals took one of three approaches to the inclusion of sexual orientation and/or gender identity in their campaigns for office:

full incorporation, full disclosure and partial incorporation, and limited incorporation. A few appeared to treat their LGBTQ identity as an integral part of their political persona, discussing their candidacy as a continuation of their LGBTQ-related activism or as an effort to promote public awareness of sexual minorities. One racial minority politician saw elected office as a chance to represent the policy interests of the social and geographical communities to which the individual belonged. Jennifer McCreath, a transgendered white woman who ran for Forces et Démocratie in Newfoundland and Labrador in the 2015 federal election, viewed her candidacy as an opportunity to demonstrate to others that transgendered individuals are not only capable but also interested in sharing the responsibility of governance. She also sought to increase the visibility of trans people in Canadian society.

However, most of the participants treated their sexual orientation as one part of their identity as individuals and politicians. Like those who made their LGBTQ identity a key part of their political persona, these individuals did not hesitate to discuss their sexual orientation, the role they expected it to play if they became candidates, and their experiences on the campaign trail. But the extent to which they emphasized their LGBTQ identity during the interviews varied from one person to the next, with some offering several LGBTQ-related examples to explain their perspectives on political candidacy and others mentioning it only briefly. Members of the latter group tended to prioritize other social identities, such as gender, in narratives about their political activities and priorities. Some preferred to focus their campaigns on non-LGBTQ-related issues such as the environment or the economy. Cyrille Giraud, an ethnic-minority gay man who had been active in both municipal and federal politics, did not want to be known simply as the gay candidate when he ran for the Green Party in the 2015 federal election. "I didn't want to be reduced to just my sexuality when my political approach is based on economics," he said. "I work in finance. For me it's really important fighting tax avoidance. I wanted to be taken seriously on this point." A number of individuals took a relaxed approach to disclosure because increased acceptance of sexual minorities had made their sexual orientation far less politically dangerous than it had been for previous generations of LGBTQ candidates. "I've never really faced a lot of obstacles because of my sexual orientation," said Jeffrey Rock, a white gay man who ran for the Liberals in the 2015 general election. "I'm in a pretty good place about it, I guess, in a lot of ways." Personal comfort probably lay behind the decision of many participants to publicly disclose their sexuality as part of their overall campaign communications, which included the typical mixture of biographical details, professional background, and policy ideas.

In contrast, some participants avoided the subject of sexual orientation during their campaigns, though for different reasons. Jasmine Joyce Sapphire Leicester did not reveal her sexual orientation or gender identity during her 2013 bid for municipal office in Newfoundland and Labrador because "at the time I was still questioning what it was." Known then as Jordan Willis Lester, she came out as transgender prior to seeking a provincial nomination with the Progressive Conservatives in 2014. Shazad Shah decided to downplay his queer identity when he sought a municipal seat in 2015, hoping to better appeal to voters in his religious British Columbia town. Although this ethnic-minority man was publicly out, he deleted all of his old social media accounts – which included photographs of him in costumes, highlighting his queerness – and created new accounts to project what he viewed as a more appropriate image for a candidate.[3] The new photographs that he posted were either head shots or depictions of him engaging in campaign activities. He left it up to voters to raise the issue of sexuality: "I let it slide and hoped that it wouldn't come up, and it didn't." His reluctance to address sexuality because of the religious views of many local voters affirms the role of religiosity found in evaluations of LGBTQ candidates in other political contexts (Doan and Haider-Markel 2010; Merolla, Schroedel, and Waller 2011). His actions also speak to the power of heteronormativity in politics. LGBTQ individuals who aspire to become politicians or to be seen as legitimate political actors are expected to conform to, or at least not challenge, the assumption of heterosexuality in the ideal leader.

The religious character of the local electorate was not the only factor that influenced candidate disclosure. Some political hopefuls kept quiet about their LGBTQ status due to apprehension regarding the public's view of alternative sexual orientations and gender identities. One woman chose not to publicly reveal her bisexuality during her campaign in part because she was concerned about voter response. She explained, "I think people are more uncomfortable around bisexuality than they are around clearly definable sexual orientations," such as homosexuality and heterosexuality. Although she was out to close family and friends, her bisexuality had gone undetected by others because her current partner was male. "I think because of that, people make assumptions," she said. "It's an assumption that, while it's both comfortable [and] easy, it's also uncomfortable because I feel like I'm passing under the radar as straight when that's not really how I see myself." Her experience suggests that all LGBTQ candidates need to answer two key questions when contemplating a bid for office. Do they publicly declare their sexual and/or gender identities? To what extent should they emphasize, or downplay, these identities in campaign communications with voters, journalists, and opponents? Limited research on LGBTQ individuals in electoral politics means we have few definitive answers. Nonetheless, it does suggest that their choices reflect not only their degree of comfort with publicly disclosing their sexuality but also the nature of their riding (Haider-Markel 2010). For example, candidates who run in socially conservative areas might feel compelled to downplay their sexuality, whereas this might not even be a consideration for those who campaign in liberal ridings.

Reaction to Disclosure

Regardless of the characteristics of their electorates, several LGBTQ individuals expected to experience a major backlash because of their sexual orientation. Yet it rarely materialized. Few candidates reported any overt discrimination from, or sexual stereotyping by, voters, journalists, or opponents (the same was true for LGBT candidates in the 2015 UK election; Reynolds 2015). When they canvassed door-to-door, they usually received a polite welcome. Although this civility pleased them, it did not lull them into believing that they would not suffer an electoral penalty because of their sexual orientation or gender identity, a view supported by voter studies (Herrick and Thomas 1999, 2002). "Especially with the area that I ran in, it definitely, I'd say, would have cost me a few votes. It is a very older neighbourhood, which tends to be a bit more conservative," said Tyler Murnaghan, a white bisexual man who ran for municipal council in Prince Edward Island in 2014. "But," he added, with "a lot of people, it never came up as an issue." Murnaghan believed that the protective nature of Prince Edward Islanders was a key factor here: "I think Islanders have this thing with protecting their [own] regardless of who they are." An alternative explanation might be that they were already accustomed to seeing an LGBTQ individual in politics. The then provincial premier, Wade MacLauchlan, is openly gay.

Not all voters were quiet about their anti-LGBTQ views, however. Some stated they would not vote for an LGBTQ candidate. This prompted at least some candidates to practise a form of respectability politics. Jennifer McCreath, a white transgender woman, became hyper-polite when interacting with such voters, hoping to end the conversation on a positive note and, one presumes, to prevent it from spiralling out of control. Ethnic-minority candidates have used this tactic for similar purposes. When yelled at by a racist heckler during his 2017 campaign for leadership of the federal NDP, Jagmeet Singh told her that he "supports and loves her." He went on to win the leadership (Canadian Press 2017). During their campaigns, out ethnic- and religious-minority study participants sometimes used humour to deal with the twin threats of racism and homophobia. El-Farouk Khaki, a gay Muslim of African heritage who ran federally for the NDP in 2008, found that the diversity of his riding meant that some voters disliked his sexuality, others his Muslim faith, and others his race. As he recalled,

I was at one door where the guy said, "Oh, don't like this guy, not going to vote for him." It was a whole anti-Muslim thing that he was on. I looked at him and said, "The guy is *me*." I said, "If you don't like the Taliban, then you should be voting for me because they like me even less than they like you."

Khaki's use of wit to try to dispel the voter's racist notions and McCreath's use of hyper-politeness to address homophobia were two coping mechanisms that came to the fore in the LGBTQ narratives of campaign experiences.

Other participants engaged in a subtler form of respectability politics, monitoring their dress to be more acceptable to voters. Derrick Biso, a white queer candidate for the Green Party in the 2015 Prince Edward Island election, made the difficult decision to wear only masculine attire during the campaign to conform – at least outwardly – to the heterosexist norms of society:

I never wore a dress as a candidate, and that really bothered me. That was a negotiation I had to make. I didn't think maybe it was the time [to express my queerness in such a way]. I didn't feel exactly comfortable. As someone who is genderqueer and who feels much more comfortable in feminine attire, having to dress more masculine in order to be more well accepted, to pass for people, to be accepted as someone who is legitimate and who is valued and who is knowledgeable and who is powerful and who is worthy, that's difficult. Every day was a greater struggle because of that, because I was putting myself out there.

Biso later noted that even female politicians attempt to project a masculine image in their dress, character, and behaviour. The queer candidate viewed these practices as a manifestation of heterosexist assumptions in society that reject alternative expressions of gender identity. But they also reflect the specifically masculinist nature of politics (Sapiro 1993, 145), in which real or perceived expressions of femininity by any politician, regardless of gender identity, are often rejected as inappropriate (Ducat 2004). Extensive research on gender in politics suggests that the depreciation of femininity shapes the sartorial expectations, and choices, of candidates.

If some of our participants struggled with gender norms, others had to navigate anti-LGBTQ attitudes among members of their own ethnic or religious group. El-Farouk Khaki encountered a double standard among Muslim voters: "They're happy to squeeze the palms of white gay and lesbian politicians who are not Muslim, but they're not so thrilled by somebody who claims a Muslim identity and is gay." Some Muslim community leaders even refused to meet with him because he was an openly gay Muslim. Perhaps they took this stance because they shared the belief of some members of ethnic-minority and religious groups that alternative sexualities are a trait of white communities, not their own (Harris 2009, 435). Although the LGBTQ and politics literature has not examined this issue, extensive research on race in politics suggests that views about race probably mediate voter reception of LGBTQ candidates. Non-white voters might reject ethnic-minority LGBTQ candidates on the basis of their sexuality, whereas white voters might do so because of their race or religion. In comparison, the sexuality penalty that white LGBTQ candidates might suffer could be alleviated, to some degree, by their whiteness. The experiences of minority LGBTQ candidates thus demonstrate that voter bias cannot always be attributed solely to sexuality. More often, the stereotyping that candidates reported experiencing related to their personal characteristics other than sexuality.

LGBTQ candidates who were subject to disturbing attacks from voters dispensed with respectability politics and confronted homophobia head on. Although vandalism of campaign signs is not unusual during Canadian elections (Woo 2015), the materials of some participants were defaced with homophobic slurs. When vandals wrote "faggot" on Ted Mouradian's signs during the 2004 federal election, he decided to turn it to his advantage. Instead of quietly replacing the signs, the Ontario NDP candidate told his staff to contact the news media to denounce the vandalism. He stated, "So we called the press and did the interview, and that actually got me more votes because of people saying, 'Why should that matter?'" In British Columbia, Jacqui Gingras had her NDP election signs defaced during the 2015 federal election and also encountered an aggressive voter who strongly disliked the fact that she was a lesbian. "We had to call the police because he kept coming into the campaign office, and it got more and more aggressive and hateful," said Gingras. "It was one time I was getting a little concerned, not for myself but for my family, for my children." Although politicians in Canada and other Western countries are not uncommonly the target of aggressive behaviour (Adams et al. 2009; James et al. 2016; Narud and Dahl 2015), the voter backlash that our participants typically experienced were verbal or electoral in nature.

In researching media treatment of LGBTQ politicians in Canada, Joanna Everitt and Michael Camp (2009a, 2009b) found that journalists could display bias against them due to their sexual orientation or gender identity. By contrast, our study participants found that journalists generally did not exhibit an overt bias (see also Chapter 3 in this volume). Only a few mentioned sexualized news content as a (potential) issue. Jennifer McCreath originally welcomed national media attention to her historic candidacy as the first openly trans individual to appear on a federal ballot (Strapagiel 2015). As she recalled, however, "I was unable to parlay that attention into a second wave of, now that we've gotten that story out of the way, let's actually talk about this great new party [Forces et Démocratie] that has some completely different ways of thinking in terms of how we do politics and how we do this engagement." A lesbian participant was aware that the news media might stereotype her on the basis on her gender and LGBTQ-related activism, though she did not say whether this had occurred. Shazad Shah was concerned about the kind of coverage that would arise if the news media obtained the photographs of him dressed in costume. Although Paul Harris was not concerned that the news media would concentrate on his sexuality, he was disappointed that the local newspaper ran hateful letters to the editor from a preacher and allowed readers to anonymously post homophobic comments regarding its online stories.

These examples aside, LGBTQ candidates were especially alert to the potentially harmful effects of well-established media practices such as focusing on mayoral races, star candidates, or highly competitive ridings. Some mentioned the tendency of journalists to ask personal questions, to take sides in partisan contests, and to pay extra attention to favourite candidates. In fact, participants saw the *lack* of media attention as a greater issue than sexualized coverage. Those who did receive news coverage and who offered an assessment generally found journalists to be fair and balanced in their reporting. "I was very much impressed with them in terms of how much integrity they brought to their work," said Jacqui Gingras. Participant observations regarding limited news coverage (Haider-Markel and Bright 2014, 265) and balanced reporting in what was provided (Haider-Markel 2010, 58–59) echo those made by many American LGBT candidates.

Like the journalists, rival candidates avoided targeting LGBTQ candidates on the basis on their sexual orientation or gender identity, though candidate competitiveness was probably a factor here. Shazad Shah noted that he never faced public scrutiny over his sexual orientation during his municipal campaign. He offered two possible reasons for this: his ability to defend himself and his lack of electoral viability. He explained,

> I think nobody wanted to touch it. Because of my past experience working within the queer community and fighting for queer rights, they were reluctant to bring it up because I would be strong in responding to it. I also think because I was a nobody, people didn't think that I would do so well, so they didn't feel that they needed to bring it up to knock me down.

Had he been perceived as a strong contender for town council, things might have gone differently. He suspected that his sexual orientation could be used against him if he were to run a more competitive campaign in the future.

A lack of electoral competitiveness did not protect all LGBTQ candidates from opponent attacks. Running as a Liberal in a Conservative stronghold, Jeffery Rock was the target of dog-whistle politics – the use of coded language – during the 2015 federal election. His Conservative opponent used this approach to remind voters of Rock's sexual orientation, even while ostensibly downplaying it. As Rock explained, "The Conservative candidate made a point to point out that he would not do any name calling or mud slinging, but in so doing was subtly name calling and mud slinging ... He was trying to reference things without referencing things." Rock remained unperturbed by this tactic: "I knew that there was a risk that that would become a weapon for the opposition to use against me, but I'm comfortable enough in my own skin that – my belief is that if you've got a problem with me, that's your problem, not mine. I'm quite self-assured." Other participants expressed similar self-confidence.

Partisan Factors

In addition to disclosure and backlash, some participants had to contend with partisanship and party competitiveness. Parties are a defining feature of Canadian politics at the federal and provincial levels, as well as in certain municipalities such as Montreal and Vancouver. In this context, a candidate's chance of winning a seat is strongly influenced by the party's electoral viability. Many out candidates run for left-wing parties such as the NDP and Greens (Everitt and Camp 2014), which are less likely to form government than the centrist Liberals and the right-wing Conservatives. One candidate chose a riding where she believed her party had a shot at winning, but her campaign was handicapped by the complacent attitude of members of the riding executive, coupled with their disappointment that they could not field the traditional white, heterosexual male whom local religious voters preferred. On election day, she was defeated, which raised the question of whether her sexual orientation or her party was responsible. Jennifer McCreath was left pondering the same question after her loss. She ran for a new party that had little hope of winning a single seat, let alone forming the federal government, and was thus unable to determine what role her trans identity had played in the viability of her campaign.

The concentration of LGBTQ individuals in urban centres suggests that sexual orientation could be an *advantage* in some electoral contests (Button, Wald, and Rienzo 1999). However, study participants held mixed opinions regarding this subject. When George Smitherman first sought provincial office in 1999, he ran in a Toronto riding that had the country's largest concentration of gays. In such a context, he felt that his sexuality was a strength: "What for a gay person in a different part of the country might be a disadvantage was for me almost exclusively an advantage." But Cyrille Giraud, a similarly situated gay candidate, did not share this view. Although his riding was home to Montreal's gay village, he did not believe that his sexuality won him the so-called gay vote. He observed that the LGBTQ community was ideologically diverse, and thus LGBTQ voters split their support among the various parties. His statement is in line with research by James Button, Kenneth Wald, and Barbara Rienzo (1999, 201), which indicates that a high concentration of gays in an electoral district does not automatically translate into greater gay political representation. Giraud's party had little chance of forming the government, probably another reason that many LGBT individuals might not have voted for him. He noted that the gay village was only one neighbourhood in his riding. Like all other candidates, LGBTQ individuals who wish to win an election must appeal to a broad spectrum of the population (for the impact of voting system on the election of LGBT candidates, see Chapter 4 in this volume).

Still, this imperative encourages parties to field diverse candidates. As Joanna Everitt (2015b) and Everitt and Camp (2014) write, the NDP has been particularly active in seeking more women and minority candidates. Although the Conservatives reject the use of a formal recruitment strategy, a white gay man who ran for the party pointed out that it has fielded candidates who challenge its image as "the party of old, white, rural men." He stated,

> That's the stereotype that gets perpetuated by political opponents. It couldn't be further from the reality, demonstrated by the diversity that you would have seen in the House of Commons. Stephen Harper's majority government, if you look at the diversity of that caucus from the geographic, gender, and ethnocultural [aspects], it was quite diverse. And [it's] true of the Conservative movement across the province, and that's something that's going to become even more so as our diversity continues to grow.

As predicted by voting studies on gender and party stereotypes (Dolan 2004, 2014), voter expectations regarding the typical Conservative candidate proved the biggest hurdle that this gay man encountered in his unsuccessful campaign. He was routinely required to dispel these assumptions. Yet he insisted that his sexual orientation was never an issue for his party.

Conclusion

LGBTQ perspectives on the challenges of political candidacy remain underexamined in political science in general and in Canadian research in particular. By interviewing recent and prospective candidates for office at all three levels of government, I have identified some of the ways in which sexual orientation and/ or gender identity shaped LGBTQ individuals' expectations of and experiences with electoral politics. Four main conclusions can be drawn from the rich qualitative data. First, though the improvement in public attitudes has enabled more candidates to campaign openly as LGBTQ, it can still complicate the process. Even those with widely understood orientations such as homosexuality expressed trepidation at the potential for encountering homophobia on the campaign trail. Yet most voters were polite, and homophobic incidents were rare and isolated.

Second, candidates varied in the degree to which they emphasized their sexual orientation and/or gender identity. Most treated these characteristics merely as two among the many that constituted their identities. Only a few made LGBTQ identity a key part of their political personas. Fear of a voter backlash led some to downplay or hide their sexual orientation and to modify their behaviour and attire. This finding suggests that homophobia not only shapes voter evaluations but also candidate tactics regarding disclosure and accommodation. Rather than challenge societal assumptions regarding gender and sexuality, some LGBTQ candidates probably just submit to heterosexist norms.

Third, sexual orientation or gender identity were not always the most important drivers of voter bias against LGBTQ candidates. Individuals who did not conform – in whole or in part – to the traditional image of a politician as a white, middle-aged, Christian man were most likely to encounter negative voter comments regarding their race/ethnicity or religion. Some ethnic-minority LGBTQ candidates thought that racism was a larger issue than anti-LGBT attitudes. The experiences of LGBTQ candidates with multiple minority identities provide important insights into the limitations of sexual orientation and/or gender identity in shaping voter attitudes. Depending upon the composition of the local electorate, other aspects of an LGBTQ individual's social background might be viewed as more problematic or threatening to the status quo. This demonstrates the importance of taking an intersectional approach to political research in general and to LGBTQ-focused research in particular (Swank and Fahs 2013). The LGBTQ community is not monolithic. It is composed of individuals who are diverse in terms of race/ethnicity, religion, age, class, occupation, political ideology, and geographical location, characteristics that influence their perspectives of and experiences with electoral politics.

Finally, the study participants did not view their sexual orientation and/or gender identity as a significant barrier to pursuing office at any level of government in Canada. It was one challenge among the many that they were required to address. This qualitative exploration of LGBTQ views on political candidacy thus reveals that sexuality and gender identity play complex roles in contemporary campaigns for office.

These insights point to a number of important avenues of research. First, the polite welcome that most candidates received and the public confusion that greeted those who represented right-wing parties illustrate the need to update experimental studies on voter assessments of LGBTQ candidates. Public attitudes toward sexual and gender minorities have improved since the turn of the century, suggesting that voter assessments might have followed suit. Research on gender and politics also points to the possibility that sexual stereotypes will matter less than party stereotypes when it comes to voter evaluations of LGBTQ candidates. Second, LGBTQ candidates who espouse right-wing views on fiscal matters but not on social matters will face unique challenges in running for socially conservative parties. Future research needs to explore how LGBTQ candidates help reshape both party views on LGBT issues and public views on right-wing parties. Third, the involvement of LGBTQ individuals in left-wing parties also warrants further examination to determine how they influence party positions in a range of policy domains as well as in internal party dynamics. Fourth, scholars should investigate whether differences between federal and provincial parties on LGBTQ-related issues and representation might be a function of who has been involved at each level and at what time in the organization's history. Finally, the experiences of ethnic-minority candidates demonstrate the need for the LGBTQ and politics literature to undergo an intersectional turn to determine how race/ethnicity, religion, gender, class, and age influence voter evaluations as well as the political perspectives and participation of LGBTQ individuals. An intersectional approach will help reveal the ways in which sexuality does, and does not, complicate the electoral environment for various types of LGBTQ candidates.

Notes

1 Closeted LGBTQ politicians who represent right-wing parties will face few, if any, difficulties caused by a clash between party and sexuality stereotypes because socially conservative voters will probably be unaware of their sexual orientation.
2 Participants were asked for their views on various types of challenges, including seeking a party nomination, fundraising, family responsibilities, and media treatment. For a fuller discussion of the federal nomination process, see Chapter 9 in this volume.
3 Scrubbing a candidate's social media sites before an election has become common practice in Canadian politics. In many cases, individuals who seek nomination are required to hand over their social media passwords to the party so their online posts can be thoroughly vetted. Cybervetting has grown in importance as parties seek to avoid the social media scandals that discredited candidates in previous elections and sabotaged party efforts to control the campaign message (Trottier 2017).

References

Adams, Susan J., Tracey E. Hazelwood, Nancy L. Pitre, Terry E. Bedard, and Suzette D. Landry. 2009. "Harassment of Members of Parliament and the Legislative Assemblies in Canada by Individuals Believed to Be Mentally Disordered." *Journal of Forensic Psychiatry and Psychology* 20 (6): 801–14. https://doi.org/10.1080/14789940903174063

Andersen, Robert, and Tina Fetner. 2008. "Cohort Differences in Tolerance of Homosexuality: Attitudinal Change in Canada and the United States, 1981–2000." *Public Opinion Quarterly* 72 (2): 311–30. https://doi.org/10.1093/poq/nfn017

Anderson, Joel, and Yasin Koc. 2015. "Exploring Patterns of Explicit and Implicit Anti-Gay Attitudes in Muslims and Atheists." *European Journal of Social Psychology* 45 (6): 687–701. https://doi.org/10.1002/ejsp.2126

Button, James W., Kenneth D. Wald, and Barbara A. Rienzo. 1999. "The Election of Openly Gay Public Officials in American Communities." *Urban Affairs Review* 35 (2): 188–209. https://doi.org/10.1177/10780879922184356

Canadian Press. 2017. "Heckler at NDP Jagmeet Singh Event Demonstrates Why Minorities Are Deterred from Politics, Prof Says." *Toronto Star*, September 11. https://www.thestar.com/news/canada/2017/09/11/heckler-at-ndp-jagmeet-singh-event-demonstrates-why-minorities-are-deterred-from-politics-prof-says.html

Crawford, Jarret T., Lee Jussim, Stephanie Madon, Thomas R. Cain, and Sean T. Stevens. 2011. "The Use of Stereotypes and Individuating Information in Political Person Perception." *Personality and Social Psychology Bulletin* 37 (4): 529–42. https://doi.org/10.1177/0146167211399473. Medline:21343439

Doan, Alesha E., and Donald P. Haider-Markel. 2010. "The Role of Intersectional Stereotypes on Evaluations of Gay and Lesbian Political Candidates." *Politics and Gender* 6 (1): 63–91. https://doi.org/10.1017/s1743923x09990511

Dolan, Kathleen. 2004. *Voting for Women: How the Public Evaluates Women Candidates*. Boulder: Westview Press.

–. 2014. "Gender Stereotypes, Candidate Evaluations, and Voting for Women Candidates: What Really Matters." *Political Research Quarterly* 67 (1): 96–107. https://doi.org/10.1177/1065912913487949

Ducat, Stephen J. 2004. *The Wimp Factor: Gender Gaps, Holy Wars, and the Politics of Anxious Masculinity*. Boston: Beacon Press.

Dunlap, Andy. 2016. "Changes in Coming Out Milestones across Five Age Cohorts." *Journal of Gay and Lesbian Social Services* 28 (1): 20–38. https://doi.org/10.1080/10538720.2016.1124351

Eidhamar, Levi Geir. 2014. "Is Gayness a Test from Allah? Typologies in Muslim Stances on Homosexuality." *Islam and Christian-Muslim Relations* 25 (2): 245–66. https://doi.org/10.1080/09596410.2013.869882

Eisenhardt, Kathleen M., and Melissa E. Graebner. 2007. "Theory Building from Cases: Opportunities and Challenges." *Academy of Management Journal* 50 (1): 25–32. https://doi.org/10.5465/amj.2007.24160888

Everitt, Joanna. 2015a. "Gender and Sexual Diversity in Provincial Election Campaigns." *Canadian Political Science Review* 9 (1): 177–92.

–. 2015b. "Mobilization on the Periphery: LGBT Activism and Success in Atlantic Canada." In *Queer Mobilizations: Social Movement Activism and Canadian Public Policy*, ed. Manon Tremblay, 125–41. Vancouver: UBC Press.

Everitt, Joanna, and Michael Camp. 2009a. "Changing the Game Changes the Frame: The Media's Use of Lesbian Stereotypes in Leadership versus Election Campaigns." *Canadian Political Science Review* 3 (3): 24–39.

–. 2009b. "One Is Not Like the Others: Allison Brewer's Leadership of the New Brunswick NDP." In *Opening Doors Wider: Women's Political Engagement in Canada*, ed. Sylvia Bashevkin, 127–44. Vancouver: UBC Press.

–. 2014. "In versus Out: LGBT Politicians in Canada." *Journal of Canadian Studies* 48 (1): 226–51. https://doi.org/10.3138/jcs.48.1.226

Golebiowska, Ewa A. 2002. "Political Implications of Group Stereotypes: Campaign Experiences of Openly Gay Political Candidates." *Journal of Applied Social Psychology* 32 (3): 590–607. https://doi.org/10.1111/j.1559-1816.2002.tb00232.x

Golebiowska, Ewa A., and Cynthia J. Thomsen. 1999. "Group Stereotypes and Evaluations of Individuals: The Case of Gay and Lesbian Political Candidates." In *Gays and Lesbians in the Democratic Process: Public Policy, Public Opinion, and Political Representation*, ed. Ellen D.B. Riggle and Barry L. Tadlock, 192–219. New York: Columbia University Press.

Haider-Markel, Donald P. 2010. *Out and Running: Gay and Lesbian Candidates, Elections, and Policy Representation*. Washington, DC: Georgetown University Press.

Haider-Markel, Donald P., and Chelsie Lynn Moore Bright. 2014. "Lesbian Candidates and Officeholders." In *Women and Elective Office: Past, Present, and Future*, 3rd ed., ed. Sue Thomas and Clyde Wilcox, 253–72. New York: Oxford University Press.

Harris, Angelique. 2009. "Marginalization by the Marginalized: Race, Homophobia, Heterosexualism, and 'the Problem of the 21st Century.'" *Journal of Gay and Lesbian Social Services* 21 (4): 430–48. https://doi.org/10.1080/10538720903163171

Herrick, Rebekah, and Sue Thomas. 1999. "The Effects of Sexual Orientation on Citizen Perceptions of Candidate Viability." In *Gays and Lesbians in the Democratic Process: Public Policy, Public Opinion, and Political Representation*, ed. Ellen D.B. Riggle and Barry L. Tadlock, 170–91. New York: Columbia University Press.

–. 2002. "Gays and Lesbians in Local Races." *Journal of Homosexuality* 42 (1): 103–26. https://doi.org/10.1300/j082v42n01_06

James, David V., Frank R. Farnham, Seema Sukhwal, Katherine Jones, Josephine Carlisle, and Sara Henley. 2016. "Aggressive/Intrusive Behaviours, Harassment and Stalking of Members of the United Kingdom Parliament: A Prevalence Study and Cross-National Comparison." *Journal of Forensic Psychiatry and Psychology* 27 (2): 177–97. https://doi.org/10.1080/14789949.2015.1124908

Langstaff, Amy. 2011. "A Twenty-Year Survey of Canadian Attitudes towards Homosexuality and Gay Rights." In *Faith, Politics, and Sexual Diversity in Canada and the United States*, ed. David Rayside and Clyde Wilcox, 49–66. Vancouver: UBC Press.

McGregor, Janyce. 2016. "'Freedom and Respect': Conservatives Strike Marriage Definition from Party Policy." *CBC News*, May 28. http://www.cbc.ca/news/politics/conservative-convention-saturday-votes-1.3604990

Merolla, Jennifer, Jean Reith Schroedel, and Scott Waller. 2011. "Evangelical Strength and the Political Representation of Women and Gays." In *Evangelicals and Democracy in America*, ed. Steven Brint and Jean Reith Schroedel, 159–86. New York: Russel Sage Foundation.

Morales, Edward S. 1989. "Ethnic Minority Families and Minority Gays and Lesbians." *Marriage and Family Review* 14 (3–4): 217–39. https://doi.org/10.1300/j002v14n03_11

Mosley, Layna, ed. 2013. *Interview Research in Political Science*. Ithaca: Cornell University Press.

Narud, Kjersti, and Alv A. Dahl. 2015. "Stalking Experiences Reported by Norwegian Members of Parliament Compared to a Population Sample." *Journal of Forensic Psychiatry and Psychology* 26 (1): 116–31. https://doi.org/10.1080/14789949.2014.981564

Norton, Aaron T., and Gregory M. Herek. 2013. "Heterosexuals' Attitudes toward Transgender People: Findings from a National Probability Sample of U.S. Adults." *Sex Roles* 68 (11): 738–53. https://doi.org/10.1007/s11199-011-0110-6

Rayside, David. 2015. "Queer Advocacy in Ontario." In *Queer Mobilizations: Social Movement Activism and Canadian Public Policy*, ed. Manon Tremblay, 85–105. Vancouver: UBC Press.

Reynolds, Andrew. 2013. "Representation and Rights: The Impact of LGBT Legislators in Comparative Perspective." *American Political Science Review* 107 (2): 259–74. https://doi.org/10.1017/s0003055413000051

–. 2015. "LGBT MPs and Candidates in the UK General Election May 2015: Results." UNC Global, May 13. http://global.unc.edu/news/lgbt-mps-and-candidates-in-the-uk-general-election-may-2015/

Röder, Antje. 2015. "Immigrants' Attitudes toward Homosexuality: Socialization, Religion, and Acculturation in European Host Societies." *International Migration Review* 49 (4): 1042–70. https://doi.org/10.1111/imre.12113

Sapiro, Virginia. 1993. "The Political Uses of Symbolic Women: An Essay in Honour of Murray Edelman." *Political Communication* 10 (2): 141–54. https://doi.org/10.1080/10584609.1993.9962972

Strapagiel, Lauren. 2015. "Jennifer McCreath Could Be the First Trans Person to Be on a Federal Ballot in Canada." *Buzzfeed*, August 12. https://www.buzzfeed.com/laurenstrapagiel/this-could-be-the-first-trans-person-to-be-on-a-federal-ball?utm_term=.baRdEpz5z#.synd7RaVa

Swank, Eric, and Breanne Fahs. 2011. "Pathways to Political Activism among Americans Who Have Same-Sex Sexual Contact." *Sexual Research and Social Policy* 8 (2): 126–38. https://doi.org/10.1007/s13178-011-0034-5

–. 2013. "An Intersectional Analysis of Gender and Race for Sexual Minorities Who Engage in Gay and Lesbian Rights Activism." *Sex Roles* 68 (11): 660–74. https://doi.org/10.1007/s11199-012-0168-9

Tasker, John Paul. 2016. "Conservative Leadership Contenders to Join Toronto Pride Parade." *CBC News*, July 2. http://www.cbc.ca/news/politics/conservative-contenders-gay-pride-1.3659699

Tolley, Erin. 2016. *Framed: Media and the Coverage of Race in Canadian Politics*. Vancouver: UBC Press.

Trottier, Daniel. 2017. "Scandal Mining: Political Nobodies and Remediated Visibility." *Media, Culture and Society* 40 (6): 1–16. https://doi.org/10.1177/0163443717734408. Medline:30111900

Wagner, Angelia. 2019. "Avoiding the Spotlight: Public Scrutiny, Moral Regulation, and LGBTQ Candidate Deterrence." *Politics, Groups, and Identities*. Advance publication: 1–17. https://doi.org/10.1080/21565503.2019.1605298

Woo, Andrea. 2015. "Campaign Lawn Signs a Symbol of Support, Target for Theft and Vandalism." *Globe and Mail*, October 19, S1.

11
Out to Win
The ProudPolitics Approach to LGBTQ Electoralism

Curtis Atkins

IN ONTARIO, CANADA's first lesbian premier, Kathleen Wynne, came to power at the head of a Liberal government in February 2013. Two years later, she was joined by Wade MacLauchlan in Prince Edward Island, who, upon becoming leader of the governing Liberal Party, became the first openly gay man to head a provincial administration. Meanwhile, in Ottawa, the country's first openly gay cabinet minister, Scott Brison, was returned to federal government in October 2015 and was shortly thereafter made president of the Treasury Board. Alongside him in the new Parliament sat five other out LGBTQ members – three men and two women. On the east coast, the first transgender candidate to appear on a federal ballot, Jennifer McCreath of Newfoundland and Labrador's small Strength in Democracy party, made her debut in the same election. With such high-profile electoral achievements in recent years, one might think there is little need for any type of special organization dedicated to electing LGBTQ candidates in Canada. Yet that is precisely the stated mission of ProudPolitics, a Toronto-based non-profit founded in early 2012.

Established by a small group of professionals and activists who were mostly in their thirties, ProudPolitics has carved out a space within the constellation of Canadian LGBTQ political organizations that is decidedly election-oriented and explicitly multi-partisan. According to its founding documents, ProudPolitics is dedicated to the notion that advancing LGBTQ equality is dependent on increasing the number of "viable, inspirational, and competent" LGBTQ leaders serving in public office (ProudPolitics 2013a). It therefore focuses on recruiting, training, and electing LGBTQ people to all levels of government in Canada.

Rather than concerning itself with advocacy around specific causes, as most movement-oriented organizations have done, ProudPolitics schools potential candidates in the nuts and bolts of running their own campaigns, promotes out candidates during elections, and defends out elected officials from homophobia. Its central idea is that the more LGBTQ persons that are present when public policy is being made, the more attention will be given to LGBTQ issues and the farther the community will advance. Although ProudPolitics is a recent addition to the Canadian LGBTQ political scene, its essential premise is not new. As far back as 1978, Harvey Milk, the first openly gay elected official in California, emphasized the importance of gay candidates running and winning. "A gay person in office," he said, "can set a tone, can command respect not only from the larger community, but from the young people in our own community who need both examples and hope" (quoted in Shilts 1982, 362; see also Chapter 8 in this volume).

ProudPolitics is loosely modelled on the Gay and Lesbian Victory Fund, a fundraising and networking group in the United States that concentrates exclusively on electing out politicians. In adopting this electoral-focused approach, ProudPolitics has differentiated itself from the liberationist organizations, legal advocacy groups, and party-based gay caucuses that have long typified Canada's LGBTQ political scene (Smith 2015). Unlike them, ProudPolitics organizes across party boundaries and is agnostic with regard to candidates' ideological viewpoints or positions in most public policy debates. It is committed to an assimilationist/post-liberationist mission that its leaders call "lived equality." With mixed results, it has endeavoured to apply a strategic orientation that was developed for the American polity, where big money drives campaigns, to the Canadian environment, in which election finance rules and non-profit regulations provide distinct sets of hurdles and incentives (Boatright 2014; Matthews 2013).[1]

This chapter analyzes the history and strategic model of ProudPolitics in terms of its place within the larger historical context of LGBTQ politics in Canada and as a particular application of an American electoral model in Canada. The achievements and setbacks of the latter process will be reviewed for their insights into the nature of post-marriage equality politics in the LGBTQ community. I conclude by outlining the possible trajectories and challenges that the ProudPolitics model faces going forward.

Lived Equality – A Post-Liberation World

During the first years after Stonewall, most organizational manifestations of LGBTQ politics in North America were liberationist in orientation (Adam 1995; Tom Warner 2002). Differentiating themselves from the homophile groups of the 1950s and 1960s that had pleaded for tolerance, organizations such as the Gay Liberation Front demanded their right to exist in the face of a hostile society (D'Emilio 1998). Liberationists saw the oppression of sexual minorities as inevitably bound up with the political and socio-economic superstructure of capitalism. In the words of Benjamin Shepard (2001), it was a divide between the "suits" and the "sluts," between respectability and rebellion. As Nicholas Benton (2013, 50), an early spokesperson for gay liberation in the United States, wrote in 1970, adherents of the gay freedom movement saw "themselves as oppressed – politically oppressed by an oppressor that not only is down on homosexuality, but equally down on all things that are not white, straight, middle class, pro-establishment." The gay movement, he said, "should harken to a greater cause – that cause of human liberation, of which homosexual liberation is just one aspect" (ibid., 113).

Gaining recognition by heterosexual society or integrating into its sexual and relationship norms – assimilation – was not high on the list of liberationist concerns. Instead, the Marxist roots of the early liberationist tendencies inspired nothing less than social and sexual revolution. If the oppressive power of heteronormativity (a term that was coined only later) was to be overturned, this would occur as just one component of the larger fight for socio-economic transformation. Tom Warner (2002, 13), for instance, summarizes gay liberation as "a revolutionary struggle that seeks the eradication of heterosexism and the overthrow of the dictatorship of compulsory heterosexuality."

Canada had its own unique manifestations of the liberationist perspective. These included the University of Toronto Homophile Association, the pioneering role played by *Body Politic* magazine, and the Gay Alliance Toward Equality (Adam 1999, 13). Adopting an outlook similar to the suits versus sluts binary that pitted assimilation against liberation, the Coalition for Lesbian and Gay Rights in Ontario, as David Rayside (2008, 69) observes, was "averse to seeking more inclusion in existing relationship regimes" and instead sought to radically challenge prevailing social norms. Pan-Canadian efforts were always hampered, however, by the challenge of organizing across the cultural and geographic bounds of a multi-national state (Smith 2015, 59). The coalition model, for instance, was never matched by a federal counterpart during its more than three decades of existence (Rayside 2015, 87).

With the onset of the prolonged economic crisis in the late 1970s, however, many movements that were born in the social upsurges of the post-war period entered a time of retrenchment. Conservative political forces were on the ascent in much of the Western world, and neoliberal economics largely eclipsed the social democratic interlude in which liberationist tendencies – whether of the national/ethnic, gender, or sexual variety – had flourished (Wolf 2009, 138–39). Gary Teeple (2000) refers to the trend as the long and slow "decline of social reform." For gays and lesbians, the 1980s were a period of intense political struggle, but that decade and the one that followed also saw the reappearance (and updating) of the reformist outlooks of the pre-Stonewall days.

A new focus on relationship recognition and equality under the law was fuelled by a number of developments at this time. For many couples, AIDS forced concerns onto the agenda about hospital visitation rights, decision-making authority for medical treatments, funerals, inheritance, and other issues (Chauncey 2004). The heightened attention to individual liberties and protections brought on by the debate around the Charter of Rights and Freedoms in Canada, as well as efforts to entrench gay rights into various provincial human-rights codes, signalled a new era marked by courtroom litigation that dealt largely with legal rights (Herman 1994, 27). The Charter encouraged a discourse in which policy was discussed almost exclusively in terms of rights and legal acceptance, an orientation that was no longer in line with a general critique of liberal society (Smith 2007, 32; see also Chapter 6 in this volume). The growing backlash of Christian and other conservative organizations against the push for gay and lesbian visibility reinforced the shift of activist energies toward legal recognition and a liberal rights discourse. As Peter Knegt (2011, 42) summarizes the situation, "Rights were no longer a means to an end as the liberationists had sought, but an end in themselves."

By the time marriage equality was achieved, first in Ontario in 2003, subsequently in other provinces, and across Canada in 2005, the assimilationist agenda had largely overshadowed the liberationist thrust that had characterized the earlier gay and lesbian movement. Queer theorists such as Michael Warner (2000, 143) may have lamented the "normalizing" effect that this search for respectability and public acceptance had on gay politics, but by the mid-2000s, post-liberation assimilationism had become the norm. The liberal paradigm of rights, rather than the radical outlook associated with social revolution, was the predominant lens through which most LGBTQ organizing took place.

ProudPolitics was born into this post-liberation world. Its founders came of age in a Canada where gays and lesbians were recognized as citizens under the law, and their relationships had been officially granted equal status to those of heterosexuals for nearly a decade. It was a fundamental dissatisfaction with the shortcomings of the assimilationist promise, however, that motivated the search for a new model of politics. Legal equality might have been achieved, but the practical reality of inequality in social and, especially, political life continued to make itself felt. Legislation and litigation alone had failed to produce actual "lived" equality.

This non-liberationist but not-quite-assimilationist middle ground perspective was a result also of the ideological diversity of the ProudPolitics conveners. Orientations among the initial group stretched from dissident conservatism, unsatisfied with the homophobia of right-wing party politics in Canada, to classical liberalism and all the way to Marxism. In the tradition of 1930s Popular Front politics, establishing a program of action required a settling on minimum points of unity.[2] The unfulfilled promises of the rights-based paradigm were apparent to all involved, but with a significant portion of the ProudPolitics leadership feeling ambivalent toward broader societal transformation, electing more LGBTQ persons to office on a meritocratic basis became the foundation for programmatic unity. This premise exposes the organization, however, to the charge of perpetuating the status quo of an LGBTQ community divided by unequal privilege, with a strategy that is essentially neoliberal and homonormative.[3] Probably only the disorganized state of the liberationist movement and the relative newness of ProudPolitics have shielded it from such critiques so far. At the same time, the lived equality concept provided the basis for eliciting participation and co-operation from ideologically diverse individuals who might otherwise find themselves on opposite sides of the liberation versus assimilation divide.

From Whisper Campaigns to a New Organization

The ProudPolitics idea had its genesis in a failed election bid for a seat on Mississauga City Council in 2010. In October of that year, twenty-seven-year-old Louroz Mercader, a Philippines-born and Canadian-raised out gay man, challenged long-time incumbent Nando Iannicca for the council seat in Ward 7. Earning 34 percent of the votes in a three-way race, Mercader did not make his sexual orientation a public aspect of his campaign, but neither did he attempt to hide it.[4] However, as his staff canvassed door-to-door, constituents often mentioned a rumour that they had heard about Mercader – he was a homosexual – with the clear implication being that they should not vote for him (on voter attitudes toward LGBTQ politicians, see Chapter 2 in this volume). The campaign workers did not know how to respond. Though the source of this whisper campaign was never conclusively ascertained, the incident highlighted how vastly unprepared Mercader and his staff had been to address the issue of sexual orientation.[5]

After reviewing several draft plans, a core group of young leaders who had worked on the Mercader campaign and others, and who had experience in a range of fields – from social entrepreneurship and finance to engineering and academia – coalesced around the idea of setting up an organization to coach LGBTQ candidates on how to engage questions about their sexual orientation.[6] Over the next two years, this group held a series of conversations with a network of approximately twenty currently serving and former elected officials, ranging from MPs and provincial ministers to mayors and school trustees, as well as a range of LGBTQ personalities in the non-profit and business sectors.[7] The group, now beginning to call itself ProudPolitics, sent a delegation to the International LGBT Leadership Conference and candidate training school hosted by the Victory Fund in Long Beach, California, during the fall of 2012.[8]

The Mississauga race exposed the uncomfortable reality that, despite the strides made toward equality from a constitutional and legal perspective, LGBTQ persons who wished to occupy positions of public leadership still face considerable hurdles. Not only must they prove their qualifications, but like any other candidate, they must also deal with the issues of sexuality that inevitably arise during an electoral contest. Questions such as how and when to involve a same-sex partner, how vocal to be on LGBTQ political issues, and how to avoid becoming pigeon-holed as "the gay candidate" were all central concerns (on the media's role in presenting the image of LGBTQ politicians, see Chapter 3 in this volume).

Set up in the spring of 2012, the steering committee of ProudPolitics carried out the new group's first major project. It held a series of meetings with LGBTQ organizations in Washington, DC, the most important of which was with the Victory Fund, upon which ProudPolitics would most closely model itself. Desiring to be multi-partisan and to ascertain best practices from a range of ideological and political orientations, the committee had additional exchanges with officials from the Human Rights Campaign, Stonewall Democrats, Log Cabin Republicans, and the now-defunct GOProud. At the same time, it also consulted with veteran Canadian LGBTQ groups, such as Egale Canada, the LGBTQ caucuses of the major political parties, and others.

Out of this process, the leaders of ProudPolitics honed their organizational focus and chose a set of strategic priorities. Lobbying and issue advocacy were eschewed in favour of attention to leadership development and candidate incubation. The experience of the Victory Fund, which had encountered a backlash from members after taking a stand on non-LGBTQ-specific issues, was a key motivator. The prior decision to be firmly multi-partisan was reinforced, and the lack of engagement between gay conservatives and the mainline LGBTQ organizations was noted as a problem to be overcome. According to the initial plans of the ProudPolitics founders, central attention would be given to supporting and promoting viable LGBTQ candidates – as measured by criteria such as the prior electoral performance of their party in the office or riding in which they were running, name recognition, likely level of community support, volunteer base capacity, and résumé strength – without regard to ideology or political affiliation (ProudPolitics 2012).

Learning from, and Adapting, an American Model

As mentioned, the organizers of ProudPolitics took as their inspiration the approach pioneered by the Victory Fund. Founded as a non-partisan political action committee in 1991, the Victory Fund is dedicated to the goal of electing LGBTQ persons to office at all levels of government across the US. It is solidly in the post-liberation tradition and has hewed closely to a liberal-rights-based agenda (Rimmerman 2000, 71). A book published by the Victory Fund in 1994 proclaimed that "gay men and lesbians are the most underrepresented group in electoral politics" and added that getting more of them into office was the key to achieving further equality (DeBold 1994, xiii). If gay and lesbian issues were going to be more adequately addressed by policymakers, the Victory Fund reasoned, there would have to be more gay people in the halls of power.

At the core of this logic is the notion that when power is shared with members of a particular under-represented group, their interests will be more strongly reflected in policy making. Academic verification of this argument as it applies to sexual orientation is still in its early stages, but significant evidence demonstrates its veracity for other marginalized groups. For instance, Beth Reingold (2008, 128) shows that an empirical link exists between women holding office and their "substantive representation" in policy. In an examination of US state legislatures, Donald Haider-Markel (2007, 107) reaches a similar conclusion for LGBTQ officeholders, noting that "higher LGBT representation ... leads to greater substantive representation." Andrew Reynolds (2013) reveals a similar correlation between the presence of LGBTQ legislators in national assemblies and parliaments and the advancement of issues concerning sexual orientation equality. In a study of ninety-six countries, Reynolds (2013, 267) finds that those with out LGBTQ members in their national legislature were fourteen times more likely to have marriage equality or civil union laws. "LGBT legislators have an effect on two levels," he wrote. "They have a direct impact on colleagues who promote and draft laws" dealing with LGBTQ issues, and "their visibility affects the views on equal rights and perceptions of gay people held by the electorate writ large" (ibid., 269).

Getting these out LGBTQ individuals into office, especially in the United States, takes money, and lots of it. This reality of American politics was the reason for the Victory Fund's establishment. "If we don't support our own," it asked (DeBold 1994, xiii), "who will be there for us?" Its founder, William Wayburn, modelled the group on EMILY's List, an organization created during the 1980s to collect money for pro-choice Democratic women candidates. "EMILY" stands for "early money is like yeast," an indication of its purpose. EMILY's List saw the early provision of campaign cash to female candidates as essential to establishing their credentials as viable and electable. Bundling money from large contributors early in a race was intended to be the "yeast" that would "raise the dough" from other donors in later stages of a campaign (Malcolm and Unger 2016).

So, like EMILY's List and the Victory Fund, ProudPolitics is premised on the assumption that securing "a place at the table" for potential political leaders is necessary, as Bruce Bawer (1993) suggests. Essentially, in the two US cases, that meant endeavouring to have voters judge prospective leaders on the basis of merit, without concern for their particular gender or sexual identity – even though that same identity would help inspire the demographics of women or LGBTQ people and be leveraged to drum up financial support from them.

EMILY's List and the Victory Fund sought to capture this place at the table by targeting a limited number of candidates in each election cycle and using the power of nationwide donor networks to funnel financial contributions into their local campaigns.

In the US context, this model has been eminently successful. Since its 1985 founding, EMILY's List has grown into a network of more than 100,000 donors that has helped elect hundreds of women to Congress, governor's seats, and state and local offices.[9] Its most prominent early beneficiary was Ann Richards, who became governor of Texas in 1990. In 2012, the Victory Fund's training operation – the Gay and Lesbian Victory Institute – collected revenue and support totalling nearly $3 million, and its parallel, yet legally separate, endorsement operation saw 123 of its 180 candidates win their races.[10]

Copying the Victory Fund model in Canada, however, presented challenges. As David Rayside (1998, 287) notes, "The Victory Fund is a peculiarly American formation, one that illustrates the prominence of money in United States elections and the need for candidates to raise funds outside party channels." Canadian campaign and candidate financing laws, as well as the rules governing the operations of non-profit corporations, have required ProudPolitics to make major adjustments to this model.

Under the US Internal Revenue Code (26 U.S.C. s. 527), the Victory Fund is categorized as a "527" group, which grants it tax-exempt status and the ability to raise and spend unlimited amounts of funds. This section of US tax law covers most political action committees (PACs) and many of the so-called super-PACs. Although at the federal level, 527s are not permitted to co-ordinate directly with a candidate, the laxness of the rules allows them to allocate promotional spending and make endorsements that reveal their preference in a race (Gerken 2014). Furthermore, the patchwork of state and local laws provides many openings for even more direct funding and support of candidates.

In Canada, there is no equivalent to the 527-type group. After the passage of the campaign finance reform amendments to the Canada Elections Act and the Income Tax Act in 2003, it seemed unlikely that any similar-style organization could develop (Boatright 2011, 186), though public unease over the activities by PAC-like groups in Canada has increased in recent years (especially at the provincial level). For ProudPolitics, the amendments to the acts meant that although it could pursue the candidate promotion and leadership incubation functions that the Victory Fund carried out, there could be no imitating its direct campaign funding operations. Training, networking, public announcement of candidacies, and defences against homophobic/transphobic attacks would be the extent of the help it could provide directly to individual candidates.

Along with this tax legality, the realities of available financing for Canadian political not-for-profits were also a factor. For much of its history, the Victory Fund had cultivated a network of wealthy private LGBTQ donors. For example, each member of its founding board of directors was required to pledge $10,000 up front as seed money for the organization (Rimmerman 2002, 40). Such a model was simply unrealistic for ProudPolitics, given the much smaller donor base in Canada and the general difficulty of raising funds for LGBTQ causes following the achievement of marriage equality. Thus, ProudPolitics relies largely on charitable grants and government social investment funds to cover its programming and operational costs. Being registered as a non-profit corporation in Ontario and depending on grants has meant that, even if it wanted to, Proud-Politics could not make direct candidate endorsements or serve as a fundraising funnel for electoral campaigns.

Further, the persistent sense that LGBTQ equality has "arrived" in Canada – that the battle has been won – produced a greater reticence on the part of some donors who might otherwise have provided funds for such efforts in the past.[11] This is despite the fact that even in countries where same-sex marriage has been legalized, as in Canada, increasingly sophisticated opposition movements are attempting to roll back the advancements already achieved (Browne and Nash 2014). Though ProudPolitics has held public fundraising events and put out calls for donors, grants have remained its primary funding source. By publicizing LGBTQ candidates through its network of advisers and supporters, as well as through its social media channels, however, it does aim to present opportunities for donors to become aware of candidates whom they may wish to support. As of now, the selection criteria for receiving promotion by Proud-Politics is simply being a candidate who is publicly known as an out LGBTQ person. There is no rigorous endorsement selection procedure like the one employed by the Victory Fund, which takes into account some of the viability criteria mentioned earlier.

Another difference that has limited the extent to which ProudPolitics could simply copy the Victory Fund is the fact that the partisan distribution of LGBTQ politicians and potential candidates is wider in Canada than in the United States. In the United States, out gay or lesbian Republican candidates are less common than Democratic ones, so the question of partisanship and the perception of being largely a Democratic Party–aligned organization was not much of a concern for the Victory Fund when raising money or making endorsements. In a number of instances, it did endorse and fund Republican candidates, but this was not the general pattern (it had more to do with the lower number of out Republican candidates than with any partisan bias by the Victory Fund). In Canada, however, out candidacies were no longer unexpected under the

NDP, Liberal, or Green Party banners by the time that ProudPolitics was founded, and they also emerged occasionally from the Conservative Party, at least in the Greater Toronto Area, where ProudPolitics initially operated. The group LGBTory, in particular, has worked to remedy the anti-gay image of the Conservatives that prevails among many in the LGBTQ community (see Chapter 5 in this volume).[12] However, the 2017 election of Andrew Scheer as federal party leader, with the backing of social conservatives, suggests that progress toward this goal has been uneven. Scheer's 2005 opposition to marriage equality and his 2016 vote against extending civil rights and Criminal Code protections to transgender persons left even LGBTory cool to his candidacy for party leadership (LGBTory Canada 2017). The increased visibility of LGBTQ members in all the major parties simply reinforces the necessity of ProudPolitics' multi-partisan commitment.

It is also the case that Canadian elections, at least at the federal and provincial levels, tend to be much more party-centred than candidate-centred, unlike in the United States. Canada's Westminster parliamentary system, with its fusion of executive and legislative powers, in contrast to America's separation of powers, is characterized by comparatively stronger party organizations, with candidates who are more dependent on their local constituency riding associations and the party apparatus for access to funding and volunteer networks. Although contests for seats at lower levels of government – such as Mercader's race in Mississauga, which prompted the establishment of ProudPolitics – bear a closer resemblance to their American equivalents, financial intervention by grant-funded groups remains a non-starter.

So, although ProudPolitics has been considerably limited in its ability to copy the candidate endorsement and funding work of the Victory Fund, it has adapted other elements of its leadership training and candidate incubation model. Its focus on preparing potential leaders for the rigours of campaigning and its strict adherence to a multi-partisan lens have set it apart as a novel approach to LGBTQ electoral politics in Canada.

Successes

After its official launch in April 2013, ProudPolitics engaged in a flurry of activity, including fundraisers, networking events, public forums, and candidate training schools. Ontario's minister of transportation and infrastructure, Glen Murray, headlined its inaugural public event (ProudPolitics 2013b). Murray was the first openly gay mayor of a major North American city, having presided over Winnipeg, Manitoba, from 1998 to 2004. His address to the gathering focused on his personal battles with homophobia as he grew up and the challenges he had faced as a public official. A multi-partisan panel discussion on similar topics followed Murray, featuring former Ontario MPP Phil Gillies of the Progressive Conservatives, federal MP Craig Scott of the NDP, and federal Liberal Party nomination candidate Tatum Wilson.

Ontario premier Kathleen Wynne sent official greetings on behalf of the province, stating that, "as a gay woman," she was very pleased to welcome the founding of ProudPolitics, which she characterized as "an important partner" in building a more inclusive and diverse Ontario (Wynne 2013). In this, its first major public event, ProudPolitics demonstrated the political star power of its network, a commitment to showcasing LGBTQ leaders from all the major partisan affiliations, and an intention to operate at multiple levels of government.

At a fundraiser held in the fall of the same year, an address by gay conservative political operative Jaime Watt was the main attraction. Selecting Watt was a further signal of ProudPolitics' determination to reach across partisan boundaries, and particularly its intention to support the work of gay conservatives as they pushed for greater acceptance within their own ideological camp. In 2009, when Egale Canada presented a leadership award to Watt for his "outstanding contribution to LGBT human rights in Canada" (Rau 2009), many gay organizations protested. Watt had worked as an adviser to the Progressive Conservative government of Mike Harris in Ontario and to the Canadian Alliance party at the federal level, a track record that prompted groups such as AIDS Action Now to denounce Egale's decision (ibid.). Perhaps the fact that ProudPolitics only provided Watt a platform to speak rather than a political honour, as Egale had, explains why it was not the target of a significant backlash or criticism.

The fundraiser also saw the debut of the lived equality theme, which would become the hallmark slogan of ProudPolitics. In his speech to open the event, Chris Matthews (2013), a member of the executive board, laid out the components of the organization's central mission and drew parallels between its ideals and those of other equality-seeking movements:

> Over the years, our community has fought for and achieved many of the same rights as our fellow citizens: from non-discrimination and inclusion policies to equal treatment in the workplace, and from the privilege to adopt and raise children to the right to marry the one we love. These are great achievements, but when such victories are achieved, it is easy to ... feel we've "made it" in Canada. We have some gay politicians in important positions after all. We can get married. The struggle is over, right? But legislative achievements gained on paper do not always translate into the actual lived experience of equality for people. To make it a little clearer, we can draw some parallels with other movements for equality. Take the African-American freedom struggle for instance. Great

legislative victories were achieved in the 1960s in the U.S., but no one doubts that the fight against prejudice, unequal access, and discrimination is an ongoing battle – a battle for *lived equality* ... Our achievement of legal equality is just one step in the struggle, not the final goal. It is an opportunity, not an endpoint. Legal equality is just the opening of a door. (emphasis in original)

Since 2013, ProudPolitics has regularly conducted public campaigns to promote out LGBTQ candidates in municipal and provincial elections in Alberta, British Columbia, Ontario, Nova Scotia, and other provinces. In addition, it launched other initiatives to maintain its public profile between elections and to expand awareness of its existence among members of the LGBTQ community. One of these is an educational program under the title of "Spotlight." A series of mini-documentaries circulated online and through social media, Spotlight tells the stories of LGBTQ elected officials such as Toronto city councillor Kristyn Wong-Tam (see Chapter 12 in this volume), Ontario MPP Glen Murray, and others (Okafor 2014).[13] Additionally, a rapid-response operation, known unofficially as ProudWatch, uses press releases and op-eds to challenge homophobic rhetoric in the press and public debate that targets out public officials (ProudPolitics 2013c, 2013d, 2013e, 2014b, 2014c). Whereas many of these have defended ProudPolitics advisers and allies from homophobia and transphobia, they have also defended people who were not connected with the group.

The most widely circulated ProudWatch press release was issued in the summer of 2015, expressing disagreement with the efforts of some gay groups to block LGBTory's participation in Pride Parades and commemorations. Striking a dual note of critique for the anti-LGBTQ policies of Conservative leaders and support for the reform efforts of the party's gay rank and file, ProudPolitics urged others in the community to give LGBTory a chance. The press release blasted some of the positions taken by Ontario Progressive Conservative leader Patrick Brown, who marched with LGBTory in the Toronto Pride Parade that summer, particularly his vote against adding gender identity to the list of protections under the Canadian Human Rights Act and the Criminal Code. The federal Conservative Party's continued commitment to defining marriage as one man, one woman was also targeted as an attack on equality. But the statement urged that "jumping so quickly to condemn groups like LGBTory may not be the best way to go" and added that achieving "lived equality" would require an increase in the number of LGBTQ leaders among Conservatives (ProudPolitics 2015). It encouraged LGBTory to push its party along the route of more openness, but it also placed the burden on Conservatives to "prove that their intentions go beyond strategic posturing" (ProudPolitics 2015).

To date, the premier ProudPolitics program has been its candidate training school, called "Out to Win." The first instalment of the bootcamp-style strategy and communications course spanned two days in the fall of 2014 and enrolled twenty-five students. It was aimed at self-identified LGBTQ candidates, straight candidates who wished to become better allies to the community, and campaign managers and staff. It devoted special attention to factors surrounding disclosure and management of LGBTQ identity during electoral campaigns. Strategies for calculating the benefits and risks of addressing sexuality and gender identity were discussed, as were methods for relating those factors to a candidate's larger policy platform. Methods for dealing with bigotry and rumours on the campaign trail while still maintaining privacy were the subject of another panel. Financing for an LGBTQ candidate was discussed as both a unique challenge and a unique opportunity, as the LGBTQ community outside a candidate's electoral constituency presents a target group for fundraising requests. Several big political names shared advice and experiences, including former Toronto mayor and head of the Ontario Human Rights Commission Barbara Hall, MP Rob Oliphant, former Ontario deputy premier George Smitherman, and several candidates or serving officials at the provincial, municipal, and school trustee levels (ProudPolitics 2014a).

The second iteration of the school, held in February 2018 and oriented around the impending Ontario election, focused on the experience of "coming out again," which is encountered by many LGBTQ candidates and some elected officials while in office. Having come out to family and friends, they must now come out publicly, a step that entails particular challenges around voter perception and possible distractions from the other issues in their platform. On the basis of feedback from attendees at the 2014 school, questions of intersectionality – the interplay of multiple identities – were given increased attention, and the unique challenges of transgender candidates were a highlighted topic. The 2018 school also significantly widened the geographical diversity of panelists and speakers, stretching from Nova Scotia, represented by former Liberal provincial cabinet minister Joanne Bernard, to British Columbia, represented by provincial NDP vice president and candidate Morgane Oger, and points in between (ProudPolitics 2018).

Challenges

Though ProudPolitics scored significant successes in its first years, it also dealt with setbacks and challenges as it sought to maintain and grow its network and programming. In addition to the problems that arose from applying the Victory Fund model, ProudPolitics has encountered other difficulties. Although its network of advisers expanded rapidly, and it easily identified LGBTQ candidates to support in the urban core of Toronto and a few other large cities, extending its efforts into other regional hubs and rural areas proved difficult. It had enough support to establish a small operation in Atlantic Canada, but other regions and provinces still lack dedicated directors or on-the-ground contacts. The reverse of that situation, however, is found in Toronto's Ward 27, which covers the Church-Wellesley gay village, where there has sometimes been an overabundance of out LGBTQ candidates competing against each other for the same municipal seat.

Also, the core leadership cadre is still younger than that of most LGBTQ organizations. Although this factor may bring a certain amount of energy to the work of ProudPolitics, it also means that the organization has less institutional memory or long-term experience upon which to draw. Fortunately, this has been partially mitigated by the consolidation of an advisory board whose broad range of members possess decades of collective experience at the federal, provincial, municipal, and other levels. From a diversity perspective, the leadership of ProudPolitics is characterized by a range of racial and ethnic identities. Nonetheless, the group has struggled to recruit and retain more females for roles on the executive board – an iteration of the male domination problem that has long plagued mixed female and male LGBTQ political groups (Cruikshank 1992, 4; Retter 2000, 199).

The 2015 federal election brought mixed results for ProudPolitics. Andrew Reynolds (2015, 1) characterizes the election as a story of "progress stalled" for out LGBTQ candidates. Although an out LGBTQ person was returned to cabinet, only six out MPs were elected, the same absolute number as in the 2011, 2008, and 2006 contests. However, because the number of seats in Parliament had increased during this period, there was actually a net decline in representation proportionally. In 2006, 6 seats out of 308 amounted to 1.95 percent LGBTQ representation, but by 2015, in a Parliament of 338 members, the same number of 6 resulted in 1.78 percent. All of the 6 were white, and only 2 were female – a reflection of the under-representation of women generally. At 33 percent of this LGBTQ cohort, though, the 2 lesbians actually performed better than women candidates overall, who made up just 26 percent of the original members of the 42nd Parliament.[14] The total number of out candidates (including successful and unsuccessful ones) increased by only two, and some of ProudPolitics' most supportive allies lost their seats. MPs such as Dany Morin from Quebec and Craig Scott from Toronto (both of the NDP) were active in their public support of ProudPolitics, but both went down to defeat. Another ally, Liberal MP Rob Oliphant, however, was returned to Parliament after a four-year absence. The stagnant outcome of the 2015 polls represented not just a setback to the programs of ProudPolitics, but also a lack of progress – at least on the federal level – toward its goal of increasing the numbers of out public officials.

Conclusion

For a small grassroots start-up, ProudPolitics made an impressive initial splash, gathering an extensive group of experienced advisers and instructors for its training program. Over fifty students have gone through its two candidate training schools. Its concerted focus on multi-partisanship has won it support across ideological boundaries. Active candidate promotion and rapid-response defence programs have been developed.

Inconsistent funding and a reliance on an all-volunteer leadership cadre, however, have meant that activities and public presence remain spotty, especially between elections. Organizational finances are not yet sufficient to support paid staff. The 2015 federal election cost many allies, but a consistent set of supporters remains in place, as does a network of current and prospective public leaders who lend their names and time.

From a historical and philosophical perspective, ProudPolitics was founded at a moment when the divisiveness of the liberation versus assimilation schism had subsided among a younger generation and nearly a decade after the victory of marriage equality in Canada. It represents a post-liberationist perspective in a post-marriage world. As a result of this and of the ideological diversity of its founders, its political perspective does not draw heavily from the liberationist critique of heteronormative society, for it does not challenge the foundations of the existing social order. But neither is it simply a continuation of the focus on litigation and the achievement of legal equality – gains that, in Canada, have mostly been attained.

Working to give substance to the promise of lived equality, ProudPolitics is committed to winning the right for LGBTQ people to run for office and to be judged on merit – a pragmatic concept around which broad organizational participation could be achieved. Although it seeks acceptance for LGBTQ leaders as a legitimate part of political society, it does so not through direct appeals to the LGBTQ collective or intra-community solidarity, but with a focus on what Tony Kushner (2000, 312) once referred to as "homosexual individualism." The ProudPolitics candidate training and incubation model aims to put living flesh onto the abstract promise of equality of opportunity that lies at the heart of the liberal paradigm.

Notes

1 From the founding of ProudPolitics in 2012 to the time of writing, the author has served as its director of research and deputy executive director. Thus, this chapter is written from the perspective of a participant observer.
2 The idea of the Popular Front is rooted in the efforts of communist parties and other left-wing groups to broaden the constituency for social change across class and ideological lines through the pursuit of shared incremental objectives and the indefinite delay of

more far-reaching demands. In gay politics, the coalition work of Harry Hay, founder of the Mattachine Society and other early gay-rights groups in the United States, has been cited as an example of the Popular Front's influence. Hay's tactics were largely modelled on his experience in the Communist Party USA during the Depression years. On the Popular Front, see James Barrett (2009); on Hay's particular application of it, see the introductory and concluding remarks in Will Roscoe (1996).

3 For a discussion of homonormativity and the assimilationist, conservative thrust of gay politics under neoliberalism, see Lisa Duggan (2002).
4 For the full official election results, see City of Mississauga, "Vote! October 25, 2010: Mississauga Municipal Election," https://www.mississaugavotes.ca/Download/Election-Results/Results2010.pdf.
5 Author interview with Louroz Mercader, ProudPolitics chair, Toronto, June 25, 2016.
6 Author interview with Arthur Kong, ProudPolitics executive director, Toronto, June 25, 2016.
7 ProudPolitics, "Our Team: National Advisory Council," http://www.proudpolitics.org/ourteam.
8 See ProudPolitics, "Victory Fund International LGBT Leadership Conference," http://www.proudpolitics.org/victory_fund_international_lgbt_leadership_conference.
9 EMILY's List, "Our History," https://www.emilyslist.org/pages/entry/our-history/. For a list of successful candidates, see EMILY's List, "Women We Helped Elect," http://www.emilyslist.org/pages/entry/women-we-helped-elect.
10 For the 2012 financial information, see Gay and Lesbian Victory Fund, Inc., "Financial Statements and Independent Auditors' Report, December 31, 2013 and 2012," https://victoryfund.org/wp-content/uploads/sites/2/2017/01/GLVF-13-FS-Final.pdf. Candidate victory numbers are detailed at Victory Fund, "Our History," https://www.victoryfund.org/our-story/victory-fund-brief-history.
11 Author interview with Louroz Mercader, June 25, 2016. It should be noted, however, that tight budgets have been a perennial problem for LGBTQ organizations in Canada, as Paul Mazur (2002, 50) notes.
12 Other than newspaper articles, the literature on LGBTory remains sparse. Named for a similar organization associated with the UK Conservative Party, it was officially founded in Toronto in 2015 by members of the Progressive Conservative Party of Ontario.
13 See also ProudPolitics, "ProudPolitics Spotlight!" http://www.proudpolitics.org/spotlight.
14 The same situation prevails for visible-minority women MPs, who are more strongly represented within the visible-minority cohort than are white women among white MPs. It has been suggested that, to win nominations, women who have intersecting identities must often be more "highly qualified" than other candidates – a hurdle that can carry over into better electoral outcomes (Black 2000, 2008).

References

Adam, Barry. 1995. *The Rise of a Gay and Lesbian Movement*. New York: Twayne.
–. 1999. "Moral Regulation and the Disintegrating Canadian State." In *The Global Emergence of Gay and Lesbian Politics: National Imprints of a Worldwide Movement*, ed. Barry Adam, Jan Willem Duyvendak, and André Krouwel, 12–29. Philadelphia: Temple University Press.
Barrett, James. 2009. "Rethinking the Popular Front." *Rethinking Marxism* 21 (4): 531–50. https://doi.org/10.1080/08935690903145671.

Bawer, Bruce. 1993. *A Place at the Table: The Gay Individual in American Society.* New York: Poseidon Press.

Benton, Nicholas. 2013. *Extraordinary Hearts: Reclaiming Gay Sensibility's Central Role in the Progress of Civilization.* Maple Shade, NJ: Lethe Press.

Black, Jerome. 2000. "Entering the Political Elite in Canada: The Case of Minority Women as Parliamentary Candidates and MPs." *Canadian Review of Sociology and Anthropology* 37 (2): 143–66. https://doi.org/10.1111/j.1755-618x.2000.tb01262.x.

–. 2008. "Ethnoracial Minorities in the 38th Parliament: Patterns of Change and Continuity." In *Electing a Diverse Canada: The Representation of Immigrants, Minorities, and Women,* ed. Caroline Andrew, John Biles, Myer Siemiatycki, and Erin Tolley, 229–54. Vancouver: UBC Press.

Boatright, Robert. 2011. "Lessons from the American Campaign Finance Reform Experience." In *Money, Politics, and Democracy: Canada's Party Finance Reforms,* ed. Lisa Young and Harold J. Jansen, 173–97. Vancouver: UBC Press.

–. 2014. *Interest Groups and Campaign Finance Reform in the United States and Canada.* Ann Arbor: University of Michigan Press.

Browne, Katherine, and Catherine J. Nash. 2014. "Resisting LGBT Rights Where 'We Have Won': Canada and Great Britain." *Journal of Human Rights* 13 (3): 322–36. https://doi.org/10.1080/14754835.2014.923754.

Chauncey, George. 2004. *Why Marriage? The History Shaping the Debate over Gay Equality.* New York: Basic Books.

Cruikshank, Margaret. 1992. *The Gay and Lesbian Liberation Movement.* New York: Routledge, Chapman and Hall.

DeBold, Kathleen, ed. 1994. *Out for Office: Campaigning in the Gay Nineties.* Washington, DC: Gay and Lesbian Victory Fund.

D'Emilio, John. 1998. *Sexual Politics, Sexual Communities: The Making of a Homosexual Minority in the United States, 1940–1970.* Chicago: University of Chicago Press. Originally published 1983.

Duggan, Lisa. 2002. "The New Homonormativity: The Sexual Politics of Neoliberalism." In *Materializing Democracy: Toward a Revitalized Cultural Politics,* ed. Russ Castronovo and Dana Nelson, 175–94. Durham: Duke University Press.

Gerken, Heather K. 2014. "Boden Lecture – The Real Problem with Citizens United: Campaign Finance, Dark Money, and Shadow Parties." *Marquette Law Review* 97 (4): 903–23.

Haider-Markel, Donald P. 2007. "Representation and Backlash: The Positive and Negative Influence of Descriptive Representation." *Legislative Studies Quarterly* 32 (1): 107–33. https://doi.org/10.3162/036298007x202001.

Herman, Didi. 1994. *Rights of Passage: Struggles for Lesbian and Gay Legal Equality.* Toronto: University of Toronto Press.

Knegt, Peter. 2011. *About Canada: Queer Rights.* Halifax: Fernwood.

Kushner, Tony. 2000. "A Socialism of the Skin (Liberation, Honey!)." In *The Best of the Nation: Selections from the Independent Magazine of Politics and Culture,* ed. Victor Navasky and Katrina Vanden Heuvel, 307–15. New York: Thunder's Mouth Press/Nation Books. Originally published 1994.

LGBTory Canada. 2017. "Statement on the Election of Andrew Scheer as Leader of the Conservative Party of Canada." Press release, May 28. Document in possession of author.

Malcolm, Ellen, and Craig Unger. 2016. *When Women Win: EMILY's List and the Rise of Women in American Politics.* New York: Houghton Mifflin.

Matthews, Chris. 2013. "Lived Equality." Speech delivered at the ProudPolitics Inaugural Fundraiser, November 14. Final draft in possession of author.

Mazur, Paul. 2002. "Gay and Lesbian Rights in Canada: A Comparative Study." *International Journal of Public Administration* 25 (1): 45–62. https://doi.org/10.1081/pad-120006538.

Okafor, Udoka. 2014. "ProudPolitics Spotlight Program: Political and Social Visibility for the LGBT Community." *Huffington Post*, September 2. http://www.huffingtonpost.com/udoka-okafor/proudpolitics-spotlight-p_b_5738916.html.

ProudPolitics. 2012. Steering Committee Agenda and Notes, June 12. Document in possession of author.

–. 2013a. "About Us." http://www.proudpolitics.org/about.

–. 2013b. "LGBT Leaders, Proud to Lead." Program from the official launch of ProudPolitics. Document in possession of author.

–. 2013c. "ProudPolitics Applauds Foreign Minister for Standing Up for Canadian Values." Press release, August 8. http://www.proudpolitics.org/proudpolitics_applauds_foreign_minister_for_standing_up_for_canadian_values.

–. 2013d. "ProudPolitics Calls Out Toronto Star." Press release, January 23. http://www.proudpolitics.org/proudpolitics_calls_out_toronto_star.

–. 2013e. "ProudPolitics Calls Out Toronto Sun Columnist over Flippant Remarks on Ontario Premier Wynne." Press release, June 27. http://www.proudpolitics.org/proudpolitics_calls_out_toronto_sun_columnist_over_flippant_remarks_on_ontario_premier_wynne.

–. 2014a. "Out to Win 2014 Strategy and Communications Training Program – September 6–7." Document in possession of author.

–. 2014b. "ProudPolitics Condemns CBC's Robert Fisher's 'Lifestyle Choice' Comment." Press release, June 12. http://www.proudpolitics.org/proudpolitics_condemns_cbc_robert_fisher_s_lifestyle_choice_comment.

–. 2014c. "ProudPolitics Condemns Cowardly Attack against Toronto Councillor Kristyn Wong-Tam." Press release, September 26. http://www.proudpolitics.org/proudpolitics_condemns_cowardly_attack_against_toronto_councillor_kristyn_wong_tam.

–. 2015. "Why Banning Conservative LGBT Groups Is the Wrong Way to Go." Press release, August 27. http://www.proudpolitics.org/why_banning_conservative_lgbt_groups_is_the_wrong_way_to_go.

–. 2018. "Out to Win 2018 – LGBTIQ+ Candidate and Campaign Training Program – February 10." Document in possession of author.

Rau, Krishna. 2009. "Gay Leaders Denounce Egale Award to Jaime Watt." *Daily Xtra*, June 3. http://www.dailyxtra.com/canada/news-and-ideas/news/gay-leaders-denounce-egale-award-jaime-watt-52640.

Rayside, David. 1998. *On the Fringe: Gays and Lesbians in the Political Process*. Ithaca: Cornell University Press.

–. 2008. *Queer Inclusions, Continental Divisions: Public Recognition of Sexual Diversity in Canada and the United States*. Toronto: University of Toronto Press.

–. 2015. "Queer Advocacy in Ontario." In *Queer Mobilizations: Social Movement Activism and Canadian Public Policy*, ed. Manon Tremblay, 85–105. Vancouver: UBC Press.

Reingold, Beth. 2008. "Women as Officeholders: Linking Descriptive and Substantive Representation." In *Political Women and American Democracy*, ed. Christina Wolbrecht, Karen Beckwith, and Lisa Baldez, 128–47. Cambridge: Cambridge University Press.

Retter, Yolanda. 2000. "Lesbian Activism in Los Angeles, 1970–1979." In *Queer Frontiers: Millennial Geographies, Genders, and Generations*, ed. Joseph Boone, Martin Dupuis, Martin Meeker, Karin Quimby, Cindy Sarver, Debra Silverman, and Rosemary Weatherston, 196–221. Madison: University of Wisconsin Press.

Reynolds, Andrew. 2013. "Representation and Rights: The Impact of LGBT Legislators in Comparative Perspective." *American Political Science Review* 107 (2): 259–74. https://doi.org/10.1017/s0003055413000051.

–. 2015. "LGBTQ Candidates in the 2015 Canadian Federal Election: Stalled Progress?" Research report from the LGBT Representation and Rights Research Initiative, University of North Carolina at Chapel Hill. https://lgbtqrightsrep.files.wordpress.com/2015/10/canadalgbtmpcoct21.pdf.

Rimmerman, Craig. 2000. "Beyond Political Mainstreaming: Reflections on Lesbian and Gay Organizations and the Grassroots." In *The Politics of Gay Rights*, ed. Craig Rimmerman, Kenneth Wald, and Clyde Wilcox, 54–78. Chicago: University of Chicago Press.

–. 2002. *From Identity to Politics: The Lesbian and Gay Movements in the United States*. Philadelphia: Temple University Press.

Roscoe, Will, ed. 1996. *Radically Gay: Gay Liberation in the Words of Its Founder, Harry Hay*. Boston: Beacon Press.

Shepard, Benjamin. 2001. "The Queer/Gay Assimilationist Split: The Suits vs. the Sluts." *Monthly Review* 53 (1): 49–62. https://doi.org/10.14452/mr-053-01-2001-05_4.

Shilts, Randy. 1982. *The Mayor of Castro Street: The Life and Times of Harvey Milk*. New York: St. Martin's Press.

Smith, Miriam. 2007. "The Impact of the *Charter*: Untangling the Effects of Institutional Change." *International Journal of Canadian Studies* 36: 17–40. https://doi.org/10.7202/040775ar.

–. 2015. "LGBTQ Activism: The Pan-Canadian Political Space." In *Queer Mobilizations: Social Movement Activism and Canadian Public Policy*, ed. Manon Tremblay, 45–63. Vancouver: UBC Press.

Teeple, Gary. 2000. *Globalization and the Decline of Social Reform: Into the Twenty-First Century*. Aurora, ON: Garamond Press.

Warner, Michael. 2000. *The Trouble with Normal: Sex, Politics, and the Ethics of Queer Life*. Cambridge: Harvard University Press.

Warner, Tom. 2002. *Never Going Back: A History of Queer Activism in Canada*. Toronto: University of Toronto Press.

Wolf, Sherry. 2009. *Sexuality and Socialism: History, Politics, and Theory of LGBT Liberation*. Chicago: Haymarket Books.

Wynne, Kathleen. 2013. "A Personal Message from the Premier." Letter of greetings to ProudPolitics on the occasion of its official launch, April 18. Document in possession of author.

12

LGBT Place Management
Representative Politics and Toronto's Gay Village

Catherine J. Nash and Andrew Gorman-Murray

IN 2014, KRISTYN WONG-TAM was the city councillor for what was then Ward 27, Toronto Centre–Rosedale, containing the city's well-known gay village ("the Village").[1] First elected in October 2010 and re-elected in 2014 and 2018, she identifies as an openly queer Chinese Canadian. In this chapter, we explore how Wong-Tam's election and tenure on city council reveal that being a queer-identified municipal politician does not necessarily equate with unproblematic acceptance by the LGBT community, in the context of Wong-Tam's efforts to revitalize the Village in anticipation of World Pride, which Toronto hosted in June 2014. In particular, we consider critiques that brand some revitalization activities as exclusionary, neoliberal, and homonormative to demonstrate that queer politicians represent a diverse and not necessarily unified LGBT community. Taken together, these examples support our contention that the hurdles encountered by queer politicians often differ from those of their heterosexual counterparts. That is, perceptions about their political decision making are typically grounded in their sexual orientation.

The Politics of Queer Representation

When she ran for election in Ward 27, Kristyn Wong-Tam faced particular challenges that were directly related to her identity as an openly queer candidate. This was complicated not only by the fact that the Village was part of her constituency but also by the nature of her ward. Toronto Centre–Rosedale was (and remains) politically, economically, and demographically diverse and complex. It was bounded on the south by Queen Street and on the west by University Avenue, Queen's Park Crescent, and Avenue Road. The provincial legislature lay at its western border. Its northern portion encompassed the upscale and affluent neighbourhoods of Rosedale, Moore Park, and Yorkville, and its eastern boundary followed Bayview Avenue and Sherwood Street down to Queen Street. The gay village is centred at the intersection of Church and Wellesley Streets (on the link between voting systems and the representation of geographic clusters of LGBT voters, see Chapter 4 in this volume). The ward contained major civic and tourism landmarks, including the Toronto Eaton Centre, Nathan Phillips Square, and Dundas Square, but its numbers of homeless people, shelters, and related health and welfare services were among the highest in the city. Overall, its population was younger than the city average and was the fastest growing, with fewer households with children and a larger number of single-person households (DeMara 2014). At the time, the entire ward was experiencing a development boom in condominium and office construction, raising concerns about access to affordable housing, gentrification, heritage preservation, and the provision of sufficient open space (City of Toronto 2016).

Prior to Wong-Tam's 2010 election, the ward had been represented by an openly gay man, Kyle Rae, for some nineteen years. Rae's relationship with the LGBT community was often fraught, but his presence as the ward's openly gay councillor was arguably a positive indicator for non-LGBT individuals about the ability of a queer candidate to represent a broad range of interests (Houston 2010). Further, in the 2010 election, the two front-running candidates, Wong-Tam and Ken Chan, were openly gay.[2]

Kristyn Wong-Tam has a long association with Toronto. Born in 1972, she emigrated with her family from Hong Kong during the mid-1970s and grew up in the inner-city neighbourhood of Regent Park. As an out, queer Asian, she initially came to public attention as a community activist for various issues related to the LGBT and Asian communities. By the early 2000s, Wong-Tam was working as a real estate agent in a downtown office, gaining important first-hand knowledge about the development and real estate activities in the downtown core. In 2002, she opened Timothy's Coffee Shop in the Village at Church and Maitland Streets, and she acquired a reputation as an engaged local businessperson who was active in the LGBT community. She was instrumental in co-founding the Church and Wellesley Business Improvement Association (BIA), an organization committed to enhancing the business climate in the neighbourhood that includes the Village (Nash and Gorman-Murray 2015). This early involvement in activism and in local business associations ensured that Wong-Tam was seen as both an entrepreneur and a community activist, positions that are not necessarily compatible on all issues.

In her public presentations during her election campaigns, Wong-Tam promoted both representations, albeit with somewhat contradictory results given her past engagement with local pride organizations (McCann 2010). For example, in the early 2000s, prior to her election, she found herself at odds with the local Pride organization. During Pride week, temporary vendors were permitted to set up stalls in front of competing Church Street businesses, including Timothy's Coffee Shop. Wong-Tam objected. As she explained, "when Pride shoots a vendor in front of my store, I take offence to it" (Cooney 2004). She was also very critical of Pride's corporate focus, arguing that "the key to reinvigorating support from businesses is rediscovering the week's political roots" (Cooney 2004; see also Nash 2014). She challenged Pride organizers to live up to "our lineage as a strong and proud community" rather than concentrating on "acceptance and partying" (Cooney 2004). Such a stance tries to make positive links between business promotion and community strength, something that many might see as a self-serving attempt to reconcile business and community interests. Her comments echo critiques from many LGBT political organizations and queer scholarship about the corporatization and depoliticization of Toronto Pride, placing her in potential conflict with local LGBT political organizations who promoted setting up stalls on Church Street (see, for example, Grundy 2004; Kates and Belk 2001; Nash 2014).

When she ran for municipal office in 2010, Wong-Tam's engagements in both community and business ventures could have been viewed as a strength. Yet despite what some saw as her clear business bona fides, several of her opponents described her as "a leftist radical, an anti-development NIMBY, a wealthy one-note political neophyte" (McCann 2010). In part, such sentiments reflect assumptions that the LGBT community is largely left-leaning in its politics, overlooking the existence of conservative gays and lesbians, particularly those in the business community (see Perrella, Brown, and Kay 2012; Chapter 1 in this volume). At a personal level, this unflattering image of Wong-Tam strings together accusations that she is "wealthy" and anti-development while ignoring her business experience and the fact that she is a self-made entrepreneur.

Upon being elected in October 2010, Wong-Tam had the difficult task of navigating a fractious city council and a combative mayor, the late Rob Ford, who also won his seat in 2010. One might expect that anti-LGBT sentiments would be muted and covert, given Canada's record on legislating LGBT equality rights and the social and political climate of inner-city Toronto. Nevertheless, Ford's tenure was marred by documented accounts of his racist and homophobic slurs, as well as by myriad allegations of drug use and criminal associations. Generally positioned right of centre politically, Ford pressed for lower taxes, smaller government, and the "end of the gravy train" for agencies that provided social and public services (McDonald 2012; on the various currents that animate the right, see Chapter 5 in this volume). Although he clashed with Wong-Tam on ideological issues, it was perhaps his relationship, or lack thereof, with the Toronto LGBT community that most highlighted the complications she experienced as a queer politician. As city councillor for Toronto Centre–Rosedale, she was seen as representing the interests of the LGBT community – a community recognized as having important tourist and marketing value for the city (see Toronto Now 2019). This positioned her in an antagonistic relationship with the mayor and certain councillors, and arguably complicated her ability to deal with wider issues.

Perhaps the most prominent controversy in the mayor's relationship with the LGBT community was his refusal to attend Pride celebrations, including the Pride flag raising at Toronto City Hall, the parade itself, and related events, many of which were attended by other city councillors. He took this stance from his first year in office, absenting himself from Pride in June 2011, citing a long-standing family tradition of going to the cottage (Salerno 2011). In 2012, he also chose not to attend Pride events, and in a conciliatory gesture, Wong-Tam offered to host a "Pride reception" with local business leaders to create a "safer space" for him. Expressing some sympathy for his apparent discomfort, she suggested that he was a "shy man" who might be more amenable to attending a small, private event, "as opposed to coming out to the parade which has a million people staring at him" (Grant 2012). Ford did not accept Wong-Tam's offer.

By 2013, Ford's refusal to attend Pride had become a major sore point between Wong-Tam, the LGBT community, and the mayor's office. This was exacerbated by two years of often vitriolic debates on LGBT issues, such as the very public controversy over the inclusion of Queers against Israeli Apartheid in the Pride Parade, which prompted some city councillors to threaten to cut Pride funding (Nash 2015). In November 2013, Wong-Tam announced that Ford had been "uninvited" to an official City of Toronto World Pride event that would host international elected officials and global human-rights leaders. She was bluntly critical of Ford:

> His time has passed. He has never acknowledged our community. We have these [homophobic and racist] comments ... He doesn't represent the values of this city ... LGBTQ people have reached out to me, and it is their preference that the mayor is not there. So, I will not be asking the mayor to receive our international dignitaries ... He should not be the face of the community when he has done nothing for this community. (quoted in Houston 2013b)

Ford's seeming animosity toward the LGBT community and its issues was on full display in the winter of 2014, during the Sochi Olympics, when cities across the country flew the Pride flag in protest against Russian anti-LGBT legislation. When Toronto city officials and community leaders raised the flag, Ford put up a large Canadian flag in his office window, purportedly in retaliation, and attempted to have the Pride flag removed. Wong-Tam stated that Ford was "clearly demonstrating that he is homophobic, that he is bigoted" (Spurr 2014).

By the election of fall 2014, Wong-Tam was holding the mayor's behaviour responsible for broader homophobic attitudes when she went public about an anonymous homophobic letter that had been sent to her office. She blamed

Ford and his supporters (nicknamed "Ford Nation") for exacerbating such "negative attitudes," which had permeated "from the top" (Csanady 2014). Others agreed, including local journalist Heer Jeet, who stated that such comments were a "natural by-product of the type of politics the Fords practice" (Csanady 2014).

Because Kyle Rae had been the Ward 27 councillor for so many years, thus setting a precedent, many of its voters were relatively unconcerned about Wong-Tam's ability to represent the wider interests of Toronto Centre–Rosedale, not just those of the LGBT community. However, as we have illustrated, her relationship with both the mainstream and LGBT communities required some delicate negotiating, given her dual position as a businessperson and an LGBT activist. Finally, although the political and social landscape in Canada might suggest that queer politicians have been fully integrated and accepted, the difficulties that Wong-Tam experienced with Mayor Ford reveal that such is not the case (for additional examples, see Chapter 10 in this volume).

Representing the Village: Planning the Future, and for Whom?

In the remainder of this chapter, we examine the debates around the revitalization initiatives that were proposed for the Village in the lead-up to World Pride 2014, including the Church Street Murals Project. We demonstrate that being a queer-identified politician does not automatically convey unproblematic engagements with the local LGBT community (representing an electorate is a multi-faceted responsibility; see Chapter 8 in this volume). Here, we draw on the concept of homonormative entrepreneurialism (HE), as formulated by Juan Miguel Kanai (2014, 1) and Juan Miguel Kanai and Kai Kenttamaa-Squires (2015), which considers how LGBT neoliberal revitalization efforts, often promoted by local LGBT politicians, might be viewed as privileging the interests and values of certain members of the LGBT community. Events such as World Pride arguably increase the circulation and influence of these (Western) mainly white, normative sexual and gendered citizens – who are commodified and monogamously coupled, with a middle-class consumeristic aesthetic (Oswin 2015). These homonormative gay persons and lesbians are constituted through LGBT landscapes, such as traditional gay villages, that reflect their understanding of sexual and gendered identities and that support their consumptive practices (Duggan 2002; Richardson 2004).

We assert that whereas Wong-Tam's interventions in the Village revitalization schemes might be understood as benefitting the local LGBT community, they could also be critiqued as privileging homonormative gays and lesbians in ways that deny or overlook the existence of queer individuals who do not share this identity (Nash 2013a, 244). Wong-Tam again attempted to walk a fine line by promoting the Village while simultaneously claiming that "queers" belonged everywhere and tried to negotiate competing interests through her initiatives. Finally, as a queer politician, she asserted a perspective that was not necessarily shared by the LGBT community as a whole.

Toronto's gay village emerged in the late 1970s, consolidating around Church and Wellesley Streets during the late 1980s (Nash 2006). By the early 1990s, neoliberal governance processes had drawn the Village into the commodified fabric of the cosmopolitan, entrepreneurial city, and it is now marketed by the City of Toronto and local LGBT interests as a tourist destination for LGBT people and heterosexuals alike (Grundy 2004; Kates and Belk 2001; Nash 2015).

Many contemporary North American gay villages, once firmly established in neoliberal landscapes, are currently in a state of flux, undergoing uneven political, social, and economic transformations. Marketed as unique locations in which to experience quintessential, cosmopolitan urban lifestyles, gay villages attract a diverse range of consumers (Gorman-Murray and Waitt 2009; Nash 2013b). Not only does this result in increased tensions in particular venues but it also contributes to a "degaying" of various queer locations (Collins 2004; Ruting 2008; Visser 2003). Social and political changes that enable queers to be increasingly comfortable in myriad inner-city locations (as well as suburban and rural ones) render gay villages no longer essential for queer political and social life (Gorman-Murray 2006; Nash and Gorman-Murray 2015). Further, some scholars argue that the internet and social media, including so-called dating apps such as Grindr, are contributing to the diminishing importance of the gay village for LGBT social life (Nash and Gorman-Murray 2016a, 2016b; see also, for example, Usher and Morrison 2010). Some scholars state that queer youth are moving away from a sexuality- and gender-based politics in favour of various "post-gay" identifications (Nash 2013a, 243–44).

Although the Toronto Village has not been immune to these trends, it has maintained a vibrant commercial and residential scene, and it provides important queer institutional infrastructure, including 519 Church Street Community Centre (the 519), Buddies in Bad Times Theatre, the Canadian Lesbian and Gay Archives, health and welfare services, homeless shelters, and queer youth and seniors outreach programs (Gallant 2013). Concerns about its decline surfaced in the mid-2000s, particularly with the loss of older, independent LGBT-owned businesses, the influx of chain stores, and the exodus of older gay men to other inner-city neighbourhoods. Today, the Village is home to an increasingly diverse non-LGBT demographic, including heterosexual single-person and family households, retirees, and students. It has also attracted growing numbers of people who are considered "undesirable," such as homeless youth, sex workers, and drug dealers and users (Gallant 2013; Goldsbie 2014; Kennedy 2010; Leong 2011).

As Kanai (2014, 1) writes, we are currently seeing a "city-based globalization of queerness" in which local neoliberal urban governance models support homonormative landscapes such as Toronto's gay village. The concept of HE describes certain urban revitalization efforts that reflect this "sexualized genre of economic and cultural interventions at the local level," that is, the commodification of a particular homonormative gay and lesbian identity (Kanai 2014, 1–2). As we suggest, an HE analysis would support critiques of Wong-Tam's initiatives as capital engagements that benefit certain homonormative gay and lesbian actors in ways that "privilege corporatization and easily marketable kinds of queer spaces and subjects to the exclusion of certain others" (Kanai and Kenttamaa-Squires 2015, 386).

World Pride 2014: Saving the Village

An international event, World Pride is designed to raise the profile of LGBT and queer issues transnationally while promoting local LGBT initiatives, including tourism and development (Luongo 2002, 168). Critiques of World Pride celebrations parallel those often made in scholarship about local Pride festivals, including claims that the festivals are no longer about political activism and social change but have been conscripted as a marketing tool for tourism, resulting in the commodification of particular people and landscapes (Grundy 2004; Johnston 2007; Kates and Belk 2001).

World Pride 2014 permits us to examine local activities, including those of Wong-Tam, through an HE lens to determine how they might privilege some members of the LGBT community over others (Kanai 2014; Kanai and Kenttamaa-Squires 2015). Prior to her election in 2010 and as a city councillor, Wong-Tam was in favour of bringing World Pride to Toronto. Our goal here is not to judge whether she "succeeded" in balancing economic and social interests (a dubious effort at best), but to detail the complexities that were in play during the lead-up to World Pride 2014.

In October 2009, Toronto's World Pride Committee, made up of representatives from the Toronto Police Services, Pride Toronto, the TD Bank, and Tourism Toronto, celebrated its successful bid to host World Pride. The original bid suggests that HE was at work, given its claims about the potential monetary benefits and opportunities for obtaining federal, provincial, and municipal funding to underwrite the event. Mainstream news reports stated that World Pride 2014 was expected to generate about three thousand jobs and bring in more than $236 million in revenue (*CBC News* 2009). After the event ended, final estimates from Tourism Toronto put attendance at more than 1 million people (*CBC News* 2014).

Hosting World Pride offered an opportunity for various stakeholders including the LGBT community, the City of Toronto, and local businesses to reflect on what role, if any, the Village should play for the LGBT community in both the short and longer term. In framing their bid to host World Pride, organizers clearly focused on the potential economic benefits of appealing to the global queer tourism market, and local businesses certainly wanted to market the Village as the "hub" for World Pride events. As Kanai and Kenttamaa-Squires (2015) argue, HE is often deployed through the concerted efforts of elected municipal officials (such as Wong-Tam), city policymakers and planners, and the LGBT business community. Although HE is often a joint effort between a city council and queer businesses, the considerable acrimony that existed between Mayor Rob Ford and various factions of city council meant that municipal support could not be taken for granted.

From the mid-2000s onward, there was considerable debate about whether the Village needed to be preserved and for whom (Nash 2013b). Some Torontonians saw it as an anachronistic area that reflected a commodified and consumerist LGBT identity politics, one that had outlived its usefulness. Others felt that the Village must remain the social and political heart of queer life – a space that was necessary to preserve community and to foster appreciation for the past in meeting the needs of the future (Nash 2013a, 2013b). When Wong-Tam ran in the 2010 election, she supported both the dispersal of queer residents throughout the city and the need for a strong and vibrant Village. She argued that although the growing number of queer-friendly neighbourhoods showed important political and social gains, the Village was "queer 24 hours a day, seven days a week" (LaRiviere 2010), making it a safe and comfortable queer location. After her election, Wong-Tam suggested that the Village, though welcoming to everyone, should never lose its LGBT character, because "we do need a geographic place to call the heart of the lesbian and gay community" (Leong 2011). Attracting large numbers of tourists and local visitors to the Village while simultaneously attempting to maintain the commercial and residential dominance of the queer Torontonians who live there are somewhat conflicting goals, as too many non-LGBT visitors could potentially "degay" the Village. Yet both goals were advocated in revitalization discussions ahead of World Pride. As a key player in efforts to rejuvenate the Village, Wong-Tam engaged in HE processes, supporting neoliberal governance initiatives as a member of council while expressing a desire to preserve the political and social edge that the Village represented for the LGBT community.

After Toronto's bid for World Pride succeeded, local businesses and members of the LGBT community developed initiatives to revitalize the Village. To determine the future of the Village, Wong-Tam was a strong proponent of developing goals and objectives through community engagement efforts (McCann 2010). In 2013, she participated in a somewhat traditional urban renewal process by supporting a Village planning study. The Village Study, spearheaded by a group composed of representatives from 519 Church Street Community Centre, a local architect, a Toronto planning firm called Planning Partnership, a community activist, and World Pride Human Rights conference co-chairs, was assembled to conduct the study. Its carefully mixed membership demonstrates an attempt to balance business and community interests (Houston 2013a; Planning Partnership 2014).

In its uncritical assumptions about the benefits of engaging in neoliberal commodification practices grounded in local economic and business development, the study's mandate highlighted HE process. A central concern of the study was to determine "how best to prepare for, and capitalize on, the upcoming international festivals and determine what kind of neighbourhood the Village can be in the coming decades" (Houston 2013a). This goal neatly encapsulates the tension between focusing on short-term business opportunities related to World Pride and concentrating on the longer-term future of the Village. This tension is located in assumptions that economic benefits are compatible with broader community development (Gallant 2013). As an HE framework suggests, LGBT entrepreneurial interests benefit the businesses that cater to normative gendered and sexual identities. They create economic and political landscapes in which the "queer unwanted" (poor, homeless, non-normatively gendered, and racialized) are not welcomed by either the normative gay and lesbian community or the heterosexuals who expect a particular experience in LGBT villages (Binnie 2004).

At various points in the planning study, the disconnections and conflicts between planning for economic growth and preserving the LGBT community in the Village became visible. For example, an online survey conducted by Planning Partnership asked individuals to consider the importance of "preserving [the Village's] history as a gay village *or* courting future economic development" (Houston 2013a, emphasis added). The use of "or" in this passage suggests that the two alternatives are mutually exclusive. The BIA, which Wong-Tam co-founded and with which she retained close ties, argued that to remain viable, the Village needed to appeal to "a wide variety of people, not just LGBT people" (Costa 2013). This perspective failed to recognize the potential "degaying" of queer places and was evidently unaware that they might appeal only to certain normative LGBT community members.

Various LGBT business owners also contemplated the impact of the proposed changes. For example, the late Peter Bochove of Spa Excess, a gay bathhouse, pointed out that maintaining the "sex-friendly appeal" of the Village would be very difficult, given that the initiatives were designed to appeal to both heterosexual consumers and homonormative gays and lesbians (Costa 2013). This degaying of the Village might lead to the eradication of an expressly sexual gay sensibility, so as not to offend some consumers of Village spaces. Bochove, who had been an activist since the bathhouse raids in 1981, asserted that the battle to "freely express one's sexuality" had been hard-fought and that attempts to create a "family-friendly" Church Street would lead to the formation of a sanitized (read: homonormative) queer neighbourhood (Costa 2013). So, although some business interests strove to maximize the monetary and marketing potential generated by World Pride, others recognized that the creation of a particular streetscape might render certain aspects of LGBT life, and some queer people, invisible.

Planning Partnership's (2014) final report, supported by Wong-Tam, concluded that the Village retained significant political, social, and cultural importance for a large number of people in the LGBT community, although some questioned whether it remained relevant. Proposed preservation techniques were intended to keep the Village "in the Village," a reference to classic planning principles to "reinforce the Village's pedestrian scale, mixed use, heritage and affordability" (Planning Partnership 2014, 18). Final recommendations included the creation of pedestrian-friendly streetscapes with markets, cultural venues, and festivals to bring a broad range of people (not just LGBT people) into the neighbourhood. The report also recommended a campaign "for the [LGBT] community to take pride in the Village as a distinct, vital place and to invest in its revitalization" – a call for community members to spend more time (and money) in the Village (Planning Partnership 2014, 2).

The report advocated revitalization by various means, including projects to position the Village as an important location for LGBT history and heritage. One example, spearheaded by Wong-Tam, was the Church Street Murals Project: through the placement of highly visible queer art, it celebrated various historical events linked to the Village as well as to "queer" Village landscapes. The murals would be part of short-term efforts to "clean up" the Village for World Pride and would also encourage its longer-term viability as a "queer" place of interest to both the LGBT community and the broader public (Salerno 2013).

As scholars contend, "heritage" initiatives and discourses often embed a particular iconography into landscapes to commemorate what some might see as an idealized past. They may accord prominence to the activities of certain individuals while neglecting others. Thus, they can help to solidify a particular historical narrative that is exclusionary (see Andersson 2012; Ingram, Bouthillette, and Retter 1997). Geographical scholarship has often been critical of such efforts, suggesting that they contribute to the corporatization of public spaces, where a certain type of "heritage" is presented and consumed. The Church Street Murals Project can be seen as part of the reclaiming of queer spaces while simultaneously operating to domesticate public locations to promote orderliness and middle-class (homonormative) consumeristic activities (Andersson 2012,

1085). Here too, we can assert that Wong-Tam's political engagements in HE impulses facilitated the commodification of queer space while creating a particular (and exclusionary) queer history for commemoration.

The Church Street Murals Project was initiated by Wong-Tam and the BIA in December 2012. Billed as the "largest mural project in Canada" (Church Street Murals Project 2013b), its aim was to showcase the talents of local queer artists who would create large murals on buildings along Church Street to commemorate Canada's sexual liberation and gay-rights movement (Salerno 2013). In proposing the project, Wong-Tam suggested that it would attract both Torontonians and "visitors from all over the world" (Costa 2013) to the Village, a comment that again reflects the desire to lure people of all kinds to the neighbourhood. The project was also presented as supporting the local LGBT community by "invigorating the visual appeal of The Church-Wellesley Village by connecting public spaces with community organizations and visual artists" (Church Street Murals Project 2013a). Overall, Wong-Tam's project sought to celebrate the diversity of the LGBT and queer community while ensuring that the murals did not further commercialize the space (Skinner 2013). In this case, "commercialization" referred to commercial advertising, not to the wider sense of space being commodified for consumption.

The mural project certainly can be seen as functioning within HE processes operating within neoliberal governance models. As Kanai and Kenttamaa-Squires (2015) argue, commemorative projects are one way that HE initiatives seek to beautify, commodify, and (re)claim particular areas as queer for the benefit of certain members of the LGBT community and local business interests. Wong-Tam, working with the BIA, regarded the mural project as a way to revitalize the Village in advance of World Pride so as to attract a variety of visitors to local businesses. However, the murals contributed to efforts to maintain the Village as a queer space through the creation of visibly queer memories embedded in the landscape, which would counter degaying processes. So, though many visitors to the Village might not be queer, their presence would be offset by the queered qualities of the streetscape and the visible reminders of the Village's queer history.

Concerns about what sort of queer landscape would be generated and supported through the mural project also surfaced. Some people feared that queer history might be desexualized via the approval of bland and "safe" murals to create a palatable (homo)normative and commodified streetscape. BIA executive David Wootton tried to allay this fear, stating that the intent of the project was not to "sanitize the area by desexualizing it" and that part of its goal was to ensure that the Village maintained its "sexy" image (Costa 2013). Despite these claims, some observers state that the murals diminish the visibility of queer sexualities and practices to avoid offending heterosexual visitors (including families). Historical commemoration is a complicated project in terms of determining whose history is celebrated, which events are reified, and how they are depicted. For example, some assert that trans people and people of colour are often excluded from mainstream accounts of Toronto's LGBT history. Recent activities by Black Lives Matter in Toronto attest to this ongoing issue (Walcott 2016). Therefore, although the murals illustrate a wide range of people and events, it remains to be seen whether everyone will be satisfied with the portrayals.

Queering Politics and Place

In this chapter, we drew on the experiences of city councillor Kristyn Wong-Tam to show that the hurdles encountered by queer politicians while serving in public office can differ from those of their heterosexual counterparts. She faced difficult challenges in working with a sharply divided municipal council led by an arguably homophobic mayor who offered little to no support to the LGBT community. For example, Mayor Ford was the only person on council to vote against funding shelter beds for homeless LGBT youth, and he worked to revoke funding for Pride in light of concerns about the participation of Queers against Israeli Apartheid (Nash 2015). Furthermore, by focusing on Village revitalization efforts and the Church Street Murals Project, we showed that being a queer politician does not guarantee support from the LGBT community, which has myriad interests in play. Using the concept of HE, we argued that research needs to carefully trace the "complex, open-ended negotiations ... that produce diverse outcomes and spatial variations" and to recognize the "culturally-mediated, socio-sexual conditions" that shape outcomes in specific locations (Kanai 2014, 4). In the case of the Village, though HE processes were at work, queer politicians and members of the LGBT community were aware of and attempted to address their potentially negative outcomes, including the exclusions and/or erasures of certain subjects and histories through the commodification of queer landscapes.

Our review also suggests areas for future research. Currently, LGBT and queer identities are in a state of flux, and some "identities" are seen as more acceptable than others. Wong-Tam arguably fits the homonormative mould, offering an acceptable representation of sexual orientation that may diminish the importance of her queerness for voters. Second, some young queers have shifted to "post-gay" identities and thus do not connect with gendered and sexual identity politics, which raises the question of how queer politicians might appeal to them. Third, and as mentioned, some of Wong-Tam's opponents suggested that her political position is left-wing or socialist, which, some might argue, mirrors the views of the LGBT community in general. Further research into LGBT political leanings, including the growth of conservatism in some quarters, such as LGBTory (see Chapter 5 in this volume), could throw light on whether queer politicians will be able to rely unquestioningly on the support of the LGBT community.

Notes

1 Since the time of writing, Ward 27 Toronto Centre–Rosedale and its boundaries have changed to become Ward 13 Toronto Centre as part of a highly contentious reorganizing of ward boundaries during the 2018 elections (Beattie 2018).
2 Although he was a champion of the LGBT community, Rae also found himself at odds with it on some LGBT issues. For example, although he was a strong supporter of Buddies in Bad Times Theatre, 519 Church Street, and the Canadian Lesbian and Gay Archives, he also supported preventing Queers against Israeli Apartheid from marching in the Pride Parade (Nash 2015). He was accused of overspending taxpayer money on a retirement party (Houston 2010). His tenure demonstrates that being a queer politician is no guarantee of unfailing support from the LGBT community.

References

Andersson, Johan. 2012. "Heritage Discourse and the Desexualisation of Public Space: The 'Historical Restorations' of Bloomsbury's Squares." *Antipode* 44 (4): 1081–98. https://doi.org/10.1111/j.1467-8330.2011.00960.x.

Beattie, Samantha. 2018. "What You Need to Know about Toronto's 25 New Wards." *Toronto Star*. September 21. https://www.thestar.com/news/toronto-election/2018/09/21/what-you-need-to-know-about-torontos-25-new-wards.html.

Binnie, Jon. 2004. *The Globalization of Sexuality*. London: Sage.

CBC News. 2009. "Toronto to Host World Pride 2014." *CBC News*, October 19. http://www.cbc.ca/news/canada/toronto/toronto-to-host-world-pride-2014-1.833198.

–. 2014. "WorldPride: Toronto Streets 'Overflowing.'" *CBC News*, June 28. http://www.cbc.ca/news/canada/toronto/World Pride -toronto-streets-overflowing-1.2690801.

Church Street Murals Project. 2013a. "About." https://churchstreetmurals.wordpress.com/about/.

–. 2013b. "The Church Street Mural Project Launch Presented by BMO." October 16. https://churchstreetmurals.wordpress.com.

City of Toronto. 2016. "Ward 27 Toronto Centre–Rosedale Profile." https://www.toronto.ca/city-government/data-research-maps/neighbourhoods-communities/ward-profiles/44-ward-model/ward-profiles-ward-27/.

Collins, Alan. 2004. "Sexual Dissidence, Enterprise and Assimilation: Bedfellows in Urban Regeneration." *Urban Studies* 41 (9): 1789–806. https://doi.org/10.1080/0042098042000243156.

Cooney, Darren. 2004. "A Hotdog Here, a Hotdog There." *Xtra Toronto*, June 23. http://www.dailyxtra.com/toronto/hotdog-hotdog-54656.

Costa, Daniela. 2013. "The Changing Face of Toronto's Village." *Xtra Toronto*, April 3. http://www.dailyxtra.com/toronto/news-and-ideas/news/the-changing-face-toronto%E2%80%99s-village-53862.

Csanady, Ashley. 2014. "Letter to Toronto City Councillor Kristyn Wong-Tam: 'I Hope You Get AIDS and Die in Public Office.'" *Canada.com*. September 24. http://o.canada.com/news/letter-to-toronto-city-councillor-kristyn-wong-tam-i-hope-you-get-aids-and-die-in-public-office.

DeMara, Bruce. 2014. "Kristyn Wong-Tam Easily Wins Ward 27, Toronto Centre-Rosedale." *Toronto Star*, October 27. https://www.thestar.com/news/city_hall/toronto2014 election/2014/10/27/toronto_centrerosedale_kristyn_wongtam_easily_wins_ward_27.html.

Duggan, Lisa. 2002. "The New Homonormativity: The Sexual Politics of Neoliberalism." In *Materializing Democracy: Towards a Revitalized Cultural Politics*, ed. R. Castronovo and D. Nelson, 175–94. Durham: Duke University Press.

Gallant, Paul. 2013. "Ready for a Renaissance." *IN Magazine*, June. https://issuu.com/intorontomag/docs/in_toronto_june_2013.

Goldsbie, Jonathan. 2014. "Cawthra Square Park to Be Renamed?" *Now Toronto*, May 20. https://nowtoronto.com/news/cawthra-square-park-to-be-renamed.

Gorman-Murray, Andrew. 2006. "Imagining Sydney's Sexual Geography through the Gay/Lesbian Media." *M/C Journal* 9 (3). http://journal.media-culture.org.au/0607/04-gorman-murray.php.

Gorman-Murray, Andrew, and Gordon Waitt. 2009. "Queer-Friendly Neighbourhoods: Interrogating Social Cohesion across Sexual Difference in Two Australian Neighbourhoods." *Environment and Planning A: Society and Space* 41 (12): 2855–73. https://doi.org/10.1068/a41356.

Grant, Kelly. 2012. "Rob Ford to Skip Parade, but Urged to Attend Other Pride Events." *Globe and Mail*, April 18. http://www.theglobeandmail.com/news/toronto/rob-ford-to-skip-parade-but-urged-to-attend-other-pride-events/article4101008/.

Grundy, John. 2004. "Staging Queer Difference." *Canadian Dimension* 38 (4). https://canadiandimension.com/articles/view/staging-queer-difference-marketing-diversity-in-toronto-john-grundy.

Houston, Andrea. 2010. "Kyle Rae Retires after 19 Years on Toronto City Council." *Xtra Toronto*, November 1. http://www.dailyxtra.com/toronto/news-and-ideas/news/kyle-rae-retires-19-years-toronto-city-council-5837.

–. 2013a. "Study of Toronto's Gay Village Underway." *Xtra Toronto*, April 30. http://www.dailyxtra.com/toronto/news-and-ideas/news/study-torontos-gay-village-underway-58844.

–. 2013b. "Toronto Mayor Rob Ford Uninvited to WorldPride Event: Wong-Tam." *Xtra Toronto*, November 5. http://www.dailyxtra.com/toronto/news-and-ideas/news/toronto-mayor-rob-ford-uninvited-worldpride-event-wong-tam-73045.

Ingram, George Brent, Ann-Marie Bouthillette, and Yolanda Retter, eds. 1997. *Queers in Space: Communities, Public Places, Sites of Resistance*. Seattle: Bay Press.

Johnston, Lynda. 2007. *Queering Tourism: Paradoxical Performances of Gay Pride Parades*. London: Routledge.

Kanai, Juan Miguel. 2014. "Whither Queer World Cities? Homo-Entrepreneurialism and Beyond." *Geoforum* 56: 1–5. https://doi.org/10.1016/j.geoforum.2014.06.012.

Kanai, Juan Miguel, and Kai Kenttamaa-Squires. 2015. "Remaking South Beach: Metropolitan Gaybourhood Trajectories under Homonormative Entrepreneurialism." *Urban Geography* 36 (3): 385–402. https://doi.org/10.1080/02723638.2014.970413.

Kates, Steven M., and Russell W. Belk. 2001. "The Meanings of Lesbian and Gay Pride Day." *Journal of Contemporary Ethnography* 30 (4): 392–429. https://doi.org/10.1177/089124101030004003.

Kennedy, John. 2010. "Gay Strip on the Block." *NOW Magazine*, January 13. https://nowtoronto.com/news/gay-strip-on-the-block/.

LaRiviere, Serafin. 2010. "Bar Chats Tackle Toronto's Church St." *Xtra Toronto*, February 10. http://www.dailyxtra.com/toronto/arts-and-entertainment/bar-chats-tackle-torontos-church-st-6699.

Leong, Melissa. 2011. "Queer and Far: As Many in the Community Move Elsewhere, the Gay Village Works to Develop a New Identity." *National Post*, February 19. http://news.nationalpost.com/posted-toronto/queer-and-far-as-many-in-the-community-move-elsewhere-the-gay-village-works-to-develop-a-new-identity.

Luongo, Michael. 2002. "Rome's World Pride: Making the Eternal City an International Gay Tourism Destination." *GLQ: A Journal of Lesbian and Gay Studies* 8 (1): 167–81. https://doi.org/10.1215/10642684-8-1-2-167.

McCann, Marcus. 2010. "Blend of Business and Activism Marks Ward 27 Candidate Kristyn Wong-Tam." *Xtra Toronto*, October 6. http://www.dailyxtra.com/toronto/news-and-ideas/news/blend-business-and-activism-marks-ward-27-candidate-kristyn-wong-tam-5937.

McDonald, Marci. 2012. "The Weirdest Mayoralty Ever – The Inside Story of Rob Ford's City Hall." *Toronto Life*, May 15. http://torontolife.com/city/toronto-politics/rob-ford-the-weirdest-mayoralty-ever/.

Nash, Catherine J. 2006. "Contesting Identity: Politics of Gays and Lesbians in Toronto in the 1970s." *Gender, Place and Culture* 12 (1): 113–35. https://doi.org/10.1080/09663690500083115.

–. 2013a. "The Age of the 'Post-Mo'? Toronto's Gay Village and a New Generation." *Geoforum* 49: 243–52. https://doi.org/10.1016/j.geoforum.2012.11.023.

–. 2013b. "Queering Neighbourhoods: Politics and Practice in Toronto." *Acme* 12 (2): 193–219.

–. 2014. "Consuming Sexual Liberation: Gay Business, Politics and Toronto's Barracks Bathhouse Raids." *Journal of Canadian Studies* 48 (1): 82–105. https://doi.org/10.3138/jcs.48.1.82.

–. 2015. "Gay and Lesbian Political Mobilization in Urban Spaces: Toronto." In *Queer Mobilizations: Social Movement Activism and Canadian Public Policy*, ed. Manon Tremblay, 208–26. Vancouver: UBC Press.

Nash, Catherine J., and Andrew Gorman-Murray. 2015. "Recovering the Gay Village: A Comparative Historical Geography of Urban Change and Planning in Toronto and Sydney." *Historical Geography* 43: 84–105.

–. 2016a. "Digital Sexualities: Section Introduction." In *The Routledge Research Companion to Geographies of Sex and Sexualities*, ed. K. Browne and G. Brown, 353–57. London: Routledge.

–. 2016b. "Digital Technologies and Sexualities in Urban Space." In *The Routledge Research Companion to Geographies of Sex and Sexualities*, ed. K. Browne and G. Brown, 399–405. London: Routledge.

Oswin, Natalie. 2015. "World, City, Queer." *Antipode* 47 (3): 557–65. https://doi.org/10.1111/anti.12142.

Perrella, Andrea, Steven Brown, and Barry Kay. 2012. "Voting Behaviour among the Gay, Lesbian, Bisexual and Transgendered Electorate." *Canadian Journal of Political Science* 45 (1): 89–117. https://doi.org/10.1017/S000842391100093X.

Planning Partnership. 2014. "Phase Two Report." http://churchandwellesley.com/wp-content/uploads/2016/12/The_State_of_the_Village_Study_and_Neighbourhood_Plan_Report.pdf.

Richardson, Diane. 2004. "Locating Sexualities: From Here to Normalcy." *Sexualities* 7 (4): 391–409. https://doi.org/10.1177/1363460704047059.

Ruting, Brad. 2008. "Economic Transformations of Gay Urban Spaces: Revisiting Collins' Evolutionary Gay District Model." *Australian Geographer* 39 (3): 259–69. https://doi.org/10.1080/00049180802270465.

Salerno, Rob. 2011. "Mayor Ford's Face Shows Up at Toronto Pride." *Xtra Toronto*, July 2. http://www.dailyxtra.com/toronto/news-and-ideas/news/mayor-fords-face-shows-at-toronto-pride-5040.

—. 2013. "Church Street Murals Project Brings Colour to Toronto's Village." *Xtra Toronto*, October 21. https://www.dailyxtra.com/church-street-murals-project-brings-colour-to-torontos-village-54777.

Skinner, J. 2013. "Church Street Murals Welcome World Pride." *Inside Toronto*, October 23. http://www.insidetoronto.com/news-story/4169069-church-street-murals-will-welcome-world-pride/#_jmpo.

Spurr, Ben. 2014. "Rob Ford Fails in Bid to Remove Pride Flag." *Now Toronto*, February 7. https://nowtoronto.com/news/rob-ford-fails-in-bid-to-remove-pride-flag/.

Toronto Now. 2019. "Neighbourhood: The Gay Village." https://www.seetorontonow.com/explore-toronto/neighbourhoods/the-gay-village/#sm.0001ycsk9g1abud40xn7rkc679zl5.

Usher, Nikki, and Eleanor Morrison. 2010. "The Demise of the Gay Enclave, Communication Infrastructure Theory, and the Transformation of Gay Public Space." In *LGBT Identity and Online New Media*, ed. Christopher Pullen and Margaret Cooper, 271–87. New York: Routledge.

Visser, Gustav. 2003. "Gay Men, Tourism and Urban Space: Reflections on Africa's Gay Capital." *Tourism Geographies* 5 (2): 168–89. https://doi.org/10.1080/1461668032000068261.

Walcott, Rinaldo. 2016. "Black Lives Matter and Misconceptions." *Now Toronto*, July 13. https://nowtoronto.com/news/black-lives-matter-and-misconceptions/.

Afterword
The Champion

Graeme Truelove

Svend Robinson was not the first gay man to sit in the House of Commons. There was at least one before him: the late Progressive Conservative MP Heward Grafftey, whose homosexuality wasn't publicly known during his time in office. We assume that there were others, through rumours, conjecture, and pure statistical probability. But when Grafftey was elected in 1958, a homosexual act was a criminal offence punishable by up to fourteen years in prison, and it would remain so until 1969. Even after decriminalization, bald-faced discrimination against gays and lesbians remained legal. Hate propaganda urging their extermination was legal, too. With police forces across the country conducting violent raids on places where gay men met, it is no surprise that neither Grafftey nor any other federal politician had ever publicly acknowledged being homosexual (on homosexuality as a criterion preventing electoral eligibility for LGBT people, see Chapter 9 in this volume). Without a natural champion, gay and lesbian equality was not an issue that commanded attention in the Parliament of Canada.

Svend Robinson changed that. Elected as a member of the New Democratic Party to represent Burnaby, British Columbia, in 1979, the presumed-straight twenty-seven-year-old thrust equality issues onto the agenda (on the long relationship between LGBT people and the NDP, see Chapter 7 in this volume). Whether by lobbing pointed questions at the government during the daily Question Period, by carefully analyzing bills with his lawyer's training, or by crafting his own legislative proposals, whenever Robinson saw opportunities to address inequalities, he took them. A few years after Robinson's election, Kevin Orr (1983, 15) wrote in the *Body Politic* that "the consistency and tenacity of his attacks on government policy affecting lesbians and gay men have been unique among federal politicians and, as a result of his work, gay issues have come up more often in the current session of Parliament than in all sessions since 1867 combined."

In Chapter 8 of this volume, Manon Tremblay notes the role played by individuals who possess strong LGBT social capital in connecting the state with LGBT social movements. Robinson became the first real link between the unassailable halls of power and the gay and lesbian activists in the streets outside. When in 1981 the Toronto Police launched Operation Soap, a series of brutal raids on gay bathhouses that resulted in the largest mass arrest in Canada since the October Crisis, the gay community was mobilized as never before. The Right to Privacy Committee raised money, co-ordinated a legal response, developed a media profile, and created a Gay Street Patrol. Massive protests were planned. But no matter how well organized, protests, rallies, and marches from fringe social movements risk being dismissed by the political mainstream. The gay community was particularly accustomed to this; typically, the only response to its protests was the thunder of police batons. But a speech from Robinson, an up-and-coming MP, at the Gay Freedom Rally in Toronto that year helped to provide credibility. More importantly, Robinson returned to the House and argued for concrete changes to federal bawdy house laws. What had been chanted on the streets of Toronto was now being transformed into policy proposals in the House of Commons.

Acting as something of a broker, Robinson helped to create a network of like-minded gay- and lesbian-rights activists who were seeking to lobby the government. He not only voiced their concerns in the House, but also brought activists to Ottawa so they could provide that voice themselves. It became a pattern: he would compile lists of groups and individuals, and would arrange for them to appear before parliamentary committees to express their views. This network was an important – and recurring – element in one of his first legislative missions: to ensure that sexual orientation became a prohibited ground for discrimination.

Led by Prime Minister Pierre Trudeau and Justice Minister Jean Chrétien, during Trudeau's final term in office, the Liberal government proposed a Charter of Rights and Freedoms that would revolutionize the Canadian legal landscape (for more details, see Chapter 6 in this volume). Among other things, the draft they prepared listed several specific grounds where discrimination would be prohibited, allowing that the courts could define further grounds as society evolved over the years. For now, sexual orientation would be left off the list, which meant that anyone who wanted to see it included would have to hire some very good lawyers. When the Special Joint Committee on the Constitution of Canada met to refine and eventually ratify the Charter, Robinson, who sat on the committee, arranged for key advocates to appear as witnesses. There they made the case that gay and lesbian Canadians shouldn't have to wait for the courts, and that parliamentarians should enshrine their rights immediately. After the committee heard their testimony, Robinson moved an amendment to include sexual orientation in the list of prohibited grounds for discrimination.

That motion was defeated, with the Liberals and Progressive Conservatives (PCs) unanimous in their opposition, but Robinson had other strategies at his disposal. In fact, he had already raised the issue in Question Period by asking

Trudeau to implement a recommendation from the Canadian Human Rights Commission to make the change. Trudeau replied that he hadn't yet read the commission's report, but he was considering appointing a committee to study the matter. He never did appoint the committee, but Robinson was undeterred. After his attempt to amend the draft Charter in committee failed, he introduced a bill to amend the Canadian Human Rights Act instead. An amendment to the law wouldn't have quite the same weight as a constitutional protection, but it would be a good start. In addition to adding sexual orientation to the list of prohibited grounds for discrimination laid out in the act, his bill would require a review of all existing legislation to determine if there were other areas in which gay and lesbian issues could be addressed (Robinson had hate propaganda in mind). "What we are talking about here is a fundamental question of human rights, of the right to live and the right to love without fear," he said in the House (British Columbia 1981, 10824).

At the time, a backbench MP needed the unanimous consent of the House to have a bill proceed any farther than second reading, and there was no shortage of MPs who were willing to block it. As he expected, his bill was stymied after the debate, but after the Liberals were defeated in 1984 and Brian Mulroney's Progressive Conservatives swept to power, he tried again, launching another bill. "Such changes are an essential first step toward the creation of a society in which each individual is recognized for his or her inherent worth and dignity as a human being," he said (British Columbia 1985, 3392).

He expected this bill to be defeated, too, but Parliament Hill has always had its share of surprises. What happened next hints at the answer to a question posed by Manon Tremblay in her chapter: Exactly how *did* Robinson ensure that sexual orientation became a prohibited ground for discrimination? The answer involves several tactics that she discusses: the role of allies, the shrewd use of connections with social movements, and the employment of emotion as a strategic resource. It wouldn't be known until years later, but in the privacy of the PC caucus room, Prime Minister Mulroney made a passionate speech condemning discrimination against homosexuals. Mulroney's brother was gay, a fact previously unknown to his caucus colleagues. This time, when Robinson's bill came up for debate, the PCs agreed to have the matter studied by the subcommittee on equality rights, which counted Robinson as a member. Robinson could recognize an opportunity when he saw one. He called once again upon the like-minded advocates he'd encountered over the previous years and reoriented his campaign toward the subcommittee.

When the Charter was signed in 1982, the government was given three years to ensure that existing legislation conformed to the new equality rights provisions in the Charter. The subcommittee was tasked with reviewing the government's work and offering recommendations. Now, its assignment explicitly included studying whether discrimination against homosexuals should be included in the legislation, too. Chaired by PC MP Patrick Boyer and consisting of five PCs, one Liberal, and Robinson representing the NDP, the subcommittee would travel the length of the country and hear hours of testimony from thousands of witnesses. Crucially, everywhere they went, Robinson made sure that gay and lesbian witnesses appeared. The other MPs took notice. Boyer recalled,

> We had barely begun our work as a committee when a surge of submissions from groups across Canada advocating for gay and lesbian rights made it clear to me that either this had been an untapped vein of public opinion waiting to express itself, or that someone had been orchestrating a wide-spread campaign to our committee, or both. After a couple public hearings, given the close similarity I saw in the wording of many presentations and written submissions and what I witnessed of Svend's tight rapport with these groups appearing before us, it was clear he was making sure spokespeople for Canada's homosexual communities would flood the committee's time and attention. (Truelove 2013, 93)

As University of Toronto political science professor David Rayside (1998, 104–39) would describe it, this was the first large-scale mobilization of gay- and lesbian-rights activists in pursuit of a federal policy goal.

Robinson's talent for networking paid off, and the trip transformed members of the subcommittee. According to its Liberal representative, Sheila Finestone, prior to undertaking the trip many of the members weren't necessarily sure they'd even met gay or lesbian people before. Suddenly, there they were at the other end of the table. "In all honesty and all candour, we were a bit shocked. First, we were shocked by the number of people we met. In every city we went to, in all the towns and villages, there were people who had chosen a lifestyle that we had not chosen," she said in the House, describing the experience. The language she used is telling: few Canadian politicians today would describe sexual orientation as a choice, but awareness of the issue was still in its nascence. "We heard details about physical abuse and psychological oppression from which they have suffered. We heard about the hate propaganda which had been targeted toward them, and that they had been demonized in many ways. We heard about the outright discrimination they faced in employment, in housing and in services," Finestone continued (British Columbia 1966a, 2444).

Robinson had hoped that the presentations would have a dramatic, eye-opening effect. It was no coincidence that the first stop on the tour was his hometown of Burnaby, where lesbian mothers showed photos of their kids, heightening the emotional impact of their stories of discrimination. "Most politicians, like most people in Canada, are touched by human reality more quickly and deeply than by theoretic discussion," Boyer noted (Truelove 2013, 93). Thanks to these meetings – meetings that, at the time, probably only Robinson had the connections to make possible – the MPs truly understood the need for change. Their final report, *Equality for All*, included the unanimous recommendation to prohibit discrimination against homosexuals (Canada, Subcommittee on Human Rights and Justice 1985). A few months later, the Department of Justice released its response:

> The Government believes that one's sexual orientation is irrelevant to whether one can perform a job or use a service or facility. The Department of Justice is of the view that the courts will find that sexual orientation is encompassed by the guarantees in section 15 of the Charter. The Government will take whatever measures are necessary to ensure that sexual orientation is a prohibited ground of discrimination. (quoted in Rayside 1998, 110)

This was a big win. In itself, the promise to "take whatever measures are necessary" didn't change the law. But until that day came, it did mean that when citizens went to court to challenge discriminatory policies against homosexuals – the ban on homosexuals serving in the Canadian military, for example – government lawyers wouldn't argue against them. In the years that followed, there would be several victories for gay and lesbian equality that can be directly traced to this commitment. "That was what was really, absolutely revolutionary," Robinson reflected years later. "That's what really changed things" (Truelove 2013, 96).

It may seem strange today that winning a promise *not* to spend taxpayer dollars fighting against equality should be seen as a great achievement. But in 1986, it was. As this progress was occurring, some MPs were still making virulently homophobic statements in the House. PC MP Ron Stewart once thundered, "Homosexuality is anti-biological. It is anti-medical, anti-biblical and I quote 'Go ye forth and multiply.' It is anti-family and it is anti-social. It is pro-deviate and it is absolutely disgusting to most Canadians ... It is hygienic insanity. It is a crime against humanity" (British Columbia 1986, 1665). Such language may not have been typical, but many people found it acceptable. Robinson's opponents could unleash as much fire, brimstone, and vitriol as they wanted in their speeches, but Robinson had to tread far more carefully. Although he often spoke with passion, he generally approached the issue like the lawyer he was. For example, during debate on one of his bills, he went out of his way to assure colleagues that accepting gays and lesbians as equal before the law was not the same thing as endorsing homosexuality. As he explained,

It is clear that the bill is not suggesting that the majority does or does not endorse homosexuality as a way of life, but rather that we genuinely accept the principle of supporting the rights of a minority. It is one thing to recognize that someone has a right to do something, and something quite different to say that it is the right thing for that particular person to do. (British Columbia 1985, 3392)

But what reads today like unnecessary placating of reactionary opponents was groundbreaking at the time. In response to that very speech, Robinson's NDP colleague Ian Waddell rose to express his admiration for Robinson's bravery. "I was listening to the words of the honourable member for Burnaby. He said that just as the native Indians need protection from racism, and women need protection from sexism, gay people need protection in law from homophobia," Waddell said. "It still takes courage to say those kinds of things in the Canadian Parliament. People will read Hansard of today years in the future and will wonder why I am saying this. However, it is a fact of life that it is still very courageous for someone to take on those issues" (British Columbia 1985, 3392).

Waddell was right, which makes Robinson's next step all the more remarkable – and necessary. He had made significant progress, but a new, stronger approach was needed. As Tremblay states, "Only out (and proud) lesbian and gay politicians can descriptively and symbolically represent LGBTQ people, and in terms of substantive representation, only they have the legitimacy to perform a politics of emotion with regard to LGBTQ representation" (page 221). As important as allies can be, she notes, they cannot harness their own life experiences, become role models, or embody hope in the way that out LGBT politicians can. In other words, if Robinson could speak as an out gay man, his words would have far more emotional impact. Furthermore, he would demonstrate to gay and lesbian Canadians that there was someone like them in the Parliament of Canada and that there were no limits to their ambitions. He'd even show Canadians who were uneasy with homosexuality that gay people were not monsters hiding in the shadows but were instead friends, neighbours, and people from all walks of life. But simply affirming that he was gay would not be enough. If it cost him his seat, Robinson might have looked courageous, but rather than serving as an inspiration to gays and lesbians, his disclosure would be a grim warning of the consequences of being openly gay. Robinson's ambition was bigger. MPs such as Ron Stewart, who claimed that homosexuality was "disgusting to most Canadians," needed to be proven unequivocally wrong. Once he came out, Robinson had to run in the next election, and he had to win.

It was a calculation years in the making. As he recalled,

I knew if I was going to do it right, if I was going to be open, I had to have established a reputation in many different areas, so then when people discovered I happened to be gay as well, their positive perception of me would enable them to say, "Well, we may not be that excited about that, but we know him. He's like a member of the family. We trust him, we respect him, so it doesn't make that much difference."[1]

By 1988, Robinson had achieved that credibility. Known at least as much for his environmental and human-rights advocacy as for his work on behalf of gays and lesbians, he was the rare Opposition MP who was a household name across the country. If Burnaby voters were, in effect, granted a referendum on homosexuality, Robinson would be in a very strong position when they cast their ballots.

On February 29, 1988, Robinson gave an exclusive interview to the CBC's Barbara Frum. In the years to come, he would call it "The Big A" – the Big Announcement. "Yes, yes, I am gay," he said. "I am proud to be a part of a community of very beautiful men and women," he continued, before acknowledging the political dimension of his announcement:

I'm using this as, hopefully, a means of telling Canadians that there are many other gays and lesbians in this country who are not able to live up to their full potential as human beings, who are subject to discrimination, who can lose their jobs, who can be thrown out of their homes, who can be the subject of violence. I guess it's a plea for understanding, for acceptance and laws which will say that we as a society don't tolerate this type of discrimination.

Finally, he added the emotive element: "If, on a beautiful, sunny, Sunday afternoon, I'm walking through Stanley Park, I'd like to be able to walk perhaps hand in hand with the man that I care a lot about, and yet somehow that barrier is still there and very real" (Truelove 2013, 128).

That image hit home for both allies and adversaries. Writing for the *Globe and Mail*, Orland French (1988) aligned himself with the latter when he suggested that the totem poles in Stanley Park "would droop in embarrassment" at the sight of an openly gay couple. A few political opponents made intolerant remarks to the media. Robinson got some hate mail. But for many, his use of relatable imagery had been masterful. "The precedent setting pronouncement had been professional, dignified, and yet passionate. This wasn't amateur hour and Robinson knew it. If the gay community had hand-picked someone to break the ice, they couldn't have done better," wrote Stan Persky (1988) in *Q Magazine*. "It had been a remarkably delicate task, calling for candour, but not cockiness, dignity without dogmatics. He had to get vastly diverse audiences to respond with a 'So What?' and simultaneously to see that it did indeed matter, not an easy trick."

In the next election, held less than a year later, Robinson won by well over seven thousand votes. Such a convincing endorsement from the electorate, and the implicit acceptance of Robinson's sexuality that came with it, made him an important role model. As Tremblay notes, this gave him an influence that an ally or a closeted LGBT politician wouldn't have. Among the letters of support he received were many from young people who had been inspired by his example. One was from teenager Aidan Johnson, whose 1996 letter eloquently described the impact of the Big A:

> Of all the people whose courage and political ideas have led me to where I am today as an openly gay teenager, none have even come close to matching the inspiration I've taken from your example. When I was fourteen years old, I remember sitting in a barber's shop fumbling through a mountain of magazines for something to read while my dad finished getting his haircut. I bypassed *Sports Illustrated* and *Reader's Digest*, and finally came to a copy of *Maclean's* that leapt into my hand and jump-started my mind. I'm sure you can guess the cover-boy! I glanced around to make sure no one had observed my choice of reading material, and then dove into the article "MP Svend Robinson: Gay and Proud." The story churned up thoughts I had never entertained before, and then, very much akin to the Loch Ness Monster, the Big One surfaced: if he can do it, why can't I?[2]

Meanwhile, back in the House, when engaging on gay and lesbian issues, Robinson could now employ an important change in syntax: instead of saying "they," he could now say "we." "Frankly, I, as a gay man and as a member of Parliament, am tired of hearing that somehow our relationships are not just as strong and just as committed and just as loving and caring as any other relationship in our society, that somehow we are incapable of being families," he told the House. "We should be entitled to full equality" (British Columbia 1992, 11926). He actively embraced his role as a symbol: "I don't think there are many people who bracket my gayness. I try to make sure that people are aware of that, and if they forget, I remind them of it – that's an important part of who I am," he said. "It's not invisible. My gayness is just as visible as [American civil rights activist] Jesse Jackson's blackness or [former NDP leader] Audrey McLaughlin's womanhood" (Rayside 1998, 194).

Robinson's eloquence and persistent work on equality issues put him in the spotlight. The media loved him (on media coverage of LGBT politicians, see Chapter 3 in this volume). Even *This Hour Has 22 Minutes* took notice of his status as the most significant gay icon in the country. When Liberal MP Roseanne Skoke railed against homosexuals, calling homosexuality an "immoral and unnatural" act that was "undermining the rights and values of our Canadian families," comedian Rick Mercer (1998, 39) responded with a satire in which he compared the statistical anomaly of being homosexual with the statistical anomaly of being Roseanne Skoke:

> How many four-foot-five, female members of Parliament are there in Canada? Not many. I'd guess ... one. It's not like I don't know what I'm talking about. I've never admitted this before, but I once experimented with being short, but then I realized that being a short grown man was unnatural, immoral, and perhaps a threat to Canadian families. So, Roseanne, I think you should just do what I did. Do what Svend Robinson did. When we were four feet tall, we made a conscious lifestyle decision to keep growing. And if you're not up for it physically, you should consider it mentally.

When an issue affecting gay and lesbian Canadians hit the news, reporters consistently turned to Robinson for his opinion, and that gave him influence. As a result, where once he was a lonely voice nagging the government from the far corner of the House, winning some fights and losing many, he now began to shape the discourse. The Liberals returned to power in 1993; asked if Robinson influenced the Jean Chrétien government's direction on gay and lesbian issues, former Liberal MP Bill Graham was quick to acknowledge him. "For sure his advocacy played a role," he said. "There were horrendous fights in the party, fights in caucus, fights all over the place ... Where Svend was great was, he was consistent through the whole piece," he added. "It was a principled position, he was articulate, and he fought for it. It was great."[3] In addition to influencing Liberal policies, Robinson affected mainstream perceptions of the Reform Party, which had supplanted the PCs as Canada's primary conservative party (for more details, see Chapter 5 in this volume). His rhetoric against Reform positions on equality issues was fierce. Perhaps just as importantly, a tip from Robinson to *Vancouver Sun* reporter Peter O'Neil led to a story that revealed that two Reform MPs believed business owners should be allowed to fire employees whose sexual orientation or skin colour caused discomfort for bigoted customers. According to O'Neil, this was one of the most controversial news stories of the period, and some Reformers blamed it for their inability to break out of Western Canada. Similar bad press plagued the Reform Party's successor, the Canadian Alliance, in part thanks to Robinson. A tip from him led to an O'Neil story about an Alliance MP who supported the recriminalization of homosexuality. Conservative lobby group REAL Women's Gwen Landolt accused O'Neil of bias, alleging that he was a member of the Gay Journalists of Canada, even though O'Neil was not gay and the organization didn't exist. Nevertheless, stories like this, and the corresponding attacks from Robinson, strengthened a perception among many Canadians that both Reform and the Canadian Alliance harboured a hidden agenda of hard-right social conservatism.

Robinson's importance to the discourse was undeniable, but equally crucial for gay and lesbian equality was the tireless policy work that he did in the House, debating with colleagues and crafting bills, motions, and amendments. He worked with an ad hoc parliamentary committee to combat the AIDS epidemic that was ravaging the gay community and helped to spur the government into announcing a national strategy. He helped to convince the Canadian Radio-television and Telecommunications Commission to prohibit hateful programming directed against homosexuals. He tried to change the definition of "spouse" in the Income Tax Act and the Canada Pension Plan to ensure that same-sex couples received the same benefits as heterosexual couples. His bill didn't pass, but they helped to lay the groundwork for a government bill passed by the Liberals in 2000 that did just that. And when that Liberal bill came up for debate, Robinson pushed the Liberals even farther, adding an amendment that would have legalized same-sex marriage. The amendment garnered few votes from the Liberals and none from the Canadian Alliance, so it was defeated. One Liberal who voted in favour, Bill Graham, recalled, "It was a funny thing to be voting in favour of Svend's amendment against the government, I'll tell you. I did get a fair bit of shit from the Whip, but it was worth it in the long run, because it was certainly the right side to be on" (Truelove 2013, 217). It wasn't the first time that Robinson had proposed legalizing same-sex marriage to the House, and it wouldn't be the last. This sort of groundwork was important. When the Liberals finally passed a bill legalizing same-sex marriage in 2005, they'd already had the issue thrust upon them for years. Graham related a conversation between one of his caucus colleagues and her kids prior to voting on the bill: "Surely you're not *still* talking about that!" they said.[4]

Not until Robinson came out publicly did some of his groundwork from years earlier, laid as a presumed-straight man, finally bear results. Early in his career, he had questioned the government on its policy of prohibiting gays and lesbians from serving in the military. At the time, the army's rationale was that the presence of gay or lesbian soldiers would affect morale and therefore diminish operational efficiency. As noted, the Mulroney government's commitment to ending such discrimination was a game-changer. Even if the government hadn't actually revised any policies then and there, that commitment made it impossible to argue against equality later in the courts. After coming out, Robinson met Captain Michelle Douglas, a lesbian soldier who was in the process of being discharged from the military because of her sexual orientation. It was a perfect example of how the government's commitment, though encouraging, hadn't yet changed the situation on the ground. Robinson convinced her to take her case to the courts in order to force the government's hand. That he had already taken the bold step of coming out himself was part of what convinced Douglas to act. "It is important for me to thank those who were always there for me. That is why I write this first letter of thanks to you. You singularly gave me the guidance and support I needed to start this battle. Through your own personal example of strength, I realized that I too could stand up against the military," she wrote to Robinson. "Words do not seem enough to express my emotion in thanking you for your support, guidance and leadership" (Truelove 2013, 137). As Tremblay points out, "LGBTQ politicians hold [a] capital of legitimacy, which flows from their life experiences" (page 222). By this point, Robinson could claim an abundant stock of this capital. He also introduced Douglas to lawyer Clayton Ruby, who represented her for free. Dusting off his courtroom skills, Robinson acted as Ruby's co-counsel. In 1992, just before the Federal Court hearings on the Douglas case were to begin, the government repealed the ban on gays and lesbians serving in the military.

For Robinson, it was a double victory: not only had he played an instrumental role in securing the government's 1986 promise to end discrimination; he had now helped force the government to keep its promise, in one area of discrimination at least. In 1996, the Chrétien government took the next step and amended the Canadian Human Rights Act, finally adding sexual orientation to the list of prohibited grounds of discrimination. "I thank the Minister of Justice for moving ahead with this legislation. It is an important step forward. For 16 long years I have been battling for this," Robinson said (British Columbia 1996b, 2543).

But his most important legislative contribution was yet to come. He'd been pushing to prohibit anti-homosexual hate propaganda since his early days in Parliament, and now he launched Bill C-250, which would accomplish just that. It was illegal to incite the extermination of members of a racial minority. Why was it legal to incite the extermination of gays and lesbians? But in 2002, the thought of adding sexual orientation to hate propaganda laws still put the Canadian Alliance and some members of the Liberal Party on the warpath. According to Alliance MP and future Conservative justice minister Vic Toews (Walberg 2006), Robinson's bill represented "the jackboot of fascism on the necks of our people." These MPs were supported by a chorus of religious or social conservative lobby groups, including the Canadian Conference of Catholic Bishops, the Catholic Civil Rights League, the Evangelical Fellowship of Canada, Focus on the Family, and the Canadian Family Action Coalition. Many of these opponents believed that the bill could lead to the Bible being banned as hate literature.

Such an outcome was unlikely in the extreme and certainly not what Robinson was seeking. He was confident that provisions in the Charter would protect religious texts, but opposition to his proposal was furious nevertheless. Furthermore, during Chrétien's tightly controlled majority government, bills from Opposition MPs simply didn't pass. In the previous session of Parliament, for example, not one bill sponsored by an Opposition MP had become law.

But Robinson wasn't just any MP. After more than twenty years on Parliament Hill, he had a solid understanding of parliamentary procedure and strong interpersonal relationships with members of all parties. When his bill reached the Justice Committee in May 2003, it stood a real chance of passing. Then it hit a snag. After the public hearings had finished, on the day the bill was scheduled for clause-by-clause debate, four of the Liberals on the committee didn't show up. Instead, they'd been replaced by four Liberals who opposed the bill. Along with the Canadian Alliance MPs, opponents to the bill now held the majority, and Toews proposed a motion to kill it. Robinson was incensed:

> As I look around the committee table, I have to say that I have seldom felt as great a sense of anger and betrayal as I feel today with respect to this bill. I look at members on the other side of this table, who have never attended a meeting of this committee when it considered this bill on hate propaganda, who showed up today to vote against the bill. (Canada, Standing Committee on Justice 2003; on obstacles to representing LGBT issues, see Chapter 12 in this volume)

According to Liberal MP Hedy Fry, the Liberal leadership was not behind the attempt to scuttle the bill. "What these four people did was they – without us knowing – started a concerted, strategic plan to check with everybody before that meeting," she explained. The rogue Liberals had done their homework. They'd found out who was likely to support the bill, and in the guise of a favour, offered to replace them at the meeting, surreptitiously shifting the balance of power. "Everybody was so happy to get somebody [else] to do their duty for them that they didn't stop to think," Fry said (Truelove 2013, 255). Regardless of the government's intention, Robinson knew that if the bill came to a vote that day, it would lose. But there was a way around the problem. Private members' bills have deadlines at the committee stage. Robinson realized that if he took the unusual step of filibustering his own bill, he could force it to miss the deadline. Then it would be sent back to the House, and he'd have a chance to pass it at third reading. This strategy worked. Back in the House, Robinson then agreed to a compromise: a clause guaranteeing an exemption for religious texts. This still wasn't good enough for the Canadian Alliance or a sizable chunk of the Liberal caucus, but the bill passed and was sent to the Senate.

The Senate should have posed an even bigger problem. Fundamentally opposed to the concept of an unelected upper chamber, the NDP has never had a lot of friends there. But according to his friend and former caucus colleague Libby Davies, Robinson did. "I made phone calls for him to Senators, and I was blown away by the people he knew in the Senate. Like, Conservatives, Liberals – this is where he was so brilliant, his personal relations," she said. "He had friends in every party, and to me that was his brilliance: his ability to know how the system worked, and to be able to work with people when he needed to get something through. And his bill is an absolute testament to that" (Truelove 2013, 256). With an election call looming, Robinson worked quickly to get key senators onside so that the bill could be brought to a vote before Parliament was dissolved, when any legislation still in progress would be scrapped. Despite stalling tactics by a handful of Liberal and Conservative senators, Robinson and his allies prevailed. On April 28, 2004, with eight sitting days to spare, the bill passed by an overwhelming margin.

"One of my regrets is that gender identity wasn't part of that package," Robinson said years later, lamenting that his bill did not provide protection for those whose gender is not the one assigned at birth. "But at that particular point, it would have been impossible, and it would have just meant that the bill would not have moved anywhere."[5] During his twenty-five years in the House, Robinson had pushed his colleagues as far as they could go on equality issues, at least at that time. Although important matters still needed to be addressed, he had undeniably changed the political landscape. Five years after Robinson came out, Bloc Québécois MP Réal Ménard became the second openly gay MP. Like Robinson, Ménard was handily re-elected several times in a row after coming out. Unlike Robinson's, Ménard's sexuality didn't have to become a major front-page news story across the country; that trail had already been blazed.

In 2001, Libby Davies became the first female MP to publicly acknowledge being in a same-sex relationship. While walking with Robinson from West Block to Centre Block, where she was to speak on his same-sex marriage bill, Davies told him that she intended to mention her relationship in her remarks. Robinson was surprised. He asked if she needed to plan it a little more, to lay the groundwork with the media and with her constituents, as he had. But it was a different time, and Davies didn't think she needed to. "We either have equality in the country or we do not. We cannot have half equality," she said in a stirring speech. But her affirmation itself was almost an aside, in matter-of-fact language. "I was involved with Bruce Eriksen for 24 years in a common-law relationship ... I am now involved in a same-sex relationship," she said (British Columbia 2001, 6641).

Her revelation was not greeted with gasps or stunned silence, but instead with the normal, ambient noise of members shuffling papers, the Speaker conferring with the clerks about the next day's debates, and maybe a cough or two from the public galleries. Adhering to the growing practice of reading from prepared speeches rather than responding to points raised by the previous speaker, the MPs who spoke after Davies addressed Robinson's same-sex marriage bill and did not refer to her statement. The next speaker, a Liberal who opposed same-sex marriage, got up to explain why he believed that, on balance, heterosexual couples made better parents than homosexual couples. Then an Alliance MP expressed his dissatisfaction with the House bureaucracy's use of "travelling partner" rather than "spouse" or "wife" when reimbursing travel claims, a matter he believed had some relevance to the legislation being debated. Then the House moved on. Media coverage the next day was limited. "It was a totally different time," Robinson said years later.[6]

Scott Brison became the next openly gay MP when he came out in 2002. Bill Siksay and Mario Silva followed in 2004, and Raymond Gravel in 2006. Of these MPs, only Brison might be considered a household name, though probably for his ministerial career, not his sexuality. Robinson's success had sent a message. Gays and lesbians throughout the political spectrum knew that the barriers that had prevented them from full participation in the democratic process could be broken down. They could run, they could win, and they could engage in gay and lesbian issues – or on any issues they chose (on running as out LGBT candidates, see Chapters 10 and 11 in this volume).

In 2004, Robinson shocked the political world by disclosing that he had stolen a valuable diamond ring from an auction house in British Columbia and then returned it; he was later diagnosed with cyclothymia, a form of bipolar disorder. He abandoned his candidacy in the election of later that year and focused on his recovery. He ran again in 2006, in Vancouver instead of Burnaby and in a riding known for its large gay and lesbian population, but he was soundly beaten (on the LGBT electorate and the impact of voting systems on its representation, see Chapters 1 and 4 in this volume). There are a number of likely reasons for his defeat: the victor, Hedy Fry, was popular and seen as a valuable ally by gays and lesbians; the prosperous riding had never been NDP-friendly; and Robinson's image had been hurt by the ring theft. But it may also be fair to argue that, by 2006, rightly or wrongly, many in the gay and lesbian community felt they no longer needed him in the way that they had before. There had been a time when gays and lesbians across the country saw Robinson as "their" MP, regardless of what riding they lived in. But times had changed. In the 2006 election, both Fry and the Conservative candidate in the riding were supporters of same-sex marriage, a far cry from Robinson's early campaigns in which he couldn't even acknowledge being gay. And with other gay MPs being elected to the House, equality issues seemed unlikely to disappear from the political radar screen.

More gay men won their seats in the 2011 federal election. In 2013, Kathleen Wynne became the first openly lesbian premier in Canadian history. "What was unthinkable back in 1988 when I came out is now reality. That is progress we can all celebrate," wrote Robinson (2013) in an op-ed article for the *Globe and Mail*. And what of Aidan Johnson, the teenager who mustered the courage to come out after reading the *Maclean's* piece on Robinson? In 2014, he was elected as a city councillor in Hamilton, Canada's tenth-largest city. When Burnaby residents first voted for Svend Robinson in 1979, thousands of Canadians who had never had a voice in Parliament got a champion. He fought for decades, and the country hasn't been the same since.

Notes

1 Author interview with Svend Robinson, 2011–12. For the same perspective, see Chapter 2 in this volume, which discusses Kathleen Wynne.
2 Letter on file in Svend Robinson's personal archives.
3 Author interview with Bill Graham, 2011–12.
4 Author interview with Bill Graham, 2011–12.
5 Author interview with Svend Robinson, 2011–12.
6 Author interview with Svend Robinson, 2011–12.

References

British Columbia. 1981. *Debates of the Legislative Assembly*, June 19, 10824.
–. 1985. *Debates of the Legislative Assembly*, March 26, 3392.
–. 1986. *Debates of the Legislative Assembly*, December 1, 1665.
–. 1992. *Debates of the Legislative Assembly*, June 12, 11926.
–. 1996a. *Debates of the Legislative Assembly*, May 7, 2444.
–. 1996b. *Debates of the Legislative Assembly*, May 9, 2543.
–. 2001. *Debates of the Legislative Assembly*, October 29, 6641.
Canada, Standing Committee on Justice. 2003. "Evidence." May 14.
Canada, Subcommittee on Human Rights and Justice. 1985. *Equality for All: Report of the Subcommittee on Human Rights and Justice*. Ottawa: Queens Printer.
Debates (Hansard): June 19, 1981, 10824; March 26, 1985, 3392; December 1, 1986, 1665; June 12, 1992, 11926; May 7, 1996, 2444; May 9, 1996, 2543; October 29, 2001, 6641.
French, Orland. 1988. "Coming Out of the Closet to Crusade." *Globe and Mail*, March 3.
Mercer, Rick. 1998. *Streeters*. Toronto: Seal Books.
Orr, Kevin. 1983. "Svend Robinson: Speaking Out on Capital Hill." *Body Politic*, March, 15.
Persky, Stan. 1988. "Svend Robinson Speaks with Stan Persky." *Q Magazine*, April.
Rayside, David. 1998. *On the Fringe: Gays and Lesbians in Politics*. Ithaca: Cornell University Press.
Robinson, Svend. 2013. "Wynne's Victory 'a Tremendous Signal of Hope and Empowerment.'" *Globe and Mail*, January 28.
Truelove, Graeme. 2013. *Svend Robinson: A Life in Politics*. Vancouver: New Star.
Walberg, David. 2006. "Look Who's Waiting in the Wings." *Xtra*, January 18, 13. https://www.dailyxtra.com/look-whos-waiting-in-the-wings-22655.

Contributors

Curtis Atkins holds a PhD in political science from York University in Toronto. He has a research and teaching background in political economy and the politics and ideas of the American left. His publications are largely in the area of US Democratic Party factionalism, social democracy, and welfare reform. He formerly taught at the School of Public Policy and Administration at York and was a researcher at Ryerson University. He currently serves as managing editor of *People's World*, a daily political and labour news publication. He is also deputy executive director of ProudPolitics Canada.

After earning his doctorate from Université Laval, **Frédéric Boily** became a professor of political science at Faculté St-Jean, University of Alberta. His areas of specialization are Canadian political ideologies, more specifically conservatism and populism. He is the author of many books, such as *Le conservatisme au Québec. Retour sur une tradition oubliée* (2010), which received the 2011 Donald Smiley award from the Canadian Political Science Association. His most recent works are *Stephen Harper. La fracture idéologique d'une vision du Canada* (2016) and *La Coalition Avenir Québec. Une idéologie à la recherche du pouvoir* (2018).

Steven D. Brown is an associate professor emeritus of political science at Wilfrid Laurier University. His areas of specialization are electoral and political behaviour, public opinion, political psychology, and survey methodology. In addition to research about LGBT political orientations, his recent publications have focused on public opinion regarding the criminal justice system – factors affecting the public's preference for punitive treatment of criminal offenders and the impact of anti-immigrant attitudes on the imputation of criminality to immigration populations.

Alexa DeGagne is an assistant professor in women's and gender studies at Athabasca University. Her research, teaching, and community engagement are focused on LGBTQ social justice movements and activisms in Canada and the United States. Her current research project examines the changing relationships between LGBTQ communities and police organizations across Canada. She has published works on LGBTQ politics in Alberta, homonationalism and the Canadian criminal justice system, LGBTQ refugees in the Canadian refugee system, the uses of anger as a tool in Canadian LGBTQ activism, and the politics of police in LGBTQ communities.

The only woman to sign the "We Demand" statement in 1971, **Cheri DiNovo** has been an LGBTQ2S activist for almost fifty years. She performed the first legalized same-sex marriage in Canada, and after being elected to the Ontario legislature in 2006, she had more LGBTQ2S legislation passed than anyone in Canadian history. Toby's Law added trans rights to the Ontario Human Rights Code. Another bill banned conversion therapy for Ontario minors, and Cy and Ruby's Law achieved parental equality for lesbian and trans parents. Finally, the Trans Day of Remembrance was established in 2017. That year, DiNovo returned to the ministry and is now minister at Trinity–St. Paul's Centre for Faith, Justice and the Arts in Toronto.

Joanna Everitt is a professor of political science at the University of New Brunswick in Saint John. She specializes in Canadian politics, gender differences in public opinion, media coverage of male and female party leaders and its impact on leadership evaluations, identity politics, and voting behaviour in Canadian elections. She is the co-editor of *Gendered Mediation: Identity and Image Making in Canadian Politics* (2019) and *The Blueprint: Conservative Parties and Their Impact on Canadian Politics* (2017), and is co-author of *Dominance and Decline: Making Sense of Recent Canadian Elections* (2012). She has also published over forty essays in national and international journals and edited collections.

Andrew Gorman-Murray is a professor of geography at Western Sydney University, Australia. His research encompasses gender, sexuality and space, homemaking and households, place making and mobilities, and social planning and the politics of belonging. His books include *Material Geographies of Household Sustainability* (2011, with Ruth Lane), *Sexuality, Rurality and Geography* (2013, with Barbara Pini and Lia Bryant), *Masculinities and Place* (2014, with Peter Hopkins), and *Queering the Interior* (2017, with Matt Cook). He is co-editor of the journal *Emotion, Space and Society* and an editorial board member for *Gender, Place and Culture* and *Social and Cultural Geography*.

Brooke Jeffrey is a professor of political science at Concordia University and a long-serving director of the graduate program in public administration. A former federal public servant, she worked on the drafting of the Canadian Human Rights Act and the Charter of Rights and Freedoms, and was research co-ordinator for the subsequent parliamentary report on visible minorities, *Equality Now*. She later served as research director and policy adviser to a succession of federal Liberal leaders. Her book *Divided Loyalties: The Liberal Party of Canada, 1984–2008* has been described as the "definitive record," which "stands alone in the literature on Canadian political parties."

Barry Kay was born in Toronto and educated at McMaster University (BA), the University of Pennsylvania (MA), and the University of Rochester (PhD). He taught at the University of Saskatchewan and the University of Windsor before coming to Wilfrid Laurier University in 1978. A member of the 1984 National Election Study team, he also developed a national seat projection model based on electoral data and opinion polls. He has authored or co-authored some 40 academic articles and book chapters, and over 270 newspaper op-ed columns. Since 2004, he has served as an election analyst and headed the election decision desk for Global Television.

Mireille Lalancette is a professor of political communication at the Université du Québec à Trois-Rivières. She has published about the construction of the mediatized image of politicians, gender, and representation, and about the use of social media by citizens, grassroots organizations, and political actors. She is the author of *ABC de l'argumentation pour les professionnels de la santé ou toute autre personne qui souhaite convaincre* (2019, with Marie-Josée Drolet and Marie-Ève Caty) and the editor of *Selfies and Stars: Politique et culture de la célébrité en France et en Amérique du Nord* (2019, with Pierre Leroux and François Hourmant). She is also the editor of *What's Trending in Canadian Politics? Understanding Transformations in Power, Media, and the Public Sphere* (2019, with Vincent Raynauld and Erin Crandall).

Catherine J. Nash is a professor in the Department of Geography at Brock University. Her research interests include sexuality/queer/feminist and trans geographies, mobilities, and digital technologies. Her work examines the historical geographies of Toronto's gay village, queer women's bathhouse spaces, trans urban spaces, and new LGBTQ neighbourhoods. She is also interested in methodologies and pedagogical issues. Her recent work considers intergenerational LGBT issues, new LGBT mobilities, and the impacts of digital technologies and new social media on urban places. She has published in a wide range of journals, including *Acme, Antipode, Area, Canadian Geographer, Environment and Planning D, Geoforum, International Journal of Urban and Regional Research,* and *Urban Studies*.

Andrea M.L. Perrella is an associate professor of political science at Wilfrid Laurier University and a member of the Laurier Institute for the Study of Public Opinion and Policy. He holds a doctorate from the Université de Montréal. He has published research in political behaviour, electoral politics, and political participation. Some of his more recent work examines attitudes toward public health policy and the structural basis of populism.

Dennis Pilon is an associate professor in the Department of Politics at York University. His research interests include Canadian and comparative democratization, voting systems, diverse representation, and class analysis. He has published in the *Canadian Political Science Review*, the *Journal of Canadian Studies*, *Labour/Le Travail*, *Studies in Political Economy*, the *Journal of Parliamentary and Political Law*, *Inroads*, and the *Socialist Register*, contributed chapters to eleven edited collections, and written two books and co-edited one other. His most recent book is *Wrestling with Democracy: Voting Systems as Politics in the Twentieth Century West*.

Tracey Raney is an associate professor in the Department of Politics and Public Administration at Ryerson University in Toronto. Her research deals with Canadian politics and women and politics. Her work focuses mainly on questions of identity and representation, including women's political representation (Canada and Ontario), sexual harassment and violence against women in politics, Canadian national identity, and sub-national/regional political identities in Canada. She has published in several journals, including the *Canadian Journal of Political Science*, *International Journal of Canadian Studies*, *Nations and Nationalism*, and *Social Politics: International Studies in Gender, State and Society*. She was awarded the 2013 Jill Vickers Prize for her paper entitled "Leaving Parliament: Gender and Exit in the Ontario Legislature."

Ève Robidoux-Descary holds a master's of Canadian studies from the University of Alberta's Campus Saint-Jean. She took her bachelor's degree in geography at Université du Québec à Montréal. Her research focuses on gender stereotyping of women in politics, especially by the Alberta and Quebec media. She is the co-author of "Entre réappropriation et neutralisation du genre: le cas de Christy Clark," a chapter in *Genre et politique dans la presse en France et au Canada* (2014), edited by Anne-Marie Gingras. She is currently a writer and editor with Alberta Education.

Manon Tremblay is a professor in the School of Political Studies at the University of Ottawa. Her research interests are gender/women in politics and LGBTQ politics and social activism. Her current research looks at LGBTQ people elected in Canadian politics. Her written work includes *100 Questions about Women and Politics* (2018); *The Ashgate Research Companion to Lesbian and Gay Activism* (2015, co-edited with D. Paternotte); *Genre et professionnalisation de la politique municipale* (2016, co-authored with A. Mévellec); *Stalled: The Representation of Women in Canadian Governments* (2013, co-edited with

L. Trimble and J. Arscott); and *The Lesbian and Gay Movement and the State: Comparative Insights into a Transformed Relationship* (2011, co-edited with D. Paternotte and C. Johnson).

Graeme Truelove is a writer and editor. He is the author of the critically acclaimed *Svend Robinson: A Life in Politics* (2013), which appeared on the BC Bookworld Bestseller List and was nominated for a 2014 BC Book Prize for the book that "contributes the most to the enjoyment and understanding of the province of British Columbia." He also contributed to the second and third editions of *House of Commons Procedure and Practice* (2009 and 2017), which was called "the most important book on the Hill" by *Maclean's* magazine. His next book, *UN-Canadian: Islamophobia in the True North*, will be published by Nightwood Editions in the fall of 2019.

Angelia Wagner is a postdoctoral fellow in the Department of Political Science at the University of Alberta. Her postdoctoral research examines how the potentially differing attitudes of women and men regarding a career in politics influence the candidate emergence process in Canada. She began this research while she was a Social Sciences and Humanities Research Council of Canada postdoctoral fellow with the Centre for the Study of Democratic Citizenship at McGill University. In addition to political candidacy, Wagner's research interests include gender and politics, Canadian politics, political communication, and representation.

Index

Note: For an overview of terminology, see the main entry "terminology, LGBTQ." Although LGBTQ acronyms vary in the text, only the abbreviation LGBTQ is used in the index. Page numbers with (t) refer to tables and those with (f) refer to figures.

abortion issue, 18, 63(t), 64, 172, 180–81. *See also* ideological spectrum, specific issues

activism. *See* social-movement activism

age: homophobia, xi, 16, 260–61

age, socio-demographics: by electoral engagement, 58–62, 59(t)–61(t), 73–74; by gender, 55, 56(t)–57(t), 73–74; by vote choice (2006–15), 69(t)–72(t), 71–74; by vote choice in Ontario election (2014), 90, 91(t)–92(t)

Ahmad, Cameron, 197

Alberta: gay-straight alliances in schools, 166, 168; human rights legislation, 188, 198n6; LGBTQ candidates, 247–49, 249(t), 252; LGBTQ councillors, 265; LGBTQ MLAs, 248, 252, 254; NDP Alberta, 252, 262; Progressive Conservatives, 35, 161, 165, 166–67, 252; same-sex marriage, 191–92, 198n7; sexual health education, 167; trans people, 166, 167, 168; United Conservative Party, 168; *Vriend v Alberta*, 188, 195, 198n6; Wildrose Party, 159, 167–68, 248. *See also* provinces and territories

Alliance Party. *See* Reform/Alliance Party

allies for LGBTQ people: about, 3, 226–27; emotions and representation, 222, 316; in House of Commons, 319; importance of, 226–27; key questions, 220; non-LGBTQ voters, 111; political parties as, 23–24; as political representatives, 220, 222, 226–28, 234; ProudPolitics as, 291; Svend Robinson's networks, 326

Ambrose, Rona, 160, 163, 211

Anders, Rob, 211

Atlantic Canada, socio-demographics: by electoral engagement, 58–62, 59(t)–61(t), 73–74; by gender and LGB/non-LGB, 55, 56(t)–57(t), 73–74; by vote choice (2006–15), 69–70, 69(t), 71–74, 71(t). *See also* New Brunswick; Newfoundland and Labrador; Nova Scotia; Prince Edward Island

Australia: demographics, 55, 76n3; representation by voting system, 128(t), 129, 132–36, 134(t)–35(t); same-sex marriage, 3

Bailey, Robert, 13, 30
Baird, John, 161–62
Bartolini, Stefano, 158
Bawer, Bruce, 285
Belgium: representation by voting system, 128(t), 132–36, 134(t)–35(t), 136; same-sex marriage, 3
Benson, Sheri, 140(t), 251
Benton, Nicholas, 280
Bernard, Joanne, 4, 291
Best, Lisa, 95
Beuhler, Sarah, 207
binaries and polarities, 5–6, 29–30, 114–15, 116–17. *See also* LGBTQ people and communities; sexuality
Bird, Karen, 138, 143
bisexuals: about, 6–7, 53–55; biphobia, 233; candidates, 267; competitiveness, 254; heteronormative assumptions, 267; ideological spectrum, 74; media framing, 119n1; municipal candidates, 268; political involvement, 62; political representation, 235n2, 236n3; self-identification, 6, 52–55; terminology,

5–7, 38n1, 119n1; voter behaviour, 53. *See also* LGBTQ people and communities; political representation; terminology, LGBTQ
bisexuals, demographics: attention to media news, 59, 59(t)–61(t); percentage of population, 13, 53–54, 76n3, 77n4; socio-demographics by electoral engagement, 58–62, 59(t)–61(t), 73–74; socio-demographics by gender, 54–55, 56(t)–57(t), 73–74
Biso, Derrick, 269
Bjarnegård, Elin, 236n4
Black, Jerome, 137–38
Blain, Raymond, 141
Blakeman, Laurie, 157
Blakeney, Allan, 186
Bloc Québécois (BQ): LGBTQ candidates, 247–49, 248(t); LGBTQ MPs, 139–40, 140(t), 252, 326; LGBTQ support in elections (2006–15), 64–67, 66(f), 68–69, 68(f); same-sex marriage, 194; socio-demographics by vote choice (2006–15), 70(t), 72(t), 73–74. *See also* Quebec
Blue Tent events, 161
Bochove, Peter, 306–7
Boisclair, André: about, 102, 105–6, 117–18; absence of pride, 112–13; cocaine use, 105, 110, 116–17, 118; election (2007), 106, 110; first elected gay politician, 34, 108, 117; homophobia, 110; likeability, 113–14; media framing of, 29–30, 34, 80, 102, 105, 250; as not a threat to heteronormativity, 117–18; personal history, 113–14, 116, 119n3; PQ leadership, 98n1, 106; research project on sexual mediation, 105–7, 117–18; respectability issues, 105, 110, 113–14, 116–17; substantive representation, 112–13, 117–18
Boissonnault, Randy, 118, 140(t), 251, 254
Bombardier, Denise, 116
Boulerice, André, 119n7
Boyer, Patrick, 187, 317–18
BPM (Beats per Minute) (film), 235
BQ. *See* Bloc Québécois (BQ)
Brazil, 24–25, 27, 28
Brewer, Allison, 30, 80, 82, 98n1, 104–5, 119n8, 250, 262

Bright, Chelsie, 228
Brison, Scott, 140(t), 251–52, 254, 255, 255n5, 279, 327
Britain. *See* United Kingdom
British Columbia: Gay Alliance Toward Equality party, 244, 281; LGBTQ candidates, 247–49, 249(t), 267, 270; LGBTQ MLAs, 252; Liberal Party, 161; NDP party, 262, 270; socio-demographics by gender and LGB/non-LGB, 55, 56(t)–57(t), 73–74; socio-demographics by vote choice and LGB/non-LGB, 69–74, 69(t), 71(t); voting systems, 136. *See also* provinces and territories; Robinson, Svend
Broadbent, Ed, 184, 204
Brown, Patrick, 168–69, 171, 290
Brown, Steven, 6, 53, 64
Buckley, William F., Jr., 172
Butler, Judith, 14, 255n1
Button, James, 20, 32, 273
Byrne, Christopher, 26

Cameron, David, 39n15, 143, 171–72
Camp, Michael, 25, 29, 30, 82, 141, 142, 250, 262, 264, 270, 273
campaigns. *See* candidates
Campbell, Kim, 188
Canadian Bill of Rights, 204, 205
Canadian Charter of Rights. *See* Charter of Rights and Freedoms
Canadian Human Rights Act (CHRA): about, 183; conservativism, 169; gender identity and expression, 169, 196, 201, 208, 209–12, 216n6, 290; sexual orientation as prohibited ground, 188–89, 231, 316, 324; trans rights, 209–12
Canadian Women Voters Congress, 245
candidates: about, 36–37, 103–4, 240–41, 254–55; competitiveness, 29, 37, 131–32, 249, 252–54, 255n1, 262; election campaigns, 249–54; eligibility, 37, 242–44, 254; feminine vs masculine traits, 16–17, 84–85, 87, 93, 103, 269; first election, challenger vs inheritor vs open-seat, 253, 253(t); first election, rural vs urban, 29; heteronormative assumptions, 103–5, 242; historical background, 240–41, 243; ideological spectrum, 242, 254; LGBTQ candidates

by party, 247–49, 248(t)–49(t);
LGBTQ MPs by party (1979–2015),
139–41, 140(t); out vs closeted, 251–52,
254; political ambition, 244–46;
public opinion trends, 3–4, 83–84,
94–95; quality candidates, defined, 29;
recruitment, 242, 244–47; resistance
to LGBTQ candidates, 260–61; role
models for, 30–31; scholarship on, 263;
self-starters, 245–47; social context,
241–42, 254–55; supply and demand,
242, 255n1, 263; theoretical framework,
241–42; unknown information, 28,
247; urban/rural areas, 29, 254–55.
See also political parties; political
representation; ProudPolitics; ridings
and districts; stereotypes of politicians
candidates, disclosure of sexual
orientation. See candidates,
perspectives on sexual orientation;
closeted politicians; out politicians; out
and proud politicians
candidates, perspectives on sexual
orientation: about, 37, 259, 273–75;
avoidance as strategy, 267; campaign
communications, 267–68; coming
out process, 264–68; competitiveness,
271–72; homophobia, 260–61, 274;
humour as strategy, 268–69; ideological
spectrum, 272–73; intersectional
approach, 266, 274–75; key questions
for candidate, 267; media practices, 271;
municipal candidates, 271; personal
comfort, 266, 268, 272; public response
to disclosure, 268–72; research project
on, 259, 263–64, 275n2; respectability
politics, 268; sexual vs party
stereotypes, 275; social context, 259–61;
social media, 267, 275n3
capital punishment, 18, 63(t), 64, 162.
See also ideological spectrum, specific
issues
Carbert, Louise, 137
Carignan, Claude, 211
Carroll, Susan, 245
Cauchon, Martin, 192, 193
Caul, Miki, 125, 136–37, 141
Celis, Karen, 220
Chambers, Stuart, 181
Chan, Ken, 299

Chaney, Paul, 25–26
Charter of Rights and Freedoms: about,
36, 184–88, 191–93; constitutional
negotiations, 315–18; *Equality for
All*, 187–88; equality rights, 182,
184–85, 233; historical background,
186–88, 232, 281–82; notwithstanding
clause, 186–87, 192; public opinion,
197; religious freedom, 191, 193, 194,
325; right to vote and to run, 243;
same-sex marriage, 191–93; sexual
orientation and equality rights,
184–88, 191–93, 198n6, 314–19. See also
human rights
CHRA. See Canadian Human Rights Act
(CHRA)
Chrétien, Jean, government: Charter
rights, 185–86, 188, 189, 193; CHRA
prohibited grounds, 324; diverse
representation, 179; refugee claims,
196; same-sex marriage, 183, 189–93;
Svend Robinson's influence, 322; voting
system reforms, 137
Christianity. See religion
cities. See municipalities; Toronto; urban/
suburban/rural areas
citizenship, substantive, 35, 38
citizenship (born in Canada),
socio-demographics: by electoral
engagement, 58–62, 59(t)–61(t), 73–74;
by gender and LGB/non-LGB, 55,
56(t)–57(t), 73–74
Civil Marriage Act (2005), 194
civil society vs state, 8, 9, 32–33, 39n9.
See also media; social-movement
activism
Clavet, Alain, 165
clientelism, 143
closeted politicians: about, 12, 251, 259,
314; candidates, 247; Conservatives,
252, 275n1; forced outing of, 12, 39n11;
historical background, 251, 259, 260–61;
in *The Normal Heart* (film), 39n11;
outing after retirement or death, 251;
recent trends, 254; as representatives,
226–27; unknown information, 251,
254. See also out politicians; out and
proud politicians
Coalition for Lesbian and Gay Rights in
Ontario, 281

coming out. *See* closeted politicians; out politicians
Comparative Provincial Election Project (CPEP), 80, 85, 89–90, 96–98
competitiveness of candidates, 29, 37, 131–32, 249, 252–54, 255n1, 262. *See also* candidates
conservatism: about, 35–36, 157–60, 171–73; diverse representation, 157–58; government role in society, 159–60, 180–81; homonationalism, 164–65; intellectual tensions in, 158–60, 172–73; key questions, 157; LGBTQ candidates, 263; LGBTQ support, xi, 36, 158, 171, 201–2; municipal politics, 300; neoliberal right, 36, 158–60; Pride events, 169–70, 173, 263; provincial politics, 157–58, 165, 171; public vs private domain, 180–81; resistance to LGBTQ candidates, 16; social conservatism, 36, 65, 158–60, 171–73, 182–83, 288; stereotypes, 275; terminology, 77n5, 158–59. *See also* Conservative Party of Canada; ideological spectrum, right (conservative); ideological spectrum, specific issues; Progressive Conservative Party of Canada; Reform/Alliance Party
Conservative Party of Canada: about, 157–58, 171–73; Blue Tent events, 161; Charter rights, 186–88; citizenship guide, 163; diverse representation, 145, 158; election defeat (2015), 160, 263; homonationalism, 162–65, 214; LGBTQ candidates by party, 247–49, 248(t)–49(t), 254, 263; LGBTQ legislators, 251–52; LGBTQ MPs by party and district (1979–2015), 139–40, 140(t), 251–52; LGBTQ support for, elections (2006–15), 64–69, 66(f)–68(f); LGBTQ support for, weakness of, 12, 53, 64–65, 70–74, 202; platform (2013, 2016), 160–61; Pride events, 263; same-sex marriage, 19, 26, 65, 160–61, 162, 163, 169, 194, 206, 208, 263; Scheer's leadership, 65, 171, 173, 288; socio-demographics by vote choice (2006–15), 69–74, 69(t)–72(t); trans rights, 211, 214; voter stereotypes of, 273; women candidates and leaders, 137. *See also* ideological spectrum, right (conservative); ideological spectrum, specific issues; LGBTory Canada; Progressive Conservative Party of Canada; Reform/Alliance Party
Conservative Party of Canada, prime ministers. *See* Harper, Stephen, government; Mulroney, Brian, government
Conservative Party, provincial parties. *See specific provinces*
conversion therapy, xi–xii, 230
Cook, Robert Douglas, 244
Cooper, Davina, 15, 26
Cortes-Vargas, Estefania, 248, 254
councillors. *See* municipalities
Court Challenges Program, 186, 188, 194
Cowperthwaite, Phil, 115
CPEP (Comparative Provincial Election Project), 80, 85, 89–90, 96–98
Criminal Code: age of consent, 196, 205, 209, 236n6; amendments (1968), 179, 197, 203; bathhouse raids (1981), 205; decriminalization of private acts, 180–82, 203, 205; expunging of criminal records, 196–97, 209; gender identity and expression, conservative views, 288, 290; gender identity and expression, NDP support, 169, 196, 201, 209, 210, 211, 212, 214–15; hate-crimes, 189, 196, 201, 210–12, 214–15, 324–26; homosexual acts (until 1969), 205, 314–15. *See also* law and legal issues
critical mass theory, 11, 31, 131
Crosbie, John, 188, 232

da Silva, Luiz Inacio "Lula," 24–25
Daily Xtra, 106, 110, 112, 115, 119n3
Damien, John, 184
David, Michel, 117
Davies, Libby, 140(t), 201, 207, 254, 326–27
Davis, Paul, 170
Day, Stockwell, 183, 189
de la Dehesa, Rafael, 21, 24–25, 28
Deckman, Melissa, 246
Declaration of Montreal on LGBT Human Rights, 210, 213
decriminalization. *See* law and legal issues

democracy and LGBTQ engagement, 30–31, 33, 109, 228
demographics. *See* LGBTQ demographics
Denier, Nicole, 39n12
Denmark: decriminalization of homosexuality, 3; representation by voting system, 128(t), 132–35, 134(t)–35(t), 136; visible minority representation, 138; women's representation, 138
descriptive approach to political representation. *See* political representation, descriptive
Diefenbaker, John, 181–82
DiNovo, Cheri, xi–xii, 230
Dirks, Gordon, 166
disabilities, people with: Charter rights, 188–89; political representation, 137
disclosure of LGBTQ identity. *See* closeted politicians; out politicians; out and proud politicians
disgust, politics of, 5, 15, 29, 30. *See also* homo-, bi-, and transphobia; stigma
districts, electoral. *See* ridings and districts
diverse representation. *See* political representation
Doan, Alesha, 16–17, 103, 261
Douglas, Michelle, 323–24
Douglas, T.C., 203
Dovi, Suzanne, 225, 233, 235
Dumont, Mario, 165

Eady, Keith, 244
Edelman, Murray, 13, 54, 62
Edge, Simon, 27
education, socio-demographics: by electoral engagement, 58–62, 59(t)–61(t), 73–74; by gender and LGB/non-LGB, 55, 56(t)–57(t), 73–74; by LGB/non-LGB, 240; by vote choice (2006–15), 69(t)–72(t), 71–74; by vote choice in Ontario election (2014), 85–86, 90, 91(t)–92(t), 97
education issues: anti-bullying initiatives, 168, 201, 210; gay-straight alliances in schools, 157, 166, 168; sex-education curriculum, 14–15, 169–70, 240; social conservatism, 168–70; trans bathroom access, 166, 172–73, 211

Egale Canada, 196, 197, 223, 284, 289
Egan, Patrick, 13, 54, 58, 62
election campaigns. *See* candidates
electoral districts. *See* ridings and districts
electoral engagement: about, 58–62, 59(t)–61(t), 73–76; by gender and LGB/non-LGB, 58–59, 59(t)–61(t); GSS survey, 58–62, 59(t)–61(t), 75–76; news attention, 58, 59(t)–61(t), 76; political interest, 58, 59(t)–61(t), 75; political involvement, 59(t)–61(t), 75–76; socio-demographics, 58–62, 59(t)–61(t), 73–74; vote choice in Ontario election (2014), 85–86, 90, 91(t)–92(t), 97; voting index, 58–59, 59(t)–61(t), 75
electoral politics: as "institutions, actors, processes, and activities," 8, 32–33. *See also* candidates; electorate; ideological spectrum; political parties; political representation; ridings and districts; voting systems
electorate: about, 17–22, 33–34, 51, 58; demographic weight of, 17, 33–34, 51, 73, 76n3, 145–46; descriptive approach, 12–17; distinctiveness of, 58; diversity within groups, 11–12, 19; geographical concentration, 20–21, 129–31, 138–39, 142–44, 223–24, 250, 254–55, 272–73; group memberships and voting behaviour, 58, 73–74; key questions on, 12, 51; "lavender vote," 12–13; pink money, 13, 39n12, 55; research assumption of heterosexuality, 22; research needed, 51–52; right to vote, 243; scholarship on, 10, 12–22, 51; self-identification in surveys, 52–55; substantive approach, 17–19; unknown information on, 21, 28, 130, 142, 145–46; visibility/invisibility, 130–31, 142, 145. *See also* ideological spectrum; LGBTQ demographics; political representation; voting systems; *and specific political parties, regions, provinces, and territories*
electorate, demographics and voting behaviours: about, 12, 51–54, 73–74; distinctiveness of, 58; electoral engagement by gender and LGB/non-LGB, 58–59, 59(t)–61(t), 73–74; group memberships, 58; GSS data, 52–54, 75–76; Ipsos Election Day

data, 52–54, 76; key questions on, 12, 51; LGB vs non-LGB people, 52; percentage of population, 53–54, 76n3; ratios, female-to-male, 54; research methods, 52–54; scholarship on, 12, 51; self-identification, 52–55, 75; size of electorate, 53–54, 73; socio-demographics by gender and LGB/non-LGB, 54–55, 56(t)–57(t), 73–74. *See also* age; education issues; electoral engagement; employment, socio-demographics; French language, socio-demographics; General Social Survey (GSS); immigrants and refugees; income; Ipsos Election Day surveys; religion; urban/suburban/rural areas
Ellerton, Jamie, 161
EMILY's List, 245, 285–86
emotions and political representation: about, 36–37, 221–22, 234–35; affect, 221; allies' emotional support, 316; anger and frustration, 235; courage of candidates, 244; emotional management, 234; expression of, 221; key questions, 234; Milk's Hope Speech, 22, 30, 225–27, 235; out and proud politicians, 221; political representation of LGBTQ people, 36–37, 220–21, 234–35; pride, 235; research needed on, 234–35; scholarship on, 221–22; in social movements, 222; symbolic aspects, 10, 36–37, 109, 223, 227; terminology, 221. *See also* out and proud politicians; Pride events; social-movement activism
employment, socio-demographics: by electoral engagement, 58–62, 59(t)–61(t), 73–74; by gender and LGB/non-LGB, 55, 56(t)–57(t), 73–74
England. *See* United Kingdom
Equal Voice, 245
Equality for All, 187–88, 318
Erickson, Lynda, 203, 205
Escobar-Lemmon, Maria, 220
Europe: conservatism, 26; LGBTQ electorate, 13–14. *See also* Belgium; Denmark; Finland; France; Germany; Netherlands; Norway; Sweden; United Kingdom
Everitt, Joanna, 10–11, 16, 25, 29, 30, 141, 142, 205, 250, 262, 264, 270, 273

Faderman, Lilian, 18
Fahs, Breanne, 18
Fairclough, Norman, 106
Farney, James, 182, 203
Federation of Canadian Municipalities, 245
females. *See* sex/gender; women
feminism, 18, 30, 64, 92(t), 98, 204
Filipinos, 27
Finestone, Sheila, 317
Finland: representation by voting system, 128(t), 132–35, 134(t)–35(t), 136; same-sex marriage, 3
first-past-the-post, 11, 224, 251. *See also* voting systems, plurality
Flanagan, Tom, 159
Forces et Démocratie party, 266, 279
Ford, Doug, 169–70
Ford, Rob, 300–2, 305, 309
Foster, Emma, 26
France: ideological spectrum, 18; LGBTQ electorate, 13–14, 18; representation by voting system, 128(t), 132–36, 134(t)–35(t); same-sex marriage, 3
French, Orland, 320
French language, socio-demographics: by electoral engagement, 58–62, 59(t)–61(t), 73–74; by gender and LGB/non-LGB, 55, 56(t)–57(t), 73–74
Fry, Hedy, 325, 327
Fugues, 106, 110, 112, 119n3

Garrison, Randall, 140(t), 211, 213, 214
Gates, Gary, 13, 76n3
Gaudet, Derek, 95
Gaudreault, Sylvain, 255
Gay Alliance Toward Equality (GATE), 244, 281
Gay and Lesbian Victory Fund, 245, 280, 283–88, 291
Gay Pride. *See* Pride events
gay-straight alliances in schools, 157, 165, 166–67, 168
gays: about, 5–7; age of consent, 196, 205, 209, 236n6; blood donations, 209, 210, 236n6; as candidates, 16, 84–85; feminine vs masculine traits, 16–17, 87, 93, 103; gay villages, 21, 131, 135, 143, 250, 254, 255, 292, 298–99, 302–9; historical tensions, 6, 21; ideological

spectrum, 74; income, 21, 39*n*12; media framing, 29; political involvement, 62; self-identification in surveys, 52–55; stereotypes, 16, 29, 84–85; terminology, 5–7, 38*n*1, 119*n*9. *See also* LGBTQ people and communities; political representation; terminology, LGBTQ

gays, demographics: attention to media news, 59, 59(t)–61(t), 62; LGBTQ MPs, gays vs lesbians, 4, 28, 54; ratio of gays to lesbians, 4, 54; socio-demographics by electoral engagement, 58–62, 59(t)–61(t), 73–74; socio-demographics by gender and LGB/non-LGB, 55, 56(t)–57(t), 73–74

gender. *See* sex/gender

genderqueer politicians, 249. *See also* queer people

General Social Survey (GSS), 52–55, 56(t)–57(t), 59(t)–61(t), 75–76. *See also* LGBTQ demographics

generational differences. *See* age

Germany: LGBTQ MPs, 4; representation by voting system, 128(t), 132–36, 134(t)–35(t)

Gillies, Phil, 289

Gingras, Jacqui, 270, 271

Giraud, Cyrille, 266, 272–73

Globe and Mail, 106, 112, 113, 115, 116

Goertz, Gary, 14

Golebiowska, Ewa, 15, 16, 39*n*14

Goodwin, Jeff, 222

Goodyear-Grant, Elizabeth, 118

Gould, Deborah, 221–22

government role in society: about, 62–64, 63(t); conservative views, 159–60; decriminalization of private acts, 180–81, 205; ideological spectrum, 62–64, 63(t); liberal views, 179–83, 191; private vs public domain, 180–81; secular state, 179–83, 191, 198*n*1. *See also* ideological spectrum, specific issues

Grafftey, Heward, 314

Graham, Bill, 322, 323

Granic Allen, Tanya, 169–70

Gravel, Raymond, 140(t), 327

Greckol, Sheila, 195

Green, James, 27

Green Party: competitiveness, 40*n*19, 252, 254, 272; first out party leader, 119*n*8; Gay pride events, 139; LGBTQ candidates, 247–49, 248(t)–49(t), 254, 266, 269

Groulx, Lionel, 159

GSS. *See* General Social Survey (GSS)

Guardian, 106, 110, 113–14, 119*n*3

Haider-Markel, Donald, 16–17, 18, 23, 25, 28, 30, 31, 32, 37, 103, 227, 228, 230–31, 255, 261, 285

Hall, Barbara, 291

Halpern v Canada (2002), 192

Hanagan, Michael, 23–24

Hansen, Eric, 13, 31

Harper, Laureen, 161

Harper, Stephen, government: cancellation of Court Challenges, 194; diversity of MPs, 273; federal election (2006), 64; foreign policy on LGBTQ rights, 161–62, 164–65; prostitution issue, 159; refugee claimants, 195–96; same-sex marriage, 65, 172, 182, 183, 194. *See also* conservatism; Conservative Party of Canada

Harris, Mike, 198*n*7, 289

Harris, Paul, 265, 271

Hatfield, Richard, 12, 98*n*1, 243, 251

HE (homonormative entrepreneurialism), 302–9

Hehr, Kent, 166

Henderson, Doug, 244

Herek, Gregory, 13

Herrick, Rebekah, 16, 31, 111, 231

Hertzog, Mark, 12–13, 17–18, 20, 226

heteronormativity and homonormativity: about, 14, 103; candidates, 103–5, 242, 267, 268, 269; critique of, 293; hegemonic ideology, 103; heteronormative allies, 226–27, 234; historical background, 280–82; homonormativity, 113, 114, 117–18, 233; media framing, 30, 103–4, 117, 118, 250; model and social capital, 236*n*4; oppressive power of, 267, 281; and respectability, 93, 113–17; sexual mediation, 103, 105; stereotypes, 14, 30. *See also* respectability

heterosexuality: assumptions in research methods, 22; cultural

dominance, 226, 236n7; gender construction, 14; ideological spectrum and norms, 263; income, 39n12; self-identification in surveys, 52–53. *See also* heteronormativity and homonormativity; sexual orientation
Hiebert, Janet, 186
HIV/AIDS pandemic, 222, 235, 281
homo-, bi-, and transphobia: attacks on effeminate straight men, 119n10; biphobia, 233; coded language, 272; coping strategies, 268–70; hate propaganda, 314, 317, 324–26; in House of Commons, 318–19, 322; and immigrants, 260; media framing of, 270–71; ProudPolitics as strategy against, 279, 286, 290, 291; public opinion trends, 83–84, 260–61; Reform/Alliance members, 322–23; Rob Ford as Toronto's mayor, 300–2, 305, 309; stereotypes of politicians, 83–84; transphobia, 211–12, 214, 233, 235n1, 290; UN international day against, 196. *See also* stigma
homonationalism: about, 212–15; conservative support, 161–62, 164–65, 214; countries with anti-LGBTQ laws, 161–62, 213–14; NDP support, 36, 202, 210, 212–15; sexual mediation of Boisclair, 116
homonormative entrepreneurialism (HE), 302–9
homosexuality: decriminalization, 3, 181–82, 196–97, 203, 243, 314; historical background, 3, 203; self-identification in surveys, 52–55; terminology, 5–7, 119n9. *See also* LGBTQ people and communities
homosocial capital, 236n4
Horne, Sharon, 19
Horwath, Andrea: agentic vs communal traits, 82, 86–88, 87(t), 89(t), 96; gender stereotypes, 94; issue competencies, 87(t), 88–89, 89(t), 96; leadership traits, 86–88, 87(t), 89(t); likeability of, 86, 86(t), 96; media framing (2014 election), 80–81; NDP leader in Ontario, 85; partisan stereotypes, 93; research project on, 80–81, 85–89, 96–98; voter pre-election knowledge of, 85–86, 93, 97
House of Commons: federal apology (2017), 197; historical background, 4; homophobia, 318–19, 322; LGBTQ allies, 319; LGBTQ female-to-male ratio, 251; LGBTQ MPs, 4, 251–52, 292; LGBTQ MPs by party (1979–2015), 139–41, 140(t); LGBTQ underrepresentation, 240
Howard, Jennifer, 254
Htun, Mala, 228
Huberman, Michael, 107
Hudak, Tim: agentic vs communal traits, 82, 86–88, 87(t), 89(t), 96; issue competencies, 87(t), 88–89, 89(t), 96; leadership traits, 82, 86–88, 87(t), 89(t); likeability of, 86, 86(t), 96; media framing (2014 election), 80–81; partisan stereotypes, 93; research project on, 80–81, 85–89, 96–98; voter pre-election knowledge of, 85–86, 93, 97
human rights: about, 179–80; and civil rights, 183; conservative approach, 158, 171; historical background, 183, 281–82; international conventions, 183; liberal approach, 179–80; rights discourse, 191, 196; sexual orientation as prohibited ground, 171, 183–89, 198n6. *See also* Canadian Human Rights Act (CHRA); Charter of Rights and Freedoms
Hunsperger, Allan, 167–68, 171
Hunter College poll, 76n3

Iacobucci, Frank, 198n6
Iannicca, Nando, 283
Iceland: first out lesbian prime minister, 104, 108; same-sex marriage, 3
identity: about, 14; intersectional identities, 130–31, 232–33; "post-gay" identities, 309; Pride events, 7–8; terminology, LGBTQ people vs communities, 7–8; unknown information, 28, 130. *See also* intersectionality; Pride events; social-movement activism; terminology, LGBTQ
ideological spectrum: about, 26–27, 35, 62–64, 63(t); diverse representation, 25, 124–26, 127–29, 136–37; emotional

aspects, 222; intersectional identities, 132; issues by gender and LGB/non-LGB, 62–64, 63(t); leaders' competencies on issues, 87(t), 88–89, 89(t); LGBTQ diversity, 201–2; LGBTQ electorate, 17–18; LGBTQ legislators, 251–52, 254; parties and stereotypes, 82, 87(t), 88–89, 89(t); policies as distinction in, 158; socio-demographics by vote choice and LGB/non-LGB (2006–15), 69(t)–72(t), 71–74; socio-demographics of voters in Ontario election (2014), 90, 91(t)–92(t), 96–98; terminology, 77n5. See also ideological spectrum, specific issues

ideological spectrum, left (liberal): about, 26–27, 179–80, 197; agentic vs communal traits, 86–88, 87(t), 89(t), 96; diverse representation, 24–25, 27, 124–29, 141–42, 254; feminism, 18, 92(t), 98, 204; human rights, 179; ideological tensions, 201–2; issues by gender and LGB/non-LGB, 62–64, 63(t); leaders' competencies on issues, 87(t), 88–89, 89(t); LGBTQ candidates, 141, 254, 262; LGBTQ electorate, 17–18; LGBTQ support by, strength, 17–19, 62; parties and diverse representation, 24–25, 127–29, 136–37, 141, 251–52; party caucuses, 127; party stereotypes, 82; scholarship on, 62; secular state, 179–83, 191, 198n1; socio-demographics by vote choice and LGB/non-LGB (2006–15), 69(t)–72(t), 71–74; terminology, liberal vs left, 77n5; tolerance of diversity, 179. See also Liberal Party of Canada; liberalism; New Democratic Party (NDP)

ideological spectrum, right (conservative): about, 26–27, 35–36, 158–60, 171–73; agentic vs communal traits, 86–88, 87(t), 89(t), 96; diverse representation, 25, 124–26, 137, 157–58; heterosexual norms, 263; leaders' competencies on issues, 87(t), 88–89, 89(t); LGBTQ candidates, 263; LGBTQ electorate, 17–18; LGBTQ groups, 26; LGBTQ legislators, 254; LGBTQ support, weakness of, 17–18, 25, 53, 64, 70–74, 202; political parties, 25, 82, 137; stereotypes, 82, 263; tensions between social conservatives and neoliberals, 158–60, 172–73; terminology, 77n5, 158–60. See also conservatism; Conservative Party of Canada; LGBTory Canada

ideological spectrum, specific issues: abortion, 18, 63(t), 64, 172, 180–81; about, 62–64, 63(t); anti-bullying laws, 210; anti-globalization, 206–7; capital punishment, 18, 63(t), 64; conversion therapy, xi–xii, 230; equality rights, 168; gay-straight alliances in schools, 157, 166–67, 168; government role in society, 62–64, 63(t), 159–60, 179–83, 191, 198n1; prostitution, 159; same-sex marriage, 19, 36, 65, 160–61; sex-education curriculum, 14–15, 169–70; trans bathroom access, 166–67, 172–73, 211. See also same-sex marriage and rights

Ignatieff, Michael, 188

immigrants and refugees: Conservative Party policies, 162–63, 195–96; homophobia, 260; Immigration and Refugee Protection Act (IRPA), 189, 255n2; inadmissible classes and LGBTQ people, 189, 255n2; LGBTQ refugees, 162–63, 189–90, 195–96; same-sex partners, 189. See also citizenship (born in Canada), socio-demographics

income: lesbians vs gays, 21; pink money stereotype, 13, 39n12, 55

income, socio-demographics: by electoral engagement, 58–62, 59(t)–61(t), 73–74; by gender and LGB/non-LGB, 55, 56(t)–57(t); by vote choice and LGB/non-LGB (2006–15), 69(t)–72(t), 71–74

Indigenous peoples: Charter rights, 188–89; diverse representation, 126–27, 137; geographical concentration, 138–39, 143; LGBTQ candidates, 248; Maori people, 126–27; marginalization, 236n5; right to vote, 243; voting systems, 138–39, 143

International LGBT Leadership Conference, 283

international LGBTQ people and communities: about, 3–4; conventions, declarations, and celebrations, 183, 196, 210, 213; criminalization of sexual acts, 241; demographics, 76n3; diverse representation, 126–27;

homonationalism, 212–15; human rights violations, 189–90; LGBTQ MPs, 4, 28, 40*n*18; LGBTQ political parties, 130; same-sex marriage/partners, 3, 189–90; scholarship on, 4, 28; under-representation of lesbians, 28; voting systems, LGBTQ representation (1985–2015), 132–35, 134(t)–35(t), 250; women's diverse representation, 124–29; women's representation by voting systems (1965–2015), 128(t), 129, 133, 136. *See also* homonationalism; World Pride, Toronto; *and specific countries*
intersectionality: about, 261, 274; to gender and sexual orientation, 16–17; intersectional identities, 130–32, 232–33; resistance to candidates, 268–70; stereotypes of politicians, 84–85, 261. *See also* identity
Ipsos Election Day surveys, 52–54, 62–64, 63(t), 69(t)–72(t), 76, 76*n*2, 77*n*5. *See also* LGBTQ demographics

Jasper, James, 222
Jean, Brian, 168
Jeet, Heer, 302
Jeffery-Poulter, Stephen, 26
Johnson, Aidan, 321, 328
Joslyn, Mark, 31

Kanai, Juan Miguel, 302, 303, 305, 308
Kay, Barry, 6, 53, 64
Kay, Jonathan, 164
Kenney, Jason, 161, 162–63, 168
Kent, Steve, 170, 171
Kenttamaa-Squires, Kai, 302, 305, 308
Kerr, Peter, 26
Khaki, El-Farouk, 268–70
Kirchick, James, 172
Klippert, Everett George, 203
Kluttz, Billy, 23
Knegt, Peter, 282
Kniss, Chad, 31
Kraus, François, 13–14, 18
Krook, Mona, 255*n*1
Kushner, Tony, 293
Kuykendall, Russ, 168

La Presse, 106, 112, 113
L'actualité, 106

Lafontaine, Yves, 110
Landau, Jamie, 103
language, French. *See* French language, socio-demographics
LaPierre, Laurier, 251
Lapointe, Charles, 39*n*5
Latin America, 21, 24–25, 27, 28
law and legal issues: age of consent, 196, 205, 209, 236*n*6; bathhouse raids (1981), 205; Court Challenges Program, 186, 188, 194; criminal law and secular state, 180–81; decriminalization of homosexuality, 3, 181–82, 196–97, 203, 243, 314; expunging of criminal records, 196, 209; federal apology (2017), 197; gender identity and expression, 210, 216*n*6; hate-crimes, 189, 196, 201, 209, 210–12, 324–25; historical background, 203; implementation of law in society, 32; NDP platforms, 209–10; public opinion, 197, 208; same-sex marriage, 65, 189–94; training in LGBTQ rights, 196. *See also* Canadian Human Rights Act (CHRA); Charter of Rights and Freedoms; Criminal Code; human rights
Laycock, David, 203, 205
Layland and Beaulne v. Ontario, 191
Layton, Jack, 207–8, 210
Le Devoir, 106, 110, 114, 115–16, 117
Lea, Chris, 119*n*8
left parties. *See* ideological spectrum, left (liberal); liberalism; political parties
legal issues. *See* law and legal issues
Leicester, Jasmine Joyce Sapphire, 267
Lemieux, Julie, 6
Lenti, Erica, 230
lesbians: about, 5–7; adoption of own children, xii; assumptions of heteronormativity, 103; feminine vs masculine traits, 16–17, 84–85, 87, 93, 103; historical tensions, 6, 21; ideological spectrum, 74; income, 21, 39*n*12; MPs, 326–27; self-identification in surveys, 52–55; stereotypes, 16; terminology, 5–7, 38*n*1, 119*n*9. *See also* LGBTQ people and communities; political representation; stereotypes of politicians; terminology, LGBTQ

lesbians, demographics: percentage of population, 13, 53–54, 76n3; ratio of gays to lesbians, 4, 54; socio-demographics by electoral engagement, 58–62, 59(t)–61(t), 73–74; socio-demographics by gender and LGB/non-LGB, 55, 56(t)–57(t)
Lester, Jordan Willis, 267
Lévesque, René, 198n3
Lewis, Gregory, 18
LGBTory Canada: historical background, 294n12; homonationalism, 163–65; Pride events, 290; same-sex marriage, 160–61, 163–64; sex-education curriculum, 170; support for Scheer, 173, 288; tensions in conservatism, 158. *See also* conservatism; Conservative Party of Canada; ideological spectrum, right (conservative)
LGBTQ demographics: about, 33–34; demographic weight of LGBTQ voters, 17, 33–34, 51, 73, 76n3, 145–46; income, 21, 39n12; Ipsos election surveys, 52–54, 62–64, 63(t), 69(t)–72(t), 76, 76n2, 77n5; key questions, 28, 51; percentage of population, 51, 53–54, 76n3, 77n4; scholarship on, 51; Statistics Canada GSS survey, 52–55, 56(t)–57(t), 59(t)–61(t), 75–76; trans people, 13, 53–54, 76n3; unknown information, 28, 130, 142, 145–46. *See also* bisexuals, demographics; electorate, demographics and voting behaviours; gays, demographics; General Social Survey (GSS); Ipsos Election Day surveys; lesbians, demographics
LGBTQ international community. *See* international LGBTQ people and communities
LGBTQ movements and organizations: about, 280–83; assimilationists, 7, 36, 281–83, 293; Egale Canada, 196, 197, 223, 284, 289; emotional aspects, 112–13; funding, 294n11; historical background, 120n15, 280–83, 293; LGBTQ political parties, 130, 141, 146, 244; liberationists, 281–83, 293; lived equality, 37, 282–83; male domination, 292; publications, 119n3; respectability, 114; rights discourse, 281–82; terminology, 119n9, 120n15. *See also* allies for LGBTQ people; ProudPolitics
LGBTQ people and communities: binaries and polarities, 5–6, 29–30; criminalization, 241; diversity of, 6, 33, 36, 38, 53, 232–33, 235; goals of equality and inclusion, 198n9; government apology (2017), 197; historical background, 203–8; intersectional identities, 21, 130–31, 132, 232–33; legitimacy of personal experience, 36–37, 222, 234, 236n3, 319; LGBTQ and women as gendered minorities, 11–12; as object of representation, 232–33, 235; political elites, 242; political influence, 145–46; privileged vs deprived subgroups, 208, 212, 233–35, 306; public opinion trends, 3–4, 83–84, 94–95, 197; research needed, 234–35, 309–10; self-identification, 5, 52–55; shared life experience, 223–27, 229–30; terminology, LGBTQ, 5–7, 119n9; terminology, people vs communities, 7–8; unknown information, 21, 28, 130, 142, 145–46; visibility/invisibility, 7, 130–31, 142, 145, 321. *See also* allies for LGBTQ people; heterosexuality; homo-, bi-, and transphobia; homosexuality; stigma; terminology, LGBTQ
LGBTQ people and communities, specific. *See* bisexuals; gays; intersectionality; lesbians; queer people; terminology, LGBTQ; trans people
LGBTQ places. *See* ridings and districts; urban/suburban/rural areas
LGBTQ political representation. *See* candidates; closeted politicians; electorate; ideological spectrum; out politicians; out and proud politicians; political representation; voting systems
LGBTQ terminology. *See* terminology, LGBTQ
Liberal Party, provincial parties, 172. *See also specific provinces*
Liberal Party of Canada: about, 36; competitiveness, 252–53; Criminal Code amendments (1968), 179, 197, 203; diverse representation, 137,

144–45; diversity within, 36; Gay pride events, 139; gender identity and expression, 214–15; homonationalism, 214; LGBTQ candidates, 247–49, 248(t)–49(t), 252–53, 266; LGBTQ MPs by party and district (1979–2015), 139–41, 140(t), 251–52; LGBTQ support, 201–2; LGBTQ support in elections (2006–15), 64–69, 66(f)–68(f), 73–74; same-sex marriage, 36, 65, 189–93, 208; socio-demographics by vote choice (2006–15), 69–74, 69(t)–72(t); trans rights, 214–15; voting system reform, 139; women's representation within, 136–37. *See also* political parties

Liberal Party of Canada, prime ministers. *See* Chrétien, Jean, government; Martin, Paul, government; Trudeau, Justin, government; Trudeau, Pierre, government

liberalism: about, 179–80, 197; conservative voices, 36; equality rights, 183, 189–90, 196, 198*n*9; human rights and equality, 179–80, 183–88; secular state, 179–83, 191, 198*n*1; terminology, liberal vs left, 77*n*5; tolerance of diversity, 179, 183, 194–97. *See also* ideological spectrum, left (liberal); Liberal Party of Canada; New Democratic Party (NDP); same-sex marriage and rights

Liebman, Marvin, 172
Litwin, Fred, 173
Lombardo, Emanuela, 9
Lukaszuk, Thomas, 166–67, 171
Lyon, Sterling, 186

M v H (1999), 189, 198*n*7
MacLauchlan, Wade: about, 102, 117–18; first elected out gay politician in PEI, 34, 108, 109–10, 111–12, 117; Liberal leader, 106–7; media framing of, 29–30, 34, 102, 109–10, 250; orientation as a non-issue, 111–12, 115, 118, 268; personal history, 109–10, 114, 115; premier of PEI, 98*n*1; research project on sexual mediation, 105–8, 117–18, 119*n*3; respectability, 34, 113, 114–15, 117; sexual mediation, 111–12, 250; substantive representation, 111–12, 117–18; symbolic representation, 109–10, 111–12, 117–18

Maclean's, 106, 109, 110–11, 116
Magni, Gabriele, 15, 19, 28–29, 37
majoritarian system. *See* voting systems, majoritarian
males. *See* men; sex/gender
Malone, Peter, 141
Maltais, Agnès, 254
Manitoba: LGBTQ candidates by party, 247–49, 249(t); LGBTQ mayors, 5, 288; LGBTQ MLAs, 252, 254; NDP opposition, 262; PC government, 171. *See also* provinces and territories
Manning, Preston, 160, 182–83
Mansbridge, Jane, 225, 229
Marchand, Len, 143
marginalized people: LGBTQ people as, 36, 226–27; NDP solidarity with, 203; political representation by, 224–25, 229–30; privileged vs deprived LGBTQ subgroups, 208, 212, 233–35, 306; research challenges, 142; shared life experiences, 224–25, 229–30. *See also* LGBTQ people and communities; race/ethnicity; visible minorities
Markle, Tristan, 207
marriage equality. *See* same-sex marriage and rights
Marsiaj, Juan, 24, 25
Martin, Paul, government, 137, 179, 182, 194
Massé, Manon, 5, 119*n*9, 223
Matland, Richard, 136, 242
Matthews, Chris, 289–90
mayors. *See* municipalities
Mazur, Amy, 14
McCreath, Jennifer, 6, 247, 266, 268–72
McGuigan, Mark, 180
McIntosh, Duncan, 115
McIver, Ric, 166–67, 171
McLaughlin, Audrey, 205
McLellan, Anne, 190, 192
McNaughton, Monte, 14–15
McSweeney, Lucy, 195
media: about, 29–30, 102–4, 117–18, 249–50; attention to news, by gender and LGB/non-LGB, 58, 59(t)–61(t); bisexuals, 119*n*1; explicit vs implicit bias, 104; "first elected," 34, 102, 104–5, 108–11, 117–18; heteronormative

assumptions, 103–4, 117, 118, 250; key questions, 15; lack of attention to LGBTQ candidates, 271; LGBTQ identity as non-issue, 94, 108, 112–13, 115, 118, 268; LGBTQ representation, 111–14, 117–18; research needed, 118; respectability of LGBTQ politicians, 34, 93, 114–18; scholarship on, 14, 102–5; sexual mediation, as concept, 103–4, 107–8; stereotypes, 29–30, 262; trans candidates, 270–71. See also heteronormativity and homonormativity; respectability; sexual mediation of politicians; stereotypes of politicians

media and individual politicians: research projects on, 80–81, 85–89, 96–98, 105–8, 117–18. See also Boisclair, André; Horwath, Andrea; Hudak, Tim; MacLauchlan, Wade; Wynne, Kathleen; Wynne, Kathleen, media framing (2014 election)

Meier, Petra, 9

Members of Parliament. See House of Commons; political representation

men. See bisexuals; gays; heteronormativity and homonormativity; identity; intersectionality; queer people; sex/gender; sexual orientation; sexuality; terminology, LGBTQ; trans people; *and entries beginning with* LGBTQ

men, demographics: ideological issues by gender, 62–64, 63(t); income, 39n12; ratios, female-to-male, 54; socio-demographics by electoral engagement, 58–62, 59(t)–61(t), 73–74; socio-demographics of LGB/non-LGB, 55, 56(t)–57(t), 73–74; socio-demographics of vote choice (2006–15), 53, 67–74, 67(f)–68(f), 69(t)–72(t), 72–73

Ménard, Réal, 5, 140(t), 223, 326

Mercader, Louroz, 283, 288

Mercer, Rick, 322

Merolla, Jennifer, 261

metropolitan areas. See municipalities; Toronto; urban/suburban/rural areas

Mexico, 20, 21, 24, 25

Miles, Matthew, 107

military service, 205, 209, 318, 323–24

Milk, Harvey: Hope Speech, 22, 30, 225–27, 235; out and proud politicians, 226–27; on political representation, 279–80; stereotypes, 15; voting system in San Francisco, 130

Mill, John Stuart, 181

Miller, Patrick, 18

minorities. See sexual orientation; visible minorities

Monro, Surya, 6

Montgomery, Kathleen, 242

Montreal, 273

Montreal Declaration on LGBT Human Rights, 210, 213

Morin, Dany, 140(t), 292

Mouradian, Ted, 270

Mulroney, Brian, government, 187–88, 316, 323

Mundy, Dean E., 108

municipalities: about, 37–38; at-large vs single-member districts, 126, 130; challenges of, 283; diverse representation, 126, 137, 141; gay villages, 131, 135, 302–9; heritage projects, 307–9; homonormative policies, 302–7; LGBTQ councillors, 5, 10, 265, 298–301, 328; LGBTQ diverse communities, 38; LGBTQ electoral engagement, 58–59, 59(t)–61(t); LGBTQ mayors, 5, 6, 288; "one-issue representative," 38; political representation, 223–24; substantive citizenship, 35, 38; visible minority representation, 137; voting systems, 130, 136. See also Toronto; Wong-Tam, Kristyn

Murnaghan, Tyler, 268

Murray, Glen, 5, 255, 288–89, 290

Muslims, 268–70

National Gay Rights Coalition, 205

National Post, 106, 119n6

Nebbeling, Ted, 4

neoliberal right, 158–60. See also conservatism; ideological spectrum, right (conservative)

Netherlands: LGBTQ MPs, 4; representation by voting system, 128(t), 132–36, 134(t)–35(t); same-sex marriage, 3; visible minority representation, 138

New Brunswick: Brewer as candidate, 30, 80, 82, 98*n*1, 104–5, 119*n*8, 250, 262; Hatfield as closeted premier, 12, 98*n*1, 243, 251; LGBTQ candidates by party, 247–49, 249(t). *See also* provinces and territories

New Democratic Party (NDP): about, 36, 40*n*19, 201–3, 215; ally for LGBTQ people, 40*n*19, 201–2, 208, 215; anti-globalization, 206–7; assimilationists, 36; competitiveness, 252–53, 272; contagion effect, 145; diverse representation, 136–37, 144; economic inequality, 202–6; equality rights, 203, 209–10; Gay Caucus, 204; Gay pride events, 139; gender identity and expression, 208; hate-crimes, 201, 209, 210–12, 324–25; historical background, 36, 203–8; homonationalism, 36, 202, 210, 212–15; ideological tensions, 201–2; incremental change, 202, 207–8; institutional inclusion of minorities, 136–37, 141, 205, 245–47; LGBTQ candidates, 25, 205, 216*n*7, 245, 247–49, 248(t)–49(t), 252–54; LGBTQ Commission, 24; LGBTQ legislators, 252; LGBTQ MPs by party and district (1979–2015), 139–41, 140(t); LGBTQ support, 24, 64–69, 66(f)–68(f), 73–74, 201–2; marginalized groups, 203, 204–5, 215; New Politics Initiative (NPI), 206–7; privileged vs deprived LGBTQ subgroups, 208, 212, 215, 233; research project on, 209, 216*n*5; same-sex marriage, 194, 202, 206, 207–8; social movements, 203–8, 215; socio-demographics by vote choice (2006–15), 69–74, 69(t)–72(t); trans candidates, 216*n*7; trans rights, 202, 209–12, 214–15, 216*n*4; Waffle group, 204, 206–7, 216*n*3. *See also* Robinson, Svend

New Democratic Party (NDP), provincial parties: competitiveness, 252–53, 262. *See also specific provinces*

New Politics Initiative (NPI), 206–7

New Zealand: Maori representation, 126–27, 139; representation by voting system, 128(t), 132–36, 134(t)–35(t), 139

Newfoundland and Labrador: LGBTQ candidates by party, 247–49, 249(t); LGBTQ MLAs, 252; LGBTQ municipal candidates, 267; Pride events, 170; Progressive Conservative Party, 165, 170, 267; Strength in Democracy party, 266, 279; trans candidates, 6, 247, 266–72, 279. *See also* provinces and territories

Nohlen, Dieter, 22

non-binary people, 248, 249. *See also* sexual orientation

The Normal Heart (film), 39*n*11

Norris, Pippa, 241–42

Northwest Territories: LGBTQ candidates, 247–49, 249(t); LGBTQ Independent, 252

Norway: diverse representation, 127–28, 138; Labour Party, 127–28; representation by voting system, 126, 127, 128(t), 132–36, 134(t)–35(t), 138

Nova Scotia: Brison as MP, 140(t), 251–52, 254, 255, 255*n*5, 279; LGBTQ candidates by party, 247–49, 249(t); LGBTQ MLAs, 252. *See also* provinces and territories

Nunavut: LGBTQ candidates, 247–49, 249(t)

Nussbaum, Martha, 5, 15, 29, 30

Oger, Morgane, 291

Oliphant, Rob, 140(t), 291, 292

O'Neil, Peter, 322–23

Ontario: Conservative Party, 80–81, 168–71; conversion therapy, xi–xii, 230; elections (2011, 2014), 80–81, 85; historical background, 94–95; human rights legislation, 184; LGBTQ candidates, 247–49, 249(t), 270; LGBTQ MPPs, 94–95, 252, 255; Liberal Party, 80–81, 198*n*2, 255; municipal politics, 283; NDP party, 35, 80–81, 85, 201; ProudPolitics, 291; same-sex benefits, 201; same-sex marriage, 35, 94, 169, 191–92, 198*n*7, 282; sexual orientation as prohibited ground, 184; socio-demographics by gender and LGB/non-LGB, 55, 56(t)–57(t); Toby's Law, xii; trans rights, xii; visible minority representation, 137; voting systems, 136; Wynne as first out gay premier, 95. *See also* provinces and territories; Toronto

Ontario, politicians. *See* Horwath, Andrea; Hudak, Tim; Wong-Tam, Kristyn; *and entries beginning with* Wynne, Kathleen
openly LGBTQ politicians. *See* out politicians; out and proud politicians
O'Regan, Seamus, 140(t), 251
Orr, Kevin, 314
out politicians: about, 244, 259–61; candidates as out vs closeted, 247; coming-out process, 58, 141, 230, 264–66, 291, 319–21, 326–27; competitiveness, 253–54; full vs partial or limited disclosure, 265–66; historical background, 132, 244, 259–61; MPs by election date and out date (1979–2015), 139–41, 140(t); personal comfort, 266, 268, 272; public opinion, 260–61; recent trends, 94–95, 264–65; shift to running as out candidates, 132, 259, 319–20; timing of disclosure, 15, 16, 261–62. *See also* candidates, perspectives on sexual orientation; closeted politicians; out and proud politicians
out and proud politicians: about, 5, 227–28; as best representatives, 5, 221, 229–30, 234–35; emotional aspects, 227–28; Harvey Milk's Hope Speech on, 225–27; identity politics, 227; legitimacy and shared experience, 222, 229–30, 319; as role models, 5, 30–31, 227–28, 265, 319; symbolic representation, 227, 319. *See also* closeted politicians; out politicians; Robinson, Svend
Out and Running (Haider-Markel), 31

Pallister, Brian, 171
parliamentary government: compared with US system, 288. *See also* House of Commons; Senate
Parti Québécois (PQ): LGBTQ candidates by party, 247–49, 249(t); LGBTQ legislators, 252; support for LGBTQ rights, 35, 198n3. *See also* Boisclair, André
parties, political. *See* political parties
Pearson, Lester, 180–81
Perrella, Andrea, 6, 19, 53, 64
Persky, Stan, 320–21
Peru, 22

Philippines, 27, 130
Phillips, Anne, 224, 229
Pilon, Dennis, 224, 250
Pitkin, Hanna, 8–9, 111, 223, 229, 233
plurality system. *See* voting systems, plurality
political engagement. *See* electoral engagement; social-movement activism
political parties: about, 25–27, 35, 146; caucuses, 127, 130, 284; compared with US parties, 288; competitiveness, 131–32, 252–53; contagion effect across parties, 136–37, 142, 144–45; differentiation by issues, 158; diverse representation, xi, 124–27; electoral capture theory, 17; first out party leader, 119n8; historical background, 141; LGBTQ activism, 23–24, 26–28; LGBTQ MPs by party (1979–2015), 139–41, 140(t); LGBTQ parties, 130, 141, 146, 244; LGBTQ political representatives, 23–25; LGBTQ support in elections (2006–15), 66–69, 66(f)–68(f); new parties for minorities, 127–28, 130, 141, 146; party discipline, 231; party quotas, 126; recruitment of candidates, 242–43; scholarship on, 23–24; under-representation of minorities, 11; women's representation within, 136–37. *See also* ideological spectrum
political parties, provincial: about, 35; competitiveness, 252–53, 262; issue competencies of leaders, 82–83, 87(t), 88–89, 90, 91(t)–92(t); leadership traits of leaders, 82, 86–88, 87(t), 89(t); LGBTQ candidates by party, 247–49, 249(t); LGBTQ parties, 244, 281; partisan stereotypes, 93; stereotypes of parties, 82; under-representation of minorities, 11. *See also* provinces and territories; *and specific provinces and territories*
political parties, specific federal. *See* Bloc Québécois (BQ); Conservative Party of Canada; Green Party; Liberal Party of Canada; New Democratic Party (NDP); Reform/Alliance Party
political representation: about, 8–10, 33, 36–37, 129–35, 220–23, 234–35, 240–41; allies as representatives,

220–22, 226–27, 234; best qualifications, 221, 225, 234–35; competitiveness, 131–32; as creative performance, 229; critical mass theory, 11, 31, 131; descriptive representation, 12, 22–23, 27–28, 36–37, 108–9, 223–24, 230; diverse representation, 124–31, 136–39, 141–45; emotional aspects, 36–37, 221–22, 225–27, 230, 234–35; formalistic representation, 9, 12, 19–23, 27, 33; "gay agenda," 84, 93, 103–4, 111; Harvey Milk's Hope Speech on, 225–27; historical background, 132; intersectional identities, 232–33; key questions, 28, 220, 234; legitimacy of personal experience, 36–37, 222, 234, 236n3, 319; male dominance, 28; as mediation, 225; object of representation, 232–33, 235; out and proud politicians, 221, 230, 234–35; parliamentary activities, 229–34; Pitkin's concepts, 8–9; political will, 138, 142, 250–51; privileged vs deprived LGBTQ subgroups, 233–35; recent trends, 141; research needed, 35, 234–35; role models, 30–31, 109–13, 223–24, 226–28, 319; scholarship on, 9–12, 28, 222–25; sexual orientation as non-issue, 94, 108, 112–13, 115, 118, 268; shared life experiences, 223–27, 229–30; state vs civil representation, 8, 9, 32–33, 39n9; substantive representation, 12, 17–19, 22–23, 36–37, 221, 230–32, 234, 285; symbolic representation, 9–10, 36–37, 230; types of, 9–10; under-representation, 28, 240–41; unknown information, 28, 130; voting systems, 19–22, 124, 223–24; Westminster parliamentary system, 231; of women vs LGBTQ people, 240–41. *See also* candidates; electorate; emotions and political representation; ideological spectrum; political parties; stereotypes of politicians; voting systems
political representation, descriptive: about, 9, 22–23, 27–30, 108–9, 223–24; collective aspects, 108–9, 223; as "first LGBTQ elected," 108–11; individuals as symbolic, 108–9, 223–24; media framing, 27, 29–30; relation to symbolic representation, 9–10; scholarship on, 4, 10, 111; sexual mediation themes, 108–9; "who they are," 23, 27, 223–24; of women, 28. *See also* political representation, symbolic (descriptive)
political representation, formalistic: about, 9, 19–20, 22–23, 27; ideological spectrum, 24–27; LGBTQ movement activists, 23–24; LGBTQ political representatives, 233; political parties, 9, 23–27; scholarship on, 10, 19–20. *See also* political parties; voting systems
political representation, substantive: about, 10, 12, 17–19, 22–23, 31–33, 111–14, 229; activities and strategies, 23, 32, 111, 229–34; allies' effectiveness, 226–27; critical mass theory, 11, 31, 131; by LGBTQ representatives, 31–33, 111–14, 285; "one-issue representatives," 38, 103–4, 111; relation to descriptive representation, 9–10; responsive to interests, 285; role models, 30–31, 33, 110–11, 223–24; scholarship on, 10, 17–19, 111, 285; visibility/invisibility, 11, 130–31, 285, 321; Wynne on, 109
political representation, symbolic (descriptive): about, 9–10, 33; emotional aspects, 36–37, 223, 227; as "first" elected, 108–11, 227; out and proud politicians, 227; relation to descriptive representation, 9–10; role models, 30–31, 33, 38, 109–13, 223–24, 227–28, 230, 319. *See also* out and proud politicians; political representation, descriptive; Robinson, Svend
political ridings. *See* ridings and districts
political spectrum. *See* ideological spectrum
politicians: scholarship on, 10–12. *See also* candidates; closeted politicians; House of Commons; out politicians; out and proud politicians; political representation
Polletta, Francesca, 222
PQ. *See* Parti Québécois (PQ)
PR system. *See* voting systems, proportional
prairie provinces, socio-demographics: by gender and LGB/non-LGB, 55, 56(t)–57(t), 73–74; by vote choice and

LGB/non-LGB (2006–15), 69–70, 69(t), 71–74, 71(t). *See also* Alberta; Manitoba; provinces and territories; Saskatchewan premiers, LGBTQ. *See* Hatfield, Richard; MacLauchlan, Wade; Wynne, Kathleen
Prentice, Jim, 157, 166
Price, Gordon, 141
Pride events: conservative participation, 169–70, 173, 263; criticism of, 120*n*12; emotional aspects, 112–13, 221–22, 223; Gay Pride parades, 112–13, 120*n*12, 139, 169–70, 263; identity and communities, 7–8; liberal participation, 112–13, 195; out and proud politicians, 221; protests against Russian laws, 301; symbolic representation, 112–13; World Pride, 209, 298, 301, 302, 304, 307
Prince Edward Island: LGBTQ candidates, 247–49, 249(t), 269; LGBTQ MLAs, 252; voting systems, 136. *See also* MacLauchlan, Wade; provinces and territories
Progressive Conservative Party of Canada, 182, 203, 206. *See also* conservatism; Conservative Party of Canada; ideological spectrum, right (conservative)
proportional system (PR). *See* voting systems, proportional
prostitution, 159
ProudPolitics: about, 37, 279–80, 293; all levels of government, 37, 245, 290, 291; allies of LGBTQ candidates, 291; American models, 280, 283–88; defences against homophobia, 279, 286, 290, 291; funding, 285–88, 291, 293; historical background, 280–81, 283–84, 293, 293*n*2; ideological diversity, 282–83, 284, 293; intersectionality, 291; lived equality, 37, 280–83, 289–90, 293; mission, 289–90; multi-partisan body, 37, 279–80, 284, 288–90, 293; successes, 288–91; training, 279–80, 284, 286, 288, 291, 293; urban/rural areas, 291–92; Victory Fund model, 245, 280, 283–88, 291. *See also* candidates; candidates, perspectives on sexual orientation
provinces and territories: about, 35; Comparative Provincial Election Project data, 80, 85, 89–90, 96–98; conservatism, 157–58, 165, 171, 252; historical background, 4–5, 141; human rights legislation, 188; LGBTQ candidates, 247–49, 249(t), 252–53, 262; LGBTQ competitiveness, 262; LGBTQ legislators, 4, 251–52; LGBTQ parties, 244; LGBTQ premiers, 4–5; marriage jurisdiction, 180, 191–94; notwithstanding clause, 186–87, 192; research needed, 35; right to vote and to run, 243; same-sex marriage, 189; sexual orientation as prohibited ground, 171, 184, 186, 188; visible minority representation, 137–38; voting systems, 136. *See also* political parties, provincial; *and specific provinces and territories*
Puar, Jasbir, 213
Purewal, Shinder, 120*n*12
Putin, Vladimir, 162

Quebec: Action démocratique du Québec (ADQ), 165; Coalition Avenir Québec (CAQ), 165; human rights charter, 35; LGBTQ candidates by party, 247–49, 249(t); LGBTQ legislators, 252, 255; LGBTQ mayors, 6; Liberal Party, 252; NDP party, 252; Québec Solidaire, 252; rural areas, 255; same-sex marriage, 65, 165; trans politicians, 6. *See also* Bloc Québécois (BQ); Boisclair, André; Parti Québécois (PQ); provinces and territories
Quebec, demographics: by gender and LGB/non-LGB, 55, 56(t)–57(t); LGB support in elections (2006–15), 64–67, 66(f), 68–69, 68(f); partisan choices, 64–73, 66(f), 68(f), 70(t), 72(t); socio-demographics by electoral engagement, 58–62, 59(t)–61(t), 73–74; socio-demographics by vote choice (2006–15), 70(t), 72(t), 73–74
queer people: about, 5–7; candidates, 248, 267, 269; gendered attire, 267, 269, 271; municipal candidates, 267, 271; politicians, 249; social movement activism, 5–6; terminology, 5–7, 38*n*1, 39*n*6; visibility/invisibility, 7, 267, 269. *See also* LGBTQ people and communities; terminology, LGBTQ

Queers against Israeli Apartheid, 301, 309, 310*n*2

race/ethnicity: candidates, 28, 246, 248, 266; diverse representation, 124–26, 224–25; hyper-politeness, 268; political ambition, 246; racism, 274; right to vote and to run, 243; stereotypes, 14; voter bias, 270, 274. *See also* intersectionality
Rae, Kyle, 299, 302, 310*n*2
Rayside, David, 28, 131, 189, 228, 231, 232, 234, 281, 286, 317
REAL Women, 162, 322–23
recruitment of candidates, 244–47. *See also* candidates; ProudPolitics
Redford, Alison, 167
Reform/Alliance Party: hate propaganda, 324–26; media coverage, 322–23; same-sex marriage, 323; social conservatism, 160, 182–83, 189–90, 206, 322–23, 327. *See also* conservatism; Conservative Party of Canada; ideological spectrum, right (conservative)
refugees. *See* immigrants and refugees
regions. *See* ridings and districts; urban/suburban/rural areas
regions, socio-demographics: by electoral engagement, 58–62, 59(t)–61(t), 73–74; by gender and LGB/non-LGB, 55, 56(t)–57(t), 73–74; by vote choice and LGB/non-LGB (2006–15), 68–74, 68(t)–72(t). *See also* Atlantic Canada, socio-demographics; British Columbia; Ontario; prairie provinces, socio-demographics; provinces and territories; Quebec
Rehfeld, Andrew, 229
Reingold, Beth, 285
religion: Calgary March for Jesus, 166–67; Catholics, 113, 166, 181, 182; diverse representation, 126; Evangelical Christians, 172, 182–83, 261, 324; hate propaganda and religious texts, 324–26; Muslims, 268–70; religious freedom, 191, 193, 194; resistance to LGBTQ candidates, 260–61, 267–71; same-sex marriage, 113, 182, 191, 193, 194; secular state, 179–83, 191, 198*n*1. *See also* government role in society

religion, socio-demographics: by gender and LGB/non-LGB, 55, 56(t)–57(t), 73–74; by LGB/non-LGB, 240; by vote choice and LGB/non-LGB (2006–15), 69(t)–72(t), 71–74; by vote choice in Ontario election (2014), 90, 91(t)–92(t), 97
representation, political. *See* candidates; electorate; political representation
research methods: assumption of heterosexuality, 22; challenges in, 142; commercial surveys, 53; discourse analysis, 106; grounded theory principles, 107; interactive and contextual approaches, 144; Interactive Voice Response (IVR), 53; qualitative research analysis, 107–8, 118; voting systems, 144; web-based surveys, 53
residency. *See* urban/suburban/rural areas
respectability: about, 114–17; binaries and polarities, 5–6, 29–30, 114–15, 116–17; defined, 114; heteronormativity, 103–4; homonormativity, 113, 114, 117–18, 233; hyper-politeness of candidates, 268; LGBTQ politicians as role models, 30–31; lifestyle issues, 103–5, 114; of women, 93, 108. *See also* heteronormativity and homonormativity
Reynolds, Andrew: diverse representation, 28–29, 31, 142, 145, 228; electorate, 15–16, 19; voting systems, 22, 132–35, 133(t)–35(t), 224, 250
Richard, Maurice, 141, 244, 252
Richards, Ann, 286
Richardson, Diane, 6
ridings and districts: at-large vs single-member districts, 126; boundary revisions, 136; candidate as challenger vs inheritor vs open-seat, 253, 253(t); competitiveness, 37, 131–32, 145, 249, 252–53, 262; geographical concentration of LGBTQ voters, 20–21, 129–31, 142–45, 223–24, 250, 254–55, 272–73; geographical concentration of visible minorities, 129, 138–39; non-traditional parties, 252. *See also* urban/suburban/rural areas; voting systems
Rienzo, Barbara, 20, 32, 273
Riggle, Ellen, 19

right parties. *See* conservatism; ideological spectrum, right (conservative); political parties

Robinson, Svend: about, 38, 230, 314–28; activist networks, 315, 317; age of consent laws, 205; allies with, 38, 326; Charter rights, 185, 315–19; coming out process (1988), 141, 244, 319–21; elections (1979–2006), 20, 140(t), 244, 254, 314, 319–21, 327, 328; first out MP, 38, 139, 141, 320–21; hate-crimes, 316; homophobia, 120n14; legitimacy of personal experience, 319, 324; LGBTQ representation, 228; media coverage, 120n14, 321–22, 328; mental health, 327; out and proud, 5, 230; parliamentary activities, 11, 230–32, 234, 321–27; as role model, 38, 230, 319, 321, 324; same-sex marriage, 323, 327; sexual mediation, 105; trans rights, 326; We Demand protests, 205

Rock, Jeffrey, 266, 272
Rogers, Marc, 18
Rosenblum, Darren, 20–22, 130–31
Rostosky, Sharon, 19
Rounthwaite, Jane, 113, 115
Rubin, Gayle, 114–17
Ruby, Clayton, 324
run, right to, 243. *See also* candidates
rural areas. *See* urban/suburban/rural areas
Russia, 162, 213–14
Ruth, Nancy, 251, 252

Saguil, Paul, 195
same-sex marriage and rights: about, 65, 182–83, 189–94; benefits, employment, 189, 206, 208; Charter rights, 182; conservative views, 65, 160–64, 169, 173, 182–83, 189–90, 206, 208, 288, 290, 323; debate issues, 190–93; election issue (2006), 19, 58, 65, 73, 160–61; federal/provincial jurisdiction, 180, 191–94; historical background, 3, 58, 65, 183, 206, 208, 231, 282, 323; international rights, 3; legalization (2005), 65, 183; LGBTory views, 160–61, 163–64, 288; LGBTQ politicians in marriages, 94, 236n9; Liberal support, 36, 65, 189–93, 208; liberal views, 182–83; *M v H* (1999), 189; marriage, as term, 190–91, 193–94; NDP support, 194, 202, 206–8, 210; public opinion, 190, 197; religious freedom, 191, 193, 194; Supreme Court reference, 194, 208

Sanbonmatsu, Kira, 245
Saskatchewan: conservatism, 165; gay-straight alliances in schools, 165; LGBTQ candidates by party, 247–49, 249(t); NDP opposition, 262; neoliberalism, 165; Saskatchewan Party, 248. *See also* provinces and territories

Saward, Michael, 9, 222, 229
Schaffner, Brian, 62
Scheer, Andrew, 65, 171, 173, 288. *See also* Conservative Party of Canada
schools. *See* education issues
Schroedel, Jean, 261
Scotland, 129, 172. *See also* United Kingdom
Scott, Craig, 140(t), 289, 292
Scott, Ian, 255
secular state, 179–83, 191, 198n1. *See also* government role in society
Senate: LGBTQ members, 4, 251, 252
Senic, Nenad, 62
separation of church and state. *See* government role in society
Severs, Eline, 229
sex/gender: gender of voters and candidates, 16–17; and heterosexuality, 14; LGBTQ and women as gendered minorities, 11–12; stereotypes, 13–14, 16–17. *See also* heteronormativity and homonormativity; identity; intersectionality; sexual orientation; sexuality; terminology, LGBTQ; *and entries beginning with* LGBTQ

sex/gender, demographics: ideological issues by gender and LGB/non-LGB, 62–64, 63(t); ratios, female-to-male, 4, 54; socio-demographics by electoral engagement, 58–62, 59(t)–61(t), 73–74; socio-demographics by gender and LGB/non-LGB, 55, 56(t)–57(t), 73–74; vote choice by gender (2006–15), 67–69, 67(f)–68(f), 69(t)–72(t), 71–73

sexual mediation of politicians: about, 102–4, 117–18; anglophone and francophone coverage, 119n4; explicit vs implicit, 104; first LGBTQ elected (theme), 34, 102, 104–5, 108–11, 117–18; heteronormative assumptions, 103–4, 117, 250; LGBTQ representation (theme), 111–14, 117–18; as non-issue, 94, 108, 112–13, 115, 118, 268; research project on, 105–8, 117–18; respectability (theme), 115–18; scholarship on, 104; sexual mediation, as concept, 103–4, 107–8. *See also* media; Wynne, Kathleen, media framing (2014 election) by sexual mediation

sexual orientation: self-identification in surveys, 52–55, 75. *See also* bisexuals; gays; heterosexuality; intersectionality; lesbians; LGBTQ people and communities; queer people; terminology, LGBTQ; trans people

sexuality: age of consent, 196, 205, 209, 236n6; binaries and polarities, 5–6, 29–30, 114–15, 116–17; good (normal) vs bad (abnormal) sex, 114–15, 117; non-binary people, 248, 249; and respectability, 93, 114–17. *See also* sexual orientation

Shah, Shazad, 267, 271
Shepard, Benjamin, 280
Sherrill, Kenneth, 13, 18, 54, 62
Siemiatycki, Myer, 137
Sigurðardóttir, Jóhanna, 104, 108
Siksay, Bill, 140(t), 210–11, 212–13, 244, 327
Silva, Mario, 140(t), 327
Simpson, Jeffrey, 198n5
Singh, Jasmeet, 268
Skoke, Roseanne, 322
Smith, Danielle, 159, 167–68, 171
Smith, Donna, 29, 104, 115, 118
Smith, Miriam, 27, 185
Smith, Raymond, 30
Smitherman, George, 94–95, 255, 265, 272, 291
Snell, Paul, 13
social media, 267, 275n3
social-movement activism: about, 33; anti-gay ballot initiatives, 19; collective identity, 19; diverse representation, 124–26, 223; electoral politics, 8; emotional aspects, 221–23; historical background, 204–7; identity and communities, 7–8; ideological spectrum and gender, 64; models of, 23–24; and political parties, 23–24, 206–7; terminology, 5, 7–8; women's movements, 11. *See also* LGBTQ movements and organizations

socio-demographics. *See* LGBTQ demographics

Stanford, Jim, 207
Stangor, Charles, 14
Statistics Canada, 52. *See also* General Social Survey (GSS)
Stein, Marc, 5, 6, 233
stereotypes of politicians: about, 14–17, 34, 80–85, 93–95, 102, 261–62; bisexuals, 7; feminine vs masculine traits, 16–17, 84–85, 87, 93, 103, 269; "gay agenda," 84, 93, 103–4, 111; gender-based stereotypes, 82–83, 93–95, 102–3; heteronormative aspects, 14, 30, 84; homophobia, 83–84; influence of factual information, 83, 85–86; intersection of gender and sexual orientation, 16–17, 34, 84–85, 261; key questions, 15, 84–85; leader's agentic vs communal traits, 82–84, 86–88, 87(t), 89(t), 96; leader's competencies on issues, 82–83, 87(t), 88–89, 89(t), 96; media framing, 82, 102; negative aspects, 81–85; political parties, 82, 93; politics of disgust, 5, 15, 29, 30; "recruitment of children," 15, 39n13, 236n6; research project, 96–98; role congruity theory, 82; scholarship on, 14–17, 81–85, 102–5; sexual-orientation–based stereotypes, 93–95; of sitting office-holders, 83, 95. *See also* heteronormativity and homonormativity; identity; media; sexual mediation of politicians; Wynne, Kathleen, media framing (2014 election); Wynne, Kathleen, media framing (2014 election) by sexual mediation

Stewart, Ron, 318, 319
stigma: about, 260; heterosexist assumptions, 260; historical background, 11; politics of disgust, 5, 15, 29, 30; public opinion trends, 83–84, 94–95, 260–61; self-identification in surveys, 53–54. *See also* homo-, bi-, and transphobia

Stone, Amy, 19

Strength in Democracy party, 266, 279
Studlar, Donley, 136
substantive citizenship, 35, 38
substantive political representation. *See* political representation, substantive
suburbs. *See* municipalities; urban/suburban/rural areas
support for LGBTQ rights. *See* allies for LGBTQ people
Swank, Eric, 18
Sweden: LGBTQ MPs, 4; representation by voting system, 127–28, 128(t), 132–35, 134(t)–35(t), 136
Syria, 214

Taylor-Robinson, Michelle, 220
Teeple, Gary, 281
terminology: conservative right, 77n5, 158–60; emotion and affect, 221; liberal left, 77n5; marriage, as term, 190–91, 193–94; MLA, generic sense, 255n4
terminology, LGBTQ: about, 5–10, 38n1, 119n9; binary classifications, 5–6, 29–30; gender identity vs expression, 216n6; historical tensions, 6; inclusiveness, 7, 119n9; people vs communities, 7–8; self-identification in surveys, 52–55, 75; use in this book, 6–7, 38n1, 76n1, 119n1, 216n1; visibility/invisibility, 7. *See also* bisexuals; gays; lesbians; queer people; trans people
territories: socio-demographics by gender and LGB/non-LGB, 55, 56(t)–57(t). *See also* Northwest Territories; Nunavut; provinces and territories; Yukon
Thatcher, Margaret, 26, 39n15, 172
Thomas, Sue, 16
Thomsen, Cynthia, 15
Tobin, Ann, 26–27
Toby's Law, xii
Toews, Vic, 324–25
Tolley, Erin, 102, 103, 118, 264
Toone, Philip, 140(t)
Toronto: bathhouse raids (1981), 205, 314–15; Church St. Murals Project, 302, 307–9; 519 Church St. Community Centre, 302, 303, 306, 310n2; gay village, 254, 255, 292, 298–99, 302–9; heritage projects, 307–9; homonormative entrepreneurialism (HE), 302–9; LGBTQ councillors, 298–301; Pride events, 120n12, 169–70, 209, 263, 290, 299–301, 304, 309, 310n2; queer institutions, 303; Rob Ford as mayor, 300–2, 305, 309; Toronto Centre-Rosedale, 255, 298–99, 302, 310n1; tourism and gay community, 300, 304–5, 308; World Pride, 209, 298, 301, 302, 304, 307. *See also* municipalities; Ontario; Wong-Tam, Kristyn
towns. *See* municipalities; urban/suburban/rural areas
training of candidates. *See* candidates; ProudPolitics
trans people: about, 6–7; adoption of own children, xii; bathroom access, 166–67, 172–73, 211; birth certificates, 167; candidates, 6, 216n7, 247, 266, 268–72, 279; demographics, 13, 53–54, 76n3; gender identity and expression, 169, 196, 201, 208–12, 216n6; gender surgery, 168, 170; hate-crimes, 210–12; historical background, 210; mayors, 6; municipal/provincial issues, 195; NDP support, 208–12; as object of representation, 232–33, 235n2, 236n3; privileged vs deprived LGBTQ subgroups, 208, 212, 233–35; ProudPolitics support, 290, 291; public opinion trends, 260; self-identification in surveys, 52–54; terminology, 5–7, 38n1, 39n6, 216n6; Toby's Law, xii; transphobia, 211–12, 214, 233, 235n1, 290; visibility/invisibility, 7, 266. *See also* LGBTQ people and communities; terminology, LGBTQ
Tremblay, Manon, 11, 20, 22, 319, 324
Treul, Sarah, 13, 31
Trimble, Linda, 120n14
Trudeau, Justin, government: diverse representation, 194–95; government apology (2017), 197; liberal policies, 194–97, 214; Pride events, 195, 222; voting system reforms, 139
Trudeau, Pierre, government: Charter of Rights, 179, 315–16; constitutional negotiations, 184, 186; decriminalization (1968), 179, 180–82, 197, 314; human rights, 183–84, 315–16;

notwithstanding clause, 186–87; private vs public domain, 180–81
Turner, John, 181

Uganda, 161–62, 213–14
UN International Convention on Civil and Political Rights, 183
UN International Day against Homophobia, Transphobia and Biphobia, 196
United Conservative Party (Alberta), 168
United Kingdom: Conservative Party, 19, 25–26, 39n15, 143, 171–72, 181; diverse representation, 127; elections (2015, 2017), 4, 26; historical background, 172, 181; ideological spectrum and LGBTQ people, 19, 26; Labour Party, 15–16, 19, 25–27, 127–29, 172; legality of homosexuality, 3, 181; LGBTQ candidates, 26, 37; LGBTQ electorate, 18–19; LGBTQ MPs, 4, 26, 28, 142, 171–72; LGBTQ representation by voting system (1985–2015), 132–35, 134(t)–35(t); LGBTQ stereotypes, 15; Liberal Democrat Party, 25–26; media framing, 29; political parties and diverse representation, 25–26, 127–28; political will for diverse representation, 142–43, 171–72; same-sex marriage, 172; Scottish National Party, 172; single-member plurality (SMP) system, 128, 142; Socialist Workers' Party, 27; trans politicians, 172; voting system, 34, 127–29, 142; women's representation by voting system (1965–2015), 127–29, 128(t), 133, 136
United States: anti-gay activism, 19, 23, 172; bisexuals, 53; closeted politicians, 12; competitiveness, 262; Congressional LGBT Equality Caucus, 13; conservatives, 26, 172, 261; constitutional rights, 185; Democratic Party, 17–18, 25, 262, 287; demographics, 13, 53–55, 76n3; diverse representation, 126; diversity in LGBTQ communities, 53; electoral capture theory, 17; electoral engagement, 58; electorate, 12–13, 51; EMILY's List, 245, 285–86; Evangelical Christians, 182, 261; Gay and Lesbian Victory Fund, 245, 280; geographical concentration of LGBTQ people, 20–21, 129–30, 140, 223–24; geographical concentration of visible minorities, 126, 129; historical background, 172, 185, 280–81, 293n2; HIV/AIDS activism, 222; ideological spectrum, 17–19, 25, 62; "lavender vote," 12–13; legality of homosexuality, 3, 39n2, 140; LGBTQ candidates, 25, 37, 255; LGBTQ electorate, 17–19; LGBTQ groups, 26; LGBTQ political representation, 31–32; LGBTQ representation by voting system (1985–2015), 132–35, 134(t)–35(t); LGBTQ state legislators, 28; LGBTQ stigma, 261; Log Cabin Republicans, 26, 284; mayors, 245; media coverage, 271; political parties and diverse representation, 25; public opinion trends, 3–4, 260–61; recruitment of candidates, 245; Republican Party, 18, 25, 26, 39n15, 172–73, 284, 287; resistance to LGBTQ candidates, 16, 260–61; same-sex marriage, 3; scholarship on, 51; state's role in government, 172; stereotypes of candidates, 261–62; substantive representation, 285; timing of disclosure, 261–62; trans people, 53, 76n3, 172–73; Victory Fund model, 245, 280, 283–88, 291; Voting Rights Act, 126; women's representation by voting system (1965–2015), 128(t), 133, 136
urban/suburban/rural areas: diverse representation, 130, 138–39, 143; electoral engagement, 58–62, 59(t)–61(t), 73–74, 138–39; gay villages, 131, 135, 143, 250, 302–9; geographical concentration, 20–21, 142–44, 223–24, 250, 254–55, 272–73; Indigenous peoples, 138–39; intersectional identities, 130; LGBTQ candidates, 248, 254–55, 262; ProudPolitics, 291–92; rural areas, 29, 138–39, 248, 255; urban areas, 13, 29, 141, 240, 250, 254, 262, 272; US ideological spectrum, 16; voting systems, 138–39. *See also* electorate; ridings and districts
urban/suburban/rural areas, socio-demographics: by gender and LGB/non-LGB, 55, 56(t)–57(t), 60(t)–61(t), 73–74; by vote choice and LGB/non-LGB (2006–15), 69(t)–72(t), 71–74; by

vote choice in Ontario election (2014), 90, 91(t)-92(t), 97

Vallée, Stéphanie, 220, 223, 235
Victory Fund, Gay and Lesbian, 245, 280, 283–88, 291
visible minorities: clientelism, 143; diverse representation, 124–26, 129–30, 137; geographical concentration, 126, 129, 138–39; intersectional identities of LGBTQ politicians, 294n14; LGBTQ people as, 321; representation and voting systems, 137–39, 143, 146; sociodemographics by electoral engagement, 58–62, 59(t)–61(t), 73–74; sociodemographics by gender and LGB/non-LGB, 55, 56(t)–57(t). *See also* Indigenous peoples; intersectionality; race/ethnicity
Von Lichtenberg, Doc, 161, 163
vote, right to, 243. *See also* electorate
voting groups. *See* electorate; electorate, demographics and voting behaviours
voting systems: about, 34, 124–26, 144–46; clientelism, 143; dedicated seats, 126–27; districting approach, 126–29; diverse representation, 21–22, 124–30, 136–39, 141–45; institutional factors, 125–26; key questions, 124; LGBTQ representation by system and country (1983–2015), 129–35, 133(t)–35(t); political parties, 126–29; political will, 138, 142, 250–51; quotas in parties, 126–29; reform efforts, 136; research needed, 250; right to vote, 243; scholarship on, 22, 124, 144–45, 224, 250; social factors, 125–26; velocity of change in diverse representation, 129; visibility/invisibility of minorities, 130–31, 142, 145–46; visible minority representation, 126–27, 129, 137–39; women's representation, 125, 128(t), 133, 136, 250. *See also* electorate; political representation; ridings and districts
voting systems, majoritarian: about, 34, 124, 136–37, 146; benefits for LGBTQ people, 11, 34; in Canada, 141–43; compared with proportional, 144–45, 224, 250; diverse representation, 34, 136–39; LGBTQ representation by system and country (1983–2015), 132–35, 133(t)–35(t); for majority party government, 21; women candidates, 20; women's representation (1965–2015), 128(t), 133, 136
voting systems, plurality: about, 124, 137; clientelism, 143; diverse representation, 138–39, 142–44; first-past-the-post system, 11, 224, 251; LGBTQ representation by system and country (1983–2015), 132–35, 133(t)–35(t); single- and multi-member plurality, 136; single-member plurality (SMP), 124, 126, 128, 128(t), 137–39, 141–43, 146
voting systems, proportional: about, 20–22, 34, 124, 132–33, 144–46; benefits for LGBTQ people, 11, 20–22, 34, 125, 132–33, 145–46, 224, 250; compared with majoritarian, 144–45, 224, 250; diverse representation, 21–22, 34, 125, 127, 136–39, 144–46; geographical concentration of LGBTQ people, 20–21, 223–24, 250; LGBTQ representation by system and country (1983–2015), 132–35, 133(t)–35(t); mixed-member variants, 145; party lists, 20, 22, 125, 127, 145, 224, 250–51; transferable votes, 145; visible minorities, 138–39; women's representation (1965–2015), 128(t), 133, 136
Vriend v Alberta, 188, 195, 198n6

Waaldijk, Kees, 3
Waddell, Ian, 319
Waite, Sean, 39n12
Wald, Kenneth, 20, 32, 273
Wall, Brad, 165
Waller, Scott, 261
Warner, Michael, 282
Warner, Tom, 281
Watt, Jaime, 289
Wayburn, William, 285
Wildrose Party of Alberta, 159, 167–68, 171, 248
Williams, Melissa, 224–25, 229
Wilson, Doug, 140
Wilson, Tatum, 289
Wilson-Raybould, Jody, 196
women: about, 10–12; Charter rights, 188–89; gender of voters and candidates, 16–17; LGBTQ and women as gendered minorities, 11–12;

media framing, 102–3; right to vote, 243; scholarship on, 102, 240–41; stereotypes, 13–14, 16–17. *See also* bisexuals; identity; intersectionality; lesbians; LGBTQ people and communities; sex/gender; sexual orientation; sexuality; terminology, LGBTQ; trans people; *and entries beginning with* LGBTQ

women, candidates: agentic vs communal traits, 82–84, 86–88, 87(t), 89(t), 96; EMILY's List, 245, 285–86; in federal election (2015), 247; feminine vs masculine traits, 16–17, 84–85, 87, 93, 103, 269; "first" elected, 108–9; political parties, 136–37; protection of women as issue, 87(t), 88–89, 89(t); recruitment, 244–45; right to run, 37. *See also* candidates

women, demographics: electoral engagement, 58–62, 59(t)–61(t), 73–74; electorate and voting behaviours, 52, 54–55, 56(t)–57(t), 73–74; ideological issues, 62–64, 63(t); ideological spectrum by vote choice, 69(t)–72(t), 71–74; ratios, female-to-male, 54; sociodemographics of LGB/non-LGB, 55, 56(t)–57(t), 73–74; socio-demographics of vote choice (2006–15), 69–74, 69(t)–72(t); socio-demographics of voters in Ontario election (2014), 90, 91(t)–92(t), 97; urban/suburban/rural areas, 55, 56(t)–57(t), 60(t)–61(t), 73–74

women, political representation: about, 10–12, 240–41; by allies, 220–21, 227; candidate recruitment and selection, 242–43, 245–47; critical mass theory, 11, 131; diverse representation, 124–26, 130, 194–95; federal parties, 136–37; "first" elected, 109; LGBTQ and women as gendered minorities, 10–12; NDP policies of inclusion, 205–6; as object of representation, 232–33; political representatives of, 224–25, 234; proportional voting systems, 22; provincial parties, 11; scholarship on, 10–12, 17, 240–41; substantive representation, 17, 111; under-representation, 10–11, 28, 109, 137, 240, 242–43, 292; by voting system

(1965–2015), 128(t), 129, 133, 136. *See also* political representation

Wong-Tam, Kristyn: about, 38, 298–301; business community, 38, 299–300, 302, 305; Church St. Murals, 302, 307–9; city councillor in Toronto, 5, 298–300; gay village, 298–99, 302–9; homonormative policies, 38, 302–9; life of, 298–99; Pride events, 299–301; ProudPolitics support, 290; Rob Ford as mayor, 300–2, 305, 309; Toronto Centre-Rosedale, 298–99, 302, 310*n*1; World Pride, 298, 301, 302, 304, 307

Wootton, David, 308

World Pride, Toronto, 209, 298, 301, 302, 304, 307

Wynne, Kathleen: about, 80–81; on coming out, 230; firsts as politician, 80–81, 95, 110–11; homophobia, 14–15; as MPP, 81, 110–11, 119*n*3; personal history, 81, 93–94, 98*n*2, 114, 115–16; Pride events, 112; ProudPolitics support, 289; respectability, 34, 93, 114–17; as role model, 81, 109–13; same-sex marriage, 94; school trustee, 15, 81, 113; sex-education curriculum, 14–15

Wynne, Kathleen, media framing (2014 election): about, 34, 80–81, 90–95; agentic vs communal traits, 82–84, 86–88, 87(t), 89(t), 90, 91(t)–92(t), 94, 96; as centrist, 91(t)–92(t), 93; gender and sexual orientation, 34, 94–95; issue competencies, 34, 87(t), 88–89, 89(t), 90, 91(t)–92(t), 94, 96; leadership traits, 82, 86–88, 87(t), 89(t), 90, 91(t)–92(t), 96; likeability of, 86, 86(t), 96; research project on, 80–81, 85–89, 96–98; respectability, 34, 93–94, 114–17; same-sex marriage, 94; scholarship on stereotypes, 81–85; socio-demographic profile of voters, 90, 91(t)–92(t), 96–98; stereotypes, 29–30, 34, 80, 90, 93–95; terminology, LGBTQ, 119*n*9; vote choice by gender, 80, 90; voter pre-election knowledge of, 85–86, 90, 93, 97; voter reliance on stereotypes, 80, 90–95, 91(t)–92(t)

Wynne, Kathleen, media framing (2014 election) by sexual mediation: about,

102; heteronormativity, 93, 98*n*2, 112, 117–18; orientation as a non-issue, 94, 108, 112, 113, 118; research project on, 105–8, 117–18; respectability, 93, 113; substantive representation, 10, 112–13, 117–18; symbolic representation, 110–11, 112, 117–18; "the first" frame, 34, 108, 110–11, 112, 117–18. *See also* media; sexual mediation of politicians

Yeager, Ken, 28
Young, Iris Marion, 225
Yukon: LGBTQ candidates by party, 247–49, 249(t); LGBTQ MLAs, 252. *See also* provinces and territories